mypoliscilab ™

Where participation leads to action!

Welcome to MyPoliSciLab, where participation leads to action!

MyPoliSciLab is a state-of-the-art, interactive, and instructive online solution for introducing students to American Government. Designed to amplify and supplement a traditional lecture course or completely administer an online course, MyPoliSciLab combines multimedia — simulations, videos, news feeds and archives, quizzes and tests — to make teaching and learning more effective and fun!

WHAT STUDENTS ARE SAYING ABOUT ONLINE EXAMS AND QUIZZES

"I love it. I keep trying until I get a perfect grade and after a couple times you know the content like the back of your hand!"

"I liked being able to view the results of the quizzes immediately instead of having to wait for them to be graded by the instructor."

WHAT STUDENTS ARE SAYING ABOUT ONLINE ACTIVITIES

"The activities were my favorite part of the course. They took a different approach to an interesting subject, and made it more applicable to real-life situations. This made the subject seem even more real than before."

"I think they are a great tool to get students to interact with the material in a way you couldn't really do in class."

ONE PLACE.
Everything your students need to succeed.

MyPoliSciLab is a state-of-the-art, interactive, and instructive online solution for your American Government course.

> **Pre-Test, Post Test, and Chapter Exam**

For each chapter of the printed textbook, students will navigate through a pre-test, post-test, and a full-chapter exam — all fully integrated with the online E-book so students can assess, review, and improve their understanding of the material in each chapter.

> **Chapter Review**

For each chapter, students will find additional resources such as a complete study guide, learning objectives, a summary.

> **E-book.**

Matching the exact layout of the printed textbook, the E-book contains multimedia icons in the margins that launch a wealth of exciting resources.

> **The New York Times Online Feed & The New York Times Search by Subject™ Archive**

Both provide free access to the full text of The New York Times and articles from the world's leading journalists of the Times. The online feed provides students with updated headlines and political news on an **hourly** basis.

> **Online Administration**

Instructors can easily track students' work on the site and monitor their progress on each activity. The Instructor Gradebook, which now includes upgraded functionality, provides maximum flexibility for allowing instructors to sort by student, activity, or to view the entire class in spreadsheet view.

> **Research Navigator™**

This database provides thousands of articles from journals as well as popular periodicals, such as Newsweek and USA Today, that give students and professors access to scholarly and topical content from a variety of sources.

> **Interactive Activities**

Students will find over 100 simulations, interactive timelines, videos, comparative exercises, and more — all integrated with the online E-book through icons that appear in the margins. Now fully updated with brand-new activities!

SIMULATION. Students are given a role to play — such as congress member, lobbyist, or police officer — so they can experience the challenges and excitement of politics firsthand.

TIMELINE. With an abundance of media and graphics, students can step through the evolution of an aspect of our political system.

VISUAL LITERACY. Students interpret and apply data about intriguing political topics. Each activity begins with an interactive primer on reading graphs and charts.

PARTICIPATION. Bringing the importance of politics home, these activities appear as three types: 1) Debates, 2) Surveys, and 3) "Get Involved" activities.

COMPARATIVE. Students compare the U.S. political system to those of other countries.

CONTINUOUSLY UPDATED MULTIMEDIA MAPPED TO CHAPTER CONTENT

NEW FEATURES

Student Polling

Updated weekly with timely, provocative questions, this new feature allows students to participate in nationwide polls on hot topics. Students are asked to vote on questions such as "Should flag burning be permitted?" Results of student responses around the country are immediately displayed.

PoliSci News

PoliSci News contains 1) an online feed from The *New York Times* that is updated hourly, 2) an exclusive *New York Times* database that allows students to browse by subject area or search for a specific topic, and 3) PoliSci News Review — a series of articles selected by a political science professor that recap the previous week's most important political events and are followed by quizzes.

Roundtable Discussion Video Clips

Video clips consist of three professors discussing important concepts covered in the text. Key concepts such as campaign finance reform and critical questions such as "Is Federalism Dead?" are discussed from a wide range of perspectives and viewpoints — providing students with a balanced review of key course material. Each discussion is accompanied by critical thinking prompts, multiple choice questions, and a transcript for reference.

Debate Video Clips

Offering lively, challenging debates from two sides of an issue, these clips feature two professors discussing hot-button issues and answering pressing questions such as "Did George Bush steal the election?" Each discussion is accompanied by critical thinking prompts, multiple choice questions, and a transcript for reference.

INSTRUCTOR: WE CAN HELP YOU EASILY INTEGRATE THESE AMAZING ASSETS INTO YOUR COURSE...HOW?

Author's Choice

With so many incredible activities to assign, we have asked our authors to hand select one or two activities that best complement or amplify each chapter. You have the work done for you in easy-to-use, pre-packaged MyPoliSciLab assignments. If you only have time to assign and complete one activity for the chapter, the Author's Choice designation makes it easy!

Go to mypoliscilab.com to see a sample chapter!

Student Survey Results

Recently, Longman Publishers conducted a nationwide survey of students to determine just how useful they find MyPoliSciLab and its individual features. The sample included hundreds of students from both 2-year and 4-year schools.

The results are impressive. Not only do they show that students find MyPoliSciLab to be an effective supplement, but they show how each specific feature of MyPoliSciLab enhances students' learning experience and engages them with the course material. See for yourself!

Very low learning value →

Very high learning value ←

	1	2	3	4	5	4s & 5s
Online Quizzes	1.3%	1.3%	8.8%	26.8%	61.9%	88.7%
Chapter Exams	0.8%	5.0%	8.4%	18.4%	67.4%	85.8%
Debate Videos	2.2%	3.5%	15.8%	27.6%	50.9%	78.5%
Roundtable Videos	3.0%	3.0%	16.5%	32.0%	45.5%	77.5%
Chapter Activities	0.9%	5.2%	16.5%	23.9%	53.5%	77.4%
Online E-Book	5.4%	8.3%	15.1%	17.6%	53.7%	71.2%
PS News Review	5.0%	4.5%	23.2%	23.2%	44.1%	67.3%
Homepage Updates	8.0%	11.7%	16.9%	23.9%	39.4%	63.4%
Polling Questions	7.6%	9.0%	27.0%	20.9%	35.5%	56.4%

WHAT STUDENTS ARE SAYING ABOUT ONLINE E-BOOK

"It helped a lot, especially since you could magnify the words. Also, it was great to be able to type in a key word and see exactly where it appears in the text."

WHAT STUDENTS ARE SAYING ABOUT DEBATE VIDEOS

"All videos were fantastic and allowed each topic to be discussed from each viewpoint but was kept objective by the moderator."

WHAT STUDENTS ARE SAYING ABOUT POLISCI NEWS

"I really liked this feature. I don't get a chance to catch up on political news very often, so this was very helpful."

WHAT STUDENTS ARE SAYING ABOUT POLLING QUESTIONS

"The polling questions are fun. Sometimes I was very surprised at other students' responses."

PEARSON

Longman

The Essentials
of American
GOVERNMENT

The Essentials of American GOVERNMENT

CONTINUITY AND CHANGE ★ 2008 Edition ★

KAREN O'CONNOR

Jonathan N. Helfat Distinguished Professor of Political Science
American University

LARRY J. SABATO

University Professor and
Robert Kent Gooch Professor of Politics
University of Virginia

PEARSON
Longman

New York San Francisco Boston
London Toronto Sydney Tokyo Singapore Madrid
Mexico City Munich Paris Cape Town Hong Kong Montreal

Editor-in-Chief: Eric Stano
Development Editor: Melissa Mashburn
Senior Marketing Manager: Elizabeth Fogarty
Supplements Editor: Brian Belardi
Senior Media Editor: Beth Strauss
Production Manager: Eric Jorgensen
Project Coordination, Text Design, Art Studio, and
    Electronic Page Makeup: Electronic Publishing Services Inc., NYC
Cover Design Manager: Nancy Danahy
Cover images: Clockwise from upper left: American flag fence in Nebraska © Corbis; Stars and
Stripes © Veer/Getty Images; American flags, New York City, New York © Photodisc/Getty
Images; High angle view of a group of people holding a large American flag © Rubberball Produc-
tions/Getty Images; American flag draped over a rural mailbox © Jupiter Images. Photo of boxes
© Nancy Danahy
Photo Research: Photosearch, Inc.
Senior Manufacturing Buyer: Alfred C. Dorsey
Printer and Binder: RR Donnelley & Sons, Co.
Cover Printer: Phoenix Color Corp.

For permission to use copyrighted material, grateful acknowledgment is made to the copyright
holders on the pages where the material appears.

Library of Congress Cataloging-in-Publication Data

The essentials of American government : continuity and change / Karen O'Connor . . . [et al.].
        p. cm.
    Prev. ed. entered under O'Connor, Karen, 1952-
    Includes bibliographical references and index.
    ISBN 0-205-52683-7 (paperbound)
    1. United States—Politics and government.   2. Texas—Politics and government.
I. O'Connor, Karen, 1952–

JK276.O36 2008
320.473—dc22

                                                        2006034942

Visit us at http://www.ablongman.com

ISBN 0-205-52683-7
ISBN 13 978-0-205-52683-3

4 5 6 7 8 9 10—DOW—10 09 08

★★★ Brief Contents

★★★ Detailed Contents

★★★ Preface

It has happened again. As we prepared this new, essentials version of our best-selling American government text, we found ourselves again surprised, challenged, and ultimately riveted by the dramatic changes that continue to take place across our political landscape. In 1992, we experienced the "Year of the Woman" that produced record numbers of women elected to national office. Then, in 1994, we were greeted with the "Year of the Angry Male Voter" that produced a Republican revolution in Congress. The editions that followed those years appeared during various phases of the Clinton scandals, including the second impeachment trial of a U.S. president in American history. Then came the 2000 election, with an outcome that remained in question until December and appeared to be decided by a single Supreme Court justice; the terrorist attacks of September 11, 2001; and the history-bucking 2002 midterm elections that returned control of both houses of Congress to the Republicans.

Little did we realize that, not long after those midterm elections, one of the longest, most expensive, divisive, and impassioned campaigns ever waged for the presidency was about to get underway. The 2004 national elections were dominated by heated discussion of the preemptive war in Iraq and debates about security and terrorism, the economy, and social issues such as same-sex marriage. A closely divided and hotly charged electorate returned George W. Bush to office for a second term with a majority of the popular vote and a solid win in the Electoral College. And, in 2006, concern over conduct of the war and corruption in Congress resulted in House and Senate Democrats winning control of both bodies and the election of the first female Speaker of the House.

It can never be said that American politics is boring. For every edition of this text, something unexpected or extraordinary has occurred, giving question to the phrase "politics as usual." At least on the national level, there appears to be little that is usual. Politics and policy form a vital, fascinating process that affects all our daily lives, and we hope that this text reflects that phenomenon as well as provides you with the tools to understand politics as an evolutionary process where history matters.

Teaching introductory American government presents special challenges and rewards. It is a challenge to introduce a new discipline to students. It is a challenge to jump from topic to topic each week. Above all, it is a challenge to motivate large and disparate groups of students to master new material and, one hopes, to enjoy it in the process. The rewards of success, however, are students who pay more attention to their government, who participate in its workings as more informed citizens, and who better understand the workings of democracy as practiced in the United States.

We have witnessed some of these rewards in the classroom. With this book, we hope to offer our experiences in written form. This brief, lower-priced text should work well in classes that are shorter, where a more inexpensive text is desired, or where instructors want to use a basic text supplemented by diverse readings that amplify specific topics. We believe that students need perspective and motivation; they also need to be exposed to information that will withstand the test of time. Our goal with this text is to transmit just this sort of information while creating and fostering student interest in American politics despite growing national skepticism about government and government officials at all levels. We hope that this brief text will explain the national mood about politics and put it in better context for students, to allow them to understand their role in a changing America.

Approach

WE BELIEVE THAT ONE cannot fully understand the actions, issues, and policy decisions facing the U.S. government, its constituent states, or the people unless these issues are examined from the perspective of how they have evolved over time. Consequently, the full title of this book is *The Essentials of American Government: Continuity and Change*. In its pages, we try to examine how the United States is governed today by looking not just at present structures and behavior but also at the Framers' intentions and how they have been implemented and adapted over the years. For example, we believe that it is critical to an understanding of the role of political parties in the United States to understand the Framers' fears of factionalism, how parties evolved, and when and why realignments in party identification occurred.

To understand all levels of American government, students must appreciate its constitutional underpinnings. Our text includes a full, *annotated* Constitution of the United States and a boxed feature, "The Living Constitution," to ensure that students understand and appreciate the role of the Constitution in American government and their everyday lives. (For more on this, see the "Features" section of this Preface.)

In addition to the constitutional and historical origins of American government, we explore issues that the Framers could never have envisioned, and how the basic institutions of government have changed in responding to these new demands. For instance, no one more than two centuries ago could have foreseen election campaigns in an age when nearly all American homes contain television sets, and the Internet allows instant access to information from across the nation and across the globe. Moreover, citizen demands and expectations routinely force government reforms, making an understanding of the dynamics of change essential for introductory students.

Our overriding concern is that students understand their government as it exists today, so that they may become better citizens and make better choices. Careful updating in every edition to reflect the significant events that affect government and citizens alike is crucial to insuring a book that accurately communicates where the United States is as a nation. We believe that by providing students with information about government, and by explaining why it is important and why their participation counts, students will come to see that politics can be a good thing.

In writing this book, we chose to put the institutions of government (Part II) before political behavior (Part III). Both sections, however, were written independently, making them easy to switch for those who prefer to teach about the actors in government and elections before discussing its institutions.

What's Changed in This Edition?

IN THIS 2008 EDITION of *The Essentials of American Government: Continuity and Change*, we have retained our basic approach to the study of politics as a constantly changing and often unpredictable enterprise. But, we also discuss the dizzying array of important events that have taken place since the preceding edition of the book was published. Most importantly, we include in-depth coverage of the 2006 midterm elections and results. We also discuss the issues that have been the subject of heated debate through the 2004 and 2006 elections and are likely to continue to be debated as we head toward the 2008 presidential election, including the wars in Iraq and Afghanistan, the treatment of those suspected of or accused of terrorism, the federal deficit, and issues such as same-sex marriage. We examine the lobbying and ethics scandals that shook Congress prior to the 2006 elections, as well as government's failed response to Hurricane Katrina, as of November 2006 the most significant disaster to face the United States since the September 11, 2001, terrorist attacks.

CHAPTER CHANGES

Many of these changes and others are reflected in this 2008 Edition. **Chapter 1** now includes a subsection that discusses the importance of religious faith as an element of shared political culture in the United States, along with updated demographic data and an expanded discussion of the aging U.S. population. The ideology section now discusses the functions of ideology and contrasts traditional conservatism with social conservatism.

Chapter 2 includes new coverage of the Iraqi Constitution and how it compares with the U.S. Constitution. **Chapter 3** opens with a new vignette about governmental responses to Hurricane Katrina and includes an updated discussion of judicial devolution and the Roberts Court. **Chapter 4** includes an expanded discussion of freedom of assembly in light of protests related to the Iraq War, immigration policy, and genocide in Darfur, Sudan. Key 2006 Supreme Court rulings related to civil liberties (including *Hamdan* v. *Rumsfeld*) and congressional response to those decisions (including the Military Commissions Act) are also covered. **Chapter 5** has been revised to include coverage of civil rights enforcement at the U.S. Department of Justice, 2006 Supreme Court rulings related to civil rights, and living wage campaigns on college campuses. **Chapter 6** includes complete coverage of the outcome of the 2006 midterm elections and the makeup of the 110th Congress. **Chapter 7** considers the impact of approval ratings on President George W. Bush's second-term policy initiatives. **Chapter 8** begins with a new vignette on avian flu planning. It also reflects second-term Bush administration Cabinet reshuffling, including the resignation of Secretary of Defense Donald Rumsfeld following the 2006 elections. **Chapter 9** offers updates on the Supreme Court's 2005–2006 term, including the addition of Chief Justice John G. Roberts Jr. as well as Justice Samuel A. Alito to the Court. **Chapter 10** features a new vignette regarding the rocky relationship between the media and the Bush administration and a new section discussing the rules governing the media. **Chapter 11** has been updated to reflect the impact of technology and campaign finance reform on party activities. Realignment, critical elections, and secular realignment are now discussed in this chapter, which also includes coverage of lobbying and ethics scandals in the 109th Congress. **Chapter 12** features new data and updated figures on election results, voter turnout, and demographics in the 2006 midterm elections, and includes an updated and expanded campaign finance discussion. **Chapter 13** includes updated coverage of social welfare policies today, including a discussion of the new Medicare Prescription Drug Improvement and Modernization Act and coverage of President George W. Bush's efforts to privatize Social Security. **Chapter 14** reflects recent Bush foreign policy efforts, including developments in the Middle East and Asia. Updated discussions of homeland security efforts, the controversy over the NSA surveillance program, and the impact of reorganization efforts on U.S. intelligence operations are also included.

NEW DESIGN

This edition marks the first time that *Essentials of American Government* has been available with both a full color design and a larger trim size. We hope that the new, colorful, and more open look and feel will engage students and make the text a more accessible and effective study tool.

Features

THE 2008 EDITION has retained the best features and pedagogy from previous editions, enhanced or revised others, and added exciting new ones.

HISTORICAL PERSPECTIVE

Every chapter uses history to serve three purposes: first, to show how institutions and processes have evolved to their present states; second, to provide some of the color that makes information memorable; and third, to provide students with a more thorough appreciation that our government was born amid burning issues of representation and power, issues that continue to smolder today. A richer historical texture helps to explain the present.

COMPARATIVE PERSPECTIVE

Changes in the Middle East, Russia and Eastern Europe, North America, South America, and Asia all remind us of the preeminence of democracy, in theory if not always in fact. As new democratic experiments spring up around the globe (e.g., Iraq), it becomes increasingly important for students to understand the rudiments of presidential versus parliamentary government and of multiparty versus two-party systems. *Global Perspective* boxes, all of which have been substantially revised or written new for this edition, compare issues, politics, and institutions in the United States with those of both industrialized democracies and non-Western countries such as Iraq and North Korea.

ENHANCED PEDAGOGY

We have revised and enhanced many pedagogical features to help students become stronger political thinkers and to echo the book's theme of evolution and change.

Preview and Review To pique students' interest and draw them into each chapter, we begin each chapter with a contemporary vignette. These vignettes deal with current issues of high interest to students and are intended to whet their appetites to read the rest of the chapter. Each vignette is followed by a bridge paragraph linking the vignette with the chapter's topics and by an outline previewing the chapter's major headings. Chapter summaries at the conclusion of each chapter restate the major points made under each of these same major headings.

Key Terms All boldfaced key terms are defined in the margin of the text where the term appears. Key terms are listed at the end of each chapter, with page references for review and study. An end-of-text glossary of the text's key terms is also provided.

Special Features The text is supported and enhanced by a number of boxed features. These features are designed to enhance student understanding of the political processes, institutions, and policies of American government. Features include:

- *American Values/American Voices.* New to this edition, these features examine the shared values that unite American citizens. American political culture, with its emphasis on liberty, equality, and individualism, as well as other values, is the glue that holds Americans together. Differing views of what it means to adhere to these values, however, often create conflict and division—especially in the policy arena. American Values/American Voices boxes are intended to help students understand the passionate beliefs and common concerns that underlie the controversies being debated on Capitol Hill, in the media, and in statehouses and homes across the United States. Topics discussed include U.S. efforts to promote democracy abroad and changes in government policy related to the establishment clause.

- *Annotated Constitution of the United States.* Appearing between chapters 2 and 3, this copy of the Constitution features comprehensive commentary on the meaning and context of the most significant articles, sections, and amendments. These annotations allow students to understand not only the Constitution's language, but also *why* it was fashioned as it was and its continued relevance today. For instance, students learn everything from why Article I is the longest and most detailed portion of the Constitution to why the "full faith and credit" clause, rarely controversial, now becomes so in the context of same-sex marriage. The Constitution was annotated with the significant help of a constitutional expert and dedicated undergraduate teacher, Gregg Ivers, of American University.

- *The Living Constitution.* These boxes, which appear in every chapter, examine the constitutional context of each chapter's topic. Every box excerpts and explains a relevant portion of the Constitution, analyzes what the Framers were responding to when it was written, and examines how it is still relevant today. For instance, chapter 4 includes a box on the Ninth Amendment, a discussion of the impossibility of enumerating every fundamental liberty and right, and the Supreme Court's ruling—nonetheless—in favor of a host of fundamental liberties since 1965.

- *On Campus.* These popular boxes, which appear in most chapters, focus in particular on material that we believe will be of great interest to college students. To that end, this feature examines issues of concern to college campuses, as well as issues, events, and legislation that were initiated on college campuses and that had an impact on the larger arena of American politics. Chapter 5, for example, discusses living wage campaigns on campus.

- *Join the Debate.* To engage students in critical thinking, foster interest in important issues, and help inspire their participation through involvement in decision making, we developed the Join the Debate feature. Heavily revised to remain current and resonant to both instructors and students, this feature introduces provocative issues under debate today and explores those issues by suggesting arguments for and against them. Topics such as chapter 6's minority party rights in Congress and chapter 9's Senate advise and consent are accompanied by supporting questions and selected reading suggestions from the authors. These features are designed to prompt students to examine various arguments in the debate, consider larger context, and take a position on issues that matter in American government today.

- *Global Perspective.* Recognizing that students benefit from understanding the commonalities and differences between the United States and other nations, Global Perspective boxes provide students with a comparative perspective on a range of issues. Some features examine a key topic such as freedom of the press, economic freedom, or American exceptionalism, while others focus on comparing an element of a foreign nation with a corresponding aspect of the United States. Features new to this edition include examinations of the Iraqi Constitution (chapter 2), the Mexican federal system (chapter 3), the Israeli Knesset (chapter 6), and the North Korean executive (chapter 7).

- *Politics Now.* These boxes provide in-depth examinations of contemporary issues, showcasing the book's currency and serving as a counterbalance to the text's thorough treatment of America's origins and history. Chapter 6, for example, discusses the efforts of a group of Muslim congressional staffers to educate members of Congress about their religion, while chapter 9 examines the new Roberts Court and its likely impact on American jurisprudence.

- *Analyzing Visuals.* These boxed features appear in every chapter and ask students to closely examine and assess a variety of different types of images, including photographs, tables, bar graphs, line graphs, and maps. Students are encouraged to analyze and interpret the visual information themselves, using the introductory paragraph and critical thinking questions provided to guide them. An introductory primer, *Analyzing Visuals: A Brief Guide* (see pages xxxii–xxxv), offers a foundation for analyzing and interpreting different kinds of visuals that students will encounter in the text and in their daily lives.

- *Web Explorations.* The end of each chapter contains relevant links to the World Wide Web. Web Explorations encourage students to learn more and think critically about the key concepts in each chapter.

- *MyPoliSciLab Icons.* Throughout the text, students will find icons (see page xxvii for samples) in the text margins that direct them to relevant simulations, visual literacy exercises, and other activities that appear in Longman's online resources, MyPoliSciLab and LongmanParticipate.com 3.0 (see below).

The Ancillary Package

THE ANCILLARY PACKAGE for *Essentials of American Government: Continuity and Change,* 2008 Edition, provides instructors and students with materials that allow them to augment, review, and better understand the materials covered in the textbook. We strive for comprehensiveness and accuracy, while seeking to provide a range of options suited for instructors and students at a variety of institutions.

INSTRUCTOR SUPPLEMENTS FOR QUALIFIED COLLEGE ADOPTERS

Instructor's Manual   (ISBN 0-205-56776-2) Written by Sue Davis of Denison University, this comprehensive manual is designed to help instructors prepare lectures, classroom activities, and assignments. The manual features chapter outlines and summaries, a broad range of teaching suggestions, ideas for student research, and suggestions for discussion that complement text themes..

Test Bank written by author Karen O'Connor of American University   (ISBN 0-205-56774-6) Contains hundreds of multiple choice, true-false, and essay questions along with an answer key. The test bank has been completely rewritten for this edition, and all questions have been written, reviewed, and class tested by Karen O'Connor herself. The test questions offer a range of difficulty from which instructors can choose, and they cover each chapter (including boxed features) comprehensively.

TestGen-EQ Computerized Testing System   (ISBN 0-321-48298-0) This flexible, easy-to-master computerized test bank includes all the test items in the printed test bank. The software allows professors to edit existing questions and to add their own items. Tests can be printed in several different formats and can include features such as graphs and tables. It is available for Windows and Macintosh computers.

Instructor Resource Center (www.ablongman.com/IRC)   A helpful Website where instructors can download supplements including: Instructor's Manuals, Test Banks, TestGens, and PowerPoint® presentations, as well as CourseCompass®, WebCT, and Blackboard materials. Instructors will need to request a password from their sales representative to gain access.

Digital Media Archive CD-ROM   (ISBN 0-205-53156-1) This complete multimedia presentation tool for instructors includes more than 150 maps, graphs, and charts; 100 photos; and 50 video clips—all on one CD-ROM and ready for inclusion in an instructor's online course, PowerPoint® presentations, and websites. It was developed in consultation with Kurt Cline, California State University, Fresno; Martin S. Edwards, Texas Tech University; Scott R. Furlong, University of Wisconsin, Green Bay; James M. Lutz, Indiana University Purdue University, Fort Wayne; and John David Rausch, Jr., West Texas A&M University.

Longman Political Science Video Program   Qualified adopters can peruse our list of videos for the American government classroom. Contact your local Allyn & Bacon/Longman representative for more information.

PowerPoint® Presentation   A lecture-outline presentation to accompany all the chapters of this new edition along with complete graphics from the book. Visit the Instructor Resource Center at **www.ablongman.com/irc** to download the presentations. Contact your local Longman representative to gain access to the site.

Transparencies (ISBN 0-321-48134-8)   Full-color acetates of the figures from all chapters of the book.

STUDENT SUPPLEMENTS FOR QUALIFIED COLLEGE ADOPTERS

Longman's MyPoliSciLab   This state-of-the-art, interactive, online solution for the American government course, fully integrated in the course management system of your choice—CourseCompass®, WebCT, or Blackboard—or as an independent website free of a course management system altogether, is available at no additional charge when bundled with a copy of this text and contains the following features:

- **Assessment.** For each chapter of the text, students will navigate through a comprehensive pre-test, post-test, and a full chapter exam, all fully integrated with an online e-book version of this text so students can assess, review, and improve their understanding of the text chapters.

■ **Interactive Activities.** Developed and revised by a team of more than 15 political science faculty, MyPoliSciLab features more than 100 highly interactive activities, all updated and revised—including comparative activities, visual literacy exercises, interactive timelines, participation exercises, and **more than 30 simulations**—for all of the major topics in the course.

■ **Roundtable Discussion Video Clips.** Added and updated throughout the semester, these 10- to 12-minute video clips consist of three professors discussing important concepts covered in the text. Dozens of key concepts (such as campaign finance reform) and critical questions (such as, "Is Federalism Dead?") are discussed from a wide range of perspectives and viewpoints, providing students with a balanced review of key course material. Each discussion is accompanied by critical thinking prompts, multiple-choice questions, and transcripts for reference.

■ **Debate Video Clips.** Updated throughout the semester and offering lively, challenging debates from two sides of an issue, these 10- to 12-minute clips feature two professors discussing hot-button issues and answering pressing questions such as, "Does the Patriot Act Violate American Civil Liberties?" Each discussion is accompanied by critical thinking prompts, multiple-choice questions, and transcripts for reference.

■ **Student Polling.** Updated weekly with timely, provocative questions, this new feature allows students to participate in nationwide polls on hot topics. Students are asked to vote on questions such as, "Should flag burning be permitted?" Results of the thousands of student responses around the country are immediately displayed.

■ **PoliSci News.** PoliSci News contains an online feed from the New York Times that is updated hourly; an exclusive New York Times database that allows students to browse by subject area or search for a specific topic; and PoliSci News Review, a series of articles selected by a political science professor that recaps the previous week's most important political events and are followed by quizzes and critical thinking questions.

■ **Author's Choice.** With so many incredible activities to assign, the authors of this book have hand selected one or two activities that best complement or amplify each chapter. You have the work done for you in easy-to-use, prepackaged MyPoliSciLab assignments. If you only have time to assign and complete one activity for the chapter, the Author's Choice designation makes it easy!

■ **Author Podcasts.** Throughout the 2007-2008 academic year, podcasts of author lectures will be added to MyPoliSciLab, giving you the opportunity to expose your students to dynamic new voices and offer "guest lecturers" on key topics. Contact your local Longman representative for more information.

■ **Research Navigator™.** The EBSCO ContentSelect Academic Journal Database content is collected from thousands of articles organized by discipline and fully searchable. Articles in popular periodicals such as Newsweek and USA Today are included as well, giving students and professors access to topical content from a variety of sources.

■ **Link Library.** Offers editorially selected "Best of the Web" sites. Libraries are continually scanned and kept up-to-date, providing the most relevant and accurate links for research assignments.

■ **Writing Resources.** Topics include Avoiding Plagiarism, Finding Sources, Using Your Library, Start Writing, Internet Research, and Citing Sources.

■ **Online e-Book.** Matching the exact layout of the printed textbook, the online e-book contains multimedia icons in the margins that launch to exciting resources (e.g., simulations or videos), which expand on key topics students encounter as they read through the text.

■ **Online Administration.** Instructors can easily track student work on the site and monitor students' progress on each activity. The Instructor Gradebook, which includes upgraded functionality to ensure a truly seamless experience for users, provides maximum flexibility allowing instructors to sort by student, activity, or to view the entire class in spreadsheet view.

See the advertisement at the front of this text for more information.

Study Guide (ISBN 0-205-56271-X) Written by John Ben Sutter of Houston Community College. The printed study guide features chapter outlines, key terms, a variety of practice tests, and critical thinking questions to help students learn.

Great Questions in Politics Written by some of the most influential scholars and thinkers in political science, each book in this series examines a major question in American politics, offers a new perspective on our political system, and challenges conventional wisdom and prevailing attitudes.

Package any of the Great Questions in Politics books with this book and receive a 10 percent discount.

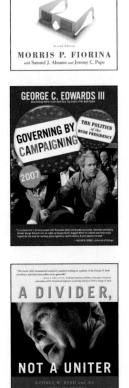

- *Culture War? The Myth of a Polarized America,* Morris. P. Fiorina, Stanford University; Samuel J. Abrams, Harvard University; and Jeremy C. Pope, Stanford University (ISBN 0-321-36606-9) This text combines polling data with a compelling narrative to debunk commonly believed myths about American politics—particularly the claim that Americans are deeply divided in their fundamental political views.

- *Governing by Campaigning: The Politics of the Bush Presidency,* 2007 Edition, George C. Edwards III, Texas A&M University (ISBN 0-205-52962-3) This brief volume, by one of the foremost experts on the presidency, explores how the Bush administration has attempted sweeping changes in public policy—without broad support for doing so—by taking its case to the American public more than any other president in history.

- *A Divider, Not a Uniter: George W. Bush and the American People: The 2006 Election and Beyond,* Gary C. Jacobson, University of California, San Diego (ISBN 0-205-52974-7) This brief, engaging book is rich in data and analyzes the reasons the public is so divided along party lines about George W. Bush.

- *Is Voting for Young People? with Postscript on New Forms of Citizen Engagement,* Martin P. Wattenberg, University of California, Irvine (ISBN 0-205-51807-9) This accessible, provocative, and brief book explores the reasons the young are less and less likely to follow politics and vote in the United States, as well as many other established democracies, and suggests ways of changing that.

- *Seven Sins of American Foreign Policy,* Loch K. Johnson, University of Georgia (ISBN 0-321-41585-X) This brief, accessible book by renowned intelligence and foreign policy expert, Loch Johnson, examines seven major shortcomings—"sins"—in American foreign policy over several administrations that have generated pervasive negative attitudes toward the United States, cost us friendship and support, and impaired our ability to advance our international interests.

- *Congressional Travels: Places, Connections, and Authenticity,* Richard F. Fenno Jr., University of Rochester (ISBN 0-321-47071-0) This book argues that authenticity—knowing what a representative is like in his or her district and looking beyond mere roll-call voting—contributes significantly to understanding the full body of work done by our members of Congress. It further posits, by recounting Fenno's life's work, that the best way to gain a sense of authenticity is to do what Fenno is most famous for—making multiple trips and spending a great deal of time observing representatives at home, with their constituents, in their districts.

Study Site for American Government (www.longmanamericangovernment.com) This online course companion provides a wealth of resources for students and instructors using Longman American government texts. Containing practice tests, flashcards, and Web explorations, the Study Site for American government helps students quickly master the fundamentals, review a subject for understanding, or prepare for an exam.

Research Navigator and Research Navigator Guide Research Navigator is a comprehensive website comprising four exclusive databases of credible and reliable source material for research and for student assignments: EBSCO's ContentSelect Academic Journal Database, the New York Times Search by Subject Archive, the Financial Times Article Archive and Company Financials, "Best of the Web" Link Library. The site also includes an extensive help section. The Research Navigator Guide provides your students with access to the Research Navigator website and includes reference material and hints about conducting online research. Available at no additional charge to qualified college adopters when packaged with the text.

Voices of Dissent: Critical Readings in American Politics, **Seventh Edition** (ISBN 0-205-56001-6) Edited by William F. Grover, St. Michael's College, and Joseph G. Peschek, Hamline University, this collection of critical essays goes beyond the debate between mainstream liberalism and conservatism to fundamentally challenge the status quo. Available at a discount when ordered packaged with the text.

You Decide! Current Debates in American Politics, **2007 Edition** (ISBN: 0-321-43016-6) Edited by John T. Rourke, University of Connecticut, this exciting debate-style reader is updated annually and examines provocative issues in American politics today. The topics have been selected for their currency, importance, and student interest, and the pieces that argue various sides of a given issue come from recent journals, congressional hearings, think tanks, and periodicals.

American Government: Readings and Cases, **Seventeenth Edition** (ISBN: 0-321-47314-0) Edited by Peter Woll, Brandeis University, this longtime best-selling reader provides a strong, balanced blend of classic readings and cases that illustrate and amplify important concepts in American government, alongside extremely current selections drawn from today's issues and literature. Available at a discount when ordered packaged with this text.

Ten Things That Every American Government Student Should Read (ISBN 0-205-28969-X) We asked American government instructors across the country to vote for 10 things beyond the text that they believe every student should read and put them in this brief and useful reader edited by Karen O'Connor of the American University. Available at no additional charge when ordered packaged with the text.

Choices: An American Government Database Reader This customizable reader allows instructors to choose from a database of more than 300 readings to create a reader that exactly matches their course needs. Go to:

www.pearsoncustom.com/database/choices.html for more information.

Newsweek **Magazine Discount Subscription**   Students receive 12 issues of Newsweek at more than 80 percent off the regular price. An excellent way for students to keep up with current events.

New York Times **Discount Subscription**   A 10-week subscription for only $20! Contact your local Allyn & Bacon/Longman representative for more information.

Penguin-Longman Value Bundles Longman offers 25 Penguin Putnam titles at more than a 60 percent discount when packaged with any Longman text. A totally unique offer and a wonderful way to enhance students' understanding of concepts in American government. Please go to www.ablongman.com/penguin for more information.

Writing in Political Science, **Third Edition** (ISBN 0-321-21735-7) Written by Diane Schmidt, California State University-Chico, this guide takes students step-by-step through all aspects of writing in political science. Available at a discount when ordered packaged with any Longman textbook.

LONGMAN STATE POLITICS SERIES

Texas, **Fourth Edition** (ISBN 0-321-38459-8) Written by Debra St. John, this is a 90-page primer on state and local government and political issues in Texas. Available at no additional cost when shrink-wrapped with the text.

Annotated 1876 Texas Constitution (ISBN 0-321-35533-4) Annotated by Stefan D. Haag, Austin Community College, this supplement offers the full 1876 Texas

Constitution integrated with a detailed primer examining the meaning and context of the Constitution's most significant language. This ancillary helps give students a deep understanding of what the 1876 Texas Constitution says, why it included the language it did, and what role this seminal document plays in the lives of Texans today.

California, **Fifth Edition** (ISBN 0-321-42764-5) Written by Barbara Stone, this is a 70-page primer on state and local government and political issues in California. Available at no additional cost when shrink-wrapped with the text.

Florida (ISBN 0-321-42763-7) Written by George Gonzalez, this is a 50-page primer on state and local government and political issues in Florida. Available at no additional cost when shrink-wrapped with the text.

Georgia (ISBN 0-321-42765-3) Written by Said L. Sewell and F. Carl Walton, this is a 70-page primer on state and local government and political issues in Georgia. Available at no additional cost when shrink-wrapped with the text.

Acknowledgments

Karen O'Connor thanks the thousands of students in her American Government courses at Emory and American University who, over the years, have pushed her to learn more about American government and to have fun in the process. She especially thanks her American University colleagues who offered books and suggestions for this most recent revision—especially David Lublin. Her former professor and longtime friend and co-author, Nancy E. McGlen, has offered support for more than two decades. Her former students, too, have contributed in various ways to this project, especially John R. Hermann, Paul Fabrizio, Bernadette Nye, Sue Davis, Laura van Assendelft, and Sarah E. Brewer.

For the last two editions of the book, Alixandra B. Yanus of the University of North Carolina, Chapel Hill, has offered invaluable assistance and unflagging support. Her fresh perspectives on politics and ideas about things of interest to students, as well as her keen eye for the typo, her research abilities, and her unbelievably hard work, have made this a much better book.

Larry J. Sabato would like to acknowledge his students at the University of Virginia and the many student interns at the UVA Center for Politics who have offered valuable suggestions and thoughtful feedback, as well as Howard Ernst, associate professor of political science at the United States Naval Academy; Zach Courser, a former University of Virginia graduate student who is now teaching at Claremont McKenna College; and Drew Kurlowski, a Ph.D. candidate at the University of Virginia.

Particular thanks from both of us go to Christopher Borick, who helped with updates to chapter 13 (Social and Economic Policy), and Kiki Caruson of the University of South Florida, who helped with updates to chapter 14 (Foreign and Defense Policy). We also thank Brian Bearry of the University of Texas at Dallas for his help with many of the Join the Debate and Global Perspective features.

In the now many years we have been writing and rewriting this book, we have been blessed to have been helped by many people at Macmillan, Allyn & Bacon, and now Longman. Eric Stano has been a fantastic editor as well as fun to work with. Our new development editor, Melissa Mashburn, has been a stern taskmaster with a political junkie's eye for extensive updating. We also thank our production editor at Electronic Publishing Services, Inc., Lake Lloyd, and marketing manager, Elizabeth Fogarty, as well as the Longman sales force. In the end, we hope that all of these talented people see how much their work and support have helped us to write a better book.

Many of our peers reviewed past editions of the book and earned our gratitude in the process:

Danny Adkinson, *Oklahoma State University*
Weston H. Agor, *University of Texas– El Paso*

James Anderson, *Texas A&M University*
Vincent A. Auger, *Western Illinois University*

Judith Baer, *Texas A&M University*
Ruth Bamberger, *Drury College*
Christine Barbour, *Indiana University*
Jon Bond, *Texas A&M University*

Stephen A. Borrelli, *University of Alabama*

Ann Bowman, *University of South Carolina*

Gary Brown, *Montgomery College*

John Francis Burke, *University of Houston–Downtown*

Gregory A. Caldeira, *Ohio State University*

David E. Camacho, *Northern Arizona University*

David Cingranelli, *SUNY–Binghamton*

Steve Chan, *University of Colorado*

Richard Christofferson Sr., *University of Wisconsin–Stevens Point*

Myles L. Clowers, *San Diego City College*

Clarke E. Cochran, *Texas Tech University*

Anne N. Costain, *University of Colorado*

Cary Covington, *University of Iowa*

Lane Crothers, *Illinois State University*

Abraham L. Davis, *Morehouse College*

Holly Dershem-Bruce, *Dawson Community College*

Robert DiClerico, *West Virginia University*

Khalil Dokhanchi, *University of Wisconsin–Superior*

John Domino, *Sam Houston State University*

Craig F. Emmert, *Texas Tech University*

Alan S. Engel, *Miami University*

Frank B. Feigert, *University of North Texas*

Evelyn C. Fink, *University of Nebraska–Lincoln*

John Fobanjong, *University of Massachusetts*

Sean D. Foreman, *Union Institute and University*

Scott R. Furlong, *University of Wisconsin–Green Bay*

Christopher P. Gilbert, *Gustavus Adolphus College*

James D. Gleason, *Victoria College*

Sheldon Goldman, *University of Massachusetts–Amherst*

Doris Graber, *University of Illinois at Chicago*

Roger W. Green, *University of North Dakota*

Charles Hadley, *University of New Orleans*

William K. Hall, *Bradley University*

Robert L. Hardgrave Jr., *University of Texas–Austin*

Chip Hauss, *George Mason University/ University of Reading*

Stacia L. Haynie, *Louisiana State University*

John R. Hermann, *Trinity University*

Marjorie Randon Hershey, *Indiana University*

Cornell Hooton, *Emory University*

Johanna Hume, *Alvin Community College*

Jon Hurwitz, *University of Pittsburgh*

Joseph Ignagni, *University of Texas–Arlington*

Dennis Judd, *University of Missouri–St. Louis*

Carol J. Kamper, *Rochester Community College*

Kenneth Kennedy, *College of San Mateo*

Donald F. Kettl, *University of Wisconsin*

John Kincaid, *University of North Texas*

Jonathan E. Kranz, *John Jay College of Criminal Justice*

Mark Landis, *Hofstra University*

Sue Lee, *North Lake College*

Brad Lockerbie, *University of Georgia*

Larry Martinez, *California State University–Long Beach*

Lyn Mather, *Dartmouth College*

Steve J. Mazurana, *University of Northern Colorado*

Clifton McCleskey, *University of Virginia*

William P. McLauchlan, *Purdue University*

Joseph Nogee, *University of Houston*

Mary Alice Nye, *University of North Texas*

John O'Callaghan, *Suffolk University*

Bruce Oppenheimer, *Vanderbilt University*

William C. Overton, *Boise State University*

Richard Pacelle, *University of Missouri–St. Louis*

Marian Lief Palley, *University of Delaware*

Richard M. Pious, *Barnard College*

David H. Provost, *California State University–Fresno*

Lawrence J. Redlinger, *University of Texas–Dallas*

Leroy N. Riescelbach, *Indiana University*

David Robertson, *Public Policy Research Centers, University of Missouri–St. Louis*

David Robinson, *University of Houston–Downtown*

David W. Rohde, *Duke University*

Frank Rourke, *Johns Hopkins University*

Donald Roy, *Ferris State University*

Ronald Rubin, *City University of New York, Borough of Manhattan Community College*

Bonita A. Sessing-Matcha, *Hudson Valley Community College*

Jocelyn D. Shadforth, *North Central College*

Daniel M. Shea, *University of Akron*

Mark Silverstein, *Boston University*

James R. Simmons, *University of Wisconsin–Oshkosh*

Elliot E. Slotnick, *Ohio State University*

Daniel A. Smith, *University of Denver*

Frank J. Sorauf, *University of Minnesota*

Gerald Stanglin, *Cedar Valley College*

Richard J. Timpone, *SUNY–Stony Brook*

Shirley Anne Warshaw, *Gettysburg College*

James A. White, *Concord College*

Martin Wiseman, *Mississippi State University*

Finally, we'd also like to thank our peers who reviewed and aided in the development of the current edition:

Sean Anderson, *Idaho State University*

Stephen Bennett, *University of Southern Indiana*

Sean Foreman, *Barry University*

Madhavi McCall, *San Diego State University*

Analyzing Visuals: A Brief Guide

The information age requires a new, more expansive definition of literacy. Visual literacy—the ability to analyze, interpret, synthesize, and apply visual information—is essential in today's world. We receive much information from the written and spoken word, but much also comes from visual forms. We are used to thinking about reading written texts critically—for example, reading a textbook carefully for information, sometimes highlighting or underlining as we go along—but we do not always think about "reading" visuals in this way. We should, for images and informational graphics can tell us a lot if we read and consider them carefully. In order to emphasize these skills, this edition of *American Government: Continuity and Change* contains an *Analyzing Visuals* feature in each chapter. The features are intended to prompt you to think about the images and informational graphics you will encounter throughout this text, as well as those you see every day in the newspaper, in magazines, on the Web, on television, and in books. We provide critical thinking questions to assist you in learning how to analyze visuals. Though we focus on one visual in each chapter, we encourage you to examine carefully and ask similar questions of *all* the visuals in this text, and those you encounter elsewhere in your study of and participation in American government.

We look at several types of visuals in the chapters: tables, graphs and charts, maps, news photographs, and political cartoons. This brief guide provides some information about these types of visuals and offers a few questions to guide your analysis of each type.

Tables

Tables are the least "visual" of the visuals we explore. Tables consist of textual information and/or numerical data arranged in tabular form, in columns and rows. Tables are frequently used when exact information is required and when orderly arrangement is necessary to locate and, in many cases, to compare the information.

TABLE 10.8 THE SUPREME COURT AND THE AMERICAN PUBLIC			
In recent years, the Court's rulings have agreed with or diverged from public opinion on various questions, such as:			
Issue	*Case*	*Court Decision*	*Public Opinion*
Should homosexual relations between consenting adults be legal?	*Lawrence* v. *Texas* (2003)	Yes	Maybe (50%)
Should members of Congress be subject to term limits?	*U.S. Term Limits* v. *Thornton* (1995)	No	Yes (77% favor)
Is affirmative action constitutional?	*Grutter* v. *Bollinger* (2003) *Gratz* v. *Bollinger* (2003)	Yes	Yes (64%)
Before getting an abortion, whose consent should a teenager be required to gain?	*Williams* v. *Zbaraz* (1980)	One parent	Both parents (38%) One parent (37%) Neither parent (22%)
Is the death penalty constitutional?	*Gregg* v. *Georgia* (1976)	Yes	Yes (72% favor)
Source: Table compiled from Lexis-Nexis RPOLL.			

For example, a table comparing Supreme Court decisions to public opinion poll information makes comparisons of the data visually accessible.

Here are a few questions to guide your analysis:

- What is the purpose of the table? What information does it show? There is usually a title that offers a sense of the table's purpose.

- What information is provided in the column headings (provided in the top row)? How are the rows labeled?

- Is there a time period indicated, such as January to June 2007? Or, are the data as of a specific date, such as June 30, 2007?

- If the table shows numerical data, what do these data represent? In what units? Dollars a special interest lobby provides to a political party? Percentages of men and women responding in a particular way to a poll question about the president's performance? Estimated life expectancy in years?

- What is the source of the information presented in the table?

Charts and Graphs

Charts and graphs depict numerical data in visual forms. The most common kinds of graphs plot data in two dimensions along horizontal and vertical axes. Examples that you will encounter throughout this text are line graphs, pie charts, and bar graphs. These kinds of visuals emphasize data relationships: at a particular point in time, at regular intervals over a fixed period of time, or, sometimes, as parts of a whole. Line graphs show a progression, usually over time (as in Social Security Costs and Revenues, 1970–2080). Pie charts (such as the distribution of federal civilian employment) demonstrate how a whole (total federal civilian employment) is divided into its parts (employees in each branch). Bar graphs compare values across categories, showing how proportions are related to each other (as in the numbers of women and minorities in Congress). Bar graphs can present data either horizontally or vertically.

Here are a few questions to guide your analysis:

- What is the purpose of the chart or graph? What information does it provide? Or, what is being measured? There is usually a title that indicates the subject and purpose of the figure.

- Is there a time period shown, such as January to June 2007? Or, are the data as of a specific date, such as June 30, 2007? Are the data shown at multiple intervals over a fixed period, or at one particular point in time?

- What do the units represent? Dollars a candidate spends on a campaign? Number of voters versus number of nonvoters in Texas? If there are two or more sets of figures, what are the relationships among them?

- What is the source? Is it government information? Private polling information? A newspaper? A private organization? A corporation? An individual?

- Is the type of chart or graph appropriate for the information that is provided? For example, a line graph assumes a smooth progression from one data point to the next. Is that assumption valid for the data shown?

- Is there distortion in the visual representation of the information? Are the intervals equal? Does the area shown distort the actual amount or the proportion?

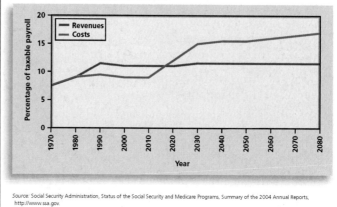

FIGURE 17.2 SOCIAL SECURITY COSTS AND REVENUES, 1970–2080 (AS PERCENTAGE OF TAXABLE PAYROLL)

Source: Social Security Administration, *Status of the Social Security and Medicare Programs, Summary of the 2004 Annual Reports*, http://www.ssa.gov.

FIGURE 9.1 DISTRIBUTION OF FEDERAL CIVILIAN EMPLOYMENT, 2004

Total Employment: 2,713,200

- Executive: 1,881,700 (69.3%)
- U.S. Postal Service: 767,600 (28.3%)
- Judicial: 33,800 (1.2%)
- Legislative: 30,000 (1.1%)

Source: Office of Personnel Management, *2005 Fact Book.*

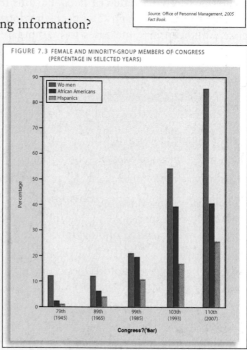

FIGURE 7.3 FEMALE AND MINORITY-GROUP MEMBERS OF CONGRESS (PERCENTAGE IN SELECTED YEARS)

Maps

Maps—of the United States, of particular regions, or of the world—are frequently used in political analysis to illustrate demographic, social, economic, and political issues and trends.

Here are a few questions to guide your analysis:

- Is there a title that identifies the purpose or subject of the map?

- What does the map key/legend show? What are the factors that the map is analyzing?

- What is the region being shown?

- What source is given for the map?

- Maps usually depict a specific point in time. What is the point in time being shown on the map?

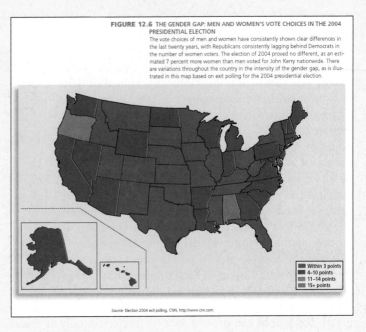

FIGURE 12.6 THE GENDER GAP: MEN AND WOMEN'S VOTE CHOICES IN THE 2004 PRESIDENTIAL ELECTION

The vote choices of men and women have consistently shown clear differences in the last twenty years, with Republicans consistently lagging behind Democrats in the number of women voters. The election of 2004 proved no different, as an estimated 7 percent more women than men voted for John Kerry nationwide. There are variations throughout the country in the intensity of the gender gap, as is illustrated in this map based on exit polling for the 2004 presidential election.

Within 3 points
4–10 points
11–14 points
15+ points

Source: Election 2004 exit polling, CNN, http://www.cnn.com.

News Photographs

If a picture is worth a thousand words, it is no wonder that our newspapers, magazines, and television news broadcasts rely on photographs as well as words to report and analyze the news. Photos can have a dramatic—and often immediate—impact on politics and government. Think about some photos that have political significance. For example, do you remember photos from the September 11, 2001, terrorist attack on the World Trade Center? Visual images usually evoke a stronger emotional response from people than do written descriptions. For this reason, individuals and organizations have learned to use photographs as a means to document events, make arguments, offer evidence, and even in some cases to manipulate the viewer into having a particular response.

Here are a few questions to guide your analysis:

- When was the photograph taken? (If there is no date given for the photograph in its credit line or caption, you may be able to approximate the date according to the people or events depicted in the photo. If the photograph appears in a newspaper, you can usually assume that the shot is fairly current with publication.)

- What is the subject of the photograph?

- Why was the photo taken? What appears to be the purpose of the photograph?

- Is it spontaneous or posed? Did the subject know he or she was being photographed?

- Who was responsible for the photo? (An individual, an agency, or organization?) Can you discern the photographer's attitude toward the subject?

- Is there a caption? If so, what kind of information does it provide? Does it identify the subject of the photo? Does it provide an interpretation of the subject?

AP Photo/J. Scott Applewhite

Political Cartoons

Political cartoons have a long history in America. Some of the most interesting commentary on American politics takes place in the form of political cartoons, which usually exaggerate physical and other qualities of the persons depicted and often rely on a kind of visual shorthand to announce the subject or set the scene—visual cues, clichés, or stereotypes that are instantly recognizable. For example, a greedy corporate executive might be depicted as an individual in professional clothing with paper currency sticking out of his or her pockets. In another cartoon, powdered wigs and quill pens might signal a historical setting. The cartoonist's goal is to comment on and/or criticize political figures, policies, or events. The cartoonist uses several techniques to accomplish this goal, including exaggeration, irony, and juxtaposition. For example, the cartoonist may point out how the results of governmental policies are the opposite of their intended effects (irony). In other cartoons, two people, ideas, or events that don't belong together may be joined to make a point (juxtaposition). Because cartoons comment on political situations and events, you generally need some knowledge of current events to interpret political cartoons.

Here are a few questions to guide your analysis:

- Study the cartoon element by element. Political cartoons are often complex. If the cartoon is in strip form, you also need to think about the relationship of the frames in sequence.

- What labels appear on objects or people in the cartoon? Cartoonists will often label some of the elements. For example, a building with columns might be labeled "U.S. Supreme Court." Or, an individual might be labeled "senator" or "Republican."

- Is there a caption or title to the cartoon? If so, what does it contribute to the meaning or impact of the cartoon?

- Can you identify any of the people shown? Presidents, well-known members of Congress, and world leaders are often shown with specific characteristics that help to identify them. Jimmy Carter was often shown with an exaggerated, toothy smile. George W. Bush is often shown with large ears, small eyes, and bushy eyebrows—sometimes with a "W" or a "43" label.

- Can you identify the event being depicted? Historical events, such as the American Revolution, or contemporary events, such as the 2004 presidential election, are often the subject matter for cartoons.

- What are the elements of the cartoon? Objects often represent ideas or events. For example, a donkey is often used to depict the Democratic Party. Or, an eagle is used to represent the United States.

- How are the characters interacting? What do the speech bubbles contribute to the cartoon?

- What is the overall message of the cartoon? Can you determine what the cartoonist's position is on the subject?

The Essentials
of American
GOVERNMENT

THE POLITICAL LANDSCAPE

1

WE THE PEOPLE OF THE UNITED STATES, in Order to form a more perfect Union, establish Justice, insure domestic Tranquility, provide for the common defence, promote the general Welfare, and secure the Blessings of Liberty to ourselves and our Posterity, do ordain and establish this Constitution for the United States of America.

THESE ARE THE WORDS that begin the Preamble to the United States Constitution. Written in 1787 by a group of men we today refer to as the Framers, this document has guided our nation, its government, its politics, its institutions, and its inhabitants for over 200 years.

When the Constitution was written, the phrases "We the People" and "ourselves" meant something very different from what they do today. After all, voting largely was limited to property-owning white males. Indians, slaves, and women could not vote. Today, through the expansion of the right to vote, the phrase "the People" encompasses men and women of all races, ethnic origins, and social and economic statuses—a variety of peoples and interests. The Framers could not have imagined the range of people today who are eligible to vote.

In the goals it outlines, the Preamble to the Constitution describes what the people of the United States can expect from their government. Still, some citizens question how well the U.S. government can deliver on the goals set out in the Preamble. Few Americans today classify the union as "perfect"; many feel excluded from "Justice" and the "Blessings of Liberty," and even our leaders do not believe that our domestic situation is particularly tranquil, as evidenced by the creation of the Department of Homeland Security and the appointment of a national intelligence director. Furthermore, recent poll results and economic statistics indicate that many Americans believe their general welfare is not well promoted by their government. Others simply do not care much at all about government. Many believe that they have no influence in its decision making, or they do not see any positive benefits from it in their lives. Yet, ironically, in times of emergency—be it a terrorist attack or the devastation of a hurricane or earthquake—many people immediately look to their government for help.

If there has been one constant in the life of the United States, it is change. The Framers would be astonished to see the current forms and functions of the institutions they so carefully outlined in the Constitution, as well as the number of additional political institutions that have arisen to support and fuel the functioning of the national government. The Framers also would be amazed at the array of services and programs the government—especially the national government—provides. They further would be surprised to see how the physical boundaries and the composition of the population have changed over the past 200 plus years. And, they might well wonder, "How did we get here?"

It is part of the American creed that each generation should hand down to the next not only a better America, but an improved economic, educational, and social status. In general, Americans long have been optimistic about our nation, its institutions, and its future. Thomas Jefferson saw the United States as the world's "best hope"; Abraham Lincoln echoed these sentiments when he called it the "last, best hope on earth."[1] But, while most Americans' lives are better than their parents', in the aftermath of natural disasters such as Hurricane Katrina, and with continuing violence in Iraq, many Americans are uncertain about what the future holds and concerned about the direction of the nation—a fact that was underscored by the outcome of the 2006 congressional elections.

IN THIS TEXT, WE PRESENT you with the tools that you need to understand how our political system has evolved and to prepare you to understand the changes that are yet to come. If you approach the study of American government and politics with an open mind, it should help you become a better citizen. We hope that you learn to ask questions, to understand how various issues have come to be important, and to see why a particular law was enacted and how it was implemented. With such understanding, we further hope that you will learn not to accept at face value everything you see on the television news, hear on the radio, or read in the newspaper and on the Internet, especially in the blogosphere. Work to understand your government, and use your vote and other forms of participation to help ensure that your government works for you.

We recognize that the discourse of politics has changed dramatically in the last few years, and that many Americans—especially the young—are turned off by politics, especially at the national level. We also believe that a thorough understanding of the workings of government will allow you to question and think about the system—the good parts and the bad—and decide for yourself the advantages and disadvantages of possible changes and reforms. Equipped with such an understanding, we hope you will become better informed and more active participants in the political process.

Every long journey begins with a single step. In this chapter, we will discuss the function and structure of government: what it is and why we need it. After looking at the origins of American government, we will explore American political culture and the characteristics of American democracy, and the changing characteristics of the American people. We will also discuss the political ideologies of the American public and its current attitudes toward American government and toward the role that government plays in people's lives.

Government: What It Is and Why We Need It

THROUGHOUT HISTORY, ALL SORTS OF SOCIETIES have organized themselves into a variety of governments, small and large, simple and complex, democratic and nondemocratic, elected and unelected. **Governments** are the vehicles through which policies are made and affairs of state are conducted. In fact, the term "government" is derived from the Greek for "to pilot a ship," which is appropriate, since we expect governments to guide "the ship of state." As we explore throughout this text, however, governments are often a result of trial and error, experiment, compromise, and sometimes bloodshed.

Unlike schools, banks, or corporations, the actions of government are binding on all of its citizens. **Citizens,** by law, are members of the political community who by nature of being born in a particular nation or having become a naturalized citizen are entitled to all of the freedoms guaranteed by the government. In exchange for these freedoms, citizens must obey the government, its laws, and its constitution. Citizens also are expected to support their governments through exercising their right to vote, serving on juries, paying taxes due, and, if they are eligible, signing themselves up for military service.

A variety of external forces such as the media, political parties, and interest groups influence the day-to-day workings of governments. Thus, we study governments in the context of **politics,** the study of what has been called "who gets what, when, and how," or more simply, the process of how policy decisions get made. All governments share to greater or lesser degrees the need to provide certain key functions, but to whom they provide these benefits, which benefits they provide, when they provide them, and how they are provided vary tremendously across as well as within nations.

FUNCTIONS OF GOVERNMENT

The Framers of the U.S. Constitution clearly recognized the need for a new government. As our opening vignette underscores, in attempting "to form a more perfect Union," the Framers set out several key functions of government that continue to be relevant today. As discussed below, several of the Framers' ideas centered on their belief that the major function of government was creating mechanisms to allow individuals to solve conflicts in an orderly and peaceful manner.

Establishing Justice One of the first things expected from governments is a system of laws that allows individuals to abide by a common set of principles. Societies adhering to what is called the rule of law allow for the rational dispensing of justice by acknowledged legal authorities. Thus, today, the Bill of Rights entitles people to a trial by jury, to know what the charges against them are, and to be tried in a courtroom presided over by an impartial judge. The U.S. Constitution created a federal judicial system to dispense justice, but the Bill of Rights specified a host of rights guaranteed to all citizens in an effort to establish justice.

Ensuring Domestic Tranquility As we will discuss throughout this text, the role of government in ensuring domestic tranquility is a subject of much debate. Following the terrorist attacks of September 11, 2001, for example, the U.S. government, as well as states and local governments, took extraordinary measures to contain the threat of terrorism from abroad as well as within the United States. Moreover, local governments have police forces, the states have national guards, and the federal government can call on the military to respond to threats against national security.

Providing for the Common Defense The U.S. Constitution calls for the president to be the commander in chief of the armed forces, and the Congress was given the authority to raise an army. The Framers recognized that one of the major purposes of government was to provide for the defense of its citizens, who alone had no ability to protect themselves from other governments. As highlighted in Figure 1.1, the defense budget is a considerable proportion of all federal outlays.

Promoting the General Welfare When the Framers added "promoting the general welfare" to their list of key government functions, they never envisioned how the

government
The formal vehicles through which policies are made and affairs of state are conducted.

citizen
Member of the political community to whom certain rights and obligations are attached.

politics
The study of who gets what, when, and how—or how policy decisions are made.

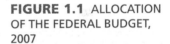

FIGURE 1.1 ALLOCATION OF THE FEDERAL BUDGET, 2007

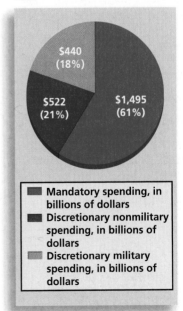

- ■ Mandatory spending, in billions of dollars
- ■ Discretionary nonmilitary spending, in billions of dollars
- ■ Discretionary military spending, in billions of dollars

Source: Fiscal Year 2007 Budget, http://www.whitehouse.gov.

Photo courtesy: David Furst/Pool/epa/Corbis

■ Former Iraqi President Saddam Hussein ruled Iraq as a totalitarian state. Here in court, Hussein objects to the lengthy list of charges against him. In November of 2006, he was convicted by an Iraqi tribunal of more than 2,500 crimes against humanity and sentenced to death by hanging.

monarchy
A form of government in which power is vested in hereditary kings and queens who govern in the interests of all.

totalitarianism
A form of government in which power resides in a leader who rules according to self-interest and without regard for individual rights and liberties.

oligarchy
A form of government in which the right to participate is conditioned on the possession of wealth, social status, military position, or achievement.

democracy
A system of government that gives power to the people, whether directly or through their elected representatives.

involvement of the government at all levels would expand so tremendously. In fact, promoting the general welfare was more of an ideal than a mandate for government. Over time, however, our notions of what the government should do have expanded along with the size of government. As we discuss throughout this text, however, there is no universal agreement on the scope of what governments should do.

Securing the Blessings of Liberty   A well-functioning government that enjoys the support of its citizenry is one of the best ways to secure the blessings of liberty for its people. In a free society, citizens enjoy a wide range of liberties and freedoms and feel free to prosper. They are free to criticize the government as well as to petition it when they disagree with its policies or have a grievance.

Taken together, these principal functions of government permeate our lives. Whether it is your ability to obtain a low-interest student loan, buy a formerly prescription-only drug over the counter, or drive a car at a particular age, government has played a major role. Similarly, without government-sponsored research, we would not have cellular telephones or the Internet.

TYPES OF GOVERNMENT

As early as Plato and Aristotle, theorists have tried to categorize governments by who participates, who governs, and how much authority those who govern enjoy. As revealed in Table 1.1, a **monarchy,** the type of government explicitly rejected by the Framers, is defined by the rule of one in the interest of all of his or her subjects. The Framers also rejected adopting an aristocracy: government by the few in the service of the many.

The least appealing of Aristotle's classifications of government is the **totalitarian** form, which he classified as rule by tyranny. Tyrants rule their countries in order to benefit themselves. In tyrannical or totalitarian systems, the leaders exercise unlimited power, and individuals have no personal rights or liberties. Generally, these systems tend to be ruled in the name of a particular religion or orthodoxy, an ideology, or a personality cult organized around the supreme leader.

Another unappealing form of government, an **oligarchy,** occurs when a few people rule in their own interest. In an oligarchy, participation in government is conditioned on the possession of wealth, social status, military position, or achievement.

A **democracy,** from the Greek words *demos* (the people) and *kratia* (power or authority), is a system of government that gives power to the people either directly or through their elected representatives Aristotle called rule of the many for the benefit of all citizens a "polity" and referred to rule of the many to benefit themselves as a "democracy." Ironically, Aristotle was quite troubled by the idea of democracy, although he believed it better than tyranny or oligarchy. He strongly believed that the collective judgment of the many was preferable to that of a few.

The majority of governments worldwide are democracies to one extent or another. In most democracies, contrary to Aristotle's fears, the "many"—or in the case of the United States and as noted in our chapter opener, "the People"—are the ruling power, albeit through their elected leaders.

TABLE 1.1	ARISTOTLE'S CLASSIFICATIONS OF GOVERNMENT		
		In Whose Interests?	
		Public	Self
Rule by:	One	Monarchy	Tyranny
	The few	Aristocracy	Oligarchy
	The many	Polity	Democracy

Source: Aristotle, *Politics* 3, 7.

The Origins of American Government: Where Did the Ideas Come From?

THE CURRENT AMERICAN POLITICAL SYSTEM did not spring into being overnight. It is the result of philosophy, trial and error, and even luck. To begin our examination of why we have the type of government we have today, we will look at the theories of government that influenced the Framers who drafted the Constitution and created the United States of America.

THE REFORMATION AND THE ENLIGHTENMENT: QUESTIONING THE DIVINE RIGHT OF KINGS

In the third century, as the Roman Empire began to fall, kings throughout Europe began to rule their countries absolutely, claiming their right to govern came directly from God. Thus, since it was thought to be God's will that a particular monarch ruled a country, it was assumed that the people in that country had no right to question their monarch's authority or agitate for a voice in their government's operation.

The intellectual and religious developments of the Reformation and Enlightenment periods of the sixteenth and seventeenth centuries encouraged people to seek alternatives to absolute monarchies and to ponder new methods of governance. In the late sixteenth century, radical Protestants split from the Church of England (which was created by King Henry VIII when the Roman Catholic Church forbade him to divorce and remarry). These Protestants or Puritans believed in their ability to speak one on one to God and established self-governing congregations. They were persecuted for their religious beliefs by the English monarchy. The Pilgrims were the first group of these Protestants to flee religious persecution and settle in America. There they established self-governing congregations and were responsible for the first widespread appearance of self-government in the American colonies. The Mayflower Compact, the document setting up the new government, was deemed sufficiently important to be written while the Pilgrims were still at sea. It took the form of a social contract, or agreement between the people and their government signifying their consent to be governed.

VIDEO ROUNDTABLE
Self-Government

HOBBES, LOCKE, AND A SOCIAL CONTRACT THEORY OF GOVERNMENT

Two English theorists of the seventeenth century, Thomas Hobbes (1588–1679) and John Locke (1632–1704), built on conventional notions about the role of government and the relationship of the government to the people in proposing a **social contract theory** of government. They argued that all individuals were free and equal by natural right. This freedom, in turn, required that all men and women give their consent to be governed.

In Hobbes's *Leviathan* (1651), he argued pessimistically that humanity's natural state was war. Government, Hobbes theorized, particularly a monarchy, was necessary to restrain humanity's bestial tendencies because life without government was but a "state of nature." Without written, enforceable rules, people would live like animals—foraging for food, stealing, and killing when necessary. To escape the horrors of the natural state and to protect their lives, Hobbes argued, people must give up certain rights to government. Without government, Hobbes warned, life would basically be "solitary, poor, nasty, brutish, and short"—a constant struggle to survive against the evil of others. For these reasons, governments had to intrude on people's rights and liberties to better control society and to provide the necessary safeguards for property.

social contract theory
The belief that people are free and equal by God-given right and that this in turn requires that all people give their consent to be governed; espoused by John Locke and influential in the writing of the Declaration of Independence.

Global Perspective

AMERICAN UNIQUENESS IN THE WORLD: ARE WE NUMBER ONE?

Is the United States unique—or is it merely ordinary? Most Americans consider this question at some point in their lives as they ponder the meaning and significance of their citizenship and identity. After all, if the United States is ordinary, then by implication Americans are probably ordinary, too. Most Americans, not satisfied with this answer, prefer to think of their country as unique.

In fact, American uniqueness—or exceptionalism—has been a pervasive theme in American political rhetoric since before the founding. Americans in the nineteenth century routinely described the nation as a "City on a Hill"—a reference to a passage in the New Testament in which Jesus urges his followers to be an example for the rest of the world. U.S. foreign policy has for many years been guided by the idea that America is "bound to lead"—in the dual sense that America's leadership is both an obligation it owes to the world and an inevitable role, given the nation's size, wealth, and power.

How does the United States compare to the rest of the world in key areas, and what do these comparisons tell us about America's role in the world? The United States is one of the top ten countries with regard to land mass, population, gross domestic product (GDP), and GDP per capita. Surprisingly given the tremendous amount of wealth, technology, and natural resources at the United States' disposal, the health and well-being of the American people in many respects are merely average. As of 2006, for example, life expectancy at birth is lower in the United States than in more than forty other nations, and the United States has a higher unemployment rate than forty-eight other nations. It seems odd that the United States, one of the world's leaders in medical technology research, should rank forty-second in infant mortality deaths, with countries such as Cuba and Slovenia having lower rates. Can the American people, acting privately or through government, change these rankings, or are they the product of structural forces that are impervious to change?

Throughout this text, we will consider questions similar to these as we compare and contrast features of U.S. politics to politics in other nations. As you study each chapter of this text, consider whether the differences between the United States and other countries stem from choice, unique circumstance, or some combination of the two.

QUESTIONS

1. What surprised you about the rankings discussed above? What rankings didn't come as a surprise? Is the United States better or worse off than you originally thought?
2. What in your own experience suggests that America is exceptional? What in your experience discounts this notion?

Source: CIA World Factbook, http://www.cia.gov.

Hobbes argued strongly for a single ruler, no matter how evil, to guarantee the rights of the weak against the strong. Leviathan, a biblical sea monster, was his characterization of an all-powerful government. Strict adherence to Leviathan's laws, however all-encompassing or intrusive on liberty, was but a small price to pay for living in a civilized society.

In contrast to Hobbes, John Locke, like many other political philosophers of the era, took the basic survival of humanity for granted. He argued that a government's major responsibility was the preservation of private property, an idea that ultimately found its way into the U.S. Constitution. In two of his works, *Second Treatise on Civil Government* (1689) and *Essay Concerning Human Understanding* (1690), Locke not only denied the divine right of kings to govern but argued that individuals were born equal and with natural rights that no king had the power to void. Under Locke's conception of social contract theory, the consent of the people is the only true basis of any sovereign's right to rule. According to Locke, people form governments largely to preserve life, liberty, and property, and to assure justice. If governments act improperly, they break their contract with the people and therefore no longer enjoy the consent of the governed. Because he believed that true justice comes from laws, Locke argued that the branch of government that makes laws—as opposed to the one that enforces or interprets laws—should be the most powerful.

VIDEO DEBATE

American Democracy and Human Rights

Locke believed that having a chief executive to administer laws was important, but that the executive should necessarily be limited by law or by the social contract with the governed. Locke's writings influenced many American colonists, especially Thomas Jefferson, whose original draft of the Declaration of Independence noted the rights to "life, liberty, and property" as key reasons to split from England.[2]

DEVISING A NATIONAL GOVERNMENT IN THE AMERICAN COLONIES

Comparing Political Landscapes

The American colonists rejected a system with a strong ruler, as in the British monarchy, as soon as they declared their independence. The colonists also were fearful of replicating the landed and titled system of the British aristocracy. They viewed the formation of a representative form of government as far more in keeping with the ideas of social contract theorists and their own traditions.

The earliest forms of government in the colonies, such as the New England town meeting, where all citizens gather to discuss and decide issues facing the town, were characterized by **direct democracy.** This tradition, however, soon proved unworkable as more and more settlers came to the New World. Therefore, many town meetings were replaced by mechanisms of **indirect democracy** (this is also called representative democracy), which call for the election of representatives to a governmental decision-making body. The Virginia House of Burgesses, created in 1619, exemplifies this tradition.

Still, many colonists were uncomfortable with the term democracy because it conjured up Hobbesian fears of the people and mob rule. Instead, they preferred the term **republic,** which implied a system of government in which the interests of the people were represented by more educated or wealthier citizens who were responsible to those who elected them. Today, representative democracies are more commonly called republics, and the words democracy and republic often are used interchangeably.

direct democracy
A system of government in which members of the polity meet to discuss all policy decisions and then agree to abide by majority rule.

indirect (representative) democracy
A system of government that gives citizens the opportunity to vote for representatives who will work on their behalf.

republic
A government rooted in the consent of the governed; a representative or indirect democracy.

American Political Culture and the Characteristics of American Democracy

AS SHOWN ABOVE, the Framers devised a representative democratic system to govern the United States. This system is based on a number of underlying concepts and distinguishing characteristics that sometimes conflict with one another. Taken together, these ideas lie at the core of American political culture. More specifically, **political culture** can be defined as commonly shared attitudes, beliefs, and core values about how government should operate. American political culture emphasizes the values of personal liberty, equality, popular consent and majority rule, popular sovereignty, civil society, and individualism.

political culture
Commonly shared attitudes, beliefs, and core values about how government should operate.

PERSONAL LIBERTY

Personal liberty is perhaps the single most important characteristic of American democracy. The Constitution itself was written to ensure life and liberty. Over the years, however, our concepts of liberty have changed and evolved from freedom *from* to freedom *to*. The Framers intended Americans to be free from governmental infringements. The addition of the Fourteenth Amendment to the Constitution and its emphasis on equal protection of the laws and subsequent passage of laws guaranteeing civil rights, however, expanded Americans' concept of liberty to include demands for freedom to work or go to school without discrimination.

personal liberty
A key characteristic of U.S. democracy. Initially meaning freedom from governmental interference, today it includes demands for freedom to engage in a variety of practices free from governmental discrimination.

EQUALITY

political equality

The principal that all citizens are equal in the political process; implied by the phrase "one person, one vote."

Another key characteristic of our democracy is **political equality.** This emphasis reflects Americans' stress on the importance of the individual. Although some individuals clearly wield more political clout than others, the adage "one person, one vote" implies a sense of political equality for all.

POPULAR CONSENT AND MAJORITY RULE

popular consent

The idea that governments must draw their powers from the consent of the governed.

Popular consent, the idea that governments must draw their powers from the consent of the governed, is one distinguishing characteristic of American democracy. Derived from John Locke's social contract theory, the notion of popular consent was central to the Declaration of Independence. A citizen's willingness to vote represents his or her consent to be governed and is thus an essential premise of democracy.

majority rule

The central premise of direct democracy in which only policies that collectively garner the support of a majority of voters will be made into law.

    Majority rule, another core political value, means that the majority (normally 50 percent of the total votes cast plus one) of citizens in any political unit should elect officials and determine policies. This principle holds for both voters and their elected representatives. Yet, the American system also stresses the need to preserve minority rights, as evidenced by the myriad protections of individual rights and liberties found in the Bill of Rights.

POPULAR SOVEREIGNTY

popular sovereignty

The notion that the ultimate authority in society rests with the people.

natural law

A doctrine that society should be governed by certain ethical principles that are part of nature and, as such, can be understood by reason.

Popular sovereignty, or the notion that the ultimate authority in society rests with the people, has its basis in **natural law.** Ultimately, political authority rests with the people, who can create, abolish, or alter their governments. The idea that all governments derive their power from the people is found in the Declaration of Independence and the U.S. Constitution, but the term popular sovereignty did not come into wide use until pre–Civil War debates over slavery. At that time, supporters of popular sovereignty argued that the citizens of new states seeking admission to the union should be able to decide whether or not their states would allow slavery within their borders.

CIVIL SOCIETY

civil society

Society created when citizens are allowed to organize and express their views publicly as they engage in an open debate about public policy.

Several of these hallmarks of our political culture also are fundamental to what many commentators now term **civil society.** This term is used to describe the society created when citizens are allowed to organize and express their views publicly as they engage in an open debate about public policy.[3] The U.S. government routinely makes grants to nongovernmental organizations, professional associations, civic education groups, and women's groups to encourage the kind of participation in the political system that Americans often take for granted. (See American Values/American Voices: Exporting Democracy.)

INDIVIDUALISM

SIMULATION

What Are American Civic Values?

Although many core political values concern protecting the rights of others, tremendous value is placed on the individual in American democracy. All individuals are deemed rational and fair, and endowed, as Thomas Jefferson proclaimed in the Declaration of Independence, "with certain unalienable rights." Although many view individualism, which holds that the primary function of government is to enable the individual to achieve his or her highest level of development, as a mixed blessing, this concept has been essential throughout American history.

RELIGIOUS FAITH

Most Americans profess to have strong religious beliefs, and the United States is the most churchgoing nation in the world. While diverse in its religious traditions,

American Values/American Voices

EXPORTING DEMOCRACY

During his second inaugural address delivered in January 2005, President George W. Bush made it clear that spreading democracy abroad was a major goal of the United States. The president's goal is not a new one for the United States. President Woodrow Wilson tried and failed after World War I to establish a democratic world order through the League of Nations. Harry Truman's administration had greater success after World War II when both Japan and West Germany were transformed into democratic nations. Supporters of U.S. efforts to export democracy to other nations cite scholarship that suggests democracies are less likely to go to war with one another.[a] Critics, however, charge that America's democratic impulse in foreign policy matters has led in the past and is likely to lead again to unforeseen and disastrous consequences.[b] Since President Bush identified spreading democracy as one of the United States' major goals, many oppressed peoples have been given hope. However, the idealism of the president's agenda has often conflicted with U.S. foreign policy realities and other policy priorities.[c]

In the Middle East, for example, the administration has promoted elections in Afghanistan and Iraq to mixed success. The Iraqi Parliament's failure initially to agree on key ministerial positions dealing with foreign policy is just one indicator that American democracy might not work for everyone. And, in the Palestinian territories, the U.S. efforts to prevent the radical Islamic group Hamas from winning control of the government were rebuffed by the electorate in a carefully monitored democratic election. As a result, the United States found itself in the ironic position of refusing to negotiate with a democratically elected government, albeit one with a history of terrorist attacks.

In other places, however, the United States has enjoyed greater success. In Kyrgyzstan, the U.S. government funded pro-democracy groups and provided generators to print an opposition newspaper before its peaceful revolution. Edil Baisalov, director of the Coalition for Democracy and Civil Society, can quote extensively from the Bush inaugural speech. "The Kyrgyz people are much, much better off today than they were a year ago, and I think the U.S. government should take pride in taking credit for that," he said. "And [it] should never apologize that it wants the people to be free."[d]

"The administration deserves credit," said Jennifer Windsor, executive director of Freedom House, a group that promotes democracy "but it's just a start."[e] At the same time, however, Human Rights Watch criticized the Bush administration for undermining its credibility in promoting democracy and freedom abroad by attempting to identify terrorists and gain information through the use of abusive interrogation tactics at Guantanamo Bay, and by deporting detainees to countries where more brutal interrogation techniques could be used.

Outside the United States, officials also question the sincerity of the Bush administration's rhetoric while commending their efforts to speak out. "All they do is talk right now," said Gulam Umarov, the son of the leader of Uzbekistan's opposition, the Sunshine Coalition. "I don't know what actual moves they take. But they are talking, which is really good."[f]

QUESTIONS

1. Is America's brand of democracy easily exportable? What pitfalls exist for nations with little experience in democracy?
2. Do highly religious Muslim nations or factions pose special problems to American efforts to bring democracy to the Middle East?

[a]G. John Ikenberry, "Why Export Democracy? The 'Hidden Grand Strategy' of American Foreign Policy," *Wilson Quarterly* 23 (Spring 1999): 2.

[b]Paul D. Carrington, "Exporting Democracy to Iraq," *Perspectives* 4 (March 31, 2003), http://www.oycf.org.

[c]This feature draws heavily on Peter Baker, "The Realities of Exporting Democracy," *Washington Post* (January 25, 2006): A1.

[d]Quoted in Baker, "The Realities of Exporting Democracy."

[e]Quoted in Baker, "The Realities of Exporting Democracy."

[f]Quoted in Baker, "The Realities of Exporting Democracy."

it is overwhelmingly Christian, with a growing number of Christian evangelicals who, since 1980, have played an exceptionally important role in American politics, defining the political positions of the Republican Party, in particular. People of religious faith often have very firm beliefs on social issues such as contraception and abortion, same-sex marriage, the right of homosexual people to adopt children, and the use of stem cells for medical research. The concerns of people of strong religious faith continue to play a major role in shaping the political agenda of the nation.

Changing Characteristics of the American People

VISUAL LITERACY
Understanding Who We Are

AMERICANS HAVE MANY THINGS IN COMMON in addition to political culture. Most Americans share a common language—English—and have similar aspirations for themselves and their families. Most agree that they would rather live in the United States than anywhere else, and that democracy, with all of its warts, is still the best system of government. Most Americans highly value education and want to send their children to the best schools possible, viewing an education as the key to success.

Despite these similarities, politicians, media commentators, and even the citizenry itself tend to focus on differences among Americans, in large part because these differences contribute to political conflicts among the electorate. Although it is true that the United States and its population are undergoing rapid change, this is not necessarily a new phenomenon.

CHANGING SIZE AND POPULATION

One year after the Constitution was ratified, fewer than 4 million Americans lived in the thirteen states. They were united by a single language, most shared a similar Protestant-Christian heritage, and those who voted were white male property owners. The Constitution mandated that each of the sixty-five members of the original House of Representatives should represent 30,000 people.

As the nation grew with the addition of new states, as revealed in Figure 1.2, the population also grew. Although the physical size of the United States has remained stable since the addition of Alaska and Hawaii in 1959, in 2007 there were more than 300 million Americans. In 2004, a single member of the House of Representatives from Montana represented more than 927,000 people.

CHANGING DEMOGRAPHICS OF THE U.S. POPULATION

As the physical size and population of the United States have changed, so have many of the assumptions on which it was founded. Much of the dynamism of American government and politics actually stems from changes in the demographics, the characteristics of the American population, that have occurred throughout our history. Below, we look at some demographic facts and then discuss some of the implications of these changes for how our nation is governed.

PARTICIPATION
The Debate Over Immigration

Changes in Racial and Ethnic Composition From the start, the American population has been altered constantly by the arrival of immigrants from various regions—Western Europeans fleeing religious persecution in the 1600s to early 1700s, Chinese laborers arriving to work on the railroads following the Gold Rush in 1848, Irish Catholics escaping the potato famine in the 1850s, Northern and Eastern Europeans from the 1880s to 1910s, and, most recently, Southeast Asians, Cubans, and Mexicans, among others.

Immigration to the United States peaked in the first decade of the 1900s, when nearly 9 million people, many of them from Eastern Europe, entered the country. The United States did not see another major wave of immigration until the late 1980s, when nearly 2 million immigrants were admitted in one year.

While immigration has been a continual source of changing demographics in America, race has also played a major role in the development and course of politics in the United States. As revealed in Figure 1.3, the racial and ethnic balance in America is changing dramatically, with the proportion of Hispanics growing at the quickest rate. More importantly, what the figure does not show is that 40 percent of Americans

FIGURE 1.2 U.S. POPULATION, 1790–2050

Since around 1890, when large numbers of immigrants began arriving in America, the United States has seen a sharp increase in population. The major reasons for this increase are new births and increased longevity, although immigration has also been a contributing factor.

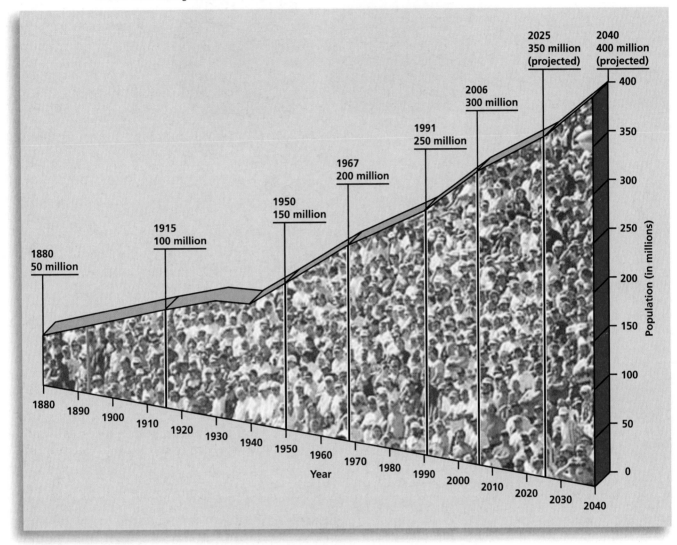

Source: *USA Today* (July 5, 2006): 1A.

under age twenty-five are members of minority groups, a fact that will permanently change the demographics of the American polity.

Changes in Age Cohort Composition Just as the racial and ethnic composition of the American population is changing, so is the average age of the population. The United States was long considered a "nation of the young" with its under-twenty population greatly outnumbering those sixty-five and older, but because of changes in patterns of fertility, life expectancy, and immigration, the nation's age profile has changed drastically.[4] When the United States was founded, the average life expectancy was thirty-five years; by 2006, it was eighty years for women and seventy-five years for men.

FIGURE 1.3 RACE AND ETHNICITY IN AMERICA: 2005 AND BEYOND

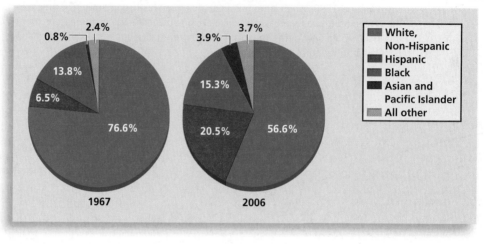

Source: U.S. Census Bureau.

An aging population produces a host of new and costly demands on the government. In 2008, the first of the Baby Boomers (the 76.8 million people who grew up from 1946 to 1964) will reach age sixty-two and begin qualifying for Social Security; in 2011, they will reach sixty-five and qualify for Medicare.[5] By the time many current college students are in their peak economic years, more than 60 percent of the American population will be over sixty-five years old. Medical care for seniors will cost more and more as science improves and the longevity of those over sixty-five increases. (See Analyzing Visuals: Health Improvements Costly in the Long Run.)

This dramatic change could potentially pit younger people against older people and result in dramatic cuts in benefits to the elderly and increased taxes for younger workers. Moreover, the elderly often vote against programs favored by younger voters, such as money for new schools and parks, and other items that they no longer view as important. At the same time, younger voters are less likely to support some things important

SIMULATION

How to Satisfy Aunt Martha

■ Concern over immigration is not a new phenomenon, as this cartoon from the early 1900s depicts.

THE HIGH TIDE OF IMMIGRATION—A NATIONAL MENACE.

Analyzing Visuals

HEALTH IMPROVEMENTS COSTLY IN THE LONG RUN

One often thinks of advances in society as improving society. And, on one level, for the individual, that is often true. If you or your parents or grandparents are the victim of a stroke, you will be thrilled with recent advances such as the development of a new drug that reduces cell death after a stroke and thus minimizes overall brain damage and resultant physical impairments. But, the availability of new treatments such as this come with huge societal costs. As people live longer but continue to retire in their sixties, the cost of just this one new intervention will add over $28,000 per year per life of additional costs to Medicare. As you examine the costs associated with each new medical intervention, which ones do you think the government should supply for its citizens? Should access to the newest technologies be limited to those who can afford them? What about making treatments available to those who have smoked or otherwise abused their health?

COSTS PER NEW MEDICAL INTERVENTION

Treatment	What It Does or Would Do	Cost to Medicare per Additional Year of Life
Anti-aging compound for healthy people	$1-a-day compound adds 10 years to life	$11,245
Treatment for acute stroke	New drug reduces cell death after stroke	$28,024
Anti-aging compound for unhealthy people	$1-a-day compound adds 10 years to life	$38,105
Alzheimer's prevention	New drug delays onset of disease	$102,774
Implantable cardioverter defibrillator	Controls heart rhythm	$131,892
Diabetes prevention	Insulin-sensitizing drug reduces disease	$188,316
Pacemakers for atrial fibrillation	New generation of pacemakers	$1,795,850

Source: Rand and *USA Today* (October 25, 2005): 2B.

to seniors, such as Medicaid and prescription drug reform, and have favored the Bush administration's plans for Social Security reform in higher numbers than seniors.

Changes in Family and Family Size In the past, familial and gender roles were clearly defined. Women did housework and men worked in the fields. Large families were imperative; children were a source of cheap farm labor. Industrialization and knowledge of birth control methods began to put a dent in the size of American families by the early 1900s. No longer needing children to work for the survival of the household unit on the farm, couples began to limit the sizes of their families. The look of American households also changed dramatically. In 1940, nine out of ten households were traditional family households. By 2004, just 67.8 percent of children under eighteen lived with both parents. In fact, almost 20 percent of children under eighteen lived with just one of their parents; the majority of these children (more than 80 percent) lived with their mother. Moreover, by 2004, more than 26 percent of all households consisted of a single person, a trend that is in part illustrative of the aging American population.

IMPLICATIONS OF THESE CHANGES

Today, 90 percent of Americans believe that illegal immigration is a serious problem, and several states have attempted to deny drivers licenses or access to other public services to undocumented immigrants.[6] (See Join the Debate: The Huntington Theory of Hispanization.) Many believe that the numbers of immigrants, legal and illegal, arriving at our shores will lead to disastrous consequences.

VIDEO DEBATE

Illegal Immigration

Join the Debate

THE HUNTINGTON THEORY OF HISPANIZATION

OVERVIEW: Many observers of American culture and politics argue that one of the United States' greatest strengths is its ability to absorb and assimilate into the social body the diverse customs and values of different peoples. These commentators highlight the contributions to politics, the arts and sciences, national defense, and the common good by various waves of immigrants—and by those brought against their will during the years of slavery. Traditionalists such as Harvard professor Samuel Huntington contend that the American "melting pot" has been successful in part because, historically, the new Americans have absorbed the fundamental political principles of the United States as their own. Though there are numerous cultures within the country, Huntington insists that there is one shared American culture based on the values espoused in the Declaration of Independence—that is, American political culture is based on the fundamental principles of equality, individual rights, and government by consent. In order for the love of freedom and self-government to be nurtured and maintained, American core principles must be accepted and protected by all citizens.

Huntington argues that during the latter part of the twentieth and into the twenty-first century, there has been a new wave of immigration into the United States unlike any other; he considers immigration from Mexico in particular, and Latin America, in general, to be detrimental to original American political principles. According to Huntington's highly controversial thesis, this immigration wave is unique in that there is a political agenda within part of the Hispanic community to "reclaim" the lands ceded to the United States after the Texas war for independence and the Mexican-American War.

Furthermore, Huntington argues, no other nation has had to contend with a long, contiguous border that immigrants can cross rather freely to maintain familial, economic, and cultural ties, thereby fostering a type of dual national or cultural allegiance (or, at worst, immigrant loyalty to the home country) that can weaken ties to American core values. Finally, he contends, Hispanic immigrants have created linguistic and cultural enclaves within the United States (Los Angeles and Miami, for example) in which there is no need to learn the language, history, and political values of their adopted nation, thus further eroding social and political bonds between citizens.

Huntington's thesis raises serious questions. Are American core ideals so exceptional that only people who share those values should be allowed citizenship? Can immigrants whose political and social beliefs differ from or oppose America's core values be assimilated into American society? If not, what corrective policy measures should be implemented? Has American history shown that, ultimately, most immigrants and their descendents embrace the principles that underlie the U.S. Constitution and American political culture?

ARGUMENTS FOR HUNTINGTON'S THESIS

- The core political values found in the Declaration of Independence and Constitution are essential to **maintain freedom and protect rights**. It may be that original

---

Such anti-immigration sentiments are hardly new. In fact, American history is replete with examples of Americans set against any new immigration. In the 1840s, for example, the Know Nothing Party arose in part to oppose immigration from Roman Catholic nations, charging that the pope was going to organize the slaughter of all Protestants in the United States. In the 1920s, the Ku Klux Klan, which had over 5 million members, called for barring immigration to stem the tide of Roman Catholic and Jewish immigrants into the nation.

Demographics affect politics and government because an individual's perspective influences how he or she hears debates on various issues. In 2006 African Americans, for example, viewed the government's initial slow response to the plight of the poor and displaced after Hurricane Katrina more unfavorably than whites.[7]

These cleavages and the emphasis many politicians put on our demographic differences play out in many ways in American politics. Baby Boomers and the elderly object to any changes in Social Security or Medicare, while those born in the 1960s and 1970s vote for politicians who support change, if they vote at all. Many policies

American principles run the risk of being replaced by ideals that advocate forms of government or politics opposed to liberty, self-government, and individual rights, thus changing the character of the American regime.

- **American institutions and political culture pursue "Justice as the end of government . . . as the end of civil society."** American ideals can be a guide for all to live together effectively in peace and harmony, rather than an end in themselves. These principles allow most individuals to pursue their unique conception of the American dream, relatively free from interference by the government and others.
- **A shared language and civic education bind citizens together.** Teaching multiple languages and cultural viewpoints while denying a common civic education and political origin can create competing sources of identity that will weaken citizens' attachments to one another and to their government.

ARGUMENTS AGAINST HUNTINGTON'S THESIS

- **Historically, certain waves of immigrants were incorrectly thought to be opposed to American values.** Benjamin Franklin expressed concerns that German immigrants could not be assimilated into colonial American life because of their culture and history, and Irish-Catholic immigrants were accused of both giving allegiance to the pope and of being anti-republican in political outlook—fears that proved to be unfounded.
- **Bilingualism in the Hispanic community does not indicate the creation of competing sources of social and political identity.** According to an opinion poll coordi-

nated by the *Washington Post* in 2000, a mere 10 percent of second-generation Hispanic immigrants rely on speaking only Spanish, which follows the pattern of English language adoption by previous waves of immigration to the United States.

- **American political culture is more than its Anglo-Protestant core.** A strength of the American experience is its ability to absorb different cultures and values and transform them into one unique political society. It took both the successive waves of immigration and the freeing of the slaves to move the United States toward the realization of the ideals espoused in the Declaration of Independence.

QUESTIONS

1. Does the issue of Hispanic immigration threaten American sovereignty and values? Do demonstrations by pro- and anti-immigrant groups signal a significant shift in U.S. history?
2. Is American political culture more than its core principles and institutions? If so, what other values and institutions add to the United States' claim that it is a true "melting pot?"

SELECTED READINGS

Daniels, Roger. *Guarding the Golden Door: American Immigration Policy and Immigrants Since 1882.* New York: Hill and Wang, 2004.

Huntington, Samuel. *Who Are We? The Challenges to America's National Identity.* New York: Simon and Schuster, 2004.

are targeted at one group or the other, further exacerbating differences—real or imagined—and lawmakers often find themselves the target of many different factions. This diversity can make it difficult to devise coherent policies to "promote the general welfare," as promised in the Constitution.

Political Ideology

IDEOLOGIES ARE SETS OR SYSTEMS OF BELIEFS that shape the thinking of individuals and how they view the world, especially in regard to issues of "race, nationality, the role and function of government, the relations between men and women, human responsibility for the natural environment, and many other matters."[8] Isaiah Berlin, a noted historian and philosopher, believed that two factors shaped the twentieth century. One was science and technology. The other was "the great ideological storms that have altered the lives of virtually all mankind: the Russian Revolution and its aftermath—totalitarian tyrannies of both right and left and the explosions of nationalism, racism, and in places, of religious bigotry, which interestingly enough, not one among the most perceptive social thinkers of the nineteenth century had ever predicted."[9]

Political scientists note that ideologies perform four key functions:

1. *Explanation.* Ideologies provide us with reasons for why social and political conditions are the way they are, especially in time of crisis.
2. *Evaluation.* Ideologies can provide the standards for evaluating social conditions and political institutions and events.
3. *Orientation.* An ideology can provide a sense of identity. Much like compasses, ideologies provide an orientation toward issues as well as to each individual's position within the world.
4. *Political Program.* An ideology helps people to make political choices and guides their political actions.

political ideology
A coherent set of values and beliefs about the purpose and scope of government.

libertarian
One who favors a free market economy and no governmental interference in personal liberties.

conservative
One thought to believe that a government is best that governs least and that big government can only infringe on individual, personal, and economic rights.

PREVAILING AMERICAN POLITICAL IDEOLOGIES

A **political ideology** is a set of values and beliefs about the purpose and scope of government. If they profess to have a political ideology, most Americans characterize themselves as liberal, conservative, or moderate (see Figure 1.4). A small proportion of Americans refer to themselves as **libertarians,** but pollsters rarely offer respondents the opportunity to label themselves as such. In the American context, political ideologies are often tied into which political party an individual supports, which in turn affects how one votes at the polls and the outcome of elections.

Conservatism **Conservatives** tend to believe that a government is best that governs least, and that big government can only infringe on individual, personal, and economic rights. They want less government, especially in terms of regulation of the economy. Conservatives favor local and state action over federal action, and

FIGURE 1.4 ADULT SELF-IDENTIFICATION AS LIBERAL, MODERATE, OR CONSERVATIVE, 1974–2006

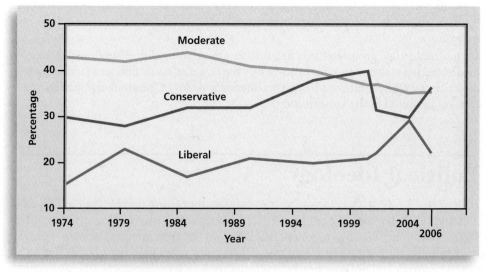

Source: Roper Center at the University of Connecticut, *Public Opinion Online.*

they emphasize fiscal responsibility, most notably in the form of balanced budgets. Conservatives are likely to support smaller, less activist governments and believe that domestic problems such as homelessness, poverty, and discrimination are better dealt with by the private sector than by the government. Since the 1970s, **social conservatives** (sometimes referred to as the Religious Right) have increasingly affected politics and policies in the United States. Social conservatives believe that moral decay must be stemmed and that the moral teachings of fundamentalism should be supported and furthered by the government. Social conservatives support government intervention to regulate sexual and social behavior and have mounted efforts to make abortion illegal and to ban same-sex marriage. While a majority of social conservatives are evangelical Christians, some Jews and many Muslims are also social conservatives.

Liberalism **Liberals** are defined as those who seek to change the political, economic, and social status quo to foster the development of equality and the well-being of individuals.[10] The meaning of the words liberal and liberalism have changed over time, but in the modern United States, liberals generally value equality over other aspects of shared political culture. They are supportive of well-funded government social welfare programs that seek to protect individuals from economic disadvantages or correct past injustices, and they generally oppose government efforts to regulate private behavior or infringe on civil rights and liberties.

PROBLEMS WITH POLITICAL LABELS

In a perfect world, liberals would be liberal and conservatives would be conservative. Studies reveal, however, that many people who call themselves conservative actually take fairly liberal positions on many policy issues. In fact, anywhere from 20 percent to 60 percent will take a traditionally conservative position on one issue and a traditionally liberal position on another.[11] Perhaps because of this difficulty with labels, many people prefer to be categorized as moderates, those who hold a range of beliefs on issues that conservatives and liberals hold to more steadfastly.

social conservative
One who believes that traditional moral teachings should be supported and furthered by the government.

VISUAL LITERACY
Who Are Liberals and Conservatives?

liberal
One considered to favor extensive governmental involvement in the economy and the provision of social services and to take an activist role in protecting the rights of women, the elderly, minorities, and the environment.

■ Speaker of the House Nancy Pelosi (D–CA) and House Minority Leader John Boehner (R–OH) represent vastly different ideological perspectives.

Photo courtesy: left: Greg Whitesell/UPI/Landov; right, Dennis Brack/Bloomberg News/Landov

Current Attitudes Toward American Government

AMERICANS' VIEWS ABOUT AND EXPECTATIONS OF government and democracy affect the political system at all levels. It has now become part of our political culture to expect negative campaigns, dishonest politicians, and political pundits who make their living bashing politicians and the political process. How Americans view politics, the economy, and their ability to achieve the **American dream**—an American ideal of a happy and successful life, which often includes wealth, a house, a better life for one's children, and, for some, the ability to grow up to be president—also is influenced by their political ideology as well as by their social, economic, educational, and personal circumstances.

Since the early 1990s, the major sources of most individuals' on-the-air news—the four major networks (ABC, CBS, FOX, and NBC) along with CNN and C-SPAN—have been supplemented dramatically as the number of news and quasi-news outlets has grown exponentially. First there were weekly programs such as *Dateline* on the regular networks. Next came FOX News, MSNBC, and CNBC—all competing for similar audiences. During the 2006 election, for example, more people turned to a cable news program than to the regular networks for their political coverage. In addition, the Internet has quickly developed as an instantaneous source of news, as well as rumor, about politics. The growth of online diaries, or blogs, has accelerated this phenomenon.

The competition for news stories, as well as the instantaneous nature of these communications, still often highlights the negative, the sensational, the sound bite, and the extreme. It's hard to remain upbeat about America or politics amidst the media's focus on personality and scandal. It's hard to remain positive about the fate of Americans and their families if you watch talk news shows that feature guests trying to outshout each other or watch campaign ads that highlight only the negative.

We also cannot ignore how Americans are now viewed abroad. For centuries, immigrants have come to our shores to be part of the American dream. But, to some people in Europe, the Middle East, and elsewhere, America is no longer the beacon it once was. The spread of American culture as embodied by fast-food chains and American television programs, along with the United States' unpopular involvement in Iraq, has intensified the stereotype of the "ugly American." Negative perceptions of America increasingly are affecting the United States' ability to improve relations at home and abroad.

HIGH EXPECTATIONS

In roughly the first 150 years of our nation's history, the federal government had few responsibilities, and its citizens had few expectations of it beyond national defense, printing money, and collecting tariffs and taxes. The state governments were generally far more powerful than the federal government in matters affecting the everyday lives of Americans (see chapter 3).

As the nation and its economy grew in size and complexity, the federal government took on more responsibilities, such as regulating some businesses, providing poverty relief, and inspecting food. Then, in response to the Great Depression of the 1930s, President Franklin D. Roosevelt's New Deal government programs proliferated in almost every area of American life, including job creation, income security, and aid to the poor. Since then, many Americans have looked to the government for solutions to all kinds of problems.

A MISSING APPRECIATION OF THE GOOD

If you don't have faith in America, its institutions, or symbols (and Figure 1.5 shows that many of us don't), it becomes even easier to blame the government for all kinds of woes—personal as well as societal—or to fail to credit governments for the things they do well.

American dream
An American ideal of a happy, successful life, which often includes wealth, a house, a better life for one's children, and, for some, the ability to grow up to be president.

Major Technological Innovations that Have Changed the Political Landscape

Exporting American Democracy

FIGURE 1.5 FAITH IN INSTITUTIONS

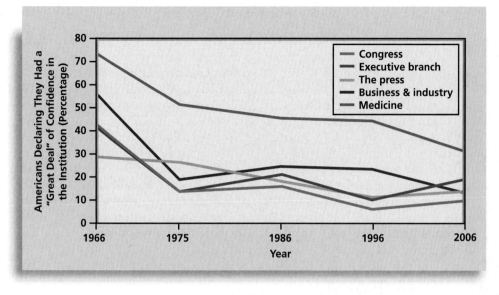

Sources: *Newsweek* (January 8, 1996): 32; *Public Perspective* 8 (February/March 1994): 4; and Lexis-Nexis RPOLL.

Whether the water you use as you brush your teeth contains fluoride is a state or local governmental issue. The federal Food and Drug Administration inspects your breakfast meat and sets standards for the advertising on your cereal box, orange juice carton, and other food packaging.

Although all governments have problems, it is important to stress the good they can do. In the aftermath of the Great Depression in the United States, for example, the government created the Social Security program, which dramatically decreased poverty among the elderly. Contract laws and the federal and state judicial systems provide an efficient framework for business, assuring people that they have recourse in the courts should someone fail to deliver as promised. Moreover, government-guaranteed student loan programs make it possible for many students to attend college. (See Table 1.2 for quality of life measures.)

MISTRUST OF POLITICIANS

One 2005 poll conducted by the Roper Center for Public Opinion Research at the University of Connecticut found that only 23 percent of the respondents trust politicians.[12] And, a recent glance at the pages of any major newspaper offers a number of

VIDEO ROUNDTABLE

Political Corruption

TABLE 1.2 HOW ARE AMERICANS REALLY DOING?

	1945	1970	2005
Life expectancy	65.9	70.8	77.8
Per capita income (1999 constant dollars)	$6,367	$12,816	$27,240
Adults who are high school grads	25%[a]	52.3%	85.2%
Adults who are college grads	5%[a]	10.7%	27.7%
Households with phones	46%	87%	95.5%
Households with cable TV	0%	4%	69.8%
Women in labor force	29%	38%	58.9%
Own their own home	46%	63%	69%
Below poverty line	39.7%[b]	12.6%	12.7%

[a]1940 figure.

[b]1949 figure.

Source: U.S. Census Bureau, *2006 Statistical Abstract of the United States*.

Photo courtesy: Chip Somodevilla/Getty Images

■ Former House Majority Leader Tom DeLay (R–TX) was forced to resign in the wake of an ethics scandal. Behavior such as DeLay's fuels Americans' mistrust of many politicians.

illustrations why this might be the case. Scandals involving advisers to President George W. Bush, K Street lobbyists (see chapter 11), and members of Congress are continually in the news.

In one particularly striking example, House Majority Leader Tom DeLay (R–TX) was forced to resign first from his leadership position and later from the House altogether following allegations about the legality of a series of financial deals made by his associate, lobbyist Jack Abramoff, and several members of DeLay's congressional staff. These allegations came on the heels of a redistricting scandal in DeLay's home state of Texas that led several Democratic incumbents to lose their seats in the November 2004 general elections when they were pitted against Republican incumbents in newly redrawn districts. DeLay's former seat in a heavily Republican district was one of a number of Republican seats taken by Democrats in the 2006 midterm elections.

Despite scandals such as these, it is important to remember that most politicians do not conform to this mold. Instead, the great majority of politicians are hard-working individuals who pride themselves on being able to deliver programs and services to their constituents.

VOTER APATHY

Americans, unlike voters in most other societies, get an opportunity to vote on a host of candidates and issues, but some say those choices may be too overwhelming. Responsible voters may opt not to go to the polls, fearing that they lack sufficient information on the vast array of candidates and issues facing them. Some citizens think their votes will not make a difference.

REDEFINING OUR EXPECTATIONS

Just as it is important to recognize that government serves many important purposes, it is also important to recognize that government and politics are not static. Politics, moreover, involves conflicts over different and sometimes opposing ideologies, and these ideologies are very much influenced by one's racial, ethnic, cultural, economic, and historical experiences. These divisions are real and affect the political process at all levels. It is clear to most Americans today that politics and government no longer can be counted on to cure all of America's ills. Government, however, will always play a major role. True political leaders will need to help Americans come to terms with America as it is today—not as it was in the past.

Summary

GOVERNMENTS, WHICH ARE MADE UP of individuals and institutions, are the vehicles through which policies are made and affairs of state are conducted. Governments have many functions. In the U.S. context, most are included in the preamble to the Constitution. Governments take many forms depending on the number who rule as well as whose interests are represented.

The American political system was based on several notions that have their roots in classical Greek ideas. The ideas of British social contract theorists John Locke and

Thomas Hobbes, who held the belief that people are free and equal by God-given right, have continuing implications for our ideas of the proper role of government in our indirect democracy.

Key characteristics of American political culture are personal liberty, equality, popular consent and majority rule, popular sovereignty, civil society, individualism, and religious faith.

Several characteristics of the American electorate can help us understand how the system continues to evolve and change. Chief among these are changes in size, population, and demographics.

Ideologies and ideas play a powerful role in politics. Most Americans identify themselves as conservatives, liberals, or moderates.

Americans have high and often unrealistic expectations of government. At the same time, they often fail to appreciate how much their government actually does for them. Some of this failure may be due to Americans' general mistrust of politicians, which may explain some of the apathy evidenced in the electorate.

KEY TERMS

American dream, p. 20
citizen, p. 5
civil society, p. 10
conservative, p. 18
democracy, p. 6
direct democracy, p. 9
government, p. 5
indirect (representative) democracy, p. 9
liberal, p. 19
libertarian, p. 18
majority rule, p. 10
monarchy, p. 6
natural law, p. 10
oligarchy, p. 6
personal liberty, p. 9
political culture, p. 9
political equality, p. 10
political ideology, p. 18
politics, p. 5
popular consent, p. 10
popular sovereignty, p. 10
republic, p. 9
social conservative p. 19
social contract theory, p. 7
totalitarianism, p. 6

SELECTED READINGS

Almond, Gabriel A., and Sidney Verba. *Civic Culture: Political Attitudes and Democracy in Five Nations.* Princeton, NJ: Princeton University Press, 1963.

Ball, Terence, and Richard Dagger. *Political Ideologies and the Democratic Ideal, 6th ed.* New York: Longman, 2005.

Craig, Stephen C., and Stephen Earl Bennett, eds. *After the Boom: The Politics of Generation X.* Lanham, MD: Rowman and Littlefield, 1997.

Dahl, Robert A. *Polyarchy: Participation and Opposition.* New Haven, CT: Yale University Press, 1971.

Elshtain, Jean Bethke. *Democracy on Trial.* New York: Basic Books, 1995.

Fiorina, Morris P. *Culture War? The Myth of a Polarized America.* New York: Longman, 2004.

Grossman, Lawrence K. *The Electronic Republic: Reshaping Democracy in the Information Age.* New York: Viking, 1995.

Hobbes, Thomas. *Leviathan.* Richard Tuck, ed. New York: Cambridge University Press, 1996.

Hochschild, Jennifer L. *Facing Up to the American Dream: Race, Class, and the Soul of the Nation.* Princeton, NJ: Princeton University Press, 1995.

Jamieson, Kathleen Hall. *Everything You Think You Know About Politics . . . and Why You're Wrong.* New York: Basic Books, 2000.

Locke, John. *Two Treatises of Government.* Peter Lasleti, ed. New York: Cambridge University Press, 1988.

Nye, Joseph S., Jr. *The Paradox of American Power: Why the World's Superpower Can't Go It Alone.* New York: Oxford University Press, 2002.

Putnam, Robert D. *Bowling Alone: Collapse and Revival of the American Community.* New York: Simon and Schuster, 2000.

Skocpol, Theda, and Morris P. Fiorina, eds. *Civic Engagement in American Democracy.* Washington, DC: Brookings Institution Press, 1999.

Verba, Sidney, Kay Schlozman, and Henry Brady. *Voice and Equality: Civic Volunteerism in American Politics,* 2nd ed. Cambridge, MA: Harvard University Press, 2002.

Zakaria, Fareed. *The Future of Freedom: Illiberal Democracy at Home and Abroad.* New York: Norton, 2003.

WEB EXPLORATIONS

To connect with others who are interested in politics, see
http://www.pbs.org/news/news_government.html

For more on Thomas Hobbes and John Locke, see
http://www.iep.utm.edu/h/hobmoral.htm and
http://www.utm.edu/research/iep/l/locke.htm

To get a minute by minute update on U.S. population, see
http://www.census.gov

For more detail on population projections, see
http://www.census.gov/population/www/projections/natsum.html

For more information on families and household composition, see
http://www.census.gov/population/socdemo/hh-fam/98ppla.txt

For more information on conservatives, see
http://www.conservative.org

For more information on liberals, see
http://www.liberaloasis.com

For more information on libertarians, see
http://www.lp.org and http://www.cato.org

To find out your ideological stance, go to
www.politicalcompass.org

For more information on the American electorate, see
http://www.census.gov/population/www/socdemo/voting/p20-542.html

We the People ... insure domestic Tranquility, provide for the common ... and our Posterity, do ordain and establish this Consti...

Article. I.

Section. 1. All legislative Powers herein granted shall be vested in a Congress of the United States, which shall consist of a Se... of Representatives.

Section. 2. The House of Representatives shall be composed of Members chosen every second Year by the People of the several Sta... in each State shall have the Qualifications requisite for Electors of the most numerous Branch of the State Legislature.

No Person shall be a Representative who shall not have attained to the Age of twenty five Years, and been seven Years a Citizen ... and who shall not, when elected, be an Inhabitant of that State in which he shall be chosen.

Representatives and direct Taxes shall be apportioned among the several States which may be included within this Union, according ... Numbers, which shall be determined by adding to the whole Number of free Persons, including those bound to Service for a Term of Years, ... not taxed, three fifths of all other Persons. The actual Enumeration shall be made within three Years after the first Meeting of the Congress ... and within every subsequent Term of ten Years, in such Manner as they shall by Law direct. The Number of Representatives shall not ... thirty Thousand, but each State shall have at Least one Representative; and until such enumeration shall be made, the State of New Ham... entitled to chuse three, Massachusetts eight, Rhode-Island and Providence Plantations one, Connecticut five, New York six, New Jersey ...

Photo courtesy: Joseph Sohm/Visions of America/Corbis

THE CONSTITUTION

AT AGE EIGHTEEN, all American citizens are eligible to vote in state and national elections. This has not always been the case. It took an amendment to the U.S. Constitution—one of only seventeen that have been added since the Bill of Rights was ratified in 1791—to guarantee the franchise to those under twenty-one years of age.

In 1942, during World War II, Representative Jennings Randolph (D–WV) proposed that the voting age be lowered to eighteen, believing that since young men were old enough to be drafted to fight and die for their country, they also should be allowed to vote. He continued to reintroduce his proposal during every session of Congress, and in 1954 President Dwight D. Eisenhower endorsed the idea in his State of the Union message. Presidents Lyndon B. Johnson and Richard M. Nixon—men who had also called upon the nation's young men to fight on foreign shores—echoed his appeal.[1]

During the 1960s, the campaign to lower the voting age took on a new sense of urgency as hundreds of thousands of young men were drafted to fight in Vietnam and thousands of men and women were killed in action. "Old Enough to Fight, Old Enough to Vote," was one popular slogan of the day. By 1970, four states—who under the U.S. Constitution are allowed to set the eligibility requirements for their voters—had lowered their voting ages to eighteen. Later that year, Congress passed legislation lowering the voting age in national, state, and local elections to eighteen.

The state of Oregon, however, challenged the constitutionality of the law in court, arguing that Congress had not been given the authority to establish a uniform voting age in state and local government under the Constitution. The U.S. Supreme Court agreed.[2] The decision from the sharply divided Court meant that those under age twenty-one could vote in national elections but that the states were free to prohibit them from voting in state and local elections. The decision presented the states with a logistical nightmare. States setting the voting age at twenty-one would be forced to keep two sets of registration books: one for voters twenty-one and over, and one for voters under twenty-one.

Jennings Randolph, by then a senator from West Virginia, reintroduced his proposed amendment to lower the national voting age to eighteen.[3] Within three months of the Supreme Court's decision, Congress sent the proposed Twenty-Sixth Amendment to the states for their ratification. The

CHAPTER OUTLINE

- ✪ The Origins of a New Nation

- ✪ The First Attempt at Government: The Articles of Confederation

- ✪ The Miracle at Philadelphia: Writing a Constitution

- ✪ The U.S. Constitution

- ✪ The Drive for Ratification

- ✪ Methods of Amending the Constitution

required three-fourths of the states ratified the amendment within three months—making its adoption on June 30, 1971, the quickest in the history of the constitutional amending process.

However, young people never have voted in large numbers. In spite of issues of concern to those under the age of twenty-five, including a possible draft, Internet privacy, reproductive rights, credit card and cell phone rules and regulations, rising college tuition, and the continuance of student loan programs, until 2004 voter turnout among those age eighteen to twenty-four continued to decline. Voter registration drives and voter awareness campaigns by groups like Rock the Vote and Hip-Hop Summit Action Network produced record numbers of young voters in 2004. And, according to exit polls after the 2006 elections, the number of young voters was up by 2% over the youth turnout for the 2002 elections.

THE CONSTITUTION INTENTIONALLY WAS WRITTEN to forestall the need for amendment, and the process by which it could be changed or amended was made time consuming and difficult. Over the years, thousands of amendments—including those to prohibit child labor, provide equal rights for women, grant statehood to the District of Columbia, balance the federal budget, and ban flag burning—have been debated or sent to the states for their approval, only to die slow deaths. Only twenty-seven amendments have successfully made their way into the Constitution. What the Framers came up with in Philadelphia has continued to work, in spite of increasing demands on and dissatisfaction with our national government. Perhaps Americans are happier with the system of government created by the Framers than they realize.

The ideas that went into the making of the Constitution and the ways in which the Constitution has evolved to address the problems of a growing and ever-changing nation are at the core of our discussion in this chapter. First, we will examine the origins of the new nation and the circumstances surrounding the Declaration of Independence and the break with Great Britain. After discussing the first attempts at American government created by the Articles of Confederation, we will examine the circumstances surrounding writing a constitution and will review the results of the Framers' efforts—the U.S. Constitution. Finally, we will address methods of amending the Constitution.

The Origins of a New Nation

STARTING IN THE EARLY SEVENTEENTH CENTURY, colonists came to the New World for a variety of reasons. Often, as detailed in chapter 1, it was to escape religious persecution. Others came seeking a new start on a continent where land was plentiful. The independence and diversity of the settlers in the New World made the question of how best to rule the new colonies a tricky one. More than merely an ocean separated England from the colonies; the colonists were independent people, and it soon became clear that the crown could not govern its subjects in the colonies with the same close rein used at home. King James I thus allowed some local participation in decision making through arrangements such as the first elected colonial assembly, the Virginia House of Burgesses, and the elected General Court that governed the Massachusetts Bay colony after 1629. Almost all of the colonists agreed that the king ruled by divine right, but English monarchs allowed the colonists significant liberties in terms of self-government, religious practices, and economic organization. For 140 years, this system worked fairly well.[4]

By the early 1760s, however, a century and a half of physical separation, development of colonial industry, and the relative self-governance of the colonies led to weakening ties with—and loyalties to—the crown. By this time, each of the thirteen colonies had drafted its own written constitution, which provided the fundamental rules or laws for each colony. Moreover, many of the most oppressive British traditions—feudalism, a rigid class system, and the absolute authority of the king—were absent in the New World. Land was abundant. The guild and craft systems that severely limited entry into many skilled professions in England did not exist in the colonies. Although religion was central to the lives of most colonists, there was no single state church.

TRADE AND TAXATION

Mercantilism, an economic theory designed to increase a nation's wealth through the development of commercial industry and a favorable balance of trade, justified Britain's maintenance of strict import/export controls on the colonies. After 1650, for example, Parliament passed a series of navigation acts to prevent its chief rival, Holland, from trading with the English colonies. From 1650 until well into the 1700s, England tried to regulate colonial imports and exports, believing that it was critical to export more goods than it imported as a way of increasing the gold and silver in its treasury. These policies, however, were difficult to enforce and often were ignored by the colonists, who saw little self-benefit in them. Thus, for years, an unwritten agreement existed. The colonists relinquished to the crown and the British Parliament the authority to regulate trade and conduct international affairs, but they retained the right to levy their own taxes.

This fragile agreement was soon put to the test. The French and Indian War, fought from 1756 to 1763 on the western frontier of the colonies and in Canada, was part of a global war initiated by the British. This American phase of the Seven Years War was fought between England and France with its Indian allies. In North America, its immediate cause was the rival claims of those two European nations for the lands between the Allegheny Mountains and the Mississippi River. The Treaty of Paris, signed in 1763, signaled the end of the war. The colonists expected that with the Indian problem on the western frontier now under control, westward migration and settlement could begin in earnest. In 1763, they were shocked when the crown decreed that there was to be no further westward movement by British subjects. Parliament believed that expansion into Indian territory would lead to new expenditures for the defense of the settlers, draining the British treasury.

To raise money to pay for the war as well as the expenses of administering the colonies, Parliament enacted the Sugar Act in 1764, which placed taxes on sugar, wine, coffee, and other products commonly exported to the colonies. A postwar colonial depression heightened resentment of the tax. Major protest, however, failed to materialize until imposition of the Stamp Act by the British Parliament in 1765. This law required that all paper items bought and sold in the colonies carry a stamp mandated by the crown. The tax itself was not offensive to the colonists. However, they feared this act would establish a precedent for the British Parliament not only to regulate commerce in the colonies, but also to raise revenues from the colonists without the approval of the colonial governments. Around the colonies, the political cry "no taxation without representation" became prominent.

Colonists were outraged. Men throughout the colonies organized the Sons of Liberty, under the leadership of Samuel Adams and Patrick Henry. Women formed the Daughters of Liberty. Protests against the Stamp Act were violent and loud. Riots, often led by the Sons of Liberty, broke out. They were especially violent in Boston, where the colonial governor's home was burned by an angry mob, and British stamp agents

mercantilism
An economic theory designed to increase a nation's wealth through the development of commercial industry and a favorable balance of trade.

■ Today, Samuel Adams (1722–1803) is well known for the beer that bears his name. His original claim to fame was as a leader against the British and loyalist oppressors (although he did bankrupt his family's brewery business). As a member of the Massachusetts legislature, he advocated defiance of the Stamp Act. With the passage of the Townshend Acts in 1767, he organized a letter-writing campaign urging other colonies to join in resistance. Later, in 1772, he founded the Committees of Correspondence to unite the colonies.

charged with collecting the tax were threatened. A boycott of goods needing the stamps as well as British imports also was organized.

FIRST STEPS TOWARD INDEPENDENCE

In 1765, nine of the thirteen colonies sent representatives to a meeting in New York City, where a detailed list of crown violations of the colonists' fundamental rights was drafted. Known as the **Stamp Act Congress,** this gathering was the first official meeting of the colonies and the first step toward a unified nation. Attendees defined what they thought to be the proper relationship between colonial governments and the British Parliament; they ardently believed Parliament had no authority to tax them without representation in that body. In contrast, the British believed that direct representation of the colonists was impractical and that members of Parliament represented the best interests of all the English, including the colonists.

The Stamp Act Congress and its petitions to the crown did little to stop the onslaught of taxing measures. Parliament did, however, repeal the Stamp Act and revise the Sugar Act in 1766, largely because of the uproar made by British merchants who were losing large sums of money as a result of the boycotts. Rather than appeasing the colonists, however, these actions emboldened them to increase their resistance. In 1767, Parliament enacted the Townshend Acts, which imposed duties on all kinds of colonial imports, including tea. Responses from the Sons and Daughters of Liberty were immediate. Another boycott was announced, and almost all colonists gave up their favorite drink in a united show of resistance to the tax and British authority.[5]

Tensions continued to run high, especially after the British sent 4,000 troops to Boston. On March 5, 1770, English troops opened fire on a mob that included disgruntled dock workers, whose jobs had been taken by British soldiers, and members of the Sons of Liberty, who were taunting the soldiers in front of the Boston Customs House. Five colonists were killed in what became known as the Boston Massacre. Following this confrontation, all duties except those on tea were lifted. The tea tax, however, continued to be a symbolic irritant.

In 1773, despite dissent in England over the treatment of the colonies, Parliament passed the Tea Act, granting a monopoly to the financially strapped East India Company to sell the tea imported from Britain. The company was allowed to funnel business to American merchants loyal to the crown, thereby undercutting colonial merchants.

When the next shipment of tea arrived in Boston from Great Britain, the colonists responded by throwing the Boston Tea Party. Similar tea parties were held in other colonies. When the news of these actions reached King George III, he flew into a rage against the actions of his disloyal subjects. "The die is now cast," the king told his prime minister. "The colonies must either submit or triumph."

King George's first act of retaliation was to persuade Parliament to pass the Coercive Acts in 1774. Known in the colonies as the Intolerable Acts, they contained a key provision calling for a total blockade of Boston Harbor until restitution was made for the tea. Another provision reinforced the Quartering Act. It gave royal governors the authority to house British soldiers in the homes of private citizens, allowing Britain to send an additional 4,000 soldiers to patrol Boston.

THE CONTINENTAL CONGRESSES

The British could never have guessed how the cumulative impact of these actions would unite the colonists. **Committees of Correspondence**—organizations in each of the American colonies created to keep colonists informed—spread the word, and food and money were sent to the people of Boston from all over the thirteen colonies. The tax itself was no longer the key issue; now the extent of British authority over the colonies was the far more important question. At the request of the colonial

Stamp Act Congress
Meeting of representatives of nine of the thirteen colonies held in New York City in 1765, during which representatives drafted a document to send to the king listing how their rights had been violated.

Committees of Correspondence
Organizations in each of the American colonies created to keep colonists abreast of developments with the British; served as powerful molders of public opinion against the British.

assemblies of Massachusetts and Virginia, all but Georgia's colonial assembly agreed to select a group of delegates to attend a continental congress authorized to communicate with the king on behalf of the now-united colonies.

The **First Continental Congress** met in Philadelphia from September 5 to October 26, 1774. It was made up of fifty-six delegates from all of the colonies except Georgia. The colonists had yet to think of breaking with Great Britain; at this point, they simply wanted to iron out their differences with the king. By October, they had agreed on a series of resolutions to oppose the Coercive Acts and to establish a formal organization to boycott British goods. The Congress also drafted a Declaration of Rights and Resolves, which called for colonial rights of petition and assembly, trial by peers, freedom from a standing army, and the selection of representative councils to levy taxes.

King George refused to yield, tensions continued to rise, and a **Second Continental Congress** was deemed necessary. Before it could meet, fighting broke out early in the morning of April 19, 1775, at Lexington and Concord, Massachusetts, with what Ralph Waldo Emerson called "the shot heard round the world." Eight colonial soldiers, called Minutemen, were killed, and 16,000 British troops besieged Boston.

When the Second Continental Congress convened in Philadelphia on May 10, 1775, delegates were united by their increased hostility to Great Britain. In a final attempt to avert conflict, the Second Continental Congress adopted the Olive Branch Petition on July 5, 1775, asking the king to end hostilities. King George rejected the petition and sent an additional 20,000 troops to quell the rebellion.

THE DECLARATION OF INDEPENDENCE

In January 1776, Thomas Paine, with the support and encouragement of Benjamin Franklin, issued (at first anonymously) *Common Sense*, a pamphlet forcefully arguing for independence from Great Britain. *Common Sense* galvanized the American public against reconciliation with England. On May 15, 1776, Virginia became the first colony to call for independence, instructing one of its delegates to the Second Continental Congress to introduce a resolution to that effect. On June 7, 1776, Richard Henry Lee of Virginia rose to move "that these United Colonies are, and of right ought to be, free and independent States, and that all connection between them and the State of Great Britain is, and ought to be, dissolved." His three-part resolution—which called for independence, the formation of foreign alliances, and preparation of a plan of **confederation**—triggered hot debate among the delegates. A proclamation of independence from Great Britain was treason, a crime punishable by death. Although six of the thirteen colonies had already instructed their delegates to vote for independence, the Second Continental Congress was suspended to allow its delegates to return home to their respective colonial legislatures for final instructions. Independence was not a move to be taken lightly.

Committees were set up to consider each point of Richard Henry Lee's proposal. A committee of five was selected to begin work on a **Declaration of Independence.** The Congress selected Benjamin Franklin of Pennsylvania, John Adams of Massachusetts, Robert Livingston of New York, and Roger Sherman of Connecticut as members of the committee. Adams lobbied hard for a Southerner to add balance. Thus, owing to his southern origin as well as his "peculiar felicity of expression," Thomas Jefferson of Virginia was selected as chair.

On July 2, 1776, twelve of the thirteen colonies (with New York abstaining) voted for independence. Two days later, the Second Continental Congress voted to adopt the Declaration of Independence penned by Thomas Jefferson. On July 9, 1776, the Declaration, now with the approval of New York, was read aloud in Philadelphia.[6]

In simple but eloquent language, Jefferson set out the reasons for the colonies' separation from Great Britain. Most of his stirring rhetoric drew heavily on the works of seventeenth- and eighteenth-century political philosophers, particularly the

First Continental Congress
Meeting held in Philadelphia from September 5 to October 26, 1774, in which fifty-six delegates (from every colony except Georgia) adopted a resolution in opposition to the Coercive Acts.

Second Continental Congress
Meeting that convened in Philadelphia on May 10, 1775, to make one last effort to avert conflict with England. It adopted the Declaration of Independence in 1776.

confederation
Type of government where the national government derives its powers from the states; a league of independent states.

Declaration of Independence
Document drafted by Thomas Jefferson in 1776 that proclaimed the right of the American colonies to separate from Great Britain.

English philosopher John Locke, who argued that individuals who give their consent to be governed have the right to resist or remove rulers who violate the rights of citizens.

It is easy to see the colonists' debt to John Locke. In ringing language, the Declaration of Independence proclaims:

> We hold these truths to be self-evident, that all men are created equal, that they are endowed by their Creator with certain unalienable Rights, that among these are Life, Liberty and the pursuit of Happiness.

The Declaration also justified the colonists' break with the crown, clarified their notions of the proper form of government, and enumerated the wrongs that the colonists had suffered under British rule. After the Declaration was signed and transmitted to the king, the Revolutionary War waged on, and the Continental Congress attempted to fashion a new united government.

The First Attempt at Government: The Articles of Confederation

Articles of Confederation
The compact among the thirteen original states that was the basis of their government. Written in 1776, the Articles were not ratified by all the states until 1781.

VIDEO ROUNDTABLE

The Articles of Confederation

THE BRITISH HAD NO WRITTEN CONSTITUTION. The delegates to the Second Continental Congress were attempting to codify arrangements that had never before been put into legal terminology. To make things more complicated, the delegates had to arrive at these decisions in a wartime atmosphere. Nevertheless, in late 1777, the **Articles of Confederation,** creating a loose "league of friendship" between the thirteen sovereign or independent states, were passed by the Congress and presented to the states for their ratification. The Articles were finally ratified by all thirteen states in March 1781.[7]

Unlike Great Britain's unitary system of government, wherein all of the powers of the government reside in the national government, the national government in a confederation derives all of its powers directly from the states. Thus, the national government in a confederacy is weaker than the sum of its parts, and the states often consider themselves independent nation-states linked together only for limited purposes such as national defense. So, the Articles of Confederation proposed the following:

- A national government with a Congress empowered to make peace, coin money, appoint officers for an army, control the post office, and negotiate with Indian tribes.
- Each state's retention of its independence and sovereignty, or ultimate authority, to govern within its territories.
- One vote in the Continental Congress for each state, regardless of size.
- The vote of nine states to pass any measure (a unanimous vote for any amendment).
- The selection and payment of delegates to the Congress by their respective state legislatures.

PROBLEMS UNDER THE ARTICLES OF CONFEDERATION

By 1784, just one year after the Revolutionary Army was disbanded, governing the new nation under the Articles of Confederation proved unworkable.[8] Congress rarely could assemble the required quorum of nine states to conduct business. Even when it did meet, there was little agreement among the states on any policies. To raise revenue to pay off war debts and run the government, various land, poll, and liquor taxes were proposed. But, since Congress had no specific power to tax, all these proposals were rejected. At one point, Congress was even driven out of Philadelphia (then the capital of the new national government) by its own unpaid army.

Although the national government could coin money, it had no resources to back up the value of its currency. Continental dollars were worth little, and trade between states became chaotic as some states began to coin their own money. Another weakness was that the Articles of Confederation did not allow Congress to regulate commerce among the states or with foreign nations. As a result, individual states attempted to enter into agreements with other countries, and foreign nations were suspicious of trade agreements made with the Congress of the Confederation.

The Articles of Confederation, moreover, had no provision for a judicial system to handle the growing number of economic conflicts and boundary disputes among the individual states. Several states claimed the same lands to the west, and Pennsylvania and Virginia went to war with each other.

The Articles' greatest weakness was the lack of a strong central government. Although states had operated independently before the war, during the war they acceded to the national government's authority to wage armed conflict. Once the war was over, however, each state resumed its sovereign status and was unwilling to give up rights, such as the power to tax, to an untested national government. Consequently, the government was unable to force the states to abide by the provisions of the Treaty of Paris, signed in 1783, which officially ended the war.

Photo courtesy: Bettmann/CORBIS

■ With Daniel Shays in the lead, a group of farmers and Continental Army veterans marched on the courthouse in Springfield, Massachusetts, to stop the state court from foreclosing on the mortgages on their farms. Unrest such as this prompted quick action to remedy the weaknesses of the Articles of Confederation.

The Miracle at Philadelphia: Writing a Constitution

ON FEBRUARY 21, 1787, in the throes of economic turmoil and with domestic tranquility gone haywire, the Congress passed an official resolution. It called for a Constitutional Convention in Philadelphia for "the sole and express purpose of revising the Articles of Confederation."

However, many delegates that gathered in sweltering Philadelphia on May 25, 1787, were prepared to take potentially treasonous steps to preserve the union. For example, on the first day the convention was in session, Edmund Randolph and James Madison of Virginia proposed fifteen resolutions creating an entirely new government (later known as the Virginia Plan). Their enthusiasm was not universal. Many delegates, including William Paterson of New Jersey, considered these resolutions to be in violation of the convention's charter and proposed the New Jersey Plan, which took greater steps to preserve the Articles. These proposals met heated debate on the convention's floor.

THE CHARACTERISTICS AND MOTIVES OF THE FRAMERS

The fifty-five delegates who attended the Constitutional Convention labored long and hard that hot summer. Owing to the high stakes of their action, all of the convention's work was conducted behind closed doors. George Washington of

VIDEO ROUNDTABLE

Intent of the Framers

Virginia, who was unanimously elected the convention's presiding officer, cautioned delegates not to reveal details of the convention even to their family members.

All of the delegates to the Constitutional Convention were men; hence, they often are referred to as the "Founding Fathers." Most of them, however, were quite young; many were in their twenties and thirties, and only one—Franklin, at eighty-one—was quite old. Several owned slaves. Here, we generally refer to the delegates as the Framers, because their work provided the framework for our new government. The Framers brought with them a vast amount of political, educational, legal, and business experience. It is clear that they were an exceptional lot who ultimately produced a brilliant **constitution,** or document establishing the structure, functions, and limitations of a government. (See Analyzing Visuals: Who Were the Framers?)

However, debate about the Framers' motives filled the air during the ratification struggle and has provided grist for the mill of historians and political scientists over the years. In his *Economic Interpretation of the Constitution of the United States* (1913), Charles A. Beard argued that the 1780s were a critical period not for the nation as a whole, but rather for businessmen who feared that a weak, decentralized government could harm their economic interests.[9] Beard argued that the merchants wanted a strong national government to promote industry and trade, to protect private property, and most importantly, to ensure payment of the public debt—much of which was owed to them.

By the 1950s, this view had fallen into disfavor when other historians were unable to find direct links between wealth and the Framers' motives for establishing the Constitution and others faulted Beard's failure to consider the impact of religion and individual views about government.[10] In the 1960s, however, another group of historians began to argue that social and economic factors were, in fact, important motives for supporting the Constitution. Jackson Turner Main for example, posited that while the Constitution's supporters might not have been the united group of creditors suggested by Beard, they were wealthier, came from higher social strata, and had greater concern for maintaining the prevailing social order than the general public.[11] Gordon S. Wood deemphasized economics to argue that major social divisions explained different groups' support for (or opposition to) the new Constitution. He concluded that the Framers were representatives of a class that favored order and stability over some of the more radical ideas that had inspired the American Revolutionary War and the break with Britain.[12]

THE VIRGINIA AND NEW JERSEY PLANS

The **Virginia Plan,** proposed by James Madison and Edmund Randolph, called for a national system based heavily on the European nation-state model, wherein the national government derives its powers from the people and not from the member states.

Its key features included:

- Creation of a powerful central government with three branches—the legislative, executive, and judicial.
- A two-house legislature with one house elected directly by the people, the other chosen from among persons nominated by the state legislatures.
- A legislature with the power to select the executive and the judiciary.

In general, smaller states such as New Jersey and Connecticut felt comfortable with the arrangements under the Articles of Confederation. These states offered another model of government, the **New Jersey Plan.** Its key features included:

- Strengthening the Articles, not replacing them.
- Creating a one-house legislature with one vote for each state with representatives chosen by state legislatures.
- Giving Congress the power to raise revenue from duties and postal service.
- Creating a Supreme Court with members appointed for life by the executive officers.

constitution
A document establishing the structure, functions, and limitations of a government.

Virginia Plan
The first general plan for the Constitution, proposed by James Madison and Edmund Randolph. Its key points were a bicameral legislature, an executive chosen by the legislature, and a judiciary also named by the legislature.

New Jersey Plan
A framework for the Constitution proposed by a group of small states; its key points were a one-house legislature with one vote for each state, the establishment of the acts of Congress as the "supreme law" of the land, and a supreme judiciary with limited power.

Analyzing Visuals

WHO WERE THE FRAMERS?

Who were the Framers of the U.S. Constitution? Of the fifty-five delegates who attended some portion of the Philadelphia meetings, seventeen were slaveholders who owned approximately 1,400 slaves. (George Washington, George Mason, and John Rutledge held the greatest number of slaves at the time of the convention.) In terms of education, thirty-one went to college; twenty-four did not. Most of those who did not attend college were trained as business, legal, and printing apprentices. Seven delegates signed both the U.S. Constitution and the Declaration of Independence. After studying the graph and the material on writing and signing the Constitution in this chapter, answer the following critical thinking questions: What is the relationship, if any, between the number of a state's delegates who served in the Continental Congresses and the number of the state's signers of the Constitution? What is the relationship, if any, between a state's population (shown in parentheses in the bar graph) and the number of the state's signers of the U.S. Constitution? What does that suggest about the conflict between the large states and small states? What is the relationship, if any, between the number of a state's delegates who were slaveholders and the number of the state's signers of the U.S. Constitution? What does that suggest about the conflicts over slavery at the convention?

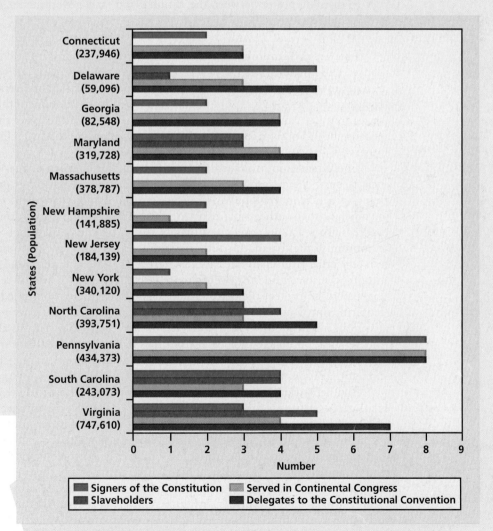

Sources: Clinton Rossiter, *The Grand Convention* (New York: Macmillan, 1966); National Archives and Records Administration, "The Founding Fathers: A Brief Overview," http://www.archives.gov.

CONSTITUTIONAL COMPROMISES

The most serious disagreement between the Virginia and New Jersey plans concerned state representation in Congress. When a deadlock loomed, Connecticut offered its own compromise. Representation in the House of Representatives would be determined by population, and each state would have an equal vote in the Senate. Again, there was a stalemate.

A committee to work out an agreement soon reported back what became known as the **Great Compromise.** Taking ideas from both the Virginia and New Jersey plans, it recommended:

- In one house of the legislature (later called the House of Representatives), there would be fifty-six representatives—one representative for every 30,000 inhabitants. Representatives would be elected directly by the people.
- That house should have the power to originate all bills for raising and spending money.
- In the second house of the legislature (later called the Senate), each state should have an equal vote, and representatives would be selected by the state legislatures.
- In dividing power between the national and state governments, national power would be supreme.[13]

The Great Compromise ultimately met with the approval of all states in attendance. The smaller states were pleased because they got equal representation in the Senate; the larger states were satisfied with the proportional representation in the House of Representatives. The small states then would dominate the Senate while the large states, such as Virginia and Pennsylvania, would control the House. But, because both houses had to pass any legislation, neither body could dominate the other.

The Great Compromise dealt with one major concern of the Framers—how best to treat the differences in large and small states—but other problems stemming largely from regional differences remained. Slavery, which formed the basis of much of the southern states' cotton economy, was one of the thorniest issues to address. To reach an agreement on the Constitution, the Framers had to craft a compromise that balanced southern commercial interests with comparable northern concerns. Eventually the Framers agreed that Northerners would support continuing the slave trade for twenty more years, as well as a twenty-year ban on taxing exports to protect the cotton trade, while Southerners consented to a provision requiring only a majority vote on navigation laws, and the national government was given the authority to regulate foreign commerce. Moreover, it was also agreed that the Senate would have the power to ratify treaties by a two-thirds majority, which assuaged the fears of southern states, who made up more than one-third of the nation at that time.

Another sticking point concerning slavery remained: how to determine state population for purposes of representation in the House of Representatives. Slaves could not vote, but the southern states wanted them included for purposes of determining population. After considerable dissension, it was decided that population for purposes of representation and the apportionment of direct taxes would be calculated by adding the "whole Number of Free Persons" to "three-fifths of all other Persons." "All other Persons" was the delegates' euphemistic way of referring to slaves. Known as the **Three-Fifths Compromise,** this highly political deal assured that the South would hold 47 percent of the House—enough to prevent attacks on slavery but not so much as to foster the spread of slavery northward.

Great Compromise
A decision made during the Constitutional Convention to give each state the same number of representatives in the Senate regardless of size; representation in the House was determined by population.

Three-Fifths Compromise
Agreement reached at the Constitutional Convention stipulating that each slave was to be counted as three-fifths of a person for purposes of determining population for representation in the U.S. House of Representatives.

UNFINISHED BUSINESS AFFECTING THE EXECUTIVE BRANCH

The Framers next turned to fashioning an executive branch. While they agreed on the idea of a one-person executive, they could not settle on the length of the term of office, nor on how the chief executive should be selected. The delegates feared putting too much power, including selection of a president, into the hands of the lower classes. At the same time, representatives from the smaller states feared that the selection of the chief executive by the legislature would put additional power into the hands of the large states.

Amid these fears, the Committee on Unfinished Portions, whose sole responsibility was to iron out problems and disagreements concerning the office of chief executive, conducted its work. The committee recommended that the presidential term of office be fixed at four years instead of seven, as had earlier been proposed. By choosing not to mention a period of time within which the chief executive would be eligible for reelection, they made it possible for a president to serve more than one term.

The Framers also created the Electoral College. The Electoral College system gave individual states a key role, because each state would select electors equal to the number of representatives it had in the House and Senate. It was a vague compromise that removed election of the president and vice president from both the Congress and the people and put it in the hands of electors whose method of selection would be left to the states.

In drafting the new Constitution, the Framers also were careful to include a provision for removal of the chief executive. The House of Representatives was given the sole responsibility of investigating and charging a president or vice president with "Treason, Bribery, or other high Crimes and Misdemeanors." A majority vote then would result in issuing articles of impeachment against the president or vice president. In turn, the Senate was given sole responsibility to try the president or vice president on the charges issued by the House. A two-thirds vote of the Senate was required to convict and remove the president or the vice president from office.

The U.S. Constitution

AFTER THE COMPROMISE ON THE PRESIDENCY, work proceeded quickly on the remaining resolutions of the Constitution. The Preamble to the Constitution, the last section to be drafted, contains exceptionally powerful language that forms the bedrock of American political tradition. Its opening line, "We the People of the United States," boldly proclaimed that a loose confederation of independent states no longer existed. Instead, there was but one American people and nation. And, the opening explained the source of the government's power: it came directly from the people.

The Constitution then explained the need for the new outline of government: "in Order to form a more perfect Union" indirectly acknowledged the weaknesses of the Articles of Confederation in governing a growing nation. Next, the optimistic goals of the Framers for the new nation were set out: to "establish Justice, insure domestic Tranquility, provide for the common defence, promote the general Welfare, and secure the Blessings of Liberty to ourselves and our Posterity"; followed by the formal creation of a new government: "do ordain and establish this Constitution for the United States of America." The Constitution was approved by the delegates from all twelve states in attendance on September 17, 1787.

Comparing Constitutions

THE BASIC PRINCIPLES OF THE CONSTITUTION

The proposed structure of the new national government owed much to the writings of the French philosopher Montesquieu (1689–1755), who advocated distinct func-

separation of powers
A way of dividing power among three branches of government in which members of the House of Representatives, members of the Senate, the president, and the federal courts are selected by and responsible to different constituencies.

checks and balances
A governmental structure that gives each of the three branches of government some degree of oversight and control over the actions of the others.

tions for each branch of government, called **separation of powers,** with a system of **checks and balances** between each branch. The Constitution's concern with the distribution of power between states and the national government also reveals the heavy influence of political philosophers, as well as the colonists' experience under the Articles of Confederation.[14] (Table 2.1 compares the major features of the Articles of Confederation and the Constitution.)

Federalism   The question before and during the convention was how much power states would give up to the national government. Given the nation's experiences under the Articles of Confederation, the Framers believed that a strong national government was necessary for the new nation's survival. However, they were reluctant to create a

---

TABLE 2.1   COMPARING THE ARTICLES OF CONFEDERATION AND THE CONSTITUTION

The United States has operated under two constitutions. The first, the Articles of Confederation, was in effect from March 1, 1781, when Maryland ratified it. The second, the Constitution, replaced the Articles when it was ratified by New Hampshire on June 21, 1788. The two documents have much in common—they were established by the same people (sometimes literally the same exact people, though mostly just in terms of contemporaries). But, they differ more than they resemble each other, when one looks at the details.

	Articles	Constitution
Formal name of the nation	The United States of America	Not specified, but referred to in the Preamble as "the United States of America"
Legislature	Unicameral, called Congress	Bicameral, called Congress, divided into the House of Representatives and the Senate
Members of Congress	Between two and seven members per state	Two senators per state, representatives apportioned according to population of each state
Voting in Congress	One vote per state	One vote per representative or senator
Appointment of members	All appointed by state legislatures, in the manner each legislature directed	Representatives elected by popular vote; senators appointed by state legislatures
Term of legislative office	One year	Two years for representatives, six for senators
Term limit for legislative office	No more than three out of every six years	None
Congressional pay	Paid by states	Paid by the federal government
When Congress is not in session	A Committee of States had the full powers of Congress	The President of the United States can call for Congress to assemble
Chair of legislature	President of Congress	Speaker of the House of Representatives; U.S. vice president is president of the Senate
Executive	None	President
National judiciary	Maritime judiciary established—other courts left to states	Supreme Court established, as well as other courts Congress deems necessary
Adjudicator of disputes between states	Congress	U.S. Supreme Court
New states	Admitted upon agreement of nine states (special exemption provided for Canada)	Admitted upon agreement of Congress
Amendment	When agreed upon by all states	When agreed upon by three-fourths of the states
Navy	Congress authorized to build a navy; states authorized to equip warships to counter piracy	Congress authorized to build a navy; states not allowed to keep ships of war
Army	Congress to decide on size of force and to requisition troops from each state according to population	Congress authorized to raise and support armies
Power to coin money	United States and the states	United States only
Ex post facto laws	Not forbidden	Forbidden of both the states and the Congress
Bills of attainder	Not forbidden	Forbidden of both the states and the Congress
Taxes	Apportioned by Congress, collected by the states	Laid and collected by Congress
Ratification	Unanimous consent required	Consent of nine states required

powerful government after the model of Britain, the country from which they had just won their independence. Its unitary system was not even considered by the colonists. Instead, they employed a system (now known as the **federal system**) that divides the power of government between a strong national government and the individual states.

federal system
Plan of government created in the U.S. Constitution in which power is divided between the national government and the state governments and in which independent states are bound together under one national government.

Separation of Powers Separation of powers is simply a way of parceling out power among the three branches of government. Its three key features are:

1. Three distinct branches of government: the legislative, the executive, and the judicial.
2. Three separately staffed branches of government to exercise these functions.
3. Constitutional equality and independence of each branch.

As illustrated in Figure 2.1, the Framers were careful to create a system in which law-making, law-enforcing, and law-interpreting functions were assigned to independent branches of government. On the national level (and in most states), only the legislature has the authority to make laws; the chief executive enforces laws; and the judiciary interprets them. Moreover, initially, members of the House of Representatives, members of the Senate, the president, and members of the federal courts were selected by and were therefore responsible to different constituencies.

The Framers could not have foreseen the intermingling of governmental functions that has since evolved. Locke, in fact, cautioned against giving a legislature the

VISUAL LITERACY

The American System of Checks and Balances

FIGURE 2.1 SEPARATION OF POWERS AND CHECKS AND BALANCES UNDER THE U.S. CONSTITUTION

LEGISLATIVE BRANCH POWERS
Pass all federal laws
Pass the federal budget
Declare war
Approve treaties and presidential appointments
Establish lower federal courts and the number of judges

Legislative Checks on the Executive
Impeach the president
Reject legislation or funding the president wants
Refuse to confirm nominees or approve treaties
Override the president's veto by a two-thirds vote

Executive Checks on the Legislative
Veto legislation
Call Congress into special session
Implement (or fail to implement) laws passed by Congress

EXECUTIVE BRANCH POWERS
Enforce federal laws and court orders
Propose legislation to Congress
Make foreign treaties
Nominate officers of the United States government and federal judges
Serve as commander in chief of the armed forces
Pardon people convicted in federal courts or grant reprieves

Judicial Checks on the Legislative
Rule federal and state laws unconstitutional

Judicial Checks on the Executive
Declare executive branch actions unconstitutional
Chief justice presides over impeachment trial

Legislative Checks on the Judicial
Change the number and jurisdiction of federal courts
Impeach federal judges
Propose constitutional amendments to override judicial decisions

Executive Checks on the Judicial
Appoint federal judges
Refuse to implement decisions

JUDICIAL BRANCH POWERS
Interpret federal laws and U.S. Constitution
Review the decisions of lower state and federal courts

ability to delegate its powers. In Article I of the Constitution, the legislative power is vested in the Congress. But, the president is also given legislative power via his ability to veto legislation, although his veto can be overridden by a two-thirds vote in Congress. Judicial interpretation, including judicial review, a process cemented by *Marbury* v. *Madison* (1803), then helps to clarify legislation passed by Congress and implemented by the executive branch. So, instead of a pure system of separation of powers, a symbiotic, or interdependent, relationship among the three branches of government has existed from the beginning. Or, as one scholar has explained, there are "separated institutions sharing powers."[15]

Checks and Balances   The separation of powers among the three branches of the national government is not complete. According to Montesquieu and the Framers, the powers of each branch (as well as the two houses of the national legislature and between the states and the national government) could be used to check the powers of the other two branches of government. The power of each branch of government is checked, or limited, and balanced because the legislative, executive, and judicial branches share some authority and no branch has exclusive domain over any single activity. The creation of this system allowed the Framers to minimize the threat of tyranny from any one branch. Thus, for almost every power granted to one branch, an equal control was established in the other two branches.

THE ARTICLES OF THE CONSTITUTION

The document finally signed by the Framers condenses numerous resolutions into a Preamble and seven separate articles. The first three articles establish the three branches of government, define their internal operations, and clarify their relationships with one another. The four remaining articles define the relationships among the states, declare national law to be supreme, and set out methods of amending the Constitution.

Article I: The Legislative Branch
Article I vests all legislative powers in the Congress and establishes a bicameral legislature, consisting of the Senate and the House of Representatives. It also sets out the qualifications for holding office in each house, the terms of office, the methods of selection of representatives and senators, and the system of apportionment among the states to determine membership in the House of Representatives.

One of the most important sections of Article I is section 8. It carefully lists the powers the Framers wished the new Congress to possess. These specified or **enumerated powers** contain many key provisions that had been denied to the Continental Congress under the Articles of Confederation.

After careful enumeration of seventeen powers of Congress in Article I, section 8, a final, general clause authorizing Congress to "make all Laws which shall be necessary and proper for carrying into Execution the foregoing Powers" was added to Article I. Often referred to as the elastic clause, the **necessary and proper clause** has been a source of tremendous congressional activity never anticipated by the Framers, including the passage of laws that regulate the environment, welfare programs, education, and communication. The necessary and proper clause is also the basis for the **implied powers** that Congress uses to execute its other powers.

Article II: The Executive Branch
Article II vests the executive power, that is, the authority to execute the laws of the nation, in a president of the United States. Section 1 sets the president's term of office at four years and explains the Electoral College. It also states the qualifications for office and describes a mechanism to replace the president in case of death, disability, or removal.

enumerated powers
Seventeen specific powers granted to Congress under Article I, section 8, of the U.S. Constitution; these powers include taxation, coinage of money, regulation of commerce, and the authority to provide for a national defense.

necessary and proper clause
The final paragraph of Article I, section 8, of the U.S. Constitution, which gives Congress the authority to pass all laws "necessary and proper" to carry out the enumerated powers specified in the Constitution; also called the elastic clause.

implied powers
Powers derived from the enumerated powers and the necessary and proper clause. These powers are not stated specifically but are considered to be reasonably implied through the exercise of delegated powers.

The powers and duties of the president are set out in section 3. Among the most important of these are the president's role as commander in chief of the armed forces, the authority to make treaties with the consent of the Senate, and the authority to "appoint Ambassadors, other public Ministers and Consuls, the Judges of the supreme Court, and all other Officers of the United States." Other sections of Article II instruct the president to report directly to Congress "from time to time," in what has come to be known as the State of the Union Address, and to "take Care that the Laws be faithfully executed." Section 4 provides the mechanism for removal of the president, vice president, and other officers.

Because Article II limits the presidency to natural-born citizens, a new amendment would be needed to change that qualification. (See Join the Debate: The "Equal Opportunity to Govern" Amendment.)

Article III: The Judicial Branch

Article III establishes a Supreme Court and defines its jurisdiction. During the Philadelphia meeting, the small and large states differed significantly as to the desirability of an independent judiciary and on the role of state courts in the national court system. The smaller states feared that a strong unelected judiciary would trample on their liberties. In compromise, Congress was permitted, but not required, to establish lower national courts. Thus, state courts and the national court system would exist side by side with distinct areas of authority. Federal courts were given authority to decide cases arising under federal law. The Supreme Court was also given the power to settle disputes between states, or between a state and the national government.

Although some delegates to the convention urged that the president be allowed to remove federal judges, ultimately judges were given appointments for life, presuming "good behavior." And, like the president's, their salaries cannot be lowered while they hold office. This provision was adopted to ensure that the legislature did not attempt to punish the Supreme Court or any other judges for unpopular decisions.

Articles IV Through VII

The remainder of the articles in the Constitution attempted to anticipate problems that might occur in the operation of the new national government as well as its relations to the states. Article IV begins with what is called the full faith and credit clause, which mandates that states honor the laws and judicial proceedings of the other states. Article IV also includes the mechanisms for admitting new states to the union.

Article V (discussed in greater detail on p. 45) specifies how amendments can be added to the Constitution. The Bill of Rights, which added ten amendments to the Constitution in 1791, was one of the first items of business when the First Congress met in 1789.

Article VI contains the supremacy clause, which asserts the basic primacy of the Constitution and national law over state laws and constitutions. The **supremacy clause** provides that the "Constitution, and the laws of the United States" as well as all treaties are to be the supreme law of the land. All national and state officers and judges are bound by national law and take oaths to support the federal Constitution above any state law or constitution. Because of the supremacy clause, any legitimate exercise of national power supersedes any state laws or action, in a process that is called preemption. Without the supremacy clause and the federal court's ability to invoke it, the national government would have little actual enforceable power; thus, many commentators call the supremacy clause the linchpin of the entire federal system.

Article VI also specifies that no religious test shall be required for holding any office. This mandate strengthens the separation of church and state guarantee that was quickly added to the Constitution when the First Amendment was ratified.

The seventh and final article of the Constitution concerns the procedures for ratification of the new Constitution: nine of the thirteen states would have to agree to, or ratify, its new provisions before it would become the supreme law of the land.

supremacy clause
Portion of Article VI of the U.S. Constitution mandating that national law is supreme to (that is, supersedes) all other laws passed by the states or by any other subdivision of government.

VIDEO DEBATE

Church and State

Join the Debate

THE "EQUAL OPPORTUNITY TO GOVERN" AMENDMENT

OVERVIEW: Article II, section 1, clause 5, of the U.S. Constitution declares: "No person except a natural-born citizen, or a citizen of the United States at the time of the Adoption of this Constitution, shall be eligible to the Office of President." Why would the Framers put such a restriction on the qualifications for president of the United States? In a letter to George Washington, John Jay argued that the duty of commander in chief was too important to be given to a foreign-born person—the potential for conflict of interest, danger, and appearance of impropriety in matters of war and foreign policy should not be left to chance. Charles Pinckney, a South Carolina delegate to the Constitutional Convention, expressed concern that foreign governments would use whatever means necessary to influence international events, and he cited the example of Russia, Prussia, and Austria manipulating the election of Stanislaus II to the Polish throne—only to divide Polish lands among themselves. Furthermore, Pinckney contended that the clause would ensure the "experience" of American politics and principles and guarantee "attachment to the country" so as to further eliminate the potential for mischief and foreign intrigue.

The election of Austrian-born Arnold Schwarzenegger and of Canadian-born Jennifer Granholm to the governorships of California and Michigan, respectively, reopened the debate concerning the citizenship requirement for president. Why shouldn't naturalized citizens be eligible for president? Many naturalized citizens have performed great service to their adopted country; both Henry Kissinger (born in Germany) and Madeleine Albright (born in Czechoslovakia) performed admirably as secretary of state, and over 700 foreign-born Congressional Medal of Honor recipients have demonstrated patriotism and the willingness to die for the country they embraced. With these viewpoints in mind, in July 2003, Senator Orrin Hatch (R–UT) introduced the Equal Opportunity to Govern Amendment to strike the natural-born-citizen clause from the Constitution. The proposed amendment takes into account the Framers' fear of foreign intervention and of divided loyalty by placing a lengthy citizenship requirement—twenty years—before naturalized citizens become eligible to run for presidential office.

Should a nation whose fundamental principle is equality of citizens have a constitutional clause that denies some citizens the presidency? Doesn't the Constitution allow the means to adapt to changes in history and social mores? On the other hand, doesn't the clause help prevent corruption from foreign sources?

ARGUMENTS FOR THE EQUAL OPPORTUNITY TO GOVERN AMENDMENT

- **The United States is in part composed of its immigrant population, and they should have a share in all political offices.** America is a nation of immigrants and many of the original Framers were foreign born, notably Alexander Hamilton, who helped shape the Washington administration and the executive branch. The Constitution allows for naturalized citizens to attain other high political office such as Speaker of the House, senator, or Supreme Court justice; why should

The Drive for Ratification

THE SECOND CONTINENTAL CONGRESS immediately accepted the work of the convention and forwarded the proposed Constitution to the states for their vote. It was by no means certain, however, that the new Constitution would be adopted. From the fall of 1787 to the summer of 1788, the proposed Constitution was debated hotly around the nation.

FEDERALISTS VERSUS ANTI-FEDERALISTS

Federalists
Those who favored a stronger national government and supported the proposed U.S. Constitution; later became the first U.S. political party.

Almost as soon as the ink was dry on the last signature to the Constitution, those who favored the new strong national government chose to call themselves **Federalists.**

naturalized citizens be denied the right to seek the presidency?

- **The natural-born-citizen clause has outlived its usefulness.** The problems that existed in 1787 either have changed or do not exist in the twenty-first century. The amendment process was created to allow for historical and political change, and ratification of the Equal Opportunity to Govern Amendment will increase the talent pool of presidential nominees, thus increasing the quality and choice of presidential aspirants for the American people.
- **The natural-born-citizen clause is discriminatory.** The clause is un-American in that it denies equality of opportunity for all American citizens. Naturalized citizens serve in the military, pay taxes, run for local, state, and federal office, endure the same national hardships and crises, and add to the overall quality of American life; thus, naturalized citizens should have the same rights and privileges as the native born.

ARGUMENTS AGAINST THE EQUAL OPPORTUNITY TO GOVERN AMENDMENT

- **Foreign governments still attempt to have undue influence in American politics.** The Framers were correct in assuming foreign governments attempt to manipulate American politics. For example, in 1999, the Democratic National Committee returned over $600,000 in campaign contributions to Chinese nationals attempting to gain influence with the Clinton administration. The clause was meant to be another institutional safeguard against presidential corruption.
- **Running for president is not a right.** The presidency is an institution designed for republican purposes. The

Framers strongly believed that foreign influence within the U.S. government must be restricted (the language was unanimously adopted by the Constitutional Convention) and thus they did not grant a right to run for presidential office.

- **There is no public movement or outcry to remove this clause from the Constitution.** Many constitutional scholars argue the Constitution should be amended only for pressing reasons, and amendments should be construed with a view to the well-being of future generations. Foreign policy and events are too fluid and too volatile to risk undermining the president's foreign policy and commander-in-chief authority. Until the American people determine otherwise, the clause should remain.

QUESTIONS

1. Is the natural-born clause discriminatory? Why or why not? If so, should the Constitution be amended to realize the principle of political equality?
2. Were the Framers wise in their analysis of foreign influence on American politics? Did they create a true institutional barrier to help prevent corruption by foreign governments? Explain your answers.

SELECTED READING

Amar, Akhil Reed. "Natural Born Killjoy: Why the Constitution Won't Let Immigrants Run for President, and Why That Should Change," *Legal Affairs* (March/April 2004), http://www.legalaffairs.org.

Breyer, Stephen. *Active Liberty: Interpreting Our Democratic Constitution.* New York: Knopf, 2005.

They were well aware that many still generally opposed the notion of a strong national government. Thus, they did not want to risk being labeled nationalists, so they tried to get the upper hand in the debate by nicknaming their opponents **Anti-Federalists.** Those put in the latter category insisted that they were instead Federal Republicans, who believed in a federal system. As noted in Table 2.2, Anti-Federalists argued that they simply wanted to protect state governments from the tyranny of a too powerful national government.[16]

Federalists and Anti-Federalists participated in the mass meetings that were held in state legislatures to discuss the pros and cons of the new plan. Tempers ran high at public meetings, where differences between the opposing groups were highlighted. Fervent debates were published in newspapers, which played a powerful role in the adoption process.

Anti-Federalists
Those who favored strong state governments and a weak national government; opposed the ratification of the U.S. Constitution.

Global Perspective

THE IRAQI CONSTITUTION

The United States and its allies invaded Iraq and over-threw Saddam Hussein and his governing Baath Party in 2003. In 2005, members of the Iraqi Transitional Government drafted a constitution to replace the Law of Administration for the State of Iraq for the Transitional Period that had been put in force by the Coalition Provisional Authority after the overthrow of Hussein's government. Iraqi voters ratified the constitution in October 2005.

On a basic level, the Iraqi Constitution is quite similar to the U.S. Constitution. Both constitutions set up a federal form of government in which power rests with the people and is shared between the states—or, in Iraq, "governorates"—and a central government. Iraqi federalism is designed to accommodate Iraq's ethnic and religious diversity at the governorate level while securing national interests such as defense and trade at the federal level. Similarly, the American Framers sought to balance the interests of large and small and northern and southern states while also providing for a strong central government that would protect the new nation from internal and external strife. Both constitutions also guarantee democratic forms and institutions. For example, Article 2 of the Iraqi Constitution promises that no law will contravene "the principles of democracy," and Article IV of the U.S. Constitution assures the American people that states must conform to "republican government."

Though both constitutions share certain fundamental, representative principles, there are significant differences, as well. Most of these differences relate to the significant religious and cultural differences between the two nations. While the First Amendment of the U.S. Constitution guarantees there will be no state establishment of religion, Article 2 of the Iraqi Constitution makes Islam "the official religion of the State and . . . a fundamental source of legislation," and notes, "no law that contradicts the established provisions of Islam may be established." Another significant difference between the two constitutions is that the Iraqi Constitution speaks to the social and economic welfare of the polity, while America's Constitution does not. Article 30 guarantees the Iraqi people "social and health security" and "a suitable income and appropriate housing," and Article 31 gives "every citizen . . . the right to health care." These provisions are at least partly indicative of the contemporary nature of the Iraqi Constitution, but more importantly they reflect Islam's traditional emphasis on caring for the less fortunate.

Like the Framers of the U.S. Constitution, the men and women who drafted the new Iraqi Constitution face great uncertainty and an uphill battle to secure their new nation's stability and sovereignty. It was nearly a hundred years before divisions in the United States led to the U.S. Civil War, but the Iraqi people were already facing what many experts considered a civil war at the time of their constitution's ratification.

QUESTIONS

1. What principles must a constitution embrace for a government to be considered truly democratic?
2. To what extent can a written constitution help a people overcome obstacles to sovereignty and stability?

Sources: The U.S. Constitution and the Iraqi Constitution, Draft Document Ratified in a Popular Referendum on October 15, 2005, translated from the Arabic by the United Nations' Office for Constitutional Support, http://www.washingtonpost.com.

THE FEDERALIST PAPERS

One name stood out from all the rest: "Publius" (Latin for "the people"). Between October 1787 and May 1788, eighty-five articles written under that pen name routinely appeared in newspapers in New York, a state where ratification was in doubt. Most were written by Alexander Hamilton and James Madison. Hamilton, a young, fiery New Yorker born in the British West Indies, wrote fifty-one; Madison, a Virginian who later served as the fourth president, wrote twenty-six; and jointly they penned another three. John Jay, also of New York, and later the first chief justice of the United States, wrote five of the pieces. These eighty-five essays became known as ***The Federalist Papers.***

The Federalist Papers
A series of eighty-five political papers written by John Jay, Alexander Hamilton, and James Madison in support of ratification of the U.S. Constitution.

Forced on the defensive, the Anti-Federalists responded to *The Federalist Papers* with their own series of letters written by Anti-Federalists adopting the pen names of "Brutus" and "Cato," two ancient Romans famous for their intolerance of tyranny. These letters (actually essays) undertook a line-by-line critique of the Constitution.

Anti-Federalists argued that a strong central government would render the states powerless.[17] They stressed the strengths the government had been granted under the

TABLE 2.2 FEDERALISTS AND ANTI-FEDERALISTS COMPARED

	Federalists	Anti-Federalists
Who were they?	Property owners, landed rich, merchants of Northeast and Middle Atlantic states	Small farmers, shopkeepers, laborers
Political philosophy	Elitist: saw themselves and those of their class as most fit to govern (others were to be governed).	Believed in the decency of the "common man" and in participatory democracy; viewed elites as corrupt; sought greater protection of individual rights.
Type of government favored	Powerful central government; two-house legislature; upper house (six-year term) further removed from the people, whom they distrusted.	Wanted stronger state governments (closer to the people) at the expense of the powers of the national government; sought smaller electoral districts, frequent elections, referendum and recall, and a large unicameral legislature to provide for greater class and occupational representation.
Alliances	Pro-British, Anti-French	Anti-British, Pro-French

Articles of Confederation, and argued that the Articles, not the proposed Constitution, created a true federal system. Moreover, they argued that the strong national government would tax heavily, that the Supreme Court would overwhelm the states by invalidating state laws, and that the president eventually would have too much power, as commander in chief of a large and powerful army.[18]

In particular, the Anti-Federalists feared the power of the national government to run roughshod over the liberties of the people. They proposed that the taxing power of Congress be limited, that the executive be curbed by a council, that the military consist of state militias rather than a national force, and that the jurisdiction of the Supreme Court be limited to prevent it from reviewing and potentially overturning the decisions of state courts. But, their most effective argument concerned the absence of a bill of rights in the Constitution. James Madison answered these criticisms in

■ Alexander Hamilton (left), James Madison (center), and John Jay (right) were important early Federalist leaders. Jay wrote five of *The Federalist Papers* and Madison and Hamilton wrote the rest. Hamilton became the first secretary of the treasury (1789–1795). He was killed in 1804 in a duel with Vice President Aaron Burr, who was angered by Hamilton's negative comments about his character. Madison served in the House of Representatives (1789–1797) and as secretary of state in the Jefferson administration (1801–1808). In 1808, he was elected fourth president of the United States and served two terms (1809–1817). Jay became the first chief justice of the United States (1789–1795) and negotiated the Jay Treaty with Great Britain in 1794. He then served as governor of New York from 1795 to 1801.

Federalist Nos. 10 and *51*. (The texts of these two essays are printed in Appendices II and III.)

In *Federalist No. 10*, Madison pointed out that the voters would not always succeed in electing "enlightened statesmen" as their representatives. The greatest threat to individual liberties would therefore come from factions within the government, who might place narrow interests above broader national interests and the rights of citizens. While recognizing that no form of government could protect the country from unscrupulous politicians, Madison argued that the organization of the new government would minimize the effects of political factions. The great advantage of a federal system, Madison maintained, was that it created the "happy combination" of a national government too large to be controlled by any single faction, and several state governments that would be smaller and more responsive to local needs. Moreover, he argued in *Federalist No. 51* that the proposed federal government's separation of powers would prohibit any one branch from either dominating the national government or violating the rights of citizens.

RATIFYING THE CONSTITUTION

Debate continued in the thirteen states as votes were taken from December 1787 to June 1788, in accordance with the ratifying process laid out in Article VII of the proposed Constitution. Three states acted quickly to ratify the new Constitution. Two small states, Delaware and New Jersey, voted to ratify before the large states could rethink the notion of equal representation of the states in the Senate. Pennsylvania, where Federalists were well organized, was also one of the first three states to ratify. Massachusetts assented to the new government but tempered its support by calling for an immediate addition of amendments, including one protecting personal rights. New Hampshire became the crucial ninth state to ratify on June 21, 1788. This action completed the ratification process outlined in Article VII of the Constitution and marked the beginning of a new nation. But, New York and Virginia, which at that time accounted for more than 40 percent of the new nation's population, had not yet ratified the Constitution. Thus, the practical future of the new nation remained in doubt.

SIMULATION

You Are James Madison

Alexander Hamilton in New York and James Madison in Virginia worked feverishly to convince delegates to their state conventions to vote for the new government. In New York, sentiment against the Constitution was high. In Albany, fighting resulting in injuries and death broke out over ratification. When news of Virginia's acceptance of the Constitution reached the New York convention, Hamilton finally was able to convince a majority of those present to follow suit by a narrow margin of three votes. Both states also recommended the addition of a series of structural amendments and a bill of rights.

ADDING A BILL OF RIGHTS

Once the Constitution was ratified, elections were held. When Congress convened, it immediately sent a set of amendments to the states for their ratification. An amendment authorizing the enlargement of the House of Representatives and another to prevent members of the House from raising their own salaries failed to garner favorable votes in the necessary three-fourths of the states. (See On Campus: A Student's Revenge: The Twenty-Seventh [Madison] Amendment.) The remaining ten amendments, known as the **Bill of Rights,** were ratified by 1791 in accordance with the procedures set out in the Constitution. The ten amendments are summarized in Table 2.3. Sought by Anti-Federalists as a protection for individual liberties, they offered numerous specific limitations on the national government's ability to interfere with a wide variety of personal liberties, some of which were already guaranteed by many state constitutions (see chapters 4 and 5).

Bill of Rights

The first ten amendments to the U.S. Constitution.

TABLE 2.3 **THE BILL OF RIGHTS**	
First Amendment	Freedom of religion, speech, press, and assembly
Second Amendment	The right to bear arms
Third Amendment	Prohibition against quartering of troops in private homes
Fourth Amendment	Prohibition against unreasonable searches and seizures
Fifth Amendment	Rights guaranteed to the accused: requirement for grand jury indictment; protections against double jeopardy, self-incrimination; due process
Sixth Amendment	Right to a speedy and public trial before an impartial jury, to cross-examine witnesses, and to have counsel
Seventh Amendment	Right to a trial by jury in civil suits
Eighth Amendment	Prohibition against bail fines, and cruel and unusual punishment
Ninth Amendment	Rights not listed in the Constitution retained by the people
Tenth Amendment	States or people reserve those powers not denied to them by the Constitution or delegated to the national government

Methods of Amending the Constitution

THE FRAMERS DID NOT WANT to fashion a government that could be too influenced by the whims of the people. Therefore, they made the formal amendment process a slow one to ensure that the Constitution was not impulsively amended. In keeping with this intent, only seventeen amendments have been added since the addition of the Bill of Rights. However, informal amendments, prompted by judicial interpretation and cultural and social change, have had a tremendous impact on the Constitution.

FORMAL METHODS OF AMENDING THE CONSTITUTION

Article V of the Constitution creates a two-stage amendment process: proposal and ratification.[19] The Constitution specifies two ways to accomplish each stage. As illustrated in Figure 2.2, amendments to the Constitution can be proposed by: (1) a vote of two-thirds of the members in both houses of Congress; or (2) a vote of two-thirds of the state legislatures specifically requesting Congress to call a national convention to propose amendments.

The second method has never been used. Historically, it has served as a fairly effective threat, forcing Congress to consider amendments that might otherwise never

You Are Proposing a Constitutional Amendment

FIGURE 2.2 METHODS OF AMENDING THE CONSTITUTION

On Campus

A STUDENT'S REVENGE: THE TWENTY-SEVENTH (MADISON) AMENDMENT

On June 8, 1789, in a speech before the House of Representatives, James Madison stated:

there is a seeming impropriety in leaving any set of men without controul to put their hand into the public coffers, to take out money to put into their pockets. . . . I have gone therefore so far as to fix it, that no law, varying the compensation, shall operate until there is a change in the legislation.

When Madison proposed that any salary increase for members of Congress could not take effect until the next session of Congress, he had no way of knowing that more than two centuries would pass before his plan, now known as the Twenty-Seventh Amendment, would become an official part of the Constitution. In fact, Madison deemed it worthy of addition only because the conventions of three states (Virginia, New York, and North Carolina) demanded that it be included.

By 1791, when the Bill of Rights was added to the Constitution, only six states had ratified Madison's amendment, and it seemed destined to fade into obscurity. In 1982, however, Gregory Watson, a sophomore majoring in economics at the University of Texas–Austin, discovered the unratified compensation amendment while looking for a paper topic for an American government class. Intrigued, Watson wrote a paper arguing that the proposed amendment was still viable because it had no internal time limit and, therefore, should still be ratified. Watson received a C on the paper.

Despite his grade, Watson began a ten-year, $6,000 self-financed crusade to renew interest in the compensation amendment. Watson and his allies reasoned that the amendment should be revived because of the public's growing anger with the fact that members of Congress had sought to raise their salaries without going on the record as having done so. Watson's perseverance paid off.

■ Gregory Watson with a document that contains the first ten amendments to the Constitution, as well as the compensation amendment ("Article the second: No law varying the compensation for services of the Senators and Representatives shall take effect until an election of Representatives shall have intervened"), which finally was ratified in 1992 as the Twenty-Seventh Amendment.

On May 7, 1992, the amendment was ratified by the requisite thirty-eight states. On May 18, the United States Archivist certified that the amendment was part of the Constitution, a decision that was overwhelmingly confirmed by the House of Representatives on May 19 and by the Senate on May 20. At the same time that the Senate approved the Twenty-Seventh Amendment, it also took action to ensure that a similar situation would never occur by declaring four other amendments dead.

Source: Fordham Law Review (December 1992): 497–539; and Anne Marie Kilday, "Amendment Expert Agrees with Congressional Pay Ruling," Dallas Morning News (February 14, 1993):13A.

have been debated. (The Living Constitution feature discusses the amendment process laid out in Article V.)

The ratification process is fairly straightforward. When Congress votes to propose an amendment, the Constitution specifies that the ratification process must occur in one of two ways: (1) a favorable vote in three-fourths of the state legislatures; or, (2) a favorable vote in specially called ratifying conventions in three-fourths of the states.

The Constitution itself was ratified by the favorable vote of nine states in specially called ratifying conventions. The Framers feared that the power of special interests in state legislatures would prevent a positive vote on the new Constitution. Since ratification of the Constitution, however, only one ratifying convention has been called. The Eighteenth Amendment, which caused the Prohibition era by outlawing nationwide the sale of alcoholic beverages, was ratified by the first method—a vote in state legislatures. Millions broke the law, others died from drinking homemade liquor,

The Living Constitution

The Congress, whenever two thirds of both houses shall deem it necessary, shall propose amendments to this Constitution, or, on the application of the legislatures of two thirds of the several states, shall call a convention for proposing amendments, which, in either case, shall be valid to all intents and purposes, as part of this Constitution, when ratified by the legislatures of three fourths of the several states, or by conventions in three fourths thereof, as the one or the other mode of ratification may be proposed by the Congress.

—ARTICLE V

With this article, the Framers acknowledged the potential need to change or amend the Constitution. This article provides for two methods to propose amendments: by a two-thirds vote of both houses of Congress or by a two-thirds vote of the state legislatures. It also specifies two alternative methods of ratification of proposed amendments: by a three-quarters vote of the state legislatures, or by a similar vote in state ratifying conventions.

During the Constitutional Convention in Philadelphia, the Framers were divided as to how frequently or how easily the Constitution was to be amended. The original suggestion was to allow the document to be amended "when soever it shall seem necessary." Some delegates wanted to entrust this authority to the state legislatures; however, others feared that it would give states too much power. James Madison alleviated these fears by suggesting that both Congress and the states have a role in the process.

In the late 1960s and early 1970s, leaders of the new women's rights movement sought passage of the Equal Rights Amendment (ERA). Their efforts were rewarded when the ERA was approved in the House and Senate by overwhelming majorities in 1971 and then sent out to the states for their approval. In spite of tremendous lobbying, a strong anti-ERA movement emerged and the amendment failed to gain approval in three-quarters of the state legislatures.

It is not unusual to have over one hundred potential amendments introduced in each session of Congress. Actions that would ban same-sex marriage, stop flag burning, and allow naturalized citizens to become president are some of the most frequently mentioned proposals.

The failed battles for the ERA as well as other amendments, including one to prohibit child labor and another to grant statehood to the District of Columbia, underscore how difficult it is to amend the Constitution. Thus, unlike the constitutions of individual states or many other nations, the U.S. Constitution rarely has been amended.

and still others made their fortunes selling bootleg or illegal liquor. After a decade of these problems, Congress decided to act. An additional amendment—the Twenty-First—was proposed to repeal the Eighteenth Amendment. It was sent to the states for ratification, but with a call for ratifying conventions, not a vote in the state legislatures.[20] Members of Congress correctly predicted that the move to repeal the

TIMELINE

The History of Constitutional Amendments

American Values/American Voices

BASEBALL, APPLE PIE, AND THE FLAG: THE POLITICS OF AMENDING THE CONSTITUTION

The American flag symbolizes the United States and is held as near and dear to most Americans as baseball and certainly apple pie. We salute the flag at sporting events, begin the school day and many events pledging our allegiance to it, and men and women have died defending its honor. Thus, it should not be surprising that many people were outraged when the U.S. Supreme Court ruled in *Texas v. Johnson* (1989) that a law prohibiting burning of the American flag was a form of speech protected under the First Amendment.

Since the Court's initial ruling, passing a constitutional amendment to prohibit flag burning has become one of the social issues Republicans have used to mobilize their base. So far, Republicans have been unsuccessful at passing an anti-flag burning amendment. While the House of Representatives passed such an amendment, it has yet to garner the required two-thirds vote necessary for passage in the more moderate Senate.

In 2006, many political observers were surprised when a Republican bill that would ban some forms of flag burning had one Democratic co-sponsor: Senator Hillary Rodham Clinton (D–NY). Many political observers believe that

Clinton is carefully positioning herself to the center in preparation for a run for the presidency in 2008, and thus is supporting a bill that would make it a crime to burn a flag to intimidate someone, burn someone else's flag, or destroy a flag on federal property. The bill co-sponsored by Clinton does not mention a constitutional amendment, and critics are divided as to whether this bill, written to meet many of the criticisms voiced by the majority of the Supreme Court, will withstand judicial review. Still, it is a bill popular with the general public, many of whom view the Court's decision as an attack on American patriotic values.

QUESTIONS

1. Why are flags, national or state, the object of such emotional attachment?
2. If the First Amendment protects political speech, can you think of a way that could justify special protections for the flag beyond the ones currently in force, such as how it is to be displayed or disposed of, which ironically, is by burning?

■ For all its moral foundation in groups such as the Women's Christian Temperance Union (WCTU), whose members invaded bars to protest the sale of alcoholic beverages, the Eighteenth (Prohibition) Amendment was a disaster. Among its side effects was the rise of powerful crime organizations responsible for illegal sales of alcoholic beverages. Once proposed, it took only ten months to ratify the Twenty-First Amendment, which repealed the Prohibition Amendment.

Eighteenth Amendment would encounter opposition in the statehouses, which were largely controlled by conservative rural interests.

The intensity of efforts to amend the Constitution has varied considerably, depending on the nature of the change proposed. Whereas the Twenty-First Amendment took only ten months to ratify, an equal rights amendment (ERA) was introduced in every session of Congress from 1923 until 1972, when Congress finally voted favorably for it. Even then, years of lobbying by women's groups were insufficient to garner necessary state support. By 1982, the congressionally mandated date for ratification, only thirty-five states—three short of the number required—had voted favorably on the amendment.[21] One of the most recent, concerted efforts would amend the Constitution to prohibit flag burning, as described in American Values/American Voices: Baseball, Apple Pie, and the Flag: The Politics of Amending the Constitution.

INFORMAL METHODS OF AMENDING THE CONSTITUTION

The formal amendment process is not the only way that the Constitution has been changed over time. Judicial interpretation and cultural and social change also have had a major impact on the way the Constitution has evolved.

Politics Now

AMENDING THE CONSTITUTION

"The union of a man and a woman is the most enduring human institution, honored and encouraged in all cultures and by every religious faith." So spoke President George W. Bush in announcing his initial support of congressional action to amend the Constitution to ban same-sex marriages. He did not endorse a specific amendment but instead called upon Congress to take action and endorse an amendment in the wake of the specter of the thousands of same-sex marriages that were conducted in San Francisco, California in early 2004 (these were later ruled invalid by that state's Supreme Court).

At the time of the president's announcement, a resolution prohibiting same-sex marriage was already pending before the 108th Congress. This bill, which defined marriage as a union between a man and a woman, had first been introduced in the House of Representatives in May of 2003. A companion resolution was introduced in the Senate in November of 2003.

In the Senate, the amendment was killed for the 108th session in July when a procedural vote to get the resolution to the floor failed on a 48–50 vote—12 votes shy of the 60 votes required by Senate rules. (Sixty-seven votes are necessary for a constitutional amendment to be approved by the Senate.) Six Republicans and one Independent voted with 43 Democrats to kill the amendment. The White House issued a statement noting the president's "disappointment" and urged the House to take up the measure, which it did a few days later. The resolution did come to a floor vote there, but the 227–186 vote tally failed to reach the two-thirds required.

The measure was reintroduced in the 109th Congress. With an extremely competitive election on the horizon, many conservative Republicans saw the amendment as an opportunity to energize their base for the upcoming contest.[a] Prohibiting same-sex marriage was a staple of the Republican Party's "American Values Agenda" for the 2006 midterm elections, and leaders believed that even if the amendment did not pass both houses, forcing incumbent members of Congress to take a position on the bill could pay big dividends in the November elections.[b]

As expected, the amendment once again failed on a procedural vote in the Senate, and did not receive a two-thirds majority in the House of Representatives. Although President Bush expressed his disappointment at the amendment's defeat, he noted his continued dedication to putting such a provision in the constitution, noting, "Our nation's founders set a high bar for amending our Constitution—and history has shown us that it can take several tries before an amendment builds the two-thirds support it needs in both houses of Congress."[c]

Opponents of same-sex marriage have had greater success in amending state constitutions. In 2004, for example, eleven states approved varying forms of state constitutional amendment provisions, all by significant margins. Moreover, efforts to prohibit same-sex marriage in crucial swing states such as Ohio and Michigan are credited with delivering a victory for President Bush. Studies conducted after the election concluded that focus on same-sex marriage and moral values drew some African American voters who generally opposed same-sex marriage to the polls—diminishing traditional Democratic Party strength and energizing in all eleven states the Republican Party's conservative base.

Eight additional states—Arizona, Colorado, Idaho, South Carolina, South Dakota, Tennessee, Virginia, and Wisconsin—considered gay marriage amendments in the 2006 midterm elections. The Arizona amendment failed and a number of the other amendments passed by smaller margins than those passed in 2004. Many commentators prior to the election noted the increasing organization of gay rights groups.[d] Perhaps as a result of this increased organization, public support for prohibitions on same-sex marriage was also dropping in the general public. One survey by the Pew Research Center conducted in March 2006, for example, showed that only 51 percent of respondents favored prohibiting gay marriage. Two years earlier, that number stood at 63 percent of respondents.[e]

The increasing favorability of state supreme courts to gay rights claims also affected groups' efforts to prohibit same-sex marriage. The 2003 Massachusetts Supreme Judicial Court decision that legalized same-sex marriage in that state and the October 2006 New Jersey Supreme Court decision granting same sex couples expanded benefits, although not actual marriage, put gay rights groups' arguments for marriage equality squarely in the public eye.

Finally, some observers have suggested that the general public is simply "burned out" on the issue of same-sex marriage.[f] Increasing violence in Iraq and a series of ethics scandals in Washington, D.C. took attention away from the gay marriage issue in 2006 and allowed congressional Democrats to win majorities in the House and Senate. The implications of these and other changes for the future of a federal marriage amendment, however, remain to be seen.

QUESTIONS

1. Historically, issues about marriage have been left to the states. How appropriate do you think it is to alter the Constitution to take authority over marriage away from the states? Can you think of other instances in which authority has been taken away from the states?

2. Why do you think that ballot measures prohibiting same sex marriage in individual states lost steam between 2004 and 2006? What effect did the defeat of the federal marriage amendment have on this change?

[a]Andrea Stone, "GOP Still Plans to Make Issue of Gay Marriage: Amendment Falls Far Short in Senate Vote." *USA Today* (June 8, 2006): 6A.

[b]Mike Soraghan, "Musgrave's Gay Marriage Ban Defeated: Democrats Called the Vote Political Posturing." *Denver Post* (July 29, 2006): A8.

[c]Quoted in Craig Gilbert, "Gay Marriage Amendment Fails in Senate: Measure Falls Far Short of 60 Votes Needed to Keep it Alive." *Milwaukee Journal Sentinel* (June 8, 2006): A3.

[d]Kirk Johnson, "Gay Marriage Losing Punch as Ballot Issue." *New York Times* (October 14, 2006): A5.

[e]Stone, "GOP Still Plans to Make Issue of Gay Marriage."

[f]Johnson, "Gay Marriage Losing Punch"

Judicial Interpretation As early as 1803, the Supreme Court declared in *Marbury* v. *Madison* that the federal courts had the power to nullify acts of the nation's government when they were found to be in conflict with the Constitution.[22] Over the years, this check on the other branches of government and on the states has increased the authority of the Court and significantly has altered the meaning of various provisions of the Constitution, a fact that prompted Woodrow Wilson to call the Supreme Court "a constitutional convention in continuous session." (More detail on the Supreme Court's role in interpreting the Constitution is found in chapters 4, 5, and 9 especially, as well as in other chapters in this book.)

Today, some analysts argue that the original intent of the Framers, as evidenced in *The Federalist Papers*, as well as in private notes taken by James Madison at the Constitutional Convention, should govern judicial interpretation of the Constitution.[23] Others argue that the Framers knew that a changing society needed an elastic, flexible document that could adapt to the ages.[24] In all likelihood, the vagueness of the document was purposeful. Those in attendance in Philadelphia recognized that they could not agree on everything and that it was wiser to leave interpretation to future generations.

SIMULATION

Yor Are Attempting to Revise the California State Constitution

Social and Cultural Change Even the most far-sighted of those in attendance at the Constitutional Convention could not have anticipated the vast changes that have occurred in the United States. For example, although many were uncomfortable with the Three-Fifths Compromise and others hoped for the abolition of slavery, none could have imagined that Colin Powell and Condoleezza Rice would serve consecutive terms as the U.S. secretary of state. Likewise, few of the Framers could have anticipated the diverse roles that women would play in American society. The Constitution often has evolved to accommodate such social and cultural changes. Thus, although there is no specific amendment guaranteeing women equal protection of the law, the federal courts have interpreted the Constitution to prohibit many forms of gender discrimination, thereby recognizing cultural and societal change. But, some change is resisted, as illustrated in Politics Now: Politics and Amending the Constitution.

Social change has also caused changes in the way institutions of government act. As problems such as the Great Depression appeared national in scope, Congress took on more and more power at the expense of the states to solve the economic and social crisis. In fact, Yale law professor Bruce Ackerman argues that on certain occasions, extraordinary times call for extraordinary measures such as the New Deal that, in effect, amend the Constitution. Thus, congressional passage (and the Supreme Court's eventual acceptance) of sweeping New Deal legislation that altered the balance of power between the national government and the states truly changed the Constitution without benefit of amendment.[25] Still, in spite of massive changes such as these, the Constitution survives, changed and ever changing after more than 200 years.

Summary

THE U.S. CONSTITUTION has proven to be a remarkably enduring document. While settlers came to the New World for a variety of reasons, most remained loyal to Great Britain and considered themselves subjects of the king. Over the years, as new generations of Americans were born on colonial soil, those ties weakened. A series of taxes levied by the king ultimately led the colonists to convene a Continental Congress and to declare their independence.

The Articles of Confederation (1781) created a loose league of friendship between the new national government and the states. Numerous weaknesses in the new government became apparent by 1784. Among the major flaws were Congress's inability to tax or regulate commerce, the absence of an executive to administer the government, and a weak central government.

When the weaknesses under the Articles of Confederation became apparent, the states called for a meeting to reform them. The Constitutional Convention (1787) quickly threw out the Articles of Confederation and fashioned a new, more workable form of government. The Constitution was the result of a series of compromises, including those over representation, over questions involving large and small states, and over how to determine population. Compromises were also made about how members of each branch of government were to be selected. The Electoral College was created to give states a key role in the selection of the president.

The proposed U.S. Constitution created a federal system that drew heavily on Montesquieu's ideas about separation of powers. These ideas concerned a way of parceling out power among the three branches of government, and checks and balances to prevent any one branch from having too much power.

The drive for ratification became a fierce fight between Federalists and Anti-Federalists. Federalists lobbied for the strong national government created by the Constitution; Anti-Federalists favored greater state power.

The Framers wanted a government that would be immune to the whims of the people. Therefore, they designed a two-stage formal amendment process that required approval on the federal and state levels. Formal amendments are not the only way that the Constitution changes. Judicial interpretation, especially by the Supreme Court, also affects the living Constitution, as do social and cultural change.

KEY TERMS

SELECTED READINGS

Ackerman, Bruce. *We the People: Transformations.* Cambridge, MA: Belknap Press, 2000.
Bailyn, Bernard. *The Ideological Origins of the American Revolution.* Cambridge, MA: Belknap Press, 1967.
Beard, Charles A. *An Economic Interpretation of the Constitution of the United States,* reissue ed. Mineola, NY: Dover, 2004.
Bernstein, Richard B., with Jerome Agel. *Amending America,* reissue ed. Lawrence: University Press of Kansas, 1995.
Bowen, Catherine Drinker. *Miracle at Philadelphia.* Boston: Little, Brown, 1986.
Brinkley, Alan, Nelson W. Polsby, and Kathleen M. Sullivan. *New Federalist Papers: Essays in Defense of the Constitution.* New York: Norton, 1997.
Dahl, Robert A. *How Democratic is the American Constitution?* New Haven, CT: Yale University Press, 2002.
Hamilton, Alexander, James Madison, and John Jay. *The Federalist Papers.* New York: Bantam Books, 1989 (first published in 1788).
Kyvig, David E. *Explicit and Authentic Acts: Amending the U.S. Constitution, 1776–1995.* Lawrence: University Press of Kansas, 1996.
Lynch, Joseph M. *Negotiating the Constitution: The Earliest Debates over Original Intent.* Ithaca, NY: Cornell University Press, 2005.
Main, Jackson Turner. *The Anti-Federalists: Critics of the Constitution, 1781–1788.* Chapel Hill: University of North Carolina Press, 2004.
———. *The Social Structure of Revolutionary America.* Princeton, NJ: Princeton University Press, 1965.
Rossiter, Clinton. *1787: Grand Convention,* reissue ed. New York: Norton, 1987.
Simon, James F. *What Kind of Nation: Thomas Jefferson, John Marshall, and the Epic Struggle to Create a United States.* New York: Simon and Schuster, 2003.
Stoner, James R., Jr. *Common Law and Liberal Theory.* Lawrence: University Press of Kansas, 1992.
Storing, Herbert J. *What the Anti-Federalists Were For.* Chicago: University of Chicago Press, 1981.
Sunstein, Cass R. *Designing Democracy: What Constitutions Do.* New York: Oxford University Press, 2001.
Tushnet, Mark. *Taking the Constitution Away from the Courts.* Princeton, NJ: Princeton University Press, 2000.
———, ed. *The Constitution in Wartime: Beyond Alarmism and Complacency.* Durham, NC: Duke University Press, 2005.
Vile, John R. *Encyclopedia of Constitutional Amendments, and Amending Issues, 1789–1995.* Santa Barbara, CA: ABC-CLIO, 1996.
Wood, Gordon S. *The Creation of the American Republic, 1776–1787,* reissue ed. New York: Norton, 1993.

WEB EXPLORATIONS

For more information on the work of the Continental Congress, see
http://lcweb2.loc.gov/ammem/bdsds/intro01.html
For a full text of the Articles of Confederation, see
http://www.usconstitution.net/articles.html
For demographic background on the Framers, see
http://www.usconstitution.net/constframedata.html
To compare *The Federalist Papers* with *The Anti-Federalist Papers,* see
http://www.law.emory.edu/FEDERAL/federalist/ and
http://wepin.com/articles/afp/index.htm
For the text of failed amendments to the U.S. Constitution, see
http://www.usconstitution.net/constamfail.html

The Constitution of the United States of America

We the People of the United States, in Order to form a more perfect Union, establish Justice, insure domestic Tranquility, provide for the common defence, promote the general Welfare, and secure the Blessings of Liberty to ourselves and our Posterity, do ordain and establish this Constitution for the United States of America.

ARTICLE I

Section 1.

All legislative Powers herein granted shall be vested in a Congress of the United States, which shall consist of a Senate and House of Representatives.

Article I is the longest and most detailed of any of the articles, sections, or amendments that make up the United States Constitution. By *enumerating* the powers of Congress, the Framers attached limits to the enormous authority they had vested in the legislative branch. At the same time, the allocation of certain powers to Congress ensured that the legislative branch would maintain control over certain vital areas of public policy and that it would be protected from incursions by the executive and judicial branches. Moreover, by clearly vesting Congress with certain powers (for example, the power to regulate interstate commerce), Article I established a water's edge for the exercise of state power in what were now national affairs.

Originally, Article I also contained restrictions limiting the amendment of several of its provisions, a feature found nowhere else in the Constitution. Section 4 prohibited Congress from making any law banning the importation of slaves until 1808, and section 9 prohibited Congress from levying an income tax on the general population. Neither section is operative any longer. Section 4 expired on its own, and section 9 was modified by passage of the Sixteenth Amendment, which established the income tax (see page 74).

Despite the great care the Framers took to limit the exercise of congressional authority to those powers enumerated in Article I, the power of Congress has grown tremendously since the nation's founding. Under Chief Justice John Marshall (1801–1835), the U.S. Supreme Court interpreted the Constitution to favor the power of the national government over the states and to permit Congress to exercise both its *enumerated* (the power to regulate interstate commerce) and *implied* (the necessary and proper clause) powers in broad fashion. With only the occasional exception, the Court has never really challenged the legislative power vested in Congress to engage in numerous areas of public policy that some constitutional scholars (and politicians and voters) believe are the province of the states. Perhaps the only area in which legislative power has diminished over the years has been the war-making power granted to Congress, something that lawmakers, for all their occasional criticism of presidential conduct of foreign policy, have ceded to the executive branch rather willingly.

Section 2.

The House of Representatives shall be composed of Members chosen every second Year by the People of the several States, and the Electors in each State shall have the Qualifications requisite for Electors of the most numerous Branch of the State Legislature.

No person shall be a Representative who shall not have attained to the Age of twenty five Years, and been seven Years a Citizen of the United States, and who shall not, when elected, be an Inhabitant of that State in which he shall be chosen.

The qualifications clause, which sets out the age and residency requirements for individuals who wish to run for the House of Representatives, became the centerpiece of a national debate that emerged during the late 1980s and early 1990s over term limits for members of Congress. In *U.S. Term Limits* v. *Thornton* (1995), the Supreme Court ruled that section 2, clause 2, did not specify any other qualification to serve in the House other than age and residency (as did section 3, clause 3, to run for the Senate). Thus, no state could restrict an individual's right to run for Congress. The Court ruled that any modification to the qualifications clause would have to come through a constitutional amendment.

Representatives and direct Taxes shall be apportioned among the several States which may be included within this Union, according to their respective Numbers which shall be determined by adding to the whole Number of free Persons, including those bound to Service for a Term of Years, and excluding Indians not taxed, three fifths of all other Persons. The actual Enumeration shall be made within three Years after the first Meeting of the Congress of the United States, and within every subsequent Term ten Years, in such Manner as they shall by Law direct. The Number of Representatives shall not exceed one for every thirty Thousand, but each State shall have at Least one Representative; and until such enumerations shall be made, the State of New Hampshire shall be entitled to chuse three, Massachusetts eight, Rhode-Island and Providence Plantations one, Connecticut five, New-York six, New Jersey four, Pennsylvania eight, Delaware one, Maryland six, Virginia ten, North Carolina five, South Carolina five, and Georgia three.

Under the Articles of Confederation, "direct" taxes (such as taxes on property) were apportioned based on land value, not population. This encouraged states to diminish the value of their land in order to reduce their tax burden. Prior to the Constitutional Convention of 1787, several prominent delegates met to discuss—and ultimately propose—changing the method for direct taxation from land value to the population of each state. A major sticking point among the delegates on this issue was how to count slaves for taxation purposes. Southern states wanted to diminish the value of slaves for tax purposes, while northern states wanted to count slaves as closer to a full person. On the other hand, southern states wanted to count slaves as "whole persons" for purposes of representation to increase their power in the House of Representatives, but northern states rejected this proposal. Ultimately, the delegates settled on the "Three-Fifths Compromise," which treated each slave as three-fifths of a person for tax and representation purposes.

At the beginning, the Three-Fifths Compromise enhanced southern power in the House. In 1790, when the 1st Congress convened, the South held 45 percent of the seats, despite a significantly smaller free population than the North. Over time, however, the South saw its power in the House diminish. By the 1830s, the South held just over 30 percent of House seats, which gave it just enough power to thwart northern initiatives on slavery questions and territorial issues, but not enough power to defeat the growing power of the North to control commercial and economic policy. This standoff between the North and South led to such events as South Carolina Senator John C. Calhoun's doctrine of nullification and secession, which argued that a state could nullify any federal law not consistent with regional or state interests. By the 1850s, the Three-Fifths Compromise had made the South dependent on expanding the number of slaveholding territories eligible for admission to the union and a judicial system sympathetic to slaveholding interests. The Three-Fifths Compromise was repealed by section 2 of the Fourteenth Amendment (see pages 72–73).

When vacancies happen in the Representation from any State, the Executive Authority thereof shall issue Writs of Election to fill such Vacancies.

This clause permits the governor of a state to call an election to replace any member of the House of Representatives who is unable to complete a term of office due to death, resignation, or removal from the House. In some cases, a governor will appoint a successor to fill out a term; in other cases, the governor will call a special election. A governor's decision is shaped less by constitutional guidelines and more by partisan interests. For example, a Democratic governor might choose to appoint a Democratic successor if he or she believes that a Republican candidate might have an advantage in a special election.

The House of Representatives shall chuse their speaker and other Officers; and shall have the sole Power of Impeachment.

Clause 5 establishes the only officer of the House of Representatives—the Speaker. The remaining offices (party leaders, whips, and so on) are created by the House.

The House also has the sole power of impeachment against members of the executive and judicial branches. The House, like the Senate, is responsible for disciplining its own members. In *Nixon* v. *U.S.* (1993), the Supreme Court ruled that government officials who are the subject of impeachment proceedings may not challenge them in court. The Court ruled that the sole power given to the House over impeachment precludes judicial intervention.

Section 3.

The Senate of the United States shall be composed of two Senators from each State chosen by the Legislature thereof, for six Years; and each Senator shall have one Vote.

The provision of this clause establishing the election of senators by state legislatures was repealed by the Seventeenth Amendment (see page 74).

Immediately after they shall be assembled in Consequence of the first Election, they shall be divided as equally as may be into three Classes. The Seats of the Senators of the first Class shall be vacated at the Expiration of the second year, of the second Class at the Expiration of the fourth Year, and of the third Class at the Expiration of the sixth Year, so that one third may be chosen every second Year and if Vacancies happen by Resignation, or otherwise, during the Recess of the Legislature of any State, the Executive thereof may make temporary Appointments until the next Meeting of the Legislature, which shall then fill such Vacancies.

Vacancies for senators are handled the same way as vacancies for representatives—through appointment or special election. The Seventeenth Amendment modified the language authorizing the state legislature to choose a replacement for a vacant Senate position.

No Person shall be a Senator who shall not have attained to the Age of thirty Years, and been nine Years a Citizen of the United States, and who shall not, when elected, be an Inhabitant of that State for which he shall be chosen.

The Vice President of the United States shall be President of the Senate, but shall have no Vote, unless they be equally divided.

Clause 4 gives the vice president the authority to vote to break a tie in the Senate. This is the only constitutional duty the Constitution specifies for the vice president. As president of the Senate, the vice president also presides over procedural matters of that body, although this is not a responsibility that vice presidents really have ever shouldered.

The Senate shall chuse their other Officers, and also a President pro tempore, in the Absence of the Vice President, or when he shall exercise the Office of President of the United States.

Clause 5 creates the position of *president pro tempore* (the president of the time), the only Senate office established by the Constitution to handle the duties of the vice president set out in section 3, clause 4.

The Senate shall have the sole Power to try all Impeachments. When sitting for that Purpose, they shall be on Oath or Affirmation. When the President of the United States is tried, the Chief Justice shall preside: And no Person shall be convicted without the Concurrence of two thirds of the Members present.

Judgment in Cases of Impeachment shall not extend further than to removal from Office, and disqualification to hold and enjoy any Office of honor, Trust or Profit under the United States; but the Party convicted shall nevertheless be liable and subject to Indictment, Trial, Judgment and Punishment, according to law.

Just as the House of Representatives has the sole power to bring impeachment against executive and judicial branch officials, the Senate has the sole power to try all impeachments. Unless the president is facing trial in the Senate, the vice president serves as the presiding officer. In 1998, President Bill Clinton was tried on two articles of impeachment (four were brought against him in the House) and found not guilty on each count. The presiding officer in President Clinton's impeachment trial was Chief Justice William H. Rehnquist.

A conviction results in the removal of an official from office. It does not prohibit subsequent civil or criminal action against that individual. Nor does it prohibit an impeached and convicted official from returning to federal office. In 1989, Alcee Hastings, a trial judge with ten years experience on the U.S. District Court for the Southern District of Florida, was convicted on impeachment charges and removed from office. In 1992, he ran successfully for the 23rd District seat of the U.S. House of Representatives, where he continues to serve as of this writing.

Section 4.

The Times, Places and Manner of holding Elections for Senators and Representatives, shall be prescribed in each State by the Legislature thereof; but the Congress may at any time by Law make or alter such Regulations, except as to the Places of chusing Senators.

The Congress shall assemble at least once in every Year, and such Meeting shall be on the first Monday in December, unless they shall by Law appoint a different Day.

Section 4 authorizes the states to establish the rules governing elections for members of Congress, but Congress has never hesitated to exercise its law-making power in this area when it has believed that improvements were necessary to improve the electoral process. The first such action did not come until 1842, when Congress passed legislation making elections to the House based on single-member districts, not from the general population. By the turn of the twentieth century, Congress had passed legislation establishing additional criteria such as the rough equality of population among districts and territorial compactness and contiguity. Article I, section 4, is one of the three main areas from which Congress derives the power to regulate the electoral process. The other two are the necessary and proper clause of Article I, section 8, clause 3, and section 2 of the Fifteenth Amendment.

Section 5.

Each House shall be the Judge of the Elections, Returns and Qualifications of its own Members, and a Majority of each shall constitute a Quorum to do business; but a smaller Number may adjourn from day to day, and may be authorized to compel the Attendance of absent Members, in such Manner, and under such Penalties as each House may provide.

Each House may determine the Rules of its Proceedings, punish its Members for disorderly Behaviour, and with the Concurrence of two thirds, expel a Member.

Clause 2 gives power to the House and Senate to establish the rules and decorum for each chamber. Expulsion from either the House or the Senate does not preclude a member from running for congressional office again or serving in any other official capacity. In *Powell v. McCormack* (1969), the Supreme Court ruled that the House's decision to exclude an individual from the chamber despite having been elected was different from the expulsion of a sitting representative.

Each House shall keep a Journal of its Proceedings, and from time to time publish the same, excepting such Parts as may in their judgment require Secrecy; and the Yeas and Nays of the Members of either House on any question shall, at the Desire of one fifth of those present, be entered on the Journal.

The *Congressional Record* is the official journal of Congress. Justice Joseph Story, in his much praised scholarly treatment of the U.S. Constitution, *Commentaries on the Constitution* (1833), said the purpose of this clause was "to insure publicity to the proceedings of the legislature, and a correspondent responsibility of the members to their respective constituents." Recorded votes (and yea-or-nay voice votes, if agreed to by one-fifth of the House or Senate), speeches, and other public business are contained in the *Congressional Record*.

Neither House, during the Session of Congress, shall, without the Consent of the other, adjourn for more than three days, nor to any other Place than that in which the two Houses shall be sitting.

Section 6.

The Senators and Representatives shall receive a Compensation for their Services, to be ascertained by Law, and paid out of the Treasury of the United States. They shall in all Cases, except Treason, Felony and Breach of the Peace, be privileged from Arrest during their Attendance at the Session of their respective Houses, and in going to and returning from the same; and for any Speech or Debate in either House, they shall not be questioned in any other Place.

The Twenty-Seventh Amendment, ratified in 1992, now governs the procedures for compensation of members of Congress. From the nation's founding until 1967, Congress had determined the salaries of its members. Then, Congress passed legislation giving the president the responsibility to recommend salary levels for members of Congress, since the president already had the responsibility to recommend pay levels for other federal officials. In 1989, as part of the Ethics Reform Act, Congress established a new system of pay raises and cost-of-living adjustments based on a particular vote.

Clause 1 also protects the right of senators and representatives from criminal prosecution for any "Speech or Debate" made in Congress. This protection stemmed from lessons drawn from the persistent conflicts between the House of Commons and the Tudor and Stuart monarchies in Great Britain, who used their power to bring civil and criminal actions against legislators whose opinions were deemed seditious or dangerous. The 1689 English Bill of Rights contained protection for legislators to conduct their business in Parliament free from such fears, and the Framers believed that such protection was essential for Congress under the Constitution. The Supreme Court has held, however, in *Gravel* v. *U.S.* (1972), that the speech or debate clause does not immunize senators or representatives from criminal inquiry if their activities in the Senate or House are the result of alleged or proven illegal action.

The privilege from arrest clause has little application in contemporary America. The clause applies only to arrests in civil suits, which were fairly common when the Constitution was ratified. The Court has interpreted the phrase "except Treason, Felony or Breach of the Peace" to make members eligible for arrest for crimes that would fall into that category. For example, a member of Congress is eligible if he or she commits a serious traffic offense, such as drunk or reckless driving, on the way to or from legislative business.

No Senator or Representative shall, during the Time for which he was elected, be appointed to any civil Office under the Authority of the United States, which shall have been created, or the Emoluments whereof shall have been encreased during such time; and no Person holding any Office under the United States, shall be a Member of either House during his Continuance in Office.

Clause 2 prohibits any senator or representative from holding a simultaneous office in the legislative or executive branches. This is one of the least controversial provisions of the Constitution. Indeed, there is no judicial interpretation of its meaning.

The general purpose of this clause is to prevent one branch of government from having an undue influence on another by creating dual incentives. It is also another safeguard in the separation of powers.

Section 7.

All Bills for raising Revenue shall originate in the House of Representatives; but the Senate may propose or concur with Amendments as on other Bills.

The power to raise revenue found in clause 1 is unique to the House of Representatives. In *Federalist No. 58*, James Madison argued that vesting such authority in the House was a key feature of the separation of powers. No bill either raising or lowering taxes may originate in the Senate. Legislation that creates incidental revenue may begin in the Senate, as long as the legislation does not involve taxation.

Every Bill which shall have passed the House of Representatives and the Senate, shall, before it become a Law, be presented to the President of the United States; If he approve he shall sign it, but if not he shall return it, with his Objections to that House in which it shall have originated, who shall enter the Objections at large on their Journal, and proceed to reconsider it. If after such Reconsideration two thirds of that House shall agree to pass the Bill, it shall be sent, together with the Objections, to the other House, by which it shall likewise be reconsidered, and if approved by two thirds of that House, it shall become a Law. But in all such Cases the Votes of both Houses shall be determined by Yeas and Nays, and the Names of the Persons voting for and against the Bill shall be entered on the Journal of each House respectively. If any Bill shall not be returned by the President within ten Days (Sundays excepted) after it shall have been presented to him, the Same shall be a Law, in like Manner as if he had signed it, unless the Congress by their Adjournment prevent its Return, in which Case it shall not be a Law.

This clause establishes several key features of presidential-congressional relations in the flow of the legislative process. For a bill to become law, it must be passed by the House and Senate, and it must be signed by the president. The Supreme Court has ruled that the veto regulations outlined in this clause serve two purposes. First, by giving the president ten days to consider a bill for approval, clause 2 provides the president with ample time to consider legislation and protects him from having to approve legislation in the wake of congressional adjournment. But clause 2 also provides Congress with a countervailing power to override a presidential veto, a procedure that requires a two-thirds vote in each chamber.

Every Order, Resolution, or Vote to which the Concurrence of the Senate and House of Represen-tatives may be necessary (except on a question of Adjournment) shall be presented to the President of the United States; and before the Same shall take Effect, shall be approved by him, or being disapproved by him, shall be repassed by two thirds of the Senate and House of Representatives, according to the Rules and Limitations prescribed in the Case of a Bill.

Clause 3 covers the presentation of resolutions, not actual legislation. For any resolution to have the force of law, it must be presented to the president for approval. Should the president veto the resolution, Congress may override this veto in the same manner expressed in section 7, clause 2. Resolutions that do not have the force of law do not require presidential approval. Preliminary votes taken on constitutional amendments and other legislative matters covered by clause 3 do not require presentation to the president.

This clause has been the subject of two major Supreme Court decisions dealing with the separation of powers. In *I.N.S.* v. *Chadha* (1983), the Court ruled that the House-only legislative veto, a practice begun during the 1930s to give Congress power to control power delegated to a rapidly expanding executive branch, violated both the bicameralism principles of Article I, section 1, and the presentment clause of section 7, clause 3. At the time, the ruling struck down about 200 legislative vetoes that had been included in various pieces of congressional legislation. In *Clinton* v. *New York* (1998), the Court ruled that the line-item veto passed by Congress to give the president the power to veto specific provisions of legislation rather than an entire bill violated the presentment clause of Article I, section 7, clause 3. The Court claimed that the line-item veto permitted the president to "repeal certain laws," a power that belonged to Congress and not the president.

Section 8.

The Congress shall have Power To lay and collect Taxes, Duties, Imposts and Excises, to pay the Debts and provide for the common Defence and general Welfare of the United States; but all Duties, Imposts and Excises shall be uniform throughout the United States;

To borrow Money on the credit of the United States;

To regulate Commerce with foreign Nations, and among the several States, and with the Indian Tribes;

To establish a uniform Rule of Naturalization, and uniform Laws on the subject of Bankruptcies throughout the United States;

To coin Money, regulate the Value thereof, and of foreign Coin, and fix the Standard of Weights and Measures;

To provide for the Punishment of counterfeiting the Securities and current Coin of the United States;

To establish Post Offices and post Roads;

To promote the Progress of Science and useful Arts, by securing for limited Times to Authors and Inventors exclusive Right to their respective Writings and Discoveries;

To constitute Tribunals inferior to the supreme Court;

To define and punish Piracies and Felonies committed on the high Seas, and Offences against the Law of Nations;

To declare War, grant Letters of Marque and Reprisal, and make rules concerning Captures on Land and Water;

To raise and support Armies, but no Appropriation of Money to that Use shall be for a longer Term than two Years;

To provide and maintain a Navy;

To make Rules for the Government and Regulation of the land and naval Forces;

To provide for calling forth the Militia to execute the Laws of the Union, suppress Insurrections and repel Invasions;

To provide for organizing, arming, and disciplining, the Militia, and for governing such Part of them as may be employed in the Service of the United States, reserving to the States respectively, the Appointment of the Officers, and the Authority of training the Militia according to the discipline prescribed by Congress;

To exercise exclusive Legislation in all Cases whatsoever, over such District (not exceeding ten Miles square) as may, by Cession of particular States, and the Acceptance of Congress, become the Seat of the Government of the United States, and to exercise like Authority over all Places purchased by the Consent of the Legislature of the State in which the Same shall be for the Erection of Forts, Magazines, Arsenals, dock-Yards, and other needful Buildings;—And

Article I, section 8, clause 1, is, in many ways, the engine of congressional power. First, clause 1 gives Congress the power to tax and spend, a power the Supreme Court has interpreted as "exhaustive" and "reaching every subject." Second, in giving Congress the power to provide for the common defense and general welfare, it offers no specific constraint on what Congress may spend public funds for and how much it may spend. Third, section 8 gives Congress complete authority in numerous areas of policy that affect Americans at home and abroad on a massive scale. These powers include the power to regulate interstate commerce (which Congress has relied on to establish federal civil rights law), to make war (a power that Congress, since the end of World War II in 1945, has increasingly deferred to the president), and to establish the federal judicial system.

Clause 1 is often cited by constitutional scholars as an example of how the Constitution constrains legislative power by limiting the powers that Congress may exercise. To a certain extent, this is true. But, it is also true that the Court has granted Congress extensive power to legislate in certain areas that bear only a tangential relationship to the specific language of some of the provisions of clause 1. For example, in *Katzenbach* v. *McClung* (1964), the Court turned back a challenge to the constitutionality of the Civil Rights Act of 1964, which Congress had passed

under its authority to regulate interstate commerce. The Court ruled that racial discrimination had an adverse effect on the free flow of commerce.

Clause 2 establishes the seat of the federal government—first New York City, now Washington, D.C. The clause also makes Congress the legislative body of the nation's capital, a power that extends to other federal bodies, such as forts, military bases, and other places where federal buildings are located.

To make all Laws which shall be necessary and proper for carrying into Execution the foregoing Powers, and all other Powers vested by this Constitution in the Government of the United States, or in any Department or Officer thereof.

Better known as the necessary and proper clause, this provision of Article I was one of the most contested points between Federalists and Anti-Federalists during the ratification debates over the Constitution. Anti-Federalists feared that the language was too broad and all-encompassing, and, if interpreted by a Supreme Court sympathetic to the nationalist ambitions of the Federalist Party, would give Congress limitless power to exercise legislative authority over state and local matters. In *McCulloch* v. *Maryland* (1819), Chief Justice John Marshall offered what constitutional scholars believe remains the definitive interpretation of the necessary and proper clause. While *McCulloch* certainly did cement the power of Congress in the federal system, the expansive definition given the necessary and proper clause by the Court is also testament to the flexible nature of the Constitution, and why so few amendments have been added to the original document.

Section 9.

The Migration or Importation of such Persons as any of the States now existing shall think proper to admit, shall not be prohibited by the Congress prior to the Year one thousand eight hundred and eight, but a Tax or duty may be imposed on such Importation, not exceeding ten dollars for each Person.

Like the other provisions of the Constitution that refer to slavery, such as the Three-Fifths Compromise, section 9 creates policy governing the institution without ever mentioning the word. The importation clause was a compromise between slave traders, who wanted to continue the practice, and opponents of slavery, who needed southern support to ratify the Constitution. In 1808, Congress passed legislation banning the importation of slaves; until then, Congress used its power to tax slaves brought to the United States.

The Privilege of the Writ of Habeas Corpus shall not be suspended, unless when in Cases of Rebellion or Invasion the public Safety may require it.

Clause 2 is the only place where the writ of *habeas corpus*—the "Great Writ," as it was known to the Framers—is mentioned in the Constitution. Only the federal government is bound by clause 2. The writ may only be suspended in times of crisis and rebellion, and then it is Congress that has the power, not the president. Thus the Military Commissions Act, which gives power to the president to suspend the writ of *habeas corpus,* may be constitutionally suspect.

No Bill of Attainder or ex post facto Law shall be passed.

A bill of attainder is a legislative act punishing a person with "pains and penalties" without the benefit of a hearing or trial. The fundamental purpose of the ban on bills of attainder is to prevent trial by legislature and other arbitrary punishments for persons vulnerable to extra-judicial proceedings. An *ex post facto law* is one passed making a previously committed civil or criminal action subject to penalty. In *Calder* v. *Bull* (1798), the Court ruled that the ban on *ex post facto* laws applied only to penal and criminal actions. A similar restriction on the states is found in Article I, section 10, clause 1.

No Capitation, or other direct, Tax shall be laid, unless in Proportion to the Census or Enumeration herein before directed to be taken.

This clause, which originally prohibited Congress from levying an income tax, was modified by the Sixteenth Amendment, passed in 1913 (see page 74).

No Tax or Duty shall be laid on Articles exported from any State.

Clause 5 prohibits Congress from levying a tax on any good or article exported from a state to a foreign country or to another state. Many southern states feared that northern members of Congress would attempt to weaken the South's slave-based economy by taxing exports. This clause prohibited such action. Congress may prohibit the shipment of certain items from one state to another and to other countries.

No Preference shall be given by any Regulation of Commerce or Revenue to the Ports of one State over those of another: nor shall Vessels bound to, or from, one State, be obliged to enter, clear, or pay Duties in another.

Congress is prohibited from making laws regulating trade that favor one state over another. Clause 6 also prohibits Congress from establishing preferences for certain ports or trade centers over others, although it may, under its power to regulate interstate commerce, pass laws that incidentally benefit certain states or maritime outlets. The Supreme Court has ruled that states are not bound by the limitations on Congress expressed in this clause.

No money shall be drawn from the Treasury, but in Consequence of Appropriations made by Law; and a regular Statement and Account of the Receipts and Expenditures of all public Money shall be published from time to time.

Clause 7 serves two fundamental purposes. First, the clause prohibits any governmental body receiving federal funds from spending those funds without the approval of Congress. Once Congress has determined that federal funds are to be spent in a certain way, the executive branch may not exercise any discretion over that decision. Second, by restricting executive control of spending power, the clause firmly reinforces congressional authority over revenue and spending, a key feature of the separation of powers.

No Title of Nobility shall be granted by the United States: And no Person holding any Office of Profit or Trust under them, shall, without the Consent of the Congress, accept of any present, Emolument, Office, or Title, of any kind whatever, from any King, Prince, or foreign State.

This provision is among the first school-taught lessons about the Constitution. To reinforce the commitment to representative democracy, the Framers prohibited a title of nobility from being conferred on any public official. This clause also prohibits any government official from accepting compensation, gifts, or similar benefits from any foreign government for services rendered without the consent of Congress.

Section 10.

No state shall enter into any Treaty, Alliance, or Confederation; grant Letters of Marque and Reprisal; coin Money; emit Bills of Credit; make any Thing but gold and silver Coin a Tender in Payment of Debts; pass any Bill of Attainder, ex post facto Law, or Law impairing the Obligation of Contracts, or grant any Title of Nobility.

This clause denies several powers to the states that were once permissible under the Articles of Confederation, and it emphasizes the Framers' commitment under the Constitution to a strong national government with Congress as the centrifugal force. During the Civil War, the Union relied on this clause in support of its view that the Confederate states had no legal existence but instead were merely "states in rebellion" against the United States.

The restrictions on states passing either bills of attainder or *ex post facto* laws have come into play at various points in American history. During Reconstruction, several states enacted legislation prohibiting any individual who aided the Confederacy from entering certain professions or enjoying other benefits available to citizens who remained loyal to the Union. The Supreme Court struck down these laws on the grounds that they violated this clause.

The provision prohibiting states from passing any law "impairing the Obligation of Contracts," better known as the contract clause, has been the subject of considerable litigation before the Supreme Court. The contract clause was intended to bar the states from interfering in private contracts between consensual parties and was considered an important limit on the power of states to restrict the fledgling national economic order of the early republic. Early on, the Court considered many laws that restricted the terms set out in private contracts as unconstitutional. But, as the United States became a more industrial society, and as citizen demands grew for government regulation of the economy, the environment, and social welfare benefits, the Court softened its position on the contract clause to permit states to make laws that served a reasonable public interest. A key case involving the contract clause is *Home Building and Loan Association* v. *Blaisdell* (1934). In *Blaisdell*, the Court ruled that a Depression-era law passed by the Minnesota legislature forgiving mortgage payments by home owners to banks did not violate the contract clause.

No State shall, without the Consent of the Congress, lay any Imposts or Duties on Imports or Exports, except what may be absolutely necessary for executing its inspection Laws: and the net Produce of all Duties and Imposts, laid by any State on Imports or Exports, shall be for the Use of the Treasury of the United States, and all such Laws shall be subject to the Revision and Controul of the Congress.

No state may tax goods leaving or entering a state, although it may charge reasonable fees for inspections considered necessary to the public interest. The restriction on import and export taxes applies only to those goods entering from or leaving for a foreign country.

No State shall, without the Consent of Congress, lay any Duty of Tonnage, keep Troops, or Ships of War in time of Peace, enter into any Agreement or Compact with another State, or with a foreign Power, or engage in War, unless actually invaded, or in such imminent Danger as will not admit of delay.

Clause 3 cements the power of Congress to control acts of war and make treaties with foreign countries. The Framers wanted to correct any perception to the contrary gained from the Articles of Confederation that states were free to act independently of the national government on negotiated matters with foreign countries. They also wanted to ensure that any state that entered into a compact with another state—something this clause does not prohibit—must receive permission from Congress.

ARTICLE II

Section 1.

The executive Power shall be vested in a President of the United States of America. He shall hold his Office during the Term of four Years, and, together with the Vice President, chosen for the same Term, be elected as follows.

In *Federalist No. 70,* Alexander Hamilton argued for an "energetic executive" branch headed by a single, elected president not necessarily beholden to the majority party in Congress. Hamilton believed that a nationally elected president would not be bound by the narrow, parochial interests that drove legislative law-making. The president would possess both the veto power over Congress and a platform from which to articulate a national vision in both domestic and foreign affairs.

Hamilton believed that the constitutional boundaries placed on executive power through the separation of powers and the fact that the president was accountable to a national electorate constrained any possibility that the office would come to resemble the monarchies of Europe. However, most presidential scholars agree that the modern presidency has grown in power precisely because of the general nature of the enabling powers of Article II.

Each State shall appoint, in such Manner as the Legislature thereof may direct, a Number of Electors, equal to the whole Number of Senators and Representatives to which the State may be entitled in the Congress; but no Senator or Representative, or Person holding an Office of Trust of Profit under the United States, shall be appointed an Elector.

Clause 2 established the Electoral College and set the number of electors from each state at the total of senators and representatives serving in Congress.

The Electors shall meet in their respective States, and vote by Ballot for two Persons, of whom one at least shall not be an Inhabitant of the same State with themselves. And they shall make a List of all the Persons voted for, and, of the Number of Votes for each; which List they shall sign and certify, and transmit sealed to the Seat of the Government of the United States, directed to the President of the Senate. The President of the Senate shall, in the Presence of the Senate and House of Representatives, open all the Certificates, and the Votes shall then be counted. The Person having the greatest Number of Votes shall be the President, if such Number be a Majority of the whole Number of Electors appointed; and if there be more than one who have such Majority, and have an equal Number of Votes, then the House of Representatives shall immediately chuse by Ballot one of them for President; and if no Person have a Majority, then from the five highest on the List the said House shall in like Manner chuse the President. But in chusing the President, the Votes shall be taken by States, the Representation from each State having one Vote; A quorum for this Purpose shall consist of a Member or Members from two thirds of the States, and a Majority of all the States shall be necessary to a Choice. In every Case, after the Choice of the President, the Person having the greatest Number of Votes of the Electors shall be the Vice President. But if there should remain two or more who have equal Votes, the Senate shall chuse from them by Ballot the Vice President.

This provision of section 1 described the rules for calling the Electoral College to vote for president and vice president. Originally, the electors did not vote separately for president and vice president. After the 1800 election, which saw Thomas Jefferson and Aaron Burr receive the identical number of electoral votes even though it was clear that Jefferson was the presidential candidate and Burr the vice presidential candidate, the nation ratified the Twelfth Amendment (see page 71).

The Twelfth Amendment did not resolve what many constitutional scholars today believe are the inadequacies of the Electoral College system. In 1824, the presidential election ended in a four-way tie, and the House of Representatives elected second-place finisher John Quincy Adams president. In 1876, Benjamin Harrison lost the popular vote but won the presidency after recounts awarded him an Electoral College majority. But perhaps the most controversial election of all came in 2000, when George W. Bush, who lost the popular contest to Al Gore by approximately 500,000 votes, was named the presidential victor after a six-week court battle over the vote count in Florida. After the Supreme Court ruled against the position of Al Gore that a recount of the Florida popular vote should continue until all votes had been counted, an outcome that would have left the nation without a president-elect for several more weeks, Bush was awarded Florida's electoral votes, which gave him 271, just one more than he needed to win the office. Outraged Democrats pledged to mount a case for Electoral College reform, but, as was so often the case before, nothing happened.

The Congress may determine the Time of chusing the Electors, and the Day on which they shall give their Votes; which Day shall be the same throughout the United States.

No Person except a natural born Citizen, or a Citizen of the United States, at the time of the Adoption of this Constitution, shall be eligible to the Office of President; neither shall any Person be eligible to that Office who shall not have attained to the Age of thirty five Years, and been fourteen Years a Resident within the United States.

This provision of Article II is referred to as the presidential eligibility clause. In addition to setting out the age and resident requirements of presidential aspirants, this clause defines who may *not* run for president—any foreign-born individual who has nonetheless obtained United States citizenship. For example, Michigan Governor Jennifer Granholm, who has lived in the United States since she was four years old, may not run for president because she was born in Canada. The same is true for California Governor Arnold Schwarzenegger, who was born in Austria but has lived in the United States his entire adult life. Judicial interpretation of the presidential eligibility clause has not resolved the question of whether children born to U.S. citizens are eligible to run for president if they meet the residency requirements.

In Case of the Removal of the President from Office, or of his Death, Resignation, or Inability to discharge the Powers and Duties of the said Office, the Same shall devolve on the Vice President, and the Congress may by Law provide for the Case of Removal, Death, Resignation or Inability, both of the President and Vice President, declaring what Officer shall then act as President, and such Officer shall act accordingly, until the Disability be removed, or a President shall be elected.

This presidential succession clause has been modified by the Twenty-Fifth Amendment (see page 78).

The President shall, at stated Times, receive for his Services, a Compensation, which shall neither be increased nor diminished during the Period for which he shall have been elected, and he shall not receive within that Period any other Emolument from the United States, or any of them.

Presidential compensation, like compensation for members of Congress, may not be increased for the current occupant of the office. The president is not eligible for any other public compensation during time in office. However, the president may continue to receive income such as interest on investments or book royalties.

Before he enter on the Execution of his Office, he shall take the following Oath or Affirmation:—"I do solemnly swear (or affirm) that I will faithfully execute the Office of President of the United States, and will to the best of my Ability, preserve, protect and defend the Constitution of the United States."

Since George Washington's inaugural in 1789, each president has added the phrase "so help me God" to the end of the presidential oath. Although Abraham Lincoln cited the oath to justify his suspension of the writ of *habeas corpus* during the Civil War, no other president has relied on the oath to justify action that stretched the boundaries of executive power. Presidents taking extraordinary action either at home or abroad have relied on either the commander in chief clause of section 2, clause 1, or the provision of section 3 authorizing the president to "faithfully execut[e]" the laws of the United States.

Section 2.

The President shall be Commander in Chief of the Army and Navy of the United States, and of the Militia of the several States, when called into the actual Service of the United States; he may require the Opinion, in writing, of the principal Officer in each of the executive Departments, upon any Subject relating to the Duties of their respective Offices, and he shall have Power to grant Reprieves and Pardons for Offences against the United States, except in Cases of Impeachment.

Section 2, clause 1, establishes the president as commander in chief of the Army and Navy of the United States. In modern times, that authority has extended to the Air Force, the Marines, and all other branches of the armed forces operating under the command of the United States, including state militias, reserve units, and national guards. Article I provides that Congress, and not the president, has the power to declare war. But, since World War II, no American president has received or requested a declaration of war to commit the armed forces to military conflicts, including those clearly acknowledged as large-scale war (Korea, Vietnam, the 1991 Persian Gulf War, Afghanistan, and the Iraq War). For these conflicts, the president received congressional *authorization* to use force, but not an Article I declaration.

Although the Supreme Court has ruled that the president has *inherent* power—that is, power to carry out the essential functions of his office in times of crisis, war, or emergencies that are not *expressly* spelled out under Article II—it has not concluded that such power is unlimited. In *Youngstown Sheet & Tube* v. *Sawyer* (1952), the Court ruled that President Harry S Truman did not have the power to seize control of the nation's steel mills to continue the production of munitions and other war supplies without congressional authorization. More

recently, the Court ruled in *Hamdan* v. *Rumsfeld* (2006) that President George W. Bush exceeded his authority when he established military commissions that had not been approved by Congress to try detainees and other "enemy combatants" captured in the war on terror. The Court ruled that since Congress had not approved of President Bush's system of military tribunals, prisoners were entitled to the protections of the Geneva Convention and the procedural rights of the Uniform Code of Military Justice. Congress passed the Military Commissions Act to address the Court's concerns.

Clause 1 also implicitly creates the Cabinet by authorizing the president to request the opinion "in writing" of the principal officers of the executive branch. The power to create Cabinet-level offices resides with Congress, not the president.

Presidential power to pardon is broad and limited only in cases of impeachment. Perhaps the most controversial pardon in American political history was President Gerald R. Ford's decision to pardon former President Richard M. Nixon, who resigned his office on August 8, 1974, after news reports and congressional inquiries strongly implicated him in the Watergate scandal. A real possibility existed that President Nixon could be tried on criminal charges as the result of his alleged activities during the Watergate scandal.

He shall have Power, by and with the Advice and Consent of the Senate, to make Treaties, provided two thirds of the Senators present concur; and he shall nominate, and by and with the Advice and Consent of the Senate, shall appoint Ambassadors, other public Ministers and Consuls, Judges of the supreme Court, and all other Officers of the United States, whose Appointments are not herein otherwise provided for, and which shall be established by Law: but the Congress may by Law vest the Appointment of such inferior Officers, as they think proper, in the President alone, in the Courts of Law, or in the Heads of Departments.

The President shall have Power to fill up all Vacancies that may happen during the Recess of the Senate, by granting Commissions which shall expire at the End of their next Session.

Clause 2 describes several powers the president may exercise in conjunction with the advice and consent of the Senate. These powers include the power, upon the approval of two-thirds of the Senate, to make treaties with foreign countries. But, the Constitution is silent on the question of whether a president (or Congress) may terminate a treaty by refusing to honor it or simply repealing it outright. When President Jimmy Carter terminated a treaty with China over the objection of Congress, several members sought a judicial resolution

of the action; the Court, however, did not decide the case on the merits and offered no resolution on the matter. The president does not require a two-thirds majority for approval of appointments to the federal judiciary, foreign ambassadorships, Cabinet-level positions, high-ranking positions in non-Cabinet agencies, and high-level military offices. But, the fact that the Senate must approve presidential appointments in these areas provides Congress (senators often listen to the constituents of House members on controversial choices) with an important check on presidential power to shape the contours of the executive branch.

Section 3.

He shall from time to time give to the Congress Information of the State of the Union, and recommend to their Consideration such Measures as he shall judge necessary and expedient; he may, on extraordinary Occasions, convene both Houses, or either of them, and in Case of Disagreement between them, with Respect to the Time of Adjournment, he may adjourn them to such Time as he shall think proper; he shall receive Ambassadors and other public Ministers; he shall take Care that the Laws be faithfully executed, and shall Commission all the Officers of the United States.

The president is required to deliver a State of the Union message to Congress each year. The nation's first two presidents, George Washington and John Adams, delivered their addresses in person. But the nation's third president, Thomas Jefferson, believed that the practice too closely resembled the Speech from the Throne delivered by British royalty. Instead, Jefferson prepared remarks for recitation before Congress by an assistant or clerk of Congress. Every American president after Jefferson followed suit until Woodrow Wilson renewed the original practice after his first year in office. Now, the State of the Union Address is a major media event, although it is less an assessment of the nation's health and happiness and more a presidential wish list for policy initiatives and the touting of partisan accomplishments.

The final provision of section 3 authorizing the president to faithfully execute the laws of the United States has proven controversial over the years. Presidents have cited this broad language to justify such far-reaching action as the suspension of the writ of *habeas corpus*, as President Abraham Lincoln did during the Civil War before being rebuffed by the Supreme Court in *Ex parte McCardle* (1867), and the doctrine of executive privilege, which, as asserted by various presidents, permits the executive branch to withhold sensitive information from the public or the other branches of government for national security reasons. The Court has been of two minds about the doctrine of executive privilege. On the one hand, the Court has said in such cases as *New York Times* v. *U.S.* (1971) and *U.S.* v. *Nixon* (1974) that the president has the power to withhold information to protect vital secrets and the nation's security. On the other hand, the Court has said, in ruling against the assertion of executive privilege in these two cases, that only an exceptional and demonstrated case can justify allowing the president to withhold information.

Section 4.

The President, Vice President and all civil Officers of the United States, shall be removed from Office on Impeachment for, and Conviction of, Treason, Bribery, or other High Crimes and Misdemeanors.

Presidential impeachment, like impeachment of the other described offices in section 4, is the responsibility of the House of Representatives. There is no judicial definition to what constitutes a high crime or misdemeanor. Complicating the matter further is that only the House and Senate are given responsibility over the impeachment process. No federal official subject to impeachment may challenge the action in federal court, as the Supreme Court has ruled that the rules governing impeachment are not actionable in court. Only two presidents, Andrew Johnson in 1868 and Bill Clinton in 1998, have ever been impeached. Neither president was convicted by the Senate of the charges brought against them.

ARTICLE III

Section 1.

The judicial Power of the United States, shall be vested in one supreme Court, and in such inferior Courts as the Congress may from time to time ordain and establish. The Judges, both of the supreme and inferior Courts, shall hold their Offices during good Behaviour, and shall, at stated Times, receive for their Services, a Compensation, which shall not be diminished during their Continuance in Office.

Like the power of Congress and the executive branch under Articles I and II, respectively, of the Constitution, the power of the federal judiciary has developed as the result of constitutional silences and ambiguities. Article III establishes only one federal court, the Supreme Court, and leaves to Congress the power to establish "inferior" courts as it deems necessary. Many students are surprised to learn that the power of judicial review was established by Congress, not the Supreme Court. Although the Court did articulate the power of judicial review in *Marbury* v. *Madison* (1803), that decision only applied to the power of the federal courts to review federal laws. The power of the federal courts to review state laws that allegedly trespassed upon the Constitution was established by the Judiciary Act of 1789. But, on the fundamental question of what constitutes the foundation and scope of judicial power, there is little doubt that the Court, not Congress, has been the foremost exponent of its own authority. Often, the Court has justified its authority to limit the power of the other branches to regulate its affairs by pointing to other provisions of the Constitution, most notably the supremacy clause of Article VI and section 5 of the Fourteenth Amendment, as well as Article III.

Section 2.

The judicial Power shall extend to all Cases, in Law and Equity, arising under this Constitution, the Laws of the United States, and Treaties made, or which shall be made, under their Authority;—to all Cases affecting Ambassadors, other public Ministers and Consuls;—to all Cases of admiralty and maritime Jurisdiction;—to Controversies to which the United States shall be a Party;—to Controversies between two or more States;—between a State and Citizens of another State;—between Citizens of different States;—between Citizens of the same State claiming Lands under Grants of different States,—and between a State, or the Citizens thereof, and foreign States, Citizens or Subjects.

In all Cases affecting Ambassadors, other public Ministers and Consuls, and those in which a State shall be Party, the supreme Court shall have original Jurisdiction. In all the other Cases before mentioned, the supreme Court shall have appellate Jurisdiction, both as to Law and Fact, with such Exceptions, and under such Regulations as the Congress shall make.

The Trial of all Crimes, except in Cases of Impeachment, shall be by Jury; and such Trial shall be held in the State where the said Crimes shall have been committed; but when not committed within any State, the Trial shall be at such Place or Places as the Congress may by Law have directed.

Section 1 invests the judicial power in "one Supreme Court," but it is in section 2 that we find the source of much of the controversy of the exercise of this power since *Marbury* was decided. By extending the judicial power to all "Cases, in Law and Equity, arising under the Constitution, [and] the laws of the United States," section 2 authorizes the Court to both decide matters of law and, if necessary, mandate a remedy commensurate with the degree of a constitutional violation. For example, in *Swann* v. *Charlotte-Mecklenburg Board of Education* (1971), the Court ruled that a lower court, having found that a school system had failed to meet desegregation requirements, had the power to order busing and other remedies to the constitutional violations it found in *Brown* v. *Board of Education* (1954).

Federal judicial power no longer extends to cases involving lawsuits between a state and citizens of another state. This provision was superceded by the Eleventh Amendment.

Section 2 also includes the exceptions and regulations clause. This clause has been used by congressional opponents of some of the Court's more controversial and generally liberal decisions. Although most scholars believe the clause limits the power of Congress to create broad jurisdiction for the courts it creates, others have argued that it permits Congress to strip the federal courts of jurisdiction to hear particular cases. Some opponents of the Court's decisions legalizing abortion, authorizing school busing, and upholding affirmative action have attempted to curb the power of federal courts to rule in such areas by stripping them of jurisdiction in such cases. To date, no president has ever signed such legislation.

Section 3.

Treason against the United States, shall consist only in levying War against them, or in adhering to their Enemies, giving them Aid and Comfort. No Person shall be convicted of Treason unless on the Testimony of two Witnesses to the same overt Act, or on Confession in open Court.

The Congress shall have Power to declare the Punishment of Treason, but no Attainder of Treason shall work Corruption of Blood, or Forfeiture except during the Life of the Person attainted.

Article III defines the only crime mentioned by the Constitution: treason.

ARTICLE IV

Section 1.

Full Faith and Credit shall be given in each State to the public Acts, Records, and judicial Proceedings of every other State. And the Congress may by general Laws prescribe the Manner in which such Acts, Records and Proceedings shall be proved, and the Effect thereof.

The full faith and credit clause rests on principles borrowed from international law that require one country to recognize contracts made in another country absent a compelling public policy reason to the contrary. Here, this principle, referred to in the law as comity, applied to the relationship between the states. For example, a driver's license issued in Ohio is good in Montana. The full and faith credit clause also requires a state to recognize public acts and court proceedings of another state. For the most part, interpretation of the full faith and credit clause has not been controversial.

That may well change, as advocates of same-sex marriage have suggested that such a marriage performed in one state must be recognized in another state, as is the case with heterosexual marriage. A constitutional challenge to the clause may well center on the public policy exception recognized in other areas of law.

Section 2.

The Citizens of each State shall be entitled to all Privileges and Immunities of Citizens in the several States.

A Person charged in any State with Treason, Felony, or other Crime, who shall flee from Justice, and be found in another State, shall on Demand of the executive Authority of the State from which he fled, be delivered up, to be removed to the State having Jurisdiction of the Crime.

The extradition clause requires that the governor of one state deliver a fugitive from justice to the state from which that fugitive fled. Congress passed the Fugitive Act of 1793 to give definition to this provision, but the federal government has no authority to compel state authorities to extradite a fugitive from one state to another. A state may, however, sue another state in federal court to force the return of a fugitive.

No Person held to Service or Labour in one State under the Laws thereof, escaping into another, shall, in Consequence of any Law or Regulation therein, be discharged from such Service or Labour, but shall be delivered up on Claim of the Party to whom such Service or Labour may be due.

The fugitive slave clause, which required any state, including those outside the slave-holding states of the South, to return escaped slaves to their owners, was repealed in 1865 by the Thirteenth Amendment. Prior to 1865, Congress passed laws in 1793 and 1850 to enforce the clause, leaving states without power to make concurrent laws on the subject, ensuring that the southern states would always have the Constitution on their side to protect slavery.

Section 3.

New States may be admitted by the Congress into this Union; but no new State shall be formed or erected within the Jurisdiction of any other State; nor any State be formed by the Junction of two or more States, or Parts of States, without the Consent of the Legislatures of the States concerned as well as of Congress.

The Congress shall have Power to dispose of and make all needful Rules and Regulations respecting the Territory or other Property belonging to the United States; and nothing in this Constitution shall be so construed as to Prejudice any Claims of the United States, or of any particular State.

Section 4.

The United States shall guarantee to every State in this Union a Republican Form of Government, and shall protect each of them against Invasion; and on Application of the Legislature, or of the Executive (when the Legislature cannot be convened) against domestic Violence.

ARTICLE V

The Congress, whenever two thirds of both Houses shall deem it necessary, shall propose Amendments to this Constitution, or, on the Application of the Legislatures of two thirds of the several States, shall call a Convention for proposing Amendments, which, in either Case, shall be valid to all Intents and Purposes, as Part of this Constitution, when ratified by the Legislatures of three fourths of the several States, or by Conventions in three fourths thereof, as the one or the other Mode of Ratification may be proposed by the Congress; Provided that no Amendment which may be made prior to the Year One thousand eight hundred and eight shall in any Manner affect the first and fourth Clauses in the Ninth Section of the first Article; and that no State, without its Consent, shall be deprived of its equal Suffrage in the Senate.

Changes to the Articles of Confederation had required the unanimous approval of the states. But, Article V of the U.S. Constitution offers multiple options—none of which require unanimity—for constitutional change. Article V was quite crucial to the ratification of the Constitution. Federalists who supported the Constitution wanted to ensure that any additions or modifications to the nation's charter would require the approval of more than a simple majority of citizens. This is why any amendment coming out of Congress requires two-thirds of the House and Senate for approval. The same is true for the rule requiring three-fourths of the states to ratify an amendment (either through conventions or state legislative action). Anti-Federalists who either opposed the Constitution or had reservations about key sections of it were soothed by the prospect of an amending process that did not require the unanimous approval of the states.

Only twenty-seven amendments since 1789 have been added to the Constitution, the first fifteen of which were added by 1870. Since 1933, when the nation repealed Prohibition by passing the Twenty-First Amendment, the Constitution has been amended only six times. In the modern constitutional era, efforts to amend the Constitution generally have centered on unhappiness with Supreme Court decisions (on school prayer, flag burning, school busing, abortion rights) or state court rulings with national implications (such as same-sex marriage) rather than any structural defect in the original Constitution (unlike woman suffrage or presidential succession) or a seismic political event (the Civil War). To date, none of these efforts have been successful.

ARTICLE VI

All Debts contracted and Engagements entered into, before the Adoption of this Constitution, shall be as valid against the United States under this Constitution, as under the Confederation.

This Constitution, and the Laws of the United States which shall be made in Pursuance thereof; and all Treaties made, or which shall be made, under the Authority of the United States, shall be the supreme Law of the Land; and the Judges in every State shall be bound thereby, any Thing in the Constitution or Laws of any State to the Contrary notwithstanding.

The Senators and Representatives before mentioned, and the Members of the several State Legislatures, and all executive and judicial Officers, both of the United States and of the several States, shall be bound by Oath or Affirmation, to support this Constitution; but no religious Test shall ever be required as a Qualification to any Office or public Trust under the United States.

Article VI made the national government responsible for all debts incurred by the Revolutionary War. This ensured that manufacturing and banking interests would be repaid for the losses they sustained during the conflict. But the most important provisions of Article VI by far are contained in its second and third clauses.

Clause 2 took another major step forward for national power and away from the confederate approach to government structure of the Articles of Confederation. By making "this Constitution" and all laws made under its authority the "supreme Law of the Land," Article VI created what constitutional scholars call the supremacy clause. The Supreme Court has invoked the supremacy clause on several occasions to rebut challenges mounted by states to its decisions or acts of Congress. Among the more notable decisions by the Supreme Court that have cited the supremacy clause to mandate compliance with a previous ruling is *Cooper* v. *Aaron* (1958). In *Cooper*, the Court cited the supremacy clause in rejecting the argument of Governor Orval Faubus of Arkansas claiming that local schools were not obligated to follow the *Brown* v. *Board of Education* (1954) ruling. The Court said that *Brown* was the law of the land and, as such, all school boards were required to comply with its requirement to desegregate their schools.

Although most Americans rightly point to the First Amendment as the baseline for the guarantee for religious freedom, clause 3 of Article VI contains an important contribution to this principle—the ban on religious tests or qualifications to hold public office. Holders of public office, no matter how great or small, were required to affirm their allegiance to the Constitution and the laws of the United States, but they could not be required to profess a belief in God or meet any other religious qualification. Numerous states nonetheless ignored this requirement until 1961, when the Supreme Court ruled in *Torcaso* v. *Watkins* that states could not administer religious oaths to holders of public office.

ARTICLE VII

The Ratification of the Conventions of nine States, shall be sufficient for the Establishment of this Constitution between the States so ratifying the Same.

Done in Convention by the Unanimous Consent of the States present the Seventeenth Day of September in the Year of our Lord one thousand seven hundred and Eighty seven and of the Independence of the United States of America the Twelfth. IN WITNESS whereof We have hereunto subscribed our Names,

G. WASHINGTON,
Presid't. and deputy from Virginia

Attest
WILLIAM JACKSON,
Secretary

DELAWARE
George Read
Gunning Bedford, Jr.
John Dickinson
Richard Basset
Jacob Broom

MASSACHUSETTS
BAY
Nathaniel Gorham
Rufus King

CONNECTICUT
William Samuel
Johnson
Roger Sherman

NEW YORK
Alexander Hamilton

NEW JERSEY
William Livingston
David Brearley
William Paterson
Jonathan Dayton

PENNSYLVANIA
Benjamin Franklin
Thomas Mifflin
Robert Morris
George Clymer
Thomas FitzSimons
Jared Ingersoll
James Wilson
Gouverneur Morris

NEW HAMPSHIRE
John Langdon
Nicholas Gilman

MARYLAND
James McHenry
Daniel of St. Thomas
Jenifer
Daniel Carroll

VIRGINIA
John Blair
James Madison, Jr.

NORTH CAROLINA
William Blount
Richard Dobbs
Spaight
Hugh Williamson

SOUTH CAROLINA
John Rutledge
Charles Cotesworth
Pinckney
Charles Pinckney
Pierce Butler

GEORGIA
William Few
Abraham Baldwin

Articles in addition to, and amendment of the Constitution of the United States of America, proposed by Congress and ratified by the Legislatures of the several states, pursuant to the Fifth Article of the original Constitution.

(The first ten amendments were passed by Congress on September 25, 1789, and were ratified on December 15, 1791.)

AMENDMENT I

Congress shall make no law respecting an establishment of religion, or prohibiting the free exercise thereof; or abridging the freedom of speech, or of the press; or the right of the people peaceably to assemble, and to petition the Government for a redress of grievances.

For many Americans, the First Amendment represents the core of what the Bill of Rights stands for: limits on government power to limit or compel religious beliefs, the right to hold political opinions and express them, protection for a free press, the right to assemble peaceably, and the right to petition, through protest or the ballot, the government for a redress of political grievances. But it is also important to remember that the First Amendment, like most of the Bill of Rights, did not apply to state governments until the Supreme Court began to apply their substantive guarantees through the Fourteenth Amendment, a process that did not begin until 1925 in *Gitlow* v. *New York*.

Until then, state and local governments often failed to honor the rights and liberties that Congress, and by extension the national government, was expressly forbidden by the Constitution from withholding. For example, southern states, prior to the Civil War, outlawed pro-abolition literature; numerous states continued to collect taxes on behalf of state-sponsored churches and religious education; newspapers often were forbidden from publishing exposes on industry or political leaders because such speech was considered seditious and thus subject to prior restraint; and public protests on behalf of unpopular causes were often banned by state breach of peace laws.

The Supreme Court has recognized other important rights implied by the enumerated guarantees of the First Amendment. These include the right to association, even when such association might come in the form of clubs or organizations that discriminate on the basis of race, sex, or religion, and the right to personal privacy, which the Supreme Court held in *Griswold* v. *Connecticut* (1965) was based in part on the right of married couples to make decisions about contraception, a decision protected by one's personal religious and political beliefs.

AMENDMENT II

A well regulated Militia, being necessary to the security of a free State, the right of the people to keep and bear Arms, shall not be infringed.

Few issues in American politics generate as much emotional heat as the extent to which Americans have a right to keep and bear arms. Supporters of broad gun ownership rights, such as the National Rifle Association, argue that the Second Amendment protects an almost absolute individual right to own just about any small arm that can be manufactured, whether for reasons of sport or self-defense. Proponents of gun control, such as the Brady Campaign to Prevent Gun Violence, argue that the amendment creates no such individual right, but refers instead to the Framers' belief—now outdated—that citizen militias had the right to form to protect themselves against other states and, if need be, the national government. Under this view, Congress and the states are free to regulate gun ownership and use as they see fit, provided that the national and state governments are within their constitutional orbit of power to do so.

The Supreme Court has not offered much help on the meaning of the Second Amendment. It has handed down only one case truly relying on the amendment, *U.S.* v. *Miller* (1939). There, a unanimous Court upheld a federal law requiring the registration of sawed-off shotguns purchased for personal use. While the Court rejected the position that the Second Amendment established an individual right to keep and bear arms, it did not close the door on individual gun ownership. This remains the constitutional baseline from which legislative battles over gun control legislation continue to be fought.

AMENDMENT III

No Soldier shall, in time of peace be quartered in any house, without the consent of the Owner, nor in time of war, but in a manner to be prescribed by law.

Among the complaints directed at King George III in the Declaration of Independence was the colonial-era practice of quartering large numbers of troops in private homes. The practice of quartering soldiers, along with the forced maintenance of British standing armies in times of peace without the consent of the colonial legislatures, formed a major component of the political grievances directed at the British crown. The Third Amendment was intended to protect individuals and their property from the abuse common to the practice of quartering soldiers.

AMENDMENT IV

The right of the people to be secure in their persons, houses, papers, and effects, against unreasonable searches and seizures, shall not be violated, and no warrants shall issue, but upon probable cause, supported by Oath or affirmation, and particularly describing the place to be searched, and the persons or things to be seized.

Although the Fourth Amendment is often discussed in tandem with the Fifth, Sixth, and Eighth Amendments—the other major provisions of the Bill of Rights outlining the criminal due process guarantees of citizens—it shares a similar undercurrent that motivated the adoption of the Third Amendment: to eliminate the practice of British officers from using the general writ of

assistance to enter private homes, conduct searches, and seize personal property. British officers had not been required to offer a specific reason for a search or justify the taking of particular items. In most cases, the writ of assistance was used to confiscate items considered to have violated the strict British customs laws of the colonial era.

The twin pillars of the Fourth Amendment, the probable cause and warrant requirements, are a direct reflection of the disdain the Framers had for the Revolutionary-era practices of the British. But, like the First Amendment, the guarantees of the Fourth Amendment did not apply to state and local law enforcement practices until well after the ratification of the Fourteenth Amendment. Until *Wolf* v. *Colorado* (1949), when the Court ruled that the Fourteenth Amendment made the Fourth Amendment binding on the states, evidence seized in violation of the probable cause or warrant requirements could be used against a criminal suspect. The Court's best-known decision on the Fourth Amendment, *Mapp* v. *Ohio* (1961), which established the exclusionary rule, also marked the high-water point in the rights afforded to criminal suspects challenging an unlawful search. Since the late 1970s, the Court has steadily added exceptions to the Fourth Amendment to permit law enforcement officers to engage in warrantless searches and seizures, provided that such practices meet a threshold of reasonableness in the context of the circumstances under which they are undertaken.

AMENDMENT V

No person shall be held to answer for a capital, or otherwise infamous crime, unless on a presentment or indictment of a Grand Jury, except in cases arising in the land or naval forces, or in the Militia, when in actual service in time of War or public danger; nor shall any person be subject for the same offence to be twice put in jeopardy of life or limb; nor shall be compelled in any criminal case to be a witness against himself, nor be deprived of life, liberty, or property, without due process of law; nor shall private property be taken for public use, without just compensation.

The Fifth Amendment, along with the Sixth Amendment, is the legacy of the ruthless and secretive tactics that figured prominently in the colonial-era system of British justice. By requiring that no person could be held for a "capital, or otherwise infamous" crime except upon indictment by a grand jury, the Fifth Amendment took an important step toward making the criminal indictment process a public function. Along with the public trial and trial by jury guarantees of the Sixth Amendment, the grand jury provision of the Fifth Amendment established that the government would have to make its case against the accused in public. Also, by guaranteeing that no person could be compelled to testify against himself or herself in a criminal proceeding, the Fifth Amendment highlighted the adversarial nature of the American criminal justice system, a feature that is distinct from its British counterpart. "Pleading the Fifth" is permissible in any criminal, civil, administrative, judicial, or investigatory context. *Miranda* v. *Arizona* (1966), one of the most famous rulings of the Supreme Court, established a right to silence that combined the ban against self-incrimination of the Fifth Amendment with the Sixth Amendment's guarantee of the assistance of counsel. The right to silence, unlike the ban against self-incrimination, extends to any aspect of an interrogation.

The Fifth Amendment also forbids double jeopardy, which prohibits the prosecution of a crime against the same person in the same jurisdiction twice, and prevents the government from taking life, liberty, or property without due process of law. This phrase was reproduced in the Fourteenth Amendment, placing an identical set of constraints on the states. The Court has applied all the guarantees of the Fifth Amendment, with the exception of the grand jury provision, to the states through the due process clause of the Fourteenth Amendment. Some constitutional scholars also consider the due process clause of the Fifth Amendment to embrace an equal protection provision when applied to federal cases.

The final provision of the Fifth Amendment prohibits the government from taking private property for public use without just compensation. Litigation on the takings clause, as some scholars refer to this provision, has generally centered on two major questions. The first is what constitutes a taking, either by the government's decision to seize private property or by regulating it to the point where its value is greatly diminished. The second question centers on what the appropriate level of compensation is for owners who have successfully established a taking.

The Supreme Court has taken an expansive definition of what it means to "take" private land for "public use." In *Kelo* v. *New London* (2004), the Court ruled that government could take private property and then sell it to private developers so long as that property was slated for economic development that would benefit the surrounding community. This marked the first time the Court had authorized a taking for something other than public use by governmental authorities.

AMENDMENT VI

In all criminal prosecutions, the accused shall enjoy the right to a speedy and public trial, by an impartial jury of the State and district wherein the crime shall have been committed, which district shall have been previously ascertained by law, and to be informed of the nature and cause of the accusation; to be confronted with the witnesses against him; to have compulsory process for obtaining witnesses in his favor, and to have the assistance of counsel for his defence.

The centerpiece of the constitutional guarantees afforded to individuals facing criminal prosecution, the Sixth Amendment sets out eight specific rights, more than any other provision of the Bill of Rights. As with the Fifth Amendment, the core features of the Sixth Amendment build upon the unfortunate legacy of the repressive practices of colonial-era Britain. The very first provision of the Sixth Amendment mandates that individuals subject to criminal prosecution receive "a speedy and public trial"; it then requires that all such trials take place in public, with the defendant informed of the cause and nature of the accusation against him or her. The common theme underlying these sections of the Sixth Amendment, as well as those requiring witnesses for the prosecution to testify in public, allowing the defendant to produce witnesses on his or her own behalf, and securing the assistance of counsel, is that any citizen threatened with the deprivation of liberty is entitled to have the case made against him or her in public. The Fifth Amendment also required the government to produce evidence that did not rely on confessions and self-incrimination. And, it required that any such evidence must be acquired lawfully and with the knowledge of a public magistrate. The Sixth Amendment establishes, in principle, the American criminal justice system as one that is open and public.

Since the vast majority of criminal prosecutions in the United States are undertaken by state and local authorities, the parchment promises of the Sixth Amendment did not extend to most Americans until the Supreme Court began incorporating the guarantees of the Bill of Rights to the states through the Fourteenth Amendment. Perhaps the best-known case involving the Sixth Amendment is *Gideon* v. *Wainwright* (1963), which held that all persons accused of a serious crime are entitled to an attorney, even if they cannot afford one, a rule that was soon extended to cover misdemeanors as well. Three years later, the Supreme Court fused the right to counsel rule established in *Gideon* with the Fifth Amendment ban against self-incrimination to create the principles animating *Miranda* v. *Arizona*. For a long time, the Court had never interpreted the Fifth and Sixth Amendments to mean that individuals had rights to criminal due process guarantees if they did not know about them or could not afford them. Decisions such as *Gideon* and *Miranda* offered a clear departure from this position.

The speedy and public trial clauses only require that criminal trials take place in public within a reasonable amount of time after the period of indictment, and that juries in such cases are unbiased. Americans also often cite the Sixth Amendment as entitling them to a trial by a "jury of one's peers." This is true to the extent individuals are entitled to a trial in the jurisdiction where the crime is alleged to have been committed. It does not mean, however, that they are entitled to a trial by persons of a similar age or background, for example.

AMENDMENT VII

In Suits at common law, where the value in controversy shall exceed twenty dollars, the right of trial by jury shall be preserved, and no fact tried by a jury, shall be otherwise re-examined in any Court of the United States, than according to the rules of the common law.

One feature of the British courts that the Framers sought to preserve in the American civil law system was the distinction between courts of common law and courts of equity. Common law courts heard cases involving strict legal rules, while equity courts based their decisions on principles of fairness and totality of circumstances. Common law courts featured juries that were authorized to return verdicts entitling plaintiffs to financial compensation for losses incurred, whereas equity courts relied upon judges to make determinations about appropriate relief for successful parties. Relief in equity courts did not consist of monetary awards, but injunctions, cease-and-desist orders, and so on. The Seventh Amendment carried over this British feature into the Constitution.

In 1938, Congress amended the Federal Rules of Civil Procedure to combine the function of civil common law and equity courts. In cases involving both legal and equitable claims, a federal judge must first decide the issue of law before moving to the equitable relief, or remedy, component of the trial. Judges are permitted to instruct juries on matters of law and fact, and may emphasize certain facts or legal issues to the jury in their instructions to the jury. But, the jury alone decides guilt or innocence. In some extraordinary cases, a judge may overturn the verdict of a jury. This happens only when a judge believes the jury has disregarded completely the facts and evidence before it in reaching a verdict.

Congress has also changed the $20 threshold for the right to a trial by jury. The amount is now $75,000. Finally, the Seventh Amendment has never been incorporated to the states through the Fourteenth Amendment.

AMENDMENT VIII

Excessive bail shall not be required, nor excessive fines imposed, nor cruel and unusual punishments inflicted.

For an amendment of so few words, the Eighth Amendment has generated an enormous volume of commentary and litigation since its ratification. This should not be surprising, as the three major provisions of the amendment deal with some of the most sensitive and emotionally charged issues involving the rights of criminal defendants.

The origin of the excessive bail clause stems from the reforms to the British system instituted by the 1689 English Bill of Rights. Having had limited success in preventing law enforcement officials from detaining suspects by imposing outrageous bail requirements, Britain amended previous laws to say that "excessive bail ought not to be required." Much like the British model, the Eighth Amendment does not state what an "excessive bail" is or the particular criminal offense that warrants a high bail amount. The Supreme Court has offered two fundamental rules on the excessive bail clause. First, a judge has the discretion to decide if a criminal offense is sufficiently serious to justify high bail. Second, a judge has the power, under *U.S.* v. *Salerno* (1987), to deny a criminal defendant bail as a "preventative measure." In both such cases, a judge's action must be considered proportionate to the nature of the criminal offense for which an individual stands accused.

Like the excessive bail clause, the excessive fines clause is rooted in the English Bill of Rights. The clause applies only to criminal proceedings, not civil litigation. For example, a tobacco company cannot appeal what it believes is an excessive jury award under this clause. An indigent criminal defendant, however, can challenge a fine levied in connection with a criminal conviction.

The most controversial section of the Eighth Amendment is the clause forbidding cruel and unusual punishments. The absence of such a guarantee from the Constitution was a major impetus for the adoption of the Bill of Rights. While most historians agree that the Framers wanted to prohibit barbaric forms of punishment, including torture, as well as arbitrary and disproportionate penalties, there is little consensus on what specific punishments met this definition. By the late 1800s, the Supreme Court had ruled that such punishments as public burning, disembowelment, and drawing and quartering crossed the Eighth Amendment barrier. In *Weems* v. *U.S.* (1910), the Court went the additional of step of concluding that any punishment considered "excessive" would violate the cruel and unusual punishment clause. And, in *Solem* v. *Helm* (1983), the Court developed a "proportionality" standard that required punishments, even simple incarceration, to bear a rational relationship to the offense.

The Court has never ruled, however, that the death penalty per se violates the Eighth Amendment. It has developed certain rules and exceptions governing the application of the death penalty, such as requiring a criminal defendant actually to have killed, or attempted to have killed, a victim. It has also ruled that the mentally retarded, as a class, are exempt from the death penalty. But it has also issued highly controversial decisions concluding, for example, that neither racial disparities in the application of capital punishment nor juvenile status at the time the offense was committed violate the Eighth Amendment. Except for a four-year ban on the practice between 1972 and 1976, the death penalty has always been an available punishment in the American criminal justice system.

AMENDMENT IX

The enumeration in the Constitution, of certain rights, shall not be construed to deny or disparage others retained by the people.

A major point of contention between the Federalists and Anti-Federalists was the need for a bill of rights. In *Federalist No. 84,* Alexander Hamilton argued that a bill of rights was unnecessary, as there was no need to place limits on the power of government to do things that it was not authorized by the Constitution to do. Hamilton also argued that it would be impossible to list all the rights "retained by the people." Protecting some rights but not others would suggest that Americans had surrendered certain rights to their government when, in Hamilton's view, the Constitution did nothing of the sort.

Given his well-deserved reputation for unbridled national power, Hamilton's views have often been dismissed as a cynical ploy to sidestep any meaningful discussion of the Bill of Rights and speed along the ratification process. But, James Madison, along with Thomas Jefferson, held a much deeper belief in the need for a bill of rights. Madison also believed that the enumeration of certain rights and liberties in the Constitution should not be understood to deny others that exist as a condition of citizenship in a free society. Madison, the primary author of the Bill of Rights, included the Ninth Amendment to underscore this belief.

The Supreme Court has never offered a clear and definitive interpretation of the Ninth Amendment, primarily because it has been wary of giving such general language any substantive definition. The amendment has been cited in such decisions as *Griswold* v. *Connecticut* (1965) and *Richmond Newspapers* v. *Virginia* (1980) along with other constitutional amendments to bolster the case on behalf of an asserted constitutional right. The difficulty in constructing a specific meaning for the Ninth Amendment can be illustrated by the fact that both supporters and opponents of legal abortion have cited it to defend the feasibility of their respective positions.

AMENDMENT X

The powers not delegated to the United States by the Constitution, nor prohibited by it to the States, are reserved to the States respectively, or to the people.

The Tenth Amendment generated little controversy during the ratification process over the Bill of Rights. As the Supreme Court later ruled in *U.S.* v. *Darby Lumber Co.* (1941), the Tenth Amendment states a truism about the relationship between the boundaries of national and state power—that the states retain those powers not specifically set out in the Constitution as belonging to the national government. There is little in the history in the debate over the Tenth Amendment to suggest that its language is anything other than declaratory. Indeed, the refusal of the 1st Congress to insert the word "expressly" before "delegated" strongly suggests that James Madison, who offered the most thorough explanation of the amendment during the floor debates, intended to leave room for this relationship to evolve as future events made necessary.

The earliest political and constitutional developments involving the Tenth Amendment tilted the balance of power firmly in favor of national power. Alexander Hamilton's vision for a national bank to consolidate the nation's currency and trading position was realized in *McCullough* v. *Maryland* (1819), in which the Court held that Article I granted Congress broad power to make all laws "necessary and proper" to the exercise of its legislative power. By no means, however, did *McCullough* settle the argument over the power reserved to the states. Led by Chief Justice Roger B. Taney, the Court handed down several decisions in the three decades leading up to the Civil War that offered substantial protection to the southern states on the matters closest to their hearts: slavery and economic sovereignty. From the period after the Civil War until the New Deal, the Court continued to shield states from congressional legislation designed to regulate the economy and promote social and political reform. After the constitutional revolution of 1937, when the Court threw its support behind the New Deal, Congress received a blank constitutional check to engage in the regulatory action that featured an unprecedented level of federal intervention in economic and social matters once the purview of the states, one that would last almost sixty years.

Beginning in *New York* v. *U.S.* (1992), however, the Court, in striking down a key provision of a federal environmental law, began to revisit the New Deal assumptions that underlay its modern interpretation of the Tenth Amendment. A few years later, in *U.S.* v. *Lopez* (1995), it invalidated a federal gun control law on the ground that Congress lacked authority under the commerce clause to regulate gun possession. And, in *U.S.* v. *Printz* (1997), the Tenth Amendment explicitly was cited to strike down an important section of the Brady Bill, a congressional law that required states to conduct background checks on prospective gun buyers. Although the Court has not returned to the dual federalism posture on the Tenth Amendment that it built from the years between the Taney Court and the triumph of the New

Deal, these decisions make clear that the constitutional status of the states as actors in the federal system has been dramatically strengthened.

AMENDMENT XI
(Ratified on February 7, 1795)

The Judicial power of the United States shall not be construed to extend to any suit in law or equity, commenced or prosecuted against one of the United States by Citizens of another State, or by Citizens or Subjects of any Foreign State.

The Eleventh Amendment was prompted by one of the earliest notable decisions of the Supreme Court, *Chisolm* v. *Georgia* (1793). In *Chisolm*, the Court held that Article III and the enforcement provision of the Judiciary Act of 1789 permitted a citizen of one state to bring suit against another state in federal court. Almost immediately after *Chisolm*, the Eleventh Amendment was introduced and promptly ratified, as the states saw this decision as a threat to their sovereignty under the new Constitution. The amendment was passed in less than a year, which, by the standards of the era, was remarkably fast.

The Eleventh Amendment nullified the result in *Chisolm* but did not completely bar a citizen from bringing suit against a state in federal court. Citizens may bring lawsuits against state officials in federal court if they can satisfy the requirement that their rights under federal constitutional or statutory law have been violated. The Eleventh Amendment has not been extensively litigated in modern times, but the extent to which states are immune under federal law from citizen lawsuits has reemerged as an important constitutional question in recent years. For example, the Court has said in several cases that the doctrine of sovereign immunity prevents citizens from suing state agencies under the Americans with Disabilities Act of 1990. But, as recently as 2003, the Court, in *Nevada* v. *Hibbs*, ruled that the Family and Medical Leave Act of 1993 did not immunize state government agencies against lawsuits brought by former state employees. States are also free to waive their immunity and consent to a lawsuit.

AMENDMENT XII
(Ratified on June 15, 1804)

The Electors shall meet in their respective states, and vote by ballot for President and Vice-President, one of whom, at least, shall not be an inhabitant of the same state with themselves; they shall name in their ballots the person voted for as President, and in distinct ballots the person voted for as Vice-President, and they shall make distinct lists of all persons voted for as President, and of all persons voted for as Vice-President, and of the number of votes for each, which lists they shall sign and certify, and transmit sealed to the seat of the government of the United States, directed to the President of the Senate;—The President of the Senate shall, in the presence of the Senate and House of Representatives, open all the certificates and the votes shall then be counted;—The person having the greatest number of votes for President, shall be the President, if such number be a majority of the whole number of Electors appointed; and if no person have such majority; then from the persons having the highest numbers not exceeding three on the list of those voted for as President, the House of Representatives shall choose immediately, by ballot, the President. But in choosing the President, the votes shall be taken by states, the representation from each state having one vote; a quorum for this purpose shall consist of a member or members from two-thirds of the states, and a majority of all the states shall be necessary to a choice. And if the House of Representatives shall not choose a President whenever the right of choice shall devolve upon them, before the fourth day of March next following, then the Vice-President shall act as President, as in the case of the death or other constitutional disability of the President.—The person having the greatest number of votes as Vice-President, shall be the Vice-President, if such number be a majority of the whole number of Electors appointed, and if no person have a majority, then from the two highest numbers on the list, the Senate shall choose the Vice-President; a quorum for the purpose shall consist of two-thirds of the whole number of Senators, and a majority of the whole number shall be necessary to a choice. But no person constitutionally ineligible to the office of President shall be eligible to that of Vice-President of the United States.

The Twelfth Amendment was added to the Constitution after the 1800 presidential election was thrown into the House of Representatives. Thomas Jefferson and Aaron Burr, running on the Democratic-Republican Party ticket, each received seventy-three electoral votes for president, even though everyone knew that Jefferson was the presidential candidate and Burr the vice presidential candidate. This was possible because Article II, section 1, did not require electors to vote for president and vice president separately. The Twelfth Amendment remedied this deficiency by requiring electors to cast their votes for president and vice president separately.

Whether it intended to or not, the Twelfth Amendment took a major step toward institutionalizing the party system in the United States. The 1796 election yielded a president and vice president from different parties, a clear indication that partisan differences were emerging in a distinct form. The 1800 election simply highlighted the problem further. By requiring electors to make their presidential and vice presidential choices

separately, the Twelfth Amendment conceded that a party system in American politics had indeed evolved, an inevitable but nonetheless disappointing development to the architects of the original constitutional vision.

AMENDMENT XIII
(Ratified on December 6, 1865)

Section 1.

Neither slavery nor involuntary servitude, except as a punishment for crime whereof the party shall have been duly convicted, shall exist within the United States, or any place subject to their jurisdiction.

Section 2.

Congress shall have power to enforce this article by appropriate legislation.

The Thirteenth, Fourteenth, and Fifteenth Amendments are known collectively as the Civil War Amendments.

In anticipation of a Union victory, the Thirteenth Amendment was passed by Congress and sent to the states for ratification before the end of the Civil War. The amendment not only formally abolished slavery and involuntary servitude; it also served as the constitutional foundation for the nation's first major civil rights legislation, the Civil Rights Act of 1866. This law extended numerous rights to African Americans previously held in servitude as well as those having "free" status during the Civil War, including the right to purchase, rent, and sell personal property, to bring suit in federal court, to enter into contracts, and to receive the full and equal benefit of all laws "enjoyed by white citizens." The Thirteenth Amendment overturned the pre–Civil War decision of the Supreme Court, *Dred Scott* v. *Sandford* (1857), which held that slaves were not people entitled to constitutional rights, but property subject to the civil law binding them to their masters.

In modern times, the Court has ruled that the Thirteenth Amendment prohibits any action that recognizes a "badge" or "condition" of slavery, such as housing discrimination and certain forms of employment discrimination. The Department of Justice also has used the Thirteenth Amendment to file lawsuits against manufacturing sweatshops and other criminal enterprises in which persons are forced to work without compensation.

AMENDMENT XIV
(Ratified on July 9, 1868)

Section 1.

All persons born or naturalized in the United States, and subject to the jurisdiction thereof, are citizens of the United States and of the State wherein they reside. No State shall make or enforce any law which shall abridge the privileges or immunities of citizens of the United States; nor shall any State deprive any person of life, liberty, or property, without due process of law; nor deny to any person within its jurisdiction the equal protection of the laws.

Many constitutional scholars believe the Fourteenth Amendment is the most important addition to the Constitution since the Bill of Rights was ratified in 1791. In addition to serving as a cornerstone of Reconstruction policy, section 1 eliminated the distinction between the rights and liberties of Americans as citizens of their respective states and those to which they were entitled under the Bill of Rights as citizens of the United States. The Republican leadership that drafted and steered the Fourteenth Amendment to passage left no doubt that the three major provisions of section 1, which placed express limits on state power to abridge rights and liberties protected as a condition of national citizenship, were intended to make the Bill of Rights binding upon the states, thus overruling *Barron* v. *Baltimore* (1833). Although the Supreme Court has never endorsed this view, the selective incorporation of the Bill of Rights to the states during the twentieth century through the Fourteenth Amendment ultimately made the Reconstruction-era vision of the Republicans a reality. The former Confederate states were required to ratify the Fourteenth Amendment to qualify for readmission into the Union.

Section 2.

Representatives shall be apportioned among the several States according to their respective numbers, counting the whole number of persons in each State, excluding Indians not taxed. But when the right to vote at any election for the choice of electors for President and Vice President of the United States, Representatives in Congress, the Executive and Judicial officers of a State, or the members of the Legislature thereof, is denied to any of the male inhabitants of such State, being twenty-one years of age, and citizens of the United States, or in any way abridged, except for participation in rebellion, or other crime, the basis of representation therein shall be reduced in the proportion which the number of such male citizens shall bear to the whole number of male citizens twenty-one years of age in such State.

Section 2 established two major changes to the Constitution. First, by stating that representatives from each state would be apportioned based on the number of "whole" persons in each state, section 2 modified the Three-Fifths Compromise of Article 1, section 2, clause 3, of the original Constitution. Note, however, that section 2 still called for the exclusion of Indians "not taxed" from the apportionment criteria. Second, section 2, for the first time anywhere in the Constitution, mentions that only "male" inhabitants of the states age twenty-one or older would be counted toward representation in the House of Representatives and eligible to vote.

The Military Reconstruction Act of 1867 had strengthened Republican power in the southern states by stripping former Confederates of the right to vote, a law that, in conjunction with the gradual addition of blacks to the voting rolls, made enactment of the Fourteenth Amendment possible. Section 2 temporarily solidified the Republican presence in the South by eliminating from apportionment counts any person that participated in the rebellion against the Union.

Section 3.

No person shall be a Senator or Representative in Congress, or elector of President and Vice President, or hold any office, civil or military, under the United States, or under any State, who, having previously taken an oath, as a member of Congress, or as an officer of the United States, or as a member of any State legislature, or as an executive or judicial officer of any State, to support the Constitution of the United States, shall have engaged in insurrection or rebellion against the same, or given aid or comfort to the enemies thereof. But Congress may by a vote of two-thirds of each House, remove such disability.

Section 3 also reflected the power of the Reconstruction-era Republicans over the South. By eliminating the eligibility of former Confederates for public office or to serve as an elector for president or vice president, the Republicans strengthened their presence in Congress and throughout national politics. This measure also allowed African Americans to run for and hold office in the South, which they were doing by 1870, the same year the Fifteenth Amendment was ratified.

In December 1868, five months after the ratification of the Fourteenth Amendment, President Andrew Johnson declared universal amnesty for all former Confederates. This measure had the effect of returning white politicians and by extension the Democratic Party to power in the South. Republican concern over this development was a major force behind the adoption of the Fifteenth Amendment, which was viewed as an instrument to protect Republican political power by securing black enfranchisement. However, Republican president Ulysses S. Grant, who defeated Johnson in 1868, pardoned all but a few hundred remaining Confederate sympathizers by signing the Amnesty Act of 1872. Decisions such as these began the gradual undoing of Republican commitment to black civil rights in the South.

Section 4.

The validity of the public debt of the United States, authorized by law, including debts incurred for payment of pensions and bounties for services in suppressing insurrection or rebellion, shall not be questioned. But neither the United States nor any State shall assume or pay any debt or obligation incurred in aid of insurrection or rebellion against the United States, or any claim for the loss or emancipation of any slave, but all such debts, obligations and claims shall be held illegal and void.

Section 4 repudiated the South's desire to have Congress forgive the Confederacy's war debts. It also rejected any claim that former slaveholders had to be compensated for the loss of their slaves.

Section 5.

The Congress shall have power to enforce, by appropriate legislation, the provisions of this article.

By giving Congress the power to enforce the provisions of the Fourteenth Amendment, section 5 reiterated the post–Civil War emphasis on national citizenship and the limit on state power to deny individuals their constitutional rights. Section 5 also extended congressional law-making power beyond those areas outlined in Article I. But the Court has taken a mixed view of the scope of congressional power to enforce the Fourteenth Amendment. In *Katzenbach* v. *Morgan* (1966), for example, the Supreme Court offered a broad ruling on the section 5 power of Congress. It held that Congress could enact laws establishing rights beyond what the Court said the Constitution required, as long as such laws were designed to establish a remedial constitutional right or protect citizens from a potential constitutional violation. In other cases, such as *City of Boerne* v. *Flores* (1997) and *U.S.* v. *Morrison* (2000), the Court ruled that Congress may not intrude upon the authority of the judicial branch to define the meaning of the Constitution or intrude on the power of the states to make laws within their own domain.

AMENDMENT XV
(Ratified on February 3, 1870)

Section 1.

The right of citizens of the United States to vote shall not be denied or abridged by the United States or by any State on account of race, color, or previous condition of servitude.

Section 2.

The Congress shall have power to enforce this article by appropriate legislation.

The Fifteenth Amendment was the most controversial of the Civil War Amendments, both for what it did and did not do. Although the adoption of the Thirteenth and Fourteenth Amendments made clear that blacks could not be returned to their pre–Civil War slavery, enthusiasm for a constitutional right of black suffrage, even among the northern states, was another matter. On the one hand, the extension of voting rights to blacks was the most dramatic outcome of the Civil War. The former Confederate states had to ratify the Fifteenth Amendment as a condition for readmission into the Union. On the other hand, the rejection of proposed language forbidding discrimination on the basis of property ownership, education, or religious belief gave states the power to regulate the vote as they wished. And, with the collapse of Reconstruction after the 1876 election, southern states implemented laws created by this opening with full force, successfully crippling black voter registration for generations to come in the region where most African Americans lived. Full enfranchisement for African Americans would not arrive until the passage of the Voting Rights Act of 1965, almost one hundred years after the ratification of the Fifteenth Amendment.

The Fifteenth Amendment also divided woman's rights organizations that had campaigned on behalf of abolition and black enfranchisement. Feminists such as Elizabeth Cady Stanton and Susan B. Anthony were furious over the exclusion of women from the Fifteenth Amendment and opposed its ratification, while others, such as Lucy Stone, were willing to support black voting rights at the expense of woman suffrage, leaving that battle for another day. The Supreme Court sided with those who opposed female enfranchisement, ruling in *Minor* v. *Happersett* (1875) that the Fourteenth Amendment did not recognize among the privileges and immunities of American citizenship a constitutional right to vote.

AMENDMENT XVI
(*Ratified on February 3, 1913*)

The Congress shall have power to lay and collect taxes on incomes, from whatever source derived, without apportionment among the several States, and without regard to any census or enumeration.

The Sixteenth Amendment was a response to the Supreme Court's sharply divided ruling in *Pollock* v. *Farmers' Loan & Trust Co.* (1895), which struck down the Income Tax Act of 1894 as unconstitutional. The Court, by a 5–4 margin, held that the law violated Article I, section 9, which prevented Congress from enacting a direct tax (on individuals) unless in proportion to the U.S. Census. In some ways, this was a curious holding, since the Court had permitted

Congress to enact a direct tax on individuals during the Civil War. Between the *Pollock* decision and the enactment of the Sixteenth Amendment, the Court approved of taxes levied on corporations, as such taxes were not really taxes but "excises" levied on "incidents of ownership."

Anti-tax groups have claimed the Sixteenth Amendment was never properly ratified and is thus unconstitutional. The federal courts have rejected that view and have sanctioned and fined individuals who have brought such frivolous challenges to court.

AMENDMENT XVII
(*Ratified on April 8, 1913*)

The Senate of the United States shall be composed of two Senators from each State, elected by the people thereof, for six years; and each Senator shall have one vote. The electors in each State shall have the qualifications requisite for electors of the most numerous branch of the State legislatures.

When vacancies happen in the representation of any State in the Senate, the executive authority of such State shall issue writs of election to fill such vacancies: Provided, That the legislature of any State may empower the executive thereof to make temporary appointments until the people fill the vacancies by election as the legislature may direct.

This amendment shall not be so construed as to affect the election or term of any Senator chosen before it becomes valid as part of the Constitution.

The Seventeenth Amendment repealed the language in Article I, section 3, of the original Constitution, which called for the election of U.S. senators by state legislatures. This method had its roots in the selection of delegates to the Constitutional Convention, who were chosen by the state legislatures. It was also the preferred method of the Framers, who believed that having state legislatures elect senators would strengthen the relationship between the states and the national government, and also contribute to the stability of Congress by removing popular electoral pressure from the upper chamber.

Dissatisfaction set in with this method during the period leading up to the Civil War, especially by the 1850s. Indiana, for example, deeply divided between Union supporters in the northern part of the state and Confederate sympathizers in the southern part, could not agree on the selection of senators and was without representation for two years. After the Civil War, numerous Senate elections were tainted by corruption, and many more resulted in ties that prevented seating senators in a timely fashion. In 1899, Delaware's election was so mired in controversy that it did not have representation in the Senate for four years.

The ratification of the Seventeenth Amendment was the result of almost two decades of persistent efforts at reform. By 1912, twenty-nine states had changed their election laws to require the popular election of senators. In the years before that, constitutional amendments were introduced on a regular basis calling for the popular election of senators. Although many powerful legislators entrenched in the Senate resisted such change, the tide of reform, now aided by journalists and scholars sympathetic to the cause, proved too powerful to withstand. One year after the Seventeenth Amendment was sent to the states for ratification, all members of the Senate were elected by the popular vote.

AMENDMENT XVIII
(Ratified on January 16, 1919)

Section 1.

After one year from the ratification of this article the manufacture, sale, or transportation of intoxicating liquors within, the importation thereof into, or the exportation thereof from the United States and all territory subject to the jurisdiction thereof for beverage purposes is hereby prohibited.

Section 2.

The Congress and the several States shall have concurrent power to enforce this article by appropriate legislation.

Section 3.

This article shall be inoperative unless it shall have been ratified as an amendment to the Constitution by the legislatures of the several States, as provided in the Constitution, within seven years from the date of the submission hereof to the States by the Congress.

The Eighteenth Amendment was the end result of a crusade against the consumption of alcoholic beverages than began during the early nineteenth century. A combination of Christian organizations emboldened by the second Great Awakening and women's groups, who believed alcohol contributed greatly to domestic violence and poverty, campaigned to abolish the manufacture, sale, and use of alcoholic beverages in the United States. Their campaign was moderately successful in the pre–Civil War era. By 1855, thirteen states had banned the sale of "intoxicating" beverages. By the end of the Civil War, however, ten states had repealed their prohibition laws.

Another wave of anti-alcohol campaigning soon emerged, however, as the Women's Christian Temperance Union, founded in 1874 and 250,000 strong by 1911, and the Anti-Saloon League, founded in 1913, pressed the case for Prohibition. Among the arguments offered by supporters of Prohibition were that the cereal grains used in the manufacture of beer and liquor diverted valuable resources from food supplies and that the malaise of drunkenness sapped the strength of manufacturing production at home and the conduct of America's soldiers in World War I. Underneath the formal case for Prohibition was a considerable anti-immigrant sentiment, as many Prohibitionists considered the waves of Italian, Irish, Poles, and German immigrants unduly dependent on alcohol.

In 1919, Congress passed the Eighteenth Amendment over President Woodrow Wilson's veto. That same year, Congress passed the Volstead Act, which implemented Prohibition and authorized law enforcement to target illegal shipments of alcohol into the United States (mostly from Canada, which, ironically, also mandated Prohibition in most of its provinces during this time) as well as alcoholic beverages illegally manufactured in the United States. Evidence remains inconclusive over just how successful the Eighteenth Amendment was in reducing alcohol consumption in the United States. More certain was the billion-dollar windfall that Prohibition created for organized crime, as well as small-time smugglers and bootleggers.

AMENDMENT XIX
(Ratified on August 18, 1920)

The right of citizens of the United States to vote shall not be denied or abridged by the United States or by any State on account of sex.

Congress shall have power to enforce this article by appropriate legislation.

The two major woman's rights organizations of the nineteenth century most active in the battle for female enfranchisement were the National Woman Suffrage Association (NWSA) and the American Woman Suffrage Association (AWSA). NWSA campaigned for a constitutional amendment modeled on the Fifteenth Amendment, which had secured African American voting rights, while the AWSA preferred to pursue women's voting rights through state-level legislative initiatives. In 1890, the two organizations combined to form the National American Woman Suffrage Association. By 1919, the NAWSA, the newer, more radical National Woman's Party, and other activists had secured congressional passage of the Nineteenth Amendment by a broad margin. It was ratified by the states just over a year later.

The Nineteenth Amendment, however, did not free black women from the voting restrictions that southern states placed in the way of African Americans. They and other minorities were not protected from such restrictions until the passage of the Voting Rights Act of 1965.

AMENDMENT XX
(Ratified on February 6, 1933)

Section 1.

The terms of the President and Vice President shall end at noon on the 20th day of January, and the terms of Senators and Representatives at noon on the 3d day of January, of the years in which such terms would have ended if this article had not been ratified; and the terms of their successors shall then begin.

Section 2.

The Congress shall assemble at least once in every year, and such meeting shall begin at noon on the 3d day of January, unless they shall by law appoint a different day.

Section 3.

If, at the time fixed for the beginning of the term of the President, the President elect shall have died, the Vice President elect shall become President. If a President shall not have been chosen before the time fixed for the beginning of his term, or if the President elect shall have failed to qualify, then the Vice President elect shall act as President until a President shall have qualified; and the Congress may by law provide for the case wherein neither a President elect nor a Vice President elect shall have qualified, declaring who shall then act as President, or the manner in which one who is to act shall be selected, and such person shall act accordingly until a President or Vice President shall have qualified.

Section 4.

The Congress may by law provide for the case of the death of any of the persons from whom the House of Representatives may choose a President whenever the rights of choice shall have devolved upon them, and for the case of the death of any of the persons from whom the Senate may choose a Vice President whenever the right of choice shall have devolved upon them.

Section 5.

Sections 1 and 2 shall take effect on the 15th day of October following the ratification of this article.

Section 6.

This article shall be inoperative unless it shall have been ratified as an amendment to the Constitution by the legislatures of three-fourths of the several States within seven years from the date of its submission.

The Twentieth Amendment is often called the lame duck amendment because its fundamental purpose was to shorten the time between the November elections, particularly in a presidential election year, and the starting date of the new presidential term and the commencement of the new congressional session. The amendment modified section 1 of the Twelfth Amendment by moving the beginning of the annual legislative session from March 4 to January 3. This change meant that the newly elected Congress would decide any presidential election thrown into the House of Representatives. It also eliminated the possibility that the nation would have to endure two additional months without a chief executive.

The Twentieth Amendment also modified Article I of the Constitution by placing a fixed time—noon—to begin the congressional session.

AMENDMENT XXI
(Ratified on December 5, 1933)

Section 1.

The eighteenth article of amendment to the Constitution of the United States is hereby repealed.

Section 2.

The transportation or importation into any State, Territory, or possession of the United States for delivery or use therein of intoxicating liquors, in violation of the laws thereof, is hereby prohibited.

Section 3.

This article shall be inoperative unless it shall have been ratified as an amendment to the Constitution by conventions in the several States, as provided in the Constitution, within seven years from the date of the submission hereof to the States by the Congress.

The Twenty-First Amendment repealed the Eighteenth Amendment, which was the first and last time that a constitutional amendment has been repealed. The Twenty-First Amendment is also the only amendment to the Constitution approved by state ratifying conventions rather than a popular vote.

By the late 1920s, Americans had tired of Prohibition, and the arrival of the Great Depression in 1929 did nothing to lift their spirits. Few public officials, well aware of the extensive criminal enterprises that had grown up around Prohibition and had made a mockery of the practice, attempted to defend Prohibition as a success. Indeed, Franklin D. Roosevelt, in his initial bid for the presidency in 1932, made the repeal of Prohibition a campaign promise. In January 1933, Congress amended the Volstead Act to permit the sale of alcoholic beverages with an alcohol content of 3.2 percent. The ratification of the Twenty-First Amendment in December returned absolute control of the regulation of alcohol to the states. States are now free to regulate alcohol as they see fit. They may, for example, limit the quantity and type of alcohol sold to consumers, or ban alcohol sales completely. The Supreme Court, in

South Carolina v. *Dole* (1984), ruled that Congress may require the states to set a certain age for the consumption of alcohol in return for participation in a federal program without violating the Twenty-First Amendment.

AMENDMENT XXII
(Ratified on February 27, 1951)

Section 1.

No person shall be elected to the office of the President more than twice, and no person who has held the office of President, or acted as President, for more than two years of a term to which some other person was elected President shall be elected to the office of the President more than once. But this Article shall not apply to any person holding the office of President when this Article was proposed by the Congress, and shall not prevent any person who may be holding the office of President, or acting as President, during the term within which this Article becomes operative from holding the office of President or acting as President during the remainder of such term.

Section 2.

This article shall be inoperative unless it shall have been ratified as an amendment to the Constitution by the legislatures of three-fourths of the several States within seven years from the date of its submission to the States by the Congress.

Thomas Jefferson, who served as the third president of the United States, was the first person of public stature to suggest a constitutional provision limiting presidential terms. "If some termination to the services of the chief Magistrate be not fixed by the Constitution," said Jefferson, "or supplied by practice, his office, nominally four years, will in fact become for life." Until Ulysses S. Grant's unsuccessful attempt to secure his party's nomination to a third term, no other president attempted to extend the two-term limit that had operated in principle. Theodore Roosevelt, having ascended to the presidency after the assassination of William McKinley in 1901, was elected to his second term in 1904. He then sat out a term, and then ran against Woodrow Wilson in the 1912 election and lost.

The first president to serve more than two terms was Franklin D. Roosevelt, and it was his success that inspired the enactment of the Twenty-Second Amendment. In 1946, Republicans took control of Congress for the first time in sixteen years and were determined to guard against such future Democratic dynasties. A year later, Congress, in one of the most party-line votes in the history of the amending process, approved the Twenty-Second Amendment. Every Republican member of the House and Senate who voted on the amendment voted for it. The remaining votes came almost exclusively from southern Democrats, whose relationship with Roosevelt was never more than a marriage of convenience. Ironically, some Republicans began to call for the repeal of the Twenty-Second Amendment toward the end of popular Republican Dwight D. Eisenhower's second term in 1956. A similar movement emerged in the late 1980s toward the end of Republican Ronald Reagan's second term. The American public at large, however, has shown little enthusiasm for repealing the Twenty-Second Amendment.

AMENDMENT XXIII
(Ratified on March 29, 1961)

Section 1.

The District constituting the seat of Government of the United States shall appoint in such manner as the Congress may direct:

A number of electors of President and Vice President equal to the whole number of Senators and Representatives in Congress to which the District would be entitled if it were a State, but in no event more than the least populous State; they shall be in addition to those appointed by the States, but they shall be considered, for the purposes of the election of President and Vice President, to be electors appointed by a State; and they shall meet in the District and perform such duties as provided by the twelfth article of amendment.

Section 2.

The Congress shall have power to enforce this article by appropriate legislation.

Article II, section 2, of the Constitution limits participation in presidential elections to citizens who reside in the states. The Twenty-Third Amendment amended this provision to include residents of the District of Columbia. Since the District was envisioned as the seat of the national government with a transient population, the Constitution afforded no right of representation to its residents in Congress. By the time the Twenty-Third Amendment was ratified, the District had a greater population than twelve states.

In 1978, Congress introduced a constitutional amendment to give the District of Columbia representation in the House and the Senate. By 1985, the ratification period for the amendment expired without the necessary three-fourths approval from the states.

AMENDMENT XXIV
(Ratified on January 23, 1964)

Section 1.

The right of citizens of the United States to vote in any primary or other election for President or Vice

President, for electors for President or Vice President, or for Senator or Representative in Congress, shall not be denied or abridged by the United States or any State by reason of failure to pay any poll tax or other tax.

Section 2.

The Congress shall have power to enforce this article by appropriate legislation.

The Twenty-Fourth Amendment continued the work of the Fifteenth Amendment. By abolishing the poll tax, the amendment eliminated one of the most popular tools used by voting registrars to prevent most African Americans and other minorities from taking part in the electoral process. Property ownership and literacy tests as conditions of the franchise extended back to the colonial era and were not particular to any region of the United States. But, the poll tax was a southern invention, coming after the enactment of the Fifteenth Amendment. By the fall of Reconstruction in 1877, eleven southern states had enacted poll tax laws. The poll tax was disproportionately enforced against poor African American voters and, in some cases, poor whites.

Congress had begun to debate a constitutional amendment to abolish the poll tax as far back as 1939, but it took the momentum of the civil rights movement to move this process forward. Shortly after the ratification of the Twenty-Fourth Amendment, Congress enacted the Civil Rights Act of 1964, the most sweeping and effective federal civil rights law to date. By the time of ratification of the Twenty-Fourth Amendment, only five states had poll taxes on their books. Spurred on by the spirit of the times, Congress enacted the Voting Rights Act of 1965, which enforced the poll tax ban of the Twenty-Fourth Amendment and also abolished literacy tests, property qualifications, and other obstacles to voter registration. In 1966, in *Harper v. Board of Elections,* the Supreme Court rejected a constitutional challenge to the historic voting rights law.

AMENDMENT XXV
(Ratified on February 10, 1967)

Section 1.

In case of the removal of the President from office or of his death or resignation, the Vice President shall become President.

Section 2.

Whenever there is a vacancy in the office of the Vice President, the President shall nominate a Vice President who shall take office upon confirmation by a majority vote of both Houses of Congress.

Section 3.

Whenever the President transmits to the President pro tempore of the Senate and the Speaker of the House of Representatives his written declaration that he is unable to discharge the powers and duties of his office, and until he transmits to them a written declaration to the contrary, such powers and duties shall be discharged by the Vice President as Acting President.

Section 4.

Whenever the Vice President and a majority of either the principal officers of the executive departments or of such other body as Congress may by law provide, transmit to the President pro tempore of the Senate and the Speaker of the House of Representatives their written declaration that the President is unable to discharge the powers and duties of his office, the Vice President shall immediately assume the powers and duties of the office as Acting President.

Thereafter, when the President transmits to the President pro tempore of the Senate and the Speaker of the House of Representatives his written declaration that no inability exists, he shall resume the powers and duties of his office unless the Vice President and a majority of either the principal officers of the executive department or of such other body as Congress may by law provide, transmit within four days to the President pro tempore of the Senate and the Speaker of the House of Representatives their written declaration that the President is unable to discharge the powers and duties of his office. Thereupon Congress shall decide the issue, assembling within forty-eight hours for that purpose if not in session. If the Congress, within twenty-one days after receipt of the latter written declaration, or, if Congress is not in session, within twenty-one days after Congress is required to assemble, determines by two-thirds vote of both Houses that the President is unable to discharge the powers and duties of his office, the Vice President shall continue to discharge the same as Acting President; otherwise, the President shall resume the powers and duties of his office.

Several tragedies to the men who occupied the offices of president and vice president and the lack of constitutional clarity about the path of succession in event of presidential and vice presidential disability spurred the enactment of the Twenty-Fifth Amendment.

Whether the vice president was merely an acting president or assumed the permanent powers of the office for the remainder of the term upon the death of a

president was answered in 1841 when John Tyler became president upon the death of William Henry Harrison, who died only a month after his inauguration. Seven more presidents died in office before the enactment of the Twenty-Fifth Amendment, and in each case the vice president assumed the presidency without controversy. What this amendment answered that the original Constitution did not was the method of vice presidential succession. The vice presidency often went unfilled for months at a time as the result of constitutional ambiguity. Since the enactment of the amendment, there have been two occasions when the president appointed a vice president. Both took place during the second term of President Richard M. Nixon. For the first time in United States history, the nation witnessed a presidential term served out by two men, President Gerald R. Ford and Vice President Nelson A. Rockefeller, neither of whom had been elected to the position.

The Twenty-Fifth Amendment also settled the path of succession in the event of presidential disability. This provision of the amendment was prompted by the memories of James Garfield lying in a coma for eighty days after being struck by an assassin's bullet and Woodrow Wilson's bedridden state for the last eighteen months of his term after a stroke. The first president to invoke the disability provision of the Twenty-Fifth Amendment was Ronald Reagan, who made Vice President George Bush acting president for the eight hours while he underwent surgery. The only other time a president invoked this provision came in 2002, when George W. Bush underwent minor surgery and transferred the powers of his office to Vice President Dick Cheney.

The provision authorizing the vice president, in consultation with Congress and members of the Cabinet, to declare the president disabled has never been invoked.

AMENDMENT XXVI
(Ratified on July 1, 1971)

Section 1.

The right of citizens of the United States, who are eighteen years of age or older, to vote shall not be denied or abridged by the United States or by any State on account of age.

Section 2.

The Congress shall have power to enforce this article by appropriate legislation.

The Twenty-Sixth Amendment was a direct response to the unpopularity of the Vietnam War and was spurred by calls to lower the voting age to eighteen so that draft-eligible men could voice their opinion on the war through the ballot box. In 1970, Congress had amended the Voting Rights Act of 1965 to lower the voting age to eighteen in all national, state, and local elections. Many states resisted compliance, claiming that Congress, while having the power to establish the voting age in national elections, had no such authority in state and local elections. In *Oregon* v. *Mitchell* (1970), the Supreme Court agreed with that view. Congress responded by drafting the Twenty-Sixth Amendment, and the states ratified it quickly and without controversy.

AMENDMENT XXVII
(Ratified on May 7, 1992)

No law, varying the compensation for the services of the Senators and Representatives shall take effect until an election of Representatives shall have intervened.

The Twenty-Seventh Amendment originally was introduced in 1789 during the 1st Congress as one of the original twelve amendments to the Constitution. Only six of the necessary eleven (of thirteen) states had ratified the amendment by 1791. As more states came into the union, the prospect of the amendment's passage only dwindled. No additional state ratified the amendment until 1873, when Ohio approved its addition to the Constitution.

Sometime in the early 1980s, a University of Texas student discovered the amendment and launched an intensive effort to bring it to the public's attention for ratification. The amendment's core purpose, preventing members of Congress from raising their salaries during the terms in which they served, meshed well with another grassroots movement that began during this time, the campaign to impose term limits on members of the House and Senate. Nothing in the nation's constitutional or statutory law prohibited the resurrection of the Twenty-Seventh Amendment for voter approval. In 1939, the Supreme Court had ruled in *Coleman* v. *Miller* that amendments could remain indefinitely before the public unless Congress had set a specific time limit on the ratification process. By 1992, the amendment had received the necessary three-fourths approval of the states, making it the last successful effort to amend the Constitution. The Twenty-Seventh Amendment has not, however, barred Congress from increasing its compensation through annual cost-of-living-adjustments.

FEDERALISM

3

ON AUGUST 26, 2005, as New Orleans, Louisiana, and other low-lying Gulf Coast areas in Mississippi and Alabama braced for what could possibly be a Category 5 hurricane named Katrina, Louisiana Governor Kathleen Blanco declared a state of emergency and requested troop assistance from the Department of Defense. On August 27, as Governor Haley Barbour declared a state of emergency in Mississippi, Governor Blanco asked President George W. Bush to declare a federal state of emergency in Louisiana, believing that "effective response is beyond the capabilities of the State and affected local governments."

The White House responded by authorizing the Federal Emergency Management Agency (FEMA) "to identify, mobilize, and provide at its discretion, equipment and resources necessary to alleviate the impacts of the emergency." On Sunday, August 28, Mayor Ray Nagin issued the first-ever mandatory evacuation of New Orleans amid warnings that the levees, built by the U.S. Army Corps of Engineers, might not hold, thereby flooding the city. As massive evacuations of the coast occurred, Marty Bahamonde, a Boston-based FEMA official, was sent to New Orleans to be the eyes and ears of FEMA Director Michael Brown. The Louisiana National Guard asked FEMA for 700 buses to help evacuate the poor who had no other methods of transportation; FEMA sent 100.

When the storm first hit land on August 29, it looked as if it might not be as bad as predicted. Still, thousands of largely poor and elderly New Orleans citizens were forced to take refuge in the Superdome and the Convention Center. As feared, the levees gave way, flooding entire sections of New Orleans and basically destroying one of the poorest areas of the city. Many residents were stranded in their homes, some on their rooftops.

The situation quickly deteriorated even further when a large proportion of New Orleans police failed to show up for work, and Mayor Nagin and Governor Blanco seemed unable to agree on strategies to deal with the colossal disaster. Both, however, pleaded for more federal assistance, but their pleas fell on deaf ears as President Bush continued to attend to other business. Bush, for example, discussed immigration with Secretary of Homeland Security Michael Chertoff, posed for a birthday photo op with Senator John McCain, visited an Arizona resort to discuss prescription drugs, and then attended a San Diego Padres baseball game.[1]

CHAPTER OUTLINE

⭐ The Origins of the Federal System: Governmental Powers Under the Constitution

⭐ Federalism and the Marshall Court

⭐ Dual Federalism: The Taney Court, Slavery, and the Civil War

⭐ Cooperative Federalism: The New Deal and the Growth of National Government

⭐ New Federalism: Returning Power to the States

President Bush was not alone in his passive reaction. Various levels of government appeared either paralyzed or unaware of the disaster in Louisiana and other coastal areas. One government official who was not able to ignore the situation was FEMA agent Bahamonde, who sent increasingly desperate e-mails back to the FEMA director. Using his Blackberry, Bahamonde, who was in the Superdome with thousands of evacuees, told Brown: "Sir, I know that you know the situation is past critical. . . . Hotels are kicking people out, thousands gathering in the streets with no food or water. . . . Estimates are that many will die within hours. We are out of food and running out of water."

Three hours later, FEMA director Brown's press secretary responded to Bahamonde that the director needed time to eat in Baton Rouge, where good restaurants were filling up. Bahamonde wrote back, "OH MY GOD!!!!!" adding, "I just ate an MRE [a prepackaged meal used by the military] and crapped in the hallway of the Superdome along with 30,000 other close friends so I understand [the] concern about busy restaurants."

In the wake of the September 11, 2001, terrorist attacks, tremendous emphasis was put on the need for local, state, and national officials to be able to work together in a time of national emergency. Katrina was the first major disaster after 9/11, and it quickly became apparent that no level of government in the federal system was addressing the crisis adequately. By Thursday, September 1, New Orleans Homeland Security Director Terry Ebbert said, "This is a national disgrace. FEMA has been here three days yet there is not command and control." Mayor Nagin sent out another desperate plea for help to FEMA and was told by FEMA Director Brown that Brown had heard "no reports of unrest."

With many local and state employees without homes or ways to get to work, and with nearly all forms of communication failing, hundreds died in New Orleans. Although Hurricane Katrina brought out the best in many Americans, the official response made clear that there was no effective coordination between the local, state, and national governments, nor any real agreement as to which level of government was responsible for what in this tragedy. In such a crisis, what is the role of a mayor? What role should a governor play? To what extent was the president responsible for FEMA's failures? These questions continue unresolved, yet they highlight some of the difficulties related to the federal system created by the U.S. Constitution.[2]

F ROM ITS VERY BEGINNING, the challenge for the United States of America was to preserve the traditional independence and rights of the states while establishing an effective national government. The Framers, fearing tyranny, divided powers between the state and the national governments. At each level, moreover, powers were divided among executive, legislative, and judicial branches. The people are the ultimate power from which both the national government and the state governments derive their power.

Although most of the delegates to the Constitutional Convention favored a strong federal government, they knew that some compromise about the distribution of powers would be necessary. Some of the Framers wanted to continue with the confederate form of government defined in the Articles of Confederation; others wanted a more centralized system, similar to that of Great Britain. Their solution was to create the world's first federal system (although the word "federal" never appears in the U.S. Constitution), in which the thirteen sovereign or independent states were bound together under one national government.

Today, the Constitution ultimately binds more than 87,000 different governments at the national, state, and local level (see Figure 3.1). The Constitution lays out the duties, obligations, and powers of each of these units. Throughout history, however, this relationship has been continually reshaped by crises, historical evolution, public expectations, and judicial interpretation. All these forces have had tremendous influence on who makes policy decisions and how these decisions get made, as is underscored in our opening vignette.

In this chapter, we will look at the origins of the federal system and the governmental powers under the Constitution created by the Framers. After we explore federalism and how it was molded by the Marshall Court, we will examine the development of dual federalism before and after the Civil War. Following a discussion of cooperative federalism and the growth of national government, we will consider new federalism, especially the movement toward returning power to the states.

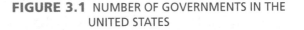

FIGURE 3.1 NUMBER OF GOVERNMENTS IN THE UNITED STATES

Source: U.S. Census Bureau, http://www.census.gov.

The Origins of the Federal System: Governmental Powers Under the Constitution

THE UNITED STATES WAS THE FIRST COUNTRY to adopt a **federal system** of government. This system of government, where the national government and state governments share powers and derive all authority from the people, was designed to remedy many of the problems experienced by the Framers under the Articles of Confederation.

The new system of government also had to be different from the **unitary system** found in Great Britain, where the local and regional governments derived all their power from a strong national government. (Figure 3.2 illustrates these different forms of government.) Having been under the rule of English kings, whom they considered tyrants, the Framers feared centralizing power in one government or institution. Therefore, they made both the state and the federal government accountable to the people at large. While the governments shared some powers, such as the ability to tax, each government was supreme in some spheres, as depicted in Figure 3.3 and described in the following section.

The federal system as conceived by the Framers has proven tremendously effective. Since the creation of the U.S. system, many other nations including Canada (1867), Mexico (1917), and Russia (1993) have adopted federal systems in their constitutions. (See Global Perspective: American and Mexican Federalism).

NATIONAL POWERS UNDER THE CONSTITUTION

Chief among the exclusive powers of the national government are the authorities to coin money, conduct foreign relations, provide for an army and navy, declare war, and establish a national court system. All of these powers set out in Article I, section 8, of the Constitution are called **enumerated powers.** Article I, section 8, also contains the **necessary and proper clause,** which gives Congress the authority to enact any laws "necessary and proper" for carrying out any of its enumerated powers. These powers derived from enumerated powers and the necessary and proper clause are known as **implied powers**.

The federal government's right to tax was also clearly set out in the new Constitution. The Framers wanted to avoid the financial problems that the national government experienced under the Articles of Confederation. If the national government was to be strong, its power to raise revenue had to be unquestionable. Although the new national government had no power under the Constitution to levy a national income tax, that was changed by the passage of the Sixteenth Amendment in 1913.

federal system
System of government where the national government and state governments share powers, derive all authority from the people, and the powers of the national government are specified in a constitution.

unitary system
System of government where the local and regional governments derive all authority from a strong national government.

enumerated powers
Seventeen specific powers granted to Congress under Article I, section 8, of the U.S. Constitution; these powers include taxation, coinage of money, regulation of commerce, and the authority to provide for a national defense.

necessary and proper clause
The final paragraph of Article I, section 8, of the U.S. Constitution, which gives Congress the authority to pass all laws "necessary and proper" to carry out the enumerated powers specified in the Constitution; also called the elastic clause.

implied powers
A power derived from an enumerated power and the necessary and proper clause. These powers are not stated specifically but are considered to be reasonably implied through the exercise of delegated powers.

FIGURE 3.2 THE FEDERAL, UNITARY, AND CONFEDERATE SYSTEMS OF GOVERNMENT

The source of governmental authority and power differs dramatically in various systems of government.

Federal System
National government and states derive authority from the people

Unitary System
Local and regional governments derive authority from the national government

Local and Regional Government

Confederate System
National government derives authority from states

States   People   National Government

COMPARATIVE
Comparing Federal and Unitary Sysrems

supremacy clause
Portion of Article VI of the U.S. Constitution mandating that national law is supreme to (that is, supersedes) all other laws passed by the states or by any other subdivision of government.

VIDEO ROUNDTABLE
Governors

Eventually, as discussed later in this chapter, this new taxing power became a powerful catalyst for further expansion of the national government.

Article VI of the federal Constitution underscores the notion that the national government is to be supreme in situations of conflict between state and national law. It declares that the U.S. Constitution, the laws of the United States, and its treaties are to be "the supreme Law of the Land; and the Judges in every State shall be bound thereby." In spite of this explicit language, the meaning of what is called the **supremacy clause** has been subject to continuous judicial interpretation.

STATE POWERS UNDER THE CONSTITUTION

Because states had all the power at the time the Constitution was written, the Framers felt no need, as they did for the new national government, to list and restate the powers of the states. Article I, however, allows states to set the "Times, Places, and Manner, for holding elections for senators and representatives." This article also guarantees each state two members in the Senate and prevents Congress from limiting the slave

FIGURE 3.3 THE DISTRIBUTION OF GOVERNMENTAL POWER IN THE FEDERAL SYSTEM

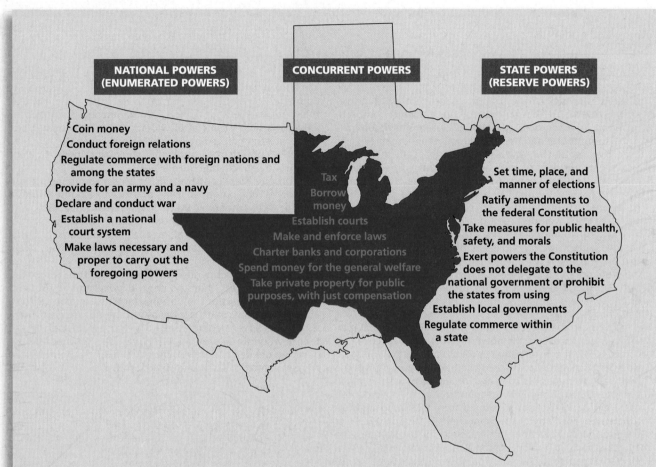

trade before 1808. Article II requires that each state appoint electors to vote for president. In addition, Article IV provides each state a "Republican Form of Government," meaning one that represents the citizens of the state. It also assures that the national government will protect the states against foreign attacks and domestic rebellion.

It was not until the **Tenth Amendment,** the final part of the Bill of Rights, that the states' powers were described in greater detail: "The powers not delegated to the United States by the Constitution, nor prohibited by it to the States, are reserved to the States respectively, or to the people." (See The Living Constitution: Tenth Amendment.) These powers, often called the states' **reserve** or **police powers,** include the ability to legislate for the public health, safety, and morals of their citizens. Today, the states' rights to legislate under their police powers are used as the rationale for many states' restrictions on abortion, including twenty-four-hour waiting requirements and provisions requiring minors to obtain parental consent before obtaining an abortion. Police powers are also the basis for state criminal laws, including varied laws concerning the death penalty.

CONCURRENT POWERS UNDER THE CONSTITUTION

As revealed in Figure 3.3, national and state powers overlap. The area where the systems overlap represents **concurrent powers**—powers shared by the national and state

Tenth Amendment
The final part of the Bill of Rights that defines the basic principle of American federalism in stating: "The powers not delegated to the United States by the Constitution, nor prohibited by it to the States, are reserved to the States respectively, or to the people."

reserve (or police) powers
Powers reserved to the states by the Tenth Amendment that lie at the foundation of a state's right to legislate for the public health and welfare of its citizens.

concurrent powers
Authority possessed by both the state and national governments that may be exercised concurrently as long as that power is not exclusively within the scope of national power or in conflict with national law.

Global Perspective

AMERICAN AND MEXICAN FEDERALISM

Like the United States, Mexico, formally known as the United Mexican States, is a federal republic with power shared between a federal government and thirty-one self-governing *estados*, or states. Mexico's *estados* have separate state constitutions, and their governments are organized into executive, legislative, and judicial branches. In the United States, the authority of each state's executive office is determined by the state's constitution; for example, the governor of Texas is constitutionally weak, whereas the governor of New York has considerably more executive authority. In Mexico, all of the governors are given significant executive clout.

Mexican municipalities, like their cousins to the north, are charged with providing public services like police and fire protection, waste and sewage management, and park and road maintenance. And, the municipalities are likewise authorized to collect user fees and local taxes, though their ability to generate revenue is considerably less than that of American local government, in part due to Mexico's high poverty rate.

For more than seventy years, the Mexican national government (in particular, the powerful office of president) was controlled by the Institutional Revolutionary Party (PRI). A national discussion regarding the devolution of power from the national government to state and local governments began in the late 1980s, primarily in reaction to the well-documented corruption and excesses stemming from PRI's long uninterrupted rule. The Party of the Democratic Revolution (PRD) lost the presidential elections under suspicious circumstances in 1988, but in 2000, the opposition National Action Party (PAN) elected its candidate, Vicente Fox, to a six-year term as president, ushering in what many hoped would be a new era of free and fair elections. The outcome of the 2006 presidential election, in which conservative candidate Felipe Calderón Hinojosa (PAN) was declared President Elect by a margin of less than one percentage point has dampened such hopes. Calderón's victory came after widespread and sometimes violent protests organized by Andrés Manuel López Obrador, the leftist PRD presidential candidate, who maintained that electoral fraud had cost him the election.

Despite these controversies, it is now commonplace for candidates running for all levels of office to espouse enthusiasm for local autonomy. State governments have also been clamoring for increased autonomy and are now beginning to receive it, albeit in very small measures in comparison to the level of autonomy of states and municipalities in America's federal system.

A significant impediment to increased state control in Mexico is the fact that the central government controls roughly 90 percent of the nation's total revenue and is thus able to mandate state action by threatening to withhold funds. Moreover, regional self-sufficiency is difficult to establish when states are competing with one another for desperately needed federal dollars. A similar though less extreme dynamic exists in the United States.

QUESTIONS

1. In what ways are American and Mexican federalism similar? In what ways are they different?
2. Does federalism necessarily guarantee the exercise of local democracy? Why or why not?

Sources: The Economist (March 27, 2003); U.S. Library of Congress, *Country Studies: Mexico; CIA World Factbook,* https://www.cia.gov/cia/publications/factbook/geos/mx.html.

VISUAL LITERACY

Explaining Differences in State Laws

SIMULATION

You Are a Restaurant Owner

bill of attainder
A law declaring an act illegal without a judicial trial.

***ex post facto* law**
Law passed after the fact, thereby making previously legal activity illegal and subject to current penalty; prohibited by the U.S. Constitution.

governments. States already had the power to tax; the Constitution extended this power to the national government as well. Other important concurrent powers include the right to borrow money, establish courts, and make and enforce laws necessary to carry out these powers.

POWERS DENIED UNDER THE CONSTITUTION

Some powers are explicitly denied to the national government or the states under Article I of the Constitution. In keeping with the Framers' desire to forge a national economy, for example, states are prohibited from entering into treaties, coining money, or impairing obligation of contracts. States also are prohibited from entering into compacts with other states without express congressional approval. In a similar vein, Congress is barred from favoring one state over another in regulating commerce, and it cannot lay duties on items exported from any state.

State governments (as well as the national government) are denied the authority to take arbitrary actions affecting constitutional rights and liberties. Neither national nor state governments may pass a **bill of attainder,** a law declaring an act illegal without a judicial trial. The Constitution also bars the national and state governments from passing *ex post facto* **laws,** laws that make an act punishable as a crime even if the

The Living Constitution

The Powers not delegated to the United States by the Constitution, nor prohibited by it to the States, are reserved to the states respectively, or to the people.

—TENTH AMENDMENT

This amendment to the Constitution—a simple affirmation that any powers not specifically given to the national government are left to the province of the states or to the citizenry—actually was unnecessary and added nothing to the original document. During the ratification debates, however, Anti-Federalists continued to be concerned that the national government would claim powers not intended for it at the expense of the states. Still, during the debates over this amendment, both houses of Congress rejected efforts to insert the word "expressly" before the word delegated. Thus, it was clear that the amendment was not intended to be the yardstick by which to measure the powers of the national government. This was reinforced by comments made by James Madison during the debate that took place over Alexander Hamilton's efforts to establish a national bank. "Interference with the power of the States was no constitutional criterion of the power of Congress," said Madison.

By the end of the New Deal, the Supreme Court had come to interpret the Tenth Amendment to allow Congress, pursuant to its authority under the commerce clause, to legislate in a wide array of areas that the states might never have foreseen when they ratified the amendment. In fact, until the 1970s, Congress's ability to legislate to regulate commerce appeared to trump any actions of the states. Since the mid-1970s, however, the Court has been very closely divided about how much authority must be reserved to the states vis-à-vis their authority to regulate commerce, especially when it involves regulation of activities of states as sovereign entities. The Court now requires Congress to attach statements of clear intention to tread on state powers. It is then up to the Court to determine if Congress has claimed powers beyond its authority under the Constitution.

action was legal at the time it was committed. (For more on civil rights and liberties, see chapters 4 and 5.)

RELATIONS AMONG THE STATES

In addition to delineating the relationship of the states with the national government, the Constitution provides a mechanism for resolving interstate disputes and facilitating relations among states. To avoid any sense of favoritism, it provides that disputes between states be settled directly by the U.S. Supreme Court under its original jurisdiction as mandated by Article III of the Constitution (see chapter 9). Moreover, Article IV requires that each state give "Full Faith and Credit . . . to the public Acts, Records and judicial Proceedings of every other State." The **full faith and credit clause** ensures

full faith and credit clause
Section of Article IV of the Constitution that ensures judicial decrees and contracts made in one state will be binding and enforceable in any other state.

On Campus

LEGISLATING AGAINST VIOLENCE AGAINST WOMEN: A CASUALTY OF THE DEVOLUTION REVOLUTION?

As originally enacted in 1994, the Violence Against Women Act (VAWA) allowed women to file civil lawsuits in federal court if they could prove that they were the victims of rape, domestic violence, or other crimes motivated by gender. VAWA was widely praised as an effective mechanism to combat domestic violence. In its first five years, $1.6 million was allocated for states and local governments to pay for a variety of programs, including a national toll-free hotline for victims of violence that averages 13,000 calls per month, funding for special police sex crime units, and civil and legal assistance for women in need of restraining orders.[a] It also provided money to promote awareness of campus rape and domestic violence and to enhance reporting of crimes such as what is often termed date rape.

Most of the early publicity surrounding VAWA stemmed from a challenge to one of its provisions. The suit brought by Christy Brzonkala was the first brought under the act's civil damages provision. While she was a student at Virginia Polytechnic Institute, Brzonkala alleged that two football players there raped her. After the university took no action against the students, she sued the school and the students. No criminal charges were ever filed in her case. The conservative Fourth Circuit Court of Appeals in Richmond, Virginia—in contrast to contrary rulings in seventeen other federal courts—ruled that Congress had overstepped its authority because the alleged crimes were "within the exclusive purview of the states."[b] The Clinton administration and the National Organization for Women's Legal Defense and Education Fund (now called Legal Momentum) appealed that decision to the Supreme Court on her behalf.

Photo courtesy: Cindy Pinkston

■ Christy Brzonkala, the petitioner in *U.S.* v. *Morrison* (2000).

In 2000, five justices of the Supreme Court, including Justice Sandra Day O'Connor, ruled that Congress had no authority under the commerce clause to provide a federal remedy to victims of gender-motivated violence, a decision viewed as greatly reining in congressional power.[c] Thus, today, students abused on campus no longer have this federal remedy.

[a] Juliet Eilperin, "Reauthorization of Domestic Violence Act Is at Risk," *Washington Post* (September 13, 2000): A6.

[b] Tony Mauro, "Court Will Review Laws of Protection," *USA Today* (September 29, 1999): 4A.

[c] *U.S.* v. *Morrison*, 529 U.S. 598 (2000).

---

privileges and immunities clause
Part of Article IV of the Constitution guaranteeing that the citizens of each state are afforded the same rights as citizens of all other states.

interstate compacts
Contracts between states that carry the force of law; generally now used as a tool to address multistate policy concerns.

PARTICIPATION

Explore Your State Constitution

that judicial decrees and contracts made in one state will be binding and enforceable in another. (See On Campus: Legislating Against Violence Against Women.)

Article IV contains the **privileges and immunities clause,** guaranteeing that the citizens of each state are afforded the same rights as citizens of all other states. Article IV also requires states to extradite, or return, criminals to states where they have been convicted or are to stand trial.

To facilitate relations among states, Article 1, section 10, clause 3, of the U.S. Constitution sets the legal foundation for interstate cooperation in the form of **interstate compacts,** contracts between states that carry the force of law. It reads, "No State shall, without the consent of Congress . . . enter into any Agreement or Compact with another state." Before 1920, interstate compacts typically were bistate compacts that addressed boundary disputes or acted to help two states accomplish some objective.

More than 200 interstate compacts exist today. While some deal with rudimentary items such as state boundaries, others help states carry out their policy objectives, and they play an important role in helping states carry out their functions. Although several bistate compacts still exist, other compacts have as many as fifty signatories.[3]

The Drivers License Compact, for example, was signed by all fifty states to facilitate nationwide recognition of licenses issued in the respective states.

States today find that interstate compacts help them maintain state control because compacts with other states allow for sharing resources, expertise, and responses that often are available more quickly than those from the federal government. The Emergency Management Assistance Compact, for example, allows states to cooperate and to share resources in the event of natural and man-made disasters. After the terrorist attacks on September 11, assistance to New York and Virginia came from a host of other states. As the Framers were aware, however, the states had differences as well as shared interests and values. (See American Values/American Voices: Legislating for One America or for Individual States?)

RELATIONS WITHIN THE STATES: LOCAL GOVERNMENT

The Constitution gives local governments, including counties, municipalities, townships, and school districts, no independent standing. Thus, their authority is not granted directly by the people, but through state governments, which establish or charter administrative subdivisions to execute the duties of the state government on a smaller scale.

Comparing State and Local Governments

Federalism and the Marshall Court

THE NATURE OF FEDERALISM, including its allocation of power between the national government and the states, has changed dramatically over the past two hundred years. Much of this change is due to the rulings of the U.S. Supreme Court, which has played a major role in defining the nature of the federal system because the distribution of power between the national and state governments is not clearly delineated in the Constitution. Few Supreme Courts have had a greater impact on the federal/state relationship than the one headed by Chief Justice John Marshall (1801–1835). In a series of decisions, he and his associates carved out an important role for the Court in defining the balance of power between the national government and the states. Two rulings in the early 1800s, *McCulloch* v. *Maryland* (1819) and *Gibbons* v. *Ogden* (1824), were particularly important.

Federalism and the Supreme Court

MCCULLOCH V. MARYLAND (1819)

McCulloh v. *Maryland* (1819) was the first major Supreme Court decision of the Marshall Court to define the relationship between the national and state governments. In 1816, Congress chartered the Second Bank of the United States. (The charter of the First Bank had been allowed to expire.) In 1818, the Maryland state legislature levied a tax requiring all banks not chartered by Maryland (that is, the Second Bank of the United States) to: (1) buy stamped paper from the state on which the Second Bank's notes were to be issued; (2) pay the state $15,000 a year; or, (3) go out of business. James McCulloch, the head cashier of the Baltimore branch of the Bank of the United States, refused to pay the tax, and Maryland brought suit against him. After losing in a Maryland state court, McCulloch appealed his conviction to the U.S. Supreme Court by order of the U.S. secretary of the treasury. In a unanimous opinion, the Court answered the two central questions that had been put to it: Did Congress have the authority to charter a bank? If it did, could a state tax it?

Chief Justice John Marshall's answer to the first question—whether Congress had the right to establish a bank or another type of corporation, given that the Constitution does not explicitly mention such a power—continues to stand as the classic exposition of the doctrine of implied powers and as a reaffirmation of the propriety of a strong national government. Although the word "bank" cannot be found in the

McCulloch v. Maryland (1819)
The Supreme Court upheld the power of the national government and denied the right of a state to tax the bank. The Court's broad interpretation of the necessary and proper clause paved the way for later rulings upholding expansive federal powers.

American Values/American Voices

LEGISLATING FOR ONE AMERICA OR FOR INDIVIDUAL STATES?

When the Framers were drafting the U.S. Constitution, they firmly believed that each state would at times exhibit its own unique political culture, a phenomenon that has been noted by many political scientists who study states within the federal system. Today, for example, we often talk about red states, blue states, and even purple states. But, how different are the states? Are those who live in the southern Bible Belt really more religious than their neighbors in other states? And, if so, how universal are "American values"?

A 2005 study published in the *Atlantic Monthly*, with tongue-in-cheek commentary by satirist P. J. O'Rourke, underscores the differences between states political cultures.[a] For example, the ratio of married to divorced people is far lower in what New Englander O'Rourke refers to as the western "flyover" states that stretch from North Dakota down to western Texas. In parts of California, Florida, Tennessee, and Maine, more than 12 percent of the population has been divorced. And, while many parts of the South contain the poorest citizens in the nation, those same people often give a higher proportion of their income to charity than citizens in wealthier parts of the country.

Crime is another area where state differences are vast. Parts of Florida, South Carolina, and California have among the highest crime rates per 100,000 residents in the country. Rourke's cheeky explanation for this pattern is that "retirees are America's secret criminal class." He continues, "this would explain the felonious Sunshine State and the great American Crescent of Crime that begins in seniors-friendly New Mexico, sweeps through the golden-age communities of Arizona and southern Nevada and continues up the Winnebago-frequented Pacific Coast."[b]

Differences in issues such as crime often lead to very different approaches to solving social problems and reflect local values. For many years New York state, often regarded as liberal, did not have the death penalty. Texas, regarded as conservative, not only has the highest proportion of inmates on death row but leads all states yearly in the number of inmates put to death. Similarly, states have very different laws on same-sex marriage, grounds for divorce, and even the ages at which children can be tried in adult courts.

QUESTIONS

1. Are there state or local values that make it difficult for us to discuss American values? Explain.
2. What basic shared attitudes are so fundamental that they must be a part of any discussion of American values?

[a] P. J. O'Rourke, "Continental Divides," *Atlantic Monthly* (January/February, 2005): 128–131.

[b] O'Rourke, "Continental Divides," 129.

Constitution, the Constitution enumerates powers that give Congress the authority to levy and collect taxes, issue a currency, and borrow funds. From these enumerated powers, Marshall found, it was reasonable to imply that Congress had the power to charter a bank, which could be considered "necessary and proper" to the exercise of its aforementioned enumerated powers.

Marshall next addressed the question of whether a federal bank could be taxed by any state government. To Marshall, this was not a difficult question. The national government was dependent on the people, not the states, for its powers. In addition, Marshall noted, the Constitution specifically calls for the national law to be supreme. "The power to tax involves the power to destroy," wrote Marshall.[4] Thus, the state tax violated the supremacy clause, because individual states cannot interfere with the operations of the national government, whose laws are supreme.

The Court's decision in *McCulloch* has far-reaching consequences even today. The necessary and proper clause is used to justify federal action in many areas, including education, health, and welfare. Furthermore, had Marshall allowed the state of Maryland to tax the Second Bank, it is possible that states could have attempted to tax all federal agencies located within their boundaries, a costly proposition that could have driven the federal government into insurmountable debt.

GIBBONS V. OGDEN (1824)

Shortly after *McCulloch*, the Marshall Court had another opportunity to rule in favor of a broad interpretation of the scope of national power. *Gibbons* v. *Ogden* (1824) involved a dispute that arose after the New York State legislature granted to Robert Fulton the

Gibbons v. Ogden (1824)
The Supreme Court upheld broad congressional power to regulate interstate commerce. The Court's broad interpretation of the Constitution's commerce clause paved the way for later rulings upholding expansive federal powers.

exclusive right to operate steamboats on the Hudson River. Simultaneously, Congress licensed a ship to sail on the same waters. By the time the case reached the U.S. Supreme Court, it was complicated both factually and procedurally. Suffice it to say that both New York and New Jersey wanted to control shipping on the lower Hudson River. But, *Gibbons* actually addressed one simple, very important question: what was the scope of Congress's authority under the commerce clause? The states argued that "commerce," as mentioned in Article I, should be interpreted narrowly to include only direct dealings in products. In *Gibbons*, however, the Supreme Court ruled that Congress's power to regulate interstate commerce included the power to regulate commercial activity as well, and that the commerce power had no limits except those specifically found in the Constitution. Thus, New York had no constitutional authority to grant a monopoly to a single steamboat operator, an act that interfered with interstate commerce.[5] Like the necessary and proper clause, today, the commerce clause is used to justify a great deal of federal legislation, including regulation of highways, the stock market, and violence against women.

Dual Federalism: The Taney Court, Slavery, and the Civil War

IN SPITE OF NATIONALIST Marshall Court decisions such as *McCulloch* and *Gibbons*, strong debate continued in the United States over national versus state power. It was under the leadership of Chief Justice Marshall's successor, Roger B. Taney (1835–1863), that the Supreme Court articulated the notions of concurrent power and **dual federalism.** Dual federalism posits that having separated and equally powerful state and national governments is the best arrangement. Adherents of this theory typically believe that the national government should not exceed its constitutionally enumerated powers, and, as stated in the Tenth Amendment, all other powers are, and should be, reserved to the states or the people.

dual federalism
The belief that having separate and equally powerful levels of government is the best arrangement.

DRED SCOTT AND THE ADVENT OF CIVIL WAR

During the Taney Court era, the comfortable role of the Supreme Court as the arbiter of competing national and state interests became troublesome when the justices were called upon to deal with the controversial issue of slavery. In cases such as *Dred Scott* v. *Sandford* (1857), the Court tried to manage the slavery issue by resolving questions of ownership, the status of fugitive slaves, and slavery in the new territories.[6] These cases generally were settled in favor of slavery and states' rights within the framework of dual federalism. In *Dred Scott*, for example, the Taney Court, in declaring the Missouri Compromise unconstitutional, ruled that Congress lacked the authority to ban slavery in the territories. This decision seemed to rule out any nationally legislated solution to the slavery question, leaving the problem in the hands of the state legislatures and the people, who did not have the power to impose their will on other states.

THE CIVIL WAR, ITS AFTERMATH, AND THE CONTINUATION OF DUAL FEDERALISM

The Civil War (1861–1865) forever changed the nature of federalism. In the aftermath of the war, the national government grew in size and powers. It also attempted to impose its will on the state governments through the Thirteenth, Fourteenth, and Fifteenth Amendments. These three amendments, known collectively as the Civil War Amendments, prohibited slavery and granted civil and political rights (including the franchise for males) to African Americans.

The U.S. Supreme Court, however, continued to adhere to its belief in the concept of dual federalism. Therefore, in spite of the growth of the national government's powers,

Photo courtesy: Missouri Historical Society

■ Dred Scott, born into slavery around 1795, became the named plaintiff in a case with major ramifications for the federal system. In 1833, Scott was sold by his original owners, the Blow family, to Dr. Emerson in St. Louis, Missouri. When Emerson died in 1843, Scott tried to buy his freedom. Before he could, however, he was transferred to Emerson's widow, who moved to New York, leaving Scott in the custody of his first owners, the Blows. Some of the Blows (Henry Blow later founded the anti-slavery Free Soil Party) and other abolitionists gave money to support a test case seeking Scott's freedom. They believed that Scott's residence with the Emerson family in Illinois and later in the Wisconsin Territory, which both prohibited slavery, made Scott a free man. After many delays, the U.S. Supreme Court ruled 7–2 in 1857 that Scott was not a citizen of the United States. "Slaves," said the Court, "were never thought of or spoken of except as property." Despite this ruling, Dred Scott was given his freedom later in 1857, when the Emerson family permanently returned him to the anti-slavery Blows. He died of tuberculosis one year later.

Sixteenth Amendment
Authorized Congress to enact a national income tax.

Seventeenth Amendment
Made senators directly elected by the people; removed their selection from state legislatures.

the importance of the state governments' powers was not diminished until 1933, when the next major change in the federal system occurred. Generally, the Court upheld any laws passed under the states' police powers, which allow states to pass laws to protect the general welfare of their citizens. These laws included those affecting commerce, labor relations, and manufacturing. After the Court's decision in *Plessy* v. *Ferguson* (1896), in which the Court ruled that state maintenance of "separate but equal" facilities for blacks and whites was constitutional, most civil rights and voting cases also became state matters, in spite of the Civil War Amendments.[7]

The Court also developed legal doctrine in a series of cases that reinforced the national government's ability to regulate commerce. By the 1930s, these two somewhat contradictory approaches led to confusion: states, for example, could not tax gasoline used by federal vehicles,[8] and the national government could not tax the sale of motorcycles to the city police department.[9] In this period, the Court, however, did recognize the need for national control over new technological developments, such as the telegraph.[10] And, beginning in the 1880s, the Court allowed Congress to regulate many aspects of economic relationships, such as monopolies, an area of regulation formerly thought to be in the exclusive realm of the states. Passage of laws such as the Interstate Commerce Act in 1887 and the Sherman Anti-Trust Act in 1890 allowed Congress to establish itself as an important player in the growing national economy.

SETTING THE STAGE FOR A STRONGER NATIONAL GOVERNMENT

In 1895, the U.S. Supreme Court found a congressional effort to tax personal incomes unconstitutional, although an earlier Court had found a similar tax levied during the Civil War constitutional.[11] Thus, Congress and the state legislatures were moved to ratify the **Sixteenth Amendment.** The Sixteenth Amendment gave Congress the power to levy and collect taxes on incomes without apportioning them among the states. The revenues taken in by the federal government through taxation of personal income "removed a major constraint on the federal government by giving it access to almost unlimited revenues."[12] If money is power, the income tax and the revenues it generated greatly enhanced the power of the federal government and its ability to enter policy areas where it formerly had few funds to spend.

The **Seventeenth Amendment,** ratified in 1913, similarly enhanced the power of the national government at the expense of the states. This amendment terminated the state legislatures' election of senators and put their election in the hands of the people. With senators no longer directly accountable to the state legislators who elected them, states lost their principal protectors in Congress. Coupled with the Sixteenth Amendment, this amendment paved the way for a drastic change in the relationship between national and state governments in the United States.

Cooperative Federalism: The New Deal and the Growth of National Government

THE ERA OF DUAL FEDERALISM came to an abrupt end in the 1930s. While the ratification of the Sixteenth and Seventeenth Amendments set the stage for expanded national government, the catalyst for dual federalism's demise was a series of economic events that ended in the cataclysm of the Great Depression:

- Throughout the 1920s, bank failures were common.
- In 1921, the nation experienced a severe slump in agricultural prices.
- In 1926, the construction industry went into decline.
- In the summer of 1929, inventories of consumer goods and automobiles were at an all-time high.
- On October 29, 1929, stock prices, which had risen steadily since 1926, crashed, taking with them the entire national economy.

Despite the severity of these indicators, Presidents Calvin Coolidge and Herbert Hoover took little action, believing that the national depression was an amalgamation of state economic crises that should be dealt with by state and local governments. However, by 1933, the situation could no longer be ignored.

THE NEW DEAL

Rampant unemployment (historians estimate it was as high as 40 to 50 percent) was the hallmark of the Great Depression. In 1933, to combat the severe problems facing the nation, newly elected President Franklin D. Roosevelt (FDR) proposed a variety of innovative programs and ushered in a new era in American politics called the **New Deal**. FDR used the full power of the president as well as his highly effective communication skills to sell the American public and Congress on a new level of federal government intervention intended to stabilize the economy and reduce suffering. Most politicians during the New Deal period agreed that to find national solutions to the Depression, which was affecting the citizens of every state in the union, the national government would have to exercise tremendous authority.

In the first few weeks of the legislative session after FDR's inauguration, Congress passed a series of acts creating new federal agencies and programs proposed by the president. These new agencies, often known by their initials, created what many termed an alphabetocracy. Among the more significant programs were the Federal Housing Administration (FHA), which provided federal financing for new home construction; the Civilian Conservation Corps (CCC), a work relief program for farmers and home owners; and the Agricultural Adjustment Administration (AAA) and the National Recovery Administration (NRA), which imposed restrictions on production in agriculture and many industries.

The New Deal programs forced all levels of government to work cooperatively with one another. Indeed, local governments—mainly in big cities—became a third partner in the federal system, as FDR relied on big-city Democratic political machines to turn out voters to support his programs. For the first time in U.S. history, in essence, cities were embraced as equal partners in an intergovernmental system and became players in the national political arena because many in the national legislature wanted to bypass state legislatures, where urban interests usually were underrepresented significantly.

New Deal programs also enlarged the scope of the national government. Those who feared this unprecedented use of national power quickly challenged the constitutionality of the programs in court.

Through the mid-1930s, the Supreme Court continued to rule that certain aspects of the New Deal went beyond the authority of Congress to regulate commerce. The Court's *laissez-faire*, or hands-off, attitude toward the economy was reflected in a series of decisions ruling various aspects of New Deal programs unconstitutional.

FDR and the Congress were outraged. FDR's frustration with the Court prompted him to suggest what ultimately was nicknamed his "Court-packing plan."

New Deal
The name given to the program of "Relief, Recovery, Reform" begun by President Franklin D. Roosevelt in 1933 to bring the United States out of the Great Depression.

VISUAL
LITERACY
**Federalism and
Regulations**

Knowing that he could do little to change the minds of those already on the Court, FDR suggested enlarging its size from nine to thirteen justices. This would have given him the opportunity to pack the Court with a majority of justices predisposed toward the constitutional validity of the New Deal.

Even though Roosevelt was popular, the Court-packing plan was not. Congress and the public were outraged that he even suggested tampering with an institution of government. Nevertheless, the Court appeared to respond to this threat. In 1937, it reversed its series of anti–New Deal decisions, concluding that Congress (and therefore the national government) had the authority to legislate in any area so long as what was regulated affected commerce in any way. Moreover, the Court also upheld the constitutionality of the bulk of the massive New Deal relief programs, such as the National Labor Relations Act of 1935, which authorized collective bargaining between unions and employees in *NLRB* v. *Jones and Laughlin Steel Co.* (1937);[13] the Fair Labor Standards Act of 1938, which prohibited the interstate shipment of goods made by employees earning less than the federally mandated minimum wage;[14] and the Agricultural Adjustment Act of 1938, which provided crop subsidies to farmers.[15] Congress then used this newly recognized power to legislate in a wide array of areas, including maximum hour and minimum wage laws and regulation of child labor.

THE CHANGING NATURE OF FEDERALISM: FROM LAYER CAKE TO MARBLE CAKE

Before the Depression and the New Deal, most political scientists likened the federal system to a layer cake: each level or layer of government—national, state, and local—had clearly defined powers and responsibilities. After the New Deal, however, the nature of the federal system changed. Government now looked something like a marble cake:

> Wherever you slice through it you reveal an inseparable mixture of differently colored ingredients. . . . Vertical and diagonal lines almost obliterate the horizontal ones, and in some places there are unexpected whirls and an imperceptible merging of colors, so that it is difficult to tell where one ends and the other begins.[16]

cooperative federalism
The relationship between the national and state governments that began with the New Deal.

The metaphor of marble cake federalism refers to what political scientists call **cooperative federalism,** a term that describes the intertwined relationship among the national, state, and local governments that began with the New Deal. States began to take a secondary, albeit important, cooperative role in the scheme of governance, as did many cities. Nowhere is this shift in power from the states to the national government clearer than in the growth of federal grant programs that began in earnest during the New Deal. Between the New Deal and the 1990s, the tremendous growth in these programs, and in federal government spending in general, changed the nature and discussion of federalism from "How much power should the national government have?" to "How much say in the policies of the states can the national government buy?" During the 1970s energy crisis, the national government initially imposed a national 55 mph speed limit on the states, for example.

FEDERAL GRANTS AND NATIONAL EFFORTS TO INFLUENCE THE STATES

As early as 1790, Congress appropriated funds for the states to pay debts incurred during the Revolutionary War. But, it wasn't until the Civil War that Congress enacted its first true federal grant program, which allocated federal funds to the states for a specific purpose.

Most commentators believe the start of this redistribution of funds began with the Morrill Land Grant Act of 1862, which gave each state 30,000 acres of public land for each representative in Congress. Income from the sale of these lands was to be earmarked for the establishment and support of agricultural and mechanical arts colleges. Sixty-nine land-grant colleges—including Texas A&M University, the University of Georgia, and Michigan State University—were founded or significantly assisted by the federal funds.

As we have seen, Franklin D. Roosevelt's New Deal program increased the flow of federal dollars to the states with the infusion of massive federal dollars for a variety of public works programs, including building and road construction. In the boom times of World War II, even more new federal programs were introduced. By the 1950s and 1960s, federal grant-in-aid programs were well entrenched. They often defined federal/state relationships and made the national government a major player in domestic policy. Until the 1960s, however, most federal grant programs were constructed in cooperation with the states and were designed to assist the states in the furtherance of their traditional responsibilities to protect the health, welfare, and safety of their citizens.

Most of these programs were **categorical grants,** ones for which Congress appropriates funds for specific purposes. Categorical grants allocate federal dollars by a precise formula and are subject to detailed conditions imposed by the national government, often on a matching basis; that is, states must contribute money to match federal funds, although the national government may pay as much as 90 percent of the total.

By the early 1960s, as concern about the poor and minorities rose, and as states (especially in the South) were blamed for perpetuating discrimination, those in power in the national government saw grants as a way to force states to behave in ways desired by the national government.[17] If the states would not cooperate with the national government to further its goals, it would withhold funds.

In 1964, the Democratic administration of President Lyndon B. Johnson (LBJ) launched its "Great Society" program, which included what LBJ called a "War on Poverty." The Great Society program was a broad attempt to combat poverty and discrimination. In a frenzy of activity in Washington not seen since the New Deal, federal funds were channeled to states, to local governments, and even directly to citizen action groups in an effort to alleviate social ills that the states had been unable or unwilling to remedy. There was money for urban renewal, education, and poverty programs, including Head Start and job training. The move to fund local groups directly was made by the most liberal members of Congress to bypass not only conservative state legislatures, but also conservative mayors and councils in cities such as Chicago, who were perceived as disinclined to help their poor, often African American, constituencies. Thus, these programs often pitted governors and mayors against community activists, who became key players in the distribution of federal dollars.

These new grants altered the fragile federal/state balance of power that had been at the core of many older federal grant programs. During the Johnson administration, the national government began to use federal grants as a way to further what federal (and not state) officials perceived to be national needs. Grants based on what states wanted or believed they needed began to decline, while grants based on what the national government wanted states to do to foster national goals increased dramatically. From pollution to economic development and law enforcement, creating a federal grant seemed like the perfect solution to every problem.[18] (See Politics Now: Bringing Home the Bacon.)

Not all federal programs mandating state or local action came with federal money, however. And, while presidents during the 1970s voiced their opposition to big government, their efforts to rein it in were largely unsuccessful.

categorical grant
Grant for which Congress appropriates funds for a specific purpose.

SIMULATION

You Are the Director of Economic Development for the City of Los Angeles, California

Politics Now

BRINGING HOME THE BACON

In the wake of the September 11, 2001, terrorist attacks on the World Trade Center in New York and the Pentagon in the Washington, D.C. area, Congress passed extraordinary appropriations bills to beef up national security at home. Many of these bills allowed the Department of Homeland Security to disperse almost unlimited funds to communities across the country.

Few small towns anticipated the federal government largess that was to flow to them as a result of the attacks.[a] Bellows Falls, Vermont, for example—a town so small that it has only eight full-time police officers—received a homeland security grant that allowed it to set up sixteen surveillance cameras costing $15,000 each. These cameras were intended to watch intersections twenty-four hours a day, as well as the town square and a local sewage plant.

In Ridgely, Maryland, population 1,300, the police chief found it "difficult to find something to use the money for." The Departments of Homeland Security and Justice were unable to compile information about how many small-town camera projects the agencies funded.[b]

Ironically, Bellows Falls was to receive only three fewer cameras than the District of Columbia, which has a population nearly 200 times that of the sleepy Vermont town! But, once the citizens of Bellows Falls recognized the possibility that "big government" could be watching them, they ended up pressuring town trustees to reject the federal funding. One trustee voiced her belief that "tapes of civic demonstrations would be kept by the federal government and used against citizens."[c] This revolt demonstrates that although the temptation of federal funds—no matter how unrelated to state and local priorities—can be tremendous, citizens across the country often stand up for their own more local political interests.

Still, in many communities, federal grants are gradually changing police practices, another irony given that policing historically has been a function of state and local governments in the federal system. Whether towns put their homeland security dollars into surveillance cameras, however, and how they use those cameras, largely depends on local mores. In Washington, D.C., for example, the police use cam-

■ Surveillance cameras like this one have been installed throughout the United States thanks to post-9/11 federal funds.

Photo courtesy: Lois Raimondo/Post Writers Group

eras only during demonstrations and emergency situations. In some areas of the United States, however, local police use cameras with little or no rationale, causing privacy advocates to worry about American civil liberties.

QUESTIONS

1. Should the federal government have more control over how homeland security dollars are spent, or should state and local governments have the power to use those grants as they see fit?
2. How do such disparities arise in the federal system when funds are disbursed to states and communities?

---

[a] This feature draws heavily on David A. Farenthold, "Federal Grants Bring Surveillance Cameras to Small Towns," *Washington Post* (January 19, 2006): A1.

[b] Farenthold, "Federal Grants Bring Surveillance Cameras to Small Towns."

[c] Diann Daniel, "No Candid Cameras: After Outcry, Vermont Village Rejects Federally Funded Security Surveillance," CSOonline.com, May 1, 2006.

New Federalism: Returning Power to the States

new federalism
Federal/state relationship proposed by Reagan administration during the 1980s; its hallmark is returning administrative powers to the state governments.

IN 1980, FORMER CALIFORNIA GOVERNOR RONALD REAGAN was elected president, pledging to advance what he called a **new federalism** and a return of power to the states. This policy set the tone for the federal/state relationship that was maintained from the 1980s until 2001. Presidents and Congresses, both Republican and Democrat, took steps to shrink the size of the federal government in favor of programs administered by state governments. President Bill Clinton lauded the demise of big government. And, on the campaign trail in 2000, George W. Bush also seemed committed to this devolution. The September 11 terrorist attacks, however, have led to substantial growth in the power and scope of the federal government.

THE REAGAN REVOLUTION

The Republican Reagan Revolution had at its heart strong views about the role of states in the federal system. While many Democrats and liberal interest groups argued that federal grants were an effective way to raise the level of services provided to the poor, others, including Reagan, attacked them as imposing national priorities on the states.

In part to curtail federal spending, Reagan almost immediately proposed massive cuts in federal domestic programs and drastic income tax cuts. Declining federal revenues dramatically altered the relationships among federal, state, and local governments. For the first time in thirty years, federal aid to state and local governments declined.[19] Reagan persuaded Congress to consolidate many categorical grants (for specific programs that often require matching funds) into far fewer, less restrictive **block grants**—broad grants to states for specific activities such as secondary education or health services, with few strings attached. He also ended general revenue sharing, which had provided significant unrestricted funds to the states.

By the end of the presidencies of Ronald Reagan and George Bush in 1993, most block grants fell into one of four categories: health, income security, education, or transportation. Yet, many politicians, including most state governors, urged the consolidation of even more programs into block grants. Calls to reform the welfare system, particularly to allow the states more latitude in an effort to get back to the Hamiltonian notion of states as laboratories of experiment, seemed popular with citizens and governments alike.

block grant
Broad grant with few strings attached; given to states by the federal government for specified activities, such as secondary education or health services.

THE DEVOLUTION REVOLUTION

In 1994, Republicans won a majority in both houses of Congress, and every Republican governor who sought reelection was victorious, while some popular Democratic governors, such as Ann Richards of Texas, lost (to George W. Bush). This Republican sweep was propelled by a campaign document known as the Contract with America.

The Contract was a campaign document proposed by then House Minority Whip Newt Gingrich (R–GA), and signed by nearly all Republican candidates (including incumbents) seeking election to the House of Representatives in 1994. In it, Republican candidates pledged to force a national debate on the role of the national government in regard to the states. A top priority was scaling back the federal government, an effort that some commentators called the devolution revolution.

Running under a clear set of priorities contained in the Contract, Republican candidates took back the House of Representatives for the first time in more than forty years. A majority of the legislative proposals based on the Contract passed the House of Representatives during the first one hundred days of the 104th Congress. However, very few of the Contract's proposals, including acts requiring a balanced budget and tax reforms, passed the Senate and became law.

On some issues, however, the Republicans were able to achieve their goals. For example, before 1995, **unfunded mandates,** national laws that direct state or local governments to comply with federal rules or regulations (such as clean air or water standards) but contain no federal funding to defray the cost of meeting these requirements, absorbed nearly 30 percent of some local budgets. Republicans in Congress, loyal to the concerns of these governments, secured passage of the Unfunded Mandates Reform Act of 1995. This act prevented Congress from passing costly federal programs without debate on how to fund them.

Another important act passed by the Republican-controlled Congress and signed into law by President Bill Clinton was the Personal Responsibility and Work

unfunded mandates
National laws that direct states or local governments to comply with federal rules or regulations (such as clean air or water standards) but contain no federal funding to defray the cost of meeting these requirements.

Michigan Democratic Governor Jennifer Granholm heads a state hard hit by cuts in some federal programs and the loss of jobs. Granholm was reelected to a second term in 2006.

VIDEO ROUNDTABLE

Contemorary Federalism

preemption
A concept derived from the Constitution's supremacy clause that allows the national government to override or preempt state or local actions in certain areas.

Opportunity Reconciliation Act of 1996. This legislation replaced the existing welfare program, known as Aid to Families with Dependent Children (AFDC), with a program known as Temporary Assistance for Needy Families (TANF). TANF returned much of the administrative power for welfare programs to the states and became a hallmark of the devolution revolution.

In the short run, these and other programs, coupled with a growing economy, produced record federal and state budget surpluses. States were in the best fiscal shape they had been in since the 1970s. According to the National Conference of State Legislatures, total state budget surpluses in 1998 exceeded $30 billion. These tax surpluses allowed many states to increase spending, while other states offered their residents steep tax cuts. Mississippi, for example, increased its per capita spending by 42.4 percent, while Alaska opted to reduce taxes by 44.2 percent.[20]

FEDERALISM UNDER THE BUSH ADMINISTRATION

On the campaign trail, George W. Bush could not have foreseen the circumstances that would surround much of his presidency. A struggling economy, terrorist attacks on the World Trade Center and the Pentagon, and the rising costs of education and welfare produced state and federal budget deficits that would have been unimaginable only a few years before.

By 2003, many state governments faced budget shortfalls of more than $30 billion. Because state governments, unlike the federal government, are required to balance their budgets, governors and legislators struggled to make ends meet. Some states raised taxes and others cut services, including school construction and infrastructure repairs. These dramatic changes helped nearly all of the states to project surpluses—albeit small—for fiscal year 2006.

The federal government was not so lucky; it struggled with a $427 billion budget deficit in 2005. This deficit had a number of sources, including President Bush's 2001 tax cuts, spending on the war in Iraq, costs associated with the dramatic expansion of the federal government after the September 11 terrorist attacks and Hurricane Katrina. In addition, the No Child Left Behind Act, which imposed a host of federal requirements on everything from class size to accountability testing, increased burdens on the federal coffers. (See Join the Debate: The No Child Left Behind Act.)

The No Child Left Behind Act was viewed by many commentators as an unprecedented usurpation of state and local powers. However, this trend of **preemption,** or allowing the national government to override state or local actions in certain areas, is not new. The phenomenal growth of preemption statutes, laws that allow the federal government to assume partial or full responsibility for state and local governmental functions, began in 1965 during the Johnson administration. Since then, Congress routinely has used its authority under the commerce clause to preempt state laws. However, until recently, preemption statutes were generally supported by Democrats in Congress and the White House, not Republicans. The Bush administration's use of these laws reflects a new era in preemption.

Photo courtesy: Jerry S. Mendoza/AP Wide World Photos

THE SUPREME COURT: A RETURN TO STATES' RIGHTS?

The role of the Supreme Court in determining the parameters of federalism cannot be underestimated. Although Congress passed sweeping New Deal legislation, it was not until the Supreme Court finally reversed itself and found those programs constitutional that any real change occurred in the federal/state relationship. From the New Deal until the 1980s, the Supreme Court's impact on the federal system generally was to expand the national government's authority at the expense of the states.

Beginning in the late 1980s, however, the Court's willingness to allow Congress to regulate in a variety of areas waned. Once Ronald Reagan was elected president, he attempted to appoint new justices committed to the notion of states' rights and to rolling back federal intervention in matters that many Republicans believed properly resided within the province of the states and not Congress or the federal courts.

Mario M. Cuomo, a former Democratic New York governor, has referred to the decisions of what he called the Reagan-Bush Court as creating "a kind of new judicial federalism." According to Cuomo, this new federalism could be characterized by the Court's withdrawal of "rights and emphases previously thought to be national."[21] Illustrative of this trend is the Supreme Court's decision in *Webster* v. *Reproductive Health Services* (1989).[22] In *Webster*, the Court first gave new latitude—and even encouragement—to the states to fashion more restrictive abortion laws. Since *Webster*, most states have enacted new restrictions on abortion, with spousal or parental consent, informed consent or waiting periods, or bans on late-term or partial birth abortions being the most common. (See Analyzing Visuals: State-by-State Report Card on Access to Abortion.) The Court consistently has upheld the authority of the individual states to limit a minor's access to abortion through imposition of parental consent or notification laws. Still, as discussed in chapter 4, in *Stenberg* v. *Carhart* (2000) the Supreme Court ruled that the state law limiting partial birth abortions without any provision to save a woman's health was unconstitutional.[23] And, in 2006, a unanimous Roberts Court ruled that states seeking to restrict minors' access to abortions must allow for some exceptions for medical emergencies.[24]

The addition of two justices by President Bill Clinton in the 1990s did little to stem the course of a Court bent on rebalancing the nature of the federal system. Since 1989, the Supreme Court has decided several major cases dealing with the nature of the federal system. Most of these have been 5–4 decisions and most have been decided against increased congressional power or in a manner to provide the states with greater authority over a variety of issues and policies. In *U.S.* v. *Lopez* (1995), for example, which involved the conviction of a student charged with carrying a concealed handgun onto school property, a five-person majority of the Court ruled that Congress lacked constitutional authority under the commerce clause to regulate guns within 1,000 feet of a school.[25] The majority concluded that local gun control in the schools was a state, not a federal, matter.

■ Since 1989, the Supreme Court has often deferred to state courts as well as judgments of the state legislatures.

Photo courtesy: Herblock/The Herb Block Foundation

Join the Debate

THE NO CHILD LEFT BEHIND ACT

OVERVIEW: The U.S. Constitution is silent in regard to educating American citizens. According to traditional interpretation of the Constitution, the Ninth and Tenth Amendments give the states and American people rights and powers not expressly mentioned or prohibited by the Constitution. It was the Framers' belief the federal principle would allow for and accommodate diverse opinions regarding life, liberty, and happiness—and it is the responsibility of the individual states to educate citizens accordingly. Historically, the states have assumed this task relatively free from federal interference, but over the last fifty years, declining educational attainment, coupled with the inability of the states to address this problem, has put education policy at the forefront of domestic policy debate. To correct this problem, the No Child Left Behind Act (NCLB) was signed into law in January 2002. NCLB was a controversial piece of legislation giving the national government substantial authority over state educational establishments; several years after enactment, NCLB is still controversial.

Though many educators and politicians agree on the goals set by the No Child Left Behind Act (NCLB)— higher educational standards, greater school accountability, ensuring qualified teachers, closing the gap in student achievement—NCLB is criticized by the two major political parties, even though significant congressional majorities of both parties voted for the act. Republicans complain that NCLB impermissibly allows federal intrusion into the educational rights of states, and Democrats worry that the federal government is not providing enough funding to

meet NCLB's strict guidelines. Nevertheless, in practice, both parties seem to have switched ideological positions in regard to the federal government's role. Though the Republicans in 1996 advocated eliminating the Department of Education and reducing education expenditures, the Bush administration has significantly increased education funding; conversely, Democrats, who traditionally have advocated an increased federal role in education, now advocate state control (though with increased federal spending as well). Four years after NCLB was signed into law, the National Assessment of Educational Progress (or NAEP, considered the nation's report card), announced general across-the-board improvement in student achievement scores. The NAEP also reported that the achievement gap between white and minority students had narrowed. Policy makers, however, continue to debate the true effectiveness of NCLB. NCLB is supported by a majority of the American people in all demographic groups.

In the Information Age, it is imperative that all citizens have the requisite skills to survive and thrive in the new economy. With this in mind, what is the best way to ensure a quality education for all Americans? Where does proper authority to educate children lie? How can the federal government determine the best way to educate children in a nation in which there are numerous ethnicities, religions, and cultures, all having differing views on what constitutes education? However, since the federal government in part funds state educational establishments, shouldn't it have a say in how its funds are spent? And, since American education achievement lags behind education in other advanced modern democracies, shouldn't school systems and teachers be held accountable?

ARGUMENTS FOR THE NO CHILD LEFT BEHIND ACT

- **NCLB gives state and local school districts the flexibility to meet its requirements.** The law gives states the

---

sovereign immunity
The right of a state to be free from lawsuit unless it gives permission to the suit. Under the Eleventh Amendment, all states are considered sovereign.

One year later, again a badly divided Court ruled that Congress lacked the authority to require states to negotiate with Indian tribes about gaming.[26] The U.S. Constitution specifically gives Congress the right to deal with Indian tribes, but the Court found that Florida's **sovereign immunity** protected the state from this kind of congressional directive about how to conduct its business. In 1997, the Court decided two more major cases dealing with the scope of Congress's authority to regulate in areas historically left to the province of the states: zoning and local law enforcement. In one, a majority of the Court ruled that sections of the Religious Freedom Restoration Act were unconstitutional because Congress lacked the authority to meddle in local zoning regulations, even if a church was liberty to define standards and the means to meet and measure them. As long as NCLB guidelines are met, the states are generally free to innovate, educate, and test according to their needs.

■ **NCLB is not an unfunded mandate.** The Government Accountability Office has ruled that NCLB does not meet the description of an unfunded mandate as defined by the 1995 Unfunded Mandates Reform Act, primarily because state school systems have the option of accepting or rejecting NCLB funding. Federal spending accounts for only 8 percent of all educational expenditures in the United States.

■ **NCLB represents federal responsiveness to the needs of parents with children in public schools.** Not only have the states failed to meet the guidelines set forth by various federal policy initiatives, but they have failed the expectations of parents as well. For example, Goals 2000 (1994) mandated a 90 percent high school graduation rate by 2000 and a number one rank in math and science for American students internationally. By 2000, the graduation rate was only 75 percent and American students ranked not first but nineteenth in math and eighteenth in science.

ARGUMENTS AGAINST THE NO CHILD LEFT BEHIND ACT

■ **NCLB requirements force school districts to teach to the test.** Rather than teaching analytical and creative thinking, the testing requirements force school districts to have students cram for the exam, thus undermining the primary goal of a true education.

■ **NCLB does not distinguish between disabled and non-English-speaking students and able students proficient in English.** A primary problem with NCLB is that it combines all students, regardless of their language level or other core educational proficiencies. This is an unfair burden on educators in school systems with a disproportionate number of disabled or non-English-speaking students, as NCLB's punitive sections assume an able, English-speaking student body.

■ **NCLB should be considered an impermissible intrusion on the prerogatives of state educational establishments.** A primary concern of the Framers was excessive federal control over state policy. NCLB erodes the line separating federal and state authority. If school systems are not addressing the concerns of parents and educational problems, it is the proper duty of the states to address these issues. Federal educational spending has increased dramatically since the passage of NCLB, and many believe this gives the federal government too much control over a traditional state policy domain.

QUESTIONS

1. Does NCLB place too many guidelines on state educational establishments? If so, what is the best way to ensure higher standards and school accountability?
2. Does NCLB give the federal government too much authority over a policy domain that traditionally has belonged to the states? Since school districts reflect local mores and attitudes, are students best educated based on local guidelines?

SELECTED READINGS

Hess, Frederick M., and Michael J. Petrilli. *No Child Left Behind*. New York: Peter Lang, 2006.

Peterson, Paul E., and Martin R. West, eds. *No Child Left Behind? The Politics and Practice of School Accountability*. Washington, DC: Brookings Institution, 2003.

involved.[27] Another 5–4 majority ruled that Congress lacked the authority to require local law enforcement officials to conduct background checks on handgun purchasers until the federal government was able to implement a national system.[28] In 1999, in another case involving sovereign immunity, a slim majority of the Supreme Court ruled that Congress lacked the authority to change patent laws in a manner that would negatively affect a state's right to assert its immunity from lawsuits.[29]

While it looked as if the Rehnquist Court (1986–2005) was well on its way to supporting Congress's devolution revolution, many commentators now question what was really happening. The addition of two new justices, Chief Justice John G.

PARTICIPATION

Is Federalism Dead and Should It Be?

Analyzing Visuals

STATE-BY-STATE REPORT CARD ON ACCESS TO ABORTION

A liberal interest group, NARAL Pro-Choice America, rates each state and the District of Columbia in fourteen categories related to abortion access, including bans on partial birth abortion procedures and counseling, clinic violence, the length of waiting periods, access for minors, and public funding, which it then translates into grades. NARAL gives an A only to states it evaluates as pro-choice on every issue on its agenda. After studying the map, answer the following critical thinking questions: What do the states that receive A's have in common? How might factors such as political culture, geography, and social characteristics of the population influence a state's laws concerning abortion? If a group that opposes abortion, such as the National Right to Life Committee, were to grade the states, would its ratings include the same categories or factors? Explain your answer. See Analyzing Visuals: A Brief Guide for additional guidance in analyzing maps.

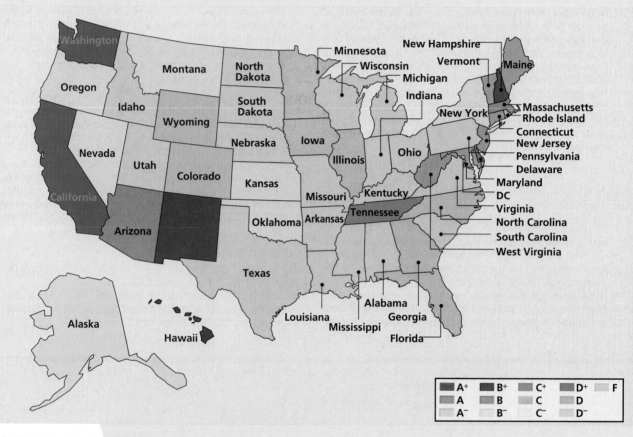

Legend: A+ B+ C+ D+ F A B C D A− B− C− D−

Source: NARAL Pro-Choice America/NARAL Foundation, "Who Decides? A State-by-State Review of Abortion and Reproductive Rights 2006." Accessed May 15, 2006, http://www.prochoiceamerica.org. Reprinted by permission.

FIGURE 3.4 THE REHNQUIST AND ROBERTS COURTS AND FEDERALISM

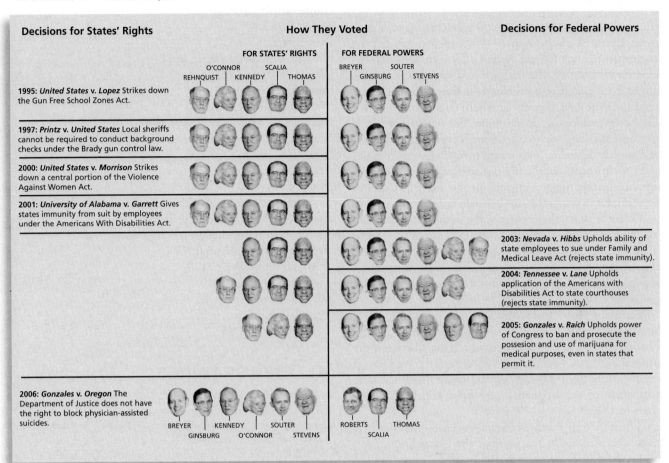

Sources: *New York Times* (June 12, 2005): 3; *New York Times* (July 2, 2006): A 18; *Legal Information Institute at Cornell University Law School*.

Roberts Jr. and Associate Justice Samuel A. Alito Jr., make the future direction of the Court less certain. As *New York Times* Supreme Court reporter Linda Greenhouse has noted, "a hallmark of the Rehnquist Court has been a re-examination of the country's most basic constitutional arrangements, resulting in decisions that demanded a new respect for the sovereignty of the states and placed corresponding restrictions on the powers of Congress."[30] Figure 3.4 demonstrates this basic pattern, but also shows that in a number of cases decided since 2003 the Court seemed to change course by supporting increased federal powers. For example, in a major case involving the distribution of power within the federal system, the Rehnquist Court upheld the ability of state employees to sue under the federal Family and Medical Leave Act.[31] And, in 2005, the Court upheld the power of Congress to prohibit states from allowing the use of medical marijuana.[32] But, as also reflected in Figure 3.4, the Roberts Court's first decision involving federalism limited the federal government's right to block Oregon's physician assisted suicide law.[33]

SIMULATION

You Are a Federal Judge

Summary

THE INADEQUACIES OF THE CONFEDERATE form of government created by the Articles of Confederation led the Framers to create a federal system of government that divided power between the national and state governments, with each ultimately responsible to the people. Both the national and state governments have both enumerated and implied powers under the Constitution. The national and state governments share some concurrent powers. Other powers are expressly denied to both governments, although the national government is ultimately declared supreme. The Constitution also lays the groundwork for the Supreme Court to be the arbiter in disagreements between states.

Over the years, the powers of the national government have increased tremendously at the expense of the states. The Supreme Court has played a key role in defining the relationship and powers of the national government through its broad interpretations of the supremacy and commerce clauses.

For many years, dual federalism, which tended to limit the national government's authority in areas such as slavery and civil rights, was the norm in relations between the national and state governments. However, the beginnings of a departure from this ideology became evident with the ratification of the Sixteenth and Seventeenth Amendments in 1913.

The notion of a limited federal government ultimately fell by the wayside in the wake of the Great Depression and Franklin D. Roosevelt's New Deal. This growth in the size and role of the federal government escalated during Lyndon B. Johnson's administration and into the mid to late 1970s. Federal grants became popular solutions for a host of state and local problems.

After his election in 1980, President Ronald Reagan tried to shrink the size and powers of the federal government through what he termed new federalism. This trend continued through the 1990s, most notably through a campaign document known as the Contract with America. Initially, George W. Bush's administration seemed committed to this devolution, but a struggling economy and the September 11 terrorist attacks led to substantial growth in the size of the federal government. Since the Reagan era, the Supreme Court often has been willing to limit Congress's authority to legislate in areas it believes are the responsibility of the states.

KEY TERMS

bill of attainder, p. 86
block grant, p. 97
categorical grant, p. 95
concurrent powers, p. 85
cooperative federalism, p. 94
dual federalism, p. 91
enumerated powers, p. 83
ex post facto law, p. 86
federal system, p. 83
full faith and credit clause, p. 87
Gibbons v. *Ogden* (1824), p. 90
implied powers, p. 83
interstate compacts, p. 88
McCulloch v. *Maryland* (1819), p. 89
necessary and proper clause, p. 83
New Deal, p. 93
new federalism, p. 96
preemption, p. 98
privileges and immunities clause, p. 88
reserve (or police) powers, p. 85
Seventeenth Amendment, p. 92
Sixteenth Amendment, p. 92
sovereign immunity, p. 100
supremacy clause, p. 84
Tenth Amendment, p. 85
unfunded mandates, p. 97
unitary system, p. 83

SELECTED READINGS

Bowman, Ann O'M., and Richard C. Kearney. *State and Local Government*, 6th ed. Boston: Houghton Mifflin, 2005.

Campbell, Tom. *Separation of Powers in Practice*. Stanford, CA: Stanford University Press, 2004.

Derthick, Martha. *The Influence of Federal Grants*. Cambridge, MA: Harvard University Press, 1970.

Elazar, Daniel J., and John Kincaid, eds. *The Covenant Connection: From Federal Theology to Modern Federalism*. Lexington, MA: Lexington Books, 2000.

Finegold, Kenneth, and Theda Skocpol. *State and Party in America's New Deal*. Madison: University of Wisconsin Press, 1995.

Grodzins, Morton. *The American System: A View of Government in the United States*. Chicago: Rand McNally, 1966.

Kincaid, John. *The Encyclopedia of American Federalism*. Washington, DC: CQ Press, 2005.

McCabe, Neil Colman, ed. *Comparative Federalism in the Devolution Era*. Lanham, MD: Rowman and Littlefield, 2003.

Nagel, Robert F. *The Implosion of American Federalism*. New York: Oxford University Press, 2002.

Stephens, G. Ross, and Nelson Wikstrom. *American Intergovernmental Relations: A Fragmented Federal Polity*. New York: Oxford University Press, 2006.

Zimmerman, Joseph F. *Interstate Cooperation: Compacts and Administrative Agreements*. New York: Praeger, 2002.

WEB EXPLORATIONS

For a directory of federalism links, see
http://www.govinfo.library.unt.edu/amcouncil/federalism.html
For more on your state and local governments, see
http://www.statelocalgov.net/

For scholarly works on federalism, see
http://www.temple.edu/federalism and
http://www.cato.org/ and
http://www.urban.org/

For perspectives on the federal system, see
http://www.usembassy.beusa/usapolitical.htm

For more information on interstate compacts, see
http://ssl.csg.org/compactlaws/comlistlinks.html

For the full text of *McCulloch* v. *Maryland* (1819), see
http://www.landmarkcases.org/mcculloch/home.html

For the full text of *Gibbons* v. *Ogden* (1824), see
http://www.landmarkcases.org/gibbons/legacy.html

For more information on the Great Depression, see
http://newdeal.feri.org

For more on the devolution revolution, see
http://www.brookings.edu/comm/policybriefs/pb03.htm

To analyze where your state stands relative to other states, see
http://www.taxfoundation.org/statefinance.html

For more information on state abortion restrictions, see
http://www.ProChoiceAmerica.org

CIVIL LIBERTIES

THE FIRST AMENDMENT TO THE CONSTITUTION—passed by the Congress on September 25, 1789, ratified by the states on December 15, 1791—boldly proclaims that "Congress shall make no law . . . abridging the freedom of speech . . . or the right of the people to peaceably assemble, and to petition the Government for a redress of grievances." However, when the Bill of Rights was drafted, approved by the Congress, and sent out to the states for their ratification, no one involved was thinking about protecting the political right to assembly as a means to petition the government about activities beyond American shores. The Framers, moreover, certainly would never have foreseen that Americans would take to the streets to petition their government and the United Nations to stop apartheid in South Africa, human rights violations in China, or genocide in Sudan's Darfur region.

While many Americans are unable to locate Darfur on maps of the African continent, for example, in late April 2006, massive "Stop Genocide" rallies were held all over the United States, urging President George W. Bush and his administration to take much stronger actions to prevent the widespread violence and killing in that region. Since 2003, thousands of people have been the target of Sudanese troops and pro-government Arab militias conducting a systematic campaign of killings and rapes. In late 2006 alone, the United Nations estimated that nearly 100,000 Darfuris had been displaced.[1]

Thousands of Americans, including approximately 250 busloads of concerned activists from forty-one states, converged on the Mall in Washington, D.C., a site of frequent national protests, to ask the president to intervene in Darfur. Other Americans held rallies in seventeen additional cities nationwide, and the combined effort resulted in the "largest public outcry for Darfur since the conflict began there."[2] Celebrities including actor George Clooney and a variety of elected representatives addressed those gathered at the rallies. Some in the crowds carried signs reading "Never Again."[3] On the Mall, Representative Michael E. Capuano (D–MA) said, "you are here today to shine a bright light on the horrors and to show the world that America will not stand quietly by while the genocide continues. I am here to tell you your leaders are listening."[4]

The rallies are not the only form of political expression that anti-genocide activists have taken. Because of student-led protest campaigns, universities

CHAPTER OUTLINE

⭐ The First Constitutional Amendments: The Bill of Rights

⭐ First Amendment Guarantees: Freedom of Religion

⭐ First Amendment Guarantees: Freedom of Speech, Press, and Assembly

⭐ The Second Amendment: The Right to Keep and Bear Arms

⭐ The Rights of Criminal Defendants

⭐ The Right to Privacy

including Stanford and Harvard divested themselves of stock in companies doing business with or investing in Sudan. In addition, more than 750,000 American citizens coordinated by the Save Darfur Coalition have petitioned the U.S. government by sending postcards to President George W. Bush requesting that his administration do more to end the genocide. Without the guarantees of the First Amendment, these efforts to convince the American government to help the citizens of another country would never have been possible.

---

civil liberties
The personal guarantees and freedoms that the federal government cannot abridge by law, constitution, or judicial interpretation.

civil rights
The government-protected rights of individuals against arbitrary or discriminatory treatment.

SIMULATION

Balancing Liberty and Security at a Time of War

WHEN THE BILL OF RIGHTS, which contains many of the most important protections of individual liberties, was written, its drafters were not thinking about issues such as abortion, gay rights, physician assisted suicide, or any of the other personal liberties discussed in this chapter, let alone the rights of those abroad, as discussed in our opening vignette. As a result, the Constitution is nonabsolute in the nature of most **civil liberties,** personal guarantees and freedoms that the government cannot abridge, either by law or by judicial interpretation. Thus, when we discuss civil liberties such as those found in the Bill of Rights, we are concerned with limits on what governments can and cannot do. **Civil rights,** in contrast, are the goverment-protected rights of individuals against arbitrary or discriminatory treatment. (Civil rights are discussed in chapter 5.)

Questions of civil liberties often present complex problems. As illustrated in the opening vignette, we must decide how to determine the boundaries of speech and assembly. We must also consider how much infringement on our personal liberties we want to give the police. Moreover, in an era of a war on terrorism, it is important to consider what liberties should be accorded to those suspected of terrorist activity.

Civil liberties cases often fall to the judiciary, who must balance the competing interests of the government and the people. Thus, in many of the cases discussed in this chapter, there is a conflict between an individual or group of individuals seeking to exercise what they believe to be a liberty, and the government, be it local, state, or national, seeking to control the exercise of that liberty in an attempt to keep order and preserve the rights (and safety) of others. In other cases, two liberties are in conflict, such as a physician's and her patients' rights to easy access to a medical clinic versus a pro-life advocate's liberty to picket that clinic. Many of the Court's recent decisions, as well as actions of the George W. Bush administration in the aftermath of the September 11, 2001, terrorist attacks are discussed in this chapter as we explore the various dimensions of civil liberties guarantees contained in the U.S. Constitution and the Bill of Rights.

In this chapter, we will discuss the Bill of Rights, the reasons for its addition to the Constitution, and its eventual application to the states. After surveying the meaning of one of the First Amendment's guarantees—freedom of religion—we will discuss the meanings of other First Amendment guarantees: freedom of speech, press, and assembly. Following a discussion of the Second Amendment and the right to keep and bear arms, we will analyze the reasons for many of the rights of criminal defendants found in the Bill of Rights and how those rights have been expanded and contracted by the U.S. Supreme Court. Finally, we will discuss the meaning of the right to privacy and how that concept has been interpreted by the Court.

The First Constitutional Amendments: The Bill of Rights

THE NOTION OF ADDING a bill of rights to the Constitution was not a popular one at the Constitutional Convention. When George Mason of Virginia proposed that such a bill be added to the preface of the proposed Constitution, his resolution was defeated unanimously.[5] In the subsequent ratification debates, Federalists argued that a bill of rights was unnecessary. Not only did most state constitutions already contain those protections, but Federalists believed it was foolhardy to list things that the national government had no power to do.

The insistence of Anti-Federalists on a bill of rights, the fact that some states conditioned their ratification of the Constitution on the addition of these guarantees, and the disagreement among Federalists about writing specific liberty guarantees into the Constitution led to prompt congressional action to put an end to further controversy. This was a time when national stability and support for the new government particularly were needed. Thus, in 1789, Congress sent the proposed Bill of Rights to the states for ratification, which occurred in 1791.

The **Bill of Rights,** the first ten amendments to the Constitution, contains numerous specific guarantees, including those of free speech, press, and religion (for the full text, see the annotated Constitution that begins on page 52). The Ninth and Tenth Amendments, in particular, highlight Anti-Federalist fears of a too-powerful national government. The **Ninth Amendment,** strongly favored by Madison, makes it clear that this special listing of rights does not mean that others don't exist. The **Tenth Amendment** reiterates that powers not delegated to the national government are reserved to the states or to the people.

THE INCORPORATION DOCTRINE: THE BILL OF RIGHTS MADE APPLICABLE TO THE STATES

The Bill of Rights was intended to limit the powers of the national government to infringe on the rights and liberties of the citizenry. In *Barron* v. *Baltimore* (1833), the Supreme Court ruled that the national Bill of Rights limited only the actions of the U.S. government and not those of the states.[6] In 1868, however, the Fourteenth Amendment was added to the U.S. Constitution. Its language suggested the possibility that some or even all of the protections guaranteed in the Bill of Rights might be interpreted to prevent state infringement of those rights. Section 1 of the Fourteenth Amendment reads: "No State shall . . . deprive any person of life, liberty, or property, without due process of law." Questions about the scope of "liberty" as well as the meaning of "due process of law" continue even today to engage legal scholars and jurists.

Until nearly the turn of the century, the Supreme Court steadfastly rejected numerous arguments urging it to interpret the **due process clause** found in the Fourteenth Amendment as making various provisions contained in the Bill of Rights applicable to the states. In 1897, however, the Court began to increase its jurisdiction over the states.[7] It began to hold states to a **substantive due process** standard whereby states had the legal burden to prove that their laws were a valid exercise of their power to regulate the health, welfare, or public morals of their citizens.

Interferences with state power, however, were rare. As a consequence, states continued to pass sedition laws (laws that made it illegal to speak or write any political criticism that threatened to diminish respect for the government, its laws, or public officials), anticipating that the Supreme Court would uphold their constitutionality. These expectations changed dramatically in 1925. Benjamin Gitlow, a member of the Socialist Party, was convicted of violating a New York law that prohibited the advocacy of the violent overthrow of the government. Gitlow had printed 16,000 copies of a manifesto in which he urged workers to rise up to overthrow the U.S. government. Although Gitlow's conviction was upheld, in *Gitlow* v. *New York* (1925), the Supreme Court noted that the states were not completely free to limit forms of political expression. The Court argued that certain "fundamental personal rights and liberties" were protected from state impairment by the Fourteenth Amendment's due process clause.[8]

Bill of Rights
The first ten amendments to the U.S. Constitution, which largely guarantee specific rights and liberties.

Ninth Amendment
Part of the Bill of Rights that reads "The enumeration in the Constitution, of certain rights, shall not be construed to deny or disparage others retained by the people."

Tenth Amendment
Part of the Bill of Rights that reiterates powers not delegated to the national government are reserved to the states or to the people.

due process clause
Clause contained in the Fifth and Fourteenth Amendments. Over the years, it has been construed to guarantee to individuals a variety of rights ranging from economic liberty to criminal procedural rights to protection from arbitrary governmental action.

substantive due process
Judicial interpretation of the Fifth and Fourteenth Amendments' due process clause that protects citizens from arbitrary or unjust laws.

incorporation doctrine
An interpretation of the Constitution that holds that the due process clause of the Fourteenth Amendment requires that state and local governments also guarantee those rights.

selective incorporation
A judicial doctrine whereby most but not all of the protections found in the Bill of Rights are made applicable to the states via the Fourteenth Amendment.

Gitlow, with its finding that states could not abridge free speech protections, was the first step in the slow development of what is called the **incorporation doctrine.** After *Gitlow,* it took the Court six more years to incorporate another First Amendment freedom—that of the press. *Near* v. *Minnesota* (1931) was the first case in which the Supreme Court found that a state law violated freedom of the press as protected by the First Amendment.[9]

SELECTIVE INCORPORATION AND FUNDAMENTAL FREEDOMS

Not all the specific guarantees in the Bill of Rights have been made applicable to the states through the due process clause of the Fourteenth Amendment. As revealed in Table 4.1. Instead, the Court has used the process of **selective incorporation** to protect the freedoms it considers most essential to order, liberty, and justice.

The rationale for selective incorporation was set out by the Court in *Palko* v. *Connecticut* (1937).[10] Frank Palko was charged with first-degree murder for killing two Connecticut police officers, found guilty of a lesser charge of second-degree murder, and sentenced to life imprisonment. Connecticut appealed. Palko was retried, found guilty of first-degree murder, and sentenced to death. Palko then appealed his second conviction, arguing that it violated the Fifth Amendment's prohibition against

TABLE 4.1	THE SELECTIVE INCORPORATION OF THE BILL OF RIGHTS		
Amendment	*Right*	*Date*	*Case Incorporated*
I	Speech	1925	*Gitlow* v. *New York*
	Press	1931	*Near* v. *Minnesota*
	Assembly	1937	*DeJonge* v. *Oregon*
	Religion	1940	*Cantwell* v. *Connecticut*
II	Bear arms		Not incorporated (A test has not been presented to the Court in recent history.)
III	No quartering of soldiers		Not incorporated (The quartering problem has not recurred since colonial times.)
IV	No unreasonable searches or seizures	1949	*Wolf* v. *Colorado*
	Exclusionary rule	1961	*Mapp* v. *Ohio*
V	Just compensation	1897	*Chicago, B&Q RR Co.* v. *Chicago*
	Self-incrimination	1964	*Malloy* v. *Hogan*
	Double jeopardy	1969	*Benton* v. *Maryland* (overruled *Palko* v. *Connecticut*)
	Grand jury indictment		Not incorporated (The trend in state criminal cases is away from grand juries.)
VI	Public trial	1948	*In re Oliver*
	Right to counsel	1963	*Gideon* v. *Wainwright*
	Confrontation of Witnesses	1965	*Pointer* v. *Texas*
	Impartial trial	1966	*Parker* v. *Gladden*
	Speedy trial	1967	*Klopfer* v. *North Carolina*
	Compulsory trial	1967	*Washington* v. *Texas*
	Criminal jury trial	1968	*Duncan* v. *Louisiana*
VII	Civil jury trial		Not incorporated (Chief Justice Warren Burger wanted to abolish these trials.)
VIII	No cruel and unusual punishment	1962	*Robinson* v. *California*
	No excessive fines or bail		Not incorporated

double jeopardy because the Fifth Amendment had been made applicable to the states by the due process clause of the Fourteenth Amendment.

The Supreme Court upheld Palko's second conviction and the death sentence. They also chose not to bind states to the Fifth Amendment's double jeopardy clause. This decision set forth principles that were to guide the Court's interpretation of the incorporation doctrine for the next several decades. The Court found that some protections found in the Bill of Rights are absorbed into the concept of due process only because they are so fundamental to our notions of liberty and justice that they cannot be denied by the states unless the state can show what is called a compelling reason for the curtailment of that particular liberty.

First Amendment Guarantees: Freedom of Religion

MANY OF THE FRAMERS were religious men, but they knew what evils could arise if the new nation was not founded with religious freedom as one of its core ideals. Although many colonists had fled Europe to escape religious persecution, most colonies actively persecuted those who did not belong to their predominant religious groups.

The Framers' distaste for a national church or religion was reflected in the Constitution. Article VI, for example, provides that "no religious Test shall ever be required as a Qualification to any Office or Public Trust under the United States." This simple statement, however, did not completely reassure those who feared the new Constitution would curtail individual liberty. Thus, the First Amendment to the Constitution soon was ratified to allay those fears.

The **First Amendment** to the Constitution begins, "Congress shall make no law respecting an establishment of religion, or prohibiting the free exercise thereof." This statement sets the boundaries of governmental action. The **establishment clause** ("Congress shall make no law respecting an establishment of religion") directs the national government not to involve itself in religion. It creates, in Thomas Jefferson's words, a "wall of separation" between church and state. The **free exercise clause** ("or prohibiting the free exercise thereof") guarantees citizens that the national government will not interfere with their practice of religion. These guarantees, however, are not absolute.

Comparing Civil Liberties

First Amendment
Part of the Bill of Rights that imposes a number of restrictions on the federal government with respect to the civil liberties of the people, including freedom of religion, speech, press, assembly, and petition.

establishment clause
The first clause in the First Amendment; it prohibits the national government from establishing a national religion.

free exercise clause
The second clause of the First Amendment; it prohibits the U.S. government from interfering with a citizen's right to practice his or her religion. Still, some forms of actual exercise of religion can be regulated.

THE ESTABLISHMENT CLAUSE

Over the years, the Court has been divided over how to interpret the establishment clause. Does this clause erect a total wall between church and state, or is some governmental accommodation of religion allowed? While the Supreme Court has upheld the constitutionality of many kinds of church/state entanglements such as public funding to provide sign language interpreters for deaf students in religious schools,[11] the Court has held fast to the rule of strict separation between church and state when issues of prayer in school are involved. In *Engel* v. *Vitale* (1962), the Court first ruled that the recitation in public school classrooms of a twenty-two-word nondenominational prayer drafted by the New Hyde Park, New York, school board was unconstitutional.[12] In 1992, the Court continued its unwillingness to allow organized prayer in public schools by finding unconstitutional the saying of prayer at a middle school graduation.[13] And, in 2000, the Court ruled that student-led, student-initiated prayer at high school football games violated the establishment clause.[14]

The Court has gone back and forth in its effort to come up with a workable way to deal with church/state questions. In 1971, in *Lemon* v. *Kurtzman*, the Court tried to carve out a three-part test for laws dealing with religious establishment issues.

According to the *Lemon* test, a practice or policy was constitutional if it: (1) had a secular purpose; (2) neither advanced nor inhibited religion; and, (3) did not foster an excessive government entanglement with religion.[15] But, since the early 1980s, the Supreme Court often has sidestepped the *Lemon* test altogether and has appeared more willing to lower the wall between church and state so long as school prayer is not involved.[16] In 1981, for example, the Court ruled unconstitutional a Missouri law prohibiting the use of state university buildings and grounds for "purposes of religious worship." The law had been used to ban religious groups from using school facilities.[17]

In 1995, the Court signaled that it was willing to lower the wall even further. In a case involving the University of Virginia, a 5–4 majority held that the university violated the free speech rights of a fundamentalist Christian group when it refused to fund the groups' student magazine. The importance of this decision was highlighted by Justice David Souter, who noted in dissent: "The Court today, for the first time, approves direct funding of core religious activities by an arm of the state.[18]

For more than a quarter century, the Supreme Court basically allowed "books only" as an aid to religious schools, noting that the books go to children, not to the schools themselves. But, in 1997, in *Agostini* v. *Felton,* the Supreme Court approved of a New York program that sent public school teachers into parochial schools during school hours to provide remedial education to disadvantaged students. The Court concluded that this was not an excessive entanglement of church and state and therefore was not a violation of the establishment clause.[19] Moreover, in 2000, the Court voted 6–3 to uphold the constitutionality of a federal aid provision that allowed the government to lend books and computers to religious schools.[20] And, in 2002, by a bitterly divided 5–4 vote, the Supreme Court in *Zelman* v. *Simmons-Harris* concluded that governments can give money to parents to allow them to send their children to private or religious schools.[21]

Establishment issues, however, do not always focus on education. In 2005, for example, the Supreme Court in a 5–4 decision narrowly upheld the continued vitality of the *Lemon* test in holding that a privately donated courthouse display that included the Ten Commandments and 300 other historical documents illustrating the evolution of American law was a violation of the First Amendment's establishment clause. Court watchers now are waiting to see how the addition of two new

■ President George W. Bush addresses an audience at The White House National Conference on Faith-Based and Community Initiatives in 2006. The Bush administration's policies have paved the way for millions of dollars in public funds to go to religious organizations. Critics contend that in many cases Bush policies run afoul of the Constitution's establishment clause.

Photo courtesy: Kimberlee Hewitt/The White House

American Values/American Voices

WHERE'S THE WALL?

In President Thomas Jefferson's view, there was to be a near impenetrable wall between church and state. Subsequent presidents and Supreme Court justices have held to that view. But, the election of President George W. Bush, the second president to claim to be a born-again Christian (Jimmy Carter was the first), brought with it a new and what many critics have called an unprecedented entanglement of church and state. Immediately after he took office in 2001, President Bush created a new Office of Faith-Based Initiatives. In January 2004, he announced, "we want to fund programs that save Americans one soul at a time."[a] In his State of the Union message, the president urged the House and Senate to make his faith-based proposals permanent. The programs administered by this office represent some of the widest ranging entanglements of church and state in the history of the United States and reflect the values of the many Americans who say that the United States would benefit from a closer connection between religious beliefs and governmental actions.

But, in making federal dollars available to religious groups for their programs, has the Bush administration left the Framers' intentions by the wayside? In 2003, for example, the administration announced that it would not withhold funding from religious groups that discriminate in hiring based on religious affiliation—thus reversing decades-old policies prohibiting religious discrimination by federally funded agencies. The Salvation Army, for example, not only received funding but was accorded greater freedom to exclude homosexuals from its workforce. And, in 2004, Americorps was able to fund a day care center for thirty-five students run by the Roman Catholic Diocese of Providence with a grant of $324,000.[b] Justice Sunday III, a lobbying event designed to bring more conservative judges to the courts, also received $1 million in federal grants, some of which may have been used indirectly to lobby for Senate approval of Roman Catholic nominees to the U.S. Supreme Court—Chief Justice John G. Roberts Jr. and Associate Justice Samuel A. Alito Jr., specifically.

Americans United for Separation of Church and State has been particularly critical of Bush's initiatives, especially those that have been accomplished through executive order and not through explicit congressional authorization. Abstinence-only sex-education programs for public schools, for example, have been a favorite of the Bush administration, but they have been barred from implementation by even some conservative state judges who believe that they contain too many references to "God, Jesus Christ, and the spiritual repercussions of sex before marriage."[c]

The separation of church and state has always been a thorny issue in American politics. On one hand, a majority of Americans clearly value the moral teachings of most major religions, especially Christianity. Our coins are embossed with "In God We Trust." The U.S. Supreme Court asks God's blessing on "This Honorable Court." Every session of the U.S. House and Senate begins with a prayer, and the House has its own chaplain. Yet, particularly when the United States is at war in an area of the world where religion often is at the core of nationalist pride and armed hostilities, it may be time to ponder once again the Framers' motives for including the establishment clause in the Constitution.

QUESTIONS

1. What reasons can you list in support of and in opposition to the United States embracing its Christian heritage more openly than ever before?
2. How does a nation founded on majority rights with protections for minorities deal with the increasing religious diversity of its citizenry and clashes caused by citizens' sometimes competing religious values?

[a]"The Rise of the Religious Right in the Republican Administration," http://www.theocracywatch.org.faith_base.htm.

[b]"The Rise of the Religious Right in the Republican Administration."

[c]http://www.theocracywatch.org.

justices to the Court will affect these closely divided opinions.[22] For example, in a case winding its way through the federal courts, a federal judge ruled in 2006 that the Prison Fellowship Ministries and the state of Iowa violated the religious establishment clause when they created a government-funded program intended to rehabilitate prisoners by total immersion in Christianity. (See American Values, American Voices: Where's the Wall?) This case, brought by Americans United for Separation of Church and State, a liberal D.C.-based advocacy group, is "widely viewed as a major challenge to President Bush's faith-based initiatives, the White House's effort to deliver more government funding to religious groups that provide social services, especially in prisons."[23]

THE FREE EXERCISE CLAUSE

The free exercise clause of the First Amendment proclaims that "Congress shall make no law . . . prohibiting the free exercise [of religion]." Although the free exercise clause of the First Amendment guarantees individuals the right to be free from government interference in the exercise of their religion, this guarantee, like other First Amendment freedoms, is not absolute. When secular law comes into conflict with religious law, the right to exercise one's religious beliefs is often denied—especially if the religious beliefs in question are held by a minority or by an unpopular or suspicious religious group.

In 1990, for example, the Supreme Court ruled that the free exercise clause allowed Oregon to ban the use of sacramental peyote (an illegal hallucinogenic drug) in some Native American tribes' traditional religious services.[24] This decision prompted a dramatic outcry. Congressional response was passage of the Religious Freedom Restoration Act, which makes it harder for states to interfere with how citizens practice their religion. Although the Supreme Court ruled portions of the act unconstitutional in 1997, it continues to have some effect.[25] For example, in 2006, the U.S. Supreme Court found that the use of Hoasca tea, which contains the controlled substance dimethyltryptamine (DMT), well-known for its hallucinogenic properties, was permissible free exercise of religion for members of the Brazilian-based O Centro Espirita Beneficente União do Vegetal church.[26]

First Amendment Guarantees: Freedom of Speech, Press, and Assembly

VISUAL LITERACY

What Speech Is Protected by the Constitution?

TODAY, SOME MEMBERS OF CONGRESS criticize the movie industry and reality television shows such as *Survivor* and *The Real World* for pandering to the least common denominator of society. Other groups criticize popular performers such as Fifty Cent for lyrics that denigrate women. Such criticism often comes with calls for increased restrictions and greater regulation of media outlets. This leads many civil libertarians to believe that the rights to speak, print, and assemble freely are being seriously threatened.[27] (For more details on content regulation, see chapter 10.)

FREEDOM OF SPEECH AND THE PRESS

A democracy depends on a free exchange of ideas, and the First Amendment shows that the Framers were well aware of this fact. Historically, one of the most volatile areas of constitutional interpretation has been in the interpretation of the First Amendment's mandate that "Congress shall make no law . . . abridging the freedom of speech or of the press." Like the establishment and free exercise clauses of the First Amendment, the speech and press clauses have not been interpreted as absolute bans against government regulation. A lack of absolute meaning has led to thousands of cases seeking both broader and narrower judicial interpretations of the scope of the amendment. Over the years, the Court has employed a hierarchical approach in determining what the government can and cannot regulate, with some items getting greater protection than others. Generally, thoughts have received the greatest protection, and actions or deeds the least. Words have come somewhere in the middle, depending on their content and purpose. (For a broader view, see Global Perspective: Freedom of the Press.)

The Alien and Sedition Acts When the First Amendment was ratified in 1791, it was considered only to protect against **prior restraint** of speech or expression, or to guard against the prohibition of speech or publication before the fact. However,

prior restraint
Constitutional doctrine that prevents the government from prohibiting speech or publication before the fact; generally held to be in violation of the First Amendment.

Global Perspective

FREEDOM OF THE PRESS

Americans are quite correctly proud of the independent voice exercised by the U.S. press. But, how do press freedoms in the United States compare with those found in other countries? And, just how free is the American press? Global comparisons can be made along three dimensions. First is the legal environment: what rules and regulations govern media content? Second is the political environment: how much political control is exercised over the content of the news media? Third is the economic environment: who owns the media and how are media outlets financed?

Using these three factors, Freedom House, a nonprofit organization that serves as a global civil liberties watchdog, issues a report each year on the degree of print, broadcast, and Internet freedom in every country in the world. The news media in each country are rated on a scale of 1–100. Those receiving a rating of 1–30 are considered free, those receiving a rating of 31–60 are considered partly free, and those receiving a rating of 61–100 are considered not free.

In 2005, the United States, as well as neighboring Canada and four other nations, received a rating of 17; twenty other nations received ratings of 16 or higher, placing the news media in these nations in the free category. Finland, Iceland, and Sweden received ratings of 9, tying them for first place. Mexico, America's southern neighbor, received a rating of 42 in 2005, placing its press in the partly free category, primarily due to intimidation and violence against journalists sponsored by drug cartels and corrupt members of the police or government. While media outlets in Mexico's large urban areas are relatively free from interference, journalists operating in more rural areas, especially along Mexico's border with the United States, are vulnerable to harassment and violence.

Russia's news media, with a rating of 68, are judged to be not free. The Russian government under the leadership of President Vladimir Putin has nearly complete control of the broadcast media; Putin's government has passed laws and used financial pressure to restrict critical coverage of its policies. These restrictions are particularly true with respect to its handling of the long and bloody war in the breakaway province of Chechnya. While Iraq's rating has improved significantly since Saddam Hussein was deposed in 2003, its media remain in the not free category. Moreover, its rating deteriorated somewhat from a 66 in 2004 to 70 in 2005, reflecting continued instability and violence, the targeting of journalists by extremists and occasionally government and coalition forces, and ambiguity surrounding the role of new institutions charged with regulating the media. Afghanistan's rating has also improved significantly since the overthrow of the Taliban regime in 2002, although its press, like Iraq's, received a rating in the "not free" range.

The five countries whose news media were rated least free in 2005 were Libya, Myanmar (Burma), Turkmenistan, Cuba, and North Korea (which came in last, with a rating of 97). Overall, seventy-five countries (39 percent) were judged to have a free press, fifty-two had a partly free press (27 percent), and sixty-seven (34 percent) did not have a free press, a slight improvement over 2003 ratings of press freedom.

QUESTIONS

1. What factors would you look at in judging whether a country had a free press? Why?
2. Are economic, political, or cultural factors most important in making the press free? Explain your answer.

Source: Freedom House, "Map of Press Freedom 2005" and "Freedom of the Press 2005: Press Freedom Rankings 1994–2005," http://www.freedomhouse.org.

---

in 1798, the Federalist Congress enacted the Alien and Sedition Acts, which were designed to ban any criticism of the Federalist government by the growing numbers of Democratic-Republicans. These acts made the publication of "any false, scandalous writing against the government of the United States" a criminal offense. Although the law clearly ran in the face of the First Amendment's ban on prior restraint, partisan Federalist judges imposed fines and jail terms on at least ten Democratic-Republican newspaper editors. The acts became a major issue in the 1800 presidential election campaign, which led to the election of Thomas Jefferson, a vocal opponent of the acts. He quickly pardoned all who had been convicted under their provisions and the Democratic-Republican Congress allowed the acts to expire.

Slavery, the Civil War, and Rights Curtailments After the public outcry over the Alien and Sedition Acts, the national government largely got out of the business of regulating speech. But, in its place, the states, which were not yet bound by the Bill of Rights, began to prosecute those who published articles critical of governmental

Civil Liberties and National Security

writ of *habeas corpus*
A court order in which a judge requires authorities to prove that a prisoner is being held lawfully and that allows the prisoner to be freed if the judge is not persuaded by the government's case. *Habeas corpus* rights imply that prisoners have a right to know what charges are being made against them.

clear and present danger test
Test articulated by the Supreme Court in *Schenck* v. *U.S.* (1919) to draw the line between protected and unprotected speech; the Court looks to see "whether the words used" could "create a clear and present danger that they will bring about substantive evils" that Congress seeks "to prevent."

direct incitement test
A test articulated by the Supreme Court in *Brandenburg* v. *Ohio* (1969) that holds that advocacy of illegal action is protected by the First Amendment unless imminent lawless action is intended and likely to occur.

policies. In the 1830s, at the urgings of abolitionists (those who sought an end to slavery), the publication or dissemination of any positive information about slavery became a punishable offense in the North. In the South, supporters of slavery enacted laws to bar publication of any anti-slavery sentiments. Southern postmasters refused to deliver northern abolitionist papers, a step that amounted to censorship.

During the Civil War, President Abraham Lincoln effectively suspended the free press provision of the First Amendment (as well as the **writ of *habeas corpus***—the right of a court to determine whether prisoners are being held lawfully and to free prisoners if the court determines they are not being held lawfully). He went so far as to order the arrest of the editors of two New York papers who were critical of him. Far from protesting against these blatant violations of the First Amendment, Congress acceded to them. In one instance, William McCardle, a Mississippi newspaper editor who had written in opposition to Lincoln and the Union occupation, was jailed by a military court without having any charges brought against him. He appealed his detainment to the U.S. Supreme Court, arguing that he was being held unlawfully. Congress, fearing that a victory for McCardle would hurt Lincoln's national standing and prompt other similarly treated Confederate editors to follow his lead, enacted legislation prohibiting the Supreme Court from issuing a judgment in any cases involving convictions for publishing statements critical of the United States. Because Article II of the Constitution gives Congress the power to determine the jurisdiction of the Court, the Court was forced to conclude in *Ex parte McCardle* (1869) that it had no authority to rule in the matter.[28]

After the Civil War, states also began to prosecute individuals for seditious speech if they uttered or printed statements critical of the government. Between 1890 and 1900, there were more than one hundred state prosecutions for sedition.[29] Moreover, by the dawn of the twentieth century, public opinion in the United States had grown increasingly hostile toward the commentary of Socialists and Communists who attempted to appeal to the growing immigrant population. Socialist and communist groups became the targets of state laws curtailing speech and the written word. By the end of World War I, over thirty states had passed laws to punish seditious speech, and more than 1,900 individuals and over one hundred newspapers were prosecuted for violations.[30] In 1925, however, states' authority to regulate speech was severely restricted by the Court's decision in *Gitlow* v. *New York*.

World War I and Anti-Governmental Speech The next major national efforts to restrict freedom of speech and the press did not occur until Congress passed the Espionage Act in 1917. Nearly 2,000 Americans were convicted of violating its various provisions, especially those that made it illegal to urge resistance to the draft or to prohibit the distribution of anti-war leaflets. In *Schenck* v. *U.S.* (1919), the Supreme Court upheld this act, ruling that Congress had a right to restrict speech "of such a nature as to create a clear and present danger that will bring about the substantive evils that Congress has a right to prevent."[31] Under this test, known as the **clear and present danger test,** the circumstances surrounding an incident are important. Under *Schenck*, anti-war leaflets, for example, may be permissible during peacetime, but during World War I they were considered to pose too much of a danger to be permissible.

For decades, the Supreme Court wrestled with what constituted a danger. Finally, in *Brandenburg* v. *Ohio* (1969), the Court fashioned a new test for deciding whether certain kinds of speech could be regulated by the government: the **direct incitement test.** Now, the government could punish the advocacy of illegal action only if "such advocacy is directed to inciting or producing imminent lawless action and is likely to incite or produce such action."[32] The requirement of "imminent lawless action" makes it more difficult for the government to punish speech and publication and is consistent with the Framers' notion of the special role played by these elements in a democratic society. Passage of the Military Commissions Act in 2006, however, leaves this ruling in question.

On Campus

POLITICAL SPEECH AND MANDATORY STUDENT FEES

In March 2000, the U.S. Supreme Court ruled unanimously in *Board of Regents* v. *Southworth* that public universities could charge students a mandatory activity fee that could be used to facilitate extracurricular student political speech as long as the programs are neutral in their application.[a]

Scott Southworth, while a law student at the University of Wisconsin, believed that the university's mandatory fee was a violation of his First Amendment right to free speech. He, along with several other law students, objected that their fees went to fund liberal groups. They particularly objected to the support of eighteen of the 125 various groups on campus that benefited from the mandatory activity fee, including the Lesbian, Gay, Bisexual, and Transgender Center, the International Socialist Organization, and the campus women's center.[b]

In ruling against Southworth and for the university, the Court underscored the importance of universities being a forum for the free exchange of political and ideological ideas and perspectives. The *Southworth* case performed that function on the Wisconsin campus even before it was argued before the Supreme Court. A student-led effort called the Southworth Project, for which over a dozen law and journalism students each earned two credits, was begun to make sure that the case was reported on campus in an accurate and sophisticated way. The Southworth Project, said a political science professor, gave "a tremendous boost to the visibility and the thinking process about the case."[c] In essence, the case made the Constitution and what it means come alive on the Wisconsin campus as students pondered the effects of First

Photo courtesy: Dave Watkins/Advance Titan/University of Wisconsin

■ Scott Southworth (right) defends his position on mandatory student fees in a 2003 debate at the University of Wisconsin with Journa Taylor (left), shared governance director of the University of Wisconsin Council.

Amendment protections on their ability to learn in a university atmosphere.

[a]*Board of Regents* v. *Southworth*, 529 U.S. 217 (2000).

[b]"U.S. Court Upholds Student Fees Going to Controversial Groups," *Toronto Star* (March 23, 2000), NEXIS.

[c]Mary Beth Marklein, "Fee Fight Proves a Learning Experience," *USA Today* (November 30, 1999): 8D.

PROTECTED SPEECH AND PUBLICATIONS

As discussed, the Supreme Court refuses to uphold the constitutionality of legislation that amounts to prior restraint of the press. Other types of speech and publication are also protected by the Court, including symbolic speech and hate speech.

Prior Restraint With only a few exceptions, the Court has made it clear that it will not tolerate prior restraint of speech. For example, in *New York Times Co.* v. *U.S.* (1971) (also called the Pentagon Papers case), the Supreme Court ruled that the U.S. government could not block the publication of secret Department of Defense documents illegally furnished to the *Times* by anti-war activists.[33] In 1976, the Supreme Court went even further, noting in *Nebraska Press Association* v. *Stuart* (1976) that any attempt by the government to prevent expression carried "'a heavy presumption' against its constitutionality."[34]

Symbolic Speech In addition to the general protection accorded to pure speech, the Supreme Court has extended the reach of the First Amendment to **symbolic speech,** a means of expression that includes symbols or signs. In the words of Justice John Marshall Harlan, these kinds of speech are part of the "free trade in ideas."[35] (For more on symbolic speech, see On Campus: Political Speech and Mandatory Student Fees.)

symbolic speech
Symbols, signs, and other methods of expression generally also considered to be protected by the First Amendment.

The Supreme Court first acknowledged that symbolic speech was entitled to First Amendment protection in *Stromberg* v. *California* (1931).[36] There, the Court overturned a communist youth camp director's conviction under a state statute prohibiting the display of a red flag, a symbol of opposition to the U.S. government. In a similar vein, the right of high school students to wear black armbands to protest the Vietnam War was upheld in *Tinker* v. *Des Moines Independent Community School District* (1969).[37]

Burning the American flag also has been held a form of protected symbolic speech. In 1989, a sharply divided Supreme Court (5–4) reversed the conviction of Gregory Johnson, who had been found guilty of setting fire to an American flag during the 1984 Republican National Convention in Dallas.[38] There was a major public outcry against the Court. Unable to pass a constitutional amendment, Congress passed the Federal Flag Protection Act of 1989, which authorized federal prosecution of anyone who intentionally desecrated a national flag. Johnson and his colleagues burned another flag and were again convicted. Their conviction was overturned by a 5–4 vote of the Supreme Court. The majority concluded that this federal law "suffered from the same fundamental flaw" as had the earlier Texas state law.[39]

Hate Speech

Hate Speech, Unpopular Speech, and Speech Zones In the 1990s, a particularly thorny First Amendment area emerged as cities and universities attempted to prohibit what they viewed as offensive hate speech. In *R.A.V.* v. *City of St. Paul* (1992), a St. Paul, Minnesota, ordinance that made it a crime to engage in speech or action likely to arouse "anger," "alarm," or "resentment" on the basis of race, color, creed, religion, or gender was at issue. The Court ruled 5–4 that a white teenager who burned a cross on a black family's front lawn, thereby committing a hate crime under the ordinance, could not be charged under that law because the First Amendment prevents governments from "silencing speech on the basis of its content."[40] In 2003, the Court narrowed this definition, ruling that state governments could constitutionally restrict cross burning when it occurred with the intent of racial intimidation.[41]

Two-thirds of colleges and universities have banned a variety of forms of speech or conduct that creates or fosters an intimidating, hostile, or offensive environment on campus. To prevent disruption of university activities, some universities have also created free speech zones that restrict the time, place, or manner of speech. Critics, including the ACLU, charge that free speech zones imply that speech can be limited on other parts of the campus, which they see as a violation of the First Amendment. They have filed a number of suits in district court, but to date none of these cases has reached the Supreme Court.

UNPROTECTED SPEECH AND PUBLICATIONS

Although the Supreme Court has allowed few governmental bans on most types of speech, some forms of expression are not protected. In 1942, the Supreme Court set out the rationale by which it would distinguish between protected and unprotected speech. According to the Court, libel, fighting words, obscenity, and lewdness are not protected by the First Amendment because "such expressions are no essential part of any exposition of ideals, and are of such slight social value as a step to truth that any benefit that may be derived from them is clearly outweighed by the social interest in order and morality."[42]

libel
False written statements or written statements tending to call someone's reputation into disrepute.

slander
Untrue spoken statements that defame the character of a person.

Libel and Slander **Libel** is a written statement that defames the character of a person. If the statement is spoken, it is **slander.** In many nations—such as Great

Britain, for example—it is relatively easy to sue someone for libel. In the United States, however, the standards of proof are much more difficult. A person who believes that he or she has been a victim of libel must show that the statements made were untrue. Truth is an absolute defense against the charge of libel, no matter how painful or embarrassing the revelations.

It is often more difficult for individuals the Supreme Court considers "public persons or public officials" to sue for libel or slander. ***New York Times Co. v. Sullivan (1964)*** was the first major libel case considered by the Supreme Court.[43] An Alabama state court found the *Times* guilty of libel for printing a full-page advertisement accusing Alabama officials of physically abusing African Americans during various civil rights protests. (The ad was paid for by civil rights activists, including former First Lady Eleanor Roosevelt.) The Supreme Court overturned the conviction and established that a finding of libel against a public official could stand only if there was a showing of "actual malice," or a knowing disregard for the truth. Proof that the statements were false or negligent was not sufficient to prove actual malice.

Fighting Words
In the 1942 case of *Chaplinsky* v. *New Hampshire,* the Court stated that **fighting words,** or words that, "by their very utterance inflict injury or tend or incite an immediate breach of peace" are not subject to the restrictions of the First Amendment.[44] Fighting words, which include "profanity, obscenity, and threats," are therefore able to be regulated by the federal and state governments.

These words do not necessarily have to be spoken; fighting words can also come in the form of symbolic expression. For example, in 1968, a California man named Paul Cohen wore a jacket that said "Fuck the Draft. Stop the War" into a Los Angeles county courthouse. He was arrested and charged with disturbing the peace and engaging in offensive conduct. The trial court convicted Cohen, and this conviction was upheld by a state appellate court. However, when the case reached the Supreme Court in 1971, the Court reversed the lower courts' decisions and ruled that forbidding the use of certain words amounted to little more than censorship of ideas.[45]

Obscenity
Through 1957, U.S. courts often based their opinions of what was obscene on an English common-law test that had been set out in 1868: "Whether the tendency of the matter charged as obscenity is to deprive and corrupt those whose minds are open to such immoral influences and into whose hands a publication of this sort might fall."[46] In *Roth* v. *U.S.* (1957), however, the Court abandoned this approach and held that, to be considered obscene, the material in question had to be "utterly without redeeming social importance," and articulated a new test for obscenity: "whether to the average person, applying contemporary community standards, the dominant theme of the material taken as a whole appeals to the prurient interests."[47]

In many ways, the *Roth* test brought with it as many problems as it attempted to solve. Throughout the 1950s and 1960s, "prurient" remained hard to define, as the Supreme Court struggled to find a standard for judging actions or words. Moreover, it was very difficult to prove that a book or movie was "*utterly* without redeeming social value." In general, even some hardcore pornography passed muster under the *Roth* test.

In light of this evidence and changes in the political climate, in 1973 the Court set out a test that redefined obscenity. To make it easier for states to regulate obscene materials, the justices concluded that lower courts must ask "whether the work depicts or describes, in a patently offensive way, sexual conduct specifically defined by state law." The courts also were to determine "whether the work, taken as a whole, lacks serious literary, artistic, political, or scientific value." And, in place of the contemporary community standards gauge used in *Roth,* the Court defined community standards to refer to the locality in question, under the rationale that what is acceptable in New York City might not be acceptable in Maine or Mississippi.[48]

Time and contexts clearly have altered the Court's and, indeed, much of America's perceptions of what works are obscene. But, the Supreme Court has allowed communities great leeway in drafting statutes to deal with obscenity and, even more important, other forms of questionable expression. In 1991, for example, the Court voted 5–4 to allow Indiana to ban totally nude erotic dancing, concluding that the statute furthered a substantial governmental interest, and therefore was not in violation of the First Amendment.[49] Since this case, the Court largely has stayed out of the fray of obscenity law. Congress, on the other hand, has continued to legislate on issues of obscenity.

Congress and Obscenity   While lawmakers have been fairly effective in restricting the sale and distribution of obscene materials, Congress has been particularly concerned with the distribution of obscenity and pornography on the Internet.

Monitoring the Internet has proven difficult for Congress. In 1996, it passed the Communications Decency Act, which prohibited the transmission of obscene materials over the Internet to anyone under age eighteen. In 1997, the Supreme Court ruled in *Reno* v. *American Civil Liberties Union* that the act violated the First Amendment because it was too vague and overbroad.[50] In reaction to the decision, Congress passed the Child Online Protection Act (COPA) in 1998. The new law broadened the definition of pornography to include any "visual depiction that is, or appears to be, a minor engaging in sexually explicit conduct." The act targeted material "harmful to minors" but applied only to World Wide Web sites, not chat rooms or e-mail. It also targeted only materials used for "commercial purposes."

VIDEO ROUNDTABLE

Political Correctness

The ACLU and online publishers immediately challenged the constitutionality of the act, and a U.S. court of appeals in Philadelphia ruled the law was unconstitutional because of its reliance on "community standards" as articulated in *Miller,* which are not enforceable on the Internet. While this case was on appeal to the Supreme Court, Congress enacted the Children's Internet Protection Act, which prohibited public libraries receiving federal funds from allowing minors access to the Web without anti-pornography filters. Meanwhile, in *Ashcroft* v. *Free Speech Coalition* (2002), the Court ruled that Congress had gone too far in a laudable effort to stamp out child pornography.[51] Six justices agreed that the law was too vague because "communities with a narrow view of what words and images are suitable for children might be able to censor Internet content, putting it out of reach of the entire country."[52]

Congressional reaction was immediate. Within two weeks of the Court's decision, lawmakers were drafting more specific legislation to meet the Court's reservations. New regulations were enacted in 2003 as part of an anti-crime bill. In this legislation, Congress further limited the kinds of cyber pornography subject to regulation and allowed those accused of creating and marketing such pornography to "escape conviction if they could show they did not use actual children to produce sexually explicit images."[53] In 2004, the Supreme Court struck down as unconstitutional Congress's latest effort to limit cyberporn. The Court also continued to block enforcement of COPA.[54]

FREEDOMS OF ASSEMBLY AND PETITION

"Peaceful assembly for lawful discussion cannot be made a crime," Chief Justice Charles Evans Hughes wrote in the 1937 case of *DeJonge* v. *Oregon*, which incorporated the First Amendment's freedom of assembly clause.[55] Despite this clear declaration, and an even more ringing declaration in the First Amendment, the fundamental freedoms of assembly and petition have been among the most controversial, especially in times of war. As with other First Amendment freedoms, the Supreme Court often has become the arbiter between the freedom of the people to express dissent and government's authority to limit controversy in the name of national security.

Because the freedom to assemble is hinged on peaceful conduct, as underscored in our opening vignette on Darfur rallies, the freedoms of assembly and petition are related directly to the freedoms of speech and of the press. If the words or actions taken at any event cross the line of constitutionality, the event itself may constitutionally no longer be protected. Absent that protection, leaders and attendees may be subject to governmental regulation and even criminal charges or civil fines.

The Second Amendment: The Right to Keep and Bear Arms

MOST COLONIES REQUIRED all white men to keep and bear arms, and all white men in whole sections of the colonies were deputized to defend their settlements against Indians and other European powers. These local militias were viewed as the best way to keep order and protect liberty. The Second Amendment was added to the Constitution to ensure that Congress could not pass laws to disarm state militias. This amendment appeased Anti-Federalists, who feared that the new Constitution would cause them to lose the right to "keep and bear arms" as well as an unstated right—the right to revolt against government tyranny.

Through the early 1920s, few state statutes were passed to regulate firearms (and generally these laws dealt with the possession of firearms by slaves). The Supreme Court's decision in *Barron* v. *Baltimore* (1833), which refused to incorporate the Bill of Rights to the state governments, prevented federal review of those state laws.[56] Moreover, in *Dred Scott* v. *Sandford* (1857) (see chapter 3), Chief Justice Roger B. Taney listed the right to own and carry arms as a basic right of citizenship.[57]

In 1934, Congress passed the National Firearms Act in response to the increase in organized crime that occurred in the 1920s and 1930s as a result of Prohibition. The act imposed taxes on automatic weapons (such as machine guns) and sawed-off shotguns. In *U.S.* v. *Miller* (1939), a unanimous Court upheld the constitutionality of the act, stating that the Second Amendment was intended to protect a citizen's right to own ordinary militia weapons and not unregistered sawed-off shotguns, which were at issue.[58] *Miller* was the last time the Supreme Court directly addressed the Second Amendment. In *Quilici* v. *Village of Morton Grove* (1983), the Supreme Court refused to review a lower court's ruling upholding the constitutionality of a local ordinance banning handguns against a Second Amendment challenge.[59]

In the aftermath of the assassination attempt on President Ronald Reagan in 1981, many lawmakers called for passage of gun control legislation. At the forefront of that effort was Sarah Brady, the wife of James Brady, the presidential press secretary who was badly wounded and left partially disabled by John Hinckley Jr., President Reagan's assailant. In 1993, her efforts helped to win passage of the Brady Bill, which imposed a federal mandatory five-day waiting period on the purchase of handguns.

PARTICIPATION

Gun Rights and Gun Control

■ President Bill Clinton signs the Brady Bill into law flanked by Vice President Al Gore, Attorney General Janet Reno, and James and Sarah Brady and their children.

Photo courtesy: Marcy Nighswander/AP Wide World Photos

VIDEO DEBATE

Gun Control

In 1997, the U.S. Supreme Court ruled 5–4 that the section of the Brady Bill requiring state officials to conduct background checks of prospective handgun owners violated principles of state sovereignty.[60] The background check provision, while important, is not critical to the overall goals of the Brady Bill because a federal record-checking system went into effect in late 1998.

Perhaps more important than the Brady Bill was the ban on assault weapons enacted by Congress as part of the Violent Crime Control and Law Enforcement Act in 1994. This provision, which prohibited Americans from owning many of the most powerful types of guns, carried a ten-year time limit. It expired just before the 2004 presidential and congressional elections. However, neither President Bush nor the Republican-controlled Congress made any serious steps toward renewal, causing many to charge that the move was political and prompted by anti-gun-control interests such as the National Rifle Association, who were major players in the Republican electoral efforts.

The Rights of Criminal Defendants

THE FOURTH, FIFTH, SIXTH, AND EIGHTH Amendments supplement constitutional guarantees against writs of *habeas corpus, ex post facto* laws, and bills of attainder by providing a variety of procedural guarantees (often called **due process rights**) for those accused of crimes. Particular amendments, as well as other portions of the Constitution, specifically provide procedural guarantees to protect individuals accused of crimes at all stages of the criminal justice process. As is the case with the First Amendment, many of these rights have been interpreted by the Supreme Court to apply to the states. In interpreting the amendments dealing with what are frequently termed "criminal rights," the courts have to grapple not only with the meaning of the amendments but also with how their protections are to be implemented.

due process rights
Procedural guarantees provided by the Fourth, Fifth, Sixth, and Eighth Amendments for those accused of crimes.

THE FOURTH AMENDMENT AND SEARCHES AND SEIZURES

Fourth Amendment
Part of the Bill of Rights that reads: "The right of the people to be secure in their persons, houses, papers, and effects, against unreasonable searches and seizures, shall not be violated, and no Warrants shall issue, but upon probable cause, supported by Oath or affirmation, and particularly describing the place to be searched, and the persons or things to be seized."

The **Fourth Amendment** to the Constitution protects people from unreasonable searches by the federal government. Moreover, in some detail, it sets out what may not be searched unless a warrant is issued, underscoring the Framers' concern with possible government abuses. (For a related discussion, see Join the Debate: The USA Patriot Act.)

The purpose of this amendment was to deny the national government the authority to make general searches. Over the years, in a number of decisions, the Supreme Court has interpreted the Fourth Amendment to allow the police to search: (1) the person arrested; (2) things in plain view of the accused person; and, (3) places or things that the arrested person could touch or reach or are otherwise in the arrestee's immediate control.

SIMULATION

You Are a Police Officer

In 1995, the Court also resolved a decades-old constitutional dispute by ruling unanimously that police must knock and announce their presence before entering a house or apartment to execute a search. But, said the Court, there may be reasonable exceptions to the rule to account for the likelihood of violence or the imminent destruction of evidence.[61] In 2006, the Court ruled in a 5–4 decision that even if police refused to knock, evidence improperly seized could be used in cases where police had a valid warrant.[62]

Warrantless searches often occur if police suspect that someone is committing or is about to commit a crime. In these situations, police may stop and frisk the individual under suspicion. In 1989, the Court ruled that there need be only a "reasonable suspicion" for stopping a suspect—a much lower standard than probable cause.[63] Thus, a suspected drug courier may be stopped for brief questioning but only a frisk search (for weapons) is permitted.

The Court also ruled in 2001 on a California policy that required individuals, as a condition of their probation, to consent to warrantless searches of their person, property, homes, or vehicles, thus limiting a probationer's Fourth Amendment protections against unreasonable searches and seizures.[64] The Court did not give blanket approval to searches; instead, a unanimous Court said that a probation officer must have a reasonable suspicion of wrongdoing—a lesser standard than probable cause afforded to most citizens. Searches can also be made without a warrant if consent is obtained, and the Court has ruled that consent can be given by a variety of persons. It has ruled, however, that the police cannot conduct a warrantless search of a home if one of the occupants objects.[65]

In situations where no arrest occurs, police must obtain search warrants from a "neutral and detached magistrate" prior to conducting more extensive searches of houses, cars, offices, or any other place where an individual would reasonably have some expectation of privacy.[66] Police cannot get search warrants, for example, to require you to undergo surgery to remove a bullet that might be used to incriminate you, since your expectation of bodily privacy outweighs the need for evidence.[67] But, courts do not require search warrants in possible drunk driving situations. Thus, the police in some states can require you to take a Breathalyzer test to determine whether you have been drinking in excess of legal limits.[68]

Homes, too, are presumed to be private. Firefighters can enter your home to fight a fire without a warrant. But, if they decide to investigate the cause of the fire, they must obtain a warrant before their reentry.[69] In contrast, under the open fields doctrine first articulated by the Supreme Court in 1924, if you own a field, and even if you post "No Trespassing" signs, the police can search your field without a warrant to see if you are illegally growing marijuana, because you cannot reasonably expect privacy in an open field.[70]

PARTICIPATION

Civil Liberties in Today's World: Privacy and the Rights of the Accused

Cars have proven problematic for police and the courts because of their mobile nature. As noted by Chief Justice William H. Taft as early as 1925, "the vehicle can quickly be moved out of the locality or jurisdiction in which the warrant must be sought."[71] Over the years, the Court has become increasingly lenient about the scope of automobile searches. In 2002, an unusually unanimous Court ruled that when evaluating if a border patrol officer acted lawfully in stopping a suspicious minivan, the totality of the circumstances had to be considered. Wrote Chief Justice William H. Rehnquist, the "balance between the public interest and the individual's right to personal security" tilts in favor of a "standard less than probable cause in brief investigatory stops." This ruling gave law enforcement officers more leeway to pull over suspicious motorists.[72]

Drug Testing While many private employers and professional athletic organizations routinely require drug tests upon application or as a condition of employment, governmental requirements present constitutional questions about the scope of permissible searches and seizures. In 1989, the Supreme Court ruled that mandatory drug and alcohol testing of employees involved in accidents was constitutional.[73] In 1995, the Court upheld the constitutionally of random drug testing of public high school athletes.[74] And, in 2002, the Court upheld the constitutionality of a Tecumseh, Oklahoma, policy that required mandatory drug testing of high school students participating in any extracurricular activities.[75] Thus, prospective band, choir, debate, or drama club members were subject to the same kind of random drug testing undergone by athletes.

Another question has arisen concerning the constitutionality of compulsory drug testing for pregnant women. In 2001, in a 6–3 decision, the Court ruled that the testing of women for cocaine use and subsequent reporting of positive tests to law enforcement officials was unconstitutional.[76]

Join the Debate

THE USA PATRIOT ACT

OVERVIEW: The Declaration of Independence forcefully espouses the principles that all individuals have "certain unalienable rights, that among these are Life, Liberty and the pursuit of Happiness," and that it is government's purpose to guarantee the secure enjoyment of these rights. To assure these liberties, government must necessarily use legitimate police force to ensure safety within its borders, and it must use military force to defend the state from outside aggression.

A considerable problem for democratic peoples in free and open societies is how to define the limits of government intervention in the private sphere. This problem becomes particularly acute during times of national crisis and armed conflict. Establishing the line between the government's constitutional duty to "provide for the common defence" and to "secure the blessings of liberty" is complicated. It becomes even more complex when those who threaten America's national security use the freedom and rights found in the United States as a means through which to wage war. To help defend against those wishing to use the openness of American society for harmful ends, the Uniting and Strengthening America by Providing Appropriate Tools Required to Intercept and Obstruct Terrorism Act of 2001, otherwise known as the USA Patriot Act, was signed into law on October 26, 2001, in response to the terrorist attacks on New York City and the Pentagon on September 11, 2001. Sunset provisions of the USA Patriot Act that included amendments designed to address civil liberties concerns

were renewed by Congress and signed into law by President George W. Bush in March 2006. Nevertheless, the act remains controversial. Does it help defend the United States against terrorist activity, or does it allow the government to abuse its power in the name of national security? Is it necessary for government to narrow the scope of civil rights and liberties in times of national distress, as has been the case throughout most of American history—for example, when Abraham Lincoln suspended *habeas corpus* in his effort to preserve the United States? Or, conversely, has American history demonstrated that injustices have been committed in the name of national security—for example, the U.S. government's internment of Japanese American citizens during World War II?

ARGUMENTS FOR THE USA PATRIOT ACT

- **The USA Patriot Act allows the government to use new technologies to address new threats.** Those engaged in terrorist activities today use sophisticated technologies. The USA Patriot Act allows the government to wage the war on terrorism by using the same and superior technologies to find and prosecute those engaged in terrorism and to help reduce the threat of terrorist attacks.
- **The USA Patriot Act dismantles the wall of legal and regulatory policies erected to limit sharply the sharing of information between intelligence, national security, and law enforcement communities.** Prior policy essentially prohibited various government agencies from communicating and coordinating domestic and national security activities, thus restricting the flow of valuable information that could prevent terrorist

VIDEO DEBATE
The Patriot Act

THE FIFTH AMENDMENT: SELF-INCRIMINATION AND DOUBLE JEOPARDY

Fifth Amendment
Part of the Bill of Rights that imposes a number of restrictions on the federal government with respect to the rights of persons suspected of committing a crime. It provides for indictment by a grand jury and protection against self-incrimination, and prevents the national government from denying a person life, liberty, or property without the due process of law. It also prevents the national government from taking property without fair compensation.

The **Fifth Amendment** provides that "No person shall be . . . compelled in any criminal case to be a witness against himself." "Taking the Fifth" is shorthand for exercising one's constitutional right not to self-incriminate. The Supreme Court has interpreted this guarantee to be "as broad as the mischief against which it seeks to guard," finding that criminal defendants do not have to take the stand at trial to answer questions, nor can a judge make mention of their failure to do so as evidence of guilt.[77] Moreover, lawyers cannot imply that a defendant who refuses to take the stand must be guilty or have something to hide.

This right not to incriminate oneself also means that prosecutors cannot use as evidence in a trial any of a defendant's statements or confessions that were not made voluntarily. As is the case in many areas of the law, however, judicial interpretation of the term voluntary has changed over time. In earlier times, it was not unusual for police to beat defendants to obtain their confessions. In 1936, however, the Supreme attacks. Now, government agencies can coordinate surveillance activities across domestic and national security policy domains.

- **The USA Patriot Act allows government agencies to use the procedures and tools already available to investigate organized and drug crime.** The USA Patriot Act uses techniques already approved by the courts in investigating such crimes as wire fraud, money laundering, and drug trafficking. These techniques include roving wire taps and judicially approved search warrants, notice of which may be delayed in certain narrow circumstances.

ARGUMENTS AGAINST THE USA PATRIOT ACT

- **Certain provisions of the USA Patriot Act may violate an individual's right to privacy.** For example, section 216 allows law enforcement officials to get a warrant to track which Web sites a person visits and to collect certain information in regard to an individual's e-mail activity. There need not be any suspicion of criminal activity—all law enforcement authorities need do is to certify that the potential information is relevant to an ongoing criminal investigation.
- **The USA Patriot Act violates the civil rights and liberties of legal immigrants.** The act permits the indefinite detention of immigrants and other noncitizens. The attorney general may detain immigrants merely upon "reasonable grounds" that one is involved in terrorism or engaged in activity that poses a danger to national security, and this detention may be indefinite until determination is made that such an individual threatens national security.

- **Safeguards to prevent direct government surveillance of citizens have been reduced.** The Patriot Act repeals certain precautions in regard to the sharing of information between law enforcement agencies and the intelligence community. These safeguards were put in place in the 1970s after revelations that the Central Intelligence Agency (CIA) and the Federal Bureau of Investigation (FBI) had been conducting joint investigations of American citizens—including surveillance of the Reverend Martin Luther King Jr.—for political purposes.

QUESTIONS

1. Does the USA Patriot Act balance liberty with security? If so, how does it strike that balance? If not, what do you think could be done to redress the imbalance?
2. Is the USA Patriot Act a necessary law? If so, what, in your view, can be done to rectify its flaws? If not, what should be done to ensure the security of the United States against terrorist activity?

SELECTED READINGS

Darmer, M. Katherine B., Robert M. Baird, and Stuart E. Rosenbaum, eds. *Civil Liberties vs. National Security in a Post 9/11 World.* Amherst, NY: Prometheus, 2004.

Etzioni, Amitai. *How Patriotic Is the Patriot Act?* New York: Routledge, 2004.

Court ruled that convictions for murder based solely on confessions given after physical beatings were unconstitutional.[78] Police then began to resort to other measures to force confessions. Defendants, for example, were given the third degree—questioned for hours on end with no sleep or food, or threatened with physical violence until they were mentally beaten into giving confessions.

Miranda v. Arizona **(1966)** was the Supreme Court's response to these creative efforts to obtain confessions that were not truly voluntary. On March 3, 1963, an eighteen-year-old girl was kidnapped and raped on the outskirts of Phoenix, Arizona. Ten days later police arrested Ernesto Miranda, a poor, mentally disturbed man with a ninth-grade education. In a police-station lineup, the victim identified Miranda as her attacker. Police then took Miranda to a separate room and questioned him for two hours. At first he denied guilt. Eventually, however, he confessed to the crime and wrote and signed a brief statement describing the crime and admitting his guilt. At no time was he told that he did not have to answer any questions or that he could be represented by an attorney.

Miranda v. Arizona **(1966)**
A landmark Supreme Court ruling that held the Fifth Amendment requires that individuals arrested for a crime must be advised of their right to remain silent and to have counsel present.

Rights of the Accused

Photo courtesy: AP Wide World Photos

■ Even though Ernesto Miranda's confession was not admitted as evidence at his retrial, his ex-girlfriend's testimony and that of the victim were enough to convince the jury of his guilt. He served nine years in prison before he was released on parole. After his release, he routinely sold autographed cards inscribed with what are called the *Miranda* rights now read to all suspects. In 1976, four years after his release, Miranda was stabbed to death in Phoenix in a bar fight during a card game. Two *Miranda* cards were found on his body, and the person who killed him was read his *Miranda* rights upon his arrest.

Miranda rights
Statements that must be made by the police informing a suspect of his or her constitutional rights protected by the Fifth Amendment, including the right to an attorney provided by the court if the suspect cannot afford one.

double jeopardy clause
Part of the Fifth Amendment that protects individuals from being tried twice for the same offense.

exclusionary rule
Judicially created rule that prohibits police from using illegally seized evidence at trial.

After Miranda's conviction, his case was appealed on the grounds that his Fifth Amendment right not to incriminate himself had been violated because his confession had been coerced. Writing for the Court, Chief Justice Earl Warren, himself a former district attorney and a former California state attorney general, noted that because police have a tremendous advantage in any interrogation situation, criminal suspects must be given greater protection. A confession obtained in the manner of Miranda's was not truly voluntary; thus, it was inadmissible at trial.

To provide guidelines for police to implement *Miranda*, the Court mandated that: "Prior to any questioning, the person must be warned that he has a right to remain silent, that any statements he does make may be used as evidence against him, and that he has a right to the presence of an attorney, either retained or appointed." In response to this mandate from the Court, police routinely began to read suspects what are now called their *Miranda* **rights,** a practice you undoubtedly have seen repeated over and over in movies and TV police dramas.

In 2000, in an opinion written by Chief Justice William H. Rehnquist, the Court reaffirmed the central holding of *Miranda*, ruling that defendants must be read *Miranda* warnings. The Court went on to say that, despite an act of Congress that stipulated that voluntary statements made during police interrogations were admissible at trial, without *Miranda* warnings, no admissions could be trusted to be truly voluntary.[79]

The Fifth Amendment also mandates: "nor shall any person be subject for the same offense to be twice put in jeopardy of life or limb." This is called the **double jeopardy clause,** and it protects individuals from being tried twice for the same offense. Thus, if a defendant is acquitted by a jury of a charge of murder, he or she cannot be retried for the offense even if new information is unearthed that could further point to guilt. In 2005, in *Smith* v. *Massachusetts*, for example, the Court in a the 5–4 majority concluded that double jeopardy applied when the trial judge ruled that the state's evidence was insufficient to maintain a prosecution but later in the trial reversed herself.[80]

THE FOURTH AND FIFTH AMENDMENTS AND THE EXCLUSIONARY RULE

In *Weeks* v. *U.S.* (1914), the U.S. Supreme Court adopted the **exclusionary rule,** which bars the use of illegally seized evidence at trial. Thus, although the Fourth and Fifth Amendments do not prohibit the use of evidence obtained in violation of their provisions, the exclusionary rule is a judicially created remedy to deter constitutional violations. In *Weeks*, for example, the Court reasoned that allowing police and prosecutors to use the "fruits of a poisonous tree" (a tainted search) would only encourage that activity.[81]

In balancing the need to deter police misconduct against the possibility that guilty individuals could go free, the Warren Court decided that deterring police misconduct was most important. In *Mapp* v. *Ohio* (1961), the Warren Court ruled that "all evidence obtained by searches and seizures in violation of the Constitution, is inadmissible in a state court."[82] This historic and controversial case put law enforcement officers on notice that if they found evidence in violation of any constitutional rights, those efforts would be for naught because the tainted evidence could not be used in federal or state trials.

More recently, Congress and the federal courts have attempted to chip away at the exclusionary rule by carving out a variety of limited "good faith exceptions." These include allowing the use of tainted evidence in a variety of situations, especially when police have a search warrant and, in good faith, conduct the search on the assumption that the warrant is valid, even if it is subsequently found invalid. Another exception to the exclusionary rule is "inevitable discovery." Evidence illegally seized may be introduced if it would have been discovered anyway in the course of continuing investigation.

Still, as recently as 2006, the Court has continued to uphold the exclusionary rule. In *U.S. v. Grubbs,* for example, the Court ruled unanimously that any evidence collected under a warrant presented by the police, yet not authorized by a judge, was inadmissible at trial.[83]

THE SIXTH AMENDMENT AND THE RIGHT TO COUNSEL

The **Sixth Amendment** guarantees to an accused person "the Assistance of Counsel in his defense." In the past, this provision meant only that an individual could hire an attorney to represent him or her in court. Since most criminal defendants are too poor to hire private lawyers, this provision was of little assistance to many who found themselves on trial. Recognizing this, Congress required federal courts to provide an attorney for defendants who could not to afford one. This was first required in capital cases (where the death penalty is a possibility); eventually, attorneys were provided to the poor in all federal criminal cases.[84]

Until the Court's 1963 decision in *Gideon* v. *Wainwright* (1963), criminal defendants were not entitled lawyers in state courts. However, writing for the Court, Justice Hugo Black explained that "lawyers in criminal courts are necessities, not luxuries." Therefore, the Court concluded, the state must provide an attorney to indigent defendants in felony cases.[85] Underscoring the Court's point, Clarence Gideon, who originally acted as his own lawyer, was acquitted when he was retried with a lawyer to argue his case.

In 1972, the Burger Court expanded the *Gideon* rule, holding that "even in prosecutions for offenses less serious than felonies, a fair trial may require the presence of a lawyer."[86] Seven years later, the Court clarified its decision by holding that defendants charged with offenses where imprisonment is a possibility but not actually imposed do not have a Sixth Amendment right to counsel.[87] Thirty years later, the Rehnquist Court expanded *Gideon* even further by revisiting the "actual imprisonment" standard announced in the 1972 and 1979 cases. In 2002, a 5–4 majority held that if a defendant received a suspended sentence and probation for a minor crime but could be sentenced in future if he or she violated the conditions of probation, then the defendant must be provided with a lawyer.[88]

The quality of counsel is an issue that has continued to vex the Court. Not everyone can afford the best attorney, but how bad must counsel be before the Sixth Amendment's right to counsel is violated? While various courts have held that lawyers who fell asleep during trial, failed to put on a defense, or were drunk during the proceedings were "adequate," in 2005 the Supreme Court ruled in a 5–4 opinion that the Sixth Amendment's guarantees required Ronald Rompilla's lawyers to examine files detailing Rompilla's criminal record that the prosecution was likely to use during the sentencing phase of his trial. Because Rompilla's defense attorneys had not done this, Rompilla was granted a new sentencing hearing.[89]

THE SIXTH AMENDMENT AND JURY TRIALS

The Sixth Amendment (and, to a lesser extent, Article III of the Constitution) provides that a person accused of a crime shall enjoy the right to a speedy and public trial by an impartial jury—that is, a trial in which a group of the accused's peers act as a fact-finding, deliberative body to determine guilt or innocence. It also provides defendants the right to confront witnesses against them.

Impartiality is a requirement of jury trials that has undergone significant change, with the method of selecting jurors being the most frequently challenged part of the process. Although potential individual jurors who have prejudged a case are not eligible to serve, no groups can be systematically excluded from serving. In 1880, for example, the Supreme Court ruled that African Americans could not be excluded from state jury pools (lists of those eligible to serve).[90] And, in 1975, the Court ruled that to bar women from jury service violated the mandate that juries be a "fair cross section" of the community.[91]

Sixth Amendment
Part of the Bill of Rights that sets out the basic requirements of procedural due process for federal courts to follow in criminal trials. These include speedy and public trials, impartial juries, trials in the state where crime was committed, notice of the charges, the right to confront and obtain favorable witnesses, and the right to counsel.

In 1986, the Court expanded the requirement that juries reflect a fair cross section of the community. Historically, lawyers had used peremptory challenges (those for which no cause needs to be given) to exclude African Americans from juries, especially when African Americans were criminal defendants. In *Batson* v. *Kentucky* (1986), the Court ruled that the use of peremptory challenges specifically to exclude African American jurors violated the equal protection clause of the Fourteenth Amendment.[92]

In 1994, the Supreme Court answered the major remaining unanswered question about jury selection: can lawyers exclude women from juries through their use of peremptory challenges? This question came up frequently because in rape trials and sex discrimination cases, one side or another often considers it advantageous to select jurors on the basis of their sex. The Supreme Court ruled that the equal protection clause prohibits discrimination in jury selection on the basis of gender. Thus, lawyers cannot strike all potential male jurors based on the belief that males might be more sympathetic to the arguments of a man charged in a paternity suit, a rape trial, or a domestic violence suit, for example.[93]

The right to confront witnesses at trial also is protected by the Sixth Amendment. In 1990, however, the Supreme Court ruled that this right was not absolute. In *Maryland* v. *Craig* (1990), the Court ruled that constitutionally the testimony of a six-year-old alleged child abuse victim via one-way closed circuit television was permissible. The clause's central purpose, said the Court, was to ensure the reliability of testimony by subjecting it to rigorous examination in an adversarial proceeding.[94]

THE EIGHTH AMENDMENT AND CRUEL AND UNUSUAL PUNISHMENT

Eighth Amendment
Part of the Bill of Rights that states: "Excessive bail shall not be required, nor excessive fines imposed, nor cruel and unusual punishments inflicted."

The **Eighth Amendment** prohibits "cruel and unusual punishments," a concept rooted in the English common-law tradition. Prior to the 1960s, however, little judicial attention was paid to the meaning of that phrase, especially in the context of the death penalty.

In the 1960s, the NAACP Legal Defense Fund (LDF), believing that the death penalty was applied more frequently to African Americans than to members of other groups, orchestrated a carefully designed legal attack on its constitutionality.[95] Public opinion polls revealed that in 1971, on the eve of the LDF's first major death sentence case to reach the Supreme Court, public support for the death penalty had fallen to below 50 percent. With the timing just right, in *Furman* v. *Georgia* (1972), the Supreme Court effectively put an end to capital punishment, at least in the short run.[96] The Court ruled that because the death penalty often was imposed in an arbitrary manner, it constituted cruel and unusual punishment in violation of the Eighth and Fourteenth Amendments.

Race and the Death Penalty

Following *Furman*, several state legislatures enacted new laws designed to meet the Court's objections to the arbitrary nature of the sentence. In 1976, in *Gregg* v. *Georgia*, Georgia's rewritten death penalty statute was ruled constitutional by the Supreme Court in a 7–2 decision.[97] Unless the perpetrator of a crime was a minor at the time of the crime or mentally retarded, the Supreme Court currently is unwilling to intervene to overrule state courts' imposition of the death penalty, even when it appears to discriminate against African Americans.

At the state level, a move to at least stay executions took on momentum in March 2000 when Governor George Ryan (R–IL) ordered a moratorium on all executions. Ryan, a death penalty proponent, became disturbed by new evidence collected as a class project by Northwestern University students. The students unearthed information that led to the release of thirteen men on the state's death row. The specter of allowing death sentences to continue in light of evidence showing so many men were wrongly convicted prompted Ryan's much publicized action. Soon thereafter, the Democratic governor of Maryland followed suit after receiving evidence that blacks were much more likely to be sentenced to death than whites; however, the Republican governor who succeeded him lifted the stay. Before leaving office in January 2003, Illinois Governor Ryan continued his anti–death penalty crusade by commuting the

Analyzing Visuals

U.S. EXECUTIONS BY YEAR, 1976–NOVEMBER 2006

The bar graph below shows the total number of executions in the United States since the Supreme Court ruled Georgia's rewritten death penalty statute constitutional in 1976. From 1976 through November 8, 2006, the United States executed 1,055 people accused of capital crimes, as defined by the various states. Looking at the data, how would you explain the very low numbers of executions from 1976 to 1983? Given what you know about the legal appeals process, can the significantly higher number of executions from 1992 to 2002 be explained? What factors may have contributed to the drop-off in the number of people executed over the past five years?

sentences of 167 death row inmates, giving them life in prison instead of death. Ryan also pardoned another four men who had given coerced confessions. This action constituted the single largest anti–death penalty action since the Court's decision in *Gregg,* and it spurred national conversation on the death penalty, which, in recent polls, has seen its lowest levels of support since 1978.

In another effort to verify that those on death row are not there wrongly, several states offer free DNA testing to death-row inmates. More than a hundred persons have been released from death row after DNA tests proved they did not commit the crimes for which they were convicted. In 2006, the Supreme Court recognized the potential exculpatory power of DNA evidence. In *House* v. *Bell,* the Court ruled a Tennessee death-row inmate who had exhausted other federal appeals was entitled to an exception to more stringent federal appeals rules due to DNA and related evidence suggesting his innocence.[98] The Court also revisited what can be considered cruel and unusual punishment in 2006. It unanimously ruled that death-row inmates could challenge the drugs and procedures involved in lethal injections.[99] (For information about the use of the death penalty, see Analyzing Visuals: U.S. Executions by Year, 1976–November 2006.)

The Living Constitution

The enumeration in the Constitution, of certain rights, shall not be construed to deny or disparage others retained by the people.

—NINTH AMENDMENT

This amendment reiterates the belief of many Federalists that it would be impossible to enumerate every fundamental liberty and right. To assuage the concerns of Anti-Federalists, the Ninth Amendment underscores that rights not enumerated are retained by the people. James Madison, in particular, feared that the enumeration of so many rights and liberties in the first eight amendments to the Constitution would result in the denial of rights that were not enumerated. So, he drafted this amendment to clarify a rule about how the Constitution and Bill of Rights were to be construed.

Until 1965, the Ninth Amendment was rarely mentioned by the Court. In that year, however, it was used for the first time by the Court as a positive affirmation of a particular liberty: marital privacy. Although privacy is not mentioned in the Constitution, it was—according to the Court—one of those fundamental freedoms that the drafters of the Bill of Rights implied as retained. Since 1965, the Court has ruled in favor of a host of fundamental liberties guaranteed by the Ninth Amendment, often in combination with other specific guarantees, including the right to have an abortion.

The Right to Privacy

TO THIS POINT, we have discussed rights and freedoms that have been derived fairly directly from specific guarantees contained in the Bill of Rights. However, the Supreme Court also has given protection to rights not enumerated specifically in the Constitution or Bill of Rights. (See The Living Constitution.)

Although the Constitution is silent about the **right to privacy,** the Bill of Rights contains many indications that the Framers expected that some areas of life were off limits to governmental regulation. As early as 1928, Justice Louis Brandeis hailed privacy as "the right to be left alone—the most comprehensive of rights and the right most valued by civilized men."[100] It was not until 1965, however, that the Court attempted to explain the origins of this right.

right to privacy
The right to be let alone; a judicially created doctrine encompassing an individual's decision to use birth control or secure an abortion.

BIRTH CONTROL

Today, most Americans take access to many forms of birth control as a matter of course. This was not always the case. *Griswold* v. *Connecticut* (1965) involved a challenge to the constitutionality of an 1879 Connecticut law prohibiting the dissemination of information about and/or the sale of contraceptives.[101] In *Griswold*, seven justices decided that various portions of the Bill of Rights, including the First, Third, Fourth, Ninth, and Fourteenth Amendments, cast what the Court called "penumbras" (unstated liberties on the fringes or in the shadow of more explicitly stated rights), thereby creating zones of privacy, including a married couple's right to plan a family. Thus, the Connecticut statute was ruled unconstitutional.

Later, the Court expanded the right of privacy to include the right of unmarried individuals to have access to contraceptives. "If the right of privacy means anything," wrote Justice William J. Brennan Jr., "it is the right of the individual, married or single, to be free from unwarranted governmental intrusion into matters so fundamentally affecting a person as the decision to bear or beget a child."[102] This right to privacy was to be the basis for later decisions from the Court, including the right to secure an abortion.

ABORTION

In 1973, the Supreme Court handed down one of its most controversial decisions, ***Roe v. Wade.*** Norma McCorvey, already a mother and an itinerant circus worker, was pregnant but unable to care for another child. Texas law allowed abortions only when they were necessary to save the life of the mother. Unable to secure a legal abortion and frightened by the conditions she found when she sought an illegal, back-alley abortion, McCorvey turned to two young Texas lawyers who were looking for a plaintiff to bring a lawsuit to challenge Texas's restrictive statute. Before a final legal decision could be reached, McCorvey gave birth and put the baby up for adoption. Nevertheless, she allowed her lawyers to proceed with the case using her as their plaintiff, under the pseudonym Jane Roe.

When the case finally came before the Supreme Court, Justice Harry A. Blackmun, a former lawyer at the Mayo Clinic, relied heavily on medical evidence to rule that the Texas law violated a woman's constitutionally guaranteed right to privacy, which he argued included her decision to terminate a pregnancy. Writing for the majority in *Roe v. Wade* (1973), Blackmun divided pregnancy into three stages. In the first trimester, a woman's right to privacy gave her an absolute right (in consultation with her physician), free from state interference, to terminate her pregnancy. In the second trimester, the state's interest in the health of the mother gave it the right to regulate abortions—but only to protect the woman's health. Only in the third trimester—when the fetus becomes potentially viable—did the Court find that the state's interest in potential life outweighed a woman's privacy interests. Even in the third trimester, however, abortions to save the life or health of the mother were to be legal.[103]

Roe v. *Wade* unleashed a torrent of political controversy. From the 1970s through the present, the right to an abortion and its constitutional underpinnings in the right to privacy have been under attack by well-organized pro-life groups. The administrations of Ronald Reagan and George Bush were strong advocates of the anti-abortion position, regularly urging the Court to overrule *Roe*. They came close to victory in *Webster* v. *Reproductive Health Services* (1989).[104] In *Webster*, the Court upheld state-required fetal viability tests in the second trimester, even though these tests would increase the cost of an abortion considerably. The Court also upheld Missouri's refusal to allow abortions to be performed in state-supported hospitals or by state-funded doctors or nurses. Perhaps most noteworthy, however, was that four justices seemed willing to overrule *Roe* v. *Wade* and that Justice Antonin Scalia publicly rebuked his colleague, Justice Sandra Day O'Connor, then the only woman on the Court, for failing to provide the critical fifth vote to overrule *Roe*.

Roe v. Wade (1973)
The Supreme Court found that a woman's right to an abortion was protected by the right to privacy that could be implied from specific guarantees found in the Bill of Rights applied to the states through the Fourteenth Amendment.

■ A once very popular anti-abortion group, Operation Rescue, staged large scale protests in front of abortion clinics across the nation gaining a surprising new member—Norma McCorvey, the "Jane Roe" of *Roe* v. *Wade* (1973). In 1995, she announced that she had become pro-life.

Photo courtesy: L.M. Otero/AP Wide World Photos

After *Webster,* states began to enact more restrictive legislation. In *Planned Parenthood of Southeastern Pennsylvania* v. *Casey* (1992), the most important abortion case since *Roe,* Justices O'Connor, Anthony Kennedy, and David Souter, in a jointly authored opinion, wrote that Pennsylvania could limit abortions so long as its regulations did not pose "an undue burden" on pregnant women.[105] The narrowly supported standard, by which the Court upheld a twenty-four-hour waiting period and parental consent requirements, did not overrule *Roe* but clearly limited its scope by abolishing its trimester approach and substituting the undue burden standard.

While President Bill Clinton was attempting to shore up abortion rights through the appointment of pro-choice judges, Republican Congresses made repeated attempts to ban—for the first time—a specific procedure used in late-term abortions.[106] Although Clinton vetoed the Partial Birth Abortion Act, many state legislatures passed their own versions. In 2000, the Supreme Court, however, ruled 5–4 in *Stenberg* v. *Carhart* that a Nebraska partial birth abortion statute was unconstitutionally vague and therefore unenforceable, calling into question the laws of twenty-nine other states with their own bans on late-term procedures.[107]

By October 2003, however, Republican control of the White House and both houses of Congress facilitated passage of the federal Partial Birth Abortion Ban Act. Pro-choice groups immediately filed lawsuits challenging the constitutionality of this law, which at this writing is awaiting a decision from the Supreme Court after oral arguments on November 8, 2006.

VIDEO DEBATE
Abortion

Also in 2003, the New Hampshire legislature enacted a law that made it illegal for physicians to perform an abortion on a woman under age eighteen unless her parents were notified in writing at least forty-eight hours before the procedure. The New Hampshire act was challenged immediately by Planned Parenthood of Northern New England. Eventually, the case was appealed to the U.S. Supreme Court. In a unanimous decision, the Court avoided the issue by sending the case back to the First Circuit, leaving questions unanswered until the Court ruled on the constitutionality of the federal Partial Birth Abortion Act.

HOMOSEXUALITY

It was not until 2003 that the U.S. Supreme Court ruled that an individual's constitutional right to privacy, which provided the basis for the *Griswold* (contraceptives) and *Roe* (abortion) decisions, prevented the state of Texas from criminalizing private sexual behavior. This monumental decision invalidated the laws of fourteen states.

In *Lawrence* v. *Texas* (2003), six members of the Court overruled its 1986 decision in *Bowers* v. *Hardwick*[108] and found that the Texas law was unconstitutional; five justices found it to violate fundamental privacy rights. Justice Sandra Day O'Connor agreed that the law was unconstitutional, but concluded that it was an equal protection violation. (See chapter 5 for a detailed discussion of the equal protection clause of the Fourteenth Amendment.) Although Justice Antonin Scalia issued a stinging dissent, charging that "the Court has largely signed on to the so-called homosexual agenda," the majority of the Court was unswayed.[109]

THE RIGHT TO DIE

In 1990, the Supreme Court ruled 5–4 that parents could not withdraw a feeding tube from their comatose daughter after her doctors testified that she could live for many more years if the tube remained in place. Writing for the majority, Chief Justice William H. Rehnquist rejected any attempts to expand the right of privacy into this thorny area of social policy. The Court did note, however, that individuals could terminate medical treatment if they were able to express, or had done so in writing via a living will, their desire to have medical treatment terminated in the event they became incompetent.[110]

Politics Now

THE RIGHT TO DIE?

In the late 1990s, assisted suicide was a hot-button issue. Politicians and the media focused on controversial Jack Kevorkian, a Michigan physician who was convicted of homicide for administering a lethal injection to a terminally ill patient. Following Kevorkian's 1999 conviction, the issue lost salience until a forty-one-year-old Florida woman thrust the right-to-die movement into the public eye once again in 2005.

Fifteen years earlier, Terri Schiavo had suffered cardiac-respiratory arrest, which left her comatose and incapacitated, although able to breathe on her own. Initially, her husband, Michael Schiavo, and her parents, Robert and Mary Schindler, worked together to pursue a variety of treatments and therapeutic options in an effort to restore Terri to her previous state. However, after about two years of experimental treatment and care that brought little improvement to Terri's mental and physical capabilities, her husband and parents began to turn against one another. The Schindlers wanted to continue as much therapy as possible, but Michael, Terri's court-appointed legal guardian, opposed such treatment, accepting the doctors' conclusion that she was in a persistent vegetative state from which she could never recover. In 1997, Michael hired a right-to-die attorney in an attempt to withdraw the feeding tube that kept his wife alive.

A series of trials and hearings in the Florida court system ensued. Most of these hearings, including one in October 2003, were decided in favor of Michael. But, following this ruling, a special session of the Florida legislature passed a law allowing Governor Jeb Bush to sign an order reinstating Terri's nutrition. Michael challenged the law as unconstitutional. The Florida Supreme Court agreed, and after the U.S. Supreme Court refused to hear an appeal of the case, Terri's feeding tube was removed for the final time on March 18, 2005. Through unprecedented congressional action that many commentators and a majority of the American public viewed as an unnecessary politicization of a very private issue, the Schindlers were able to argue their case again in federal court. Nevertheless, Terri died thirteen days later of dehydration. An autopsy supported the conclusion that she could never have recovered or improved.

The story of Terri's fight, which received almost nonstop coverage for several months on cable news, continues to live on through a reinvigorated "will to live" movement. At the forefront of this movement is the Terri Schindler Schiavo Foundation as well as the disabilities rights group Not Dead Yet.[a] Not Dead Yet, which was established following several of Dr. Kevorkian's initial assisted suicide cases and now has chapters in thirty states, has been an especially potent political force working to ensure full civil and medical rights for people with mental and physical disabilities. Members of Not Dead Yet argue that any action that jeopardizes the life of a disabled person, be it assisted suicide or violence against the disabled, violates the Americans with Disabilities Act and the Constitution's guarantee of equal protection of the law. (For more on equal protection and the civil rights of disabled Americans, see chapter 5.)

We live in an era of tremendous medical advancements that allow physicians to administer live-saving and life-preserving care to patients with severe illnesses and for a long amount of time. Questions about life and death have become more and more complicated. As one expert on these issues stated, "wonderful medical advances enable us to prolong the dying process. The first question is, Should we? And then come all the others: Who lives? Who dies? How do you decide? When do you decide? Who decides?"[b]

QUESTIONS

1. Are there any circumstances under which assisted suicide should be legal, or should the federal government prohibit assisted suicide in all cases as a way of ensuring the general welfare?
2. Do state legislatures and the U.S. Congress have the right to intervene in cases such as Schiavo? Explain your answer.

[a]See http://www.terrisfight.org and http://www.notdeadyet.org.

[b] Jeremy Pearce, "Ronald E. Cranford, 65, an Expert on Coma, Is Dead," *New York Times* (June 3, 2006): A14.

In 1997, the U.S. Supreme Court ruled unanimously that terminally ill persons do not have a constitutional right to physician assisted suicide. The Court's action upheld the laws of New York and Washington State that make it a crime for doctors to give life-ending drugs to mentally competent but terminally ill patients who wish to die.[111] But, Oregon enacted a right-to-die or assisted suicide law approved by Oregon voters that allows physicians to prescribe drugs to terminally ill patients. In November 2001, however, Attorney General John Ashcroft issued a legal opinion determining that assisted suicide is not "a legitimate medical purpose," thereby putting physicians who follow their state law in jeopardy of federal prosecution.[112] His memo also called for the revocation of the physicians' drug prescription licenses, putting the state and the national government in conflict in an area that Republicans historically have argued is the province of state authority. Oregon officials immediately (and successfully) sought a court order blocking Ashcroft's attempt to interfere with implementation of Oregon law.[113] Later, a federal judge ruled that Ashcroft had overstepped his authority on every point.[114] And, the U.S. Supreme Court agreed with the lower court on many points. In *Gonzales* v. *Oregon,* the new Attorney General, Alberto Gonzales, argued unsuccessfully that Oregon's Death with Dignity Act was a violation of the federal Controlled Substances Act of 1970 and that what was called the "Ashcroft Directive," was consistent with the public interest.[115] (See Politics Now: The Right to Die?)

Summary

MOST OF THE FRAMERS originally opposed the Bill of Rights. Anti-Federalists, however, continued to stress the need for a bill of rights during the drive for ratification of the Constitution, and some states tried to make their ratification contingent on the addition of a bill of rights. Thus, during its first session, Congress sent the first ten amendments to the Constitution, the Bill of Rights, to the states for their ratification. Later, the addition of the Fourteenth Amendment allowed the Supreme Court to apply some of the amendments to the states through a process called selective incorporation.

The First Amendment guarantees freedom of religion. The establishment clause, which prohibits the national government from establishing a religion, does not, according to Supreme Court interpretation, create an absolute wall between church and state. The Court largely has adopted an accommodationist approach when interpreting the free exercise clause by allowing some governmental regulation of religious practices.

Historically, one of the most volatile areas of constitutional interpretation has been in the interpretation of the First Amendment's mandate that "Congress shall make no law . . . abridging the freedom of speech or of the press." Some areas of speech and publication are unconditionally protected by the First Amendment. Among these are prior restraint, symbolic speech, and hate speech. Other areas of speech and publication, however, are unprotected by the First Amendment. These include libel, fighting words, and obscenity and pornography.

The freedoms of peaceable assembly and petition are directly related to the freedoms of speech and of the press. As with other First Amendment rights, the Supreme Court has often become the arbiter between the right of the people to express dissent and government's right to limit controversy in the name of security.

Initially, the right to keep and bear arms was envisioned as one dealing with state militias. Over the years, states and Congress have enacted various gun ownership restrictions, with little Supreme Court interpretation as a guide to their ultimate constitutionality.

The Fourth, Fifth, Sixth, and Eighth Amendments provide a variety of procedural guarantees to individuals accused of crimes. In particular, the Fourth Amendment prohibits unreasonable searches and seizures. The Fifth Amendment guarantees that "no person shall be compelled to be a witness against himself." The Sixth Amendment guarantees "assistance of counsel" and an impartial jury. The Eighth Amendment bans "cruel and unusual punishments."

The right to privacy is a judicially created right carved from the implications of the First, Third, Fourth, Ninth, and Fourteenth Amendments. Statutes limiting access to birth control and abortion rights and banning homosexual acts have been ruled unconstitutional violations of the right to privacy. The Court, however, appears poised to allow some states to legalize their citizens' right to die under a physician's supervision.

KEY TERMS

Bill of Rights, p. 109
civil liberties, p. 108
civil rights, p. 108
clear and present danger test, p. 116
direct incitement test, p. 116
double jeopardy, p. 126
due process clause, p. 109
due process rights, p. 122
Eighth Amendment, p. 128
establishment clause, p. 111
exclusionary rule, p. 126
Fifth Amendment, p. 124
fighting words, p. 119
First Amendment, p. 111
Fourth Amendment, p. 122
free exercise clause, p. 111
incorporation doctrine, p. 110
libel, p. 118

SELECTED READINGS

Abrams, Floyd. *Trials of the First Amendment.* New York: Viking, 2005.

Cole, David, and James X. Dempsey. *Terrorism and the Constitution: Sacrificing Civil Liberties in the Name of National Security,* 2nd ed. Washington, DC: First Amendment Foundation, 2002.

Etzoni, Amitai, and Jason H. Marsh, eds. *Rights vs. Public Safety after 9/11: America in the Age of Terrorism.* Lanham, MD: Rowman and Littlefield, 2003.

Fiss, Owen M. *The Irony of Free Speech,* reprint ed. Cambridge, MA: Harvard University Press, 1998.

Friendly, Fred W. *Minnesota Rag: Corruption, Yellow Journalism, and the Case that Saved Freedom of the Press,* reissue ed. Minneapolis: University of Minnesota Press, 2003.

Gates, Henry Louis, Jr., ed. *Speaking of Race, Speaking of Sex: Hate Speech, Civil Rights, and Civil Liberties.* New York: New York University Press, 1995.

Greenawalt, Kent. *Fighting Words: Individuals, Communities, and Liberties of Speech,* reprint ed. Princeton, NJ: Princeton University Press, 1995.

Ivers, Gregg, and Kevin T. McGuire, eds. *Creating Constitutional Change.* Charlottesville: University Press of Virginia, 2004.

Lewis, Anthony. *Gideon's Trumpet,* reissue ed. New York: Vintage Books, 1989.

———. *Make No Law: The Sullivan Case and the First Amendment,* reprint ed. New York: Random House, 1991.

O'Brien, David M. *Constitutional Law and Politics,* vol. 2: *Civil Rights and Civil Liberties,* 5th ed. New York: Norton, 2002.

———. *Animal Sacrifice and Religious Freedom:* Church of the Lukumi Babalu Age *v.* City of Hialeah. Lawrence: University Press of Kansas, 2004.

O'Connor, Karen. *No Neutral Ground: Abortion Politics in an Age of Absolutes.* Boulder, CO: Westview, 1996.

Regan, Priscilla M. *Legislating Privacy: Technology, Social Values, and Public Policy.* Chapel Hill: University of North Carolina Press, 1995.

Weddington, Sarah. *A Question of Choice,* reprint ed. New York: Grosset/Putnam, 1993.

WEB EXPLORATIONS

To view an original copy of the Bill of Rights, see
http://www.archives.gov/national_archives_experience/charters/bill_of_rights.html

For groups with opposing views on how the First Amendment should be interpreted, see
http://www.au.org and
http://www.pfaw.org and
http://www.aclj.org

For privacy issues, see
http://www.epic.org and
http://www.privacy.org

To compare the different sides of the abortion debate, go to
http://www.naral.org/
http://www.nrlc.org/

For more on gay rights and recent court cases, see
http://www.hrc.org/

To learn more about the right to die movement, see
http://www.hemlock.org/home.jsp

To learn more about the "will to live" movement, see
http://www.notdeadyet.org/

CIVIL RIGHTS

THE U.S. GOVERNMENT long has played an important role in enforcing civil rights in the nation. The passage of the Thirteenth, Fourteenth, and Fifteenth Amendments, for example, abolished slavery, guaranteed citizens equal protection of the laws, and granted the right to vote to newly free male slaves. Much later, after a prolonged civil rights movement sparked by years of discrimination against African Americans, particularly in the South, the U.S. Congress passed sweeping anti-discrimination legislation in the Civil Rights Act of 1964 and the Voting Rights Act of 1965. The Civil Rights Act, in particular, banned discrimination in employment, public accommodations, and education based on race, creed, color, religion, national origin, or sex. Over the years, Congress has added prohibitions based on pregnancy and disability to the act.

The Civil Rights Act and all federal statutes prohibiting discrimination are enforced by the Civil Rights Division of the Department of Justice. The division is headed by an assistant attorney general, a political appointee, who reports to the chief law enforcement official of the United States, the attorney general.

In 2006, the Civil Rights Division was in turmoil. Almost 20 percent of its lawyers, a record number, left in 2005 when many took advantage of a buy-out program that allowed them to retire early. Other career lawyers took positions elsewhere because they were upset by what they perceived as the politicization of the division. Many of the lawyers, all career civil servants, believed they were being pressured to leave because they "did not share the administration's conservative view on civil rights laws."[1] Veteran lawyers charged that the political appointees in the division made hiring and policy decisions without consulting staff members with more expertise.

Significant statistical support for these perceptions exists. Since President George W. Bush took office and appointed those who shared his beliefs to key division spots, prosecutions of race and sex discrimination have decreased by 40 percent. Many division lawyers found their workloads shifted to immigration and deportation cases.[2]

Voting Rights Act enforcement, too, has been politicized, according to many nonpolitical career lawyers in the division's voting rights section. According to former lawyers in the section, attorneys "who remain are barred

CHAPTER OUTLINE

- ✪ Slavery, Abolition, and Winning the Right to Vote, 1800–1890

- ✪ The Push for Equality, 1890–1954

- ✪ The Civil Rights Movement

- ✪ The Women's Rights Movement

- ✪ Other Groups Mobilize for Rights

- ✪ Continuing Controversies in Civil Rights

from offering recommendations in major voting rights cases."[3] And, when the section has involved itself in cases in Georgia, Mississippi, and Texas, it has supported actions that would favor the election of Republicans. With regard to the controversial Texas redistricting plan, for example, Attorney General Alberto Gonzales acknowledged in December 2005 that Department of Justice officials had overruled a unanimous finding by six lawyers and two analysts in the Civil Rights Division that aspects of the Texas plan would violate the Civil Rights Act of 1965.[4] In 2006, the U.S. Supreme Court ruled that states did not have to wait for a new census to redraw district lines, supporting the administration and Gonzales's position. But, the Court did find that a district that diluted the voting power of Hispanics violated the Voting Rights Act.[5]

VIDEO ROUNDTABLE

Equality

civil rights
Refers to the government-protected rights of individuals against arbitrary or discriminatory treatment by governments or individuals based on categories such as race, sex, national origin, age, religion, or sexual orientation.

THE DECLARATION OF INDEPENDENCE, written in 1776, boldly proclaims: "We hold these truths to be self-evident, that all men are created equal, that they are endowed by their Creator with certain unalienable rights." And, although the Framers considered some equality issues, one entire class of citizens—slaves—were treated in the new Constitution more as property than as people. Delegates to the Constitutional Convention put political expediency before the immorality of slavery. Moreover, the Constitution considered white women full citizens for purposes of determining state population, but voting qualifications were left to the states, and none allowed women to vote at the time the Constitution was ratified.

Since the Constitution was written, concepts of **civil rights,** the government-protected rights of individuals against arbitrary or discriminatory treatment by governments or individuals based on categories such as race, sex, national origin, age, religion, or sexual orientation, have changed dramatically. The addition of the Fourteenth Amendment, one of three Civil War Amendments ratified from 1865 to 1870, introduced the notion of equality into the Constitution by specifying that states could not deny "any person within its jurisdiction equal protection of the laws." Throughout history, the Fourteenth Amendment's equal protection guarantees have been the linchpin of efforts to expand upon the original intent of the amendment to allow its provisions to protect a variety of other groups from discrimination.

Since passage of the Civil War Amendments, there has been a fairly consistent pattern of the expansion of civil rights to more and more groups. In this chapter, we will first discuss slavery, abolition, and winning the right to vote, 1800–1890. We will then examine African Americans' and women's next push for equality, 1890–1954. These topics lead to an analysis of the civil rights movement and the Civil Rights Act of 1964. After discussing the development of a new women's rights movement, we will present the efforts of other groups to mobilize for rights. Finally, we will explore continuing controversies in civil rights.

Slavery, Abolition, and Winning the Right to Vote, 1800–1890

THE PERIOD FROM 1800 TO 1890 was one of tremendous change and upheaval in America. Despite the Civil War and the freeing of the slaves, the promise of equality guaranteed to African Americans by the Civil War Amendments failed to become a reality. Women's rights activists also began to make claims for equality, often using the arguments enunciated for the abolition of slavery, but they too fell far short of their goals.

SLAVERY AND CONGRESS

As the nation grew westward in the early 1800s, conflicts between northern and southern states intensified over the admission of new states to the union with free or slave status. The first major crisis occurred in 1820, when Missouri applied for admission to the union as a slave state—that is, one in which slavery would be legal. Missouri's admission would have weighted the Senate in favor of slavery and therefore was opposed by northern senators. To resolve this conflict, Congress passed the Missouri Compromise of 1820. The Compromise prohibited slavery north of the geographical boundary at 36 degrees latitude. This act allowed Missouri to be admitted to the union as a slave state, and to maintain the balance of slave and free states, Maine was carved out of a portion of Massachusetts.

THE FIRST CIVIL RIGHTS MOVEMENTS: ABOLITION AND WOMEN'S RIGHTS

The Missouri Compromise solidified the South in its determination to keep slavery legal, but it also fueled the fervor of those who opposed slavery. William Lloyd Garrison, a white New Englander, galvanized the abolitionist movement in the early 1830s. Garrison, a newspaper editor, founded the American Anti-Slavery Society in 1833; by 1838, it had more than 250,000 members.

Slavery was not the only practice that people began to question in the decades following the Missouri Compromise. In 1840, for example, Elizabeth Cady Stanton and Lucretia Mott, who were to found the first women's rights movement, attended the 1840 meeting of the World Anti-Slavery Society in London with their husbands. After their long journey, they were not allowed to participate in the convention because they were women. As they sat in the balcony, apart from the male delegates, they paused to compare their status to that of the slaves they sought to free. They concluded that women were not much better off than slaves, and they resolved to meet to address these issues.

The first meeting for women's rights was held in Seneca Falls, New York, in 1848. The 300 people who attended passed resolutions calling for the abolition of legal, economic, and social discrimination against women. All of the resolutions reflected the attendees' dissatisfaction with contemporary moral codes, divorce and criminal laws, and the limited opportunities for women in education, the church, medicine, law, and politics. Ironically, only the call for woman suffrage failed to win unanimous approval.

THE 1850S: THE CALM BEFORE THE STORM

By 1850, much was changing in America: the Gold Rush had spurred westward migration, cities grew as people were lured from their farms, railroads and the telegraph increased mobility and communication, and immigrants flooded into the United States. The woman's movement gained momentum, and slavery continued to tear the nation apart. Harriet Beecher Stowe's *Uncle Tom's Cabin*, a novel that depicted the evils of slavery, further inflamed the country. *Uncle Tom's Cabin* sold more than 300,000 copies in 1852.

The tremendous national reaction to Stowe's work, which later prompted President Abraham Lincoln to call Stowe "the little woman who started the big war," had not yet faded when a new controversy over the Missouri Compromise of 1820 became the lightning rod for the first major civil rights case to be addressed by the U.S. Supreme Court. As discussed in chapter 3, in *Dred Scott* v. *Sandford* (1857), the Court had ruled that the Missouri Compromise, which prohibited slavery north of a set geographical boundary, was unconstitutional. Furthermore, the Court went on to add that slaves were not U.S. citizens, and as a consequence, slaves could not bring suits in federal court.

THE CIVIL WAR AND ITS AFTERMATH: CIVIL RIGHTS LAWS AND CONSTITUTIONAL AMENDMENTS

The Civil War had many causes, but slavery was clearly a key issue. During the war (1861–1865), abolitionists continued to press for an end to slavery. They were

The Living Constitution

Neither slavery nor involuntary servitude, except as a punishment for crime whereof the party shall have been duly convicted, shall exist within the United States, or any place subject to their jurisdiction.

—THIRTEENTH AMENDMENT, SECTION 1

This amendment, the first of three Civil War Amendments, abolished slavery throughout the United States and its territories. It also prohibited involuntary servitude.

Based on his wartime authority, in 1863, President Abraham Lincoln issued the Emancipation Proclamation abolishing slavery in the states that were in rebellion against the United States. Because Congress was considered to lack the constitutional authority to abolish slavery, after one unsuccessful attempt to garner the two-thirds vote necessary, the proposed Thirteenth Amendment was forwarded to the states on February 1, 1865. With its adoption, said one of its sponsors, it relieved Congress "of sectional strifes." Initially, some doubted if any groups other than newly freed African slaves were protected by the provisions of the amendment. Soon, however, the Supreme Court went on to clarify this question by noting: "If Mexican peonage or the Chinese coolie labor system shall develop slavery of the Mexican or Chinese race within our territory, this amendment may safely be trusted to make it void."

In the early 1990s, the Supreme Court was called on several times to construe section 1 of the amendment, especially in regard to involuntary servitude. Thus, provisions of an Alabama law that called for criminal sanctions and jail time for defaulting sharecroppers were considered unconstitutional and Congress enacted a law banning this kind of involuntary servitude. More recently, however, the Court has found compulsory high school community service programs not to violate the ban on involuntary servitude. The Court and a host of lower federal and state courts, however, have upheld criminal convictions of those who, for example, psychologically coerced mentally retarded farm laborers into service or who lured foreign workers to the United States with promises of jobs and then forced them to work long hours at little or no pay. Human trafficking, in fact, has been targeted by the Bush administration as an especially onerous form of involuntary servitude. The U.S. Department of Justice has undertaken hundreds of investigations in an attempt to end this system.

rewarded when President Abraham Lincoln issued the Emancipation Proclamation, which provided that all slaves in states still in active rebellion against the United States would be freed automatically on January 1, 1863. Designed as a measure to gain favor for the war in the North, the Emancipation Proclamation did not free all slaves—it freed only those who lived in the Confederacy. Complete abolition of slavery did not occur until congressional passage and ultimate ratification of the Thirteenth Amendment in 1865. (See The Living Constitution.)

The **Thirteenth Amendment** was the first of the three Civil War Amendments. It banned all forms of "slavery [and] involuntary servitude." Although southern states were required to ratify the Thirteenth Amendment as a condition of their readmission to the union after the war, most of the former Confederate states quickly passed laws that were designed to restrict opportunities for newly freed slaves. These **Black Codes** prohibited African Americans from voting, sitting on juries, or even appearing in public places. Although Black Codes differed from state to state, all empowered local law-enforcement officials to arrest unemployed blacks, fine them for vagrancy, and hire them out to employers to satisfy their fines.

An outraged Congress enacted the Civil Rights Act of 1866 to invalidate some state Black Codes. President Andrew Johnson vetoed the legislation, but—for the first time in history—Congress overrode a presidential veto. The Civil Rights Act formally made African Americans citizens of the United States and gave the Congress and the federal courts the power to intervene when states attempted to restrict the citizenship rights of male African Americans in matters such as voting. Congress reasoned that African Americans were unlikely to fare well if they had to file discrimination complaints in state courts, where most judges were elected. Passage of a federal law allowed African Americans to challenge discriminatory state practices in the federal courts, where judges were appointed for life by the president.

Because controversy remained over the constitutionality of the act (since the Constitution gives states the right to determine qualifications of voters), the **Fourteenth Amendment** was proposed simultaneously with the Civil Rights Act to guarantee, among other things, citizenship to all freed slaves. Other key provisions of the Fourteenth Amendment barred states from abridging "the privileges or immunities of citizenship" or depriving "any person of life, liberty, or property without due process of law," or denying "any person within its jurisdiction the equal protection of the laws." Unlike the Thirteenth Amendment, which had near-unanimous support in the North, the Fourteenth Amendment was opposed by many women because it failed to guarantee suffrage for women. The **Fifteenth Amendment** was also passed by Congress in the aftermath of the Civil War. It guaranteed the "right of citizens" to vote regardless of their "race, color or previous condition of servitude." Sex was not mentioned.

Woman's rights activists were shocked. Abolitionists' continued support of the Fifteenth Amendment, which was ratified by the states in 1870, prompted many woman's rights supporters to leave the abolition movement and to work solely for the cause of women's rights. Twice burned, Susan B. Anthony and Elizabeth Cady Stanton decided to form their own group, the National Woman Suffrage Association (NWSA), to achieve that goal. (Another, more conservative group, the American Woman Suffrage Association, also was formed.) In spite of the NWSA's opposition, however, the Fifteenth Amendment was ratified by the states in 1870.

CIVIL RIGHTS, CONGRESS, AND THE SUPREME COURT

Congress was clear in its wishes that the rights of African Americans be expanded and that the Black Codes be rendered illegal. The Supreme Court, however, was not nearly so protective of those rights as it interpreted the Civil War Amendments. In the first two tests of the scope of the Fourteenth Amendment, the Supreme Court ruled that the citizenship rights guaranteed by the amendment applied only to rights of national citizenship and not to state citizenship.

Claims for expanded rights and requests for a clear definition of U.S. citizenship rights continued to fall on deaf ears in the halls of the Supreme Court. In 1875, for example, the Court ruled that a state's refusal to let a woman vote did not violate the privileges and immunities clause of the Fourteenth Amendment.[6] The justices ruled unanimously that voting was not a privilege of citizenship.

Thirteenth Amendment
One of the three Civil War Amendments; specifically bans slavery in the United States.

Black Codes
Laws denying most legal rights to newly freed slaves; passed by southern states following the Civil War.

Fourteenth Amendment
One of the three Civil War Amendments; guarantees equal protection and due process of the laws to all U.S. citizens.

Fifteenth Amendment
One of the three Civil War Amendments; specifically enfranchised newly freed male slaves.

Civil Rights Cases (1883)
Name attached to five cases brought under the Civil Rights Act of 1875. In 1883, the Supreme Court decided that discrimination in a variety of public accommodations, including theaters, hotels, and railroads, could not be prohibited by the act because such discrimination was private discrimination and not state discrimination.

poll tax
A tax levied in many southern states and localities that had to be paid before an eligible voter could cast a ballot.

grandfather clause
Voting qualification provision in many southern states that allowed only those whose grandfathers had voted before Reconstruction to vote unless they passed a wealth or literacy test.

In the same year, continued southern resistance to African American equality led Congress to pass the Civil Rights Act of 1875, designed to grant equal access to public accommodations. In 1883, however, a series of cases decided by the Supreme Court severely damaged the vitality of the 1875 act.

The *Civil Rights Cases* (1883) were five separate cases involving the convictions of private individuals found to have violated the Civil Rights Act by refusing to extend accommodations to African Americans in theaters, a hotel, and a railroad.[7] In deciding these cases, the Supreme Court ruled that Congress could prohibit only state or governmental action and not private acts of discrimination. The Court thus seriously limited the scope of the Civil Rights Act by concluding that Congress had no authority to prohibit private discrimination in public accommodations. Southern states viewed the Court's ruling as an invitation to gut the reach and intent of the Thirteenth, Fourteenth, and Fifteenth Amendments.

In devising ways to make certain that African Americans did not vote, Southerners had to avoid the intent of the Fifteenth Amendment. This amendment did not guarantee suffrage; it simply said that states could not deny anyone the right to vote on account of race or color. To exclude African Americans in a seemingly racially neutral way, southern states used three devices before the 1890s: (1) **poll taxes** (small taxes on the right to vote that often came due when poor African American sharecroppers had the least amount of money on hand); (2) some form of property-owning qualifications; and, (3) "literacy" or "understanding" tests, which allowed local voter registration officials to administer difficult reading-comprehension tests to potential voters.

To make certain that these laws did not further reduce the numbers of poor or uneducated white voters, many southern states added a **grandfather clause** to their voting qualification provisions, granting voting privileges to those who failed to pass a wealth or literacy test only if their grandfathers had voted before Reconstruction. Grandfather clauses effectively denied the descendents of slaves the right to vote.

While African Americans continued to face wide-ranging racism on all fronts, women also confronted discrimination. During this period, married women, by law, could not be recognized as legal entities. Women often were treated in the same category as juveniles and imbeciles, and in many states they were not entitled to wages, inheritances, or custody of their children.

The Struggle for Equal Protection

Plessy v. Ferguson (1896)
Plessy challenged a Louisiana statute requiring that railroads provide separate accommodations for blacks and whites. The Court found that separate but equal accommodations did not violate the equal protection clause of the Fourteenth Amendment.

The Push for Equality, 1890–1954

THE PROGRESSIVE ERA (1890–1920) was characterized by a concerted effort to reform political, economic, and social affairs. Prejudice against African Americans was just one target of progressive reform efforts. Distress over the inferior legal status of African Americans was aggravated by the U.S. Supreme Court's decision in *Plessy v. Ferguson* (1896).[8] In *Plessy*, the Court upheld the constitutionality of a Louisiana law mandating racial segregation on all public trains. The majority concluded that the Louisiana law was constitutional. The justices based their decision on their belief that separate facilities for blacks and whites provided equal protection of the laws. After all, they reasoned, African Americans were not prevented from riding the train; the Louisiana statute required only that the races travel separately. Justice John Marshall Harlan was the lone dissenter. He argued that "the Constitution is colorblind" and that it was senseless to hold constitutional a law "which, practically, puts the badge of servitude and degradation upon a large class of our fellow citizens."

The separate-but-equal doctrine enunciated in *Plessy v. Ferguson* soon came to mean only separate, as new legal avenues to discriminate against African Americans were enacted into law throughout the South. By 1900, equality for African Americans was far from the promise first offered by the Civil War Amendments. Again and again, the Supreme Court nullified the intent of the amendments and sanctioned racial segregation while the states avidly followed its lead.[9]

THE FOUNDING OF KEY GROUPS

By 1909, major race riots had occurred in several American cities, and progressive reformers were concerned about these outbreaks of violence and the possibility of others. Oswald Garrison Villard, the influential publisher of the *New York Evening Post*—and the grandson of William Lloyd Garrison—called a conference to discuss the problem. This group soon evolved into the National Association for the Advancement of Colored People (NAACP).

The NAACP was not the only new group. The struggle for women's rights was revitalized in 1890 by the merging of the National and American Woman Suffrage Associations into the National and American Woman Suffrage Association (NAWSA), devoted largely to securing woman suffrage. The **suffrage movement** was greatly facilitated by the proliferation of women's groups that emerged during the Progressive era. In addition to the rapidly growing temperance movement—the move to ban the sale of alcohol, which many women blamed for a variety of social ills—women's groups were created to seek protective legislation in the form of maximum hour or minimum wage laws for women and to work for improved sanitation, public morals, and education.

NAWSA based its claim to the right to vote largely on the fact that women, as mothers, should be enfranchised. Furthermore, although many members of the suffrage movement were NAACP members, the new women's movement—called the suffrage movement because of its focus on the vote alone and not on broader issues of women's rights—took on racist overtones. Suffragists argued that if undereducated African Americans could vote, why couldn't women?

Having roots in the Progressive movement gave the suffrage movement an exceptionally broad base that transformed NAWSA from a small organization of just over 10,000 members in the early 1890s to a true social movement of more than 2 million members in 1917. By 1920, a coalition of women's groups, led by NAWSA and the newer, more radical National Woman's Party, was able to secure ratification of the **Nineteenth Amendment** to the Constitution. It guaranteed all women the right to vote—fifty years after African American males were enfranchised by the Fifteenth Amendment.

After passage of the suffrage amendment in 1920, the fragile alliance of diverse women's groups that had come together to fight for the vote quickly disintegrated. Widespread organized activity on behalf of women's rights did not reemerge until the 1960s. In the meantime, however, the NAACP continued to fight racism and racial segregation. In fact, its activities and those of others in the civil rights movement would later give impetus to a new women's movement.

LITIGATING FOR EQUALITY

During the 1930s, leaders of the NAACP began to sense that the time was right to launch a full-scale challenge in the federal courts to the constitutionality of *Plessy*'s

suffrage movement
The drive for voting rights for women that took place in the United States from 1890 to 1920.

Nineteenth Amendment
Amendment to the Constitution that guaranteed women the right to vote.

■ W. E. B. DuBois (second from right in the second row, facing left) is pictured with the other original leaders of the Niagara Movement, an early civil rights group. This 1905 photo was taken on the Canadian side of Niagara Falls because no hotel on the U.S. side would accommodate the group's African American members. At the meeting, a list of injustices suffered by African Americans was detailed.

Photo courtesy: The New York Public Library/Art Resource, NY

■ Suffragists demonstrating in the early 1900s for the franchise. Parades like this one took place in cities all over the United States. Other women took more militant action. Women in the National Woman's Party were jailed for protesting at the White House. They faced deplorable conditions while incarcerated and were force-fed after going on hunger strikes in protest.

Photo courtesy: Library of Congress

separate-but-equal doctrine. The NAACP mapped out a long-range strategy that would first target segregation in professional and graduate education. In 1935, all southern states maintained fully segregated elementary and secondary schools. Colleges and universities also were segregated, but most states did not provide for postgraduate education for African Americans. NAACP lawyers chose to target law schools because they were institutions that judges could well understand, and integration there would prove less threatening to most whites.

Lloyd Gaines, a graduate of Missouri's all-black Lincoln University, sought admission to the all-white University of Missouri Law School in 1936. He was immediately rejected. In the separate-but-equal spirit, the state offered to build a law school at Lincoln (although no funds were allocated for the project) or, if he didn't want to wait, to pay his tuition at an out-of-state law school. Gaines rejected the offer, sued, lost in the lower courts, and appealed to the U.S. Supreme Court.

Gaines's case was filed at an auspicious time. As discussed in chapter 3, a constitutional revolution of sorts occurred in Supreme Court decision making in 1937. Before this time, the Court was most receptive to and interested in the protection of economic liberties. In 1937, however, the Court reversed itself in a series of cases and began to place individual freedoms and personal liberties on a more protected footing. Thus, in 1938, Gaines's lawyers pleaded his appeal to a far more sympathetic Supreme Court. NAACP attorneys argued that the creation of a separate law school of a lesser caliber than that of the University of Missouri would not and could not afford Gaines an equal education. The justices agreed and ruled that Missouri had failed to meet the separate-but-equal requirements of *Plessy*. The Court ordered Missouri either to admit Gaines to the school or to set up a law school for him.[10]

Recognizing the importance of the Court's ruling, in 1939 the NAACP created a separate, tax-exempt legal defense fund to devise a strategy that would build on the Missouri case and bring about equal educational opportunities for all African American children. The first head of the NAACP Legal Defense and Educational Fund, commonly referred to as the LDF, was Thurgood Marshall, who later became the first African American to serve on the U.S. Supreme Court. Sensing that the Court would be more amenable to the NAACP's broader goals if it were first forced to address a

American Values/American Voices

WHO IS ENTITLED TO VOTE?

Today, despite the significant progress that African Americans and other groups have made in securing civil rights, many voting rights advocates believe one growing group of disenfranchised individuals looms large: ex-felons. A question that goes to the heart of our criminal justice system and challenges American ideals of equality is this: once a felon is convicted, should his or her civil rights, especially the right to vote, be sacrificed?

As of 2006, the answer appears to be yes. All but two states (Maine and Vermont) prohibit incarcerated felons from voting and thirty-six states prohibit felons from voting while they are on probation. Three states deny the vote to all ex-felons who have completed their sentences, and nine other states disenfranchise some categories of ex-offenders or allow convicted felons to apply for restoration of their voting rights only after they have served their sentence and have waited a specified number of years. According to Human Rights Watch and The Sentencing Project, nearly 5 million American citizens are prevented from voting because of these state laws. Moreover, because a disproportionate percentage of ex-felons are African American males, many consider these voting prohibitions to be a form of government-sanctioned discrimination. In fact, one study estimates that nearly 15 percent of African American men cannot vote because of limitations on felons' voting rights.[a]

This issue is a concern not only to human rights groups but also to Democrats, who believe that many convicted felons would be more likely to vote Democratic. Some Republicans agree. According to Alabama Republican Party Chair Marty Connors, "As frank as I can be, we're opposed to [restoring voting rights] because felons don't tend to vote Republican." One study found that George W. Bush would have lost Florida, and therefore the presidential election in 2000, by 80,000 votes if ex-felons there had been allowed to vote.[b]

The Fourteenth Amendment, the locus of most civil rights laws, specifically allows states to deny voting rights to persons guilty of "participation in rebellion or other crimes." Supporters of voting rights for ex-felons argue that despite this constitutional authority, laws disenfranchising those who have paid their debt to society run counter to notions of equity in American society.

QUESTIONS

1. If a basic American value has been the continual expansion of voting rights, on what basis can those rights be denied to felons who have served their time? Is voting a civil right or a privilege?
2. In many states, jury service is linked to voting rights. Should convicted felons be allowed to serve on juries?

[a]Bryan Knowles, "Should Convicted Felons Have Voting Rights?" Speakout.com, June 9, 2000.

[b]Kevin Krajick, "Why Can't Ex-Felons Vote?" Washington Post (August 18, 2004): A19.

---

variety of less threatening claims to educational opportunity, Marshall and the LDF brought a series of carefully crafted test cases to the Court.

The first case involved H. M. Sweatt, a forty-six-year-old African American mail carrier, who applied for admission to the all-white University of Texas Law School in 1946. Rejected on racial grounds, Sweatt sued. The judge gave the state six months to establish a law school or to admit Sweatt to the university. The state legislature saw the handwriting on the wall and authorized $3 million for the creation of the Texas State University for Negroes. One hundred thousand dollars of that money was to be for a new law school in Austin across the street from the state capitol building. It consisted of three small basement rooms, a library of 10,000 books, access to the state law library, and three part-time first-year instructors as the faculty. Sweatt declined the opportunity to obtain an education there and instead chose to continue his legal challenge.

Eventually, the U.S. Supreme Court handled this case together with another LDF case involving graduate education.[11] The eleven southern states field an *amicus curiae* (friend of the court) brief, in which they argued that *Plessy* should govern both cases. In a dramatic departure from the past, however, the administration of President Harry S Truman filed a friend of the court brief urging the Court to overrule *Plessy*. Although the Court did not overrule *Plessy*, the justices found that the measures taken by the states in each case failed to live up to the strictures of the separate-but-equal doctrine. The Court unanimously ruled that the remedies to each situation were inadequate to afford a sound education.

Photo courtesy: BBettmann/Corbis

■ Here George McLaurin, a retired university professor and the plaintiff in one of the LDF's challenges to "separate but equal doctrine" is shown outside of the classroom. This was the university's response when a federal district court ordered his admission into the University of Oklahoma's doctoral program.

Brown v. Board of Education (1954)
U.S. Supreme Court decision holding that school segregation is inherently unconstitutional because it violates the Fourteenth Amendment's guarantee of equal protection; marked the end of legal segregation in the United States.

equal protection clause
Section of the Fourteenth Amendment that guarantees that all citizens receive "equal protection of the laws."

In 1950, after these decisions were handed down, the LDF concluded that the time had come to launch a full-scale attack on the separate-but-equal doctrine. The decisions of the Court were encouraging, and the position of the U.S. government and the population in general appeared to be more receptive to an outright overruling of *Plessy*.

The challenge came in the form of **Brown v. Board of Education (1954),** four cases involving public elementary or high school systems that mandated separate schools for blacks and whites.[12] In *Brown*, LDF lawyers, again led by Thurgood Marshall, argued that *Plessy*'s separate-but-equal doctrine was unconstitutional under the **equal protection clause** of the Fourteenth Amendment, and that if the Court was still reluctant to overrule *Plessy*, the only way to equalize the schools was to integrate them. A major component of the LDF's strategy was to prove that the intellectual, psychological, and financial damage to African Americans resulting from segregation precluded any court from finding that equality was served by the separate-but-equal policy.

On May 17, 1954, Chief Justice Earl Warren delivered the fourth opinion of the day, *Brown* v. *Board of Education*. Writing for the Court, Warren stated:

> To separate [some school children] from others . . . solely because of their race generates a feeling of inferiority as to their status in the community that may affect their hearts and minds in a way very unlikely ever to be undone. We conclude, unanimously, that in the field of public education the doctrine of "separate but equal" has no place.

Brown was the most important civil rights case decided in the twentieth century.[13] It immediately evoked an uproar that shook the nation. Some segregationists called the day the decision was handed down Black Monday. The governor of South Carolina denounced the decision, saying, "Ending segregation would mark the beginning of the end of civilization in the South as we know it."[14]

The Civil Rights Movement

VIDEO ROUNDTABLE

The Civil Rights Movement

BROWN SERVED AS A CATALYST for change, sparking the development of the modern civil rights movement. Women's work in that movement and the student protest movement that arose in reaction to the U.S. government's involvement in Vietnam gave women the experience needed to form their own organizations to press for full equality. As African Americans and women became more and more successful, they served as models for other groups who sought equality—Hispanic Americans, Native Americans, homosexuals, the disabled, and others.

SCHOOL DESEGREGATION AFTER *BROWN*

One year after *Brown*, in a case referred to as *Brown* v. *Board of Education II* (1955), the Court ruled that racially segregated systems must be dismantled "with all deliberate speed."[15] Many politicians in the South entered into a near conspiracy to avoid the mandates of *Brown II*. In Arkansas, for example, Governor Orval Faubus, who was facing a reelection bid, announced that he would not "be a party to any attempt to force acceptance of change to which people are overwhelmingly opposed."[16] The day before school was to begin, he announced that National Guardsmen would surround Little Rock's Central High School to prevent African American students from entering. While the federal courts in Arkansas continued to order the admission of African American children, the governor remained adamant. Finally, President Dwight D. Eisenhower sent federal troops to Little Rock to protect the rights of the nine students attending Central High.

In reaction to the governor's outrageous conduct, the Court broke with tradition and issued a unanimous decision in *Cooper* v. *Aaron* (1958), which was filed by the Little Rock School Board asking the federal district court for a two-and-one-half-year delay in implementation of its desegregation plans. Each justice signed the opinion individually, underscoring his individual support for the notion that "no state legislator or executive or judicial officer can war against the Constitution without violating his undertaking to support it."[17] The state's actions thus were ruled unconstitutional and its "evasive schemes" illegal. (For a current look at education equality, see Join the Debate: *Brown* v. *Board of Education* After Fifty Plus Years.)

A NEW MOVE FOR AFRICAN AMERICAN RIGHTS

In 1955, soon after *Brown II*, the civil rights movement took another step forward—this time in Montgomery, Alabama. Rosa Parks, the local NAACP's Youth Council adviser, decided to challenge the constitutionality of the segregated bus system. First, Parks and other NAACP officials began to raise money for litigation and made speeches around town to garner public support. Then, on December 1, 1955, Rosa Parks made history when she refused to leave her seat on a bus to move to the back to make room for a white male passenger. She was arrested for violating an Alabama law banning integration of public facilities, including buses. After she was freed on bond, Parks and the NAACP decided to enlist city clergy to help her cause. At the same time, they distributed 35,000 handbills calling for African Americans to boycott the Montgomery bus system.

The boycott was led by a twenty-six-year-old minister, Reverend Martin Luther King Jr. As it dragged on, Montgomery officials and local business owners began to harass the city's African American citizens. The residents held out, despite suffering personal hardship for their actions, ranging from harassment to bankruptcy to job loss. In 1956, a federal court ruled that the segregated bus system violated the equal protection clause of the Fourteenth Amendment. After a year of walking, black Montgomery residents ended their protest when city buses were ordered to integrate. The first effort at nonviolent protest had been successful. Organized boycotts and other forms of nonviolent protest, including sit-ins at segregated restaurants and bus stations, were to follow.

FORMATION OF NEW GROUPS

The recognition and respect that Reverend Martin Luther King Jr. earned within the African American community helped him to launch the Southern Christian Leadership

■ Noted civil rights leader Rosa Parks died in 2005, leaving many editorial cartoonists with the occasion to comment on her historical significance.

THE ARREST THAT CHANGED AMERICA

Rosa Parks 1913 ~ 2005

Photo courtesy: Roger Harvell/Editorial Cartoonists

Join the Debate

BROWN V. BOARD OF EDUCATION AFTER FIFTY PLUS YEARS

OVERVIEW: It is difficult to overstate the impact of the Supreme Court decision in *Brown* v. *Board of Education* (1954) on American life. The *Brown* decision was instrumental in making civil rights the highest priority on the domestic policy agenda during the 1950s and 1960s, and it held out the promise of educational equality for all Americans. The Court in *Brown* held "education is perhaps the most important function of state and local governments," and that "In these days, it is doubtful . . . any child may reasonably be expected to succeed in life if he is denied the opportunity of an education"—which the Court believed is a right that "must be made available to all on equal terms." For American society to attain justice, the Court understood segregation had to end and that equal educational opportunity is the key through which all Americans are given the tools to survive and thrive in contemporary society.

After over five decades, the results of the *Brown* decision have been mixed. The objective of *Brown* was to create equal educational opportunity; however, there is no constitutional mandate for such a prospect. The Constitution does not speak to education, so that right is given to the states to determine, and it follows that with vast discrepancies in wealth and resources between the states, educational establishments will be unequal as well. This problem is exacerbated when fewer funds are allocated to substandard school districts with significant minority populations. Additionally, many members of the predominately white middle class have been abandoning inner cities, leaving poorer, minority populations in underfunded school districts, thus engendering *de facto* segregation. The disparities in education reflect disparities in housing patterns, a problem which is outside the authority of school administrators. Segregation is seen even in integrated schools when a disproportionate number of white and Asian Americans are found in advanced placement classes and a disproportionate number of African American and Hispanic Americans are found in remedial and special-needs classes.

A principal effect of *Brown* was to highlight the disparity between the education of majority and minority America. Fifty years later, however, it seems educational segregation may still be the rule rather than the exception. What is the best way to ensure equal educational opportunity for all Americans? Does a diverse classroom necessarily mean a quality education for all? If so, what is the best way to achieve this standard, and if not, what other policy alternatives are available? The 2000 National Assessment of Education Progress (NAEP) shows vast disparities in educational achievement between white and black America. Is segregation the problem, or are there other significant factors as well? What is the best way to ensure a level playing field in the education policy domain?

ARGUMENTS FOR THE EFFECTIVENESS OF *BROWN*

- *Brown* **has reframed the way Americans view educational integration.** The Court held in *Brown* that education is "necessary for good citizenship" and the only way to make American society more just is to provide all citizens the opportunity for a quality education in order for all to realize their ideal of the American Dream. Americans now understand that an equal education for all is necessary to improve the lives of individuals and to realize fundamental American political principles.

Conference (SCLC) in 1957, soon after the end of the Montgomery bus boycott. Unlike the NAACP, which had northern origins and had come to rely largely on litigation as a means of achieving expanded equality, the SCLC had a southern base and was rooted more closely in black religious culture. The SCLC's philosophy reflected King's growing belief in the importance of nonviolent protest and civil disobedience.

Eventually, the SCLC and the Student Non-violent Coordinating Committee (SNCC), largely made up of activist college students, dominated the new civil rights movement.

While the SCLC generally worked with church leaders in a community, SNCC was much more of a grassroots organization. Always perceived as more radical than the SCLC, SNCC tended to focus its organizing activities on the young, both black and white.

- *Brown* **signaled the end of racial segregation and helped usher in the civil rights movement.** *Brown* was instrumental in creating the social context for the Civil Rights Acts of 1957, 1960, and 1964 and the Voting Rights Act of 1965. Though there is work yet to be done, the sum total of this legislation was to help further and partially realize the goals of social equality and equality before the law.
- *Brown* **set the model for other social justice movements in the United States.** The legal approach by NAACP LDF lawyers has set the standard for other groups pursuing legal and social equality and inclusion. Supporters of women's rights, Hispanic and Native American rights, gay rights, and rights of the disabled rights may be said to owe a debt of gratitude to the constitutional interpretation and legal strategies offered by the legal team that argued for *Brown* and the U.S. Supreme Court.

ARGUMENTS AGAINST THE EFFECTIVENESS OF *BROWN*

- **Fifty years later, there are still vast disparities in educational attainment between minority and white students.** According to the NAEP, 63 percent of black, inner-city fourth-graders are unable to attain basic proficiency in reading. And, according to African American educator Walter Williams, the average black high school graduate has achieved the educational equivalent of a seventh- or eighth-grade mastery of basic subjects and is thus ill prepared to enter the job market or a university.
- **The goal of *Brown* has yet to be fully realized; instead of educational and social integration, segregation between the races is still a significant problem.** In 2004, approximately 70 percent of African American children

attend public schools where greater than 50 percent of the student population is black—in Washington, D.C., the student population is 85 percent black. One effect of the *Brown* decision is "white flight"—the movement of the white middle class out of the inner cities to the suburbs and surrounding countries.

- **The *Brown* decision does not address other problems that affect educational attainment.** *Brown* does not address other factors understood to affect social and educational achievement. For example, *Brown* does not address issues such as the effect of high rates of illegitimacy in black communities on educational attainment. In a controversial speech to the NAACP, comedian Bill Cosby took black parents to task for not tending to the education of their children; after all, it is not funding or segregation keeping children from spending time doing their homework, from skipping school, and from reading.

QUESTIONS

1. Is integration in educational institutions the solution for academic achievement, or are there other, more significant solutions to help close the learning gap?
2. Will an attempt to realize educational equality across the states violate states' rights and the principle of federalism? What is the best way to ensure this equality?

SELECTED READINGS

Cottrol, Robert, et al. Brown v. Board of Education: *Caste, Culture and the Constitution.* Lawrence: University Press of Kansas, 2003.

Ogletree, Charles J. *All Deliberate Speed: Reflections on the First Half-Century of* Brown v. Board of Education. New York: Norton, 2004.

In addition to joining the sit-in bandwagon, SNCC also came to lead what were called freedom rides, designed to focus attention on segregated public accommodations. Bands of college students and other civil rights activists traveled by bus throughout the South in an effort to force bus stations to desegregate.

While SNCC continued to sponsor sit-ins and freedom rides, in 1963 the Reverend Martin Luther King Jr. launched a series of massive nonviolent demonstrations in Birmingham, Alabama, a major stronghold of segregation. Thousands of blacks and whites marched to Birmingham in a show of solidarity. Peaceful marchers were met there by the Birmingham police commissioner, who ordered his officers to use dogs, clubs, and fire hoses on the marchers. Americans across the nation were horrified as they witnessed on television the brutality and abuse heaped on the protesters. As the marchers hoped, shocking scenes such as the one shown in Analyzing Visuals: Police

Analyzing Visuals

POLICE CONFRONT CIVIL RIGHTS DEMONSTRATORS IN BIRMINGHAM

Civil rights demonstrators in the 1960s sought national attention for their cause, and photos in the print media were a powerful tool in swaying public opinion. In the May 1963 photograph by Charles Moore reprinted here, dogs controlled by police officers in Birmingham, Alabama, attack civil rights demonstrators. This photograph first appeared in the May 17, 1963, issue of the very popular *Life* magazine as part of an eleven-page spread of Moore's photographs of the demonstration in Birmingham. The photo was reprinted often and even frequently mentioned on the floor of Congress during debates on the Civil Rights Act of 1964. After examining the photograph, answer the following critical thinking questions: What do you observe about the scene and the various people shown in the photograph? What do you notice about the man who is being attacked by the dogs? The other demonstrators? The police? What emotions does the picture evoke? Why do you think this image was an effective tool in the struggle for civil rights?

Photo Courtesy: Charles Moore/Black Star/Stock Photo

Confront Civil Rights Demonstrators in Birmingham, helped convince President John F. Kennedy to propose important civil rights legislation.

THE CIVIL RIGHTS ACT OF 1964

Both the SCLC and SNCC sought full implementation of Supreme Court decisions dealing with race and an end to racial segregation and discrimination. The cumulative effect of collective actions including sit-ins, boycotts, marches, and freedom rides—as well as the tragic bombings and deaths inflicted in retaliation—led Congress to pass the first major piece of civil rights legislation since the post–Civil War era, the Civil Rights Act of 1964, followed the next year by the Voting Rights Act. Several events led to the consideration of this legislation.

In 1963, President John F. Kennedy requested that Congress pass a law banning discrimination in public accommodations. Seizing the moment, the Reverend Martin Luther King Jr. called for a monumental march on Washington, D.C., to demonstrate widespread support for far-ranging anti-discrimination legislation. It was clear that national laws outlawing discrimination were the only answer: southern legislators would never vote to repeal discriminatory laws. The March on Washington for Jobs and Freedom was held in August 1963, only a few months after the Birmingham demonstrations. More than 250,000 people heard King deliver his famous "I Have a Dream" speech from the Lincoln Memorial. Before Congress had the opportunity to vote on any legislation, however, John F. Kennedy was assassinated on November 22, 1963.

When Vice President Lyndon B. Johnson, a southern-born, former Senate majority leader, succeeded Kennedy as president, he put civil rights reform at the top of his legislative priority list, and civil rights activists gained a critical ally. Thus, through the 1960s, the movement subtly changed in focus from peaceful protest and litigation to legislative lobbying. Its focus broadened from integration of school and public fa-cilities and voting rights to issues of housing, jobs, and equal opportunity.

In spite of strong presidential support and the sway of public opinion, the Civil Rights Act of 1964 did not sail through Congress. Southern senators, led by South Carolina's Strom Thurmond, a Democrat who later switched to the Republican Party, conducted the longest filibuster in the history of the Senate. For eight weeks, Thur-mond led the effort to hold up voting on the civil rights bill until cloture (see chapter 6) was invoked and the filibuster ended. Once passed, the **Civil Rights Act of 1964:**

- Outlawed arbitrary discrimination in voter registration and expedited voting rights lawsuits.
- Barred discrimination in public accommodations engaged in interstate commerce.
- Authorized the Department of Justice to initiate lawsuits to desegregate public facilities and schools.
- Provided for the withholding of federal funds from discriminatory state and local programs.
- Prohibited discrimination in employment on grounds of race, color, religion, na-tional origin, or sex.
- Created the Equal Employment Opportunity Commission (EEOC) to monitor and enforce the bans on employment discrimination.

As challenges were made to the Civil Rights Act of 1964, other changes contin-ued to sweep the United States. African Americans in the North, who believed that their brothers and sisters in the South were making progress against discrimination, found themselves frustrated. Northern blacks were experiencing high unemployment, poverty, discrimination, and little political clout. Some, including Black Muslim leader Malcolm X, even argued that, to survive, African Americans must separate themselves from white culture in every way. These increased tensions resulted in riots in many major cities from 1964 to 1968, when many African Americans in the North took to the streets, burning and looting to vent their rage. The assassination of the Reverend Martin Luther King Jr. in 1968 triggered a new epidemic of race riots.

Civil Rights Act of 1964
Legislation passed by Congress to outlaw segregation in public facilities and racial discrimination (among other types of decison-making) in employment, education, and voting; created the Equal Employment Op-portunity Commission.

The Women's Rights Movement

JUST AS IN THE ABOLITION MOVEMENT IN THE 1800S, women from all walks of life participated in the civil rights movement. Women were important members of new groups such as SNCC and the SCLC as well as more traditional groups such as the NAACP, yet they often found themselves treated as second-class citizens. At one point during a SNCC national meeting, its chair openly proclaimed: "The only posi-tion for women in the SNCC is prone."[18] Statements and attitudes like these led some women to found early women's liberation groups that generally were quite radical but small in membership. Others founded more traditional groups such as the National Organization for Women (NOW). Groups such as NOW sought improved rights for women through lobbying for specific laws or a constitutional amendment to guaran-tee women equal rights; others, following the model of the NAACP LDF, turned to the courts.

Comparing Civil Rights

LITIGATION FOR EQUAL RIGHTS

The paternalistic attitudes of the Supreme Court, and perhaps society as well, contin-ued well into the 1970s. Said one U.S. Supreme Court justice in 1971, "Despite the enlightened emancipation of women from the restrictions and protections of bygone years, and their entry into many parts of community life formerly considered to be reserved to men, a woman is still regarded as the center of home and family life."[19]

These kinds of attitudes were in sufficient to forge a new movement for women's rights. However, three events occurred to move women to action. In 1961, soon after his election, President John F. Kennedy created the President's Commission on the Status of Women. The commission's report, *American Women,* released in 1963, documented pervasive discrimination against women in all walks of life. In addition, the civil rights movement and the publication of Betty Friedan's *The Feminine Mystique* (1963) led some women to question their lives and status in society. The passage of the Equal Pay Act in 1963 (which guaranteed women equal pay for equal work) and the Civil Rights Act of 1964, which barred discrimination in employment based on sex as well as race (and other factors), motivated women to demand workplace equity.

In 1966, after the **Equal Employment Opportunity Commission** failed to enforce the law as it applied to sex discrimination, female activists formed the National Organization for Women (NOW). NOW was modeled closely on the NAACP. Its founders sought to work within the system to prevent discrimination. Initially, most of this activity was geared toward two goals: (1) achievement of equality either by passage of an equal rights amendment to the Constitution, or (2) by judicial decision.

Not all women agreed with the notion of full equality for women. Nevertheless, from 1923 to 1972, a proposal for an equal rights amendment was made in every session of every Congress. Every president since Harry S Truman backed it. By 1972, public opinion favored its ratification, and in response to pressure from NOW, the National Women's Political Caucus, and a wide variety of other feminist groups, Congress voted in favor of the **Equal Rights Amendment** (ERA) by overwhelming majorities (84–8 in the Senate; 354–24 in the House). The amendment provided that:

> Equality of rights under the law shall not be denied or abridged by the United States or by any state on account of sex.
>
> The Congress shall have the power to enforce, by appropriate legislation, the provisions of this article.

Within a year, twenty-two states ratified the amendment, most by overwhelming margins. But, the tide soon turned. In 1974 and 1975, the amendment only squeaked through the Montana and North Dakota legislatures, and two states—Nebraska and Tennessee—voted to rescind their earlier ratifications.

By 1978, one year before the deadline for ratification was to expire, thirty-five states had voted for the amendment—three short of the three-fourths necessary for ratification. Efforts in key states such as Illinois and Florida failed as opposition to the ERA intensified. Faced with the prospect of defeat, ERA supporters heavily lobbied Congress to extend the deadline for ratification. Congress extended the ratification period by three years, but to no avail. No additional states ratified the amendment and three more rescinded their votes.

What began as a simple correction to the Constitution turned into a highly controversial proposed change. Even though large numbers of the public favored the ERA, opponents needed to stall ratification in only thirteen states while supporters had to convince legislators in thirty-eight. The success that women's rights activists were having in the courts was hurting the effort. When women first sought the ERA in the late 1960s, the Supreme Court had yet to rule that women were protected by the Fourteenth Amendment's equal protection clause from any kind of discrimination, thus clearly showing the need for an amendment. But, as the Court widened its interpretation of the Constitution to protect women from discrimination, in the eyes of many, the need for a new amendment became less urgent. The proposed amendment died without being ratified on June 30, 1982, but continues to be introduced in each session of Congress.

Equal Employment Opportunity Commission
Federal agency created to enforce the Civil Rights Act of 1964, which forbids discrimination on the basis of race, creed, national origin, religion, or sex in hiring, promotion, or firing.

Equal Rights Amendment
Proposed amendment that would bar discrimination against women by federal or state governments.

THE EQUAL PROTECTION CLAUSE AND CONSTITUTIONAL STANDARDS OF REVIEW

The Fourteenth Amendment protects all U.S. citizens from state action that violates equal protection of the laws. Most laws, however, are subject to what is called the rational basis or minimum rationality test. This lowest level of scrutiny means that governments must allege a rational foundation for any distinctions they make. As early as 1937, the Supreme Court recognized that certain freedoms were so fundamental that a very heavy burden would be placed on any government that sought to restrict those rights. When fundamental freedoms such as those guaranteed by the First Amendment or **suspect classifications** such as race are involved, the Court uses a heightened standard of review called **strict scrutiny** to determine the constitutional validity of the challenged practices, as detailed in Table 5.1.

In legal terms, this means that if a statute or governmental practice makes a classification based on race, the statute is presumed to be unconstitutional unless the state can prove the law in question is necessary to accomplish a permissible goal and that it is the least restrictive means through which that goal can be accomplished.

During the 1960s and into the 1970s, the Court routinely struck down as unconstitutional practices and statutes that discriminated on the basis of race. "Whites-only" public parks and recreational facilities, tax-exempt status for private schools that discriminated, and statutes prohibiting racial intermarriage were declared unconstitutional. In contrast, the Court refused even to consider the fact that the equal protection clause might apply to discrimination against women.

Finally, in *Reed* v. *Reed* (1971), a case argued by Ruth Bader Ginsburg (now an associate justice of the Supreme Court) as director of the Women's Rights Project of the ACLU, the Supreme Court ruled that an Idaho law granting a male parent automatic preference over a female parent as the administrator of their deceased child's estate violated the equal protection clause of the Fourteenth Amendment. Although the Court did not rule that sex was a suspect classification, it concluded that the equal protection clause of the Fourteenth Amendment prohibited unreasonable classifications based on sex.[20] In *Craig* v. *Boren* (1976), the Court carved out a new test to be used in examining claims of sex discrimination: "to withstand constitutional challenge, . . . classifications by gender must serve important governmental objectives and must be substantially related to achievement of those objectives."[21]

suspect classification
Category or class, such as race, that triggers the highest standard of scrutiny from the Supreme Court.

strict scrutiny
A heightened standard of review used by the Supreme Court to determine the constitutional validity of a challenged practice.

VIDEO ROUNDTABLE

Suspect Classifications and Gay Marriage

TABLE 5.1	THE EQUAL PROTECTION CLAUSE AND STANDARDS OF REVIEW USED BY THE SUPREME COURT TO DETERMINE WHETHER IT HAS BEEN VIOLATED			
Type of Classification (What kind of statutory classification is at issue?)	Standard of Review (What standard of review will be used?)	Test (What does the Court ask?)	Example (How does the Court apply the test?)
Fundamental freedoms (including religion, assembly, press, and privacy). Suspect classifications (including race, alienage, and national origin)	Strict scrutiny or heightened standard	Is classification necessary to the accomplishment of a permissible state goal? Is it the least restrictive way to reach that goal?	*Brown* v. *Board of Education* (1954): Racial segregation is not necessary to accomplish the state goal of educating its students.
Gender	Intermediate standard	Does the classification serve an important governmental objective, and is it substantially related to those ends?	*Craig* v. *Boren* (1976): Keeping drunk drivers off the roads may be an important governmental objective, but allowing eighteen- to twenty-one-year-old women to drink alcoholic beverages while prohibiting men of the same age from drinking is not substantially related to that goal.
Others (including age, wealth, mental retardation, and sexual orientation)	Minimum rationality standard	Is there any rational foundation for the discrimination?	*Romer* v. *Evans* (1996): Colorado state constitutional amendment denying equal rights to homosexuals is unconstitutional.

Since 1976, the Court has applied the intermediate standard of constitutional review to most claims that it has heard involving gender. Thus, the following kinds of practices have been found to violate the Fourteenth Amendment:

- Single-sex public nursing schools.[22]
- Laws that consider males adults at twenty-one years but females at eighteen years.[23]
- Laws that allow women but not men to receive alimony.[24]
- State prosecutors' use of peremptory challenges to reject men or women to create more sympathetic juries.[25]
- Virginia's maintenance of an all-male military college, the Virginia Military Institute.[26]
- Different requirements for a child's acquisition of citizenship based on whether the citizen parent is a mother or a father.[27]

In contrast, the Court has upheld the following governmental practices and laws:

- Draft registration provisions for males only.[28]
- State statutory rape laws that apply only to female victims.[29]

The level of review used by the Court is crucial. Clearly, a statute excluding African Americans from draft registration would be unconstitutional. But, because gender is not subject to the same higher standard of review that is used in racial discrimination cases, the exclusion of women from the requirements of the Military Selective Service Act was ruled permissible because the government policy was considered to serve "important governmental objectives."[30]

This history has perhaps clarified why women's rights activists continue to argue that until the passage of an equal rights amendment, women will never enjoy the same rights as men. An amendment would automatically raise the level of scrutiny that the Court applies to gender-based claims, although there are clear indications that Justices Ginsburg and Sandra Day O'Connor (who is now retired) favored requiring states to show "exceedingly persuasive justifications" for their actions.[31]

STATUTORY REMEDIES FOR SEX DISCRIMINATION

In part because of the limits of the intermediate standard of review and the fact that the equal protection clause applies only to *governmental* discrimination, women's rights activists began to bombard the courts with sex-discrimination cases. Other cases have been filed under Title VII of the Civil Rights Act, which prohibits discrimination by private (and, after 1972, public) employers, or under the Equal Pay Act that Congress passed in 1963, which requires employers to pay women and men equal pay for equal work. Nevertheless, a large wage gap between men and women continues to exist. In spite of the fact that the Equal Pay Act is more than forty years old, women in 2004 earned less than 77 percent of what men earned (see Figure 5.1). Key victories under Title VII include:

- Consideration of sexual harassment as sex discrimination.[32]
- Inclusion of law firms, which many argued were private partnerships, in the coverage of the act.[33]
- A broad definition of what can be considered sexual harassment, which includes same-sex harassment.[34]
- Allowance of voluntary affirmative action programs to redress historical discrimination against women.[35]

Title IX
Provision of the Educational Amendments of 1972 that bars educational institutions receiving federal funds from discriminating against female students.

Other victories have come under **Title IX,** which parallels Title VII and greatly expanded the opportunities for women in elementary, secondary, and postsecondary

FIGURE 5.1 THE WAGE GAP, 1990–2004

The Equal Pay Act was passed in 1963; still women's wages continue to fall short of men's although the gap is closing among all women with the exception of Hispanic women. What factors might account for these glaring inequities?

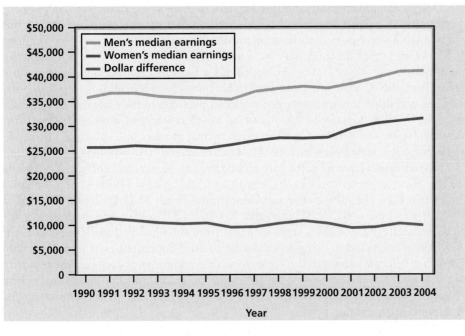

Sources: Census Bureau, Current Population Reports, Median Earning of Workers 15 Years Old and Over by Work Experience and Sex. Data from http://www.pay-equity.org/info-time.html.

institutions. It bars educational institutions receiving federal funds from discriminating against female students. Since women's groups saw eradication of educational discrimination as key to improving other facets of women's lives, they lobbied for it heavily. They have also litigated to make sure that its key provisions are enforced. (See chapter 8 for more on Title IX.)

Other Groups Mobilize for Rights

AFRICAN AMERICANS AND WOMEN are not the only groups that have suffered unequal treatment under the law. Many other disadvantaged groups have mobilized to achieve civil rights that were denied to them.

HISPANIC AMERICANS

As noted in chapter 1, Hispanic Americans now are the largest minority group in the United States. Until the 1920s, most Hispanics lived in the southwestern United States. These early groups, many of whom were from families who had owned land when parts of the Southwest were still in Mexico's control, formed the League of United Latin American Citizens (LULAC) in 1929. LULAC continues to be the largest Hispanic group in the United States, with local councils in every state and Puerto Rico.[36]

In later decades, large numbers of immigrants from Mexico and Puerto Rico came to the United States. These new immigrants quickly became a source of cheap labor. Mexicans tended to settle in the Southwest, where they most frequently were employed as migratory farm workers. Puerto Ricans mainly settled in New York City. Both groups tended to live in their own neighborhoods, where life was centered around the Roman Catholic Church and the customs of their homeland. Both groups, however, largely lived in poverty.

Despite the income and language barriers faced by these immigrants, a push for greater Hispanic rights began in the mid-1960s, just as many Cuban immigrants began to establish homes in Florida, dramatically altering the political and social climate of Miami and other neighboring towns and cities. This new movement, marked by the establishment of the National Council of La Raza in 1968, included many tactics drawn from the African American civil rights movement, including sit-ins, boycotts, marches, and other activities designed to attract publicity to their cause.[37] In one early example, in 1965, Cesar Chavez organized migrant workers into the United Farm Workers Union and led them in their strike against growers in California. This strike was eventually coupled with a national boycott of several farm products.

Hispanics also have relied heavily on litigation to secure legal change. Key groups are the Mexican American Legal Defense and Educational Fund (MALDEF) and the Puerto Rican Legal Defense and Educational Fund. MALDEF was founded in 1968 after members of LULAC met with NAACP LDF leaders and, with their assistance, secured a $2.2-million start-up grant from the Ford Foundation. MALDEF originally was created to bring test cases before the Supreme Court to force school districts to allocate more funds to schools with predominantly low-income minority populations, to implement bilingual education programs, to force employers to hire Hispanics, and to challenge election rules and apportionment plans that undercount or dilute Hispanic voting power.

MALDEF has been successful in its efforts to expand voting rights and opportunities to Hispanic Americans under the Voting Rights Act of 1965 (renewed in 2006 for ten years) and the U.S. Constitution's equal protection clause. In 1973, for example, it won a major victory when the Supreme Court ruled that multimember electoral districts (in which more than one person represents a single district) in Texas discriminated against African Americans and Hispanic Americans.[38]

MALDEF's success in educational equity cases came more slowly. In 1973, for example, the Supreme Court refused to find that a Texas law under which the state appropriated a set dollar amount to each school district per pupil, while allowing wealthier districts to enrich educational programs from other funds, violated the equal protection clause of the Fourteenth Amendment.[39]

In 1989, however MALDEF won a case in which a state district judge elected by the voters of only a single county declared the state's entire method of financing public schools to be unconstitutional under the state constitution.[40] And, in 2004, it entered into a settlement with the state of California in a case brought four years earlier to address, in MALDEF's words, "the shocking inequities facing public school children across the state."[41]

MALDEF continues to litigate in a wide range of areas of concern to Hispanics. High on its agenda today are affirmative action, the admission of Hispanic students to state colleges and universities, health care for undocumented immigrants, and challenging unfair redistricting practices that make it more difficult to elect Hispanic legislators. It also litigates to challenge many state redistricting plans to ensure that Hispanics are adequately represented. In 2005, for example, MALDEF, LULAC, and other Hispanic

■ More than a million immigrants and their supporters took to the streets across the nation to rally for immigrants' civil rights on May 1, 2006, in the wake of proposed immigration legislation in Congress. Here, an estimated 400,000 people march in Chicago, Illinois. Immigration issues continue to divide Americans. On October 26, 2006, President Bush signed a bill authorizing an additional 700 miles of fencing along the U.S. border with Mexico. While 1.2 billion dollars have been designated for enhanced border security, it remains to be seen whether these funds will be used specifically to build the fence.

Photo courtesy: John Zich/zimages.com

rights groups played a major role in challenging a redistricting plan created by the Texas legislature, charging that the legislature's plan was designed intentionally to limit Hispanic representation in south Texas.[42] The U.S. Supreme Court subsequently found in 2006 that the Texas plan improperly diluted Hispanic voting strength in Congressional District 23.[43]

MALDEF is also at the fore of legislative lobbying for expanded rights. Since 2002, it has worked to oppose restrictions concerning driver's license requirements for undocumented immigrants, to gain greater rights for Hispanic workers, and to ensure that redistricting plans do not silence Hispanic voters. It won a victory on this issue in California in 2004. MALDEF also focuses on the rights of Hispanic workers, an issue that attracted vast attention in 2006.

NATIVE AMERICANS

Native Americans are the first true Americans, and their status under U.S. law is unique. Under the U.S. Constitution, Indian tribes are considered distinct governments, a situation that has affected Native Americans' treatment by the Supreme Court in contrast to other groups of ethnic minorities. And, minority is a term that accurately describes American Indians. It is estimated that there were as many as 10 million Indians in the New World at the time Europeans arrived in the 1400s, with estimates varying from a high of 150–200 million to a low of 20–50 million throughout North and South America.[44] By 1900, the number of Indians in the continental United States had plummeted to less than 2 million. Today, there are 2.8 million.

It was not until the 1960s, at the same time women were beginning to mobilize for greater civil rights, that Indians, too, began to mobilize. Like the civil rights and women's rights movements, the movement for Native American rights had a radical as well as a more traditional branch. During this time, many Indians, trained by the American Indian Law Center at the University of New Mexico, began to file hundreds of test cases in the federal courts involving tribal fishing rights, tribal land claims, and the taxation of tribal profits. The Native American Rights Fund (NARF), founded that same year, became the NAACP LDF of the Indian rights movement when the "courts became the forum of choice for Indian tribes and their members."[45]

Native Americans have won some very important victories concerning hunting, fishing, and land rights. They continue to gain access to their sacred places and have filed lawsuits to stop the building of roads and new construction on ancient burial grounds or other sacred spots. Today, these land rights allow Native Americans to play host to a number of casinos across the country, a phenomenon that is explored in Politics Now: Reclaiming Rights. However, Native Americans have not fared particularly well in areas such as religious freedom, especially where tribal practices come into conflict with state law.

Native Americans have also found themselves locked in a controversy with the Department of the Interior over its handling of Indian trust funds, which are to be paid out to Indians for the use of their lands. In 1996, several Indian tribes filed suit to force the federal government to account for the billions of dollars it has collected over the years for its leasing of Indian land, which it took from the Indians and held in trust since the late-nineteenth century, and to force reform of the system.[46] As the result of years of mismanagement, the trust, administered by the Department of the Interior, has no records of monies taken in or how they were disbursed. The ongoing class action lawsuit includes 500,000 Indians, who claim that they are owed more than $10 billion. The trial judge found massive mismanagement of the funds, which generate up to $500 million a year, and at one time threatened to hold the secretary of the interior in contempt. In early 2004, a mediator was appointed to help bring greater resolution to the conflict.[47] At this writing, the lawsuit has yet to reach its conclusion.

Politics Now

RECLAIMING RIGHTS: INDIANS USE DIVERSE WAYS TO REVERSE THE ECONOMIC ADVERSITY OF DISCRIMINATION

Under the U.S. Constitution, Indian tribes on tribal lands are treated as foreign nations and are therefore not subject to federal or state laws, which generally have prohibited gambling. Therefore, state governments and some Indian tribes have fashioned arrangements whereby in return for settlements of longtime land disputes, states have allowed Indians to build gambling casinos on their reservations. These agreements usually grant state governments a portion of the casinos' profits.

The profit-sharing relationship has been mutually beneficial. The state of Connecticut, for example, earned more than $400 million in 2003 from its revenue-sharing agreement. And, the Thunder Valley Casino has helped members of the United Auburn Indian Community in California to improve their living conditions drastically. Before the casino opened, not one of the 250 members of the tribe had ever attended college. Members of the tribe lived in slum conditions, nearly 80 percent did not know how to write a check, and many were unable to afford basic amenities such as running water and kitchen appliances.[a] Some were homeless. Now, the tribe has financial consultants to help its members.

All get free medical, dental, and vision care. Special education and tutoring programs are helping the tribe's ninety-three children and their parents become more educated, as well as adjusted to the tremendous changes in their economic status.

These improvements in Indians' economic affairs have helped to increase their political clout. Tribes are donating to political campaigns of candidates who seem predisposed to policies favorable to tribes. The Agua Caliente Band of Cahuilla Indians, for example, donated $7.5 million to political campaigns in just one year alone. And, during the California gubernatorial recall of 2004, Indian tribes contributed over $11 million to candidates. These large expenditures, Indians claim, are legal, because as sovereign nations they are immune from federal and state campaign finance disclosure laws.[b] It is likely that the political involvement of Indian tribes will continue to grow as their casinos—and the profits of those ventures—continue to proliferate.

[a]Louis Sahagun, "Tribes Fear Backlash to Prosperity," *Los Angeles Times* (May 3, 2004): B1.

[b]Sahagun, "Tribes Fear Backlash to Prosperity."

GAYS AND LESBIANS

Until very recently, gays and lesbians have had an even harder time than other groups in achieving anything approximating equal rights.[48] However, gays and lesbians have, on average, far higher household incomes and educational levels than these other groups, and they are beginning to convert these advantages into political clout at the ballot box and through changes in public opinion. As discussed in chapter 4, gays and lesbians initially did not fare well in the Supreme Court. In the late 1970s, the Lambda Legal Defense and Education Fund, the Lesbian Rights Project, and Gay and Lesbian Advocates and Defenders were founded by gay and lesbian activists dedicated to ending legal restrictions on the civil rights of homosexuals.[49] Although these groups have won important legal victories concerning HIV/AIDS discrimination, insurance policy survivor benefits, and even some employment issues, they generally were not as successful as other historically disadvantaged groups.[50]

In 1993, for example, President Bill Clinton tried to ban discrimination against homosexuals in the armed services, who were subject to immediate discharge if their sexual orientation was discovered. Eventually, Clinton and Senate leaders compromised on what was called the "Don't Ask, Don't Tell" policy. It stipulated that gays and lesbians would no longer be asked if they were homosexual, but they were barred from revealing their sexual orientation (under threat of discharge from the service).[51] Although this policy was initially viewed as a successful compromise, it has been called into question in recent years, as the wars in Iraq and Afghanistan have increased America's need for active-duty military personnel. Since the policy was adopted in 1994, 10,000 soldiers have been discharged for their sexual orientation.[52]

The public's views toward homosexuality have changed over time, as signaled by the Court's 1996 decision in *Romer* v. *Evans*.[53] In this case, the Court ruled that a

Colorado amendment that denied homosexuals the right to seek protection from discrimination was unconstitutional under the equal protection clause of the Fourteenth Amendment. In 2000, Vermont became the first state to recognize civil unions, marking another landmark in the struggle for equal rights for homosexuals. And, in *Lawrence* v. *Texas* (2003), at discussed in chapter 4, the Court reversed an earlier ruling by finding a Texas statute that banned sodomy to be unconstitutional.[54]

In November 2003, the Massachusetts Supreme Court ruled that denying homosexuals the right to civil marriage was unconstitutional under the state's constitution. The U.S. Supreme Court later refused to hear an appeal of this case. In 2004, many conservative groups and Republican politicians made same-sex marriage a key issue. Referendums or amendments prohibiting same-sex marriage were placed on eleven state ballots and all were passed overwhelmingly by voters. With his approval ratings in freefall in the summer of 2006, President George W. Bush again renewed his call for a constitutional amendment to ban same-sex marriage. In the U.S. Senate, however, supporters failed to gain a simple majority, let alone the two-thirds vote necessary to send a proposed amendment to the states. Same-sex marriage bans were on eight state ballots in the 2006 elections. Only one, in Arizona, was defeated, but the issue received less attention than congressional scandals and the ongoing war in Iraq.

PARTICIPATION
Civil Rights and Gay Adoption

DISABLED AMERICANS

After World War II, many veterans returned to a nation unequipped to handle their disabilities. The Korean and Vietnam Wars made the problems of disabled veterans all the more clear. These disabled veterans saw the successes of African Americans, women, and other minorities, and they too began to lobby for greater protection against discrimination.[55] In 1990, in coalition with other disabled people, veterans convinced Congress to pass the Americans with Disabilities Act (ADA). The statute defines a disabled person as someone with a physical or mental impairment that limits one or more "life activities," or who has a record of such impairment. It thus extends the protections of the Civil Rights Act of 1964 to all of those with physical or mental disabilities. It guarantees access to public facilities, employment, and communication services. It also requires employers to acquire or modify work equipment, adjust work schedules, and make existing facilities accessible.

In 1999, the U.S. Supreme Court issued a series of four decisions redefining and significantly limiting the scope of the ADA. The cumulative impact of these decisions was to limit dramatically the number of people who can claim coverage under the act. Moreover, these cases "could profoundly affect individuals with a range of impairments—from diabetes and hypertension to severe nearsightedness and hearing loss—who are able to function in society with the help of medicines or aids but whose impairments may still make employers consider them ineligible for certain jobs."[56] Thus, pilots who need glasses to correct their vision cannot claim discrimination when employers fail to hire them because of their correctable vision.[57] In the 2004 case of *Tennessee* v. *Lane,* however, the Court ruled 5–4 that disabled persons could sue states that failed to make reasonable accommodations to assure that courthouses are handicapped accessible.[58] The largest national nonprofit organization lobbying for expanded civil rights for the disabled is the American Association of People with Disabilities (AAPD). Acting on behalf of the over 56 million Americans who suffer from some form of disability, it works in coalition with other disability organizations to assure that the ADA is implemented fully. AAPD was founded by activists who lobbied for the ADA and who recognized that "beyond national unity for ADA and our civil rights, people with disabilities did not have a venue or vehicle for working together for common goals."[59]

■ George Lane, the appellant in the 2004 Supreme Court case of *Tennessee* v. *Lane,* which involved the scope of the Americans with Disabilities Act, was forced to crawl up two flights of stairs to attend a court hearing on a misdemeanor charge. Had he not, Lane could have been jailed.

Photo courtesy: Jason R. Davis/AP/Wide World Photos

Global Perspective

DISABILITY RIGHTS

Securing the civil rights of people with disabilities is an increasingly important goal throughout the world. While people with disabilities still face discrimination in the United States and elsewhere, conditions have improved markedly in many nations. Redressing past discrimination is now a condition of European Union (EU) membership and is helping to raise awareness and improve conditions in nations that are seeking EU membership.

The American civil rights and women's rights movements gave rise to the U.S.-based disability rights movement in the 1960s and 1970s. The disabled in the United States first received limited protection in the Rehabilitation Act of 1973, yet it would be another seventeen years before America's disabled would receive comprehensive civil rights protection with the passage of the American with Disabilities Act (ADA). Similarly, during the European Union's 2003 "European Year of People with Disabilities," the European Parliament unveiled an action plan in which EU member states would update all disability law to be in conformity with federation policy, as well as with current understandings of human rights. The directive's goal is to "render discrimination of disabled people illegal in all areas of life." In addition to granting protections similar to those guaranteed to Americans by the ADA, the EU directive regulates consumer product design in order to make products useful and accessible to people with disabilities and regulates how people with disabilities are portrayed in the media. The action plan's objective is to integrate Europe's disabled into social and economic life by "mainstreaming" disability issues into EU policy domains by 2010.[a]

The EU's directive has provided disability rights groups with a useful bargaining chip in their efforts to further rights for the disabled in nations seeking EU membership. Mental Disability Rights International (MDRI), a nonprofit disability rights organization, released a report in September 2005 documenting the widespread use of electroshock therapy without anesthesia in Turkish psychiatric institutions. Turkey, which was just beginning membership talks with the European Union at the time of the report's release, has since ended the practice at its primary psychiatric facility and is also addressing other problems raised in the report.[b]

In May 2006, MDRI published a similar report noting the significant institutional abuse against children with mental and physical disabilities in Romania, another nation seeking EU membership.[c] Former Romanian dictator Nicolae Ceausescu's policies resulted in the neglect of nearly 200,000 children in state-run orphanages. Since Ceausescu's assassination and the end of communist rule in 1989, the number of children in orphanages has dropped to approximately 30,000. According to MDRI's report, however, many of the children who remain in institutions have physical and mental disabilities and face decrepit and unsanitary conditions and extreme neglect. In some cases, children are being confined in adult facilities where they are permanently restrained. MDRI and other human rights and disability rights groups are putting pressure on the EU to bar Romania's entrance until measures to address these problems are put in place and adequate resources are allocated to prevent further abuses. Though slow in coming, recognition of disability civil rights has gone global, and nations will increasingly have to comply with an evolving understanding of human and civil rights.

QUESTIONS

1. What additional problems are faced by the disabled community around the globe? How can these problems be addressed?
2. Is the United States truly a leader in recognizing disabled civil rights? Why or why not?

[a]European Disability Forum, news release, 2003.

[b]Craig S. Smith, "Romania's Orphans Face Widespread Abuse, Group Says," *New York Times* (May 10, 2006), http://select.nytimes.com.

[c]*Mental Disability Rights International Report,* May 2006.

SIMULATION

You Are the Mayor

Civil rights groups such as the AAPD often find themselves working in concert with more radical disability rights groups such as Not Dead Yet, which opposes assisted suicide and euthanasia laws, believing that they infringe on the civil rights of people with disabilities—especially those who, like Terri Schiavo, are too incapacitated to speak for themselves. Other groups, such as the National Right to Life Committee, work to protect the rights of the disabled and elderly, believing that any attempts to withhold nourishment or treatment or otherwise end life are basic violations of civil rights. (For a broader view, see Global Perspective: Disability Rights.)

Continuing Controversies in Civil Rights

SINCE PASSAGE OF MAJOR CIVIL RIGHTS legislation in the 1960s and the Supreme Court's continued interest in upholding the civil rights of many groups, African

Americans, women, Hispanics, Native Americans, gays and lesbians, and the disabled have come much closer to the attainment of equal rights. Yet, all of these groups still remain far from enjoying full equality under the Constitution in all areas of life. Enforcement of anti-discrimination laws varies based on administration priorities as well as the resources of private individuals to fund challenges to perceived discriminatory practices.

AFFIRMATIVE ACTION

This civil rights debate centers on the question of equality of opportunity versus equality of results. Most civil rights and women's rights organizations argue that the lingering and pervasive burdens of racism and sexism can be overcome only by taking race or gender into account in fashioning remedies for discrimination. They argue that the Constitution is not and should not be blind to color or sex.

Affirmative Action

Other groups believe that if it was once wrong to use labels to discriminate against a group, it should be wrong to use those same labels to help a group. Laws should be neutral, or color-blind. According to this view, quotas and other forms of **affirmative action,** policies designed to give special attention or compensatory treatment to members of a previously disadvantaged group, should be illegal.

affirmative action
Policies designed to give special attention or compensatory treatment to members of a previously disadvantaged group.

The debate over affirmative action and equality of opportunity became particularly intense during the presidential administration of Ronald Reagan, in the wake of two court cases that were generally decided in favor of affirmative action shortly before Reagan's election. In 1978, the Supreme Court for the first time fully addressed the issue of affirmative action. In *Regents of the University of California* v. *Bakke* (1978), a sharply divided Court ruled that the use of strict quotas in college admissions activity was inappropriate, but the school was free to "take race into account."[60] Other cases upheld this view until the later 1980s. Then, in a three-month period in 1989, the Supreme Court handed down five civil rights decisions limiting programs and making it harder to prove employment discrimination. In response, Congress passed the Civil Rights Act of 1991, which overruled these decisions. Then, in *Grutter* v. *Bollinger* (2003), the U.S. Supreme Court voted to uphold the constitutionality of the University of Michigan's law school admissions policy, which gave preference to minority applicants.[61] However, in a companion case, the Court struck down Michigan's undergraduate point system, which gave minority applicants twenty points simply because they were minorities.[62]

Taken together, these cases set the stage for a new era in affirmative action in the United States. While the use of strict quotas and automatic points is not constitutional, the Court clearly believes that there is a place for some preferential treatment, at least until greater racial and ethnic parity is achieved.

PAY EQUITY AND OTHER ISSUES OF WORKPLACE DISCRIMINATION

Race is not the only issue that continues to breed civil rights controversies. In fact, one of the largest barriers faced by minority groups living in the United States is the issue of pay equity, which, as already discussed, has an especially significant impact on female workers. The issue of pay equity for women has recently received national attention through a lawsuit filed against the nation's largest employer, Wal-Mart. Six California women filed a claim against the chain, charging that they were the victims of gender discrimination.[63] These women asserted that they were paid lower wages and offered fewer opportunities for advancement than their male colleagues. In June 2004, a federal judge broadened their class action suit to include 1.6 million women. The lawsuit is still pending before the Ninth Circuit Court of Appeals. Meanwhile, similar suits have been filed by employees at other big box stores, including Costco.

Wal-Mart has also been involved in a lawsuit seeking pay equity for Hispanics. Nine illegal immigrants who worked as janitors at Wal-Marts in New Jersey are suing the company for discriminating against them by paying them lower wages and giving them fewer benefits based solely on their ethnic origin. Another group of Wal-Mart

On Campus

CAMPAIGNING FOR A LIVING WAGE

As a college student, you cross paths with a number of adults throughout the day. There are, of course, your parents and the professors, librarians, and administrators who control your academic life. But, there are also the food service workers who prepare food in the campus dining hall and the custodians who clean dorms, classrooms, and the student union. At many colleges and universities across the country, the latter are contract workers hired through companies such as Aramark and Sodexho. These cooks and cleaners—who are often minorities and immigrants—are not university employees, so they do not enjoy the tuition remission, health care, wage levels, or guaranteed employment given to professors and office staff. In fact, at many universities, these workers' salaries are insufficient to live on; one university janitor estimated that she made about $600 a month for her full-time job.[a]

Across the country, students have become aware of the low wages and little or no benefits given to service workers and have taken steps to lobby their universities' administrations for what is known as a living wage. The amount of this wage varies from municipality to municipality. It is calculated as the minimum hourly wage a person can earn and yet afford to pay for the basic essentials of life—food, water, shelter, utilities, and transportation—with a small amount left over for other expenditures. In Charlottesville, Virginia, home of the University of Virginia, for example, the living wage is $10.72 per hour.[b] In contrast, in Washington, D.C., the living wage is $14 per hour, far above the 2006 federal minimum wage Congressional Democrats hope to raise in 2007.[c]

Currently, living wage campaigns are ongoing at about fifty universities across the country. Many of these efforts are coordinated by an interest group known as the Living Wage Action Coalition, that has field organizers who travel around the country teaching students how to deploy successful strategies at their own universities. The tactics used by living wage protestors are varied and can be extreme. At Georgetown University and the University of Miami, for example, students have gone on hunger strikes. At the University of Virginia and the University of Vermont, students have set up tent cities on their campus's main quads to bring attention to their cause. And, at Washington University in St. Louis, students set up residence inside the university's admissions building to get the attention of administrators, prospective students, and the public.

Success in adopting a living wage has been achieved at a number of campuses, including Georgetown, Stanford, Harvard, and Washington universities. A number of municipalities, including San Francisco, California; Baltimore, Maryland; and Madison, Wisconsin, also have adopted living wage provisions. Observers, however, expect that this is only the beginning for living wage campaigns across the country as students demand moral action from universities that are being run more and more like corporations.[d]

[a]Jennifer Lenhart, "Georgetown Rally Presses Pay Issue: Students Join with Labor Officials," *Washington Post* (March 23, 2005): B3.

[b]Carol Morello and Susan Kinzie, "'Living Wage' Cry Still Piercing: U-VA Protestors Plan Next Round," *Washington Post* (April 19, 2006): B1.

[c]Lenhart, "Georgetown Rally Presses Pay Issue."

[d]Susan Kinzie, "GU Protestors Savor Win—and a Meal: Nine-Day Hunger Strike Resulted in Better Compensation for Contract Workers," *Washington Post* (March 25, 2005): B4.

employees from twenty-one states are also suing the corporation, claiming that executives knowingly conspired to hire illegal immigrants and, in doing so, violated the workers' civil rights by refusing to pay Social Security and other wage compensation benefits.[64] These suits are representative of a growing trend in discrimination suits filed by immigrants who believe they have been persecuted or disadvantaged following changes in security and immigration law after the September 11, 2001, terrorist attacks. In fact, many of the Hispanics groups discussed in this chapter have been forced to devote significant portions of their time to immigration cases rather than workplace discrimination issues as the Civil Rights Division, as noted in our opening vignette, continues to allocate lawyers' resources toward immigration issues. (For more on efforts to help minorities gain pay equity, see On Campus: Campaigning for a Living Wage.)

Summary

WHILE THE FRAMERS AND OTHER AMERICANS basked in the glory of the newly adopted Constitution and Bill of Rights, their protections did not extend to all Americans.

When the Framers tried to compromise on the issue of slavery, they only postponed dealing with a volatile question that was later to rip the nation apart. Ultimately, the Civil War was fought to end slavery. Among its results were the triumph of the abolitionist position and adoption of the Thirteenth, Fourteenth, and Fifteenth Amendments. During this period, women also sought expanded rights, especially the right to vote, but to no avail.

Although the Civil War Amendments were added to the Constitution, the Supreme Court limited their application. The NAACP was founded in the early 1900s to press for equal rights for African Americans. Women's groups also were active during this period, successfully lobbying for passage of the Nineteenth Amendment, which assured them the right to vote.

In 1954, the U.S. Supreme Court ruled in *Brown* v. *Board of Education* that state-segregated school systems were unconstitutional. This victory empowered African Americans as they sought an end to other forms of pervasive discrimination. Bus boycotts, sit-ins, freedom rides, pressure for voting rights, and massive nonviolent demonstrations became common tactics. This activity culminated in the passage of the Civil Rights Act of 1964.

After passage of the Civil Rights Act, a new women's rights movement arose. Several women's rights groups were created, and while some sought a constitutional amendment, others attempted to litigate under the equal protection clause and several laws to obtain greater equality.

Building on the successes of African Americans and women, other groups, including Hispanic Americans, Native Americans, gays and lesbians, and the disabled, organized to litigate for expanded civil rights as well as to lobby for anti-discrimination laws. None of the groups discussed in this chapter have yet to reach full equality, and other groups, including immigrants, are seeking to improve their civil rights.

KEY TERMS

affirmative action, p. 161
Black Codes, p. 141
Brown v. *Board of Education* (1954), p. 146
civil rights, p. 138
Civil Rights Act of 1964, p. 151
Civil Rights Cases (1883), p. 142
Equal Employment Opportunity Commission, p. 152
equal protection clause, p. 146
Equal Rights Amendment, p. 152
Fifteenth Amendment, p. 141
Fourteenth Amendment, p. 141
grandfather clause, p. 142
Nineteenth Amendment, p. 143
Plessy v. *Ferguson* (1896), p. 142
poll tax, p. 142
strict scrutiny, p. 153
suffrage movement, p. 143
suspect classification, p. 153
Thirteenth Amendment, p. 141
Title IX, p. 154

SELECTED READINGS

Delgado, Richard. *Justice at War: Civil Liberties and Civil Rights During Times of Crisis.* New York: New York University Press, 2005.

Eastland, Terry. *Ending Affirmative Action: The Case for Colorblind Justice.* New York: Basic Books, 1997.

Featherstone, Liza. *Selling Women Short: The Landmark Battle for Worker's Rights at Wal-Mart.* New York: Basic Books, 2005.

Freeman, Jo. *The Politics of Women's Liberation.* New York: Backinprint.com, 2000.

Garcia, John A. *Latino Politics in America: Community Culture and Interests.* Lanham, MD: Rowman and Littlefield, 2003.

Guinier, Lani, and Susan Sturm. *Who's Qualified?* Boston: Beacon Press, 2001.

Kluger, Richard. *Simple Justice,* reprint ed. New York: Vintage, 2004.

Mansbridge, Jane J. *Why We Lost the ERA.* Chicago: University of Chicago Press, 1986.

McClain, Paula D., and Joseph Stewart Jr. *"Can We All Get Along?" Racial and Ethnic Minorities in American Politics,* 4th ed. Boulder, CO: Westview, 2005.

McGlen, Nancy E., et al. *Women, Politics, and American Society,* 4th ed. New York: Longman, 2004.

Nobles, Melissa. *Shades of Citizenship: Race and the Census in Modern America.* Palo Alto, CA: Stanford University Press, 2000.

Reed, Adolph, Jr., ed. *Without Justice for All: The New Liberalism and Our Retreat from Racial Equity.* Boulder, CO: Westview, 1999.

Rodriguez, Clara E. *Changing Race: Latinos, the Census, and the History of Ethnicity in the United States.* New York: New York University Press, 2000.

Rosales, F. Arturo. *Chicano! The History of the Mexican American Civil Rights Movement.* Houston, TX: Arte Publico, 1996.

Williams, Juan. *Eyes on the Prize: America's Civil Rights Years, 1954–1965.* New York: Penguin, 1987.

Wilson, William Julius. *The Bridge over the Racial Divide: Rising Inequality and Coalition Politics,* 2nd ed. Berkeley: University of California Press, 2001.

WEB EXPLORATIONS

For more on civil rights generally, see
  http://www.civilrightsproject.harvard.edu
For more on abolition, the American Anti-Slavery Society, and its leaders, see
  http://www.loc.gov/exhibits/african/afam005.html
To read the full text of *Brown* v. *Board of Education* (1954), see
  http://caselaw.lp.findlaw.com
For more about the Montgomery bus boycott and the Reverend Martin Luther King Jr., see
  http://www.stanford.edu/group/King/about_king/encyclopedia/bus_boycott.html
For more about NOW and the EEOC, see
  http://www.now.org and
  http://www.eeoc.gov
For more about the Equal Rights Amendment, see
  http://www.equalrightsamendment.org
For more about the ACLU Women's Rights Project, see
  http://www.aclu.org/WomensRights/WomensRightsMain.cfm
To learn more about MALDEF, see
  http://www.maldef.org
For more about the Native American Rights Fund, see
  http://www.narf.org
For more about gay and lesbian rights groups, see
  http://www.glaad.org
For more about disability advocacy groups, see
  http://www.aapd-dc.org

Photo courtesy: Doug Mills/The New York Times

CONGRESS

6

ON FEBRUARY 6, 2002, REPRESENTATIVE NANCY PELOSI (D–CA) broke through a glass ceiling when she was sworn in as the Democratic House whip, becoming the first woman in history to win an elected position in the formal leadership of the U.S. House of Representatives.[1] The whip position has long been viewed as a stepping stone to becoming the Speaker of the House. House Speakers Tip O'Neill (D–MA) and Newt Gingrich (R–GA) were both former whips. As whip, it was Pelosi's responsibility to convince Democratic members of the House to vote together on the full range of bills before the 107th Congress.

First elected to Congress from California in 1986, Pelosi quickly made her mark as an advocate for human rights in China and as an effective fundraiser. Her fund-raising skills and years of experience in the House, in fact, helped her win the hotly contested race for the whip position. As part of the House leadership, she became the first woman to attend critical White House meetings, where, said Pelosi, "Susan B. Anthony and others are with me."[2]

Although the president's party traditionally loses seats in midterm elections, in 2002 House Republicans actually increased their majority. Critics charged that the Democrats lacked a consistent message. Therefore, soon after the election results were in, House Minority Leader Richard Gephardt (D–MO) resigned from his position, leaving Pelosi in line to succeed him. Representative Harold Ford (D–TN), one of the youngest members of the House, threw his hat into the ring to oppose Pelosi's campaign for the leader's position. Ford charged that Pelosi, who already was being referred to by conservatives as a "San Francisco liberal," was simply too liberal to lead the Democrats back to political viability in the 2004 elections. A majority of the members of the House Democratic Caucus, however, did not appear fazed by these charges; Pelosi was elected minority leader by an overwhelming majority.

In 2006, when Democrats regained control of Congress, Pelosi was catapulted into the role of Speaker. In shattering what she termed "the marble ceiling" as Speaker of the House, Pelosi became the first woman to hold that position and is second in line of succession to the presidency. Thus, more than 150 years after women first sought the right to vote, a female member of Congress now leads the House of Representatives.

CHAPTER OUTLINE

- The Constitution and the Legislative Branch of Government
- How Congress Is Organized
- The Members of Congress
- How Members Make Decisions
- The Law-making Function of Congress
- Congress and the President
- Congress and the Judiciary

165

THE FRAMERS' ORIGINAL CONCEPTION of the representational function of Congress was much narrower than it is today. Instead of regarding members of Congress as representatives of the people, those in attendance at the Constitutional Convention were extremely concerned with creating a legislative body that would be able to make laws to govern the new nation. Over time, Congress has attempted to maintain the role of a law- and policy-making institution, but changes in the demands made on the national government have allowed the executive and judicial branches to gain powers at the expense of the legislative. Moreover, although the Congress as a branch of government has experienced a decline in its authority, the power and the importance of individual members have grown. Thus, the public doesn't think much about Congress itself, but somewhat ironically, citizens hold their own elected representatives in high esteem.

The dual roles that Congress plays contribute to this divide in public opinion. Members of Congress must combine and balance the roles of lawmaker and policy maker with being a representative of their district, their state, their party, and sometimes their race, ethnicity, or gender. Not surprisingly, this balancing act often results in role conflict.

In this chapter, we will analyze the powers of Congress and the competing roles members of Congress play as they represent the interests of their constituents, make laws, and oversee the actions of the other two branches of government. We will also see that, as these functions have changed throughout U.S. history, so has Congress itself. We will first examine what the Constitution has to say about Congress—the legislative branch of government. We will then compare the two chambers and consider how their differences affect the course of legislation. After looking at the members of Congress, including how members get elected, and how they spend their days, we will examine the various factors that influence how members of Congress make decisions. We will also examine the law-making function of Congress. Finally, we will discuss the ever changing relationship between Congress and the president, and between Congress and the judiciary.

The Constitution and the Legislative Branch of Government

ARTICLE I OF THE CONSTITUTION describes the structure of the legislative branch of government we know today. As discussed in chapter 2, the Great Compromise at the Constitutional Convention resulted in the creation of an upper house, the Senate, and a lower house, the House of Representatives. Any two-house legislature, such as the one created by the Framers, is called a **bicameral legislature.** Each state is represented in the Senate by two senators, regardless of the state's population. The number of representatives each state sends to the House of Representatives, in contrast, is determined by that state's population.

The U.S. Constitution sets out the formal, or legal, requirements for membership in the House and Senate. As agreed to at the Constitutional Convention, House members are to be at least twenty-five years of age; senators, thirty. Members of the House are required to have resided in the United States for at least seven years; those elected to the Senate, nine. Both representatives and senators must be legal residents of the states from which they are elected.

Senators are elected for six-year terms, and originally they were elected by state legislatures because the Framers intended for senators to represent their states' interests in the Senate. State legislators lost this influence over the Senate with the ratification of the Seventeenth Amendment in 1913, which provides for the direct election of senators by voters. Then, as now, one-third of all senators are up for reelection every two years.

bicameral legislature
A legislature divided into two houses; the U.S. Congress and the state legislatures are bicameral except Nebraska, which is unicameral.

VIDEO DEBATE

Congressional Term Limits

Members of the House of Representatives are elected to two-year terms by a vote of the eligible electorate in each congressional district. The Framers expected that House members would be more responsible to the people because they were elected directly by them and more responsive to the people because they were up for reelection every two years.

The U.S. Constitution requires that a census, which entails the counting of all Americans, be conducted every ten years. Until the first census could be taken, the Constitution fixed the number of representatives in the House of Representatives at sixty-five. In 1790, then, one member represented about 30,000 people. As the population of the new nation grew and states were added to the union, the House became larger and larger. In 1910, it expanded to 435 members, and in 1929, its size was fixed at that number by statute.

Each state is allotted its share of these 435 representatives based on its population. After each U.S. Census, the number of seats allotted to each state is adjusted by a constitutionally mandated process called **apportionment.** After seats are apportioned, congressional districts must be redrawn by state legislatures to reflect population shifts to ensure that each member in Congress represents approximately the same number of residents. The Supreme Court has now ruled that districts may be redrawn more frequently. This process of redrawing congressional districts to reflect increases or decreases in the number of seats allotted to a state, as well as population shifts within a state, is called **redistricting.** The legal controversies and effects of redistricting are discussed in chapter 12.

The Constitution specifically gives Congress its most important power: the authority to make laws. Both houses share this law-making power. For example, no **bill** (proposed law) can become law without the consent of both houses. Examples of other constitutionally shared powers include the power to declare war, raise an army and navy, coin money, regulate commerce, establish the federal courts and their jurisdiction, establish rules of immigration and naturalization, and "make all Laws which shall be necessary and proper for carrying into Execution the foregoing Powers." (See The Living Constitution.) As interpreted by the U.S. Supreme Court, the necessary and proper clause, found at the end of Article I, section 8, when coupled with one or more of the specific powers enumerated in Article I, section 8, has allowed Congress to increase the scope of its authority, often at the expense of the states.

Reflecting the different constituencies and size of each house of Congress (as well as the Framers' intentions), Article I gives special, exclusive powers to each house in addition to their shared role in law-making. For example, as noted in Table 6.1, the Constitution specifies that all revenue bills must originate in the House of Representatives. Over the years, however, this mandate has been blurred, and it is not unusual to see budget bills being considered simultaneously in both houses, especially since, ultimately, each must approve all bills. The House also has the power to impeach: the authority to charge the president, vice president, or other "civil officers, including federal judges, with "Treason, Bribery, or other high Crimes and Misdemeanors." Only the Senate is authorized to conduct trials of **impeachment,** with a two-thirds yea vote being necessary before a federal official can be removed from office.

The Senate has the sole authority to approve major presidential appointments, including federal judges, ambassadors, and Cabinet- and sub-Cabinet-level positions. The Senate, too, must approve all presidential treaties by a two-thirds vote.

apportionment
The process of allotting congressional seats to each state following the decennial census according to their proportion of the population.

redistricting
The redrawing of congressional districts to reflect increases or decreases in seats allotted to the states, as well as population shifts within a state.

bill
A proposed law.

impeachment
The power delegated to the House of Representatives in the Constitution to charge the president, vice president, or other "civil officers," including federal judges, with "Treason, Bribery, or other high Crimes and Misdemeanors." This is the first step in the constitutional process of removing such government officials from office.

How Congress Is Organized

EVERY TWO YEARS, a new Congress is seated. After ascertaining the formal qualifications of new members, the Congress organizes itself as it prepares for the business of the coming session. Among the first items on its agenda are the election of new

TABLE 6.1	KEY DIFFERENCES BETWEEN THE HOUSE OF REPRESENTATIVES AND THE SENATE

Constitutional Differences

House	Senate
435 voting members (apportioned by population)	100 voting members (two from each state)
Two-year terms	Six-year terms (one-third up for reelection every two years)
Initiates all revenue bills	Offers "advice and consent" on many major presidential appointments
Initiates impeachment procedures and passes articles of impeachment	Tries impeached officials Approves treaties

Differences in Operation

House	Senate
More centralized, more formal; stronger leadership	Less centralized, less formal; weaker leadership
Rules Committee fairly powerful in controlling time and rules of debate (in conjunction with the Speaker of the House)	No rules committee; limits on debate come through unanimous consent or cloture of filibuster
More impersonal	More personal
Power distributed less evenly	Power distributed more evenly
Members are highly specialized	Members are generalists
Emphasizes tax and revenue policy	Emphasizes foreign policy

Changes in the Institution

House	Senate
Power centralized in the Speaker's inner circle of advisers	Senate workload increasing and institution becoming more formal; threat of filibusters more frequent than in the past
House procedures becoming more efficient	Becoming more difficult to pass legislation
Turnover is relatively high, although those seeking reelection almost always win	Turnover is moderate

leaders and the adoption of rules for conducting its business. As illustrated in Figure 6.1, each house has a hierarchical leadership structure that is closely tied to the key role of political parties in organizing Congress.

THE ROLE OF POLITICAL PARTIES IN ORGANIZING CONGRESS

majority party
The political party in each house of Congress with the most members.

minority party
The political party in each house of Congress with the second most members.

The basic division in Congress is between majority and minority parties. The **majority party** is the party in each house with the most members. The **minority party** is the party in each house with the second most members. Some of the implications of this split are discussed in Join the Debate: Minority Party Rights in Congress. (For the party breakdowns in the 110th Congress, see Figure 6.2.) Parties play a key role in the committee system, an organizational feature of Congress that facilitates its lawmaking and oversight functions. The committees, controlled by the majority party in each house of Congress, often set the agendas.

At the beginning of each new Congress—the 110th Congress, for example, will sit in two sessions, one in 2007 and one in 2008—the members of each party gather in their party caucus or conference. Historically, these caucuses have enjoyed varied

FIGURE 6.1 ORGANIZATIONAL STRUCTURE OF THE HOUSE OF REPRESENTATIVES AND THE SENATE IN THE 110TH CONGRESS

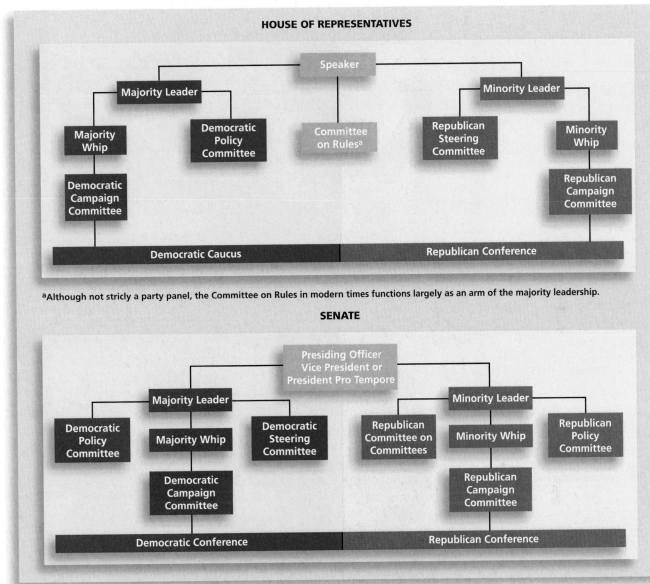

ᵃAlthough not strictly a party panel, the Committee on Rules in modern times functions largely as an arm of the majority leadership.

Source: Adapted from Roger H. Davidson and Walter J. Oleszek, *Congress and Its Members,* 10th ed. Washington, DC: CQ Press, 2006.

powers, but today the party caucuses—now called caucus by House Democrats and conference by House and Senate Republicans and Senate Democrats—have several roles, including nominating or electing party officers, reviewing committee assignments, discussing party policy, imposing party discipline, setting party themes, and coordinating media, including talk radio. Conference and caucus chairs are recognized party leaders who work with other leaders in the House or Senate.[3]

Each caucus or conference has specialized committees that fulfill certain tasks. House Republicans, for example, have a Committee on Committees that makes committee assignments. The Democrats' Steering Committee performs this function. Each party also has a congressional campaign committee to assist members in their reelection bids.

FIGURE 6.2 THE 110TH CONGRESS

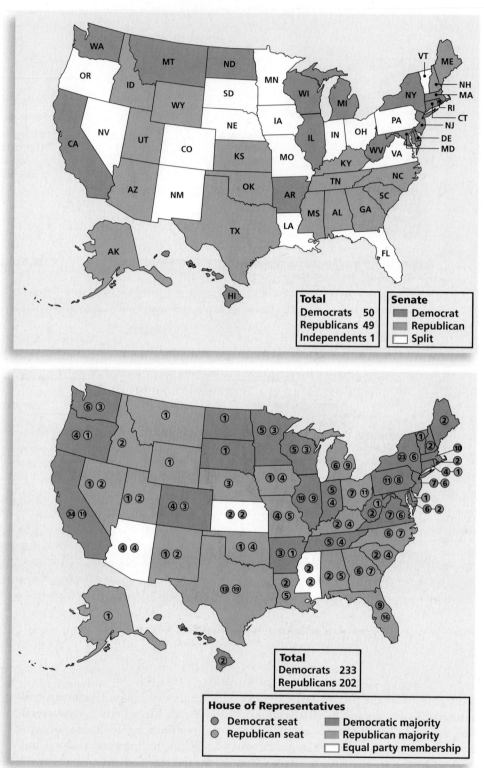

THE HOUSE OF REPRESENTATIVES

Even in the first Congress in 1789, the House of Representatives was almost three times larger than the Senate. It is not surprising, then, that from the beginning the House has been organized more tightly, structured more elaborately, and governed by

The Living Constitution

The Congress shall have Power ... To establish an uniform Rule of Naturalization.

—ARTICLE 1, SECTION 8, CLAUSE 4

This article reiterates the sovereign power of the nation and places authority to draft laws concerning naturalization in the hands of Congress.

Congress's power over naturalization is exclusive—meaning that no state can bestow U.S. citizenship on anyone. Citizenship is a privilege and Congress may make laws limiting or expanding the criteria. The word *citizen* was not defined constitutionally until ratification in 1868 of the Fourteenth Amendment, which sets forth two kinds of citizenship: by birth and through naturalization. Throughout American history, Congress has imposed a variety of limits on naturalization, originally restricting it to "free, white persons." "Orientals" were excluded from eligibility in 1882. At one time those affiliated with the Communist Party and those who lacked "good moral character" (a phrase that was construed to bar homosexuals, drunkards, gamblers, and adulterers) were deemed unfit for citizenship. These restrictions no longer carry the force of law, but they do underscore the power of Congress in this matter.

Congress continues to retain the right to naturalize large classes of individuals, as it did in 2000 when it granted automatic citizenship rights to all minor children adopted abroad as long as both adoptive parents were American citizens. Naturalized citizens, however, do not necessarily enjoy the full rights of citizenship enjoyed by other Americans. Congress at any time, subject only to Supreme Court review, can limit the rights and liberties of naturalized citizens, especially in times of national crisis. In the wake of the September 11, 2001, terrorist attacks, when it was revealed that one-third of the forty-eight al-Qaeda–linked operatives who took part in some sort of terrorist activities against the United States were lawful permanent residents or naturalized citizens, Congress called for greater screening by the Immigration and Naturalization Service for potential terrorists.

stricter rules. Traditionally, loyalty to the party leadership and voting along party lines has been more common in the House than in the Senate. House leaders also play a key role in moving the business of the House along. Historically, the Speaker of the House, the majority and minority leaders, and the Republican and Democratic House whips have made up the party leadership that runs Congress. This group now has been expanded to include deputy whips of both parties, as well as those who head the Democratic Caucus and the Republican Conference.

The Speaker of the House

The **Speaker of the House** is the only officer of the House of Representatives specifically mentioned in the Constitution. The entire House of Representatives elects the Speaker at the beginning of each new Congress. Traditionally, the Speaker is a member of the majority party, as are all committee

TIMELINE

The Power of the Speaker of the House

Speaker of the House
The only officer of the House of Representatives specifically mentioned in the Constitution; elected at the beginning of each new Congress by the entire House; traditionally a member of the majority party.

Join the Debate

MINORITY PARTY RIGHTS IN CONGRESS

OVERVIEW: After the closely contested 2000 and 2004 presidential elections, and with the outcome of the 2006 elections allowing Democrats to regain both chambers of Congress by winning what were in nearly every case close races, some political commentators have concluded that the United States may be viewed as divided into two significant minorities representing the Republican and Democratic Party faithful. It follows, so the logic goes, that in the event of close elections, the governing process should strive to reflect the policy and political desires of the relatively nonpartisan "moderate middle" of the American electorate. Representatives typically are chosen by partisans in primary elections, however, and elected officials are compelled to at least try to enact party preferences. Should law-making rules be written to prevent legislative majorities from enforcing their agendas over the objections of the minority party? What rights should the minority party in a two-party system have to pursue its interests? What does the Constitution say in regard to this dilemma?

Article I, section 5, of the Constitution gives both chambers of Congress the authority to "determine the Rules of its Proceedings" and declares that a "Majority of each [chamber] shall constitute a Quorum to do business" (a quorum is the number of members required to transact affairs). Other than giving a legislative minority the right to "compel the Attendance of absent Members" (to ensure there is a majority of representatives available to conduct legislative business), the Constitution does not speak to minority party rights. And, the language of the Constitution plainly gives each chamber the power to determine its own manners of procedure, and hence the power to make rules governing the legislative process. Thomas Jefferson and Supreme Court Justice Joseph Story, two commentators who had differing understandings of constitutional interpretation, were both in agreement that majority rule for law-making is a "natural right" and that giving legislative minorities the ability to frustrate law-making by a "natural majority" was tantamount to inviting rule by faction.

Discussions on this point in the Constitutional Convention show the Framers were concerned with legislative minorities having the ability to govern. They believed the majority principle was adequate to ensure legislation that reflected the will of the people, because in a country as large and diverse as the United States, compromise and conciliation between members of Congress would be unavoidable, given the diverse social, economic, and regional interests they would represent. This, they believed, would help foster decent law and policy. Nevertheless, the Framers did not foresee the rise of ideological political parties and their resulting political maneuvering. In fact, James Madison, in *Federalist, No. 10,* argued that the Constitution would tend "to break and control the violence of faction." Many believe that minority safeguards like the Senate's filibuster rule may be necessary to ensure that congressional governance reflects the policy desires of the broad majority of American voters.

ARGUMENTS AGAINST MINORITY PARTY RIGHTS IN CONGRESS

- **The Constitution is explicit where it requires supermajorities for political action.** The Constitution plainly states when a supermajority is necessary for an act of government, and there are seven instances in the Constitution where this is necessary. For example, Article I requires that a two-thirds vote of each chamber is necessary to override a presidential veto, and Article II requires that a two-thirds vote of the Senate is necessary

chairs. Although typically not the member with the longest service, the Speaker generally has served in the House for a long time and in other House leadership positions as an apprenticeship.

The Speaker presides over the House of Representatives, oversees House business, and is the official spokesperson for the House, as well as being second in the line of presidential succession. Moreover, the Speaker is the House liaison with the president and generally has great political influence within the chamber. The Speaker is also expected to smooth the passage of party-backed legislation through the House.

Other House Leaders After the Speaker, the next most powerful people in the House are the majority and minority leaders, who are elected in their individual **party caucuses** or **conferences.** The **majority leader** is the second most important person

party caucus or conference
A formal gathering of all party members.

majority leader
The elected leader of the party controlling the most seats in the House of Representatives or the Senate; is second in authority to the Speaker of the House and in the Senate is regarded as its most powerful member.

to ratify treaties. If the Framers wanted more than a simple majority vote to make law and policy, it would be embodied in the Constitution's text.

- **Voters have the ability to unseat members of Congress.** If voters don't care for the legislative and political agenda of the majority party in Congress, they are competent enough to vote the party out of power. Voter disaffection with forty years of Democratic Party dominance of Congress, for example, led to the party being voted out of majority status in the 1994 midterm elections. It is politically unwise to consider the electorate fools.
- **Giving a legislative minority authority to stop legislation frustrates the will of the electorate.** Even in a closely divided electorate, the majority principle remains. Echoing the sentiment expressed in the Constitutional Convention, Thomas Jefferson argued that majority rule must necessarily be the rule for democratic government because it is a self-evident part of natural justice—how else does one determine and act on the desires of the electorate? The Framers believed that giving legislative minorities rights was essentially giving democratic government over to the rule of small elites.

ARGUMENTS FOR MINORITY PARTY RIGHTS IN CONGRESS:

- **Legislative majorities can be unjust.** Many consider actions by legislative majorities to be harmful to the rights or lives of citizens. For example, some believe the Defense of Marriage Act, which gives the states the authority to deny the legitimacy of same-sex marriages made in other states, is an infringement on the rights of individual citizens to marry. Allowing a minority party the right to impede legislation could provide a means for preventing unjust or unfair legislation.
- **Giving the minority party legislative rights helps the deliberative process.** Better law would be the result of

allowing a minority party the right to slow down the legislative process. Under Republican rule, Democrats frequently are not given the final text of bills until it is nearly time to vote on them. Giving the minority party assured rights would make certain there will be compromise and negotiation in the legislative process, and as a result, law and policy would be further filtered through deliberation and conciliation.

- **Legislation should reflect the preferences of the electorate as a whole.** Representative democracy means representation for all, not just for a political majority. Giving the minority party the right to block legislation will ensure legislation and policy are crafted in such a way as to reflect the diverse and broad policy preferences of the American electorate at large. Otherwise, legislation will reflect the ideological desires of only a portion of the American people.

QUESTIONS

1. Should minority parties have the right to slow down or derail the passage of legislation sponsored by the majority party? Is this a violation of the Framers' majority principle? Why or why not?
2. Given the fact that minority-party representatives are duly elected by a majority of their constituents, what minority-party protections, if any, seem appropriate?

SELECTED READINGS

Cox, Gary W., and Matthew D. McCubbins. *Setting the Agenda: Responsible Party Government in the U.S. House of Representatives.* New York: Cambridge University Press, 2005.

Eilperin, Juliet. *Fight Club Politics: How Partisanship Is Poisoning the U.S. House of Representatives.* Lanham, MD: Rowman and Littlefield, 2006.

VIDEO ROUNDTABLE

Congressional Leadership

in the House; his or her counterpart on the other side of the aisle (the House is organized so that if you are facing the front of the chamber, Democrats sit on the left side and Republicans on the right side of the center aisle) is the **minority leader.** The majority leader helps the Speaker schedule proposed legislation for debate on the House floor. In the past, both leaders worked closely with the Speaker. In recent Congresses, however, Republicans rarely have consulted Democratic Party leadership.[4]

The Republican and Democratic **whips,** who are elected by party members in caucuses, assist the Speaker and majority and minority leaders in their leadership efforts. The position of whip originated in the British House of Commons, where it was named after the "whipper in," the rider who keeps the hounds together in a fox hunt. Party whips—who were first designated in the U.S. House of Representatives in 1899 and in the Senate in 1913—do, as their name suggests, try to whip fellow Democrats or Republicans

minority leader
The elected leader of the party with the second highest number of elected representatives in the House of Representatives or the Senate.

whip
Key representative who keeps close contact with all members and takes nose counts on key votes, prepares summaries of bills, and in general acts as a communications link within the party.

Photo courtesy: Doug Mills/The New York Times

■ Head of the Democratic Senatorial Campaign Committee, Senator Charles Schumer (D–NY) and then Senate Minority Leader Harry Reid (D–NV) strategize after the Democratic Party picked up six seats from Republicans and recaptured the Senate majority in the 2006 election. Reid was chosen as Senate Majority Leader shortly after the election.

president pro tempore
The official chair of the Senate; usually the most senior member of the majority party.

into line on partisan issues. They try to maintain close contact with all members on important votes, prepare summaries of content and implications of bills, get "nose counts" during debates and votes, and in general get members to toe the party line. Whips and their deputy whips also serve as communications links, distributing word of the party line from leaders to rank-and-file members and alerting leaders to concerns in the ranks.

THE SENATE

The Constitution specifies that the presiding officer of the Senate is the vice president of the United States. Because he is not a member of the Senate, he votes only in the case of a tie.

The official chair of the Senate is the **president pro tempore,** or pro tem, who is selected by the majority party and presides over the Senate in the absence of the vice president. The position of pro tem today is primarily an honorific office that generally goes to the most senior senator of the majority party. Once elected, the pro tem stays in that office until there is a change in the majority party in the Senate. Since presiding over the Senate can be a rather perfunctory duty, neither the vice president nor the president pro tempore actually perform the task very often. Instead, the duty of presiding over the Senate rotates among junior members of the chamber.

The true leader of the Senate is the majority leader, elected to the position by the majority party. Because the Senate is a smaller and more collegial body, operating without many of the more formal House rules concerning debate, the majority leader is not nearly as powerful as the Speaker of the House. The Republican and Democratic whips round out the leadership positions in the Senate and perform functions similar to those of their House counterparts. But, leading and whipping in the Senate can be quite a challenge. Senate rules always have given tremendous power to individual senators; in most cases senators can offer any kind of amendments to legislation on the floor, and an individual senator can bring all work on the floor to a halt indefinitely through a filibuster unless three-fifths of the senators vote to cut him or her off.[5]

THE COMMITTEE SYSTEM

The saying "Congress in session is Congress on exhibition, whilst Congress in its committee rooms is Congress at work" may not be as true today as it was when Woodrow Wilson wrote it in 1885.[6] Still, "The work that takes place in the committee and subcommittee rooms of Capitol Hill is critical to the productivity and effectiveness of Congress."[7]

Committees are especially important in the House of Representatives because of its size. The establishment of subcommittees allows for even greater specialization.

Types of Committees There are four types of congressional committees: (1) standing; (2) joint; (3) conference; and, (4) select, or special.[8]

standing committee
Committee to which proposed bills are referred.

joint committee
Includes members from both houses of Congress; conducts investigations or special studies.

1. **Standing committees,** so called because they continue from one Congress to the next, are the committees to which bills are referred for consideration.

2. **Joint committees** are set up to expedite business between the houses and to help focus public attention on major matters, such as the economy, taxation, or scandals. They include members from both houses of Congress who conduct investigations or special studies.

3. **Conference committees** are special joint committees that reconcile differences in bills passed by the House and Senate. A conference committee is made up of those members from the House and Senate committees that originally considered the bill.

4. **Select (or special) committees** are temporary committees appointed for specific purposes. Generally such committees are established to conduct special investigations or studies and to report back to the chamber that established them.

In the 109th Congress, the House had nineteen standing committees, each with an average of thirty-one members. (See Table 6.2.) Together, these standing committees had a total of eighty-six subcommittees that collectively act as the eyes, ears, and hands of the House. They consider issues roughly parallel to those of the departments represented in the president's Cabinet.

Although most committees in one house parallel those in the other, the House Committee on Rules, for which there is no counterpart in the Senate, plays a key role in the House's law-making process. Indicative of the importance of the Rules Committee, majority party members are appointed directly by the Speaker. This committee reviews most bills after they come from a committee and before they go to the full chamber for consideration. Performing a traffic cop function, the Rules Committee

conference committee
Joint committee created to iron out differences between Senate and House versions of a specific piece of legislation.

select (or special) committee
Temporary committee appointed for specific purpose, such as conducting a special investigation or study.

TABLE 6.2   COMMITTEES OF THE 109TH CONGRESS (WITH SUBCOMMITTEE EXAMPLE IN ITALICS)

Standing Committees

House	Senate
Agriculture	Agriculture, Nutrition, and Forestry
Appropriations	Appropriations
Armed Services	Armed Services
Budget	Banking, Housing, and Urban Affairs
Education and the Workforce	Budget
Energy and Commerce	Commerce, Science, and Transportation
Financial Services	Energy and Natural Resources
Government Reform	Environment and Public Works
Homeland Security	Finance
House Administration	Foreign Relations
International Relations	Health, Education, Labor, and Pensions
Judiciary	Homeland Security and Governmental Affairs
Courts, the Internet, and Intellectual Property	Judiciary
Immigration, Border Security, and Claims	*Administrative Oversight and the Courts*
Commercial and Administrative Law	*Antitrust, Competition Policy, and Consumer Rights*
Crime, Terrorism, and Homeland Security	*The Constitution, Civil Rights, and Property Rights*
Constitution	
Resources	*Corrections and Rehabilitation*
Rules	*Crime and Drugs*
Science	*Immigration, Border Security, and Citizenship*
Small Business	*Intellectual Property*
Standards of Official Conduct	*Terrorism, Technology, and Homeland Security*
Transportation and Infrastructure	Rules and Administration
Veterans Affairs	Small Business and Entrepreneurship
Ways and Means	Veterans Affairs

Select, Special, and Other Committees

House	Senate	Joint Committees on
Permanent Select Intelligence	Indian Affairs	Economics
Select Homeland Security	Select Ethics	Printing
Select Bipartisan Committee to Investigate the Preparation for and Response to Hurricane Katrina	Select Intelligence	Taxation
	Special Aging	Library

gives each bill what is called a rule, which contains the date the bill will come up for debate and the time that will be allotted for discussion, and often specifies what kinds of amendments can be offered. Bills considered under a closed rule cannot be amended.

Standing committees have considerable power. They can kill bills, amend them radically, or hurry them through the process. In the words of former President Woodrow Wilson, once a bill is referred to a committee, it "crosses a parliamentary bridge of sighs to dim dungeons of silence from whence it never will return."[9] Committees report out to the full House or Senate only a small fraction of the bills assigned to them. Bills can be forced out of a House committee by a **discharge petition** signed by a majority (218) of the House membership.

In the 109th Congress, the Senate had sixteen standing committees ranging in size from fifteen to twenty-nine members. It also had sixty-eight subcommittees, which allowed all majority party senators to chair at least one.

In contrast to the House, whose members hold few committee assignments (an average of 1.8 standing and three subcommittees), senators each serve on an average of three to four committees and seven subcommittees. Whereas the committee system allows House members to become policy or issue specialists, Senate members often are generalists. In the 109th Congress, Senator Kay Bailey Hutchison (R–TX), for example, served on several committees, including Appropriations; Commerce, Science, and Transportation; Veterans Affairs; and Rules. She served on even more subcommittees, chairing two of them, and was the vice chair of the Republican Conference.

Senate committees enjoy the same power over framing legislation that House committees do, but the Senate, being an institution more open to individual input than the House, gives less deference to the work done in committees. In the Senate, legislation is more likely to be rewritten on the floor, where all senators can participate and add amendments at any time.

Committee Membership
Many newly elected members of Congress come into the body with their sights on certain committee assignments. Others are more flexible. Many legislators seeking committee assignments inform their party's selection committee of their preferences. They often request assignments based on their own interests or expertise or on a particular committee's ability to help their prospects for reelection. One political scientist has noted that committee assignments are to members what stocks are to investors—they seek to acquire those that will add to the value of their portfolios.[10]

Representatives often seek committee assignments that have access to what is known as **pork,** legislation that allows representatives to bring money and jobs to their districts in the form of public works programs, military bases, or other programs. Many of these programs are called earmarks because they are monies earmarked for specific projects within a member's district. Legislators who bring jobs and new public works programs back to their districts are hard to defeat when up for reelection. But, ironically, these are the programs that attract much of the public criticism directed at the federal government in general and Congress in particular. Thus, it is somewhat paradoxical that pork improves a member's chances for reelection.

Pork isn't the only motivator for those seeking strategic committee assignments.[11] Some committees, such as Energy and Commerce, facilitate reelection by giving House members influence over decisions that affect large campaign contributors. Other committees, such as Education and the Workforce or Judiciary, attract members eager to work on the policy responsibilities assigned to the committee even if the appointment does them little good at the ballot box. Another motivator for certain committee assignments is the desire to have power and influence within the chamber. The Appropriations and Budget Committees provide that kind of reward for most members.

In both the House and the Senate, committee membership generally reflects the party distribution within that chamber. For example, at the outset of the 110th Congress, Democrats held a narrow majority of House seats and thus claimed about a

discharge petition
Petition that gives a majority of the House of Representatives the authority to bring an issue to the floor in the face of committee inaction.

VIDEO ROUNDTABLE

Contemporary Legislative Process

pork
Legislation that allows representatives to bring home the bacon to their districts in the form of public works programs, military bases, or other programs designed to benefit their districts directly.

54 percent share of the seats on several committees, including International Relations, Energy and Commerce, and Education and the Workforce. On committees more critical to the operation of the House or to the setting of national policy, the majority often takes a disproportionate share of the slots. Since the Rules Committee regulates access to the floor for legislation approved by other standing committees, control by the majority party is essential for it to manage the flow of legislation. For this reason, no matter how narrow the majority party's margin in the chamber, it makes up more than two-thirds of the Rules Committee membership.

Committee Chairs   Committee chairs enjoy tremendous power and prestige. They are authorized to select all subcommittee chairs, call meetings, and recommend majority members to sit on conference committees. Committee chairs may even opt to kill a bill by refusing to schedule hearings on it. They also have a large committee staff at their disposal and are often recipients of favors from lobbyists, who recognize the chair's unique position of power. Personal skill, influence, and expertise are a chair's best allies.

Historically, committee chairs were the majority party members with the longest continuous service on the committee. Committee chairs in the House, unlike the Senate, are no longer selected by **seniority,** or time of continuous service on the committee. Today, the House leadership interviews potential chairs to make certain that candidates demonstrate loyalty to the party. The seniority system was also affected by term limits enacted by the Republican House and Senate in 1995 and 1997, respectively. Chairs were held to six-year terms, forcing many longtime committee chairs to step down. It remains to be seen if Democrats will follow this practice.

seniority
Time of continuous service on a committee or within the House or Senate.

The Members of Congress

MANY MEMBERS OF CONGRESS clearly relish their work, although there are indications that the high cost of living in Washington and of maintaining two homes, political scandals, intense media scrutiny, the need to tackle hard issues, and a growth of partisan dissension are taking a toll on many members. It is also difficult to please two constituencies—party leaders, colleagues, and lobbyists in Washington, D.C., and constituents at home. Table 6.3 shows a representative day in the life of a member of Congress, both at home and in Washington.

TABLE 6.3 **A DAY IN THE LIFE OF A MEMBER OF CONGRESS**	
8:30 a.m.	Breakfast with a former member
9:30 a.m.	Science Committee: hearing
10:00 a.m.	Private briefing by NASA officials for afternoon subcommittee hearing
10:00 a.m.	Commerce Committee: markup session of pending legislation
12:00 p.m.	Photo opportunity with Miss Universe
12:00 p.m.	Lunch with visiting friend at Watergate Hotel
1:30 p.m.	Science Committee: subcommittee hearing
1:30 p.m.	Commerce Committee: subcommittee markup session of pending legislation
2:00 p.m.	House convenes
3:00 p.m.	Meeting with National Alliance for Animal Legislation officials
4:30 p.m.	Meeting with American Jewish Congress delegates
5:00 p.m.	State University reception
5:00 p.m.	Briefing by the commissioner of the Bureau of Labor Statistics on the uninsured
5:30 p.m.	Reception/fundraiser for a party whip
6:00 p.m.	Reception/fundraiser for fellow member from the same state
6:00 p.m.	"Cajun" foods reception sponsored by Louisiana member
6:00 p.m.	Winetasting reception on behalf of New York wine industry sponsored by NY member
10:45 p.m.	House adjourns

Source: http://www.c-span.org/questions/week113.asp.

■ In 2002, Representatives Loretta and Linda Sanchez (both D–CA) became the first sisters to serve together in the U.S. Congress. Since then, they have pushed for women's issues, such as enforcement of Title IX, research for breast cancer, and protections against sexual assault in the military. Here they are shown being sworn in by then Speaker of the House Dennis Hastert (R–IL).

Photo courtesy: Office of Representative Loretta Sanchez.

RUNNING FOR AND STAYING IN OFFICE

Despite the long hours, hard work, and sometimes even abuse that senators and representatives experience, thousands aspire to these jobs every year. Yet, only 535 men and women (plus five nonvoting delegates) actually serve in the U.S. Congress. Membership in one of the two major political parties is almost always a prerequisite for election, because election laws in various states often discriminate against independents (those without party affiliation) and minor-party candidates. (For a different method, see Global Perspective: Parliamentary Systems.)

Incumbency helps members stay in office once they are elected.[12] It's often very difficult for outsiders to win because they don't have the advantages enjoyed by incumbents, including name recognition, access to free media, inside track on fund-raising, and a district drawn to favor the incumbent. As illustrated in Analyzing Visuals. Approval Ratings of Congress and Individual Representatives, which compares the way poll respondents feel about their own representatives to how they feel about Congress as an institution, most Americans approve of their *own* members of Congress. It is not surprising, then, that from 1980 to 1990, an average of 95 percent of the incumbents who sought reelection won their primary and general election races.[13] More recent elections saw even higher proportions of incumbents returning to office. One study concluded that unless a member of Congress was involved in a serious scandal, his or her chances of defeat were minimal.[14] In 2006, with a few House races left undecided, at least 27 members seeking reelection lost, up from only seven in 2004.

CONGRESSIONAL DEMOGRAPHICS

Congress is better educated, richer, more male, and more white than the rest of the United States. In fact, all but three senators are college graduates; 396 representatives share that honor. Over two-thirds of the members in each body also hold advanced degrees.

Nearly two hundred of the members of Congress are millionaires. The Senate, in fact, is often called the Millionaires Club, and its members sport names including Rockefeller and Kennedy. In fact, twenty-one senators are worth at least $3.1 million. Twenty-nine members of the House have a net worth over that amount.[15]

incumbency
The fact that being in office helps a person stay in office because of a variety of benefits that go with the position.

VISUAL
LITERACY

Why Is It So Hard to Defeat an Incumbent?

Global Perspective

PARLIAMENTARY SYSTEMS: THE ISRAELI KNESSET

When most Americans think of the legislative process, they typically think of the U.S. Congress, bicameral in structure, controlled by two political parties, and limited by the Constitution's system of checks and balances. Writing in the early 1800s, Alexis de Tocqueville noted the U.S. Congress fits the "genius," or political spirit, of the American people. He also wrote that different democratic states would require representative institutions that equally matched the "genius" of their peoples.

Diverse democratic legislatures exist across the globe. Most of them are parliamentary systems in which the executive branch is dependent upon the legislative branch's—the parliament's—direct or indirect support. In the bulk of parliamentary systems, the head of government, generally referred to as the prime minister, is chosen by the governing party or coalition of parties in the parliament. This is a significant departure from America's separate and co-equal legislative and executive branches of government. Another aspect of many parliamentary systems that differs markedly from the U.S. system is the employment of an electoral system of proportional representation in which legislative seats are awarded according to the proportion each party receives of the popular vote. In America's winner-take-all system, a one-vote majority determines a contest's winner. Nations relying on proportional representation tend to have a broad array of political parties with markedly different ideological outlooks and policy positions.

Almost no legislature could be more different from the American Congress than Israel's Knesset, the Middle East's longest-lived democratic legislature. With the exception of Turkey's National Assembly, no other legislative institution in the Middle East is typified by such fairly contested elections among formal opposition parties in well-established roles, as well as established minority parties.

The Knesset is unicameral and Israel's elections guarantee proportional representation. Unlike the U.S. Congress, in which the different chambers were designed to represent different interests (those of the people in the U.S. House of Representatives and those of the state governments in the Senate), the Knesset's single chamber can be said to approximate the ideal of direct democracy. The Israeli electoral system awards seats in the legislature to political parties in exact proportion to their share of the total vote. This means that any party able to gain a small plurality of votes will have representation. In 2006, the Knesset included representatives from twelve different parties, with no party holding a majority. Since the parties are so diverse in their views, compromise is often difficult to achieve. This is a significant departure from the U.S. Congress, where Democrats and Republicans control legislative and political activity and a party with only a one-seat advantage over its opposition holds significant power to influence legislation.

Significant differences in the political authority vested in the Knesset and the Congress exist as well. The Knesset is not subject to a system of checks and balances like that established by the U.S. Constitution. For all practical purposes, the Knesset *is* the government. The Israeli prime minister cannot veto any legislative and policy action by the Knesset, and the Knesset is not subject to judicial review. In fact, the Knesset has the constitutional power to overrule Israeli Supreme Court decisions regarding legislative and governing action, even those that go against Israel's Basic Law. Despite this, in recent years Israel's Supreme Court has assumed an increased role in Israeli political affairs.

QUESTIONS

1. Does the principle of separation of powers help or hinder effective governance? In what ways?
2. What changes would be likely if the United States amended the Constitution and adopted a proportional representation electoral system?

The average age of senators is sixty. The average age of House members is fifty-four.

As revealed in Figure 6.3, the 1992 elections saw a record number of women, African Americans, and other minority-group members elected to Congress. By the 110th Congress, there were at least 70 women in the House (pending the outcome of a few races) and 16 in the Senate. In 2007, there were 40 African Americans in the House and one in the Senate. Although Hispanics now outnumber African Americans in the United States, there are but 26 Hispanics in the 110th Congress—23 of them serve in the House of Representatives and three in the Senate. All African Americans and the vast majority of Hispanics are Democrats.

Occupationally, members of Congress no longer are overwhelmingly lawyers, although lawyers continue to be the largest single occupational group. In the 109th Congress, 275 were former state legislators and 111 were former congressional

Analyzing Visuals

APPROVAL RATINGS OF CONGRESS AND INDIVIDUAL REPRESENTATIVES

For many years, political scientists have noted that approval ratings of Congress as an institution are generally quite low, rarely exceeding 50 percent. On the other hand, the public's approval rating of its own member tends to be much higher, usually above 50 percent. The line graph demonstrates the differences between these ratings since 1990. Do the data for approval of Congress and approval of one's own representative follow similar trends over the period covered in the figure?

What factors do you think account for the differences in the ratings of Congress and of one's own representative? What are the effects of the differences in these ratings?

Note that the question regarding one's own representative was a slightly different one in 2004 from the earlier question—asking not just about approval but also about reelection. Do you think that this difference in wording affected the rating positively or negatively?

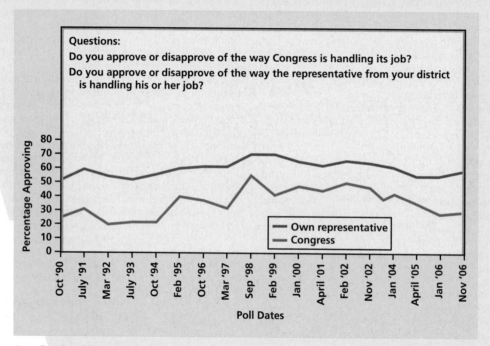

Source: Data derived from Lexis-Nexis RPOLL.

staffers. The number of veterans in Congress has continued to decline since the end of the Vietnam War. In 2006, eleven Iraq war veterans ran; in Pennsylvania alone, three Democratic veterans unseated incumbent Republicans.

THEORIES OF REPRESENTATION

Over the years, political theorists have offered various ideas about how constituents' interests are best represented in any legislative body. British political philosopher Edmund Burke (1729–1797), who also served in the British Parliament, believed that although he was elected from Bristol, it was his duty to represent the interests of the entire nation. He reasoned that elected officials were obliged to vote as they personally thought best. According to Burke, representatives should be **trustees** who listen

trustee
Role played by elected representatives who listen to constituents' opinions and then use their best judgment to make final decisions.

FIGURE 6.3 FEMALE AND MINORITY-GROUP MEMBERS OF CONGRESS, SELECTED YEARS

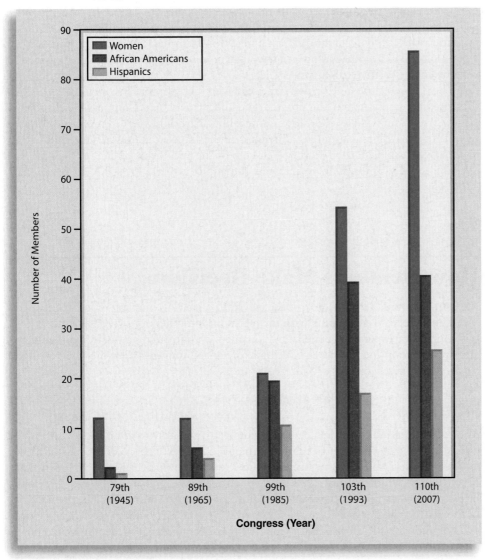

to the opinions of their constituents and then can be trusted to use their own best judgment to make final decisions.

A second theory of representation holds that representatives are **delegates.** True delegates are representatives who vote the way their constituents would want them to, whether or not those opinions are the representative's. Delegates, therefore, must be ready and willing to vote against their conscience or personal policy preferences if they know how their constituents feel about a particular issue. Not surprisingly, members of Congress and other legislative bodies generally don't fall neatly into either category. It is often unclear how constituents feel about a particular issue, or there may be conflicting opinions within a single constituency. With these difficulties in mind, a third theory of representation holds that **politicos** alternately don the hat of trustee or delegate, depending on the issue. On an issue of great concern to their constituents, representatives most likely will vote as delegates; on other issues, perhaps those that are less visible, representatives will act as trustees and use their own best judgment.

delegate
Role played by elected representatives who vote the way their constituents would want them to, regardless of their own opinions.

politico
Role played by elected representatives who act as trustees or as delegates, depending on the issue.

How a representative views his or her role—as a trustee, delegate, or politico—may still not answer the question of whether it makes a difference if a representative or senator is male or female, African American, Hispanic, or Caucasian, young or old, gay or straight. Burke's ideas about representation don't even begin to address more practical issues of representation. Can a man, for example, represent the interests of women as well as a woman? Can a rich woman represent the interests of the poor? Are veterans more sensitive to veterans' issues?

The actions of the lone Native American who served in the Senate until 2005 underscore the representative function that members can play in Congress. Senator Ben Nighthorse Campbell (R–CO), for example, not surprisingly served on the Committee on Indian Affairs. Earlier, as a member of the House, he fought successfully for legislation to establish the National Museum of the American Indian on the Mall in Washington, D.C. Only one American Indian, Tom Cole (R–OK), serves in the 110th Congress.

How Members Make Decisions

AS A BILL MAKES ITS WAY through the labyrinth of the law-making process described above, members are confronted with the question: "How should I vote?" Members adhere to their own personal beliefs on some matters, but their views often are moderated by other considerations. To avoid making any voting mistakes, members look to a variety of sources for cues.

PARTY

Members often look to party leaders for indicators of how to vote. Indeed, it is the whips' job in each chamber to reinforce the need for party cohesion, particularly on issues of concern to the party. In fact, from 1970 to the mid-1990s, the incidence of party votes in which majorities of the two parties took opposing sides roughly doubled to more than 60 percent of all roll-call votes.[16] Under unified Republican control in the 107th Congress, for example, there was perfect party unity on all major votes taken in the House.[17] In the 108th Congress, Democratic senators demonstrated unanimity in filibustering several presidential judicial nominations to the U.S. Courts of Appeals. While some charged that this was not evidence of party unity, but instead elected officials taking their direction from major liberal special interest groups, there can be no doubt that in both closely divided houses, party reigns supreme.[18]

Party loyalty is not the only reason members vote the way they do. Both parties have committees in both houses of Congress that provide extraordinary campaign assistance in the form of funding, political and media consulting, and direct mailing. Members know that if they fail to go along with the party on major votes, they risk losing this critical campaign support. Similarly, both senators and representatives can be assisted in their reelection bids by having the president (if he is of the same party) or highly popular political leaders come to their states or districts to assist them in their electioneering activities.

After years of Congress and the presidency being controlled by the Republican Party, in 2006, voters voiced their discontent over what many viewed as the excessive partisanship of the 109th Congress. A poll taken on Election Day 2006 found that 52 percent of voters would prefer **divided government,** the political condition in which different parties control the White House and Congress. Historically, divided government has lead to a situation called gridlock, which often results in very little important legislation being enacted into law. In an attempt to avert a gridlock scenario, Democratic Leader Nancy Pelosi (D–CA), soon to become the new Speaker of

divided government
The political condition in which different political parties control the White House and Congress.

the House, met with President George W. Bush two days after the election.

CONSTITUENTS

Constituents—the people who live and vote in the home district or state—are always in the member's mind when casting a vote.[19] It is rare for a legislator to vote against the wishes of his or her constituents regularly, particularly on issues of welfare rights, domestic policy, or other highly salient issues.

Gauging how voters feel about any particular issue often is not easy. Because it is virtually impossible to know how the folks back home feel on all issues, a representative's perception of their constituents' preferences is important. Even when voters have opinions, legislators may get little guidance if their district is narrowly divided. But, with regard to particularly charged topics like same-sex marriage, abortion restrictions, and flag burning—often called "wedge issues," given their ability to divide or drive a wedge between voters—members are always keenly aware of the consequences of voting against their constituents' views.

COLLEAGUES AND CAUCUSES

The range and complexity of issues confronting Congress mean that no one can be up to speed on more than a few topics. When members must vote on bills about which they know very little, they often turn for advice to colleagues who have served on the committee that handled the legislation. On issues that are of little interest to a legislator, **logrolling,** or vote trading, often occurs. Logrolling often takes place on specialized bills targeting money or projects to selected congressional districts. An unaffected member often will exchange a yea vote for the promise of a future yea vote on a similar piece of specialized legislation.

Members may also look to other representatives who share common interests. Special-interest caucuses created around issues, home states, regions, congressional class, or other commonalities facilitate this communication. Prior to 1995, the power of these groups was even more evident, as several caucuses enjoyed formal status within the legislative body and were provided staff, office space, and budgets. Today, however, all caucuses are informal in nature, although some, such as the Black and Hispanic Caucuses, are far more organized than others. The Congressional Women's Caucus, for example, has formal elections of its Republican and Democratic co-chairs and vice chairs, it provides staff to work on issues of common concern to caucus members, and staffers meet regularly to facilitate support for legislation of interest to women members.

INTEREST GROUPS, LOBBYISTS, AND POLITICAL ACTION COMMITTEES

A primary function of most lobbyists, whether they work for interest groups, trade associations, or large corporations, is to provide information to supportive or potentially supportive legislators, committees, and their staffs.[20] Pressure groups also use grassroots appeals to pressure legislators by urging their members in a particular state or district to call, write, fax, or e-mail their senators or representatives. Lobbyists can't vote, but constituents back home can and do. Lobbyists and the corporate or other

Photo courtesy: The Register Mail, Mia Algotti/AP/Wide World Photos

■ Senator Barack Obama (D–IL), seen here speaking at a church, campaigned extensively for Democratic candidates around the country in 2006 leading many to suspect he was testing the waters for a 2008 presidential run. Obama, who was elected to his first term in 2004, is the only African American senator in the 110th Congress.

logrolling
Vote trading; voting yea to support a colleague's bill in return for a promise of future support.

Politics Now

MUSLIM STAFFERS SEEK TO EDUCATE MEMBERS OF CONGRESS

As the war in Iraq unfolded, Representative Tom Tancredo (R–CO) gave a radio interview in July 2005 in which he suggested "bombing Islam's holy sites, including Mecca."[a] At that moment Nayyera Haq, a spokesperson for Representative John Salazar (D–CO), realized that as a Muslim working on Capitol Hill, she could no longer stay quiet. By fall 2005, the twenty-four-year-old Haq organized with twenty-two mostly Democratic Muslims working in Congress to start the Congressional Muslim Staffers Association. Staff associations are not unusual. They are often formed around issue areas, sports teams (softball is a favorite), and other interests, including religion.

Haq's group was not the first Muslim group to form on Capitol Hill. Muslim staff members have been meeting together each Friday for prayer since 1998. That group, however, was inward-looking and based on common interests. Haq's new group, on the other hand, comprised of a cross section of American Muslims including African Americans, South Asians, Arab Americans, and others, has an external purpose. Their goal is to educate other staffers and, through them, congressional members about Islam so that they might make more informed decisions about America's relationships with Islamic countries.

During spring 2006, for example, after the violence that was triggered around the world when cartoons caricaturizing Muhammad were printed in a Danish newspaper, the association hosted a lunchtime seminar open to other staffers and members of Congress. It dealt with the life of Muhammad and his critical importance to Muslims. The luncheon attracted over fifty non-Muslim staffers, and panelists now are regularly asked to talk to other off-Hill groups as Americans seek a better understanding of one of the world's oldest and largest religions.

The group also focuses on more general educational efforts, teaching staffers and members that Islam shares its roots with Judaism and Christianity and providing them with a broader understanding of the breadth of Islamic beliefs. The association recognizes that theirs is an uphill battle. Still, Haq contends that her group has important work to do.

"Being a Muslim staffer on the Hill is unique," says Haq. "In our offices there is a desire for knowledge about Islam. And there's a broad lack of understanding between our government and others. It's almost a responsibility to speak up

■ Staffers Sarah Bassal (left) and Amina Rubin (right) prepare for a workshop on Muhammad intended to educate policymakers about Islam.

Photo courtesy: Uri Gripas/UPI

and not be silent as a progressive Muslim."[b] The 2006 election of the first Muslim member of Congress, Representative Keith Ellison (D-MN), is likely to provide additional opportunities for education and understanding about Islam in the 110th Congress.

QUESTIONS

1. To what extent are elected representatives responsible for educating themselves on major religions like Islam?
2. Staffers routinely play a key role in helping members of Congress draft legislation and determine policy positions, as well as how to vote on specific legislation. How appropriate is it for staffers to wield such influence?

---

[a]This feature draws heavily from Nela Banerjee, "Muslim Staff Members on Mission to Educate Congress," *New York Times* (June 3, 2006): A11; and Pauline Jelinek, "Legislative Aides Aim to Lift Islam's Image," *Detroit Free Press*, (June 30, 2006)

[b]Banerjee, "Muslim Staff Members on Mission to Educate Congress."

interests they represent, however, can contribute to political campaigns and are an important source of campaign contributions. Many have political action committees (PACs) to help support members seeking reelection.

Finally, lobbyists and the interests they represent are an important source of campaign contributions. The high cost of campaigning has made members of Congress, especially those without huge personal fortunes, attentive to those who help pay the tab for the high cost of many campaigns. The almost 5,000 PACs organized by interest groups are a major source of many members' campaign funding.

STAFF AND SUPPORT AGENCIES

Members of Congress rely heavily on members of their staffs for information on pending legislation.[21] Not only do staff members meet regularly with staffers from other offices about proposed legislation or upcoming hearings, but staff members also prepare summaries of bills and brief the representative or senator based on their research and meetings. Especially if a bill is nonideological or one on which the member has no real position, staff members can be very influential. In many offices, staffers are the greatest influence on their boss's votes, and lobbyists are just as likely to contact key staffers as they are members. (See Politics Now: Muslim Staffers Seek to Educate Members of Congress.)

Congressional committees and subcommittees also have their own dedicated staff to assist committee members. Additional support for members comes from support personnel at the Congressional Research Service (CRS) at the Library of Congress, the Government Accountability Office (GAO), and the Congressional Budget Office (CBO).

The Law-making Function of Congress

THE ORGANIZATION OF CONGRESS allows it to fulfill its constitutional responsibilities, chief among which is its law-making function. It is through this power that Congress affects the day-to-day lives of all Americans and sets policy for the future. Proposals for legislation—be they about terrorism, Medicare, or tax policy—can come from the president, executive agencies, committee staffs, interest groups, or even private individuals. Only members of the House or Senate, however, can formally submit a bill for congressional consideration (although many are initially drafted by lobbyists). Once a bill is introduced by a member of Congress, it usually reaches a dead end. Of the approximately 10,000 or so bills introduced in the 109th session of Congress, approximately 250 were made into law.

HOW A BILL BECOMES A LAW

A bill must survive several stages before it becomes a law. It must be approved by one or more standing committees and both chambers, and, if House and Senate versions differ, each house must accept a conference report resolving those differences. These multiple points of approval provide many opportunities for members to revise the content of legislation and to alter their views on a particular piece of legislation several times over. Thus, it is much easier to defeat a bill than it is to get one passed. The House and Senate have parallel processes, and often the same bill is introduced in each chamber at the same time.

A bill must be introduced by a member of Congress, but, in an attempt to show support for the aims of the bill, it is often sponsored by several other members (called co-sponsors).[22] Once introduced, the bill is sent to the clerk of the chamber, who gives it a number (for example, HR 1 or S 1—indicating House or Senate bill number one for the Congress). The bill is then printed, distributed, and sent to the appropriate committee or committees for consideration.

The committee usually refers the bill to one of its subcommittees, which researches the bill and decides whether to hold hearings on it. The subcommittee hearings provide the opportunity for those on both sides of the issue to voice their opinions. Most of these hearings are now open to the public because of 1970s sunshine laws, which require open sessions. After the hearings, the bill is revised in subcommittee, and then the subcommittee votes to approve or defeat the bill. If the subcommittee votes in favor of the bill, it is returned to the full committee. There,

SIMULATION

You Are a Member of Congress

markup

A process in which committee members offer changes to a bill before it goes to the floor in either house for a vote.

during **markup,** committee members can add items to the bill and send it to the House or Senate floor with a favorable recommendation. It can also reject the bill (see Figure 6.4).

The second stage of action takes place on the House or Senate floor. As previously discussed, in the House, before a bill may be debated on the floor, it must be approved by the Committee on Rules and given a rule and a place on the calendar, or schedule. (House budget bills, however, don't go to the Rules Committee.) In the House, the rule given to a bill determines the limits on the floor debate and specifies what types of amendments, if any, may be attached to the bill. Once the Rules Committee considers the bill, it is put on the calendar.

FIGURE 6.4 HOW A BILL BECOMES A LAW

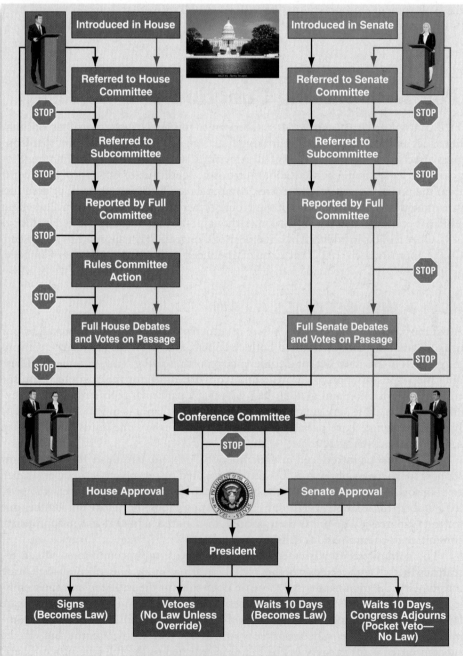

When the day arrives for floor debate, the House may choose to form a Committee of the Whole. This procedure allows the House to deliberate with only one hundred members present to expedite consideration of the bill. On the House floor, the bill is debated, amendments are offered, and a vote ultimately is taken by the full House. If the bill survives, it is sent to the Senate for consideration if it was not considered there simultaneously.

Unlike the House, where debate is necessarily limited given the size of the body, bills may be held up by a hold or a filibuster in the Senate. A **hold** is a tactic by which a senator asks to be informed before a particular bill is brought to the floor. This request signals the Senate leadership and the sponsors of the bill that a colleague may have objections to the bill and should be consulted before further action is taken.

Filibusters, which allow for unlimited debate on a bill (or a presidential appointment), grew out of the absence of rules to limit speech in the Senate. In contrast to a hold, a filibuster is a more formal and public way of halting action on a bill. There are no rules on the content of a filibuster as long as a senator keeps talking. A senator may read from a phone book, recite poetry, or read cookbooks to delay a vote. Often, a team of senators takes turns speaking to keep the filibuster going in the hope that a bill will be tabled or killed. In 1964, for example, a group of northern liberal senators continued a filibuster for eight-two days in an effort to prevent amendments that would weaken a civil rights bill. Still, filibusters often are more of a threat than an actual event on the Senate floor, although members may use them in extreme circumstances. (See American Values/American Voices: The Gang of Fourteen and the Search for Compromise.)

There is only one way to end a filibuster. Sixteen senators must sign a motion for **cloture.** This motion requires the votes of sixty members to limit debate; after a cloture motion passes the Senate floor, members may spend no more than thirty additional hours debating the legislation at issue.

The third stage of action takes place when the two chambers of Congress approve different versions of the same bill. When this happens, they establish a conference committee to iron out the differences between the two versions. The conference committee, whose members are from the original House and Senate committees, hammers out a compromise, which is returned to each chamber for a final vote. Sometimes the conference committee fails to agree and the bill dies there. No changes or amendments to the compromise version are allowed. If the bill is passed, it is sent to the president, who either signs it or **vetoes** it. If the bill is not passed in both houses, it dies.

The president has ten days to consider a bill. He has four options:

1. The president can sign the bill, at which point it becomes law.

2. The president can veto the bill, which is more likely to occur when the president is of a different party from the majority in Congress; Congress may override the president's veto with a two-thirds vote in each chamber, a very difficult task.

3. The president can wait the full ten days, at the end of which time the bill becomes law without his signature if Congress is still in session.

4. If the Congress adjourns before the ten days are up, the president can choose not to sign the bill, and it is considered pocket vetoed.

A **pocket veto** figuratively allows bills stashed in the president's pocket to die. The only way for a bill then to become law is for it to be reintroduced in the next session and be put through the process all over again. Because Congress sets its own date of adjournment, technically the session could be continued the few extra days necessary to prevent a pocket veto. Extensions are unlikely, however, as sessions are scheduled to adjourn close to the November elections or the December holidays.

hold
A tactic by which a senator asks to be informed before a particular bill is brought to the floor. This stops the bill from coming to the floor until the hold is removed.

filibuster
A formal way of halting action on a bill by means of long speeches or unlimited debate in the Senate.

cloture
Mechanism requiring sixty senators to vote to cut off debate.

veto
Formal constitutional authority of the president to reject bills passed by both houses of the legislative body, thus preventing their becoming law without further congressional activity.

pocket veto
If Congress adjourns during the ten days the president has to consider a bill passed by both houses of Congress, without the president's signature, the bill is considered vetoed.

American Values/American Voices

THE GANG OF FOURTEEN AND THE SEARCH FOR COMPROMISE

In early 2005, a bipartisan group of moderate senators came together to negotiate a compromise over what was being called the "nuclear option" to abolish the filibuster.[a] The Gang of Fourteen, composed of seven Republicans and seven Democrats, led by Senators Ben Nelson (D–NE) and John McCain (R–AZ), were sometimes called the "Mod Squad," as they were considered the Senate's moderates and often held the power to cast the deciding votes on controversial pieces of legislation. By coming together, they effectively barred any change in Senate rules concerning the filibuster and forestalled the potential use of the nuclear option that would have allowed cloture on a filibuster to be ended by a simple majority vote, not the sixty votes required by current Senate rules.[b]

The group believed that there was safety in numbers as its members often found themselves at odds with their increasingly partisan parties. As Democrats and Republicans moved to the left and right respectively, the Gang of Fourteen argued that they more truly reflected American values and that it was their responsibility to give voice and power to the wishes of most Americans whose views, as reported by public opinion polls, are far more centrist than those of most elected officials in Washington, D.C.

In 2005, as acrimony increased in the Senate over the Democrats' use of the filibuster to prevent Senate votes on several controversial Bush administration nominees for vacancies on the federal courts, the Gang of Fourteen played an important role by entering into an agreement whereby the seven Democrats would no longer vote along with their party on filibustering judicial nominees except in "extraordinary circumstances." In turn, the seven Republicans would break with the Republican leadership and vote against the nuclear option if it was invoked. Because the Republicans' majority was so slim, the agreement effectively stopped the Republican leadership from changing Senate rules. More-over, it prevented the Democrats from gaining the forty-one votes necessary to uphold a filibuster.

The informal group sprang to action again in July 2005, when it tried to advise President Bush on the choice of a nominee to replace retiring Supreme Court Justice Sandra Day O'Connor. In November 2005, the group met to discuss the nomination of Samuel A. Alito Jr. to the Supreme Court, and in January 2006, the members of the group unanimously supported a cloture vote in the Alito nomination, providing more than enough votes to prevent a filibuster. Alito was confirmed to take the much more moderate Justice O'Connor's place on the Court.

Many commentators believe that in spite of their bipartisan intentions, the Gang of Fourteen facilitated the confirmation of two conservatives to the Supreme Court—Alito and the new Chief Justice John G. Roberts Jr.—perhaps altering that Court's stance on a host of issues. Early votes by Roberts and Alito, especially in areas of criminal defendants' rights, support that view. Still, most Americans prefer not to see criminals go free over procedural issues. Thus, by facilitating the confirmation of these justices, the Gang of Fourteen may have been echoing the true voice of American values in the Senate. In 2006, two Republicans in the Gang of Fourteen were defeated—Lincoln Chafee (R–RI) and Mike DeWine (R–OH). Joe Lieberman (D–CT) lost the Democratic primary but won in the general election. While the Gang of Fourteen has dissolved, the 2006 elections showed that the American public may largely prefer more moderate values.

[a]Jackie Kucinich and Jeffrey Young, "Social Security Is Next for Gang of Fourteen," *The Hill* (May 25, 2005): 1.

[b]James Kuhnhenn, "Appeals Picks Renew Battle: 'Gang of 14' May Intercede on 2 Judicial Nominees," *Pittsburgh Post-Gazette* (May 10, 2006): A8.

[c]Kuhnhenn, "Appeals Picks Renew Battle."

Congress and the President

THE CONSTITUTION ENVISIONED that the Congress and the president would have discrete powers and that one branch would be able to hold the other in check. Over the years, and especially since the 1930s, the president often has held the upper hand. In times of crisis or simply when it was unable to meet public demands for solutions, Congress willingly has handed over its authority to the chief executive. Even though the chief executive has been granted greater latitude, legislators do, of course, retain ultimate legislative authority to question executive actions and to halt administration activities by cutting off funds for programs a president wants. Congress also wields ultimate power over the president, since it can impeach and even remove him from office.

THE SHIFTING BALANCE OF POWER

The balance of power between Congress and the executive branch has seesawed over time. Today, Congress often finds itself responding to executive branch proposals. Critics of Congress point to its slow and unwieldy nature as well as the complexity of national problems as reasons that Congress often doesn't seem to act on its own.

Comparing Legislatures

CONGRESSIONAL OVERSIGHT OF THE EXECUTIVE BRANCH

From the the 1960s through the election of President George W. Bush, Congress increased its **oversight** of the executive branch. Oversight subcommittees became particularly prominent in the 1970s and 1980s as a means of promoting investigation and program review, to determine if an agency, department, or office is carrying out its responsibilities as intended by Congress.[23] Congressional oversight also includes checking on possible abuses of power by members of the military and governmental officials, including the president. The Republican-controlled Congress was especially mindful of its oversight duties during the Clinton administration. Not only did it regularly hold oversight hearings involving Cabinet secretaries, but it also launched several investigations of the Clintons themselves, from Travelgate, to their investments in a failed Whitewater development in Arkansas, and President Bill Clinton's involvement with Monica Lewinsky that led to his impeachment in the House and trial in the Senate.

oversight
Congressional review of the activities of an agency, department, or office.

Key to Congress's performance of its oversight function is its ability to question members of the administration to see if they are enforcing and interpreting the laws as intended by Congress. These committee hearings, now routinely televised, are among Congress's most visible and dramatic actions. The hearings are not used simply to gather information. Hearings may focus on particular executive-branch actions and often signal that Congress believes changes in policy need to be made before an agency next comes before the committee to justify its budget. Hearings also are used to improve program administration. Since most members of House and Senate committees and subcommittees are interested in the issues under their jurisdiction, they often want to help and not hinder policy makers.

Although Congress, particularly under Republican leadership, abandoned some of its oversight functions members also have other means of oversight at their disposal. Legislators may augment their formal oversight of the executive branch by allowing citizens to appeal adverse bureaucratic decisions to agencies, Congress, and even the courts. The Congressional Review Act of 1996 allows Congress to nullify agency regulations by joint resolutions of legislative disapproval. This process, called **congressional review,** is another method of exercising congressional oversight.[24] The act provides Congress with sixty days to disapprove newly announced agency regulations, often passed to implement some congressional action. A regulation is disapproved if the resolution is passed by both chambers and signed by the president, or when Congress overrides a presidential veto of a disapproving resolution. To date, however, this act has been used only once—in 2001—when Congress reversed Clinton administration ergonomics regulations, which were intended to prevent job-related repetitive stress injuries.

congressional review
A process whereby Congress can nullify agency regulations by a joint resolution of legislative disapproval.

Foreign Policy and National Security The Constitution divides foreign policy powers between the executive and the legislative branches. The president has the power to wage war and negotiate treaties, whereas Congress has the power to declare war, and the Senate has the power to ratify treaties. The executive branch, however, has become preeminent in foreign affairs despite the constitutional division of powers. This supremacy is partly due to a series of crises and the development of nuclear weapons in the twentieth century; both have necessitated quick decision making and secrecy, which are much easier to manage in the executive branch. Congress, with its 535 voting members, has a more difficult time reaching a consensus and keeping secrets.

After years of playing second fiddle to a series of presidents from Theodore Roosevelt to Richard M. Nixon, a "snoozing Congress" was "aroused" and seized for itself the authority and expertise necessary to go head-to-head with the chief executive.[25] In a delayed response to Lyndon B. Johnson's conduct of the Vietnam War, Congress passed the **War Powers Act** in 1973 over President Nixon's veto. This act requires presidents to obtain congressional approval before committing U.S. forces to a combat zone. It also requires them to notify Congress within forty-eight hours of committing troops to foreign soil. In addition, the president must withdraw troops within sixty days unless Congress votes to declare war. The president also is required to consult with Congress, if at all possible, prior to committing troops.

The War Powers Act has been of limited effectiveness in claiming a larger congressional role in international crisis situations. Presidents Gerald R. Ford, Jimmy Carter, and Ronald Reagan never consulted Congress in advance of committing troops, citing the need for secrecy and swift movement, although each president did notify Congress shortly after the incidents. They contended that the War Powers Act was probably unconstitutional because it limits presidential prerogatives as commander in chief. In 2001, when Congress passed a joint resolution authorizing the president to use force against terrorists, the resolution included language that met War Powers Act requirements and waived the sixty-day limit on the president's authority to involve U.S. troops abroad.[26]

Confirmation of Presidential Appointments

The Senate plays a special oversight function through its ability to confirm key members of the executive branch, as well as presidential appointments to the federal courts. As discussed in chapters 8 and 9, although the Senate generally confirms most presidential nominees, it does not always do so. A wise president considers senatorial reaction before nominating potentially controversial individuals to his administration or to the federal courts, especially in times of divided governments when Congress and the president are of different politcal parties.

The Impeachment Process

As discussed earlier, the impeachment process is Congress's ultimate oversight of the U.S. president (as well as of federal court judges). The U.S. Constitution is quite vague about the impeachment process, and much of the debate about it concerns what is an impeachable offense. The Constitution speci-

---

War Powers Act
Passed by Congress in 1973; the president is limited in the deployment of troops overseas to a sixty-day period in peacetime (which can be extended for an extra thirty days to permit withdrawal) unless Congress explicitly gives its approval for a longer period.

■ The issue of congressional oversight of the executive branch has become particularly thorny since the terrorist attacks of September 11, 2001. As early as July 17, 2003, Senator Jay Rockefeller (D–WV), the ranking member on the Senate Intelligence Committee, wrote to Vice President Dick Cheney that he was very troubled by what he had heard at a secret intelligence briefing. At this particular briefing, Rockefeller had been apprised of the fact that the National Security Agency was monitoring Americans' phone and e-mail communications without the judicial oversight called for by law. "Clearly," wrote Rockefeller, "the activities we discussed raise profound oversight issues."

Photo courtesy: left, Alex Wong/Getty Images; right, Office of Jay Rockefeller fies that a president can be impeached for treason, bribery, or other "high crimes and misdemeanors." Most commentators agree that this phrase was meant to mean significant abuses of power. In *Federalist No. 65,* Alexander Hamilton noted his belief that impeachable offenses "are of a nature which may with peculiar propriety be denominated political, as they relate chiefly to injuries done immediately to society itself."

House and Senate rules control how the impeachment process operates. Yet, because the process is used so rarely, and under such disparate circumstances, there are few hard and fast rules. The U.S. House of Representatives has voted to impeach only seventeen federal officials—and only two of those were presidents, Andrew Johnson and Bill Clinton. (Seven of the others were convicted and removed from office and three resigned.)

Only four resolutions against presidents have resulted in further action: (1) John Tyler, charged with corruption and misconduct in 1843; (2) Andrew Johnson, charged with serious misconduct in 1868; (3) Richard M. Nixon, charged with obstruction and the abuse of power in 1974; and, (4) Bill Clinton, charged with perjury and obstruction of justice in 1998.

Congress and the Judiciary

CONGRESS EXERCISES ITS CONTROL over the judiciary in a variety of ways. Not only does it have the constitutional authority to establish the size of the Supreme Court, its appellate jurisdiction, the structure of the federal court system, and allocate its budget, but the Senate also has the authority to accept or reject presidential nominees to the federal courts (as well as executive branch appointments).

In the case of federal district court appointments, senators often have considerable say in the nomination of judges from their states through **senatorial courtesy,** a process by which presidents generally defer to the senators who represent the state where the vacancy occurs. The judicial nominees of both Presidents Bill Clinton and George W. Bush have encountered a particularly hostile Senate.

An equally potentially potent form of congressional oversight of the judicial branch, which involves both the House and the Senate, is the setting of the jurisdiction of the federal courts. Originally, the jurisdiction, or ability of the federal courts to hear cases, was quite limited. Over time, however, as Congress legislated to regulate the economy and even crime, the caseload of the courts skyrocketed. No matter how busy federal judges are, it is ultimately up to the Congress to determine the number of judges on each court.

During the 109th Congress, several members, unhappy with Supreme Court decisions and the Senate's failure to pass a proposed constitutional amendment to ban same-sex marriage, began to push for a bill to prevent federal courts from hearing challenges to the federal Defense of Marriage Act. In the House, the Republican majority leader pledged to promote similar legislation to bar court challenges to the Pledge of Allegiance and other social issues, including abortion. When Congress rears the ugly head of jurisdiction, it is signaling to the federal courts that Congress believes federal judges have gone too far.

senatorial courtesy
A process by which presidents, when selecting district court judges, defer to the senator in whose state the vacancy occurs.

Summary

THE SIZE AND SCOPE OF CONGRESS, and demands put on it, have increased tremendously over the years. The Constitution created a bicameral legislature with members of each body to be elected differently, and thus to represent different constituencies. Article I of the Constitution sets forth qualifications for office, states age minimums, and specifies how legislators are to be distributed among the states. The Constitution also requires seats in the House of Representatives to be apportioned by population. The Constitution provides a vast array of enumerated and implied powers to Congress. Some, such as law-making and oversight, are shared by each house of Congress; others are not.

Political parties play a major role in the way Congress is organized. The Speaker of the House, the most powerful person in Congress, is traditionally a member of the majority party, and members of the majority party chair all committees. In addition to the party leaders, Congress has a labyrinth of committees and subcommittees that cover the entire range of government policies, often with a confusing tangle of shared responsibilities. Each legislator serves on one or more committees and multiple subcommittees. Most business of Congress is done in committees.

Incumbency is an important factor in winning reelection—as is the kind of representation a member or senator provides to his or her district. A multitude of factors impinge on legislators as they decide policy issues. These include political party, constituents, colleagues and caucuses, interest groups, lobbyists, political action committees, and staff and support agencies.

The road to enacting a bill into law is long and strewn with obstacles, and only a small share of the proposals introduced become law. Legislation must be approved by committees in each house and on the floor of each chamber. Legislation that is passed in different forms by the two chambers must be resolved in a conference before going back to each chamber for a vote and then to the president, who can sign the proposal into law, veto it, or allow it to become law without his signature.

Although the Framers intended for Congress and the president to have discrete spheres of authority, over time, power shifted between the two branches, with Congress often appearing to lose power to the benefit of the president. Still, Congress has attempted to oversee the actions of the president and the executive branch through legislative oversight. Congress also uses congressional review to limit presidential power. Congress also has attempted to rein in presidential power through passage of the War Powers Act, to little practical effect. Congress, through the Senate, possesses the power to confirm or reject presidential appointments. Its ultimate weapon is the power of impeachment and conviction.

Congress exercises its control over the judiciary in a variety of ways. Not only does it have the constitutional authority to establish the size of the Supreme Court, its appellate jurisdiction, and the structure of the federal court system, but the Senate also has the authority to accept or reject presidential nominees to the federal courts.

KEY TERMS

apportionment, p. 167
bicameral legislature, p. 166
bill, p. 167
cloture, p. 187

conference committee, p. 175
congressional review, p. 189
delegate, p. 181
discharge petition, p. 176
divided government, p. 182
filibuster, p. 187
hold, p. 187
impeachment, p. 167
incumbency, p. 178
joint committee, p. 174
logrolling, p. 183
majority leader, p. 172
majority party, p. 168
markup, p. 186
minority leader, p. 173
minority party, p. 168
oversight, p. 189
party caucus or conference, p. 172
pocket veto, p. 187
politico, p. 181
pork, p. 176
president pro tempore, p. 174
redistricting, p. 167
select (or special) committee, p. 175
senatorial courtesy, p. 191
seniority, p. 177
Speaker of the House, p. 171
standing committee, p. 174
trustee, p. 180
veto, p. 187
War Powers Act, p. 190
whip, p. 173

SELECTED READINGS

Adler, E. Scott, and John S. Lapinski. *The Macropolitics of Congress.* Princeton, NJ: Princeton University Press, 2006.

Bianco, William T., ed. *Congress on Display, Congress at Work.* Ann Arbor: University of Michigan Press, 2000.

Binder, Sarah A. *Stalemate: Causes and Consequences of Legislative Gridlock.* Washington, DC: Brookings Institution, 2003.

Campbell, Colton C., and Paul S. Herrnson. *War Stories from Capitol Hill.* New York: Pearson, 2003.

Cox, Gary W., and Matthew D. McCubbins. *Setting the Agenda: Responsible Party Government in the U.S. House of Representatives.* New York: Cambridge University Press, 2005.

Davidson, Roger H., and Walter Oleszek. *Congress and Its Members,* 10th ed. Washington, DC: CQ Press, 2006.

Deering, Christopher J., and Steven S. Smith, *Committees in Congress,* 3rd ed. Washington, DC: CQ Press, 1997.

Dodd, Lawrence C., and Bruce I. Oppenheimer, eds. *Congress Reconsidered,* 8th ed. Washington, DC: CQ Press, 2004.

Evans, Diana. *Greasing the Wheels: Using Pork Barrel Projects to Build Majority Coalitions in Congress.* New York: Cambridge University Press, 2004.

Fenno, Richard F., Jr. *Going Home: Black Representatives and Their Constituents.* Chicago: University of Chicago Press, 2003.

———. *Home Style: House Members in Their Districts,* reprint ed. New York: Longman, 2002.

Gertzog, Irwin N. *Women and Power on Capitol Hill: Reconstructing the Congressional Women's Caucus.* Boulder, CO: Lynne Rienner, 2004.

Mayhew, David R. *Congress: The Electoral Connection.* New Haven, CT: Yale University Press, 1974.

O'Connor, Karen, ed. *Women in Congress: Running, Winning, and Ruling.* New York: Haworth, 2004.

Oleszek, Walter J. *Congressional Procedures and the Policy Process,* 6th ed. Washington, DC: CQ Press, 2004.

Polsby, Nelson W. *How Congress Evolves: Social Bases of Institutional Changes,* new ed. New York: Oxford University Press, 2005.

Price, David E. *The Congressional Experience: A View from the Hill,* 3rd ed. Boulder, CO: Westview, 2005.

Quirk, Paul J., and Sarah A. Binder, eds. *Institutions of American Democracy: The Legislative Branch.* New York: Oxford University Press, 2006.

Rosenthal, Cindy Simon, ed. *Women Transforming Congress.* Norman: University of Oklahoma Press, 2003.

Schickler, Eric. *Disjointed Pluralism: Institutional Innovation and the Development of the U.S. Congress.* Princeton, NJ: Princeton University Press, 2001.

Swers, Michele. *The Difference Women Make: The Policy Impact of Women in Congress.* Chicago: University of Chicago Press, 2002.

Thurber, James A., ed. *Rivals for Power: Congressional Presidential Relations.* Lanham, MD: Rowman and Littlefield, 2001.

WEB EXPLORATIONS

To find out who your representative is and how he or she votes, see
http://www.thomas.loc.gov

To learn more about the legislative branch, see
www.senate.gov
www.house.gov

To learn more about the 110th Congress, see
http://clerk.house.gov

For more on the offices of the Congress, including the Speaker of the House and her activities, see
http://speakernews.house.gov

To get up-to-date data on House leaders, see
http://stenyhoyer.house.gov
http://democraticleader.house.gov

For information on specific committees, see
www.senate.gov
www.house.gov

For more information on minority party rights and the Senate filibuster, see
http://www.americanprogress.org
http://www.brookings.edu

Photo courtesy: Dennis Brack

THE PRESIDENCY

WHEN RONALD REAGAN DIED on June 5, 2004, many Americans, first in California and then in Washington, D.C., lined up for hours to pay their respects to the man who had been the fortieth president of the United States. Many people were able to see, for the first time in recent memory, the grandeur of a presidential state funeral. Reagan was the first president to lie in state in the Rotunda of the Capitol since Lyndon B. Johnson did in January 1973, and one of only nine American presidents to receive that honor.

The 200 plus years of presidential funerals underscore the esteem with which most Americans accord the office of the president, regardless of its occupant. Just before the first president, George Washington, died, he made it known that he wanted his burial to be a quiet one, "without parade or funeral oration." He also asked that he not be buried for three days; at that time, it was not without precedent to make this kind of request out of fear of being buried alive. Despite these requests, Washington's funeral was a state occasion as hundreds of soldiers, with their rifles held backward, marched to Mount Vernon, Virginia, where he was interred. Across the nation, imitation funerals were held, and the military wore black arm bands for six months.[1] It was during Washington's memorial service that Henry Lee declared that the former president was "first in war, first in peace, and first in the hearts of his countrymen."[2]

When Abraham Lincoln died in 1865 after being wounded by an assassin's bullet, more than a dozen funerals were held for him. Hundreds of thousands of mourners lined the way as the train carrying his open casket traveled the 1,700 miles to Illinois, where he was buried next to the body of his young son, who had died three years earlier. Most president's bodies were transported to their final resting place by train, allowing ordinary Americans the opportunity to pay their respects as the train traveled long distances. When Franklin D. Roosevelt died in Warm Springs, Georgia, his body was transported to Washington, D.C., and then to Hyde Park, New York, where he, like Washington, was buried on his family's estate.

Today, one of the first things a president is asked to do upon taking office is to consider his funeral plans. The military alone has a book 138 pages long devoted to the kind of ceremony and traditions that were so evident in the Reagan funeral: a horse-drawn caisson; a riderless horse with boots hung backward in the stirrups to indicate that the deceased will ride no

CHAPTER OUTLINE

⭐ The Origins of and Rules Governing the Office of President of the United States

⭐ The Constitutional Powers of the President

⭐ The Development and Expansion of Presidential Power

⭐ The Presidential Establishment

⭐ The President as Policy Maker

⭐ Presidential Leadership and the Importance of Public Opinion more; a twenty-one-gun salute; a flyover by military aircraft. Each president's family, however, has personalized their private, yet also public opportunity to mourn. The Reagan family, for example, filed a 300-page plan for the funeral in 1989 and updated it regularly. Former presidents Gerald R. Ford, Jimmy Carter, and George Bush all have filed formal plans; Bill Clinton and George W. Bush have yet to do so.

The Reagan funeral also created a national time-out from the news of war, and even presidential campaigns were halted in respect for the deceased president. One historian commented that the event gave Americans the opportunity to "rediscover . . . what holds us together instead of what pulls us apart."[3] This is often the role of presidents—in life or in death.

THE AUTHORITY GRANTED to the president by the U.S. Constitution and through subsequent congressional legislation makes it a position with awesome responsibility. Not only did the Framers not envision such a powerful role for the president, but they could not have foreseen the skepticism with which many presidential actions are now greeted in the press, on talk radio, and on the Internet. Presidents have gone into policy arenas never dreamed of by the Framers. Imagine, for example, what the Framers might have thought about President George W. Bush's 2006 State of the Union Address where he asked legislators to prohibit "the most egregious abuse of medical research—human cloning."

The modern media, used by successful presidents to help advance their agendas, have brought us closer to our presidents and made them seem more human, a mixed blessing for those trying to lead. Only two photographs exist of Franklin D. Roosevelt in a wheelchair—his paralysis was a closely guarded secret. Five decades later, Bill Clinton was asked on national TV what kind of underwear he preferred (briefs). Later, revelations about his conduct with Monica Lewinsky made this disclosure seem tame. This demystifying of the president and the increased mistrust of government make governing a difficult job.

A president relies on more than the formal powers of office to lead the nation: public opinion and public confidence are key components of his ability to get his programs adopted and his vision of the nation implemented. As political scientist Richard E. Neustadt has noted, the president's power often rests on his power to persuade.[4] To persuade, he not only must be able to forge links with members of Congress, but he also must have the support of the American people and the respect of foreign leaders.

VIDEO DEBATE

Presidential Power

The abilities to persuade and to marshal the informal powers of the presidency have become more important over time. In fact, the presidency of George W. Bush and the circumstances that surround it are dramatically different from the presidency of his father George Bush (1989–1993). America is changing dramatically and so are the responsibilities of the president and people's expectations of the person who holds that office. Presidents in the last century battled the Great Depression, fascism, communism, and several wars involving American soldiers. With the Cold War over, until the war in Iraq, there were few chances for modern presidents to demonstrate their leadership in a time of crisis or threat.

The tension between public expectations about the presidency and the formal powers of the president permeate our discussion of how the office has evolved from its humble origins in Article II of the Constitution to its current stature.

First, we will examine the origins of and rules governing the office of president of the United States and the constitutional powers of the president. We will then examine the development and expansion of presidential power and a more personalized presidency. After discussing the development of the presidential establishment, we will focus on the president as policy maker. Finally, we will examine presidential leadership and the importance of public opinion.

The Origins of and Rules Governing the Office of President of the United States

AS WITH MANY OF AMERICA'S POLITICAL INSTITUTIONS, the origins of the presidency date back to the Constitutional Convention. The delegates there quickly decided to dispense with the Articles of Confederation and fashion a new government composed of three branches: the legislative (to make the laws), the executive (to execute, or implement, the laws), and the judicial (to interpret the laws). The Framers had little difficulty in agreeing that executive authority should be vested in one person, although some delegates suggested multiple executives to diffuse the power of the executive branch. Under the Articles of Confederation, there had been no executive branch of government; the eighteen different men who served as the president of the Continental Congress of the United States of America were president in name only—they had no actual authority or power in the new nation. Yet, because the Framers were so sure that George Washington—whom they had trusted with their lives during the Revolutionary War—would become the first president of the new nation, many of their deepest fears were calmed. They agreed on the necessity of having one individual speak on behalf of the new nation, and they all agreed that this one individual should be George Washington.

The manner of the president's election haunted the Framers for some time, and their solution to the dilemma—the creation of the Electoral College—is described in detail in chapter 12. We leave the resolution of that issue aside for now and turn instead to details of the issues the Framers resolved quickly.

PRESIDENTIAL QUALIFICATIONS AND TERMS OF OFFICE

The Constitution requires that the president (and the vice president, whose major function is to succeed the president in the event of his death or disability) be a natural-born citizen of the United States, at least thirty-five years old, and a resident of the United States for at least fourteen years.

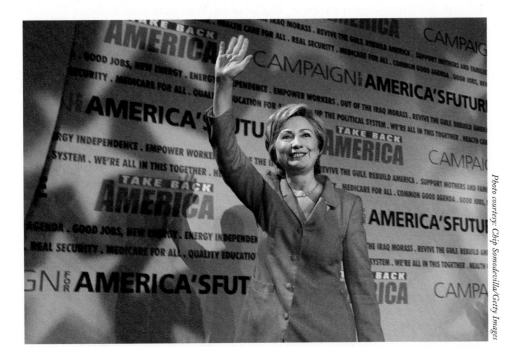

■ Senator Hillary Rodham Clinton (D–NY) waves goodbye after addressing the Campaign for America's Future 2006 "Take Back America" conference in Washington, D.C. Several women, including Senator Clinton and Secretary of State Condoleezza Rice, have been discussed as potential contenders for the presidency in 2008.

Photo courtesy: Chip Somodevilla/Getty Images

At one time the length of a president's term was controversial. Four-, seven-, and eleven-year terms with no eligibility for reelection were suggested by various delegates to the Constitutional Convention. The Framers ultimately reached agreement on a four-year term with eligibility for reelection. In the 1930s and 1940s, however, Franklin D. Roosevelt ran successfully in four elections as Americans fought first the Great Depression and then World War II. Despite Roosevelt's popularity, negative reaction to his long tenure in office ultimately led to passage (and ratification in 1951) of the **Twenty-Second Amendment.** It limits presidents to two four-year terms. A vice president who succeeds a president due to death, resignation, or impeachment is eligible for a total of ten years in office: two years of a president's remaining term and two elected terms, or more than two years of a president's term followed by one elected term.

During the Constitutional Convention, Benjamin Franklin was a staunch supporter of including a provision allowing for **impeachment,** a process by which to begin to remove an official from office. He noted that "historically, the lack of power to impeach had necessitated recourse to assassination."[5] Not surprisingly, then, he urged the rest of the delegates to formulate a legal mechanism to remove the president and vice president.

The impeachment provision ultimately included in Article II was adopted as a check on the power of the president. As we discussed in detail in chapter 6, each house of Congress was given a role to play in the impeachment process to assure that the chief executive could be removed only for "Treason, Bribery, or other high Crimes and Misdemeanors." The House is empowered to vote to impeach the president by a simple majority vote. The Senate then acts as a court of law and tries the president for the charged offenses. A two-thirds majority vote in the Senate on any count contained in the articles of impeachment is necessary to remove the president from office.

In 1974, President Richard M. Nixon resigned from office rather than face the certainty of impeachment, trial, and removal from office for his role in covering up details about a break-in at the Democratic Party's national headquarters in the Watergate office complex. What came to be known simply as Watergate also produced a major decision from the Supreme Court on the scope of what is termed **executive privilege.** In *U.S. v. Nixon* **(1974),** the Supreme Court ruled unanimously that there was no overriding executive privilege that sanctioned the president's refusal to comply with a court order to produce information for use in the trial of the Watergate defendants.

RULES OF SUCCESSION

Through 2006, eight presidents have died in office from illness or assassination. William H. Harrison was the first president to die in office—he caught a cold at his inauguration in 1841 and died one month later. (John Tyler thus became the first vice president to succeed to the presidency.) In 1865, Abraham Lincoln became the first president to be assassinated.

The Framers were aware that a system of orderly transfer of power was necessary; this was the primary reason they created the office of the vice president. To further clarify the order of presidential succession, in 1947, Congress passed the Presidential Succession Act, which lists—in order—those in line (after the vice president) to succeed the president.

1. Speaker of the House of Representatives
2. President pro tempore of the Senate
3. Secretaries of state, treasury, and defense, and other Cabinet heads in order of the creation of their department.

The Succession Act has never been used because there has always been a vice president to take over when a president died in office. The **Twenty-Fifth Amend-**

Twenty-Second Amendment
Adopted in 1951, prevents a president from serving more than two terms, or more than ten years if he came to office via the death or impeachment of his predecessor.

impeachment
The power delegated to the House of Representatives in the Constitution to charge the president, vice president, or other "civil officers," including federal judges, with "Treason, Bribery, or other high Crimes and Misdemeanors." This is the first step in the constitutional process of removing such government officials from office.

executive privilege
An implied presidental power that allows the president to refuse to disclose information regarding confidential conversations or national security to Congress or the judiciary.

U.S. v. Nixon **(1974)**
Key Supreme Court ruling on power of the president, finding that there is no absolute constitutional executive privilege to allow a president to refuse to comply with a court order to produce information needed in a criminal trial.

Twenty-Fifth Amendment
Adopted in 1967 to establish procedures for filling vacancies in the office of president and vice president as well as providing for procedures to deal with the disability of a president.

The Living Constitution

Whenever there is a vacancy in the office of the Vice President, the President shall nominate a Vice President who shall take office upon confirmation by a majority vote of both Houses of Congress.

—TWENTY-FIFTH AMENDMENT, SECTION 2

This clause of the Twenty-Fifth Amendment allows a president to fill a vacancy in the office of vice president with the consent of a simple majority of both Houses of Congress. The purpose of this amendment, which also deals with vacancies in the office of the president, was to remedy some structural flaws in Article II. At the time of this amendment's addition to the Constitution in 1965, seven vice presidents had died in office and one had resigned. For over 20 percent of the nation's history there had been no vice president to assume the office of the president in case of his death or infirmity. When John F. Kennedy was assassinated, Vice President Lyndon B. Johnson became president and the office of vice president was vacant. Since Johnson had suffered a heart attack as vice president, members of Congress were anxious to remedy the problems that might occur should there be no vice president.

Richard M. Nixon followed Johnson as president, and ironically, during Nixon's presidency, the office of the vice president became empty twice! First, Nixon's vice president, Spiro T. Agnew, was forced to resign in the wake of charges of bribe taking, corruption, and income tax evasion while an elected official in Maryland. He was replaced by popular House Minority Leader Gerald R. Ford (R–MI), who had no trouble getting a majority vote in both houses of Congress to confirm his nomination. When Nixon resigned rather than face sure impeachment, Ford became president and selected the former governor of New York, Nelson A. Rockefeller, to be his vice president. This chain of events set up for the first time in U.S. history a situation in which neither the president nor the vice president had been elected to those positions.

ment, in fact, was added to the Constitution in 1967 to assure that this will continue to be the case. Should a vacancy occur in the office of the vice president, the Twenty-Fifth Amendment directs the president to appoint a new vice president, subject to the approval (by a simple majority) of both houses of Congress. (See The Living Constitution: Twenty-Fifth Amendment, Section 2.)

The Constitutional Powers of the President

SIMULATION

Presidential Leadership: Which Hat Do You Wear?

THOUGH THE FRAMERS nearly unanimously agreed about the need for a strong central government and a greatly empowered Congress, they did not agree about the proper role of the president or the sweep of his authority. In contrast to Article I's laundry list of enumerated powers for the Congress, Article II details few presidential powers. Perhaps the most important section of Article II is its first sentence: "The executive Power shall be vested in a President of the United States of America." Nonetheless, the sum total of the president's powers, enumerated below, allows him to become a major player in the policy process.

THE APPOINTMENT POWER

To help the president enforce laws passed by Congress, the Constitution authorizes him to appoint, with the advice and consent of the Senate, "Ambassadors, other public Ministers and Consuls, judges of the supreme Court, and all other Officers of the United States, whose Appointments are not herein otherwise provided for, and which shall be established by Law." Although this section of the Constitution deals only with appointments, behind that language is a powerful policy-making tool. The president has the authority to make nearly 3,000 appointments to his administration (of which just over 1,000 require Senate confirmation),[6] and he technically appoints more than 75,000 military personnel. Many of these appointees are in positions to wield substantial authority over the course and direction of public policy. Although Congress has the authority "to make all laws," through the president's enforcement power—and his chosen assistants—he often can set the policy agenda for the nation. And, especially in the context of his ability to make appointments to the federal courts, his influence can be felt far past his term of office.

It is not surprising, then, that selecting the right people is often one of a president's most important tasks. Presidents look for a blend of loyalty, competence, and integrity. Identifying these qualities in people is a major challenge that every new president faces. Recent presidents, especially Bill Clinton and George W. Bush, have made an effort to create a Cabinet and staff that, in President Clinton's terms, looks "more like America." (See Table 7.1.)

In the past, when a president forwarded a nomination to the Senate for its approval, his selections traditionally were given great respect—especially those for the **Cabinet,** an advisory group selected by the president to help him make decisions and execute the laws. In fact, until the Clinton administration, the vast majority (97 percent) of all presidential nominations were confirmed.[7]

THE POWER TO CONVENE CONGRESS

The Constitution requires the president to inform the Congress periodically of "the State of the Union," and authorizes the president to convene either or both houses of Congress on "extraordinary Occasions." In *Federalist No. 77,* Hamilton justified the latter by noting that because the Senate and the chief executive enjoy concurrent powers to make treaties, "It might often be necessary to call it together with a view to this

SIMULATION

You Are Appointing a Supreme Court Justice

Cabinet
The formal body of presidential advisers who head the fifteen executive departments. Presidents often add others to this body of formal advisers.

TABLE 7.1	PRESIDENTIAL TEAMS (SENIOR ADMINISTRATIVE POSITIONS REQUIRING SENATE CONFIRMATION)		
	Total Appointments	*Total Women*	*Percentage Women*
Jimmy Carter	1,087	191	17.6%
Ronald Reagan	2,349	277	11.8%
George Bush	1,079	215	19.9%
Bill Clinton	2,479	1,125	45.0%
George W. Bush[a]	2,786	1,017	36.0%

[a] Bush data include all political appointees through 2005.

Sources: "Insiders Say White House Has Its Own Glass Ceiling," Atlanta Journal and Constitution (April 10, 1995): AF; Judi Hasson, "Senate GOP Leader Lott Says He'll Work with Clinton," USA Today (December 4, 1996): 8A; and U.S. House of Representatives, Committee on Government Reform—Minority Staff, "The Growth of Political Appointees in the Bush Administration," May 2006.

object, when it would be unnecessary and improper to convene the House of Representatives." The power to convene Congress was important when Congress did not sit in nearly year-round sessions. Today this power has little more than symbolic significance.

THE POWER TO MAKE TREATIES

The president's power to make treaties with foreign nations is checked by the Constitution's stipulation that all treaties must be approved by at least two-thirds of the members of the Senate. The chief executive can also "receive ambassadors," wording that has been interpreted to allow the president to recognize the existence of other nations.

The Senate may require substantial amendment of a treaty prior to its consent. When President Jimmy Carter proposed the controversial Panama Canal treaty in 1977 to turn the canal over to Panama, for example, the Senate required several conditions to be ironed out before approving the canal's return.

Presidents may also "unsign" treaties, a practice often met with dismay from other signatories. For example, the George W. Bush administration formally withdrew its support for the International Criminal Court (ICC). In a short, three-sentence letter to UN Secretary General Kofi Annan, the United States withdrew from efforts to create the first permanent court to prosecute war crimes, genocide, and other crimes against humanity. This treaty had been signed by President Bill Clinton and was scheduled to take effect July 1, 2002. Critics of the treaty argued that it could lead to politically motivated charges against U.S. troops in Afghanistan and Iraq.[8]

Presidents also often try to get around the constitutional "advice and consent" of the Senate requirement for ratification of treaties and the congressional approval requirement for trade agreements by entering into an **executive agreement,** which allows the president to form secret and highly sensitive arrangements with foreign nations without Senate approval. Presidents have used these agreements since the days of George Washington, and their use has been upheld by the courts. Although executive agreements are not binding on subsequent administrations, since 1900 they have been used far more frequently than treaties, further cementing the role of the president in foreign affairs, as revealed in Table 7.2.

executive agreement
Formal government agreement entered into by the president that does not require the advice and consent of the U.S. Senate.

veto power
The formal, constitutional authority of the president to reject bills passed by both houses of Congress, thus preventing their becoming law without further congressional action.

THE VETO POWER

In keeping with the system of checks and balances, the president was given the authority to veto any act of Congress (with the exception of joint resolutions that propose constitutional amendments), and Congress was given the authority to override an executive veto by a two-thirds vote in each house. The president's **veto power** is a powerful policy tool because Congress cannot usually muster enough votes to override a veto. Thus, in over 200 years, there have been approximately 2,500 presidential vetoes and only about a hundred have been overridden.

THE POWER TO PRESIDE OVER THE MILITARY AS COMMANDER IN CHIEF

One of the most important constitutional executive powers is the president's authority over the military. Article II states that the president is "Commander in Chief of the Army and Navy of the United States." While the Constitution

TABLE 7.2 TREATIES AND EXECUTIVE AGREEMENTS CONCLUDED BY THE UNITED STATES, 1789–2006

Years	Number of Treaties	Number of Executive Agreements
1789–1839	60	27
1839–1889	215	238
1889–1929	382	763
1930–1932	49	41
1933–1944 (F. Roosevelt)	131	369
1945–1952 (Truman)	132	1,324
1953–1960 (Eisenhower)	89	1,834
1961–1963 (Kennedy)	36	813
1964–1968 (L. Johnson)	67	1,083
1969–1974 (Nixon)	93	1,317
1975–1976 (Ford)	26	666
1977–1980 (Carter)	79	1,476
1981–1988 (Reagan)	125	2,840
1989–1992 (Bush)	67	1,350
1993–2000 (Clinton)	209	2,047
2001–2006 (G.W. Bush)	45	612

Note: Number of treaties includes those concluded during the indicated span of years. Some of these treaties did not receive the consent of the U.S. Senate. Varying definitions of what an executive agreement comprises and their entry-into-force date make the above numbers approximate.

Sources: 1789–1980: *Congressional Quarterly's Guide to Congress,* 291; 1981–2002: Office of the Assistant Legal Adviser for Treaty Affairs. U.S. Department of State; 2002–2006: www.saramitchell.org/MarshallPrins.pdf/.

THE PRESIDENT'S MANY HATS

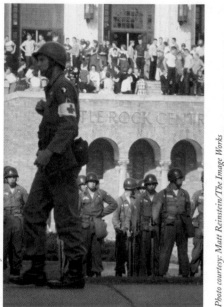

Photo courtesy: Bettmann/Corbis

■ Chief law enforcer: National Guard troops sent by President Dwight D. Eisenhower enforce federal court decisions ordering the integration of public schools in Little Rock, Arkansas.

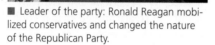

Photo courtesy: Matt Reinstein/The Image Works

■ Leader of the party: Ronald Reagan mobilized conservatives and changed the nature of the Republican Party.

Photo courtesy: Wally McNamee/Folio, Inc.

■ Commander in chief: President George Bush and his wife, Barbara, with troops in the Persian Gulf.

Photo courtesy: Bettmann/Corbis

■ Shaper of domestic policy: President Jimmy Carter announces new energy policies. Here, he wears a sweater to underscore that thermostats in the White House were turned down to save energy.

Photo courtesy: J. David Ake/AFP/Getty Images

■ Key player in the legislative process: President Bill Clinton meets with Speaker of the House Newt Gingrich (R–GA).

Photo courtesy: Bettmann/Corbis

■ Chief of state: President John F. Kennedy and his wife, Jacqueline, with the president of France and his wife during the Kennedys' widely publicized 1961 trip to that nation.

specifically grants Congress the authority to declare war, presidents since Abraham Lincoln have used the commander in chief clause in conjunction with the chief executive's duty to "take Care that the Laws be faithfully executed" to wage war (and to broaden various powers).

Modern presidents continually clash with Congress over the ability to commence hostilities. Realizing that misinformation had led Congress to defer to the executive in the conduct of the Vietnam War, Congress in 1973 passed the **War Powers Act** to limit the president's authority to introduce American troops into hostile foreign lands without congressional approval. President Richard M. Nixon vetoed the act, but it was overridden by a two-thirds majority in both houses of Congress.

Presidents since Nixon have continued to insist that the War Powers Act is an unconstitutional infringement of their executive power. Still, in 2001, President George W. Bush Complied with the act; he sought, and both houses of Congress approved, a joint resolution authorizing the use of force against "those responsible for the recent [September 11] attacks launched against the United States." This resolution actually gave the president more open-ended authority to wage war than his father had received in 1991 to conduct the Persian Gulf War or President Lyndon B. Johnson had received after the Gulf of Tonkin Resolution in 1964.[9] Later, in October 2002, after President Bush declared Iraq to be a "grave threat to peace," the House (296–133) and Senate (77–23) voted overwhelmingly to allow the president to use force in Iraq "as he determines to be necessary and appropriate," thereby conferring tremendous authority on the president to wage war. (See Join the Debate: The War Powers Act.)

> **War Powers Act**
> Passed by Congress in 1973; the president is limited in the deployment of troops overseas to a sixty-day period in peacetime (which can be extended for an extra thirty days to permit withdrawal) unless Congress explicitly gives its approval for a longer period.

THE PARDONING POWER

Presidents can exercise a check on judicial power through their constitutional authority to grant reprieves or pardons. A **pardon** is an executive grant releasing an individual from the punishment or legal consequences of a crime before or after conviction, and restores all rights and privileges of citizenship. Presidents exercise complete pardoning power for federal offenses except in cases of impeachment, which cannot be pardoned. President Gerald R. Ford granted the most famous presidential pardon when he pardoned former President Nixon—who had not been formally charged with any crime—"for any offenses against the United States, which he, Richard Nixon, has committed or may have committed while in office." This unilateral, absolute pardon prevented the former president from ever being tried for any crimes he may have committed. It also unleashed a torrent of public criticism against Ford and questions about whether Nixon had discussed the pardon with Ford before Nixon's resignation. Many analysts attribute Ford's defeat in his 1976 bid for the presidency to that pardon.

Although the pardoning power normally is not considered a key presidential power, its use by a president can get him in severe trouble with the electorate. Three presidents defeated in their reelection bids—Ford, Carter, and George Bush—all incurred the wrath of the voters for unpopular pardons.

> **pardon**
> An executive grant providing restoration of all rights and privileges of citizenship to a specific individual charged or convicted of a crime.

The Development and Expansion of Presidential Power

EACH PRESIDENT BRINGS to the position not only a vision of America, but also expectations about how to use presidential authority. The forty-two men who have held the nation's highest office have been a diverse lot. (While there have been forty-three presidents, only forty-two men have held the office: Grover Cleveland served as the twenty-second and twenty-fourth president because he was elected to nonconsecutive terms in 1884 and 1892.) Most presidents find accomplishing their goals much more

Join the Debate

THE WAR POWERS ACT

OVERVIEW: While the Constitution divides the power to wage war between Congress and the president, scholars and politicians disagree on the specifics of the division. They also disagree on how this division should play out in specific circumstances. The Constitution gives Congress the authority to declare war, to make the rules that govern military forces, and to provide appropriations to the armed services. Yet, the president's constitutional jurisdiction over war powers has steadily increased since the nation's founding. Although President James Madison would not go to war with Great Britain in 1812 without a war declaration from Congress, the last six major American conflicts—in Korea, Vietnam, the Persian Gulf, Kosovo, Afghanistan, and Iraq—were conducted without formal declarations of war.

The War Powers Act of 1973, passed in the aftermath of the Vietnam War, was an attempt to rein in the war-making authority of the president by demanding, among other things, that the executive notify Congress when committing the U.S. military to hostile action. The War Powers Act requires the president to report to Congress "in every possible instance" within forty-eight hours after deploying the armed forces in combat. Implied in the law is the understanding that the information Congress receives will be timely and accurate. President Richard M. Nixon's veto of the act was overridden by both houses of Congress, but presidential administrations since Nixon's, Democratic and Republican alike, have agreed that the act infringes on the president's constitutional duty as commander in chief.

The intelligence the president and Congress receive is critically important when determining whether or not to engage in and support armed conflict. The president's authority as commander in chief gives him access to significant intelligence resources needed to conduct foreign affairs, but sometimes these sources are flawed. For instance, in 1998,

President Bill Clinton ordered the destruction of a pharmaceutical plant in Sudan based on faulty intelligence that the site produced nerve gas. In 2002–2003, President George W. Bush made the case for invading Iraq by asserting that the country possessed weapons of mass destruction (WMDs) that posed an imminent threat to the United States. WMDs loomed large in the national debate regarding whether or not to intervene in Iraq.

Complying with the War Powers Act, the president asked for and received authorization from Congress to use military force against Iraq if diplomatic efforts failed. Critics have charged that congressional authorization would not have been as forthcoming had the president and his administration not ignored or downplayed intelligence reports that contradicted their beliefs in the existence of WMDs. The fact that such weapons were not found undermined the administration's credibility with many Americans, including members of Congress, as well as foreign nations. Some constitutional scholars have noted that intelligence failures and the rising death toll and costs related to military action in Iraq suggest it is time for Congress to increase its oversight of the executive in foreign policy matters. Other scholars disagree, siding with executive-branch officials who consider the War Powers Act an infringement on the president's constitutional authority.

Should a president, in times of crisis, be unlimited in his ability to defend the United States through the use of military force? To what extent should Congress be privy to the same intelligence reports available to the president and how much of a say should Congress have in decisions that will directly affect the lives of tens of thousands of Americans? What approach is most likely to ensure that when the United States goes to war, the war is not only necessary and just but is also conducted with the least amount of casualties and damage to all parties?

ARGUMENTS FOR THE WAR POWERS ACT

■ **The War Powers Act reflects the will of the American people.** The doctrine of civilian supremacy places ultimate war-making authority with the American people, and the

difficult than they envisioned. After President John F. Kennedy was in office two years, for example, he noted publicly that there were "greater limitations upon our ability to bring about a favorable result than I had imagined."[10] Similarly, as he was leaving office, President Harry S Truman mused about what surprises awaited his successor, Dwight D. Eisenhower, a former general: "He'll sit here and he'll say, 'Do this! Do that!' And nothing will happen. Poor Ike—it won't be a bit like the army. He'll find it very frustrating."[11]

A president's authority is limited by the formal powers enumerated in Article II of the Constitution and by the Supreme Court's interpretation of those constitutional

War Powers Act reflects the will of the people as expressed through the representative institution of Congress.

- **The War Powers Act is an attempt by Congress to restore the balance of shared control of the military with the executive.** The act's stated purpose is to "fulfill the intent of the framers . . . and insure that the collective judgment of both the Congress and the President will apply to the introduction of United States Armed Forces into hostilities . . . and to the continued use of such forces." This is an attempt to return to the constitutional principle that waging war is to be shared by both branches of government.
- **The War Powers Act is an additional check on the president's authority as commander in chief.** The act is an attempt to prevent future presidents from engaging in hostilities of questionable importance to U.S. national security and to force deliberation within the government with regard to armed conflict. For example, had Congress known of President Lyndon B. Johnson's use of faulty or intentionally misleading information to increase U.S. military involvement in Vietnam, U.S. involvement in Southeast Asia may have taken a different, less costly path in both lives and expenditures.

ARGUMENTS AGAINST THE WAR POWERS ACT

- **International relations can be so volatile that the president must be able to act quickly without hindrance.** Alexander Hamilton argued that the reasons for war are "infinite" and that the United States must have an institution that can react quickly and with force to defend the United States. He found this energy in government in the executive—and the American executive was created in part to act quickly without relative interference during exceptional times of crisis.
- **The Supreme Court has upheld an expanded interpretation of the president's authority.** In *U.S.* v. *Curtiss-Wright* (1936), the Court argued that the president and "not Congress has the better opportunity of knowing the conditions which prevail in foreign countries, and

especially this is true during times of war. He has his confidential sources of information. . . . Secrecy in respect of information gathered by them may be highly necessary and the premature disclosure of it productive of harmful results." Thus, the Court concluded that the president is uniquely responsible in the area of foreign policy and war making.

- **It is the president's duty to "preserve, protect, and defend" the Constitution, and thus the country it governs, and it is the executive's prerogative to decide the means to do so, especially in times of conflict.** During extraordinary times, the president must take extraordinary means to defend the nation without undue interference from Congress. *Federalist No. 8* argues: "It is the nature of war to increase the executive at the expense of the legislative authority" as this is considered a natural shift in power. A historical example is President Abraham Lincoln's use of presidential power during the Civil War. A current example would be the Iraq War where National Intelligence Estimates released in 2006 conflicted with the intelligence shared with Congress by Bush administration officials prior to the onset of hostilities.

QUESTIONS

1. Does Congress have the power to limit the war-making power of the executive? If so, what implications does this have for U.S. national security?
2. Should Congress have access to the same information and intelligence regarding foreign-policy matters available to the president? Are there any circumstances where such information should be restricted to just the president and his closest advisers?

SELECTED READINGS

Fisher, Louis. *Presidential War Power.* Lawrence: University Press of Kansas, 2004.

Tushnet, Mark, ed. *The Constitution in Wartime: Beyond Alarmism and Complacency.* Durham, NC: Duke University Press, 2005.

provisions. How a president wields these powers is affected by the times in which the president serves, his confidantes and advisers, and the president's personality and leadership abilities. The 1950s postwar era of good feelings and economic prosperity, presided over by the grandfatherly Eisenhower, for instance, called for a very different leader from the one needed by the Civil War–torn nation governed by Abraham Lincoln.

During that war, Lincoln argued that he needed to act quickly for the very survival of the nation. He suspended the writ of *habeas corpus*, which allows those in prison to petition to be released, citing the need to jail persons even suspected of

inherent powers
Powers of the president that can be derived or inferred from specific powers in the Constitution.

VIDEO ROUNDTABLE

Presidential Greatness

PARTICIPATION

Rate the Presidents

New Deal
The name given to the program of "Relief, Recovery, Reform" begun by President Franklin D. Roosevelt in 1933 to bring the United States out of the Great Depression.

disloyal practices. He ordered a blockade of southern ports, in effect initiating a war without the approval of Congress. He also closed the U.S. mails to treasonable correspondence. Lincoln argued that the **inherent powers** of his office allowed him to circumvent the Constitution in a time of war or national crisis. Since the Constitution conferred on the president the duty to make sure that the laws of the United States are faithfully executed, reasoned Lincoln, the acts enumerated above were constitutional. He simply refused to allow the nation to crumble because of what he viewed as technical requirements of the Constitution.

Not only do different times call for different kinds of leaders; they also often provide limits or, conversely, wide opportunities for whoever serves at that time. Crises, in particular, trigger expansions of presidential power. The danger to the nation posed by the Civil War in the 1860s required a strong leader to take up the reins of government. Because of his leadership during this crisis, Lincoln is generally ranked by historians as the best president. (See Table 7.3.)

Before the days of instantaneous communication, the nation could afford to allow Congress, with its relatively slow deliberative processes, to make most decisions. Furthermore, decision making might have been left to Congress because its members, and not the president, were closest to the people. As times and technology have changed, however, so have the public's expectations of anyone who becomes president. For example, the breakneck speed with which so many cable news networks as well as their Internet sites report national and international events has intensified the public's expectation that, in a crisis, the president will be the individual to act quickly and decisively on behalf of the entire nation. Congress often is just too slow to respond to fast-changing events—especially in foreign affairs.

In the twentieth and twenty-first centuries, the general trend has been for presidential—as opposed to congressional—decision making to be more and more important. (See Politics Now: The Expansion of Presidential Powers.) The start of this trend can be traced to the four-term presidency of Franklin D. Roosevelt (FDR), who led the nation through several crises. This growth of presidential power and the growth of the federal government and its programs in general are now criticized by many commentators.

FDR took office in 1933 in the midst of a major crisis—the Great Depression—during which a substantial portion of the U.S. workforce was unemployed. Noting the sorry state of the national economy in his inaugural address, FDR concluded: "This nation asks for action and action now." To jump-start the American economy, FDR asked Congress for and was given "broad executive powers to wage a war against the emergency, as great as the power that would be given to me if we were in fact invaded by a foreign foe."[12]

Just as Abraham Lincoln had taken bold steps on his inauguration, Roosevelt also acted quickly. He immediately fashioned a plan for national recovery called the **New Deal**, a package of bold and controversial programs designed to invigorate the failing American economy (these are discussed in detail in chapter 3).

Roosevelt served an unprecedented twelve years in office; he was elected to four terms but died shortly after beginning the last one. During his years in office, the nation went from the economic war of the Great Depression to the real international conflict of World War II. The institution of the presidency changed profoundly and permanently as new federal agencies were created to implement New Deal programs as the executive branch became responsible for implementing a wide variety of new programs.

Not only did FDR create a new bureaucracy to implement his pet programs, but he also personalized the presidency by establishing a new relationship between the president and the people. In his radio addresses, or fireside chats, as he liked to call them, he spoke directly to the public in a relaxed and informal manner about serious issues.

TABLE 7.3	THE BEST AND THE WORST PRESIDENTS

Who was the best president and who was the worst? Many surveys of scholars have been taken over the years to answer this question, and virtually all have ranked Abraham Lincoln the best. A 2000 C-SPAN survey of fifty-eight historians from across the political spectrum for example, came up with these results:

Five Best Presidents	*Five Worst Presidents*
1. Lincoln (best)	1. Buchanan (worst)
2. F. Roosevelt	2. A. Johnson
3. Washington	3. Pierce
4. T. Roosevelt	4. Harding
5. Truman	5. W. Harrison

Source: C-SPAN Survey of Presidential Leadership, www.cspan.com.

Politics Now

THE EXPANSION OF PRESIDENTIAL POWERS

The broad presidential powers claimed by Abraham Lincoln during the Civil War and Franklin D. Roosevelt (FDR) during the Great Depression illustrate just some of the ways that presidents have increased the powers of their office beyond what is explicitly written in the Constitution. President Richard M. Nixon, for example, broadly interpreted executive powers in his attempts to wiretap suspected domestic terrorists' phones without a judge's permission, to block the release of papers regarding the Vietnam War and Watergate, and to impound federal funds.[a]

Like Lincoln, FDR, and Nixon, President George W. Bush has claimed greater administrative powers for the president and his advisers. Many of these powers, including authorizing secret wiretaps administered by the National Security Agency and permitting secret military tribunals for suspected terrorists imprisoned at Guantanamo Bay, have been claimed through relatively unchecked executive orders. Before ordering the invasion of Iraq, Bush worked with leaders in Congress to secure almost unprecedented authorization to circumvent the War Powers Act and run the military intervention through the White House rather than Congress. While the Supreme Court's ruling in *Hamdan* v. *Rumsfeld* (2006) provided a temporary check on the President's approach to detaining and trying terrorism suspects, the Republican-led Congress rapidly provided Bush with the Military Commissions Act, which gave him the congressional authorization the Court had ruled he needed in order to continue his policies unabated.

How these widely criticized actions will affect the presidency as an institution—as well as President Bush's legacy—remains to be seen. Both Lincoln and FDR were criticized while in office. Today, their actions, which led to economic and military successes, receive wide praise from historians. Some scholars argue that Lincoln and FDR's actions can be viewed as an extension of presidential prerogative, a princi-

ple discussed in the works of British philosopher John Locke, whose writings informed much of the political philosophy of the Framers.[b] Under presidential prerogative, chief executives can act unilaterally in times of national emergency, as long as they have the consent of the governed and are acting in the people's best interests.

Nixon is not viewed as kindly by historians, who largely agree that even in the vague interest of national security, a number of Nixon's actions overstepped the acceptable boundaries of executive power. The Supreme Court, too, agreed with this interpretation: each of the attempts mentioned above to interpret presidential power broadly ended up before the Court; in each case, the Court ruled against Nixon.

The difference between Lincoln and FDR and Nixon seems to be one of how their expansions of presidential power fit within the big picture. As time passes, a similar standard will likely be used to examine Bush's actions. A judgment eventually will be made on whether Bush's expansion of powers provided the successful means to an important end, or whether his actions were unnecessary power-grabs with little clear justification.

QUESTIONS

1. What circumstances justify expansions of presidential power? What specific powers are most appropriate to be expanded?
2. How does the broadening of presidential powers affect the checks and balances and separation of powers systems conceived by the Framers? What can other branches do to rectify any imbalance that may exist?

[a] John W. Dean, "The U.S. Supreme Court and the Imperial Presidency," http://writ.news.findlaw.com/dean/20040116.html.

[b] Arthur M. Schlesinger, *The Imperial Presidency* (Boston: Houghton Mifflin, 1989).

To his successors, FDR left the modern presidency, including a burgeoning federal bureaucracy (see chapter 8), an active and usually leading role in both domestic and foreign policy and legislation, and a nationalized executive office that used technology—first radio, then television, and now the Internet—to bring the president closer to the public than ever before.

The Presidential Establishment

AS THE RESPONSIBILITIES AND SCOPE of presidential authority grew over the years, so did the executive branch, including the number of people working directly for the president in the White House. The vice president and his staff, the Cabinet, the first lady and her staff, the Executive Office of the President, and the White House staff all help the president fulfill his duties as chief executive.

THE VICE PRESIDENT

Historically, presidents chose their vice presidents largely to balance—politically, geographically, or otherwise—the presidential ticket, with little thought given to the possibility that the vice president would become president. Franklin D. Roosevelt, for example, a liberal New Yorker, selected John Nance Garner, a conservative Texan, to be his running mate in 1932. After serving two terms, Garner—who openly disagreed with Roosevelt over many policies, including Roosevelt's decision to seek a third term—unsuccessfully sought the 1940 presidential nomination himself.

How much power a vice president has depends on how much the president is willing to give him. Jimmy Carter was the first president to give his vice president, Walter Mondale, more than ceremonial duties. In fact, Walter Mondale was the first vice president to have an office in the White House. No vice presidents, however, have ever enjoyed the access to, and ear of, the president to the extent of Vice President Dick Cheney. Some commentators have even argued that Cheney has a more clear agenda of where the United States should be moving, especially in terms of foreign affairs. The vice president, for example, long believed it critical to end Saddam Hussein's regime in Iraq in order to build democracy in the Middle East, and there are questions as to whether Cheney and his top advisers tried to silence critics of the administration's justifications for war in Iraq.

THE CABINET

The Cabinet, which has no basis in the Constitution, is an informal institution based on practice and precedent whose membership is determined by tradition and presidential discretion. By custom, this advisory group selected by the president includes the heads of major executive departments. Presidents today also include their vice presidents in Cabinet meetings, as well as any other agency heads or officials to whom they would like to accord Cabinet-level status. As a body, the Cabinet's major function is to help the president execute the laws and assist him in making decisions.

As revealed in Table 7.4, over the years the Cabinet has grown as new departments have accommodated for new pressures on the president to act in areas that initially were not considered within the scope of concern of the national government. As interest groups, in particular, pressured Congress and the president to recognize their demands for services and governmental action, they often were rewarded by the creation of an executive department. Since each was headed by a secretary who automatically became a member of the president's Cabinet, powerful groups including farmers (Agriculture), business people (Commerce), workers (Labor), and teachers (Education) saw the creation of a department as increasing their access to the president.

The size of the president's Cabinet has increased over the years at the same time that most presidents' reliance on their Cabinet secretaries has decreased, although some individual members of a president's Cabinet may be very influential. Many commentators believe that Secretary of State Condoleezza Rice is especially influential in the George W. Bush administration. (Chapter 8 provides a more detailed discussion of the Cabinet's role in executing U.S. policy.)

THE FIRST LADY

From Martha Washington to Laura Bush, first ladies (a term coined during the Civil War) have assisted presidents as informal advisers while making other, more public contributions to American society. Until recently, the only formal national recognition given to first ladies was an exhibit of inaugural ball gowns at the Smithsonian Institution. In 1992, in keeping with renewed interest in the varied roles played by first ladies, the

■ In 1919, President Woodrow Wilson had what many believed to be a nervous collapse in the summer and a debilitating stroke in the fall that incapacitated him for several months. His wife, Edith Bolling Galt Wilson, refused to admit his advisers to his sickroom, and rumors flew about the "First Lady President," as many suspected it was his wife and not Wilson who was issuing the orders.

Photo courtesy: Stock Montage, Inc.

TABLE 7.4 THE U.S. CABINET AND RESPONSIBILITIES OF EACH EXECUTIVE DEPARTMENT

Department Head	Department	Date of Creation	Responsibilities
Secretary of State	Department of State	1789	Responsible for the making of foreign policy, including treaty negotiation
Secretary of the Treasury	Department of the Treasury	1789	Responsible for government funds and regulation of alcohol, firearms, and tobacco
Secretary of Defense	Department of Defense	1789	Responsible for national defense; current department created by consolidating the former Departments of War, the Army, the Navy, and the Air Force in 1947
Attorney General	Department of Justice	1870	Represents U.S. government in all federal courts, investigates and prosecutes violations of federal law
Secretary of the Interior	Department of the Interior	1849	Manages the nation's natural resources, including wildlife and public lands
Secretary of Agriculture	Department of Agriculture	1889	Assists the nation's farmers, oversees food-quality programs, administers food stamp and school lunch programs
Secretary of Commerce	Department of Commerce	1903	Aids businesses and conducts the U.S. Census (originally the Department of Commerce and Labor)
Secretary of Labor	Department of Labor	1913	Runs labor programs, keeps labor statistics, aids labor through enforcement of laws
Secretary of Health and Human Services	Department of Health and Human Services	1953	Runs health, welfare, and Social Security programs; created as the Department of Health, Education, and Welfare (lost its education function in 1979)
Secretary of Housing and Urban Development	Department of Housing and Urban Development	1965	Responsible for urban and housing programs
Secretary of Transportation	Department of Transportation	1966	Responsible for mass transportation and highway programs
Secretary of Energy	Department of Energy	1977	Responsible for energy policy and research, including atomic energy
Secretary of Education	Department of Education	1979	Responsible for the federal government's education programs
Secretary of Veterans Affairs	Department of Veterans Affairs	1989	Responsible for programs aiding veterans
Secretary of Homeland Security	Department of Homeland Security	2002	Responsible for all issues pertaining to homeland security

Smithsonian launched an exhibit that highlighted the personal accomplishments of first ladies since Martha Washington. The exhibit was built around three themes: (1) the political role of the first ladies, including how they were portrayed in the media and perceived by the public; (2) their contributions to society, especially their personal causes; and, (3) still, of course, their inaugural gowns.

THE EXECUTIVE OFFICE OF THE PRESIDENT (EOP)

The **Executive Office of the President (EOP)** was established by FDR in 1939 to oversee his New Deal programs. It was created to provide the president with a general staff to help him direct the diverse activities of the executive branch. In fact, it is a minibureaucracy of several advisers and offices located in the ornate Executive Office Building next to the White House on Pennsylvania Avenue, as well as in the White House itself, where the president's closest advisers often are housed.

The EOP has expanded over time to include several advisory and policy-making agencies and task forces. Over time, the units of the EOP have become the prime policy makers in their fields of expertise as they play key roles in advancing the president's

Executive Office of the President (EOP)
Establishment created in 1939 to help the president oversee the executive branch.

210 CHAPTER 7 ★ THE PRESIDENCY

policy preferences. Among the EOP's most important members are the National Security Council, the Council of Economic Advisers, the Office of Management and Budget, the Office of the Vice President, and the Office of the U.S. Trade Representative.

The National Security Council (NSC) was established in 1947 to advise the president on American military affairs and foreign policy. The NSC is composed of the president, the vice president, and the secretaries of state and defense. The chair of the Joint Chiefs of Staff and the director of the Central Intelligence Agency also participate. Others such as the White House chief of staff and the general counsel may attend. The national security adviser runs the staff of the NSC, coordinates information and options, and advises the president.

Presidents can give clear indications of their policy preferences by the kinds of offices they include in the EOP. President George W. Bush, for example, not only moved or consolidated several offices when he became president in 2001, but he created a new Office of Faith-Based and Community Initiatives to help him achieve his goal of greater religious involvement in matters of domestic policy.

THE WHITE HOUSE STAFF

Although presidents organize the White House staff in different ways, they typically have a chief of staff whose job is to facilitate the smooth running of the staff and the executive branch of government. Successful chiefs of staff also have protected the president from mistakes and helped implement policies to obtain the maximum political advantage for the president. Other key White House aides include the counselor to the president, domestic, foreign, and economic policy strategists, communications staff, White House counsel, and a lobbyist who acts as a liaison between the president and Congress.

Although White House staffers prefer to be located in the White House in spite of its small offices, many staffers are relegated to the old Executive Office Building next door because White House office space is limited. In Washington, the size of the office is not the measure of power that it often is in corporations. Instead, power in the White House goes to those who have the president's ear and the offices closest to the Oval Office.

The President as Policy Maker

WHEN FDR SENT HIS first legislative package to Congress, he broke the traditional model of law-making.[13] As envisioned by the Framers, it was to be Congress that made the laws. Now FDR was claiming a leadership role for the president in the legislative process. Said the president of this new relationship: "It is the duty of the President to propose and it is the privilege of the Congress to dispose."[14] With those words and the actions that followed, FDR shifted the presidency into a law- and policy-maker role. Now the president and the executive branch not only executed the laws but generally suggested them, too.

THE PRESIDENT'S ROLE IN PROPOSING AND FACILITATING LEGISLATION

From FDR's presidency to the Republican-controlled 104th Congress, the public looked routinely to the president to formulate concrete legislative plans to propose to Congress, which subsequently adopted, modified, or rejected his plans for the nation. Then, in 1994, it appeared for a while that the electorate wanted Congress to reassert itself in the legislative process. In fact, the Contract with America was a Republican call for Congress to take the reins of the law-making process. But, several Republican Congresses failed to pass many of the items of the contract, and President Bill Clinton's continued forceful presence in the budgetary process made a resurgent role for Congress largely illusory. The same scenario holds true for President George W. Bush, although by 2006 even some Republicans were concerned with Bush's continued deficit spending requests.

On the whole, presidents have a hard time getting Congress to pass their programs.[15] Passage is especially difficult if the president presides over a divided government, which occurs when the presidency and Congress are controlled by different political parties (see chapter 6). Recent research by political scientists, however, shows that presidents are much more likely to win on bills central to their announced agendas, such as President George W. Bush's victory on the Iraq War resolution, than to secure passage of legislation proposed by others.[16]

Because presidents generally experience declining support for policies they advocate throughout their terms, it is important that a president propose key plans early in his administration, during the honeymoon period, a time when the goodwill toward the president often allows a president to secure passage of legislation that he would not be able to gain at a later period. Even President Lyndon B. Johnson, who was able to get nearly 60 percent of his programs through Congress, noted: "You've got to give it all you can, that first year . . . before they start worrying about themselves. . . . You can't put anything through when half the Congress is thinking how to beat you."[17]

Presidents can also use **patronage** (jobs, grants, or other special favors given as rewards to friends and political allies for their support) and personal rewards to win support. Invitations to the White House and campaign visits to the home districts of members of Congress running for office are two ways to curry favor with legislators, and inattention to key members can prove deadly to a president's legislative program. Former Speaker of the House Tip O'Neill (D–MA) reportedly was quite irritated when the Carter transition team refused O'Neill's request for extra tickets to Jimmy Carter's inaugural. This incident did not exactly get the president off to a good start with the powerful Speaker.

A president can also bolster support for his legislative package is to call on his political party. As the informal leader of his party, he should be able to use that position to his advantage in Congress, where party loyalty is very important. This strategy works best when the president has carried members of his party into office on his coattails, as was the case in the Johnson and Reagan landslides of 1964 and 1984, respectively. In fact, many scholars regard President Lyndon B. Johnson as the most effective legislative leader.[18] Not only had he served in the House and as Senate majority leader, but he also enjoyed a comfortable Democratic Party majority in Congress.

patronage
Jobs, grants, or other special favors that are given as rewards to friends and political allies for their support.

THE BUDGETARY PROCESS AND LEGISLATIVE IMPLEMENTATION

Closely associated with a president's ability to pass legislation is his ability to secure funding for new and existing programs. A president sets national policy and priorities through his budget proposals and his continued insistence on their congressional passage. The budget proposal not only outlines the programs he wants but indicates the importance of each program by the amount of funding requested for each and for its associated agency or department.

Because the Framers gave Congress the power of the purse, Congress had primary responsibility for the budget process until 1930. The economic disaster set off by the stock market crash of 1929, however, gave FDR, once elected in 1932, the opportunity to assert himself in the congressional budgetary process, just as he inserted himself into the legislative process. In 1939, the Bureau of the Budget, which had been created in 1921 to help the president tell Congress how much money it would take to run the executive branch of government, was made part of the newly created Executive Office of the President. In 1970, President Nixon changed its name to the **Office of Management and Budget (OMB)** to clarify its function in the executive branch.

Office of Management and Budget (OMB)
The office that prepares the president's annual budget proposal, reviews the budget and programs of the executive departments, supplies economic forecasts, and conducts detailed analyses of proposed bills and agency rules.

The OMB works exclusively for the president and employs hundreds of budget and policy experts. Key OMB responsibilities include preparing the president's annual budget proposal, designing the president's program, and reviewing the progress, budget, and program proposals of the executive department agencies. It also supplies economic forecasts to the president and conducts detailed analyses of proposed bills and agency rules. OMB reports allow the president to attach price tags to his legislative proposals and defend the presidential budget. The OMB budget is a huge document, and even those who prepare it have a hard time deciphering all of its provisions. Even so, the expertise of the OMB directors often gives them an advantage over members of Congress.

POLICY MAKING THROUGH REGULATION

Proposing legislation and using the budget to advance policy priorities are not the only ways that presidents can affect the policy process, especially in times of highly divided government. Executive orders offer the president an opportunity to make policy without legislative approval. Major policy changes have been made when a president has issued an **executive order,** a rule or regulation issued by the president that has the effect of law. While many executive orders are issued to help clarify or implement legislation enacted by Congress, other executive orders have the effect of making new policy. President Harry S Truman ordered an end to segregation in the military through an executive order, and affirmative action was institutionalized as national policy through Executive Order 11246, issued by Lyndon B. Johnson in 1966.

executive order
A rule or regulation issued by the president that has the effect of law. All executive orders must be published in the *Federal Register*.

Executive orders have been used since the 1980s to set national policies toward abortion. President Ronald Reagan, for example, used an executive order to stop federal funding of fetal tissue research and to end federal funding of any groups providing abortion counseling. President Bill Clinton immediately rescinded those orders when he became president. One of President George W. Bush's first acts upon taking office was to issue an executive order reversing those Clinton orders.

With the Stroke of a Pen: The Executive Order Over Time

Like presidents before him, George W. Bush has used executive orders to put his policy stamp on a wide array of important issues. After much soul searching, for example, he signed an executive order limiting federal funding of stem cell research to the sixty or so cell lines currently in the possession of scientific researchers.[19] An executive order also was used to allow military tribunals to try any foreigners captured by U.S. forces in Afghanistan or linked to the terrorist acts of September 11, 2001.

Presidential Leadership and the Importance of Public Opinion

A PRESIDENT'S ABILITY to get his programs adopted or implemented depends on many factors, including his leadership abilities, his personality and powers of persuasion, his ability to mobilize public opinion to support his actions, and the public's perception of his performance, as well as Congress's perceptions of his public support.

PRESIDENTIAL LEADERSHIP

Leadership is not an easy thing to exercise, and it remains an elusive concept for scholars to identify and measure, but it is important to all presidents seeking support for their programs and policies. Moreover, ideas about the importance of effective leaders have deep roots in our political culture. The leadership abilities of the great presidents—Washington, Jefferson, Lincoln, and FDR—have been extolled over and over again, leading us to fault modern presidents who fail to cloak themselves in the armor of leadership. (See American Values/American Voices: The President and Moral Leadership.) Americans thus have come to believe that "If presidential leadership works some of the time, why not all of the time?"[20] This attitude, in turn, directly influences what we expect presidents to do and how we evaluate them. (See Table 7.5.) Research by political scientists shows that presidents can exercise leadership by increasing public attention to particular issues. Analyses of presidential State of the Union Addresses, for example, reveal that mentions of particular policies translate into more Americans mentioning those policies as the most important problems facing the nation.[21]

Frequently, the difference between great and mediocre presidents centers on their ability to grasp the importance of leadership style. Truly great presidents, such as Lincoln and FDR, understood that the White House was a seat of power from which decisions could flow to shape the national destiny. They recognized that their day-to-day activities and how they went about them should be

TABLE 7.5 BARBER'S PRESIDENTIAL PERSONALITIES

Political scientist James David Barber defines presidential character as the "way the president orients himself toward life." Barber believes that there are four presidential character types, based on energy level (whether the president is active or passive) and the degree of enjoyment a president finds in the job (whether the president has a positive or negative attitude). Barber believes that active and positive presidents are more successful than passive and negative presidents. Active-positive presidents, he argues, approach the presidency with a characteristic zest for life and have a drive to lead and succeed. In contrast, passive-negative presidents find themselves reacting to circumstances, are likely to take directions from others, and fail to make full use of the enormous resources of the executive office.

Active	Passive
Positive	
F. Roosevelt	Taft
Truman	Harding
Kennedy	Reagan
Ford	
Carter[a]	
G. Bush	
Negative	
Wilson	Coolidge
Hoover	Eisenhower
L. Johnson	
Nixon	

[a]Some scholars think that Carter better fits the active-negative typology.

Source: James David Barber, The Presidential Character: Predicting Performance in the White House, 4th ed. (Englewood Cliffs, NJ: Prentice Hall, 1992).

■ In the wake of Democratic wins that some attributed to President Bush's low approval ratings, Secretary of Defense Donald Rumsfeld surprised observers when he resigned a day after the 2006 midterm elections. Here, President Bush escorts Rumsfeld to the door of the Oval Office after the president introduced his nominee for Rumsfeld's replacement, Robert Gates.

Photo courtesy: Tim Sloan/AFP/Getty Images

American Values/American Voices

THE PRESIDENT AND MORAL LEADERSHIP

In addition to the many formal roles that come with the office, the president of the United States is often expected to be the nation's moral leader and the chief enforcer of American values. Beginning in elementary school, for example, children learn not only about the contributions of great presidents to the betterment of the nation but also about these leaders' moral behavior. Students are taught that a young George Washington cut down a cherry tree against his parents' orders but could not lie to his father about his actions. Similarly, school children learn that Abraham Lincoln embraced American values of equality and fairness and as a result fought the Civil War to free the slaves and maintain the Union. But, neither of these stories is entirely correct. Washington most likely never cut down that cherry tree, and in recent years, scholars have questioned Lincoln's motives for the conduct of the Civil War. One researcher, for example, has claimed that Lincoln used the presidency to serve his own economic interests, as well as those of the railroad companies who had supported his political campaigns.[a]

The stories we learn as children help to increase the mythology of the American presidency. By telling tales of how the greatest presidents behaved during the nation's early years, Americans perpetuate the myth that presidents are exemplary figures born with moral compasses far superior to those possessed by the average citizen. And, in setting such a high bar for presidential actions, Americans also set themselves up for inevitable disappointment, expecting a level of perfection from presidents that no man or woman could possibly achieve.

Presidents, in truth, are just as likely as other citizens to suffer lapses of morality in both their professional and personal lives. President Bill Clinton, for example, was not the first president to be accused of adultery. He was just one president in a long line of predecessors including Thomas Jefferson, Andrew Jackson, Grover Cleveland, Franklin D. Roosevelt, and John F. Kennedy.

And, while President George W. Bush has been heavily criticized for his liberal use of executive orders for a variety of purposes, including establishing military tribunals and authorizing wiretaps of suspected terrorists, he is not the first president to use executive orders to achieve his policy goals. Presidents Franklin D. Roosevelt and Harry S Truman, for example, used executive orders to seize mills, mines, and factories whose production was crucial to the World War II and Korean War efforts. Roosevelt and Truman argued that these actions were necessary to preserve national security. The Supreme Court, however, eventually disagreed with the Truman administration in *Youngstown Sheet and Tube* v. *Sawyer* (1952). In that case, the Court unequivocally stated that Truman had overstepped the boundaries of his office as provided by the Constitution.[b]

It is important to remember that, whatever Americans are socialized to believe, presidents are not necessarily morally or ethically superior to average human beings. This idea was widely acknowledged by the Framers and was part of the reason the Constitution's authors relied so heavily on the concepts of checks and balances and separation of powers. No acknowledgement of this truth is more famous than that written by James Madison in *Federalist No. 51:* "If men were angels, no government would be necessary. If angels were to govern men, neither external nor internal controls on government would be necessary."

QUESTIONS

1. Why do you think presidents are expected to be moral leaders for the citizens of the United States? Do you think this expectation is a reasonable one? Why or why not?
2. What factors should be taken into consideration when judging the morality of presidential actions? Should presidents be held to a different moral or ethical standard than ordinary American citizens?

---

[a] Thomas DiLorenzo, *The Real Lincoln: A New Look at Abraham Lincoln, His Agenda, and an Unnecessary War,* reprint ed. (New York: Three Rivers Press, 2003).

[b] *Youngstown Sheet and Tube* v. *Sawyer,* 343 U.S. 579 (1952).

---

designed to bolster support for their policies and to secure congressional and popular backing that could translate their intuitive judgment into meaningful action. Mediocre presidents, on the other hand, have tended to regard the White House as "a stage for the presentation of performances to the public" or a fitting honor to cap a career.[22]

Political scientist Richard E. Neustadt calls the president's ability to influence members of Congress and the public "the power to persuade." Neustadt believes this power is crucial to presidential leadership.[23]

Global Perspective

NORTH KOREA'S KIM JONG IL AND UNCONTROLLED EXECUTIVE AUTHORITY

One of the Framers' biggest concerns was the potential for tyranny that a strong executive branch could present. As a result, the president's powers are subject to constitutional checks by the Congress and Supreme Court, as well as the will of the people, who vote in presidential elections every four years.

The difference between the American and North Korean executive could not be more extreme. The North Korean government is widely considered one of the world's most oppressive, and this is especially evident in the structure and function of its executive in relation to North Korea's institutions of government. North Korea—or, as it is formally known, the Democratic People's Republic of Korea (DPRK)—is a communist dictatorship that has been controlled by Kim Jong Il, the son of North Korea's founder, President Kim Il Sung, since the elder's death in 1994. The position of president was essentially abolished in North Korea in 1998 when Kim Il Sung was declared "eternal president of the republic."

Executive authority, political power, and governing right are vested in North Korea's only major political party, the Korean Workers' Party (KWP). Several minor parties exist, but they are controlled by the KWP and do not oppose its rule. Since 1997, Kim Jong Il's official titles have been general secretary of the KWP and chairman of the National Defense Commission. In 1998, Kim's latter position, which places him in control of North Korea's extensive military apparatus, was declared the "highest office of state," making him North Korea's official head of state.

Like the United States' Constitution, North Korea's Constitution calls for separation of power and checks and balances. However, due to the extremely secretive nature of the North Korean regime, little is known concerning the actual relationships between the executive, legislative, and judicial branches. The legislature, known as the Supreme People's Assembly, is understood to be a rubber-stamp assembly: it simply ratifies decisions made by executive institutions subject to KWP control. Since Kim Jong Il serves as both head of state and head of the party, the legislative authority of the assembly is considered nonexistent. North Korea's executive extensively interferes with the judiciary, and judges and prosecutors at all levels are chosen by KWP members, giving Kim Jong Il and his supporters de facto control over judicial operations.

The control Kim exercises over North Korea's economy is similar to his control of the nation's political and military institutions. Kim Il Sung's emphasis on building and maintaining an army, estimated to be as large as 1 million, resulted in a nation whose people depend on international aid for basic necessities. Widespread famine continues as Kim Jong Il's government allocates resources to building long-range missiles and developing chemical, biological, and nuclear weapons—an issue of great concern to the United States and other nations. The nation's domestic woes are likely to continue after the UN ordered additional sanctions when North Korea tested a nuclear bomb in October 2006, defying a UN directive not to do so.

QUESTIONS

1. Should absolute power be entrusted to a single political institution or individual? Why or why not?
2. How does the centralization of power in North Korea affect North Korea's citizens and other nations?

Sources: Library of Congress, "Country Notes, North Korea"; Freedom House, "North Korea"; *CIA World Factbook.*

GOING PUBLIC: MOBILIZING PUBLIC OPINION

Historically, even before the days of radio, television, and the Internet, presidents tried to reach out to the public to gain support for their programs through what President Theodore Roosevelt called the bully pulpit. The development of commercial air travel and radio, newsreels, television, and computers have made direct communication to larger numbers of voters easier. Presidents, first ladies, and other presidential advisers travel all over the world to publicize their views and to build personal support as well as support for administration programs.

COMPARATIVE

Comparing Chief Executives

Direct presidential appeals to the electorate like those often made by recent presidents are referred to as "going public."[24] Going public means that a president goes over the heads of members of Congress to gain support from the people, who can then place pressure on their elected officials in Washington.

Analyzing Visuals

PRESIDENTIAL APPROVAL RATINGS SINCE 1953, BY PARTY

Presidential approval ratings tend to follow a cyclical pattern. Presidents generally enjoy their highest ratings at the beginning of their terms and experience lower ratings toward the end. Presidents also typically receive higher rates of approval from members of their own party throughout their terms than from members of the opposing party. Presidents George Bush, Bill Clinton, and George W. Bush all enjoyed popularity surges during the course of their terms, and the drop-offs from those surges were generally much steeper among members of the other party than among members of their own party. President George W. Bush received a spectacular and sustained boost after September 11, but his approval ratings later dropped dramatically among voters affiliated with the Democratic Party, and he has received low marks from members of the Republican Party as well.

After viewing the line graph and reading the related chapter material, answer the following critical thinking questions about presidential approval patterns: What explains the cyclical pattern of presidential approval? Which presidents since Eisenhower have had the lowest ratings from members of the other party? By members of their own party? Which have had the highest ratings by members of the other party? By members of their own party? Do recent presidents' approval ratings follow the same overall pattern as those for presidents in the 1960s and 1970s?

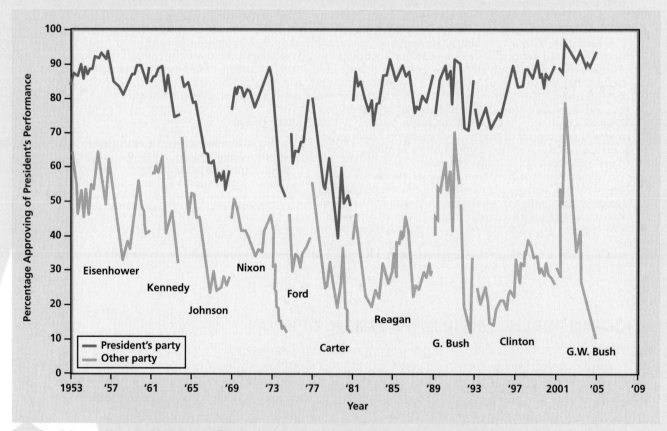

Source: Gary C. Jacobson, University of California at San Diego.

THE PUBLIC'S PERCEPTION OF PRESIDENTIAL PERFORMANCE

Presidential Success in Polls and Congress

Typically presidents enjoy their highest level of public approval at the beginning of their terms and try to take advantage of this honeymoon period to get their programs passed by Congress as soon as possible. Each action a president takes, however, is divisive—some people will approve, and others will disapprove. Disapproval tends to have a negative cumulative effect on a president's approval rating.

However, many recent presidents, including George Bush, Bill Clinton, and George W. Bush, have experienced increases in their approval ratings during the course of their presidencies. Usually coming on the heels of a domestic or international crisis such as the 1991 Persian Gulf War or the September 11, terrorist attacks, these surges generally don't last long, as the cumulative effects of governing once again catch up with the president.

President George Bush's rapid rise in popularity occurred after the major and, perhaps more important, quick victory in the 1991 Persian Gulf War. His popularity, however, plummeted as the good feelings faded and Americans began to feel the pinch of recession. In contrast, President Bill Clinton's approval scores skyrocketed after the 1996 Democratic National Convention. More interestingly, Clinton's high approval ratings continued in the wake of allegations of wrongdoing in the Oval Office, his eventual admission of inappropriate conduct, and through his impeachment proceedings. In fact, when Clinton went to the American public and admitted that he misled them about his relationship with Monica Lewinsky, an ABC poll conducted immediately after his speech showed a 10-point jump in his job approval rating.[25]

George W. Bush enjoyed one of the longest rallies in history. But, by 2005, his approval ratings once again hovered around 50 percent in the wake of personnel scandals, escalating violence in Iraq, and rising gas prices. The president's approval ratings dropped even lower in 2006; by the midterm elections they were a scant 35 percent. In many states, voters viewed the elections as a referendum on Bush, leading to widespread Democratic victories that resulted in Democrats gaining control of both the House and the Senate. The number of Democratic governors increased by seven in the 2006 elections, and Democrats also won control of nine additional chambers in the state legislatures.

Since Lyndon B. Johnson's presidency, only four presidents have left office with approval ratings of more than 50 percent. (See Analyzing Visuals: Presidential Approval Ratings Since 1953, by Party.) Many credit this trend to events such as Vietnam, Watergate, and the Iraq War, which have made the public increasingly skeptical of presidential performance.

Summary

BECAUSE THE FRAMERS FEARED a tyrannical monarch, they gave considerable thought to the office of the chief executive. Since ratification of the Constitution, the office has changed considerably—more through practice and need than from changes in the Constitution. Distrust of a too-powerful leader led the Framers to create an executive office with limited powers. They mandated that a president be at least thirty-five years old, a natural-born citizen, and a U.S. resident for at least fourteen years, and they opted not to limit the president's term of office. To further guard against tyranny, they made provisions for the removal of the president.

The Framers gave the president a variety of specific constitutional powers in Article II, including the appointment power, the power to convene Congress, and the power to make treaties. The Constitution also gives the president the power to grant pardons and to veto acts of Congress. In addition, the president derives considerable power from being commander in chief of the military.

The development of presidential power has depended on the personal force of those who have held the office. The modern presidency, though, is generally marked by the election of Franklin D. Roosevelt in 1932. As the responsibilities of the president have grown, so has the executive branch of government. FDR established the Executive Office of the President to help him govern. Perhaps the most key policy advisers are those closest to the president: the vice president, the White House staff, some members of the Executive Office of the President, and sometimes, the first lady.

Since FDR, the public has looked to the president to propose legislation to Congress. Through proposing legislation, advancing budgets, and involvement in the regulatory process, presidents make policy.

To gain support for his programs or proposed budget, the president uses a variety of skills, including personal leadership and direct appeals to the public. How the president goes about winning support is determined by his leadership and personal style, affected by his character and his ability to persuade. Since the 1970s, however, the American public has been increasingly skeptical of presidential actions, and few presidents have enjoyed extended periods of the kind of popularity needed to help win support for programmatic change.

KEY TERMS

Cabinet, p. 200
executive agreement, p. 201
Executive Office of the President (EOP), p. 209
executive order, p. 212
executive privilege, p. 198
impeachment, p. 198
inherent powers, p. 206
New Deal, p. 206
Office of Management and Budget (OMB), p. 212
pardon, p. 203
patronage, p. 211
Twenty-Fifth Amendment, p. 198
Twenty-Second Amendment, p. 198
U.S. v. *Nixon* (1974), p. 198

veto power, p. 201
War Powers Act, p. 203

SELECTED READINGS

Barber, James David. *The Presidential Character: Predicting Presidential Performance in the White House,* 4th ed. Englewood Cliffs, NJ: Prentice Hall, 1992.

Campbell, Karlyn Kohr, and Kathleen Hall Jamieson. *Deeds Done in Words: Presidential Rhetoric and the Genres of Governance.* Chicago: University of Chicago Press, 1990.

Cooper, Philip J. *By Order of the President: The Use and Abuse of Executive Direct Action.* Lawrence: University Press of Kansas, 2002.

Cronin, Thomas E., and Michael A. Genovese. *The Paradoxes of the American Presidency,* new ed. New York: Oxford University Press, 2006.

Dallek, Robert. *Hail to the Chief: The Making and Unmaking of American Presidents.* New York: Oxford University Press, 2001.

Daynes, Byron W., and Glen Sussman. *The American Presidency and the Social Agenda.* Upper Saddle River, NJ: Prentice Hall, 2001.

Edwards, George C., III, and Stephen J. Wayne. *Presidential Leadership: Politics and Policy Making,* 6th ed. New York: Bedford Books, 2002.

Greenstein, Fred I. *The Presidential Difference: Leadership Style from FDR to George W. Bush,* 2nd ed. Princeton, NJ: Princeton University Press, 2004.

Martin, Janet M. *The American Presidency and Women: Promise, Performance, and Illusion.* College Station: Texas A&M Press, 2003.

Neustadt, Richard E. *Presidential Power and the Modern Presidents.* New York: Free Press, 1991.

Pfiffner, James P. *The Character Factor: How We Judge America's Presidents.* College Station: Texas A&M University Press, 2004.

———. *The Modern Presidency,* 4th ed. Belmont, CA: Wadsworth, 2004.

Ragsdale, Lyn. *Vital Statistics on the Presidency: Washington to Clinton.* Washington, DC: CQ Press, 1998.

Rossiter, Clinton. *The American Presidency,* reprint ed. Baltimore, MD: Johns Hopkins University Press, 1987.

Skowronek, Stephen. *The Politics Presidents Make: Leadership from John Adams to Bill Clinton.* Cambridge, MA: Harvard University Press, 1997.

Warshaw, Shirley Anne. *The Keys to Power: Managing the Presidency,* 2nd ed. New York: Longman, 2004.

WEB EXPLORATIONS

To learn more about specific presidents, see
   http://www.nara.gov/nara/president/address.html
For a chronology of the Clinton impeachment proceedings, see
   http://www.washintonpost.com/wp-srv/politics/special/clinton/timeline.htm
For more on the vice president, see
   http://www.whitehouse.gov/vicepresident

To learn more about presidential pardons, go to
http://jurist.law.pitt.edu/pardons0a.htm
For more on the modern White House, see
http://www.whitehouse.gov
For more on first ladies, see
http://www.firstladies.org
To try your hand at balancing the budget, go to
http://www.nathannewman.org/nbs

For more details on Watergate, see
http://watergate.info
For more on The White House Project formed to elect a woman president, see
http://www.thewhitehouseproject.org
For more details on the controversy over the War Powers Act, see
http://www.ford.utexas.edu/library/speeches/770411.htm
http://www.fff.org/comment/com0204a.asp

THE EXECUTIVE BRANCH AND THE FEDERAL BUREAUCRACY

8

TO MAINTAIN A SECURE HOMELAND, planning is critical. And, at a time when federal resources are stretched to their limit given the high cost of military interventions in Iraq and Afghanistan, the U.S. government—especially its bureaucracy—is trying to prepare for what some are calling the next pandemic: avian flu.

Avian influenza, or H5N1—the designation scientists have given this particular strain of the influenza virus—has infected domesticated and migratory birds in more than fifty nations across Asia, Africa, and Europe. It has infected more than 250 people worldwide and has an astonishingly high death rate of more than 50 percent. Flu viruses mutate rapidly, and experts believe it is highly likely that this particular strain of avian flu could become a global threat to humanity. The last major influenza pandemic occurred in 1918 and killed tens of millions of people worldwide.

Since it takes time to culture a reliable vaccine to protect people from getting a specific strain of flu, a virus like H5N1, if it becomes easily transmittable from person to person, could outpace the abilities of governments to vaccinate their citizens or contain the outbreak. Even if the first widespread infections occurred in China, given the global travel patterns of U.S. citizens, a deadly virus likely would be on the ground in the United States within weeks. "If such an outbreak occurred, hospitals would become overwhelmed, riots would engulf vaccination clinics, and even power and food would be in short supply," concludes a draft of a plan the Bush administration developed as part of its initial planning to handle avian flu.[1]

On May 3, 2006, Frances Townsend, the White House homeland security adviser, issued the administration's Pandemic Influenza Strategic Plan to get the nation ready for a disaster as severe as the 1918 flu outbreak. The new government plan outlined the responsibilities of every federal department and agency should the flu begin to spread quickly among humans. The secretary of health and human services was given major responsibility for health issues, and nonmedical emergency efforts and coordination were given to the secretary of homeland security. The secretary of state was given responsibility for international response issues.[2]

Critics were quick to point out that none of the secretaries were given emergency powers to spend additional monies for actions such as granting emergency medical coverage to the uninsured. Priorities as to how to allot any vaccines or interventional medicines were also left unanswered, as was any potential role for the military. "The real shortcoming of the plan is that it doesn't say who's in charge," said a top health official who fears the consequences of a disorganized response from the federal government.[3]

Possibly further complicating a "national plan of action," the administration's plan places tremendous responsibility on state and local governments, who are often first responders in any emergency. And, it has been criticized by the National Association of County and City Health officials, who view the administration's plan as "the mother of all unfunded mandates."[4]

The plan, which suggests steps that state and local governments can take to prepare for a pandemic, calls for quarantine and travel restrictions, but the administration admits that such steps are largely stopgap measures. Its worst-case scenario foresees the deaths of nearly 2 million Americans and the need to hospitalize an additional 8.5 million.

---

bureaucracy
A set of complex hierarchical departments, agencies, commissions, and their staffs that exists to help a chief executive officer carry out his or her duties. Bureaucracies may be private organizations of governmental units.

IN THE AMERICAN SYSTEM, the **bureaucracy,** or the thousands of federal government agencies and institutions that implement and administer federal laws and programs, can be thought of as the part of the government that makes policy as it links together the three branches of the national government. Although Congress makes the laws, it must rely on bureaucrats in the executive branch to enforce and implement them. These agency determinations, in turn, are often challenged in the courts. Because most administrative agencies that make up part of the bureaucracy enjoy reputations for special expertise in clearly defined policy areas, the federal judiciary routinely defers to bureaucratic administrative decision makers. In fact, the federal bureaucracy often is called the "fourth branch of government."

Politicians often charge that the bureaucracy is too large, too powerful, and too unaccountable to the people or even to elected officials. Many politicians, elected officials, and voters complain that the federal bureaucracy is too wasteful. Nevertheless, few critics discuss the fact that laws and policies also are implemented by state and local bureaucracies and bureaucrats whose numbers are proportionately far larger, and often far less accountable, than those working for the federal government.

As a result, many Americans are uncomfortable with the large role of the federal government in policy making. Nevertheless, recent studies show that most users of federal agencies rate quite favorably the agencies and the services they receive. Many of those polled by the Pew Research Center were frustrated by complicated rules and the slowness of a particular agency. Still, a majority gave most agencies overall high marks. Most of those polled drew sharp distinctions between particular agencies and the government as a whole. For example, 84 percent of physicians and pharmacists rated the Food and Drug Administration favorably, whereas only one-half were positive about the government in general.[5]

Harold D. Lasswell once defined political science as the "study of who gets what, when, and how."[6] It is by studying the bureaucracy that those questions can perhaps best be answered. To understand the role of the bureaucracy, we will first examine the executive branch and the development of the federal bureaucracy. Then, after examining the modern bureaucracy by discussing bureaucrats and the formal organization of the bureaucracy, we will consider how the bureaucracy works. Finally, we will discuss making agencies accountable.

The Origins and Growth of the Federal Bureaucracy

IN 1789, ONLY THREE DEPARTMENTS EXISTED under the Articles of Confederation: Foreign Affairs, War, and Treasury. George Washington inherited those departments when he became president. Soon, the head of each department was called its secretary, and Foreign Affairs was renamed the Department of State. To provide the president with legal advice, Congress also created the office of attorney general. From the beginning, individuals appointed as Cabinet secretaries (as well as the attorney general) were subject to approval by the U.S. Senate, but they could be removed from office by the president alone. Even the First Congress realized how important it was that a president be surrounded by those in whom he had complete confidence and trust.

THE CIVIL WAR AND THE GROWTH OF GOVERNMENT

As discussed in chapter 3, the Civil War (1861–1865) permanently changed the nature of the federal bureaucracy. As the nation geared up for war, thousands of additional employees were added to existing departments. The Civil War also spawned the need for new government agencies. A series of poor harvests and distribution problems led President Abraham Lincoln (who understood that you need well-fed troops to conduct a war) to create the Department of Agriculture in 1862, although it was not given full Cabinet-level status until more than twenty years later.

After the Civil War, the need for a strong national government continued unabated. The Pension Office was established in 1866 to pay benefits to the thousands of Union veterans who had fought in the war (more than 127,000 veterans initially were eligible for benefits). Justice, headed by the attorney general, was made a department in 1870, and other departments were added through 1900.

FROM THE SPOILS SYSTEM TO THE MERIT SYSTEM

In 1831, describing President Andrew Jackson's populating the federal government with his political cronies, a New York senator commented, "To the victor belong the spoils." From his statement derives the term **spoils system** to describe the firing of public office holders of the defeated political party and their replacement with loyalists of a new administration. The spoils system was a form of **patronage,** that is jobs, grants, or other special favors given as rewards to friends and political allies for their support. Political patronage often is defended as an essential element of the party system because it provides rewards and inducements for party workers.

This system reached a high-water mark during Abraham Lincoln's presidency. By the time James A. Garfield, a former distinguished Civil War officer, was elected president in 1880, many reformers were calling for changes in the patronage system. On his election to office, thousands pressed Garfield for positions. Garfield resolved to reform the civil service, but his life was cut short by the bullets of an assassin who, ironically, was a frustrated job seeker.

Public reaction to Garfield's death and increasing criticism of the spoils system prompted Congress to pass the Civil Service Reform Act in 1883, more commonly known as the **Pendleton Act,** named in honor of its sponsor, Senator George H. Pendleton (D–OH). It established the principle of federal employment on the basis of open, competitive exams and created a bipartisan three-member Civil Service Commission, which operated until 1978. Initially, only about 10 percent of the positions in the federal **civil service system** were covered by the law, but later laws and executive orders extended coverage of the act to over 90 percent of all federal employees. This new system was called the **merit system.**

spoils system
The firing of public office holders of a defeated political party and their replacement with loyalists of the newly elected party.

patronage
Jobs, grants, or other special favors that are given as rewards to friends and political allies for their support.

Pendleton Act
Reform measure that created the Civil Service Commission to administer a partial merit system. The act classified the federal service by grades, to which appointments were made based on the results of a competitive examination. It made it illegal for federal political appointees to be required to contribute to a particular political party.

civil service system
The system created by civil service laws by which many appointments to the federal bureaucracy are made.

merit system
The system by which federal civil service jobs are classified into grades or levels, to which appointments are made on the basis of performance on competitive examinations.

The Evolution of the Federal Bureaucracy

independent regulatory commission

An agency created by Congress that is generally concerned with a specific aspect of the economy.

■ During the New Deal, President Franklin D. Roosevelt suggested and Congress enacted the Emergency Relief Appropriation Act, which authorized the Works Progress Administration (WPA) to hire thousands of unemployed workers—like these men shown widening a road—to complete numerous public work projects.

Photo courtesy: AP Wide World Photos

REGULATING THE ECONOMY AND THE GROWTH OF GOVERNMENT IN THE TWENTIETH CENTURY

As the nation grew, so did the bureaucracy. (See Analyzing Visuals: The Ebb and Flow of Federal Employees in the Executive Branch, 1789–2005.) In the wake of the tremendous growth of big business (especially railroads), widespread price fixing, and other unfair business practices that occurred after the Civil War, Congress created the Interstate Commerce Commission (ICC). In creating the ICC, Congress was reacting to public outcries over the exorbitant rates charged by railroad companies for hauling freight. It became the first **independent regulatory commission,** an agency outside a major executive department. Independent regulatory commissions such as the ICC, generally concerned with particular aspects of the economy, are created by Congress to be independent of direct presidential authority. Commission members are appointed by the president and hold their jobs for fixed terms, but they are not removable by the president unless they fail to uphold their oaths of office. In 1887, the creation of the ICC also marked a shift in the focus of the bureaucracy from service to regulation. Its creation gave the government—in the shape of the bureaucracy—vast powers over individual and property rights.

As discussed in chapter 3, the ratification of the Sixteenth Amendment to the Constitution in 1913 affected the size of government and the possibilities for growth. It gave Congress the authority to implement a federal income tax to supplement the national treasury and provided an infusion of funds to support new federal agencies, services, and governmental programs.

The bureaucracy continued to grow after the stock market crashed in 1929, ushering in the high unemployment and weak financial state of the Great Depression. President Franklin D. Roosevelt created hundreds of new government agencies to regulate business practices and various aspects of the national economy. Roosevelt believed that a national depression called for national intervention. Thus, the president proposed, and the Congress enacted, far-ranging economic legislation. The desperate mood of the nation supported these moves, as most Americans began to change their ideas about the proper role of government and the provision of governmental services. Formerly, most Americans had believed in a hands-off approach; now they considered it the government's job to get the economy going and get Americans back to work.

World War II also prompted an expansion of the federal bureaucracy. Tax rates were increased to support the war, and they never again fell to prewar levels. After the war, this infusion of new monies and veterans' demands for services led to a variety of new programs and a much bigger government. The G.I. (Government Issue) Bill, for example, provided college loans for returning veterans and reduced mortgage rates to allow them to buy homes. The national government's involvement in these programs not only affected more people but also led to its greater involvement in more regulation. Homes bought with Veterans Housing Authority loans, for example, had to meet certain specifications. With these programs, Americans became increasingly accustomed to the national government's role in entirely new areas such as affordable middle-class housing and scholarships that allowed lower- and middle-class men their first opportunities for higher education.

Within two decades after World War II, the civil rights movement and President Lyndon B. Johnson's War on Poverty pro-

Analyzing Visuals

THE EBB AND FLOW OF FEDERAL EMPLOYEES IN THE EXECUTIVE BRANCH, 1789–2005

As discussed in chapter 7, most major expansions of governmental authority occur during times of war, social crisis, or economic emergency. For example, the federal government grew slowly until the 1930s, when President Franklin D. Roosevelt's New Deal programs were created in response to the high unemployment and weak financial markets of the Great Depression. A more modest spike in the federal workforce occurred in the mid-1960s during President Lyndon B. Johnson's Great Society program.

After reviewing the data and balloons in the line graph and reading the material in this chapter on the development of the executive branch and federal bureaucracy, answer the following critical thinking questions: Before the United States' involvement in World War II, what was the principal reason for the growth in the number of federal employees? The rapid decline in federal employees between 1945 and 1950 resulted from the end of World War II, but why do you think the number of federal employees declined after 1970? What do you think caused the increase in federal employees between 1975 and 1990? Later decreases in the Clinton and George W. Bush administrations?

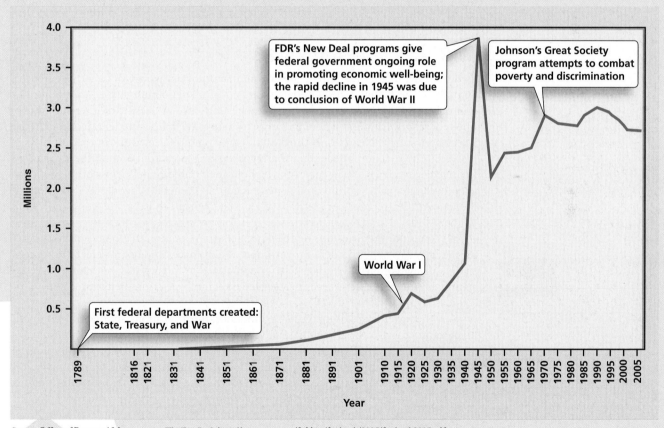

Sources: Office of Personnel Management, *The Fact Book,* http://www.opm.gov/feddata/factbook/2005/factbook2005.pdf.

duced additional growth in the bureaucracy. The Equal Employment Opportunity Commission (EEOC) was created in 1965 (by the Civil Rights Act of 1964). The Departments of Housing and Urban Development (HUD) and Transportation were created in 1965 and 1966, respectively. These expansions of the bureaucracy corresponded to increases in the president's power and his ability to persuade Congress that new agencies would be an effective way to solve pressing social problems.

The Modern Bureaucracy

THE NATIONAL GOVERNMENT differs from private business in numerous ways. Governments exist for the public good, not to make money. Businesses are driven by a profit motive; government leaders, but not bureaucrats, are driven by reelection. Businesses get their money from customers; the national government gets its money from taxpayers. Another difference between a bureaucracy and a business is that it is difficult to determine to whom bureaucracies are responsible. Is it the president? Congress? The citizenry? Still, governments can learn much from business, and recent reform efforts have tried to apply business solutions to create a government that works better and costs less.

The different natures of government and business have a tremendous impact on the way the bureaucracy operates. Because all of the incentive in government "is in the direction of not making mistakes," public employees view risks and rewards very differently from their private-sector counterparts.[7] The key to the modern bureaucracy is to understand who bureaucrats are, how the bureaucracy is organized, how organization and personnel affect each other, and how bureaucrats act within the political process. It also is key to understand that government cannot be run like a business. An understanding of these facts and factors can help in the search for ways to motivate positive change in the bureaucracy.

WHO ARE BUREAUCRATS?

Federal bureaucrats are career government employees who work in the executive branch in the Cabinet-level departments and independent agencies that comprise more than 2,000 bureaus, divisions, branches, offices, services, and other subunits of the federal government. There are approximately 2.7 million federal workers in the executive branch. Nearly one-third of all civilian employees work in the U.S. Postal Service. The remaining federal civilian workers are spread out among the various executive departments and agencies throughout the United States. Most of these federal employees are paid according to what is called the "General Schedule" (GS). They advance within fifteen GS grades (as well as steps within those grades) and move into higher GS levels and salaries as their careers progress.

VIDEO DEBATE

The Merit System

As a result of reforms during the Truman administration that built on the Pendleton Act, most civilian federal governmental employees today are selected by merit standards, which include tests (such as civil service or foreign service exams) and educational criteria. Merit systems protect federal employees from being fired for political reasons.

At the lower levels of the U.S. Civil Service, most positions are filled by competitive examinations. These usually involve a written test. Mid-level to upper ranges of federal positions do not normally require tests; instead, applicants simply submit a resume, or even apply by phone. Personnel departments then evaluate potential candidates and rank candidates according to how well they fit a particular job opening. Only the names of those deemed "qualified" are then forwarded to the official filling the vacancy. This can be a time-consuming process; it often takes six to nine months before a position can be filled in this manner.

The remaining 10 percent of the federal workforce is made up of persons not covered by the civil service system. These positions generally fall into three categories:

1. Appointive policy-making positions. Nearly 3,000 people are presidential appointees. Some of these, including Cabinet secretaries and under and assistant secretaries, are subject to Senate confirmation. These appointees, in turn, are responsible for appointing high-level policy-making assistants who form the top of the bureaucratic hierarchy. These are called "Schedule C" political appointees (see Figure 8.1).

FIGURE 8.1 CHARACTERISTICS AND RANK DISTRIBUTION OF FEDERAL CIVILIAN EMPOYEES, 2004

This bar graph depicts the percentage of the federal civilian workforce in several categories. As you review the data displayed in the graph, consider the trends you observe across GS levels, the underrepresentation of Hispanics overall, as well as women in some categories.

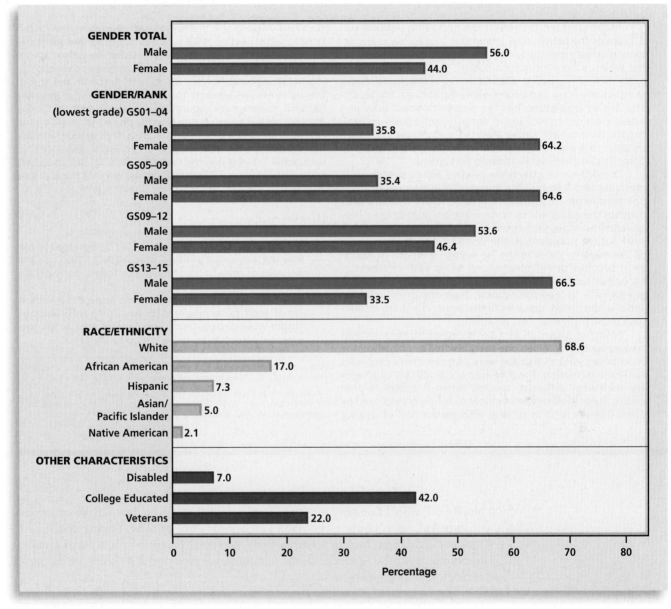

Source: Office of Personnel Management, *The Fact Book.*

COMPARATIVE

Comparing Bureaucracies

2. Independent regulatory commissioners. Although each president gets to appoint as many as one hundred commissioners, they become independent of his direct political influence once they take office.

3. Low-level, nonpolicy patronage positions. These types of positions generally concern secretarial assistants to policy makers.

More than 15,000 job skills are represented in the federal government, and its workers are among the best trained and most skilled and efficient in the world. (See Global Perspective: Bureaucratic Culture in the United Kingdom.) Government

Global Perspective

BUREAUCRATIC CULTURE IN THE UNITED KINGDOM

Bureaucracies tend to reflect the prevailing political culture of the people they administer, and bureaucratic activity is largely determined by the form of government under which a bureaucracy functions. The United Kingdom (U.K.), or as it is typically referred to, Great Britain, functions as a parliamentary democracy where Parliament, the bicameral British legislature, has the power to enact laws and where elections to Parliament determine the party controlling the government. Unlike their U.S. counterparts, who are considered a part of the executive branch, bureaucrats in Great Britain ultimately answer to Parliament.

This difference affects the relative power that the U.S. president and British prime minister have over political appointees. In the United States, presidents are free to use or discount the policy advice or recommendations of their chosen administrators, who as members of the executive branch work for the president. In the United Kingdom, the leader of the majority party in the House of Commons in Parliament becomes prime minister and works with members of his or her party to appoint the ministers who will form a government to lead the country. Thus, the prime minister and the appointed members of the government are responsible to party members in Parliament.

Both the American and British administrative systems provide continuity. When one party is voted out of office, the bureaucracy ensures that the work of government continues without interruption. The American and British bureaucracies are somewhat different, though, when it comes to free speech rights. Civil servants actively or formerly employed by Great Britain's security services who are accused of leaking classified information may be prosecuted under the British Official Secrets Act of 1989, which provides for broader safeguards of security information than exist in the United States, since the law also allows the British government to prosecute journalists who repeat such disclosures. In the United States, the right of civil servants to inform the public of possibly harmful government operations is considered by many (though not all) to be constitutionally protected based on the First Amendment ideals of a free press, free speech, and the right to petition the government for redress of grievances. No such public interest defense currently exists for British leakers and whistleblowers, unless it can be proved that the leak was intended to prevent an immediate threat to life.[a]

QUESTIONS

1. Should a president or prime minister be expected to follow the advice of political appointees? What are the benefits or drawbacks of having to follow bureaucratic advice?
2. To what extent should civil servants respect the authority of their government with regard to information? Under what circumstances would it be ethical for government information to be leaked to the press?

Sources: CIA World Factbook; U.K. Civil Service, http://www.civilservice.gov.uk; Official Secrets Act of 1989, http://www.opsi.gov.uk; BBC News online, http://news.bbc.co.uk.

[a] Sarah Lyall, "Britain Wields Legal Bludgeon in Effort to Stop Leaks," *New York Times* (July 13, 2006); Martin Bright, "Follow My Lead, Says Whistleblower," *Observer* (September 12, 2004), http://observer.guardian.co.uk.

---

employees, whose average age is forty-seven years, have an average length of service of seventeen years. Thirty-eight percent are age fifty-one or older. They include forest rangers, FBI agents, foreign service officers, computer programmers, security guards, librarians, administrators, engineers, plumbers, lawyers, doctors, postal carriers, and zoologists, among others.

The diversity of government jobs mirrors the diversity of jobs in the private sector. The federal workforce, itself, is also diverse but underrepresents African Americans and Hispanics, in particular, and the employment of women lags behind that of men. Women still make up more than 60 percent of the lowest GS levels but have raised their proportion of positions in the GS 13–15 ranks from 18 percent in 1990 to over 30 percent in 2004.[8]

The Changing Face of the Federal Bureaucracy

There are about 332,500 federal workers in the nation's capital; the rest are located in regional, state, and local offices scattered throughout the country. To enhance efficiency, the United States is broken up into several regions, with most agencies having regional offices in one city in that region. (See Figure 8.2.) The decentralization of the bureaucracy facilitates accessibility to the public. The Social Security Administration, for example, has numerous offices so that its clients can have a place nearby to take their paperwork, questions, and problems. Decentralization also helps distribute jobs and incomes across the country.

FIGURE 8.2 FEDERAL AGENCY REGIONS AND CITY HEADQUARTERS

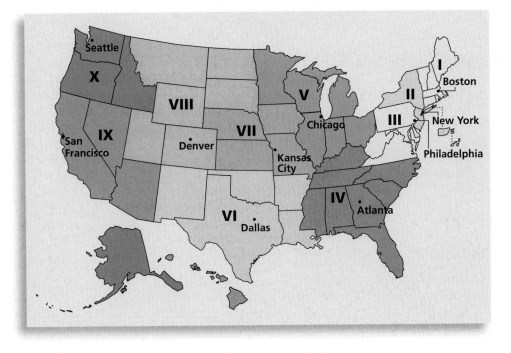

Source: Department of Health and Human Services, http://www.hhs.gov/images/regions.gif.

The graying of the federal workforce is a problem of concern to many. More than two-thirds of those in the highest nonpolitical positions as well as a large number of mid-level managers are eligible to retire.[9] Many in government hope that the Presidential Management Fellows Program which was begun in 1977 to hire and train future managers and executives will be enhanced to make up for the shortfall in experienced managers that the federal government is now facing. Agencies even are contemplating ways to pay the college loans of prospective recruits while at the same time trying to enhance benefits to attract older workers.[10] The federal government has also devoted resources to shrinking the number of federal employees by hiring outside contractors. The biggest reason for these reforms is that outside contractors may provide cheaper labor than government employees and are not eligible for government benefits and pension plans.

PARTICIPATION

Who Wants To Be a Bureaucrat?

FORMAL ORGANIZATION

While even experts can't agree on the exact number of separate governmental agencies, commissions, and departments that make up the federal bureaucracy, there are at least 1,150 civilian agencies.[11] A distinctive feature of the executive bureaucracy is its traditional division into areas of specialization. For example, the Occupational Safety and Health Administration (OSHA) handles occupational safety, and the Department of State specializes in foreign affairs. It is not unusual, however, for more than one agency to be involved in a particular issue or for one agency to be involved in myriad issues. In fact, numerous agencies often have authority in the same issue areas, making administration even more difficult. Agencies fall into four general types: (1) Cabinet departments; (2) government corporations; (3) independent agencies; and, (4) regulatory commissions.

The Cabinet Departments   The fifteen Cabinet **departments** are major administrative units that have responsibility for conducting a broad area of government operations. Cabinet departments account for about 60 percent of the federal workforce.

departments
Major administrative units with responsibility for a broad area of government operations. Departmental status usually indicates a permanent national interest in a particular governmental function, such as defense, commerce, or agriculture.

The Living Constitution

The President . . . may require the Opinion, in writing, of the principle Officer in each of the executive Departments, upon any subject relating to the Duties of their respective Office.

—ARTICLE II, SECTION 2, CLAUSE 1

This clause, along with additional language designating that the president shall be the commander in chief, notes that the heads of departments are to serve as advisers to the president. There is no direct mention of the Cabinet in the Constitution.

This meager language is all that remains of the Framers' initial efforts to create a council to guide the president. Those in attendance at the Constitutional Convention largely favored the idea of a council, but could not agree on who should be a part of that body. Some wanted to follow the British parliamentary model and create the Cabinet from members of the House and Senate who would rotate into the bureaucracy; most, however, appeared to support the idea of the heads of departments along with the chief justice, who would preside when the president was unavailable. The resulting language above depicts a one-sided arrangement whereby the heads of executive departments must simply answer in writing questions put to them by the president.

The Cabinet of today is totally different from the structure envisioned by the Framers. George Washington was the first to convene a meeting of what he called his Cabinet. Some presidents have used their Cabinets as trusted advisers; others have used them to demonstrate that they are committed to political, racial, ethnic, or gender diversity, and have relied more on White House aides than particular Cabinet members. Who is included in the Cabinet, as well as how it is used, is solely up to the discretion of the sitting president.

SIMULATION

You Are the President of MEDICORP

The vice president, the heads of all of the departments, as well as the heads of the Environmental Protection Agency (EPA), Office of Management and Budget (OMB), Office of National Drug Control Policy, the U.S. Trade Representative, and the president's chief of staff make up his formal Cabinet.

The executive branch departments depicted in Figure 8.3 are headed by Cabinet members called secretaries (except the Department of Justice, which is headed by the attorney general). The secretaries are responsible for establishing their department's general policy and overseeing its operations. As discussed in chapter 7, Cabinet secretaries are responsible directly to the president but are often viewed as having two masters—the president and those affected by their department. Cabinet secretaries also are tied to Congress, from which they get their appropriations and the discretion to implement legislation and make rules and policy.

FIGURE 8.3 THE EXECUTIVE BRANCH

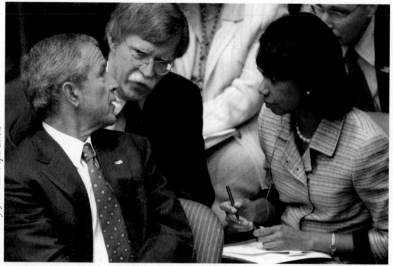

Photo courtesy: Justin Lane/epa/Corbis

■ President George W. Bush confers with Secretary of State Condoleezza Rice and U.S. Ambassador to the United Nations John R. Bolton. After the 2006 midterm elections, many questioned whether Bolton, a recess appointment in 2005 whose nomination was resubmitted by President Bush on November 9, 2006, would have the necessary votes to remain in his post.

government corporation
Business established by Congress that performs functions that could be provided by a private business (such as the U.S. Postal Service).

independent executive agency
Governmental unit that closely resembles a Cabinet department but has a narrower area of responsibility (such as the Central Intelligence Agency) and is not part of any Cabinet department.

Although departments vary considerably in size, prestige, and power, they share certain features. Departmental status generally signifies a strong permanent national interest to promote a particular function. Each department covers a broad area of responsibility generally reflected by its name. Each secretary is assisted by one or more deputies or under-secretaries who take part of the administrative burden off the secretary's shoulders, as well as by several assistant secretaries who direct major programs within the department. In addition, each secretary, just as the president, has numerous assistants who help with planning, budgeting, personnel, legal services, public relations, and their key staff functions. Most departments are subdivided into bureaus, divisions, sections, or other smaller units, and it is at this level that the real work of each agency is done. Most departments are subdivided along functional lines, but the basis for division may be geography, work processes, or clientele. Clientele agencies are particularly subject to outside lobbying from organized interests in Washington. The clientele agencies and groups also are active at the regional level, where the agencies devote a substantial part of their resources to program implementation.

Government Corporations **Government corporations** are the most recent addition to the bureaucracy. Dating from the early 1930s, they are businesses established by Congress to perform functions that could be provided by private businesses. The corporations are formed when the government chooses to engage in activities that primarily are commercial in nature, produce revenue, and require greater flexibility than Congress generally allows regular departments. Some of the better-known government corporations include Amtrak and the Federal Deposit Insurance Corporation. Unlike other governmental agencies, government corporations charge for their services.

Independent Executive Agencies **Independent executive agencies** closely resemble Cabinet departments but have narrower areas of responsibility. Generally speaking, independent agencies perform service rather than regulatory functions. The heads of these agencies are appointed by the president and serve, like Cabinet secretaries, at his pleasure.

Independent agencies exist apart from executive departments for practical or symbolic reasons. The National Aeronautics and Space Administration (NASA), for example, could have been placed within the Department of Defense. Such positioning, however, could have conjured up thoughts of a space program dedicated solely to military purposes, rather than to civilian satellite communication or scientific exploration. Similarly, the Environmental Protection Agency (EPA) could have been created within the Department of the Interior but instead was created as an independent agency in 1970 to administer federal programs aimed at controlling pollution and protecting the nation's environment. As an independent agency, the EPA is less indebted to the president on a day-to-day basis than it would be if it were within a Cabinet department, although the president still has the ability to appoint its director and may intervene on high-profile decisions.

Independent Regulatory Commissions Independent regulatory commissions are agencies created by Congress to exist outside the major departments to regulate a specific economic activity or interest. Because of the complexity of modern economic issues, Congress sought to create agencies that could develop expertise and provide continuity of policy with respect to economic issues because neither Congress nor the courts have the time or specific talents to do so. Examples include the National Labor Relations Board, the Federal Reserve Board, the Federal Communications Commission, and the Securities and Exchange Commission (SEC).[12]

Older boards and commissions, such as the SEC and the Federal Reserve Board, generally are charged with overseeing a certain industry. Most were created specifically to be free from partisan political pressure. Each is headed by a board composed of five to seven members (always an odd number, to avoid tie votes) who are selected by the president and confirmed by the Senate for fixed, staggered terms to increase the chances of a bipartisan board. Unlike executive department heads, they cannot easily be removed by the president.

Newer regulatory boards are more concerned with how the business sector relates to public health and safety. The Occupational Safety and Health Administration (OSHA), for example, promotes job safety. These boards and commissions often lack autonomy and freedom from political pressures; they are generally headed by a single administrator who can be removed by the president. Thus, they are far more susceptible to the political wishes of the president who appoints them.

GOVERNMENT WORKERS AND POLITICAL INVOLVEMENT

As the number of federal employees and agencies grew during the 1930s, many Americans began to fear that the members of the civil service would play major roles not only in implementing public policy but also in electing members of Congress and even the president. Consequently, Congress enacted the Political Activities Act of 1939, commonly known as the **Hatch Act,** named in honor of its main sponsor, Senator Carl Hatch (D–NM). It was designed to prohibit federal employees from becoming directly involved in working for political candidates. Although this act allayed many critics' fears, other people argued that the Hatch Act was too extreme.

Today, government employees' political activity is regulated by the **Federal Employees Political Activities Act** of 1993. This liberalization of the Hatch Act allows employees to run for public office in nonpartisan elections, contribute money to political organizations, and campaign for or against candidates in partisan elections. Federal employees still, however, are prohibited from engaging in political activity while on duty, soliciting contributions from the general public, or running for office in partisan elections. See Table 8.1 for more specifics about the Federal Employees Political Activities Act.

Hatch Act
Law enacted in 1939 to prohibit civil servants from taking activist roles in partisan campaigns. This act prohibited federal employees from making political contributions, working for a particular party, or campaigning for a particular candidate.

Federal Employees Political Activities Act
1993 liberalization of the Hatch Act. Federal employees now are allowed to run for office in nonpartisan elections and to contribute money to campaigns in partisan elections.

How the Bureaucracy Works

GERMAN SOCIOLOGIST MAX WEBER believed bureaucracies were a rational way for complex societies to organize themselves. Model bureaucracies, said Weber, are characterized by certain features, including:

1. A chain of command in which authority flows from top to bottom.
2. A division of labor whereby work is apportioned among specialized workers to increase productivity.
3. Clear lines of authority among workers and their superiors.
4. A goal orientation that determines structure, authority, and rules.
5. Impersonality, whereby all employees are treated fairly based on merit and all clients are served equally, without discrimination, according to established rules.
6. Productivity, whereby all work and actions are evaluated according to established rules.[13]

TABLE 8.1 THE FEDERAL EMPLOYEES POLITICAL ACTIVITIES ACT

Here are some examples of permissible and prohibited activities for federal employees under the Federal Employees Political Activities Act of 1993. Federal Employees:

- **May** be candidates for public office in nonpartisan elections
- **May** assist in voter registration drives
- **May** express opinions about candidates and issues
- **May** contribute money to political organizations
- **May** attend political fund-raising functions
- **May** attend and be active at political rallies and meetings
- **May** join and be active members of a political party or club
- **May** sign nominating petitions
- **May** campaign for or against referendum questions, constitutional amendments, and municipal ordinances
- **May** campaign for or against candidates in partisan elections
- **May** make campaign speeches for candidates in partisan elections
- **May** distribute campaign literature in partisan elections
- **May** hold office in political clubs or parties
- **May not** use their official authority or influence to interfere with an election
- **May not** collect political contributions unless both individuals are members of the same federal labor organization or employee organization and the one solicited is not a subordinate employee
- **May not** knowingly solicit or discourage the political activity of any person who has business before the agency
- **May not** engage in political activity while on duty
- **May not** engage in political activity in any government office
- **May not** engage in political activity while wearing an official uniform
- **May not** engage in political activity while using a government vehicle
- **May not** solicit political contributions from the general public
- **May not** be candidates for public office in partisan elections

Source: U.S. Special Counsel's Office.

Clearly, this Weberian idea is somewhat idealistic, and even the best-run government agencies don't always work this way, but most are trying.

When Congress creates any kind of department, agency, or commission, it is actually delegating some of its powers listed in Article I, section 8, of the U.S. Constitution. Therefore, the laws creating departments, agencies, corporations, or commissions carefully describe their purpose and give them the authority to make numerous policy decisions, which have the effect of law. Congress recognizes that it does not have the time, expertise, or ability to involve itself in every detail of every program; therefore, it sets general guidelines for agency action and leaves it to the agency to work out the details. How agencies execute congressional wishes is called **implementation,** the process by which a law or policy is put into operation.

Historically, political scientists attempting to study how the bureaucracy made policy investigated what they termed **iron triangles,** a term that was used to refer to the relatively stable relationships and patterns of interaction that occurred among federal workers in agencies or departments, interest groups, and relevant congressional subcommittees (see Figure 8.4). Today, iron triangles no longer dominate most policy processes. Some do, however, persist, such as the relationship between the Department of Veterans Affairs, the House Committee on Veterans Affairs, and the American Legion and the Veterans of Foreign Wars, the two largest veterans groups.

Many political scientists examining external influences on the modern bureaucracy prefer to examine **issue networks.** In general, issue networks, like iron triangles, include agency officials, members of Congress (and committee staffers), and interest group lobbyists. But, they also include lawyers, consultants, academics,

implementation
The process by which a law or policy is put into operation by the bureaucracy.

iron triangle
The relatively stable relationship and pattern of interaction that occurs among an agency, interest groups, and congressional committees or subcommittees.

issue network
The loose and informal relationship that exists among a large number of actors who work in broad policy areas.

public relations specialists, and sometimes even the courts. Unlike iron triangles, issue networks are constantly changing as members with technical expertise or newly interested parties become involved in issue areas.

As a result of the increasing complexity of many policy domains, many alliances have also been created within the bureaucracy. One such example is **interagency councils,** working groups that bring together representatives of several departments and agencies to facilitate the coordination of policy making and implementation. Depending on how well these councils are funded, they can be the prime movers of administration policy in any area where an interagency council exists. The U.S. Interagency Council on the Homeless, for example, was created in 1987 to coordinate the activities of the more than fifty governmental agencies and programs that work to alleviate homelessness.

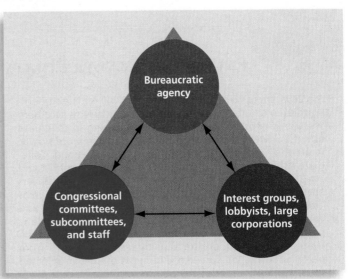

FIGURE 8.4 AN IRON TRIANGLE

In areas where there are extraordinarily complex policy problems, recent presidential administrations have created policy coordinating committees (PCCs) to facilitate interaction among agencies and departments at the subcabinet level. These PCCs gained increasing favor after the terrorist attacks on September 11, 2001. For example, the PCC on Terrorist Financing, which includes representatives from the Departments of Treasury, State, Defense, and Justice, along with the CIA and FBI, conducted a study that recommended to the president that he ask the Saudi government to take action against alleged terrorist financiers.[14] Similarly, in the wake of the 2003 *Columbia* space shuttle disaster, a PCC on space was created to review NASA's evaluation of why the disaster occurred.[15]

interagency council
Working group created to facilitate coordination of policy making and implementation across a host of governmental agencies.

MAKING POLICY

The end product of all of these decision-making bodies is policy making. Policy making and implementation take place on both informal and formal levels. Practically, many decisions are left to individual government employees on a day-to-day basis. Department of Justice lawyers, for example, make daily decisions about whether or not to prosecute individuals. Similarly, street-level Internal Revenue Service agents make many decisions during personal audits. These street-level bureaucrats make policy on two levels. First, they exercise wide discretion in decisions concerning citizens with whom they interact. Second, taken together, their individual actions add up to agency behavior.[16] Thus, how bureaucrats interpret and how they apply (or choose not to apply) various policies are equally important parts of the policy-making process.

Administrative discretion, the ability to make choices concerning the best way to implement congressional or executive intentions, also allows decision makers (whether they are in a Cabinet-level position or at the lowest GS levels) a tremendous amount of leeway. It is exercised through two formal administrative procedures: rule making and administrative adjudication.

administrative discretion
The ability of bureaucrats to make choices concerning the best way to implement congressional intentions.

rule making
A quasi-legislative administrative process that has the characteristics of a legislative act.

Rule Making **Rule making** is a quasi-legislative administrative process that results in regulations and has the characteristics of a legislative act. **Regulations** are the rules that govern the operation of all government programs and have the force of law. In essence, then, bureaucratic rule makers often act as lawmakers as well as law enforcers when they make rules or draft regulations to implement various congressional

regulations
Rules that govern the operation of a particular government program that have the force of law.

On Campus

ENFORCING GENDER EQUITY IN COLLEGE ATHLETICS

In 2004, there were approximately 150,000 female student-athletes, a number up dramatically from 1971, when there were only about 30,000 women participating in collegiate athletics.[a] Male participation has grown much more slowly, while the number of women's teams in the National Collegiate Athletic Association nearly doubled between 1971 and 2002, from 4,776 to 8,414.[b] A major source of that difference? The passage in 1972 of legislation popularly known as Title IX, which prohibits discrimination against girls and women in federally funded education, including athletic programs. This legislation mandates that "No person in the United States shall, on the basis of sex, be excluded from participation in, be denied the benefits of, or be subjected to discrimination under any education program or activity receiving federal financial assistance." It wasn't until December 1978—six years after passage of Title IX—that the Office for Civil Rights in what was then the Department of Health, Education, and Welfare released a policy interpretation of the law, dealing largely with the section that concerned intercollegiate athletics.[c] More than thirty pages of text were devoted to dealing with a hundred or so words from the statute. Football was recognized as unique, because of the huge revenues it produces, so it could be inferred that male-dominated football programs could continue to outspend women's athletic programs. The more than sixty women's groups that had lobbied for equality of spending were outraged and turned their efforts toward seeking more favorable rulings on the construction of the statute from the courts.

Increased emphasis on Title IX enforcement has led many women to file lawsuits to force compliance. In 1991, in an effort to trim expenses, Brown University cut two men's and two women's teams from its varsity roster. Several women students filed a Title IX complaint against the school, arguing that it violated the act by not providing women varsity sport opportunities in relation to their population in the university. The women also argued that cutting the two women's programs saved $62,000, whereas the men's cuts saved only $16,000. Thus, the women's varsity programs took a bigger hit, in violation of federal law.

A U.S. district court refused to allow Brown to cut the women's programs. A U.S. court of appeals upheld that action, concluding that Brown had failed to provide adequate opportunities for its female students to participate in athletics.[d] In 1997, in *Brown University* v. *Cohen,* the U.S. Supreme Court declined to review the appeals court's decision.[e] This put all colleges and universities on notice that discrimination against women would not be tolerated, even when, as in the case of Brown University, the university had expanded sports opportunities for women tremendously since the passage of Title IX.

Women have made significant strides on all college campuses, but true equity in athletics is still a long way away at many colleges and universities. Although the number of women participating in college level sports is increasing, the proportion of women coaches is decreasing (at the same

■ Soccer Olympian Julie Foudy lobbies along with female Democratic and Republican members of the Congressional Women's Caucus to save Title IX.

time the pool of women who could be coaches is increasing). Most colleges still provide far fewer opportunities to women, given their numbers in most universities, and enforcement still lags. This disparity has required groups including the National Women's Law Center to take the lead in the *Brown* case and to spend millions of dollars in legal fees to press for fuller enforcement.[f] Individual colleges and universities must comply with the law, aggrieved students must complain of inequities, and the Department of Education's Office of Civil Rights now is charged with enforcing the law.

In early 2003, after holding hearings on Title IX throughout the United States, a commission appointed by the Bush administration recommended to the secretary of education that enforcement of Title IX's requirements that provide opportunities for women in athletics be weakened to account for perceived differences in interest in athletics between male and female college students. In March 2005, the Bush administration announced new rules that would allow colleges to avoid the act's gender equity requirements if a sufficient number of women on any campus fail to return an e-mail survey expressing interest in playing sports.

---

[a] *Intercollegiate Athletics: Status of Efforts to Promote Gender Equity,* General Accounting Office, October 25, 1996.

[b] Bill Pennington, "Colleges: More Men's Teams Benched as Colleges Level the Playing Field," *New York Times* (May 9, 2002): A1.

[c] See Joyce Gelb and Marian Lief Palley, *Women and Public Policies* (Charlottesville: University of Virginia Press, 1996), ch. 5.

[d] *Cohen v. Brown University,* 101 F.3d 155 (1996).

[e] *Cohen v. Brown University,* 520 U.S. 1186 (1997).

[f] http://www.edc.org/WomensEquity/resource/title9/report/athletic.html.

statutes. Some political scientists say that rule making "is the single most important function performed by agencies of government."[17]

Because regulations often involve political conflict, the 1946 Administrative Procedures Act established rule-making procedures to give everyone the chance to participate in the process. The act requires that: (1) public notice of the time, place, and nature of the rule-making proceedings be provided in the *Federal Register;* (2) interested parties be given the opportunity to submit written arguments and facts relevant to the rule; and, (3) the statutory purpose and basis of the rule be stated. Once rules are written, thirty days generally must elapse before they take effect.

Sometimes an agency is required by law to conduct a formal hearing before issuing rules. Evidence is gathered, and witnesses testify and are cross-examined by opposing interests. The process can take weeks, months, or even years, at the end of which agency administrators must review the entire record and then justify the new rules. Although cumbersome, the process has reduced criticism of some rules and bolstered the deference given by the courts to agency decisions. Many Americans are unaware of the opportunities available to them to influence government at this stage. As illustrated in On Campus: Enforcing Gender Equity in College Athletics, women's groups and female athletes testified at hearings held around the country urging the secretary of education not to revise existing Title IX regulations, which the administration ultimately did.

SIMULATION

You Are a Federal Administrator

Administrative Adjudication **Administrative adjudication** is a quasi-judicial process in which a bureaucratic agency settles disputes between two parties in a manner similar to the way courts resolve disputes. Administrative adjudication is referred to as quasi judicial, because law-making by any body other than Congress or adjudication by any body other than the judiciary would be a violation of the constitutional principle of separation of powers.

Agencies regularly find that persons or businesses are not in compliance with the federal laws the agencies are charged with enforcing, or that they are in violation of an agency rule or regulation. To force compliance, some agencies resort to administrative adjudication, which generally is less formal than a trial. Several agencies and boards employ administrative law judges to conduct the hearings. Although these judges are employed by the agencies, they are strictly independent and cannot be removed except for gross misconduct.

administrative adjudication
A quasi-judicial process in which a bureaucratic agency settles disputes between two parties in a manner similar to the way courts resolve disputes.

Making Agencies Accountable

THE QUESTION OF to whom bureaucrats should be responsible is one that continually comes up in any debate about governmental accountability. Should the bureaucracy be answerable to itself? To organized interest groups? To its clientele? To the president? To Congress? Or to some combination of all of these? At times an agency becomes so removed from the public it serves that Congress must step in.

Although many critics of the bureaucracy argue that federal employees should be responsive to the public interest, the public interest is difficult to define. As it turns out, several factors work to control the power of the bureaucracy, and to some degree, the same kinds of checks and balances that operate among the three branches of government serve this function.

VIDEO ROUNDTABLE

Hurricane Katrina and New Orleans

EXECUTIVE CONTROL

As the size and scope of the American national government, in general, and of the executive branch and the bureaucracy, in particular, have grown, presidents have delegated more and more power to bureaucrats. But, most presidents have continued to

Politics Now

E-GOVERNMENT

In 1992, the White House first went up on the World Wide Web. Now all government agencies and bureaus have Web sites and provide a plethora of information to the American public that formerly would have taken numerous trips to the library or even Washington, D.C., to obtain.

By 1998, the Government Paperwork Elimination Act required that federal agencies allow persons transacting business with the government to have the option of submitting information or transacting business with them electronically. It is from this act that you or members of your family now have the option of submitting your tax returns electronically.

In 2002, the Bush administration took additional advantage of changing technologies and the increasing number of Americans' access to it, whether in their homes, at local public libraries, or at Internet cafes. The E-Government Act of 2002 was an effort to mandate that all government agencies use "Internet-based information technologies to enhance citizens' access to government information and services."[a]

According to the E-Gov Web site, e-government is not simply about putting forms online; its major purpose is to harness technology to make it easier for citizens to learn more about government services. Through GovBenefits.gov, for example, citizens can find answers to a range of questions dealing with their individual circumstances and will immediately receive a list of government programs for which they may be eligible. Recreation.gov allows individuals to find out about national parks and recreation sites and to make online reservations at those facilities.

One addition to the e-government effort under the Bush administration is its eRulemaking Initiative. Managed by the Environmental Protection Agency, this new use of technology is designed to transform "the federal rule-making process by enhancing the public's ability to participate in their government's regulatory decision making." Regulations.gov was launched in 2002 to allow the public to "search, view, and comment on proposed federal regulations

open for comment."[b] While the regulatory process almost exclusively involved interest groups and affected industries, this new initiative allows the public to search proposed regulations easily. Agencies are in the process of posting their proposed regulations on this central site, although some agencies still have their own sites. OMB Watch, a nonprofit group that monitors government actions as they affect citizen participation, has applauded the notion of a centralized, one-stop method to allow concerned citizens input into the policy process.

Even before revelations that the government has collected e-mails, phone records, and other information about millions of Americans, the notion of e-government had become somewhat controversial, despite its original intentions. Earlier surveys revealed that while nearly 50 percent of the public believed that it is permissible for the federal government to search its data bases for information to help track terrorists, 42 percent disagreed, believing that "privacy should be a top priority."[c]

QUESTIONS

1. Will the bureaucracy become more responsive to citizens and less captured by special interests as e-government increases?
2. Studies reveal that many Americans use e-government largely for gathering information. As the government increasingly uses the Web for collecting information about Americans, what problems do you see potentially happening with expansions of e-government?

---

[a] About E-Gov, http://www.whitehouse.gov/omb/egov/about_leg.htm.

[b] http://www.regulations.gov.

[c] Judy Sarasohn, "Survey Finds Americans Split on 'E-Government,' " *Washington Post* (April 14, 2003): A14.

---

try to exercise some control over the bureaucracy, although they have often found that task more difficult than they first envisioned.

Presidents try to appoint the best possible persons to carry out their wishes and policy preferences. Presidents make hundreds of appointments to the executive branch; in doing so, they have the opportunity to appoint individuals who share their views on a range of policies. Although presidential appointments make up a very small proportion of all federal jobs, presidents or the Cabinet secretaries usually fill most top policy-making positions. (See American Values/American Voices: Policy Making and the Role of Religion in the Executive Branch.)

Presidents, with the approval of Congress, can reorganize the bureaucracy. They also can make changes in an agency's annual budget requests and ignore legislative initiatives originating within the bureaucracy. As discussed in chapter 7, presidents also can shape policy and provide direction to bureaucrats by issuing executive

VIDEO ROUNDTABLE

Bureaucratic Reform

American Values/American Voices

EXECUTIVE CONTROL OF THE BUREAUCRACY

President George W. Bush, an evangelical Christian, consistently discusses the centrality of his religious faith and values in his life. In an interview with the *Washington Times* in January 2005, Bush said, "I fully understand that the job of the president is and must always be protecting the great right of people to worship or not worship as they see fit. . . . On the other hand, I don't see how you can be president at least from my perspective, how you can be president, without a relationship with the Lord."[a] Conservative evangelical Christians are a key component of the Republican Party's base, and the president's policies, many of them promoted through administrative actions such as political appointments and executive orders, are very much in line with his faith and values and those of his supporters, who have been known to refer to themselves, members of the GOP (the Grand Old Party), as belonging to "God's Official Party."[b]

President Bush's conservative, evangelical agenda has been furthered by his strategic use of the appointment power and is reflected in those he has appointed. In a departure from previous administrations, Bush administration Cabinet officers, who typically have been allowed to hire their own senior staffs, were given a list of candidates who had been interviewed and approved by the director of the White House Office of Personnel, thus insuring the hiring of only those with a shared commitment to the president's policy positions.[c] The former dean of evangelist Pat Robertson's Regent University was made the director of the Office of Personnel Management. High-profile Bush appointees such as Secretary of Commerce Don Evans and Attorney General John Ashcroft held weekly and sometimes daily prayer meetings in their offices to which political appointees and other staffers were invited. Lester Crawford, who served as commissioner of the Food and Drug Administration, refused to allow emergency contraception to be made available over the counter in spite of positive recommendations by staff and a panel of experts. Many attributed this to Crawford's religious beliefs.

The president, like his predecessors, has also used executive orders to further his values agenda within the bureaucracy. Countering President Bill Clinton's pro-choice policy positions, two days after taking office in 2001, President Bush issued an executive order reinstating a ban on funding nongovernmental organizations engaging in abortion-related activities. This global gag rule, which was in effect during President Bush's father's time in office, prevents money from going to any international family planning agencies that mention abortion as an alternative to pregnancy. Only groups that exclusively tout abstinence-only education can receive funding. The president also issued directives severely limiting stem cell research—a move that put him at odds with former First Lady Nancy Reagan, who lost her husband, President Ronald Reagan, to Alzheimer's disease. Stem cell research may provide a cure for Alzheimer's as well as other illnesses; nevertheless, President Bush, like other pro-life advocates, is against making use of cells from fetuses in scientific experiments because he believes that life begins at conception. One of the president's most controversial actions, discussed in American Values/American Voices: Where's the Wall? in chapter 4, was to create offices of faith-based initiatives in most federal departments. By doing so, the president added to the number of overtly religious political appointments he was able to make.

QUESTIONS

1. What role should the president and the executive branch play in defining what the American values agenda should be?
2. To what extent should the president seek to shape the bureaucracy in order to further his preferred policy agenda without the help of Congress?

[a]James G. Lakely, "President Outlines Role of His Faith," *Washington Times* (January 12, 2005), http://washingtontimes.com.

[b] Michael Crowley, "Base Ball: TNR's Republican Convention Blog," *New Republic Online* (August 30, 2004), http://www.tnr.com.

[c] Shirley Anne Warshaw, "The Administrative Strategies of President George W. Bush," *Extensions* (Spring 2006): 19–20.

orders.[18] **Executive orders** are rules or regulations issued by the president that have the effect of law. For example, even before Congress acted to protect women from discrimination by the federal government, the National Organization for Women convinced President Lyndon B. Johnson to sign a 1967 executive order that amended an earlier one prohibiting the federal government from discriminating on the basis of race, color, religion, or national origin in the awarding of federal contracts, by adding to it the category of "gender." Although the president signed the order, the Office of Federal Contract Compliance, part of the Department of Labor's Employment Standards Administration, failed to draft appropriate guidelines for implementation of the order until several years later.[19]

executive order

A rule or regulation issued by the president that has the effect of law. All executive orders must be published in the *Federal Register*.

Join the Debate

FUEL EFFICIENCY STANDARDS AND GOVERNMENT POLICY

OVERVIEW: Government bureaucracies influence life in the United States in many beneficial and, sometimes, not so beneficial ways. Government agencies are charged with securing the common good and are dedicated to serving the American public. Administrative agencies, however, do not operate in a vacuum—they have mandates from the government and are ultimately subject to congressional, executive, and judicial supervision. Bureaucratic rule-making is subject to political oversight so as to ensure agencies and departments are held accountable for their activities, though administrative units vary in the extent of their discretion and freedom of action, depending on their mandates. While considered expert in their respective policy domains, bureaucrats may receive politically motivated, ill-conceived, or poorly researched directives from the government that can interfere with an agency's mission or operating efficiency. The intersection between politics, policy, and administrative regulation can be illustrated by the battle over government-mandated fuel economy for America's vehicles under the Corporate Average Fuel Economy (CAFE) program, which was part of the 1975 Energy Policy and Conservation Act (ECPA).

In response to the 1973 Organization of Petroleum Exporting Countries (OPEC) oil embargo and the resulting energy crisis, Congress established the CAFE program to reduce America's dependence on imported oil and consumption of gasoline. The idea was to set fuel efficiency standards for American passenger automobiles and light trucks, with fines to be imposed on automakers whose vehicle lines failed to meet these standards. Congress retained the authority to determine the miles-per-gallon standard for passenger cars, but it gave the Department of Transportation (DOT) the authority to set standards for light trucks (which include minivans and SUVs) and to enforce these regulations. Automakers have opposed these standards from the beginning. The industry claims that CAFE regulations impose an undue cost on automobile production by forcing manufacturers to make products the market does not want. As a result, the Department of Transportation has been thrust into the political battles between auto industry interests, environmental and energy interests, and Congress over whether to increase or repeal the CAFE standards.

CAFE policy has had mixed results. During the 1980s, a surge of fuel efficient new cars and trucks, coupled with tighter emission controls, reduced auto pollutants. But, low gas prices throughout the 1990s and through 2004 allowed Americans to buy less efficient vehicles (notably trucks and SUVs), and this resulted in an overall increase in American gasoline consumption. As disruptions in the Middle East and global competition contribute to periods of record gas prices in the United States, CAFE standards have once again taken a prominent place in America's energy policy debate. The Bush administration has called on Congress to give the DOT the authority to set new CAFE standards for both light trucks and passenger cars, but Congress has been reluctant to increase the department's rule-making authority due to pressure from the automobile and oil and gas industries.

ARGUMENTS FOR INCREASING FUEL EFFICIENCY STANDARDS

- **Increased standards will reduce America's dependence on foreign oil.** One obvious benefit of increased standards would be to reduce the United States' depen-

CONGRESSIONAL CONTROL

Congress, too, plays an important role in checking the power of the bureaucracy. Constitutionally, it possesses the authority to create or abolish departments and agencies as well as to transfer agency functions. In addition, it can expand or contract bureaucratic discretion. The Senate's authority to confirm (or reject) presidential appointments also gives Congress a check on the bureaucracy.

Congress uses many of its constitutional powers to exercise control over the bureaucracy. These include its investigatory powers. It is not at all unusual for a congressional committee or subcommittee to hold hearings on a particular problem and then direct the relevant agency to study the problem or find ways to remedy it. Representatives of the agencies also appear before these committees on a regular basis to inform members about agency activities and ongoing investigations.

dence on foreign oil supplies. Building more fuel-efficient vehicles would allow the United States to decrease oil imports while American energy producers seek alternative fuel sources and the means for cleaner and more efficient oil extraction from U.S. territory.

- **Increased efficiency standards will reduce the effect of greenhouse gas emissions.** The Environmental Protection Agency reports that technology improvements to meet CAFE standards have resulted in cleaner vehicles that emit reduced greenhouse gas pollutants. Increasing the standards should create a more environmentally friendly vehicle fleet.
- **Increased efficiency standards will force automakers to seek improved and efficient technologies.** In order to meet increased CAFE standards and remain profitable, automakers will develop automobiles with a view to affordability and efficiency. As a response to America's oil concerns, the hybrid car was developed, and research is currently being directed to explore other alternative energy sources, such as hydrogen fuel cells.

ARGUMENTS FOR REPEALING FUEL EFFICIENCY STANDARDS

- **Efficiency standards have failed to reduce America's oil consumption.** The *Wall Street Journal* reports that as America's autos have become more fuel efficient, Americans have almost *doubled* the number of miles driven. The effect is a net increase in oil consumption, and this is contrary to CAFE's policy goals. Many argue that if the government is truly concerned with decreasing fuel consumption, it should increase gas taxes, a strategy that has proven to be effective, if unpopular, elsewhere.

- **CAFE standards have created new environmental problems.** To meet CAFE standards, automakers have made lighter-weight vehicles by using composites and plastics to replace steel, for example. But, the National Research Council has found that new vehicle materials may create a new set of environmental impacts, such as environmental problems with vehicle disposal.

- **Market mechanisms are the best way to reduce fuel consumption and pollutants.** Dramatically increased gasoline prices have created a strong demand for fuel- and energy-efficient hybrid vehicles and have caused American public opinion to coalesce around the idea of pursuing research into alternative fuels and power sources. Automakers are responding by developing the hybrid vehicles the American people are now demanding.

QUESTIONS

1. Should the federal government have a role in directing the automobile industry in regard to fuel efficiency standards? Why or why not?
2. What seems to be the best policy to reduce America's dependence on foreign energy sources? Why?

SELECTED READINGS

Bent, Robert, Lloyd Orr, and Randall Baker, eds. *Energy: Science, Policy, and the Pursuit of Sustainability.* Washington, DC: Island Press, 2002.

National Research Council. *Effectiveness and Impact of Corporate Average Fuel Economy: Standards.* Washington, DC: National Academies Press, 2003.

Legislators also augment their formal oversight of the executive branch through the power of the purse and by allowing citizens to appeal adverse bureaucratic decisions to agencies, Congress, and even the courts. Congressional review, a procedure adopted by the 104th Congress, by which agency regulations can be nullified by joint resolutions of legislative disapproval, is another method of exercising congressional oversight. This form of oversight is discussed in greater detail in chapter 6.

JUDICIAL CONTROL

Whereas the president's and Congress's ongoing control over the actions of the bureaucracy is very direct, the judiciary's oversight function is less apparent. Still, federal judges, for example, can issue injunctions or orders to an executive agency even before a rule is promulgated formally, giving the federal judiciary a potent check on the bureaucracy.

The courts also have ruled that agencies must give all affected individuals their due process rights guaranteed by the U.S. Constitution. A Social Security recipient's checks cannot be stopped, for example, unless that individual is provided with reasonable notice and an opportunity for a hearing. On a more informal, indirect level, litigation, or even the threat of litigation, often exerts a strong influence on bureaucrats. Injured parties can bring suit against agencies for their failure to enforce a law, and can challenge agency interpretations of any law. In general, however, the courts give great weight to the opinions of bureaucrats and usually defer to their expertise.[20]

Research by political scientists shows that government agencies are strategic. They often implement Supreme Court decisions "based on the costs and benefits of alternative policy choices." Specifically, the degree to which agencies appear to respond to Supreme Court decisions is based on the "specificity of Supreme Court opinions, agency policy preferences, agency age, and *amicus curiae* support."[21]

The development of specialized courts has altered the relationship of some agencies with the federal courts, apparently resulting in less judicial deference to agency rulings. Research by political scientists reveals that specialized courts such as the Court of International Trade, because of their expertise, defer less to agency decisions than do more generalized federal courts. Conversely, decisions from executive agencies are more likely to be reversed than those from more specialized independent regulatory commissions.[22]

Summary

THE BUREAUCRACY PLAYS a major role in America as a shaper of public policy, earning it the nickname the fourth branch of government. The federal bureaucracy has changed dramatically since George Washington's time, when the executive branch had only three departments—State, War, and Treasury—through the Civil War. Significant gains occurred in the size of the federal bureaucracy as the government geared up to conduct a war. As employment opportunities within the federal government increased, concurrent reforms in the civil service system assured that more and more jobs were filled according to merit and not by patronage. By the late 1800s, reform efforts led to further increases in the size of the bureaucracy, as independent regulatory commissions were created. In the wake of the Depression, many new agencies were created to get the national economy back on course as part of President Franklin D. Roosevelt's New Deal.

The modern bureaucracy is composed of more than 2.7 million civilian workers from all walks of life. In general, bureaucratic agencies fall into four general categories: departments, government corporations, independent agencies, and independent regulatory commissions. The political activity of federal employees is regulated by the Federal Employees Political Activities Act.

The bureaucracy gets much of its power from the Congress delegating its powers. A variety of formal and informal mechanisms have been created to help the bureaucracy work more efficiently. These mechanisms help the bureaucracy and bureaucrats make policy.

Agencies enjoy considerable discretion, but they also are subjected to many formal controls. The president, Congress, and the judiciary all exercise various degrees of control over the bureaucracy.

KEY TERMS

administrative adjudication, p. 237
administrative discretion, p. 235
bureaucracy, p. 222
civil service system, p. 223
departments, p. 229
executive order, p. 239
Federal Employees Political Activities Act, p. 233
government corporation, p. 232
Hatch Act, p. 233
implementation, p. 234
independent executive agency, p. 232
independent regulatory commission, p. 224
interagency council, p. 235
iron triangle, p. 234
issue network, p. 234
merit system, p. 223
patronage, p. 223
Pendleton Act, p. 223
regulations, p. 235
rule making, p. 235
spoils system, p. 223

SELECTED READINGS

Aberbach, Joel D., and Bert A. Rockman. *In the Web of Politics: Three Decades of the U.S. Federal Executive.* Washington, DC: Brookings Institution, 2000.

Borrelli, MaryAnne. *The President's Cabinet: Gender, Power, and Representation.* Boulder, CO: Lynne Rienner, 2002.

Brehm, John, and Scott Gates. *Working, Shirking, and Sabotage: Bureaucratic Response to a Democratic Public.* Ann Arbor: University of Michigan Press, 1997.

Dolan, Julie A., and David H. Rosenbloom. *Representative Bureaucracy: Continued Cases and Controversies.* Armonk, NY: M. E. Sharpe, 2003.

Felbinger, Claire L., and Wendy A. Haynes, eds. *Outstanding Women in Public Administration: Leaders, Mentors, and Pioneers.* Armonk, NY: M. E. Sharpe, 2004.

Goodsell, Charles T. *The Case for Bureaucracy: A Public Administration Polemic,* 4th ed. Washington, DC: CQ Press, 2003.

Gormley, William T., and Steven J. Balla. *Bureaucracy and Democracy: Accountability and Performance.* Washington, DC: CQ Press, 2003.

Ingraham, Patricia Wallace. *The Foundation of Merit: Public Service in American Democracy.* Baltimore, MD: Johns Hopkins University Press, 1995.

Ingraham, Patricia Wallace, and Laurence E. Lynn Jr. *The Art of Governance: Analyzing Management and Administration.* Washington, DC: Georgetown University Press, 2004.

Kerwin, Cornelius M. *Rulemaking: How Government Agencies Write Law and Make Policy,* 3rd ed. Washington, DC: CQ Press, 2003.

Peters, B. Guy. *The Politics of Bureaucracy,* 5th ed. New York: Routledge, 2001.

Richardson, William D. *Democracy, Bureaucracy and Character.* Lawrence: University Press of Kansas, 1997.

Stivers, Camilla. *Gender Images in Public Administration: Legitimacy and the Administrative State,* 2nd ed. Thousand Oaks, CA: Sage, 2002.

Twight, Charlotte. *Dependent on DC: The Rise of Federal Control over the Lives of Ordinary Americans.* New York: Palgrave Macmillan, 2002.

Wilson, James Q. *Bureaucracy: What Government Agencies Do and Why They Do It,* reprint ed. New York: Basic Books, 2000.

WEB EXPLORATIONS

To examine the federal workforce by gender, race, and ethnicity, go to
http://www.opm.gov/feddata/factbook/

To see federal agency rules and regulations contained in the *Federal Register,* go to
http://www.gpoaccess.gov/fr/index.html

For more about the IRS and its modernization efforts, see
http://www.irs.gov

To find out more about the Presidential Management Fellows Program, go to
http://www.pmf.opm.gov/

To view the scorecard of federal agencies trying implement the president's management agenda, go to
http://www.whitehouse.gov/results/agenda/scorecard.html

For contrasting views on the debate over fuel efficiency standards, go to
http://www.heritage.org/Research/EnergyandEnvironment/BG1458.cfm
http://www.ppionline.org/documents/clean_cars_0304.pdf

THE JUDICIARY

9

IN THE WAKE OF THE SEPTEMBER 11, 2001, terrorist attacks, Congress passed the Authorization for Use of Military Force, giving the president power to "use all necessary appropriate force" against "nations, organizations, or persons" that he deemed to have "planned, authorized, committed or aided" in the completion of those attacks. The president then sent U.S. troops to Afghanistan to subdue al-Qaeda and to quell the Taliban regime that was lending it support. Soon thereafter, members of the U.S.-supported Afghani Northern Alliance captured several U.S. citizens in Afghanistan, including Yaser Hamdi, who was later handed over to U.S. forces. The capture of Hamdi opened the door to a number of civil liberties questions, which were eventually resolved by the U.S. Supreme Court, underscoring the major role played by the Court in acting as the arbiter of disputes within the federal system.

After his capture, Hamdi, who although a U.S. citizen had spent much of his life in Saudi Arabia, was sent to a U.S. detention facility at Guantanamo Bay, Cuba, where he was held with no access to the outside world or to an attorney. From there, he was sent to a U.S. military base in Virginia and then to a naval brig in South Carolina. The Department of Justice declined to bring any charges against Hamdi and instead designated him an "enemy combatant."

In July 2002, Hamdi's father filed suit on his son's behalf, seeking a review of the legality of his son's detention. He alleged that the government was holding Hamdi in violation of the Fifth and Fourteenth Amendments. A federal judge ordered the United States to allow an attorney to meet with Hamdi in private. While this decision was being appealed, Hamdi was held in solitary confinement with no access to his lawyer. The case finally ended up before the U.S. Supreme Court, where Hamdi, yet to be charged with a crime, argued that his basic civil liberties as an American citizen were being denied. The U.S. government countered that by designating Hamdi an enemy combatant, it was justified holding him in the United States indefinitely—without formal charges or proceedings—until it decided that access to counsel or other actions were warranted.

In June 2004, the U.S. Supreme Court ruled in *Hamdi et al.* v. *Rumsfeld* that "a state of war is not a blank check for the president" to deny basic civil

CHAPTER OUTLINE

- ✪ The Constitution and the Creation of the Federal Judiciary

- ✪ The American Legal System

- ✪ The Federal Court System

- ✪ How Federal Court Judges Are Selected

- ✪ The Supreme Court Today

- ✪ Judicial Philosophy and Decision Making

- ✪ Judicial Policy Making and Implementation

liberties to U.S. citizens held in captivity. The Court went on to say that citizens must be apprised of the charges against them and allowed access to lawyers.[1] Although the Court affirmed the right of the president to detain citizens as enemy combatants, it reiterated that such prisoners must be given the right to challenge their captivity before a neutral fact finder.

Hamdi was released in October 2004, but as a condition of his release, he had to renounce his U.S. citizenship and return to Saudi Arabia. This outcome meant that Hamdi was never formally charged or brought to trial, despite three years of imprisonment. The question of how the U.S. government should treat enemy combatants was not, however, completely resolved. Thus, in 2006, the Supreme Court revisited the issue in *Hamdan* v. *Rumsfeld.*

Hamdan stemmed from a lawsuit filed by Guantanamo Bay detainee Salim Hamdan, a Yemeni whom the administration accused of being an agent of Osama bin Laden. Continuing the line of reasoning established in *Hamdi*, the Court ruled that the military commissions created by the Bush administration in 2001 to try suspected members of al-Qaeda went far beyond the con-stitutional powers granted to the president under the U.S. Constitution.[2] A 5–3 majority—Chief Justice John G. Roberts Jr. did not participate in the decision because he had been on the lower court that had upheld the president's actions—found that the commissions "were neither authorized by federal law nor required by military necessity"[3] and circumvented the Geneva Conventions for dealing with prisoners of war, as well as the U.S. Military Code of Justice.

The *Hamdi* and *Hamdan* cases represent a historically significant rebuke of executive authority in a time of war and underscore the growing authority of the Supreme Court in the federal system. In the past, the Court has often acquiesced to unprecedented claims of executive power, such as those claimed by President Abraham Lincoln during the Civil War, or President Franklin D. Roosevelt's internment of Japanese American citizens during World War II. Moreover, the Court's rulings underscore that in the delicate system of separation of powers established by the Framers, the Supreme Court of the United States—not the president—is the ultimate authority on what the U.S. Constitution means.

I N 1787, when Alexander Hamilton wrote to urge support of the U.S. Constitution, he firmly believed that the judiciary would prove to be the weakest of the three departments of government. In its formative years, the judiciary was, in Hamilton's words, "the least dangerous" branch. The judicial branch seemed so inconsequential that when the young national government made its move to the District of Columbia in 1800, Congress actually forgot to include any space to house the justices of the Supreme Court!

Today, the role of the courts, particularly the Supreme Court of the United States, is significantly different from that envisioned when the national government came into being. The "least dangerous branch" now is perceived by many as having too much power.

In this chapter, we will first look at the Constitution and the creation of the federal judiciary. After considering the American legal system and the concepts of civil and criminal law, we will discuss the federal court system composed of specialized courts, district courts, courts of appeals, and the Supreme Court, which is the ultimate authority on all federal law. Then, we will examine how federal court judges are selected. All appointments to the federal district courts, courts of appeals, and the Supreme Court are made by the president and are subject to Senate confirmation. Our study of the Supreme Court today will make clear that only a few of the millions of cases filed in courts around the United States every year eventually make their way to the Supreme Court through the lengthy appellate process. After an examination of judicial philosophy and decision making and how judicial decision making is based on a variety of legal and extra-legal factors, we will discuss judicial policy making and implementation.

A note on terminology: When we refer to the "Supreme Court," the "Court," or the "high Court" here, we always mean the U.S. Supreme Court, which sits at the pinnacle of the federal and state court systems. The Supreme Court is referred to by the name of the chief justice who presided over it during a particular period. For example, the Marshall Court is the Court presided over by John Marshall from 1801 to 1835, and the Roberts Court is the current Court that began in late 2005. When we use the term "courts," we refer to all federal or state courts unless otherwise noted.

The Constitution and the Creation of the Federal Judiciary

THE DETAILED NOTES James Madison took at the Constitutional Convention in Philadelphia make it clear that the Framers devoted little time to writing the content of Article III, which created the judicial branch of government. The Framers believed that a federal judiciary posed little of the threat of tyranny that they feared from the other two branches. Anti-Federalists, however, were quick to object to a judiciary whose members had life tenure and the ability to interpret what was to be "the supreme law of the land."

The Framers also debated the need for any federal courts below the level of the Supreme Court. Some argued in favor of deciding all cases in state courts, with only appeals going before the Supreme Court. Others argued for a system of federal courts. A compromise left the final choice to Congress, and Article III, section 1, begins simply by vesting "The judicial Power of the United States . . . in one supreme Court, and in such inferior Courts as the Congress may from time to time ordain and establish." Although there is some debate over whether the Court should have the power of **judicial review,** which allows the judiciary to review acts of the other branches of government and the states, the question is left unsettled in Article III—and was not finally resolved until *Marbury* v. *Madison* (1803),[4] regarding acts of the national government and *Martin* v. *Hunter's Lessee* (1816), regarding state law.[5]

Article III, section 1, also gave Congress the authority to establish other courts as it saw fit. Section 2 specifies the judicial power of the Supreme Court (see Table 9.1) and discusses the Court's original and appellate jurisdiction. This section also specifies that all federal crimes, except those involving impeachment, shall be tried by jury in the state in which the crime was committed. The third section of the article defines treason, and mandates that at least two witnesses appear in such cases.

judicial review
Power of the courts to review acts of other branches of government and the states.

TABLE 9.1   THE JUDICIAL POWER OF THE UNITED STATES SUPREME COURT

The following are the types of cases the Supreme Court was given the jurisdiction to hear as initially specified in the Constitution:

- All cases arising under the Constitution and laws or treaties of the United States
- All cases of admiralty or maritime jurisdiction
- Cases in which the United States is a party
- Controversies between a state and citizens of another state (later modified by the Eleventh Amendment)
- Controversies between two or more states
- Controversies between citizens of different states
- Controversies between citizens of the same states claiming lands under grants in different states
- Controversies between a state, or the citizens thereof, and foreign states or citizens thereof
- All cases affecting ambassadors or other public ministers

The Living Constitution

The Judges both of the supreme and inferior Courts, shall . . . receive for their Services, a Compensation, which shall not be diminished during their Continuance in Office.

—ARTICLE III, SECTION 1

This section of Article III simply posits the notion that the salaries of all federal judges cannot be reduced during their service on the bench. During the Constitutional Convention, there was considerable debate over how to treat the payment of federal judges. Some believed that Congress should have an extra check on the judiciary by being able to intimidate judges with the threat of reducing their salaries. This provision was a compromise after James Madison suggested that Congress have the authority to bar increases as well as decreases in the salaries of these unelected jurists. The delegates recognized that decreases, as well as no opportunity for raises, could negatively affect the pluses associated with life tenure.

There has not been much controversy over this clause of the Constitution. When the federal income tax was first enacted, some judges unsuccessfully challenged it as a diminution of their salaries. Much more recently, Chief Justices William H. Rehnquist and John G. Roberts Jr. repeatedly have urged Congress to increase salaries for federal judges, who earn less than some of their former clerks do as first-year associates in private law firms. As early as 1989, Rehnquist noted that "judicial salaries were the single greatest problem facing the federal judiciary today." Roberts, in his first state of the judiciary message, pointed out that the comparatively low salaries earned by federal judges drive away many well-qualified and diverse lawyers, compromising the independence of the American judiciary.

More and more federal judges are leaving the bench for more lucrative private practice, which is a relatively recent phenomenon. While a salary of $212,100 (for the chief justice) or $203,300 (for the other justices) may sound like a lot to most people, lawyers in large urban practices routinely earn more than double and often triple that amount each year. Supreme Court clerks, moreover, now regularly receive $200,000 signing bonuses (in addition to large salaries) from law firms anxious to pay for their expertise.

VIDEO DEBATE
Popular Election of Judges

Although it is the duty of the chief justice of the United States to preside over presidential impeachments, this is not mentioned in Article III. Instead, Article I, section 3, notes in discussing impeachment, "When the President of the United States is tried, the Chief Justice shall preside."

Had the Supreme Court been viewed as the potential policy maker it is today, it is highly unlikely that the Framers would have provided for life tenure with "good behavior" for federal judges in Article III. This feature was agreed on because the Framers did not want the justices (or any federal judges) subject to the whims of politics, the public, or politicians. Moreover, Alexander Hamilton argued in *Federalist No.*

78 that the "independence of judges" was needed "to guard the Constitution and the rights of individuals." Because the Framers viewed the Court as quite powerless, Hamilton stressed the need to place federal judges above the fray of politics.

Some checks on the power of the judiciary were nonetheless included in the Constitution. The Constitution gives Congress the authority to alter the Court's jurisdiction (its ability to hear certain kinds of cases). Congress can also propose constitutional amendments that, if ratified, can effectively reverse judicial decisions, and it can impeach and remove federal judges. In one further check, it is the president who, with the "advice and consent" of the Senate, appoints all federal judges. (See Join the Debate: Senate Advice and Consent and Judicial Nominations.)

THE JUDICIARY ACT OF 1789 AND THE CREATION OF THE FEDERAL JUDICIAL SYSTEM

In spite of the Framers' intentions, the pervasive role of politics in the judicial branch quickly became evident with the passage of the Judiciary Act of 1789. Congress spent nearly the entire second half of its first session deliberating the various provisions of the act to give form and substance to the federal judiciary.

The **Judiciary Act of 1789** established the basic three-tiered structure of the federal court system. At the bottom are the federal district courts—at least one in each state—each staffed by a federal judge. If the people participating in a lawsuit (called litigants) were unhappy with the district court's verdict, they could appeal their case to one of three circuit courts. Each circuit court, initially created to function as a trial court for important cases, was composed of one district court judge and two itinerant Supreme Court justices who met as a circuit court twice a year. It wasn't until 1891 that circuit courts (or, as we know them today, courts of appeals) took on their exclusively appellate function. The third tier of the federal judicial system fleshed out by the Judiciary Act of 1789 was the Supreme Court of the United States. Although the Constitution mentions "the supreme Court," it was silent on its size. In the Judiciary Act, Congress set the size of the Supreme Court at six—the chief justice plus five associate justices. After being reduced to five members in 1801, it later expanded and contracted, and finally the Court's size was expanded to nine in 1869.

Judiciary Act of 1789
Established the basic three-tiered structure of the federal court system.

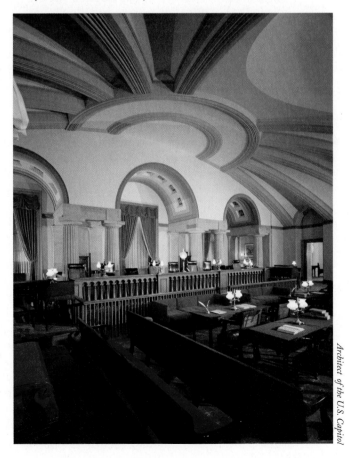

■ The Supreme Court initially met in this small room in the basement of the U.S Capitol building.

The first session of the Court—presided over by John Jay, who was appointed chief justice of the United States by George Washington—initially had to be adjourned when less than half the justices attended. Later, once a sufficient number of justices assembled, the Court decided only one major case—*Chisholm* v. *Georgia* (1793). Moreover, as an indication of its lowly status, one associate justice left the Court to become chief justice of the South Carolina Supreme Court.

In its first decade, the Court took several actions to help mold the new nation. First, by declining to give George Washington advice on the legality of some of his actions, the justices attempted to establish the Supreme Court as an independent, nonpolitical branch of government. The early Court also tried to advance principles of nationalism and to maintain the national government's supremacy over the states. Finally, in a series of circuit and Supreme Court decisions, the justices paved the way for announcement of the doctrine of judicial review by the third chief justice, John Marshall.[6]

Architect of the U.S. Capitol

Join the Debate

SENATE ADVICE AND CONSENT AND JUDICIAL NOMINATIONS

OVERVIEW: Article II of the Constitution gives the president sole authority to make judicial and executive appointments, and it gives the Senate the power to confirm the chief executive's choices. Furthermore, Article I of the Constitution gives the Senate authority to determine its own rules; this includes procedural devices such as the filibuster to slow or stop legislative and political action. Any senator can use the filibuster to delay a vote on a political nominee. A two-thirds majority vote is needed to invoke cloture, thereby ending the filibuster, while only a simple majority is needed to confirm a nominee. Historically, the Senate generally has confirmed the president's nominees, and it was only in 1955 that the tradition of judicial appointees regularly appearing before the Senate Judiciary Committee began (the first potential justice to appear before the Senate did so in 1925). Though there were battles over judicial politics (President Thomas Jefferson's supporters came close to impeaching Justice Salmon Chase for political reasons), the Senate generally has played a narrow role in the confirmation process and usually has deferred to the president's wishes.

Precedent for filibustering Supreme Court nominees was set in 1968 when President Lyndon B. Johnson's choice for chief justice, Abe Fortas, was blocked by the Republican minority. But it was with the controversial Supreme Court nomination of Judge Robert H. Bork in 1987 that confirmation politics took a contentious turn. The Senate voted against Bork's nomination after unprecedented pressure from civil and women's rights groups who believed his conservative judicial views would roll back civil liberties protections.

Senate Democrats, while in the minority argued that the use of the filibuster was necessary to help moderate the ideological make-up of the federal bench, noting that Republicans made similar arguments when they were in the minority and opposed some of former President Bill Clinton's judicial nominees. As a result, the Senate's Republican majority threatened to use the somewhat arcane rules of the chamber to bar filibusters on judicial nominations. Those opposed to judicial filibusters argued that the minority party had no right to thwart the majority's constitutional advice and consent role. They argued that the Constitution requires a simple majority to confirm nominees—the Constitution is explicit when it requires a two-thirds or three-quarters supermajority vote—and judicial filibusters have the effect of denying the Senate majority its right to exercise consent.

ARGUMENTS AGAINST ALLOWING FILIBUSTERS IN THE SENATE'S CONFIRMATION PROCESS

- **Article II of the Constitution gives the president sole authority to make judicial nominations.** Constitutional scholar John Eastman has argued based on records of the constitutional and state ratifying conventions that the president has full power over the nomination process.

THE MARSHALL COURT: *MARBURY V. MADISON* (1803) AND JUDICIAL REVIEW

John Marshall was appointed chief justice by President John Adams in 1801, three years after he declined to accept a nomination as associate justice. An ardent Federalist, Marshall has come to be considered the most important justice ever to serve on the high Court. Part of his reputation is the result of the duration of his service and the historical significance of this period in our nation's history.

Marshall began the practice of issuing opinions on behalf of the Court. For the Court to take its place as an equal branch of government, Marshall strongly believed, the justices needed to speak as a Court and not as six individuals. He also claimed the right of judicial review, from which the Supreme Court derives much of its day-to-day power and impact on the policy process.

In *Federalist No. 78*, Alexander Hamilton first publicly endorsed the idea of judicial review, noting, "Whenever a particular statute contravenes the Constitution, it

The Chief Justice of the Supreme Court

The Senate's role is to provide advice and consent on already chosen nominees.

- **Article I of the Constitution gives the House of Representatives and the Senate the authority to decide their own rules of procedure.** Article I, section 5, gives each chamber the authority to determine its own rules of procedure by a simple majority vote. If the Senate, in order to change with the times, wishes to adapt rules accordingly, it has the full authority of the Constitution behind it. There is nothing in the Constitution creating or giving protection to judicial filibusters.
- **The Constitution's Framers intended only a simple majority vote for the advice and consent clause.** Alexander Hamilton explains in *Federalist Nos. 76* and *77* that the advice and consent function would be exercised "by the whole body, by [the] entire branch of the legislature." That is, the advice and consent would reflect the majority's will. A faction should not be allowed to thwart a legitimate majority's will.

ARGUMENTS FOR ALLOWING FILIBUSTERS IN THE SENATE'S CONFIRMATION PROCESS

- **Filibusters are necessary to maintain the ideological balance of the federal courts.** Filibusters on judicial nominees allow the minority party to check a president's attempt to stack the judiciary with one political philosophy. Maintaining ideological diversity will allow different constitutional interpretations and understanding, thus adding depth to our knowledge of constitutional jurisprudence.

- **The Founders intended for the Senate to be a deliberative body.** The Constitution's writers intended for Senate debate to be slow, deliberate, and reasoned. The idea was to create a small legislative body in which all views would be aired in the marketplace of ideas. The filibuster keeps the debate open. Besides, if two-thirds of the Senate support cloture, the filibuster ends.
- **Senate rules benefit both political parties and their partisans.** No party remains in the majority forever. History shows that both parties spend significant time in both majority and minority status. Altering the rules to suit partisan politics practically ensures that minority party members will engage in the same tactics and politics once they regain majority standing.

QUESTIONS

1. Who has the better argument: those who oppose or support judicial filibusters? Why?
2. Should a president strive to place nonpartisan judges on the federal bench? Why or why not?

SELECTED READINGS

David, Richard. *Electing Justice: Fixing the Supreme Court Nomination Process.* New York: Oxford University Press, 2005.
Epstein, Lee, and Jeffrey A. Segal. *Advice and Consent: The Politics of Judicial Appointments.* New York: Oxford University Press, 2005.

will be the duty of the judicial tribunals to adhere to the latter and disregard the former." Nonetheless, because the power of judicial review is not mentioned in the U.S. Constitution, the actual authority of the Supreme Court to review the constitutionality of acts of Congress was an unsettled question. But, in *Marbury v. Madison* (1803), Chief Justice John Marshall claimed this sweeping authority for the Court by asserting that the right of judicial review was a power that could be implied from the Constitution's supremacy clause.[7]

Marbury v. Madison arose amid a sea of political controversy. In the final hours of the Adams administration, William Marbury was appointed a justice of the peace for the District of Columbia. But, in the confusion of winding up matters, Adams's secretary of state failed to deliver Marbury's commission. Marbury then asked James Madison, Thomas Jefferson's secretary of state, for the commission. Under direct orders from Jefferson, who was irate over the Adams administration's last-minute appointment of several Federalist judges (quickly confirmed by the Federalist Senate), Madison refused to turn over the commission. Marbury and three other Adams

Marbury v. Madison (1803)
Case in which the Supreme Court first asserted the power of judicial review in finding that the congressional statute extending the Court's original jurisdiction was unconstitutional.

Judicial Review

Photo Courtesy: Boston Athenaeum

■ John Marshall was an ardent Federalist and a third cousin of Democratic-Republican President Thomas Jefferson, whose administration he faced head on in *Marbury* v. *Madison* (1803). Marshall served on the Court until the day he died, participating in more than 1,000 decisions and authoring more than 500 opinions. Interestingly, he came to the Court with little legal experience and no judicial experience.

trial courts

Courts of original jurisdiction where cases begin.

appellate courts

Courts that generally review only findings of law made by lower courts.

jurisdiction

Authority vested in a particular court to hear and decide the issues in any particular case.

original jurisdiction

The jurisdiction of courts that hear a case first, usually in a trial. Courts determine the facts of a case under their original jurisdiction.

appointees who were in the same situation then filed a writ of *mandamus* (a legal motion) asking the Supreme Court to order Madison to deliver their commissions.

Political tensions ran high as the Court met to hear the case. Jefferson threatened to ignore any order of the Court. Marshall realized that he and the prestige of the Court could be devastated by any refusal of the executive branch to comply with the decision. Responding to this challenge, in a brilliant opinion that in many sections reads more like a lecture to Jefferson than a discussion of the merits of Marbury's claim, Marshall concluded that although Marbury and the others were entitled to their commissions, the Court lacked the power to issue the writ sought by Marbury. In *Marbury* v. *Madison,* Marshall further ruled that the parts of the Judiciary Act of 1789 that extended the jurisdiction of the Court to allow it to issue writs were inconsistent with the Constitution's specific enumeration of the Court's jurisdiction and therefore unconstitutional.

Although the immediate effect of the decision was to deny power to the Court, its long-term effect was to establish the principle of judicial review. Said Marshall, writing for the Court, "it is emphatically the province and duty of the judicial department to say what the law is." Through judicial review, an implied power, the Supreme Court most dramatically exerts its authority to determine what the Constitution means. Since *Marbury,* the Court has routinely exercised the power of judicial review to determine the constitutionality of acts of Congress, the executive branch, and the states.

The American Legal System

THE JUDICIAL SYSTEM in the United States can best be described as a dual system consisting of the federal court system and the judicial systems of the fifty states, as illustrated in Figure 9.1. Cases may arise in either system. Basically, both systems are three tiered. At the bottom of the system are **trial courts,** where litigation begins. In the middle are appellate courts in the state systems and the courts of appeals in the federal system. At the top of each pyramid sits a court of last resort. (Some states call their high courts supreme courts; New York and Maryland, however, call it the Court of Appeals; Oklahoma and Texas have a Supreme Court and a separate highest state court for criminal cases called the Court of Criminal Appeals.) The federal courts of appeals and Supreme Court as well as state courts of appeals and supreme courts are **appellate courts** that, with few exceptions, review on appeal only cases that already have been decided in lower courts. These courts generally hear matters of both civil and criminal law.

JURISDICTION

Before a state or federal court can hear a case, it must have **jurisdiction,** which means the authority to hear and decide the issues in that case. The jurisdiction of the federal courts is controlled by the U.S. Constitution and by statute. Jurisdiction is conferred based on issues, the amount of money involved in a dispute, or the type of offense. Procedurally, we speak of two types of jurisdiction: original and appellate. **Original jurisdiction** refers to a court's authority to hear disputes as a trial court and may occur on the federal or state level. More than 90 percent of all cases, whether state or

FIGURE 9.1 THE DUAL STRUCTURE OF THE AMERICAN COURT SYSTEM

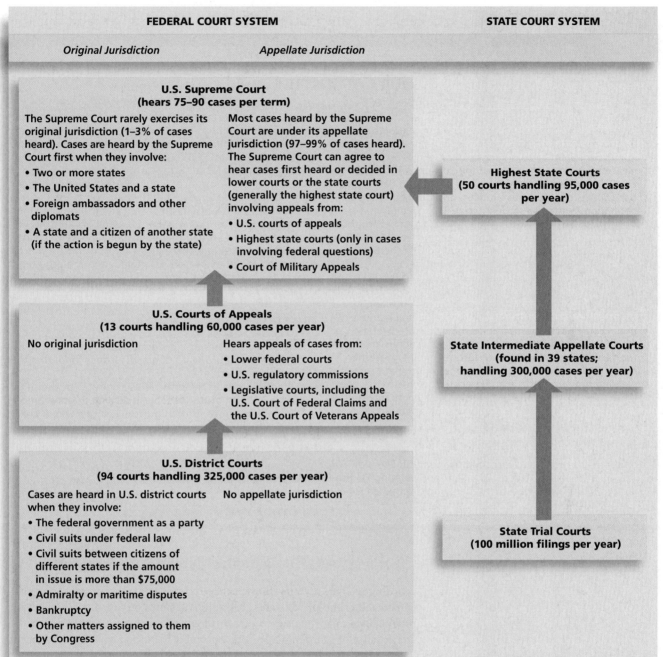

federal, end in the court of original jurisdiction. **Appellate jurisdiction** refers to a court's ability to review cases already decided by a trial court. Appellate courts ordinarily do not review the factual record; instead, they review legal procedures to make certain that the law was applied properly to the issues presented in the case.

CRIMINAL AND CIVIL LAW

Criminal law is the body of law that regulates individual conduct and is enforced by the state and national governments.[8] Crimes are graded as felonies, misdemeanors, or

appellate jurisdiction
The power vested in an appellate court to review and/or revise the decision of a lower court.

criminal law
Codes of behavior related to the protection of property and individual safety.

Global Perspective

THE EUROPEAN COURT OF JUSTICE

The European Union (EU) is composed of twenty-five member nations who have agreed to cede some of their national sovereignty in exchange for the political and economic benefits that belonging to a large, overarching organization provides. Members of the European Union turn to the Court of Justice as their highest court. The Court of Justice consists of twenty-five judges, one from each EU member nation, who serve six-year terms. These judges may sit in a Grand Chamber of thirteen judges or in chambers of three or five judges. Court of Justice proceedings may take place in any of the twenty-one official languages of the European Union.

It is the Court of Justice's role to ensure that EU law and regulations are interpreted uniformly and applied by all member states, regardless of the cultural norms and mores of those nations. For example, when a member state's national court has a question concerning the interpretation or validity of European Union law or policy, it submits a request for clarification to the Court of Justice, and the court then issues a preliminary ruling to all member national courts explaining how to construe and execute the directive in question. The U.S. Supreme Court fulfills a similar role as the ultimate interpreter of federal law but offers no advisory opinions.

Unlike the Supreme Court, however, the Court of Justice is empowered to levy sanctions, including heavy fines, on recalcitrant states to force compliance with EU rules. For example, France was fined $25 million for violating EU fishing regulations and was threatened with fines when it pro-

hibited the importation of British beef. With authority comes accountability, and citizens of some EU member nations question whether too much authority has been taken away from their national courts. For example, when German students began relocating to Austria to take advantage of lower university entrance requirements, many Austrians were outraged and appealed to the high court. The Court of Justice ruled that Austrian university admission policy must give access to citizens of all other EU members, but the Austrian government argued that educational policy is a matter of national sovereignty and that the Court of Justice was engaging in judicial overreach. EU member nation arguments such as this are similar to those offered by states' rights advocates in the United States.

QUESTIONS

1. What similarities and differences can you identify between the European Court of Justice and the U.S. Supreme Court?
2. Identify some of the difficulties associated with the European Court of Justice's role in settling disputes among member nations. Is the Court of Justice's task more or less difficult than that of the U.S. Supreme Court in settling disputes between state governments and the federal government?

Sources: CIA World Factbook, http://www.cia.gov; European Court of Justice, http://curia.europa.eu.

---

offenses, according to their severity. Some acts—for example, murder, rape, and robbery—are considered crimes in all states. Although all states outlaw murder, their penal, or criminal, codes treat the crime quite differently. Some states, for example, allow the death penalty for murder, while others prohibit the use of capital punishment. Other practices—such as gambling—are illegal only in some states.

Criminal law assumes that society itself is the victim of the illegal act. Therefore, the government prosecutes, or brings an action, on behalf of an injured party (acting as a plaintiff) in criminal but not civil cases. Criminal cases are traditionally in the purview of the states. But, a burgeoning set of federal criminal laws is contributing significantly to delays in the federal courts.

civil law
Codes of behavior related to business and contractual relationships between groups and individuals.

Civil law is the body of law that regulates the conduct and relationships between private individuals or companies. Because the actions at issue in civil law do not constitute a threat to society at large, people who believe they have been injured by another party must take action on their own to seek judicial relief. Civil cases, then, involve lawsuits filed to recover something of value, whether it is the right to vote, fair treatment, or monetary compensation for an item or service that cannot be recovered.

Each civil or criminal case has a plaintiff, or petitioner, who brings charges against a defendant, or respondent. Sometimes the government is the plaintiff. The government may bring civil charges on behalf of the citizens of the state or the national government against a person or corporation for violating the law, but it is always the government that brings a criminal case. When cases are initiated, they are known first by the name of the petitioner. In *Marbury* v. *Madison,* William Marbury was the plaintiff, suing the defendants, the U.S. government and James Madison as its secretary of state, for not delivering his judicial commission.

Before a criminal or civil case gets to court, much has to happen. Most cases involve a whole series of formal and informal proceedings before a formal trial, and most legal disputes that arise in the United States never get to court. Most individuals accused of criminal conduct plead guilty, often to a lesser charge or in exchange for a guaranteed sentence. Individuals and companies involved in civil disputes also routinely settle their disagreements out of court. Often these settlements are not reached until minutes before the case is to be tried. Many civil cases that go to trial are settled during the course of the trial—before the case can be handed over to the jury or submitted to a judge for a decision or determination of responsibility or guilt.

During trials, judges must often interpret the intent of laws enacted by Congress and state legislatures as they bear on the issues at hand. To do so, they read reports, testimony, and debates on the relevant legislation and study the results of other similar legal cases. They also rely on the presentations made by lawyers in their briefs and at trial. If it is a jury trial, the jury ultimately is the finder of fact, while the judge is the interpreter of the law.

The Federal Court System

THE FEDERAL DISTRICT COURTS, courts of appeals, and the Supreme Court are called **constitutional** (or Article III) **courts** because Article III of the Constitution either established them (as is the case with the Supreme Court) or authorizes Congress to establish them. Judges who preside over these courts are nominated by the president (with the advice and consent of the Senate), and they serve lifetime terms, as long as they engage in "good behavior."

In addition to constitutional courts, **legislative courts** are set up by Congress, under its implied powers, generally for special purposes. The U.S. territorial courts (which hear federal cases in the territories) and the U.S. Court of Veterans Appeals are examples of legislative courts, or what some call Article I courts. The judges who preside over these federal courts are appointed by the president (subject to Senate confirmation) and serve fixed, limited terms.

constitutional courts
Federal courts specifically created by the U.S. Constitution or by Congress pursuant to its authority in Article III.

legislative courts
Courts established by Congress for specialized purposes, such as the Court of Military Appeals.

DISTRICT COURTS

As we have seen, Congress created U.S. district courts when it enacted the Judiciary Act of 1789. District courts are federal trial courts of original jurisdiction (see Figure 9.1). There are currently ninety-four federal district courts staffed by a total of 678 active judges, assisted by more than 300 retired judges who still hear cases on a limited basis. No district court cuts across state lines. Every state has at least one federal district court, and the most populous states—California, Texas, and New York—each have four.[9]

Federal district courts, where the bulk of the judicial work takes place in the federal system, have original jurisdiction over only specific types of cases, as indicated in Figure 9.1. Although the rules governing district court jurisdiction can be complex, cases heard in federal district courts by a single judge (with or without a jury) generally fall into one of three categories:

1. They involve the federal government as a party.
2. They present a federal question based on a claim under the U.S. Constitution, a treaty with another nation, or a federal statute.

3. They involve civil suits in which citizens are from different states, and the amount of money at issue is more than $75,000.[10]

Each federal judicial district has a U.S. attorney, who is nominated by the president and confirmed by the Senate. The U.S. attorney in each district is that district's chief law enforcement officer. The size of the staff and the number of assistant U.S. attorneys who work in each district depend on the amount of litigation in each district. U.S. attorneys, like district attorneys within the states, have a considerable amount of discretion as to whether they pursue criminal or civil investigations or file charges against individuals or corporations.

THE COURTS OF APPEALS

The losing party in a case heard and decided in a federal district court can appeal the decision to the appropriate court of appeals. The United States courts of appeals (known as the circuit courts of appeals prior to 1948) are the intermediate appellate courts in the federal system and were established in 1789 to hear appeals from federal district courts. There are currently eleven numbered courts of appeals. A twelfth, the D.C. Circuit Court of Appeals, handles most appeals involving federal regulatory commissions and agencies, including, for example, the National Labor Relations Board and the Securities and Exchange Commission. The thirteenth federal appeals court is the U.S. Court of Appeals for the Federal Circuit, which largely deals with patents and contract and financial claims against the federal government.

In 2005, the U.S. courts of appeals were staffed by 179 active judges—assisted by almost 100 retired judges who still hear cases on a limited basis—who were appointed by the president, subject to Senate confirmation. The number of judges within each circuit varies—depending on the workload and the complexity of the cases—and ranges from six to nearly thirty. Each circuit is supervised by a chief judge, the most senior judge in terms of service below the age of sixty-five, who can serve no more than seven years. In deciding cases, judges are divided into rotating three-judge panels, made up of the active judges within the circuit, visiting judges (primarily district judges from the same circuit), and retired judges. In rare cases, all the judges in a circuit may choose to sit together (*en banc*) to decide a case by majority vote.

The courts of appeals have no original jurisdiction. Rather, Congress has granted these courts appellate jurisdiction over two general categories of cases: appeals from criminal and civil cases from the district courts, and appeals from administrative agencies. Once a decision is made by a federal court of appeals, a litigant no longer has an automatic right to an appeal. The losing party may submit a petition to the U.S. Supreme Court to review the case, but the Court grants few of these requests.

In general, courts of appeals try to correct errors of law and procedure that have occurred in lower courts or administrative agencies. Courts of appeals hear no new testimony; instead, lawyers submit written arguments in what is called a **brief** (also submitted in trial courts), and then appear to present and argue the case orally to the court.

brief
A document containing the legal written arguments in a case filed with a court by a party prior to a hearing or trial.

Comparing Judiciaries

THE SUPREME COURT

The U.S. Supreme Court, as we saw in the opening vignette, is often at the center of the storm of highly controversial issues that have yet to be resolved successfully in the political process. As the court of last resort at the top of the judicial pyramid, it reviews cases from the U.S. courts of appeals and state supreme courts (as well as other courts of last resort) and acts as the final interpreter of the U.S. Constitution. It not only decides major cases with tremendous policy significance each year, but it also ensures uniformity in the interpretation of national laws and the Constitution, resolves conflicts among the states, and maintains the supremacy of national law in the federal system.

Since 1869, the U.S. Supreme Court has consisted of eight associate justices and one chief justice, who is nominated by the president specifically for that position. There is no special significance about the number nine, and the Constitution is silent about the size of the Court. Between 1789 and 1869, Congress periodically altered the size of the Court. The lowest number of justices on the Court was six; the most, ten. Through January 2007, only 110 justices had served on the Court, and there had been seventeen chief justices (see Appendix IV).

Decisions of any court of appeals are binding on only the district courts within the geographic confines of the circuit, but decisions of the U.S. Supreme Court are binding throughout the nation and establish national **precedents**. This reliance on past decisions or precedents to formulate decisions in new cases is called *stare decisis* (a Latin phrase meaning "let the decision stand"). The principle of *stare decisis* allows for continuity and predictability in our judicial system. Although *stare decisis* can be helpful in predicting decisions, at times judges carve out new ground and ignore, decline to follow, or even overrule precedents in order to reach a different conclusion in a case involving similar circumstances. In one sense, that is why there is so much litigation in America today. Parties know that one cannot always predict the outcome of a case; if such prediction were possible, there would be little reason to go to court.

precedent
Prior judicial decision that serves as a rule for settling subsequent cases of a similar nature.

stare decisis
In court rulings, a reliance on past decisions or precedents to formulate decisions in new cases.

How Federal Court Judges Are Selected

THE SELECTION OF FEDERAL JUDGES is often a very political process with important political ramifications because judges are nominated by the president and must be confirmed by the U.S. Senate. Presidents, in general, try to select well-qualified men and women for the bench. But, these appointments also provide a president with the opportunity to put his philosophical stamp on the federal courts (see Figure 9.2). Nominees, however, while generally members of the nominating president's party, usually are vetted through the senator's offices of the states where the district court or court of appeals vacancy occurs. In the Clinton White House, candidates for district court generally came from recommendations by Democratic senators, "or in the absence of a Democratic senator, from the Democratic members of the House of Representatives or other high ranking Democratic Party politicians."[11] This process, by which presidents generally defer selection of district court judges to the choice of senators of their own party who represent the state where the vacancy occurs, is known as **senatorial courtesy.**

VIDEO ROUNDTABLE
Selecting Federal Judges

senatorial courtesy
Process by which presidents generally defer selection of district court judges to the choice of senators of their own party who represent the state where the vacancy occurs.

WHO ARE FEDERAL JUDGES?

Typically, federal district court judges have held other political offices, such as those of state court judge or prosecutor. Most have been involved in politics, which is what usually brings them into consideration for a position on the federal bench.

Increasingly, today, most judicial nominees have had prior judicial experience. White males continue to dominate the federal courts, but since the 1970s, most presidents have pledged (with varying degrees of success) to do their best to appoint more African Americans, women, and other traditionally underrepresented groups to the federal bench. (See Analyzing Visuals: Race, Ethnicity and Gender of District Court Appointees.)

APPOINTMENTS TO THE U.S. SUPREME COURT

Like other federal court judges, the justices of the Supreme Court are nominated by the president and must be confirmed by the Senate. Historically, because of the special place the Supreme Court enjoys in our constitutional system, its nominees have

FIGURE 9.2 HOW A PRESIDENT AFFECTS THE FEDERAL JUDICIARY

This figure depicts the number of judges appointed by each president and how quickly a president can make an impact on the make-up of the Court.

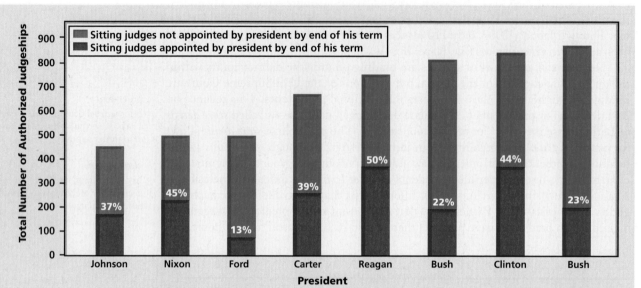

PRESIDENT	Appointed to Supreme Court	Appointed to Courts of Appeals[a]	Appointed to District Courts[b]	Total Appointed	Total Number of Judgeships[c]	Percentage of Judgeships Filled by President
Johnson (1963–1969)	2	40	122	164	449	37
Nixon (1969–1974)	4	45	179	228	504	45
Ford (1974–1977)	1	12	52	65	504	13
Carter (1977–1981)	0	56	202	258	657	39
Reagan (1981–1989)	3	78	290	368	740	50
Bush (1989–1993)	2	37	148	185	825	22
Clinton (1993–2001)	2	66	305	373	841	44
Bush (2001–2005)[d]	2	35	168	203	866	23

[a]Does not include the appeals court for the federal circuit
[b]Includes district courts in the territories
[c]Total judgeships authorized in president's last year in office
[d]Except for Supreme Court appointments, data for George W. Bush cover only his first term

Sources: "Imprints on the Bench," *CQ Weekly Report* (January 19, 2001): 173. Reprinted by permission of Copyright Clearance Center on behalf of Congressional Quarterly, Inc. Updated by author.

encountered more opposition than have district court or court of appeals nominees. As the role of the Court has increased over time, so too has the amount of attention given to nominees. With this increased attention has come greater opposition, especially to nominees with controversial views. For a discussion of the new justices on the Roberts Court, see Politics Now: The Roberts Court.

NOMINATION CRITERIA

Justice Sandra Day O'Connor once remarked that "You have to be lucky" to be appointed to the Court.[12] Although luck is certainly important, over the years

Analyzing Visuals

RACE/ETHNICITY AND GENDER OF DISTRICT COURT APPOINTEES

Traditionally, white males have dominated federal court appointments. Of President Ronald Reagan's 290 appointees to federal district courts, for example, 92.4 percent were white males. Of President Bill Clinton's 305 appointments, however, the percentage of white males was only 52.1 percent. George W. Bush reversed the trend during his first term; 67.3 percent of his appointees were white males. While most presidents in recent years have pledged to appoint more women, African Americans, and Hispanics to the federal bench, Clinton was the most successful. After reviewing the bar graph below, answer the following critical thinking questions: Is there a difference between appointments made by Democratic presidents (Carter and Clinton) and Republican presidents? Which group is most underrepresented in appointments? What factors do presidents consider, in addition to the nominee's gender, race, and ethnicity, in making appointments to the federal bench? Should gender, race, and ethnicity be considered by a president? Explain your answers.

*Through January 20, 2005.

Source: Sheldon Goldman et al., "W. Bush's Judiciary: The First Term Record," *Judicature* 88 (May/June 2005): 269.

nominations to the bench have been made for a variety of reasons. Some nominees have been friends or political allies of the president, for example, but at least six criteria are especially important: competence, ideology or policy preferences, rewards, pursuit of political support, religion, and race and gender.

Politics Now

THE ROBERTS COURT

At the end of the 2005–2006 term, the first with a new chief justice since 1986 and the first with a new justice since 1994, commentators were anxious to see if John G. Roberts Jr., and Justice Samuel A. Alito Jr., had begun to make their marks on the Court. As posed by the *New York Times* Supreme Court reporter Linda Greenhouse, the question was whether it was the Roberts Court in name as well as in practice. Her answer? "Not yet." Says Greenhouse, a keen observer of the Court, Chief Justice Roberts "was clearly in charge, presiding over the Court with grace, wit and meticulous preparation. But he was not in control."[a]

In major divided Court decisions, Roberts was in the minority nearly as frequently as he was in the majority. Therefore, he was unable to exert influence over the Court's decisions by assigning the writing of many important majority opinions. (By Supreme Court tradition, the most senior justice in the majority assigns the author of the Court's opinion.) Nor was he able to stop the public bickering that has now become a hallmark of some of the justices, particularly Justice Antonin Scalia. Even the Court's quietest member, Justice Clarence Thomas, took the opportunity to announce his dissent in *Hamdan* v. *Rumsfeld* (2006), discussed in the opening vignette. Publicly reading a dissent is a rare practice on the Court. In fact, in fifteen years on the bench, this was the first dissent Thomas delivered orally.[b]

Greenhouse argues that the justice in control on the Roberts Court appears to be Anthony Kennedy, who has a history of being the swing justice in many major cases. As a result, Justice Kennedy's votes often determine the direction of many of the 5–4 decisions that have become standard for the narrowly divided Court. Greenhouse speculates that the current Court could even be called the Stevens Court, after the most senior justice, John Paul Stevens. Justice Stevens assigns the author of the majority opinion any time Chief Justice Roberts is in the minority and Justice Stevens is in the majority. And, Justice Stevens used this authority to author many of the Court's most important decisions, including *Hamdan,* discussed in our opening vignette.

In short, says Greenhouse, Robert's first term was a time of testing, of battles joined and battles, for the moment, postponed.[c] Still, the frequent agreement of Roberts and Alito—they voted together in 88 percent of all decisions—sends a powerful signal that the Court is heading in a decidedly conservative direction.

QUESTIONS

1. What role should the chief justice play on the Supreme Court?
2. As the Supreme Court becomes more conservative, and with cases on presidential authority, the treatment of prisoners in detainee camps, and abortion on its 2006–2007 calendar, what role do you foresee the Roberts Court playing in national policy?

[a]This feature draws heavily on Linda Greenhouse, "Roberts Is at the Court's Helm, But he isn't in Control," *New York Times* (July 1, 2006): A1.

[b] *Hamdan* v. *Rumsfeld,* 548 U.S. ___ (2006).

[c] Greenhouse, "Roberts Is at the Court's Helm."

Competence Most prospective nominees are expected to have had at least some judicial or governmental experience. For example, John Jay, the first chief justice, was one of the authors of *The Federalist Papers* and was active in New York politics. In 2007, all nine sitting Supreme Court justices had prior judicial experience (see Table 9.2).

Ideology or Policy Preferences Most presidents seek to appoint to the Court individuals who share their policy preferences, and almost all have political goals in mind when they appoint a justice. Presidents Franklin D. Roosevelt, Richard M. Nixon, and Ronald Reagan were very successful in molding the Court to their own political beliefs. Roosevelt was able to appoint eight justices from 1937 to his death in 1945, solidifying support for his liberal New Deal programs. In contrast, President Reagan was extraordinarily successful in remolding the Court in a conservative image.

Rewards Historically, many of those appointed to the Supreme Court have been personal friends of presidents. Abraham Lincoln, for example, appointed one of his key political advisers to the Court. Lyndon B. Johnson appointed his longtime friend Abe Fortas to the bench. Most presidents also select justices of their own party affiliation. Chief Justice John G. Roberts Jr. and Justice Samuel A. Alito Jr., for example, both Republicans, worked in the Department of Justice during the Reagan and George Bush administrations. Roberts also served as associate White House counsel under Reagan.

TABLE 9.2 **THE SUPREME COURT, 2006**

Name	Year of Birth	Year of Appointment	Political Party	Law School	Appointing President	Religion	Prior Judicial Experience	Prior Government Experience
John G. Roberts Jr.	1955	2005	R	Harvard	G. W. Bush	Roman Catholic	U.S. Court of Appeals	Dept. of Justice, White House Counsel
John Paul Stevens	1920	1975	R	Chicago	Ford	Nondenominational Protestant	U.S. Court of Appeals	
Antonin Scalia	1936	1986	R	Harvard	Reagan	Roman Catholic	U.S. Court of Appeals	
Anthony Kennedy	1936	1988	R	Harvard	Reagan	Roman Catholic	U.S. Court of Appeals	
David Souter	1939	1990	R	Harvard	G. Bush	Episcopalian	U.S. Court of Appeals	New Hampshire assistant attorney general
Clarence Thomas	1948	1991	R	Yale	G. Bush	Roman Catholic	U.S. Court of Appeals	Chair, Equal Employment Opportunity Commission
Ruth Bader Ginsburg	1933	1993	D	Columbia	Clinton	Jewish	U.S. Court of Appeals	
Stephen Breyer	1938	1994	D	Harvard	Clinton	Jewish	U.S. Court of Appeals	Chief counsel, Senate Judiciary Committee
Samuel A. Alito Jr.	1950	2006	R	Yale	G. W. Bush	Roman Catholic	U.S. Court of Appeals	U.S. Attorney, Dept. of Justice

Pursuit of Political Support from Various Groups During Ronald Reagan's successful campaign for the presidency in 1980, some of his advisers feared that the gender gap would hurt him. Polls repeatedly showed that he was far less popular with female voters than with men. To gain support from women, Reagan announced during his campaign that should he win, he would appoint a woman to fill the first vacancy on the Court. When Justice Potter Stewart, a moderate, announced his early retirement from the bench, under pressure from women's rights groups, President Reagan nominated Sandra Day O'Connor of the Arizona Court of Appeals to fill the vacancy.

Through 2007, only two African Americans and two women have served on the Court. Race was undoubtedly a critical issue in the appointment of Clarence Thomas to replace Thurgood Marshall, the first African American justice. But, President George Bush refused to acknowledge his wish to retain a black seat on the Court. Instead, he announced that he was "picking the best man for the job on the merits," a claim that was met with considerable skepticism by many observers.

Of the 110 justices who have served on the Court, almost all have been members of traditional Protestant faiths. Only eleven have been Catholic and only seven have been Jewish. Today, more Catholics—John Roberts Jr., Antonin Scalia, Anthony Kennedy, Clarence Thomas, and Samuel Alito Jr.—serve on the Court than at any other point in history. At present the Court has no Hispanics, no evangelical Christians, and only one woman and one African American.

THE SUPREME COURT CONFIRMATION PROCESS

The Constitution gives the Senate the authority to approve all nominees to the federal bench. As detailed below, the Senate Judiciary Committee investigates the nominees,

Justice Samuel A. Alito Jr. was the subject of a high stakes confirmation battle that involved a number of interest groups in late 2005 and early 2006. Here, Justice Alito signs autographs for ardent supporters on the way to his confirmation hearing.

holds hearings, and votes on its recommendation for Senate action. At this stage, the committee may reject a nominee or send the nomination to the full Senate for a vote. The full Senate then deliberates on the nominee before voting. A simple majority vote is required for confirmation.

Investigation As a president begins to narrow the list of possible nominees to the Supreme Court, those names are sent to the Federal Bureau of Investigation before a nomination formally is made. After a formal nomination is made and sent to the Senate, the Senate Judiciary Committee begins its own investigation. (The same process is used for nominees to the lower federal courts, although such investigations generally are not nearly as extensive as for Supreme Court nominees.)

Lobbying by Interest Groups Until the 1980s, interest groups played a minor and backstage role in most appointments to the Supreme Court. Now, although interest groups generally have not lobbied on behalf of any one individual, it is common for interest groups to lobby against a prospective nominee. Even this, however, is a relatively recent phenomenon. In 1987, the nomination of Judge Robert H. Bork to the Supreme Court led liberal groups to launch the most extensive radio, television, and print media campaign against a nominee to the U.S. Supreme Court. These interest groups felt that Bork's actions as solicitor general, especially his firing of the Watergate special prosecutor at the request of President Richard M. Nixon, as well as his political beliefs, were abhorrent.

More and more, interest groups are also getting involved in district court and court of appeals nominations. They recognize that these appointments often pave the way for future nominees to the Supreme Court, as was the case with most of the members of the current Court.

The Senate Committee Hearings and Senate Vote After hearings are concluded, the Senate Judiciary Committee usually makes a recommendation to the full Senate. Any rejections of presidential nominees to the Supreme Court generally occur only after the Senate Judiciary Committee has recommended against a nominee's appointment. Few recent confirmations have been close; Clarence Thomas's 52–48 vote in 1991 and Samuel A. Alito Jr.'s 58–42 vote in 2006 were the closest in recent history.

The Supreme Court Today

GIVEN THE JUDICIAL SYSTEM'S VAST SIZE and substantial, although often indirect, power over so many aspects of our lives, it is surprising that so many Americans know next to nothing about the judicial system, in general, and the U.S. Supreme Court, in particular.

Chief Justice John Roberts

Even after the recent attention the Supreme Court received during the nominations of John G. Roberts Jr. and Samuel A. Alito Jr., more than half of those Americans surveyed in early 2006 could not name one member of the Court; virtually no one could name all nine members of the Court. As revealed in Table 9.3, Sandra Day O'Connor, the first woman appointed to the Court, was the most well-known justice. Still, only about a quarter of those polled could name her. To fill in any gaps in your knowledge of the current Supreme Court, see Table 9.2.

While much of this ignorance can be blamed on the American public's lack of interest, the Court has also taken great pains to ensure its privacy and sense of decorum. Its rites and rituals contribute to the Court's mystique and encourage a "cult of the robe."[13] Consider, for example, the way Supreme Court proceedings are conducted. Oral arguments are not televised, and deliberations concerning the outcome of cases are conducted in utmost secrecy. In contrast, C-SPAN brings us daily coverage of various congressional hearings and floor debate on bills and important national issues, and Court TV (and sometimes other networks) provides gavel-to-gavel coverage of many important state court trials. The Supreme Court, however, remains adamant in its refusal to televise its proceedings—including public oral arguments, although it now allows the release of same-day audio tapes of oral arguments.

TABLE 9.3 DON'T KNOW MUCH ABOUT . . . THE SUPREME COURT

Supreme Court Justice	Percentage Who Could Name
Sandra Day O'Connor	27
Clarence Thomas	21
John G. Roberts Jr.	16
Antonin Scalia	13
Ruth Bader Ginsburg	12
Anthony Kennedy	7
David Souter	5
Stephen Breyer	3
John Paul Stevens	3

Source: Findlaw.com poll, January 10, 2006, http://company.findlaw.com.

DECIDING TO HEAR A CASE

Over 9,600 cases were filed at the Supreme Court in its 2005–2006 term; 90 were heard, and 88 decisions were issued. In contrast, from 1790 to 1801, the Court heard only eighty-seven cases under its appellate jurisdiction.[14] In the Court's early years, the main of the justices' workload involved their circuit-riding duties. From 1862 to 1866, only 240 cases were decided. Creation of the courts of appeals in 1891 resulted in an immediate reduction in Supreme Court filings—from 600 in 1890 to 275 in 1892.[15] As recently as the 1940s, fewer than 1,000 cases were filed annually. Since that time, filings increased at a dramatic rate until the mid 1990s and then shot up again in the late 1990s, as revealed in Figure 9.3, and have, with but the exception of a few

VISUAL LITERACY

Case Overload

FIGURE 9.3 SUPREME COURT CASELOAD, 1950–2006 TERMS

Cases the Supreme Court chooses to hear (represented by red bars below) represent a tiny fraction of the total number of cases filed with the Court (represented by green bars).

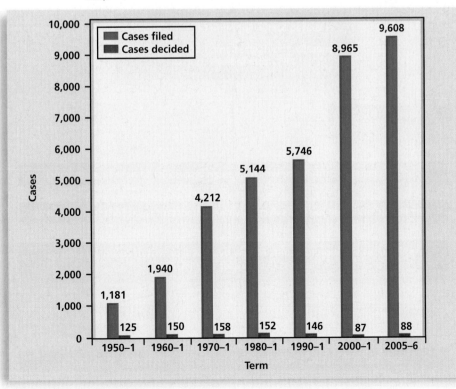

Source: Administrative Office of the Courts; Supreme Court Public Information Office.

terms, shown steady growth. The process by which cases get to the Supreme Court is outlined in Figure 9.4.

The content of the Court's docket is, of course, every bit as significant as its size. During the 1930s, cases requiring the interpretation of constitutional law began to take a growing portion of the Court's workload, leading the Court to take a more important role in the policy-making process. At that time, only 5 percent of the Court's

FIGURE 9.4 HOW A CASE GETS TO THE SUPREME COURT
This figure illustrates both how cases get on the Court's docket and what happens after a case is accepted for review.

■ The Roberts Court. Back row, from left to right: Justices Stephen Breyer, Clarence Thomas, Ruth Bader Ginsburg, and Samuel A. Alito Jr. Front row, from left to right: Justice Anthony Kennedy, Justice John Paul Stevens, Chief Justice John G. Roberts Jr., Justice Antonin Scalia and Justice David Souter.

cases involved questions concerning the Bill of Rights. By the late 1950s, one-third of filed cases involved such questions; by the 1960s, half did.[16] More recently, about half of the cases decided by the Court deal with issues raised in the Bill of Rights.[17]

As discussed earlier in the chapter, the Court has two types of jurisdiction. The Court has original jurisdiction in "all Cases affecting Ambassadors, other public Ministers and Consuls, and those in which a State shall be a party." It is rare for more than two or three of these cases to come to the Court in a year. The second kind of jurisdiction enjoyed by the Court is its appellate jurisdiction. The Court is not expected to exercise its appellate jurisdiction simply to correct errors of other courts. Instead, appeal to the Supreme Court should be taken only if the case presents important issues of law, or what is termed "a substantial federal question."

Since 1988, nearly all appellate cases that have gone to the Supreme Court arrived there on a petition for a **writ of** *certiorari* (from the Latin "to be informed"), which is a request for the Supreme Court—at its discretion—to order up the records of the lower courts for purposes of review.

Writs of *Certiorari* and the Rule of Four

The Supreme Court controls its own caseload through the *certiorari* process, deciding which cases it wants to hear, and rejecting most cases that come to it. All petitions, or writs of *certiorari*, must meet two criteria:

1. The case must come from either a U.S. court of appeals, a special three-judge district court, or a state court of last resort.

2. The case must involve a federal question. Thus, the case must present questions of interpretation of federal constitutional law or involve a federal statute, action, or treaty.

The clerk of the Court's office transmits petitions for writs of *certiorari* first to the chief justice's office, where clerks review the petitions, and then to the individual justices' offices. On the Roberts Court, all of the justices except Justice John Paul Stevens (who allows his clerks great individual authority in selecting the cases for him to review) participate in what is called the *cert* pool.[18] Pool participants review their assigned fraction of petitions and share their notes with each other. Those cases that the justices deem noteworthy are then placed on what is called the discuss list prepared by

writ of *certiorari*
A request for the Court to order up the records from a lower court to review the case.

Rule of Four
At least four justices of the Supreme Court must vote to consider a case before it can be heard.

SIMULATION

You Are a Clerk for Supreme Court Justice Judith Gray

the chief justice's clerks and circulated to the chambers of the other justices. All others are dead listed and go no further unless a justice asks that a case be removed from the dead list and discussed at conference. Only about 30 percent of submitted petitions make it to the discuss list. During one of the justices' weekly conference meetings, the cases on the discuss list are reviewed. The chief justice speaks first, then the rest of the justices, according to seniority. The decision process ends when the justices vote, and by custom, *certiorari* is granted according to the **Rule of Four**—when at least four justices vote to hear a case.

The Role of Clerks   As early as 1850, the justices of the Supreme Court beseeched Congress to approve the hiring of a clerk to assist each justice. Congress denied the request, so when Justice Horace Gray hired the first law clerk in 1882, he paid the clerk himself. Justice Gray's clerk was a top graduate of Harvard Law School whose duties included cutting Justice Gray's hair and running personal errands. Finally, in 1886, Congress authorized each justice to hire a stenographer clerk for $1,600 a year.

Clerks typically are selected from candidates at the top of the graduating classes of prestigious law schools. They perform a variety of tasks, ranging from searching for arcane facts to playing tennis or taking walks with the justices. Clerks spend most of their time researching material relevant to particular cases, reading and summarizing cases, and helping justices write opinions. The clerks also make the first pass through the petitions that come to the Court, undoubtedly influencing which cases get a second look. Just how much help they provide in the writing of opinions is unknown.[19] (See Table 9.4 for more on what clerks do.)

In 2006, the nine active justices and retired Justice O'Connor employed a total of thirty-eight clerks. This growth in the number of clerks has had many interesting ramifications for the Court. As the number of clerks has grown, so have the number and length of the Court's opinions.[20] And, until recently, the number of cases decided annually increased as more help was available to the justices.

The relationship between clerks and the justices for whom they work is close and confidential, and many aspects of the relationship are kept secret.[21] Clerks may sometimes talk among themselves about the views and personalities of their justices, but rarely has a clerk leaked such information to the press. In 1998, a former clerk to Justice Harry A. Blackmun broke the silence. Edward Lazarus published a book that shocked many Court watchers by penning an insider's account of how the Court really works.[22] He also charged that the justices give their young, often ideological, clerks far too much power.

TABLE 9.4   WHAT DO SUPREME COURT CLERKS DO?

Supreme Court clerks are among the best and brightest recent law school graduates. Almost all first clerk for a judge on one of the courts of appeals. After their Supreme Court clerkship, former clerks are in high demand. Firms often pay signing bonuses of up to $200,000 to attract clerks, who often earn over $150,000 their first year in private practice.

Tasks of a Supreme Court clerk include the following:

- Perform initial screening of the 9,000 or so petitions that come to the Court each term
- Draft memos to summarize the facts and issues in each case, recommending whether the case should be accepted by the Court for full review
- Write a "bench memo" summarizing an accepted case and suggesting questions for oral argument
- Write the first draft of an opinion
- Be an informal conduit for communicating and negotiating between other justices' chambers as to the final wording of an opinion

HOW DOES A CASE SURVIVE THE PROCESS?

It can be difficult to determine why the Court decides to hear a particular case. Sometimes it involves a perceived national emergency, as was the case with appeals concerning the outcome of the 2000 presidential election. The Court does not offer reasons, and "the standards by which the justices decide to grant or deny review are highly personalized and necessarily discretionary," noted former Chief Justice Earl Warren.[23] Political scientists nonetheless have attempted to determine the characteristics of the cases the Court accepts; not surprisingly, they are similar to those that help a case get on the discuss list. Among the cues are the following:

- The federal government is the party asking for review.
- The case involves conflict among the circuit courts.
- The case presents a civil rights or civil liberties question.

- The case involves ideological and/or policy preferences of the justices.
- The case has significant social or political interest, as evidenced by the presence of interest group *amicus curiae* briefs.

The Federal Government   One of the most important cues for predicting whether the Court will hear a case is the position the solicitor general takes on it. The **solicitor general,** appointed by the president, is the fourth-ranking member of the Department of Justice and is responsible for handling most appeals on behalf of the U.S. government to the Supreme Court. The solicitor's staff resembles a small, specialized law firm within the Department of Justice. But, because this office has such a special relationship with the Supreme Court, even having a suite of offices within the Supreme Court building, the solicitor general often is referred to as the Court's "ninth and a half member."[24] Moreover, the solicitor general, on behalf of the U.S. government, appears as a party or as an *amicus curiae* in more than 50 percent of the cases heard by the Court each term. *Amicus curiae* means friend of the court. *Amici* may file briefs or even appear to argue their interests orally before the Court. This special relationship with the Court helps explain the overwhelming success the solicitor general's office enjoys before the Supreme Court. The Court generally accepts 70 to 80 percent of the cases where the U.S. government is the petitioning party, compared with about 5 percent of all others.[25]

Conflict Among the Circuits   Conflict among the lower courts is apparently another reason that the justices take cases. When interpretations of constitutional or federal law are involved, the justices seem to want consistency throughout the federal court system.

Interest Group Participation   A quick way for the justices to gauge the ideological ramifications of a particular civil rights or liberties case is by the nature and amount of interest group participation. Richard C. Cortner has noted that "Cases do not arrive on the doorstep of the Supreme Court like orphans in the night."[26] Instead, most cases heard by the Supreme Court involve either the government or an interest group—either as the sponsoring party or as an *amicus curiae*. Liberal groups such as the American Civil Liberties Union, People for the American Way, or the NAACP Legal Defense Fund, and conservative groups including the Washington Legal Foundation, Concerned Women for America, or the American Center for Law and Justice, routinely sponsor cases or file *amicus* briefs either urging the Court to hear a case or asking it to deny *certiorari*.

The positions of both parties are often echoed or expanded in *amicus curiae* briefs filed by interested parties, especially interest groups. (The vast majority of the cases decided by the Court in the 1990s, for example, had at least one *amicus* brief.) Interest groups also provide the Court with information not necessarily contained in the major-party briefs, help write briefs, and assist in practice oral arguments during moot-court sessions. In these moot-court sessions, the lawyer who will argue the case before the nine justices goes through several complete rehearsals, with prominent lawyers and law professors role playing the various justices.

Research by political scientists has found that "not only does [an *amicus*] brief in favor of *certiorari* significantly improve the chances of a case being accepted, but two, three and four briefs improve the chances even more."[27] Clearly, it's the more the merrier, whether or not the briefs are filed for or against granting review.[28]

HEARING AND DECIDING THE CASE

Once a case is accepted for review, a flurry of activity begins. Lawyers on both sides of the case begin to prepare their written arguments for submission to the Court. In these briefs, lawyers cite prior case law and make arguments as to why the Court should find in favor of their client.

solicitor general
The fourth-ranking member of the Department of Justice; responsible for handling all appeals on behalf of the U.S. government to the Supreme Court.

amicus curiae
"Friend of the court"; *amici* may file briefs or even appear to argue their interests orally before the court.

You Are a Young Lawyer

Oral Arguments   Once a case is accepted by the Court for full review, and after briefs and *amicus* briefs are submitted on each side, oral argument takes place. Oral argument generally is limited to the immediate parties in the case, although it is not uncommon for the U.S. solicitor general to appear to argue orally as an *amicus curiae.* Oral argument at the Court is fraught with time-honored tradition and ceremony. At precisely ten o'clock every morning when the Court is in session, the Court marshal, dressed in a formal morning coat, emerges to intone "Oyez! Oyez! Oyez!" as the nine justices emerge from behind a reddish-purple velvet curtain to take their places on the raised and slightly angled bench. The chief justice sits in the middle. The remaining justices sit to the left and right alternating in seniority.

Almost all attorneys are allotted one half hour to present their cases, and this time includes that required to answer questions from the bench. Although many Court watchers have tried to figure out how a particular justice will vote based on the questioning at oral argument, most researchers find that the nature and number of questions asked do not help much in predicting the outcome of a case.

The Conference and the Vote   The justices meet in closed conference once a week when the Court is hearing oral arguments. Since the ascendancy of Chief Justice Roger B. Taney to the Court in 1836, the justices have begun each conference session with a round of handshaking. Once the door to the conference room closes, no others are allowed to enter. The justice with the least seniority acts as the doorkeeper for the other eight, communicating with those waiting outside to fill requests for documents, water, and any other necessities.

Conferences highlight the importance and power of the chief justice, who presides over them and makes the initial presentation of each case. Each individual justice then discusses the case in order of his or her seniority on the Court, with the most senior justice speaking next. Most accounts of the decision-making process reveal that at this point some justices try to change the minds of others, but that most enter the conference room with a clear idea of how they will vote on each case. Although other Courts have followed different procedures, during the Rehnquist Court, the justices generally voted at the same time they discussed each case, with each justice speaking only once. Initial conference votes were not final, and justices were allowed to change their minds before final votes were taken later. The Roberts Court is much more informal than the Rehnquist Court. The justices' regular Friday conferences now last longer, and unlike the conferences headed by Rehnquist, the new chief justice encourages discussion.[29]

Writing Opinions   After the Court has reached a decision in conference, the justices must formulate a formal opinion of the Court. If the chief justice is in the majority, he selects the justice who will write the opinion. This privilege enables him to wield tremendous power and is a very important strategic decision. If the chief justice is in the minority, the assignment falls to the most senior justice in the majority.

The opinion of the Court can take several different forms. Most decisions are reached by a majority opinion written by one member of the Court to reflect the views of at least five of the justices. This opinion usually sets out the legal reasoning justifying the decision, and this legal reasoning becomes a precedent for deciding future cases. The reasoning behind any decision is often as important as the outcome. Under the system of *stare decisis,* both are likely to be relied on as precedent later by lower courts confronted with cases involving similar issues.

In the process of creating the final opinion of the Court, informal caucusing and negotiation often take place, as justices may hold out for word changes or other modifications as a condition of their continued support of the majority opinion. This negotiation process can lead to divisions in the Court's majority. When this occurs, the Court may be forced to decide cases by plurality opinions, which attract the support of three or four justices. While these decisions do not have the precedential value of majority opinions, they nonetheless have been used by the Court to decide many major cases.

Justices who agree with the outcome of the case but not with the legal rationale for the decision may file concurring opinions to express their differing approach. Justices who do not agree with the outcome of a case file dissenting opinions. Although these opinions have little direct legal value, they can be an important indicator of legal thought on the Court and are an excellent platform for justices to note their personal and legal disagreements with other members of the Court.

The process of crafting a final opinion is not an easy one, and justices often rely heavily on their clerks to do much of the revision. Neither is the process apolitical. Today, one vote on the Court can be the difference between two very different outcomes.

Judicial Philosophy and Decision Making

JUSTICES DO NOT MAKE decisions in a vacuum. Principles of *stare decisis* dictate that the justices follow the law of previous cases in deciding cases at hand. But, a variety of legal and extra-legal factors have also been found to affect Supreme Court decision making.

JUDICIAL PHILOSOPHY, ORIGINAL INTENT, AND IDEOLOGY

Legal scholars long have argued that judges decide cases based on the Constitution and their reading of various statutes. Determining what the Framers meant—if that is even possible today—often appears to be based on an individual jurist's philosophy.

One of the primary issues concerning judicial decision making focuses on what is called the activism/restraint debate. Advocates of **judicial restraint** argue that courts should allow the decisions of other branches to stand, even when they offend a judge's own sense of principles. Restraintists defend their position by asserting that the federal courts are composed of unelected judges, which makes the judicial branch the least democratic branch of government. Consequently, the courts should defer policy making to other branches of government as much as possible.

Advocates of judicial restraint generally agree that judges should be **strict constructionists;** that is, they should interpret the Constitution as it was written and intended by the Framers. They argue that in determining the constitutionality of a statute or policy, the Court should rely on the explicit meanings of the clauses in the document, which can be clarified by looking at the intent of the Framers.

Advocates of **judicial activism** contend that judges should use their power broadly to further justice, especially in the areas of equality and personal liberty. Activists argue that it is the courts' appropriate role to correct injustices committed by the other branches of government. Explicit in this argument is the notion that courts need to protect oppressed minorities.[30]

Although judicial activists are often considered politically liberal and restraintists politically conservative, in recent years a new brand of conservative judicial activism has become prevalent. Unlike their liberal counterparts, whose activist decisions often expanded the rights of political and legal minorities, conservative activist judges view their positions as an opportunity to issue broad rulings that impose conservative political beliefs and policies on the country at large.

Some scholars argue that this increased conservative judicial activism has had an effect on the Court's reliance on *stare decisis* and adherence to precedent. Chief Justice William H. Rehnquist even noted that while "*stare decisis* is a cornerstone of our legal system . . . it has less power in constitutional cases."[31]

judicial restraint
A philosophy of judicial decision making that argues courts should allow the decisions of other branches of government to stand, even when they offend a judge's own sense of principles.

strict constructionist
An approach to constitutional interpretation that emphasizes the Framers' original intentions.

judicial activism
A philosophy of judicial decision making that argues judges should use their power broadly to further justice, especially in the areas of equality and personal liberty.

MODELS OF JUDICIAL DECISION MAKING

Most political scientists who study what is called judicial behavior conclude that a variety of forces shape judicial decision making. Of late, many have attempted to explain how judges vote by integrating a variety of models to offer a more complete picture of how judges make decisions.[32] Many of those models attempt to take into account justices' individual behavioral characteristics and attitudes as well as the fact patterns of the case.

Behavioral Characteristics Originally, some political scientists argued that social background differences, including childhood experiences, religious values, education, earlier political and legal careers, and political party loyalties, are likely to influence how a judge evaluates the facts and legal issues presented in any given case. Justice Harry A. Blackmun's service at the Mayo Clinic often is pointed to as a reason that his opinion for the Court in *Roe* v. *Wade* (1973) was grounded so thoroughly in medical evidence. Similarly, Justice Potter Stewart, who was generally considered a moderate on most civil liberties issues, usually took a more liberal position on cases dealing with freedom of the press. Why? It may be that Stewart's early job as a newspaper reporter made him more sensitive to these claims.

The Attitudinal Model The attitudinal approach links judicial attitudes with decision making.[33] Simply stated, the attitudinal model holds that Supreme Court justices decide cases according to their personal preferences toward issues of public policy. Among some of the factors used to derive attitudes are a justice's party identification,[34] the party of the appointing president, and the liberal/conservative leanings of a justice.[35]

The Strategic Model Some scholars who study the courts now are advocating the belief that judges act strategically, meaning that they weigh and assess their actions against those of other justices to optimize the chances that their preferences will be adopted by the whole Court.[36] Moreover, this approach seeks to explain not only a justice's vote but also the range of forces such as congressional/judicial relations and judicial/executive relations that also affect the outcome of legal disputes.

PUBLIC OPINION

Many political scientists have examined the role of public opinion in Supreme Court decision making.[37] Not only do the justices read legal briefs and hear oral arguments, but they also read newspapers, watch television, and have some knowledge of public opinion—especially on controversial issues.

Whether or not public opinion actually influences some justices, public opinion can act as a check on the power of the courts as well as an energizing factor. Activist periods on the Supreme Court generally have corresponded to periods of social or economic crisis. For example, the Marshall Court supported a strong national government, much to the chagrin of a series of pro-states' rights Democratic-Republican presidents in the early crisis-ridden years of the republic. Similarly, the Court capitulated to political pressures and public opinion when, after 1936, it reversed many of its earlier decisions that had blocked President Franklin D. Roosevelt's New Deal legislation.

The courts, especially the Supreme Court, can be the direct target of public opinion. When *Webster* v. *Reproductive Health Services* (1989) was about to come before the Supreme Court, the Court was subjected to unprecedented lobbying as groups and individuals on both sides of the abortion issue marched and sent appeals to the Court. Mail at the Court, which usually averaged about 1,000 pieces a day, rose to an astronomical 46,000 pieces per day, virtually paralyzing normal lines of communication.

The Supreme Court also appears to affect public opinion. Political scientists have found that the Court's initial rulings on controversial issues such as abortion or capital

American Values/American Voices

JUDICIAL INDEPENDENCE AND THE COURT OF WORLD OPINION

Although the Framers spent little time on Article III of the U.S. Constitution at the Philadelphia Convention, the provisions they did include regarding Supreme Court justices—life tenure with good behavior and fixed compensation—were included for one major reason: the need to preserve the independence of the Court from all other branches. Alexander Hamilton defended these inclusions extensively in *The Federalist Papers*. In *Federalist No. 78*, for example, Hamilton wrote: "judges under this system will be independent in the strict sense of the word. . . . [T]here is no power above them that can control their decisions, or correct their errors. There is no authority that can remove them from office for any errors or want of capacity, or lower their salaries, and in many cases their power is superior to that of the legislature."

The actions of the Court's earliest chief justices, including John Jay and John Marshall, went a long way toward maintaining an image of independence for the Supreme Court. Even today, most casual observers consider the Court a neutral arbiter of the law that is above outside influence. As this chapter shows, however, the Supreme Court is not entirely insulated from outside forces. Historically, interest groups, public opinion, and even justices' personal experiences have played a role in the justices' decisions. So, too, have the laws and customs of other countries.

As early as 1877, in the case of *Pennoyer* v. *Neff*, Justice Stephen Field used international law to help define the boundaries of the U.S. Constitution's due process clause.[a] Recently, however, drawing on other countries' laws in American courts has become a contentious issue among the justices of the Supreme Court. Justices John Paul Stevens, Ruth Bader Ginsburg, and Steven Breyer sit on one side of the issue. These justices often refer to international law in their opinions and have spoken out in defense of cautiously using international standards for guidance in their decision-making process. Justice Ginsburg, for example, has said: "If U.S. experience and decisions can be instructive to systems that have more recently instituted or invigorated judicial review for constitutionality, so we can learn from others including Canada, South Africa, and most recently the U.K.—now engaged in measuring ordinary laws and executive actions against charters securing basic rights."[b]

On the other side of the issue sit a number of federal and state judges, including Supreme Court Justices Clarence Thomas and Antonin Scalia, who argue that citing international law compromises the independence of the American courts, runs contrary to the intentions of the Framers, and ignores the uniqueness of the American nation. In a 2006 speech to the American Enterprise Institute, for example, Scalia declared: "If there was any thought absolutely foreign to the founders of our country, surely it was the notion that we Americans should be governed the way that Europeans are—and nothing has changed."[c]

The justices' opinions in the 2002 death penalty case of *Atkins* v. *Virginia* illustrate how contentious the use of international law has become on the Supreme Court. Justice Stevens penned the majority opinion, and in footnote 21 he noted, "Moreover, within the world community, the imposition of the death penalty for crimes committed by mentally retarded offenders is overwhelmingly disapproved." In dissent, Justice Scalia attacked his colleague's reference to international norms, noting, "But the Prize for the Court's Most Feeble Effort to fabricate 'national consensus' must go to its appeal (deservedly relegated to a footnote) to the views of . . . the so-called 'world community.' . . . We must never forget that it is a Constitution for the United States of America that we are expounding. . . . [W]here there is not first a settled consensus among our own people, the views of other nations, however enlightened the Justices of this Court may think them to be, cannot be imposed upon Americans through the Constitution."[d]

The *Atkins* case is just one example of the public battles over the use of international law in the U.S. Supreme Court. Justices have used comparative constitutionalism to guide their decisions on a number of civil liberties issues, including affirmative action, homosexual rights, and assisted suicide.[e] And, with an increasingly global community, this is not a trend that is likely to stop anytime soon. The question is whether this international focus compromises the independence of American courts or whether it provides enlightening evidence of progress made in other societies that can be used to make the United States a better place to live.

QUESTIONS

1. Do you think that drawing on international law in framing judicial opinions compromises the independence of American courts? Why or why not?
2. When does it become appropriate for judges and justices to turn to international law and other external factors to help them reach a decision?

[a] Tim Wu, "Should the Supreme Court Care What Other Countries Think?" *Slate* (April 9, 2004), http://www.slate.com.

[b] Ruth Bader Ginsburg, speech at the University of Cape Town, South Africa, February 7, 2006.

[c] Antonin Scalia, speech at the American Enterprise Institute, February 21, 2006.

[d] *Atkins* v. *Virginia*, 536 U.S. 304 (2002).

[e] See *Grutter* v. *Bollinger*, 539 U.S. 306 (2003); *Bowers* v. *Hardwick*, 478 U.S. 186 (1986) and *Lawrence* v. *Texas*, 539 U.S. 558 (2003); and *Washington* v. *Glucksburg*, 521 U.S. 702 (1997).

punishment positively influence public opinion in the direction of the Court's opinion. However, this research also finds that subsequent decisions have little effect.[38]

The Court is dependent on the public for its prestige as well as for compliance with its decisions. In times of war and other emergencies, for example, the Court frequently has decided cases in ways that commentators have attributed to the sway of public opinion and political exigencies. In *Korematsu* v. *U.S.* (1944), for example, the high Court upheld the obviously unconstitutional internment of Japanese American citizens during World War II.[39] Moreover, Chief Justice William H. Rehnquist himself once suggested that the Court's restriction on presidential authority in *Youngstown Sheet & Tube Co.* v. *Sawyer* (1952), which invalidated President Harry S Truman's seizure of the nation's steel mills,[40] was largely attributable to Truman's unpopularity in light of the Korean War.[41]

Public confidence in the Court, as with other institutions of government, has ebbed and flowed. Public support for the Court was highest after the Court issued *U.S.* v. *Nixon* (1974).[42] At a time when Americans lost faith in the presidency due to the Watergate scandal, they could at least look to the Supreme Court to do the right thing. Although the numbers of Americans with confidence in the courts has fluctuated over time, in 2006, 49 percent of those sampled by Gallup International had a "great deal" or "quite a lot" of confidence in the Supreme Court.[43] Recent battles over judicial opinions regarding hot-button social issues have led to blatantly hostile rhetoric toward members of the judiciary on the Internet and even in Congress. This, in turn, has led even some members of the Supreme Court to comment publicly on the continuing need for an independent judiciary. (See American Values/American Voices: Judicial Independence and the Court of World Opinion.)

Judicial Policy Making and Implementation

ALL JUDGES, whether they recognize it or not, make policy. The primary way federal judges, and the U.S. Supreme Court, in particular, make policy is through interpreting statutes or the Constitution. This occurs in a variety of ways. Judges can interpret a provision of a statute to cover matters previously not understood to be covered by the law, or they can discover new rights, such as that of privacy, from their reading of the Constitution. They also have literal power over life and death when they decide death penalty cases.

POLICY MAKING

VIDEO ROUNDTABLE

Judges and Politics

One measure of the power of the courts and their ability to make policy is that more than one hundred federal laws have been declared unconstitutional. Although many of these laws have not been particularly significant, others have.

Another measure of the policy-making power of the Supreme Court is its ability to overrule itself. Although the Court generally abides by the informal rule of *stare decisis,* by one count, it has overruled itself in more than 200 cases.[44] Moreover, in the past few years, the Court repeatedly has reversed earlier decisions in the areas of criminal defendants' rights, women's rights, and the establishment of religion, thus revealing its powerful role in determining national policy. A measure of the growing power of the federal courts is the degree to which they now handle issues that had been considered political questions more appropriately left to the other branches of government to decide.

IMPLEMENTING COURT DECISIONS

President Andrew Jackson, annoyed about a particular decision handed down by the Marshall Court, is alleged to have said, "John Marshall has made his decision; now let him enforce it." Jackson's statement raises a question: how do Supreme Court rulings translate into public policy? In fact, although judicial decisions carry legal and even moral authority, all courts must rely on other units of government to carry out their directives. If the president or members of Congress, for example, don't like a particular Supreme Court ruling, they can underfund programs needed to implement a decision or seek only lax enforcement. **Judicial implementation** refers to how and whether judicial decisions are translated into actual public policies affecting more than the immediate parties to the lawsuit.

How well a decision is implemented often depends on how well crafted or popular it is. Hostile reaction in the South to *Brown* v. *Board of Education* (1954) and the absence of precise guidelines to implement the decision meant that the ruling went largely unenforced for years. The *Brown* experience also highlights how much the Supreme Court needs the support of both federal and state courts as well as other governmental agencies to carry out its judgments. For example, you probably graduated from high school after 1992, when the Supreme Court ruled that public middle school and high school graduations could not include a prayer, yet your own commencement ceremony may have included one.

For effective implementation of a judicial decision, the first requirement is that the members of the implementing population must act to show that they understand the original decision. For example, the Supreme Court ruled in *Reynolds* v. *Sims* (1964) that every person should have an equally weighted vote in electing governmental representatives.[45] This "one person, one vote" decision might seem simple enough at first glance, but in practice it can be very difficult to understand.

The second requirement is that the implementing population actually must follow Court policy. Thus, when the Court ruled that men could not be denied admission to a state-sponsored nursing school, the implementing population—in this case, university administrators and the state board of regents governing the nursing school—had to enroll qualified male students.[46]

Judicial decisions are most likely to be implemented smoothly if responsibility for implementation is concentrated in the hands of a few highly visible public officials, such as the president or a governor. By the same token, these officials also can thwart or impede judicial intentions. Recall from chapter 5, for example, the effect of Governor Orval Faubus's initial refusal to allow black children to attend all-white public schools in Little Rock, Arkansas.

The third requirement for implementation is that the consumer population must be aware of the rights that a decision grants or denies them. Teenagers seeking an

judicial implementation
Refers to how and whether judicial decisions are translated into actual public policies affecting more than the immediate parties to a lawsuit.

PARTICIPATION
The Courts and School Vouchers

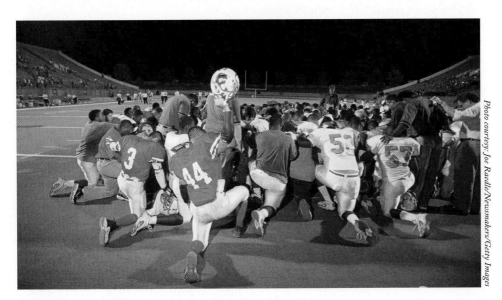

Photo courtesy: Joe Raedle/Newsmakers/Getty Images

■ This photo, taken in September 2000, illustrates the difficulty in implementing judicial decisions. Although the Supreme Court had ruled in June 2000 that pre-game prayers at public schools were unconstitutional, prayers continued at many public school sporting events across the country after the Court's decision.

abortion, for example, are consumers of the Supreme Court's decisions on abortion. They need to know that most states require them to inform their parents of their intention to have an abortion or to get parental permission to do so.

Summary

THE JUDICIARY AND THE LEGAL PROCESS—on both the national and state levels—are complex and play a far more important role in the setting of policy than the Framers ever envisioned. Many of the Framers viewed the judicial branch of government as little more than a minor check on the other two branches, ignoring Anti-Federalist concerns about an unelected judiciary and its potential for tyranny. The Judiciary Act of 1789 established the basic federal court system we have today. It was the Marshall Court (1801–1835), however, that interpreted the Constitution to include the Court's major power, that of judicial review.

Ours is a dual judicial system consisting of the federal court system and the separate judicial systems of the fifty states. In each system there are two basic types of courts: trial courts and appellate courts. Each type deals with cases involving criminal and civil law. Original jurisdiction refers to a court's ability to hear a case as a trial court; appellate jurisdiction refers to a court's ability to review cases already decided by a trial court.

The federal court system is made up of constitutional and legislative courts. Federal district courts, courts of appeals, and the Supreme Court are constitutional courts.

District court and court of appeals judges are nominated by the president and subject to Senate confirmation. Senators often play a key role in recommending district court appointees from their home state. Supreme Court justices are nominated by the president and must also win Senate confirmation. Presidents use different criteria for selection, but important factors include competence, standards, ideology, rewards, pursuit of political support, religion, race, ethnicity, and gender.

Several factors go into the U.S. Supreme Court's decision to hear a case. Not only must the Court have jurisdiction, but at least four justices must vote to hear the case, and cases with certain characteristics are most likely to be heard. Once a case is set for review, briefs and *amicus curiae* briefs are filed and oral argument scheduled. The justices meet after oral argument to discuss the case, votes are taken, and opinions are written and circulated.

Judges' philosophy and ideology have an extraordinary impact on how they decide cases. Political scientists consider these factors in identifying several models for how judges make decisions, including the behavioral, attitudinal, and strategic models.

The Supreme Court is an important participant in the policy-making process. The process of judicial interpretation gives the Court powers never envisioned by the Framers.

KEY TERMS

amicus curiae, p. 267
appellate courts, p. 252
appellate jurisdiction, p. 253
brief, p. 256
civil law, p. 254
constitutional courts, p. 255
criminal law, p. 253
judicial activism, p. 269
judicial implementation, p. 273
judicial restraint, p. 269
judicial review, p. 247
Judiciary Act of 1789, p. 249
jurisdiction, p. 252
legislative courts, p. 255
Marbury v. *Madison* (1803), p. 251
original jurisdiction, p. 252
precedent, p. 257
Rule of Four, p. 266
senatorial courtesy, p. 257
solicitor general, p. 267
stare decisis, p. 257
strict constructionist, p. 269
trial courts, p. 252
writ of *certiorari*, p. 265

SELECTED READINGS

Abraham, Henry J. *The Judiciary: The Supreme Court in the Governmental Process*, 10th ed. New York: New York University Press, 1996.

Baum, Lawrence. *The Supreme Court*, 8th ed. Washington, DC: CQ Press, 2004.

———. *The Puzzle of Judicial Behavior.* Ann Arbor: University of Michigan Press, 1997.

Clayton, Cornell, and Howard Gillman, eds. *Supreme Court Decision-Making: New Institutionalist Approaches.* Chicago: University of Chicago Press, 1999.

Epstein, Lee, and Jeffrey A. Segal. *Advice and Consent: The Politics of Judicial Appointments.* New York: Oxford University Press, 2005.

Epstein, Lee, et al. *The Supreme Court Compendium*, 3rd ed. Washington, DC: Congressional Quarterly Inc., 2002.

Goldman, Sheldon. *Picking Federal Judges: Lower Court Selection from Roosevelt Through Reagan.* New Haven, CT: Yale University Press, 1997.

Hall, Kermit L., ed. *The Oxford Companion to the Supreme Court of the United States,* 2nd ed. New York: Oxford University Press, 2005.

Hall, Kermit L., and Kevin T. McGuire, eds. *Institutions of American Democracy: The Judicial Branch.* New York: Oxford University Press, 2005.

Lazarus, Edward. *Closed Chambers: The First Eyewitness Account of the Epic Struggles Inside the Supreme Court.* New York: Times Books, 1998.

O'Brien, David M. *Storm Center: The Supreme Court in American Politics,* 7th ed. New York: Norton, 2005.

Perry, H. W. *Deciding to Decide: Agenda Setting in the United States Supreme Court,* reprint ed. Cambridge, MA: Harvard University Press, 2005.

Salokar, Rebecca Mae. *The Solicitor General: The Politics of Law.* Philadelphia: Temple University Press, 1992.

Segal, Jeffrey A., and Harold J. Spaeth. *The Supreme Court and the Attitudinal Model Revisited.* New York: Cambridge University Press, 2002.

Slotnick, Elliot E., and Jennifer A. Segal. *Television News and the Supreme Court: All the News That's Fit to Air.* Boston: Cambridge University Press. 1998.

Sunstein, Cass R. *One Case at a Time: Judicial Minimalism on the Supreme Court,* 2nd ed. Cambridge, MA: Harvard University Press, 2001.

Ward, Artemus, and David L. Weiden. *Sorcerer's Apprentices: 100 Years of Law Clerks at the United States Supreme Court.* New York: New York University Press, 2006.

Woodward, Bob, and Scott Armstrong. *The Brethren: Inside the Supreme Court,* 2nd ed. New York: Avon, 2005.

WEB EXPLORATIONS

To learn more about the workings of the U.S. justice system, see
http://www.usdoj.gov

To learn more about U.S. federal courts, see
http://www.uscourts.gov/

To take a virtual tour of the U.S. Supreme Court and examine current cases on its docket, go to
http://www.supremecourtus.gov

To learn about the U.S. Senate Judiciary Committee and judicial nominations currently under review, see
http://judiciary.senate.gov

To learn the extent of the ABA's legislative and government advocacy, go to
http://www.abanet.org

To learn more about The Federalist Society, see
http://www.fed-soc.org

To examine the major Supreme Court decisions from the past to the present, go to
http://supct.law.cornell.edu/supct/index.htm

To examine the recent filings of the office of solicitor general, go to
http://www.usdoj.gov/org/

Photo courtesy: David Guttenfelder/AP Wide World Photos

PUBLIC OPINION AND THE NEWS MEDIA

10

EMBARRASSING IMAGES have hounded President George W. Bush in a way that few other administrations have experienced. In May 2003, there was the president's landing, fully equipped with green flight suit and matching helmet, on the USS *Abraham Lincoln* and his speech under the now infamous "Mission Accomplished" banner. In October 2005, there was the White House's failed effort to pass off a staged media event as an authentic question-and-answer exchange between the president and troops in Iraq. There were the horrific images of prisoner abuse at Abu Ghraib in April 2004, and the troubling images from New Orleans following Hurricane Katrina and the government's belated response.

Beyond the images was the indictment of Lewis "Scooter" Libby, Vice President Dick Cheney's chief of staff. Libby was indicted on five charges related to a leak that exposed the identity of an undercover CIA operative whose husband had written an unflattering editorial in the *New York Times* that challenged veracity of information the president reported in his State of the Union Address. More recently, widespread reports surfaced revealing that the United States had paid Iraqi reporters to run pro-U.S. stories—stories that received less coverage than the news reports about the payments. And, in a public image nightmare, Vice President Cheney accidentally shot and wounded a fellow hunter, not reporting the incident to the press until the next day, and then only to a small local Texas newspaper. The publication of an unflattering book about the Bush White House by veteran reporter Bob Woodward in September 2006, a little over a month before the 2006 midterm elections, led to furious media attention and a parade of former officials willing to acknowledge their disagreements with the president and his Cabinet.

The Bush administration has its own complaints about the media: In June 2006, the president angrily reacted to a report in the *New York Times* and other newspapers that revealed a secret financial monitoring program the United States was operating to track the flow of terrorist funds around the world. Bush claimed the *Times* was undermining the war on terrorism and being irresponsible in choosing to print the story.

The Bush administration, despite its reputation for being one of the most media savvy and tight-lipped administrations in modern times, has time and again been stung by media that remain beyond its control. The Bush presidency has shown that in a world with twenty-four-hour news coverage and highly competitive private media outlets, there are few secrets in Washington. Moreover, attempts to control the media message stand the risk of backfiring and leading to unwanted media scrutiny, which often translates into negative effects in public opinion polls.

THE NETWORKS, MANY MAJOR NEWSPAPERS, and polling organizations routinely report on and often attempt to gauge public opinion about a wide array of events. Still, many citizens question the fairness or bias of the media in all of its forms as well as the accuracy of public opinion polls. Often, as reported by or even commissioned by the media, polls reveal much about what "the public" is thinking. The complex interactions of the media and public opinion are the focus of this chapter.

First we will discuss political socialization and other factors that influence opinion formation about political matters. After an examination of the history of public opinion research, we will examine how we form political opinions.

Looking next at the news media, we will examine the development of the press in the United States and current issues affecting the media. We will also discuss the rules under which the news media operate, how the media cover politics, and how the media influence public opinion.

Political Socialization

political socialization
The process through which an individual acquires particular political orientations; the learning process by which people acquire their political beliefs and values.

POLITICAL SCIENTISTS BELIEVE that many of our attitudes about issues are grounded in our political values. We learn these values through **political socialization.** Family, school, peers, and the mass media are often important influences or agents of political socialization. A variety of other factors, too, often influence how political opinions are formed or reinforced. These include religious beliefs, race, ethnicity, gender, age, the region of the country in which you live, and political events. Your own political knowledge may also shape your ideals.

THE FAMILY

The influence of the family on political socialization can be traced to two factors: communication and receptivity. Children, especially during their preschool years, spend tremendous amounts of time with their parents; early on they learn their parents' political values, even though these concepts may be vague. One study, for example, found that the most important visible public figures for children under the age of ten were police officers and, to a much lesser extent, the president.[1] Young children almost uniformly view both as "helpful." But, by the age of ten or eleven, children become more selective in their perceptions of the president. By this age, children raised in Democratic households are much more likely to be critical of a Republican president than are those raised in Republican households. In 1988, for example, 58 percent of children in Republican households identified themselves as Republicans, and many had developed strong positive feelings toward Ronald Reagan, the Republican president. Support for and the popularity of Ronald Reagan translated into support for the

FIGURE 10.1 THE IDEOLOGICAL SELF-IDENTIFICATION OF FIRST-YEAR COLLEGE STUDENTS

A majority of first-year college students describe themselves as middle of the road; this number has held fairly steady since the early 1990s. The number of students identifying themselves as liberal and far left declined dramatically during the 1970s and early 1980s, while the number of students identifying themselves as conservative and far right increased. But, by far, most students continue to identify their ideology as middle of the road.

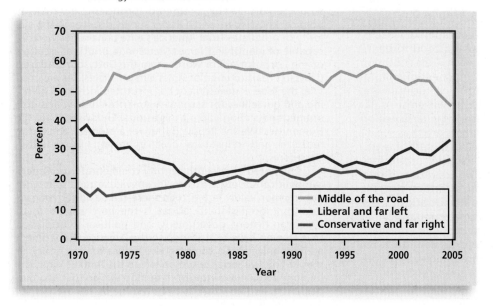

Sources: Reprinted from Howard W. Stanley and Richard G. Niemi, *Vital Statistics on American Politics, 2005–2006* (Washington, DC: CQ Press, 2006), 121. 2005 data from Cooperative Institutional Research Program (CIRP), "The American Freshman: National Norms for Fall 2005" (December 2005).

Republican Party through the 1988 presidential election and also contributed to the decline of liberal ideological self-identification of first-year college students (see Figure 10.1).

SCHOOL AND PEERS

Researchers report mixed findings concerning the role of schools in the political socialization process. There is no question that, in elementary school, children are taught respect for their nation and its symbols. Most school days begin with the Pledge of Allegiance, and patriotism and respect for country are important, although subtle, components of most school curricula. Support for flag and country create a foundation for national allegiance that prevails despite the negative views about politicians and government institutions that many Americans develop later in life. For example, though many Americans initially questioned action in Iraq in 2003, large numbers of schoolchildren prepared letters and packages to send to troops there and elsewhere. In some states, teachers were also encouraged to limit anti-war discussion.[2] Measures such as these, however controversial, help to build a sense of patriotism at a young age.

A child's peers—that is, children about the same age—also seem to have an important effect on the socialization process. Whereas parental influences are greatest from birth to age five, a child's peer group becomes increasingly important as the child gets older, especially as he or she gets into middle school or high school.[3]

Join the Debate

TEACHING CIVICS IN AMERICAN HIGH SCHOOLS

OVERVIEW: Classical, Enlightenment, and contemporary political theories assert that a primary function of the state is the education of citizens; indeed, civic education is understood to be inseparable from public education. Civic education is considered an essential component of political socialization. In many classrooms, for example, children elect the students who will erase chalkboards or serve as class leaders; by participating in classroom elections, students are thus socialized to accept electoral politics as part of legitimate political behavior. All mass democratic societies have some form of civic education, if only to teach citizens social norms, virtues, and the "rules of the game" of the democratic process. Low voter turnout and close election outcomes have been cited by supporters of civic education as a sign that more needs to be done to teach young people the importance of political participation. Recently, civic education requirements have taken on additional urgency in light of debates about immigration policy and questions regarding the extent to which civic education efforts should focus exclusively on U.S. norms or emphasize commonalities and differences among democratic nations worldwide.

It is obvious and accepted that civic education in secondary education has declined over the last thirty years. Many point to the Watergate scandal, the Vietnam War, and racial and social unrest during the civil rights movement as having a negative effect on the teaching of American history and government. The latest National Assessment of Educational Progress (NAEP) determined that only 26 percent of all high school seniors may be considered "proficient" in American political knowledge, and a Roper survey discovered the majority of graduates from America's elite universities were incapable of identifying James Madison (a principal architect of the Constitution) or words from the Gettysburg Address (Lincoln's reaffirmation of American principles). As a corrective, the federal government has instituted increased spending and guidelines for secondary American history and government education under the National Endowment for the Humanities' We the People Initiative, a program created to reaffirm and reinstitute civic education in America's classrooms.

The noted nineteenth-century commentator on American political society Alexis de Tocqueville argued that without common values and virtues, there can be no common action and social stability. What is the best way to teach American history, government, and political principles so that all who have contributed to the American experiment are recognized? Is a common civic education necessary, or should political socialization be left to the family? What can be done to increase interest in democratic politics and participation, and how can civic knowledge be restored to the American electorate?

ARGUMENTS FOR INCREASED CIVIC EDUCATION IN HIGH SCHOOLS

- **There may be a relationship between the decline in political participation and the lack of civic education.** Research indicates there may be a correlation between political participation and civic education. A Carnegie Corporation study contends that student participation in the management of schools and classrooms, as well as in simulations of democratic institutions and

High schools also can be important agents of political socialization. They continue the elementary school tradition of building good citizens and often reinforce textbook learning with trips to the state or national capital. They also offer courses on current U.S. affairs. Many high schools impose a compulsory service learning requirement, which some studies report positively affects later political participation.[4] Although the formal education of many people in the United States ends with high school, research shows that better-informed citizens vote more often as adults. Therefore, presentation of civic information is especially critical at the high school level, where it reinforces views about participation. (See Join the Debate: Teaching Civics in American High Schools.)

At the college level, teaching style often changes. Many college courses and texts like this one designed in part to provide you with the information necessary to think critically about issues of major political consequence. It is common in college for students to be called on to question the appropriateness of certain political actions processes, may increase involvement in the American political process.

- **Civic education teaches citizens how to participate in democratic society.** Students become politically socialized by taking part in school elections, activities, and extracurricular activities (such as participating in debate teams and publishing school newspapers). Civic education teaches not only cooperation but tolerance of dissent and opposing views, as well as the means of political compromise. This helps prepare students for the realities of pluralistic democratic life.
- **Civic education is a complement to political socialization.** The primary influence on one's political development comes from family and friends, and mass media and culture also help to shape political values and attitudes. The role of a formal civic education is to teach American history and governmental and political structures and principles, as well as to provide a forum for students to hone their political skills, practice public debate, and learn civic engagement.

ARGUMENTS AGAINST INCREASED CIVIC EDUCATION IN HIGH SCHOOLS

- **Civic education is innately biased by promoting certain values over others.** In a free, multicultural society, it is inherently wrong to press upon individuals a certain political and social view. Modern democratic governments gather their strength from the many diverse cultures and political views that make up their respective social bodies. Teaching one sociopolitical view would stifle the contributions of those from different cultures. To this end, the American Historical Society advocates the teaching of comparative and world history in the nation's classrooms.

- **Parents should be responsible for civic education.** One may assume a government-sanctioned education will be partial to its own interests and views. It is proper that parents introduce their children to political culture and socialization. This will help ensure a diversity of views in regard to the nature of government, thereby fostering debate and compromise in the marketplace of political ideas.
- **In a pluralist society it is difficult to determine what should constitute a civic education curriculum.** Which understanding of American history, politics, and government is to be taught? Different groups have different interpretations and understanding of the historical unfolding of American society. To promote the views of one group over another would be unfair, and to teach all views would be to overwhelm students with information; the effect may be actually to *discourage* political engagement by subjecting students to information overload.

QUESTIONS

1. Is there a correlation between the decline in civic participation and civic education? If so, why? If not, why not?
2. Is it the proper place of public schools to engage in civic education or is this the duty of family and friends?

SELECTED READINGS

Niemi, Richard G., and Jane Junn. *Civic Education: What Makes Students Learn*. New Haven, CT: Yale University Press, 2005.

Ravitch, Diane, ed. *Making Good Citizens: Education and Civil Society*. New Haven, CT: Yale University Press, 2003.

or to discuss underlying reasons for certain political or policy decisions. Therefore, most researchers believe that college has a liberalizing effect on students. Since the 1920s, studies have shown that students become more liberal each year they are in college. However, students entering college in the 1980s were more conservative than in past years. The 1992 and 1996 victories of Bill Clinton and his equally youthful running mate Al Gore, who went out of their way to woo the youth vote, probably contributed to the small bump in the liberal ideological identification of first-year college students in those years.

THE MASS MEDIA

The media today are taking on a growing role as socialization agents. Adult Americans spend nearly thirty hours a week in front of their television sets; children spend even more.[5] Television has a tremendous impact on how people view politics, government, and politicians. TV talk shows, talk radio, and online newsletters, magazines, and blogs are important sources of information about politics for many, yet the information that people get from these sources often is skewed.

Over the years, more and more Americans have turned away from traditional sources of new such as nightly news broadcasts on the major networks and daily newspapers in favor of different outlets. In 2004, one study estimated that more than 40 percent of those polled regularly learned about the election or candidates from alternative sources such as *The Tonight Show, The Late Show,* or *The Daily Show.*[6]

All of the major candidates in the 2004 presidential election as well as major party candidates in the 2006 midterms used another form of media to sway and inform voters: the Internet, a form of campaigning that was considered new in 1996. Each presidential and most other major and minor campaigns launched Internet sites, and the major networks and newspapers had their own Internet sites reporting on the election. Moreover, during the 2004 election cycle, more than 50 percent of those polled reported using the Internet to research candidates' positions on the issues.[7]

RELIGIOUS BELIEFS

Throughout our history, religion has played an extraordinary role in political life. Many colonists came to our shores seeking religious liberty, yet many quickly moved to impose their religious beliefs on others, and some made participation in local politics contingent on religiosity. Since political scientists began to look at the role of religion, numerous scholars have found that organized religion influences the political beliefs and behaviors of its adherents. The effects of organized religion are magnified in today's society, as 76 percent of all Americans consider religion an important part of their lives.

Through much of the twentieth century, social scientists found that faith-based political activity occurred largely on the left. From the civil rights movement, to efforts to improve the living standards of farmers and migrant workers, to abolition of the death penalty, religious leaders were evident. The civil rights movement, in particular, was led by numerous religious men, including the Reverend Martin Luther King Jr. and the Reverend Andrew Young and more recently the Reverend Jesse Jackson and the Reverend Al Sharpton.

In 1972, for the first time, a religious gap appeared in voting and public opinion. Richard M. Nixon's campaign was designed to appeal to what he termed "the Silent Majority," who wanted a return to more traditional values after the tumult of the 1960s. By the 1980s, conservative Christians could take credit for the election of Ronald Reagan. Throughout the 1980s, first the Moral Majority and then the Christian Coalition have played increasingly key roles in politics. Today, religion is the second largest predictor of the vote, after party identification. Regular church-goers have conservative views and vote Republican by a 2 to 1 margin.

In 2004, 54 percent of Americans identified themselves as Protestant, 25 percent as Catholic, 4 percent as Jewish, and 2 percent as other, while 15 percent claimed to have no religious affiliation. As shown in Figure 10.2, Protestants, especially evangelicals, are the most conservative and Jews the most liberal. And, as liberals, Jews tend to vote Democratic.[8] In 2004, for example, John Kerry and his running mate, John Edwards, captured 74 percent of the Jewish vote.[9]

RACE AND ETHNICITY

Differences in political socialization of African Americans and whites appear at a very early age. Young black children, for example, generally show very positive feelings about the American society and political processes, but this attachment lessens considerably over time. Black children fail to hold the president in the esteem accorded him by white children. In fact, older African American children in the 1960s viewed

FIGURE 10.2 THE IDEOLOGICAL SELF-IDENTIFICATION OF PROTESTANTS, CATHOLICS, AND JEWS

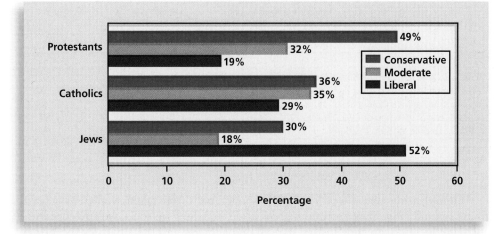

Source: Data compiled and analyzed by Alixandra B. Yanus from the 2004 American National Election Study.

the government primarily in terms of the U.S. Supreme Court.[10] These differences continue through adulthood.

Race and ethnicity are exceptionally important factors in elections and in the study of public opinion. The direction and intensity of African Americans opinions on a variety of hot-button issues often are quite different from those of whites. As revealed in Analyzing Visuals: Racial and Ethnic Attitudes on Selected Issues, whites are much more likely to support the war in Iraq than are blacks or Hispanics. Likewise, differences can be seen in other issue areas, including support for preferential treatment to improve the position of minorities.[11]

Hispanics, Asians/Pacific Islanders, and American Indians are other identifiable ethnic minorities in the United States who often respond differently to issues than do whites. Generally, Hispanics and American Indians hold similar opinions on many issues, largely because members of these groups often have low incomes and find themselves targets of discrimination. Government-sponsored health insurance for the working poor, for example, is a hot-button issue with Hispanic voters, with 94 percent favoring it. Unlike many other Americans, they also favor bilingual education and liberalized immigration policies.[12] (See chapter 1.)

Within the Hispanic community, however, existing divisions often depend on national origin. Generally, Cuban Americans who cluster in Florida and in the Miami–Dade County area, in particular, are more likely to be conservative. They fled from communism and Fidel Castro in Cuba, and they generally vote Republican. In contrast, Hispanics of Mexican origin who vote in California, New Mexico, Arizona, Texas, or Colorado are more likely to vote Democratic.[13]

GENDER

Poll after poll reveals that women hold very different opinions from men on a variety of issues, as shown in Table 10.1. Some believe that from an early age women are socialized to be more nurturing and caring while men are more aggressive. According to this argument, these differences in political socialization lead to different political orientations and often have translated into substantial gaps in the way men and women vote. Women, and particularly unmarried women, are more likely to be Democrats, while white men are increasingly becoming the core of the Republican Party.[14]

TABLE 10.1 GENDER DIFFERENCES ON POLITICAL ISSUES

Public opinion polls reveal that men and women tend to hold different views on a number of political issues. Yet, on some political issues, little difference is evident.

	Men (%)	Women (%)
Iraq War worth the cost	42	35
Increase federal spending on Social Security	57	67
Favor ban on late-term (partial birth) abortion	57	60
Federal government should make it more difficult to buy guns	48	67
Increase federal spending on war on terrorism	50	36
Voted for George W. Bush in 2004	55	48

Source: Data compiled and analyzed by Alixandra B. Yanus from the 2004 American National Election Study.

From the time that the earliest public opinion polls were taken, women have been found to hold more liberal attitudes about issues touching on social welfare concerns, such as education, juvenile justice, capital punishment, and the environment. Some analysts suggest that women's more nurturing nature and their prominent role as mothers lead them to have more liberal attitudes on issues affecting the family or children. Research by political scientists, however, finds no support for a maternal explanation.[15]

Historically, public opinion polls have also found that women hold more negative views about war and military intervention. However, the gender gap on military issues began to disappear in the late 1990s, when the United States intervened in Kosovo. Many speculated that this occurred because of the increased participation of women in the workforce and the military, the "sanitized nature of much of the war footage" shown on TV, and the humanitarian reasons for involvement.[16]

The gender gap in military affairs also was not visible following the terrorist attacks of September 11, 2001. Right after the attacks, polls showed that 47 percent of women and 53 percent of men voiced their support for the operations in Afghanistan.[17] However, as the memory of 9/11 has receded, the war in Iraq has resulted in a renewed gender gap on foreign affairs (see Table 10.1). Many commentators speculate that this gap may be the product of increasing concerns about terrorism abroad and national security at home.

AGE

Age seems to have a decided effect on one's political socialization. A person's view of the proper role of government, for example, often depends on the era in which one was born and an individual's experiences with a variety of social, political, and economic forces. Older people continue to be affected by having lived through the Great Depression and World War II. One political scientist predicts that as people now in their forties and fifties continue to age, the age gap in political beliefs about political issues, especially governmental programs, will increase.[18] Young people, for example, resist higher taxes to fund Medicare, while the elderly resist efforts to limit Medicare or Social Security. As Americans live longer, senior citizens are becoming a potent political force. In states such as Florida, to which many northern retirees have flocked seeking relief from cold winters and high taxes, the elderly have voted as a bloc to defeat school tax increases and to pass tax breaks for themselves.

In the future, the graying of America will have major social and political consequences. As we discuss in chapter 12, those between sixty and seventy vote in much larger numbers than do their younger counterparts. Moreover, the fastest growing age group in the United States is that of citizens over the age of sixty-five. Thus, not only are there more people in this category, but they are more likely to be registered to vote, and often vote conservatively.

Analyzing Visuals

RACIAL AND ETHNIC ATTITUDES ON SELECTED ISSUES

Political opinions held by racial and ethnic groups in the United States differ on many issues. In the figure below, the opinions of whites, blacks, and Hispanics are compared on a number of political issues. After studying the bar graph and the material in this chapter on race, ethnicity, and public opinion, answer the following critical think-

ing questions: What do you observe about the differences and similarities in opinions among the different groups? On which issues do blacks and whites, Hispanics and blacks, and Hispanics and whites have similar or diverging opinions? What factors might explain these similarities and differences?

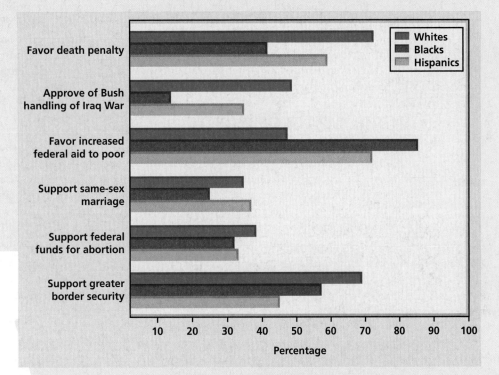

Source: Data compiled and analyzed by Alixandra B. Yanus from the 2004 American National Election Study.

REGION

Regional and sectional differences have been important factors in the development and maintenance of political beliefs since colonial times. As the United States developed into a major industrial nation, waves of immigrants with different religious traditions and customs entered the United States and often settled in areas where other immigrants from their region already lived. For example, thousands of Scandinavians settled in Minnesota, and many Irish settled in the urban centers of the Northeast, as did many Italians and Jews. All brought with them unique views about numerous issues, as well as about the role of government. These political views often have been transmitted through generations, and many regional differences continue to affect public opinion today.

Comparing Public Opinion

One of the most long-standing and dramatic regional differences in the United States is that between the South and the North. Recall that during the Constitutional

Convention most Southerners staunchly advocated a weak national government. Nearly a hundred years later, the Civil War was fought in part because of basic differences in philosophy toward government (states' rights in the South versus national rights in the North). As we know from the results of modern political polling, the South has continued to lag behind the rest of the nation on support for civil rights, while continuing to favor return of power to the states at the expense of the national government.

The South also is much more religious than the rest of the nation, as well as more Protestant. Seventy-six percent of the South is Protestant (versus 49 percent for the rest of the nation), and church attendance is highest in the South, where 38 percent report weekly visits. In contrast, only 30 percent of those living in the North and 29 percent of those residing in the West go to church or synagogue on a weekly basis.[19] Given the South's higher churchgoing rates, it is not surprising that the Christian Coalition (discussed in chapter 11) has been very successful at mobilizing voters in that region.

The West, too, is different from other sections of the nation. Some people have moved there to avoid city life; other residents have an anti-government bias. Many who have sought refuge there are staunchly against any governmental action, especially on the national level.

THE IMPACT OF EVENTS

TIMELINE

War, Peace, and Public Opinion

Key political events play a very important role in a person's political socialization. You probably have some professors who remember what they were doing on the day that President John F. Kennedy was killed—November 22, 1963. This dramatic event is indelibly etched in the minds of virtually all people who were old enough to be aware of it. Similarly, most college students today remember where they were when they heard about the September 11, attacks on the World Trade Center and the Pentagon. These attacks on American shores evoked a profound sense of patriotism and national unity as American flags were displayed from windows, doors, balconies, and cars. For many Americans, the attacks were life-changing political events.

One has to go back to 1974 to find a political event that had such a dramatic effect on what people thought about the political process. President Richard M. Nixon's resignation in 1974 made a particular impression on young people, who were forced to realize that their government was not always right or honest. This general distrust of politicians was reignited during the highly publicized investigation of President Bill Clinton and his subsequent impeachment.

Public Opinion and Polling

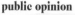

public opinion
What the public thinks about a particular issue or set of issues at any point in time.

public opinion polls
Interviews or surveys with samples of citizens that are used to estimate the feelings and beliefs of the entire population.

AT FIRST GLANCE, **public opinion** seems to be a very straightforward concept: it is what the public thinks about a particular issue or set of issues at a particular time. Since the 1930s, governmental decision makers have relied heavily on **public opinion polls**—interviews with samples of citizens that are used to estimate what the public is thinking. According to George Gallup (1901–1983), an Iowan who is considered the founder of modern-day polling, polls have played a key role in defining issues of concern to the public, shaping administrative decisions, and helping "speed up the process of democracy" in the United States.[20]

THE HISTORY OF PUBLIC OPINION RESEARCH

As early as 1824, one Pennsylvania newspaper tried to predict the winner of that year's presidential contest. Later, in 1883, the *Boston Globe* sent reporters to selected election precincts to poll voters as they exited voting booths, in an effort to predict the results of key contests. In 1916, *Literary Digest*, a popular magazine, began mailing survey postcards to potential voters in an effort to predict election outcomes. *Literary Digest* drew its survey sample from "every telephone book in the United States, from the rosters of clubs and associations, from city directories, lists of registered voters [and] classified mail order and occupational data."[21] Using data from the millions of postcard ballots it received from all over the United States, *Literary Digest* correctly predicted every presidential election from 1920 to 1932.

But, public opinion polling as we know it today did not begin to develop until the 1930s. Much of this growth was prompted by Walter Lippmann's seminal work *Public Opinion* (1922). In this piece, Lippmann observed that research on public opinion was far too limited, especially in light of its impor-

tance. Researchers in a variety of disciplines, including political science, heeded Lippmann's call to learn more about public opinion. Some tried to use scientific methods to measure political thought through the use of surveys or polls. As methods for gathering and interpreting data improved, survey data began to play an increasingly important role in all walks of life, from politics to retailing.

Literary Digest, for example, was a pioneer in the use of **straw polls**, unscientific surveys used to gauge public opinion, to predict the popular vote in those four presidential elections. Its polling methods were hailed widely as "amazingly right" and "uncannily accurate."[22] In 1936, however, its luck ran out. *Literary Digest* predicted that Republican Alfred M. Landon would beat incumbent President Franklin D. Roosevelt by a margin of 57 percent to 43 percent of the popular vote. Roosevelt, however, won in a landslide election, receiving 62.5 percent of the popular vote and carrying all but two states.

Literary Digest's 1936 straw poll had three fatal errors. First, its sample was drawn from telephone directories and lists of automobile owners. This technique oversampled the upper middle class and the wealthy, groups heavily Republican in political orientation. Moreover, in 1936, voting polarized along class lines. Thus, the oversampling of wealthy Republicans was particularly problematic because it severely underestimated the Democratic vote.

Literary Digest's second problem was timing. Questionnaires were mailed in early September. It did not measure the changes in public sentiment that occurred as the election drew closer.

Its third error occurred because of a problem we now call self-selection. Only highly motivated individuals sent back the cards—a mere 22 percent of those surveyed responded. Those who respond to mail surveys (or today, online surveys) are quite different from the general electorate; they often are wealthier and better educated and care more fervently about issues. *Literary Digest*, then, failed to observe one of the now well-known cardinal rules of survey sampling: "One cannot allow the respondents to select themselves into the sample."[23]

At least one pollster, however, correctly predicted the results of the 1936 election: George Gallup. Gallup had written his dissertation in psychology at the University of Iowa on how to measure the readership of newspapers. He then expanded his research to study public opinion about politics. He was so confident about his methods that he

straw polls
Unscientific surveys used to gauge public opinion on a variety of issues and policies.

gave all of his newspaper clients a money-back guarantee: if his poll predictions weren't closer to the actual election outcome than those of the highly acclaimed *Literary Digest,* he would refund their money. Although Gallup underpredicted Roosevelt's victory by nearly 7 percent, the fact that he got the winner right was what everyone remembered, especially given *Literary Digest*'s dramatic miscalculation.

Through the late 1940s, polling techniques became more sophisticated. The number of polling groups also dramatically increased, as businesses and politicians began to rely on polling information to market products and candidates. But, in 1948, the polling industry suffered a severe, although fleeting, setback when Gallup and many other pollsters incorrectly predicted that Thomas E. Dewey would defeat President Harry S Truman.

Nevertheless, as revealed in Figure 10.3, the Gallup Organization, now cochaired by George Gallup Jr., continues to predict the winners of the presidential popular vote successfully. In 2004, for example, Gallup predicted the winner while underpredicting George W. Bush's popular vote.

TRADITIONAL PUBLIC OPINION POLLS

Polling has several key phases, including: (1) determining the content and phrasing the questions; (2) selecting the sample; and, (3) contacting respondents.

FIGURE 10.3 THE SUCCESS OF THE GALLUP POLL IN PRESIDENTIAL ELECTIONS, 1936–2004
As seen here, Gallup's final predictions have been remarkably accurate. Furthermore, in each of the years where there is a significant discrepancy between Gallup's prediction and the election's outcome, there was a prominent third candidate. In 1948, Strom Thurmond ran on the Dixiecrat ticket; in 1980, John Anderson ran as the American Independent Party candidate; in 1992, Ross Perot ran as an independent.

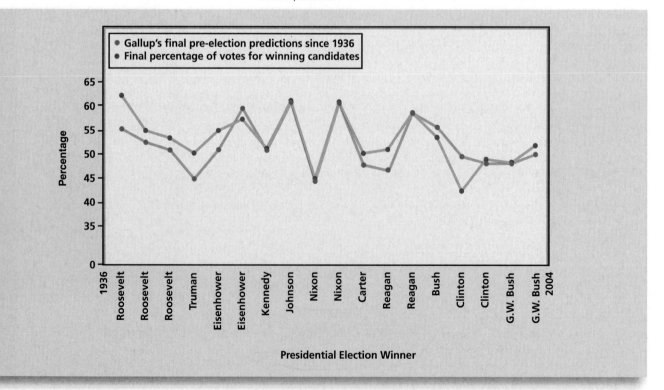

Source: Marty Baumann, "How One Polling Firm Stacks Up," *USA Today* (October 27, 1992): 13A. 1996 data from Mike Mokrzycki, "Pre-election Polls' Accuracy Varied," *Atlanta Journal and Constitution* (November 8, 1996): A12. 2000 data from Gallup Organization, "Poll Releases" (November 7, 2000). 2004 data from *USA Today* and CNN/Gallup Tracking Poll, USAtoday.com.

Determining the Content and Phrasing the Questions

Once a candidate, politician, or news organization decides to use a poll to measure the public's attitudes, special care has to be taken in constructing the questions to be asked. For example, if your professor asked you, "Do you think my grading procedures are fair?" rather than asking, "In general, how fair do you think the grading is in your American Politics course?" you might give a slightly different answer. The wording of the first question tends to put you on the spot and personalize the grading style; the second question is more neutral. Even more obvious differences appear in the real world of polling, especially when interested groups want a poll to yield particular results. Responses to highly emotional issues such as abortion, same-sex marriage, and affirmative action often are skewed depending on the wording of a particular question.

Selecting the Sample

Once the decision is made to take a poll, pollsters must determine the universe, or the entire group whose attitudes they wish to measure. This universe could be all Americans, all voters, all city residents, all Hispanics, or all Republicans. In a perfect world, each individual would be asked to give an opinion, but such comprehensive polling is not practical. Consequently, pollsters take a sample of the universe in which they are interested. One way to obtain this sample is by **random sampling.** This method of selection gives each potential voter or adult the same chance of being selected. In theory, this sounds good, but it is actually impossible to achieve because no one has lists of every person in any group. Thus, the method of poll taking is extremely important in determining the validity and reliability of the results.

Most national surveys and commercial polls use samples of 1,000 to 1,500 individuals and use a variation of the random sampling method called **stratified sampling.** Simple random, nonstratified samples are not very useful at predicting voting because they may undersample (or oversample) key populations that are not likely to vote. To avoid these problems, reputable polling organizations use stratified sampling (the most rigorous sampling technique) based on census data that provide the number of residences in an area and their location.

About twenty respondents from each primary sampling unit are picked to be interviewed. Generally four or five city blocks or areas are selected, and then four or five target families from each district are used. Large, sophisticated surveys such as the National Election Study and General Social Survey, which produce the data commonly used by political scientists, attempt to sample from lists of persons living in each household. The key to the success of the stratified sampling method is not to let people volunteer to be interviewed—volunteers as a group often have different opinions from those who do not volunteer.

Stratified sampling generally is not used by those who do surveys reported in the *New York Times* and *USA Today* or on network news programs. Instead, those organizations or pollsters working for them randomly place telephone calls to every tenth, hundredth, or thousandth person or household. If those individuals do not answer, they call the next person on the list.

Contacting Respondents

After selecting the methodology to conduct the poll, the next question is how to contact those to be surveyed. Television stations often ask people to call in, and some surveyors hit the streets. Telephone polls, however, are becoming the most frequently used mechanism by which to gauge the temper of the electorate.

The most common form of telephone polls are random-digit dialing surveys, in which a computer randomly selects telephone numbers to be dialed. Because it is estimated that as many as 95 percent of the American public have telephones in their homes, samples selected in this manner are likely to be fairly representative, although the increasing use of cell phones, especially among young adults, may eventually affect this.

Individual, in-person interviews are conducted by some groups, such as the University of Michigan for the National Election Study. Some analysts favor such in-per-

SIMULATION

You Are a Polling Consultant

random sampling
A method of poll selection that gives each person in a group the same chance of being selected.

stratified sampling
A variation of random sampling; census data are used to divide the country into four sampling regions. Sets of counties and standard metropolitan statistical areas are then randomly selected in proportion to the total national population.

■ This script provides the general format for a survey conducted by the Council for Marketing and Opinion Research. Note that even in a telephone survey drawn from a random sample, the respondent has the opportunity to self-select out of the sample.

Photo courtesy: CCouncil for Marketing and Opinion Research (CMOR)

Model Introduction

Hello, my name is _____ and I'm calling from (company). Today/Tonight we are calling to gather opinions regarding (general subject), and are not selling anything. This study will take approximately (length) and may be monitored (and recorded) for quality purposes. We would appreciate your time. May I include your opinions?

Closing

- At the conclusion of the survey, thank the respondent for his/her time.

- Express the desired intention that the respondent had a positive survey experience and will be willing to participate in future market research projects.

- Remind the respondent that his/her opinions do count.

MODEL CLOSING

Thank you for your time and cooperation. I hope this experience was a pleasant one and you will participate in other market research projects in the future. Please remember that your opinion counts! Have a good day/evening.

Alternative: Participate in collecting respondent satisfaction data to improve survey quality.

Thank you very much for taking part in this survey. Because consumers like you are such a valued part of what we do, I'd like you to think about the survey you just participated in. On a scale from 1 to 10 where ten means "it was a good use of my time", and one means "it was not a good use of my time", which number between 1 and 10 best describes how you feel about your experience today? That's all the questions I have. Please remember that your opinion counts! Have a good day/evening.

son surveys, but others argue that the unintended influence of the questioner or pollster is an important source of errors. How the pollster dresses, relates to the person being interviewed, and even asks the questions can affect responses. (Some of these factors, such as tone of voice or accent, can also affect the results of telephone surveys.)

POLITICAL POLLS

As polling has become increasingly sophisticated and networks, newspapers, and magazines compete with each other to report the most up-to-the-minute changes in public opinion on issues or politicians, new types of polls have been suggested and put into use. Each type of poll has contributed much to our knowledge of public opinion and its role in the political process. See Politics Now: Public Opinion and Political Capital for additional information on the uses of public opinion polls by politicians.

Push Polls All good polls for political candidates contain push questions. These questions produce information that helps campaigns judge their own strengths and weaknesses as well as those of their opponents.[24] They might, for example, ask if you would be more likely to vote for candidate X if you knew that candidate was a strong environmentalist. These kinds of questions are accepted as an essential part of any poll, but there are concerns as to where to draw the line. Questions that go over the line result in **push polls,** which are telephone polls with an ulterior motive. Push polls are designed to give respondents some negative or even untruthful information about a candidate's opponent in order to push them away from that candidate toward the one paying for the poll.

push polls
Polls taken for the purpose of providing information on an opponent that would lead respondents to vote against that candidate.

tracking polls
Continuous surveys that enable a campaign to chart its daily rise or fall in support.

Tracking Polls During the 2004 presidential elections, **tracking polls** were taken on a daily basis by some news organizations. These polls allow candidates to monitor short-term campaign developments and the effects of their campaign strategies.

Tracking polls involve small samples (usually of registered voters contacted at certain times of day) and are conducted every twenty-four hours. They usually are

FIGURE 10.4 A DAILY TRACKING POLL FOR THE 2004 PRESIDENTIAL ELECTION
The day-to-day fluctuations in presidential and congressional races are often shown through tracking polls. This figure shows the ups and downs of the 2004 presidential election.

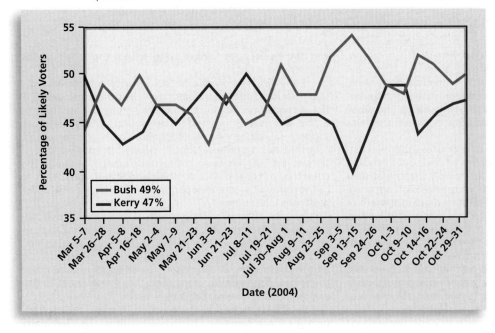

Source: USA Today and CNN/Gallup Poll results, http://www.usatoday.com/news/politicselections/nation/polls/usatodaypolls.htm.

combined statistically with some other data to produce a statistical average to boost the sample size and therefore the statistical reliability.[25] Even though such one-day surveys are fraught with reliability problems and are vulnerable to bias, many major news organizations continue their use. (See Figure 10.4.)

Exit Polls **Exit polls** are polls conducted at selected polling places on Election Day. Generally, large news organizations send pollsters to selected precincts to sample every tenth voter as he or she emerges from the polling place. The results of these polls are used to help the media predict the outcome of key races, often just a few minutes after the polls close in a particular state and generally before voters in other areas—sometimes in a later time zone—have cast their ballots. They also provide an independent assessment of why voters supported particular candidates.

In 1980, President Jimmy Carter's own polling and the results of network exit polls led him to concede defeat three hours before the polls closed on the West Coast. Many Democratic party officials and candidates criticized Carter and network predictions for harming their chances at victories, arguing that with the presidential election already called, voters were unlikely to go to the polls. In the aftermath of that controversy, all networks agreed not to predict the results of presidential contests until all polling places were closed. In 2000, exit polls led newscasters to inaccurately call Florida in the Gore column. In 2004, mid-afternoon exit poll results that were leaked on the Internet made many believe a Kerry victory was at hand. Whether Republicans voted later, Democrats were more willing to be polled, or for other reasons, the exit polls were wrong. Early reports on the 2006 midterm elections found the exit polls more reliable than in past years.

exit polls
Polls conducted at selected polling places on Election Day.

SHORTCOMINGS OF POLLING

The information derived from public opinion polls has become an extremely important part of governance. When the results of a poll are accurate, they express the feelings of

Politics Now

PUBLIC OPINION AND POLITICAL CAPITAL

In early 2006, much was made of President George W. Bush's declining approval ratings—a trajectory that is determined through a series of public opinion polls. And, while any person who has survived high school can understand the dilemmas that come with being unpopular, when you're the president of the United States, these problems are magnified exponentially.

For presidents and other public figures, approval ratings are often used as tacit measures of their political capital: their ability to enact public policy simply because of their name and their office. Presidents who have high approval ratings, as President Bush did in the immediate aftermath of September 11, are assumed to be more powerful leaders with a mandate for action that comes largely by virtue of the high levels of public support they enjoy. They are often able to use their clout to push controversial legislation, such as the USA Patriot Act or the No Child Left Behind Act, through Congress. A public appearance from a popular president can even deliver a hotly contested congressional seat or gubernatorial contest to the president's party.

In sharp contrast, presidents with low approval ratings are often crippled in the policy arena. Their low ratings can actually prevent favored policies from being enacted on Capitol Hill, even when their party controls the legislature, as many of their partisans locked in close elections shy away from being seen or affiliated with an unpopular president.

Because of the public opinion–political capital connection, President Bush's approval ratings, which hovered around 30 percent in July 2006, were a major concern for his advisers. Not only did the president hope to achieve significant legislative goals such as immigration reform, privatization of Social Security, and a constitutional amendment to ban same-marriage, but 2006 was a midterm election year

and the House and Senate were within the reach of the Democrats.

Early failures on the Social Security reform and the same-sex marriage amendment as well as the president's initial immigration bill were viewed by many as casualties of Bush's approval ratings and his newfound inability to secure support in Congress. As one Republican pollster commented, "[Bush] has no political capital. Slowly but surely it's been unraveling. There's been a direct correlation between the trajectory of his approval numbers and the—I don't want to call it disloyalty—the independence on the part of the Republicans in Congress."[a]

In spite of, or perhaps because of, these legislative failures, the president and vice president's fund-raising appearances for the Republican Party quickly eclipsed anything they had done during the 2002 midterm elections. Six months before the 2006 midterm elections, Bush had made thirty-two fund-raising stops, and Vice President Dick Cheney had made a remarkable sixty-two.[b]

By the week before the election, President Bush's approval ratings remained below 40 percent. This led many Republican candidates in close elections to ask President Bush not to campaign in their districts. The Republican National Committee sent First Lady Laura Bush and more moderate Republicans such as Rep. John McCain (R–AZ) to rally supporters. Other Republicans in close elections chose to downplay their affiliation with the president and his policies, choosing instead to tout their records of bipartisan support and cooperation with former President Bill Clinton.

[a]Quoted in Peter Baker, "In an Election Year, GOP Wary of Following Bush," Washington Post (March 10, 2006): A6.

[b]Peter Baker and Jim Vanderhei, "Elections are Crux of GOP's Strategy," Washington Post (May 22, 2006): A1.

the electorate in unique way and help guide the creation of public policy. However, when the results of a poll are inaccurate, disastrous consequences often result.

Sampling Error The accuracy of any poll depends on the quality of the sample that was drawn. Small samples, if properly drawn, can be very accurate if each unit in the universe has an equal opportunity to be sampled. If a pollster, for example, fails to sample certain populations, his or her results may reflect that shortcoming. Often the opinions of the poor and homeless are underrepresented because insufficient attention is given to making certain that these groups are sampled representatively. For example, in the case of tracking polls, if you choose to sample only on weekends or from 5 p.m. to 9 p.m., you may get more Republicans, who tend to have higher incomes and are less likely to be working shift work or multiple jobs. There comes a point in sampling, however, where increases in the size of the sample have little effect on a reduction of the **sampling error** (also called **margin of error**), the difference between the actual universe and the sample.

All polls contain errors. Standard samples of approximately 1,000 to 1,500 individuals provide fairly good estimates of actual behavior (in the case of voting, for

sampling error or margin of error
A measure of the accuracy of a public opinion poll.

example). Typically, the margin of error in a sample of 1,500 will be about 3 percent. If you ask 1,500 people "Do you like ice cream?" and 52 percent say yes and 48 percent say no, the results are too close to tell whether more people like ice cream than not. Why? Because the margin of error implies that somewhere between 55 percent (52 + 3) and 49 percent (52 − 3) of the people like ice cream, while between 51 percent (48 + 3) and 45 percent (48 − 3) do not. The margin of error in a close election makes predictions very difficult.

Limited Respondent Options Polls can be inaccurate when they limit responses. If you are asked, "How do you like this class?" and are given only like or dislike options, your full sentiments may not be tapped if you like the class very much or feel only so-so about it.

Lack of Information Public opinion polls may also be inaccurate when they attempt to gauge attitudes about issues that some or even many individuals do not care about or about which the public has little information. Most academic public opinion research organizations, such as the National Election Study, use some kind of filter question that first asks respondents whether or not they have thought about the question. These screening procedures generally allow surveyors to exclude as many as 20 percent of their respondents, especially on complex issues like the federal budget. Questions on more personal issues such as moral values, drugs, crime, race, and women's role in society get far fewer no opinion or don't know responses.

Difficulty Measuring Intensity Another shortcoming of polls concerns their inability to measure intensity of feeling about particular issues. Whereas a respondent might answer affirmatively to any question, it is likely that his or her feelings about issues such as abortion, the death penalty, or the war in Iraq are much more intense than are his or her feelings about the Electoral College or types of voting machines.

Why We Form and Express Political Opinions

OFTEN, THE SENTIMENTS we express in public opinion polls can be traced to our political socialization. However, most people are also influenced by a number of other factors, including: (1) personal benefits; (2) political knowledge; (3) cues from various leaders or opinion makers; and (4) their political ideology.

PERSONAL BENEFITS

Most polls reveal that Americans are growing more and more "I" centered. This perspective often leads people to agree with policies that will benefit them personally. You've probably heard the adage "People vote with their pocketbooks." Taxpayers generally favor lower taxes, hence the popularity of candidates pledging "No new taxes." An elderly person is likely to support Social Security increases, while a young worker worried about the continued stability of the Social Security program is not likely to be very supportive of federal retirement programs. An African American is likely to support affirmative action programs, while many whites argue that such programs are reverse discrimination.

Some government policies, however, don't really affect us individually. Legalized prostitution and the death penalty, for example, are often perceived as moral issues that directly affect few citizens. Individuals' attitudes on these issues often are based on underlying values they have acquired through the years.

When we are faced with policies that don't affect us personally and don't involve moral issues, we often have difficulty forming an opinion. Foreign policy is an area in which this phenomenon is especially true. Most Americans often know little of the world around them. Unless moral issues such as prisoner abuse in Iraq are involved, American public opinion is likely to be volatile in the wake of any new information.

POLITICAL KNOWLEDGE

Political knowledge and political participation have a reciprocal effect on one another—an increase in one will increase the other. Knowledge about the political system is essential to successful political involvement, which, in turn, teaches citizens about politics and increases their interest in public affairs.[26] And, according to Walter Lippmann, although few citizens know everything about all of the candidates and issues in a particular election, they often know enough to impose their views and values as to the general direction the nation should take.[27]

This is true despite the fact that most Americans' level of knowledge about history and politics is quite low. A 2002 Department of Education report, for example, found that most high school seniors had a poor grasp of history and that levels of knowledge haven't changed in nearly a decade.[28] Fifty-two percent didn't know that Russia was an ally of the United States in World War II, and 63 percent didn't know that President Richard M. Nixon opened diplomatic relations with China. According to the Department of Education, today's college graduates have less civic knowledge than high school graduates did fifty years ago.[29]

CUES FROM LEADERS

As early as 1966, noted political scientist V. O. Key Jr. argued in *The Responsible Electorate* that voters "are not fools."[30] Still, low levels of knowledge can lead to rapid opinion shifts on issues. The ebb and flow of popular opinion can be affected dramatically (some cynics might say manipulated) by political leaders. Given the visibility of political leaders and their access to the media, it is easy to see the important role they play in influencing public opinion. Political leaders, members of the news media, and a host of other experts have regular opportunities to influence public opinion because of the lack of deep conviction with which most Americans hold many of their political beliefs.[31]

The president, especially, is often in a position to mold public opinion through effective use of the bully pulpit, as discussed in chapter 7.[32] Political scientist John E. Mueller concludes, in fact, that there is a group of citizens—called followers—who are inclined to rally to the support of the president no matter what he does.[33]

POLITICAL IDEOLOGY

political ideology
The coherent set of values and beliefs about the purpose and scope of government held by groups and individuals.

As discussed in chapter 1, an individual's coherent set of values and beliefs about the purpose and scope of government is called his or her **political ideology.** Americans' attachment to strong ideological positions has varied over time. In sharp contrast to spur-of-the-moment responses, these sets of values, which are often greatly affected by political socialization, can prompt citizens to favor a certain set of policy programs and adopt views about the proper role of government in the policy process.

Conservatives generally are likely to support smaller, less activist governments, limited social welfare programs, and reduced government regulation of business. They also may have very strong views on social issues, including abortion and same-sex marriage. In contrast, liberals generally believe that the national government has an important role to play in a wide array of areas, including helping the poor and the disadvantaged. Unlike most conservatives, they generally favor activist governments. Most Americans however, identify themselves as moderates.

VIDEO
ROUNDTABLE
**Political
Knowledge**

VIDEO
ROUNDTABLE
**Public Opinion
and Leadership**

PARTICIPATION
**Are You a Liberal
or a
Conservative?**

The Evolution of News Media in the United States

THE MASS MEDIA—the entire array of organizations through which information is collected and disseminated to the general public—form a colossal enterprise in the United States. The mass media include the production and distribution of movies, television, radio, and Web-based material. Collectively, the mass media make use of broadcast, cable, and satellite technologies to distribute information, which reaches every corner of the United States. The mass media have become a powerful tool for both entertaining and informing the public. They serve as a reflection of American society but also as the primary lens through which citizens view American culture and American politics. The **news media,** which are one component of the larger mass media, provide the public with new information about subjects of public interest and play a vital role in the political process.[34]

PRINT MEDIA

The first example of news media in America came in the form of newspapers, which were published in the colonies as early as 1690. The number of newspapers grew throughout the 1700s, as colonists began to realize the value of a press free from government oversight and censorship. The battle between Federalists and Anti-Federalists over ratification of the Constitution, discussed in chapter 2, played out in various partisan newspapers in the late eighteenth century. Thus, it was not surprising that one of the Anti-Federalists' demands was to include an amendment guaranteeing the freedom of the press in the Constitution's final version. (See The Living Constitution: Freedom of the Press.)

The partisan press eventually gave way to what was called the penny press. In 1833, Benjamin Day founded the *New York Sun,* which cost a penny at the newsstand. Beyond its low price, the *Sun* sought to expand its audience by freeing itself from the grip of a single party. Inexpensive and politically independent, the *Sun* was the forerunner of modern newspapers, which rely on mass circulation and commercial advertising to produce profit. By 1861, the penny press had so supplanted partisan papers that President Abraham Lincoln announced that his administration would have no favored or sponsored newspaper.

Although print media were becoming less partisan, they were not necessarily becoming more respectable. Mass-circulation dailies sought wide readership, attracting readers with the sensational and the scandalous. The sordid side of politics became the entertainment of the times. One of the best-known examples occurred in the presidential campaign of 1884, when the *Buffalo Evening Telegraph* headlined "A Terrible Tale" about Grover Cleveland, the Democratic nominee.[35] In 1871, while sheriff of Buffalo, Cleveland allegedly had fathered a child. Even though paternity was indeterminate because the child's mother had been seeing other men, Cleveland had accepted responsibility, since all the other men were married, and he had dutifully paid child support for years. The strict Victorian moral code that dominated American values at the time made the story even more shocking than it would be today. Fortunately for Cleveland, another newspaper, the *Democratic Sentinel,* broke a story that helped to offset this scandal: Republican presidential nominee James G. Blaine and his wife had had their first child just three months after their wedding.

In the late 1800s and early 1900s, prominent publishers such as William Randolph Hearst and Joseph Pulitzer expanded the reach of newspapers in their control by practicing what became known as **yellow journalism**—sensationalized reporting that lowered journalistic standards to increase readership. Hearst's and Pulitzer's newspapers featured pictures and comics printed in color and sensationalized news

mass media
The entire array of organizations through which information is collected and disseminated to the general public.

news media
Media providing the public with new information about subjects of public interest.

Three Hundred Years of American Mass Media

yellow journalism
A form of newspaper publishing en vogue in the late nineteenth century that featured pictures, comics, color, and sensationalized, oversimplified news coverage.

The Living Constitution

Congress shall make no law respecting an establishment of religion, or prohibiting the free exercise thereof; or abridging the freedom of speech, or of the press; or the right of the people peaceably to assemble, and to petition the government for a redress of grievances.

—FIRST AMENDMENT

The Framers knew that no democracy is easy, that a republic requires a continuous battle for rights and responsibilities. One of those rights is the freedom of the press, preserved in the First Amendment to the Constitution. To protect the press, the Framers were wise enough to keep the constitutional language simple. Their view of the press, and its required freedom, was almost certainly less broad than we conceive of the press today.

It is difficult today to appreciate what a leap of faith it was for the Framers to grant freedom of the press when James Madison brought the Bill of Rights before Congress. Newspapers largely were run by disreputable people, since at the time editors and reporters were judged as merely purveyors of rumor and scandal, the reason Madison, as well as Alexander Hamilton and John Jay, published their newspaper articles advocating the ratification of the Constitution, *The Federalist Papers,* under the pseudonym "Publius."

The printed word was one of the few mediums of political communication in the young nation—it was critical for keeping Americans informed about issues. Therefore, the Framers had to hope that giving freedom for the press to print all content, although certain to give rise to tabloids, would also produce high-quality newspapers. Nevertheless, we should note that the Framers were not above using journalism as a way of promoting their political agendas. For example, Thomas Jefferson created a newspaper, the *National Gazette,* to report news favoring his Democratic-Republican Party. Giving the press freedom was also giving opposing politicians an open forum to attack each other.

Not much has changed since the Framers instituted the free press. We still have tabloids and partisan publications in which politicians attack each other, and we still rely on the press to give us important political information with which we make voting decisions. The First Amendment declares the priority of free expression. The Framers recognized that all kinds of information would have to be allowed in order to create as many opportunities for solid information to be reported, the fear being that regulations in response to what offends some people might be the first step on the slippery slope to censorship. In other words, protecting the *New York Times* and the *Wall Street Journal* means protecting the "paparazzi" or else we will have neither. Although the vices and virtues of a free press have not changed, the number of media has. But, the simple yet powerful protection the Framers created in the First Amendment made their invention and implementation merely a continuation of a freedom we all enjoy.

stories designed to increase their readership and to capture a share of the burgeoning immigrant population market.

The Progressive movement, discussed in chapter 5, gave rise to a new type of journalism in the early 1920s. **Muckraking** journalists—so named by President Theodore Roosevelt after a special rake designed to collect manure—were devoted to exposing misconduct by government, business, and individual politicians.[36] For Roosevelt, muckraking was a derogatory term used to describe reporters who focused on the carnal underbelly of politics rather than its more lofty pursuits. Nevertheless, much good came from these efforts. Muckrakers stimulated demands for anti-trust regulations—laws that prohibit companies, such as large steel companies, from controlling an entire industry—and exposed deplorable working conditions in factories, as well as outright exploitation of workers by business owners. An unfortunate side effect of this emphasis on crusades and investigations, however, was the frequent publication of gossip and rumor without sufficient proof.

As the news business grew, its focus increasingly shifted to maintaining and increasing its profitability. Newspapers became more careful in their reporting to avoid alienating the advertisers and readers who produced their revenues, and reporting became less harsh and more objective.

muckraking
A form of journalism, en vogue in the early twentieth century, concerned with reforming government and business conduct.

RADIO NEWS

The advent of radio in the early part of the twentieth century was a media revolution and a revelation to the average American who rarely, if ever, had heard the voice of a president, governor, or senator. The radio became the center of most homes in the evening, when national networks broadcast the news as well as entertainment shows. Calvin Coolidge was the first president to conduct radio broadcasts on a regular basis, but President Franklin D. Roosevelt made the radio appearance a must-listen by presenting "fireside chats" to promote his New Deal, to allay the fears of some citizens that his program was too radical, and to calm Americans as the country entered World War II. Roosevelt's soothing voice made it difficult for most Americans to believe that what the president wanted could be anything other than what was best for America.

News radio, which began to take a back seat to television by the mid-1950s, regained popularity with the development of AM talk radio in the mid-1980s. Controversial radio host Rush Limbaugh began the trend with his unabashed conservative views, opening the door for other conservative commentators such as Laura Ingraham, Sean Hannity, and Michael Reagan, son of the former president. Statistics show that conservative radio hosts have resurrected the radio as a news medium by giving the information that they broadcast a strong ideological bent. In 1997, 12 percent of Americans reported getting their news from talk radio; by 2004, 17 percent did.[37] As AM radio has grown in popularity, liberal groups have attempted to break into the AM market, but to date liberal programming, such as Air America, which was established in 2004 but filed for bankruptcy in 2006, has had limited success. The impact of fee-based satellite radio services on news radio remains to be seen. Sirius Satellite Radio, for example, offers both a conservative and a liberal political talk channel and received significant publicity when radio personality Howard Stern moved his show to Sirius's network in early 2006.

TELEVISION NEWS

Television was first demonstrated in the United States at the 1939 World's Fair in New York, but it did not take off as a news source until after World War II. Although television had expanded into most homes by the early 1960s, it would take several years for television to replace print and radio as the nation's chief news provider. In 1963, two major networks provided thirty minutes of news coverage while the rest provided only fifteen minutes of news per day. During this period, a substantial -

FIGURE 10.5 DISTRIBUTION OF NEWS SOURCE USAGE BY INDIVIDUALS
While the dominant, mainstream media outlets are still used by the greatest number of consumers, growth areas include ethnic, alternative, and online media.

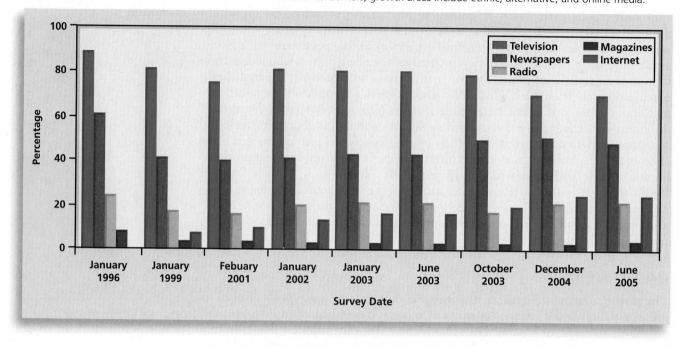

Source: Pew Research Center for the People and the Press, "Strong Opposition to Media Cross-Ownership Emerges: Public Wants Neutrality and Pro-American Point of View," http://www.stateofthenewsmedia.org.

majority of Americans still received most of their news from newspapers, but in 2005, 74 percent of Americans claimed to get their news from television, whereas only 44 percent read newspapers (see Figure 10.5).

There is, however, an important distinction between network and cable news stations. Network news has lost viewers since 1980, with the loss becoming even steeper after the advent of cable news. Between 2000 and 2004, viewership for all network news programming declined from 45 percent to 35 percent.[38] Cable news has seen an increase in viewership, from 34 percent in 2000 to 38 percent in 2004. This uptick is due in large part to the increased availability of services providing twenty-four-hour news channels. By 2006, 58 percent of all U.S. households subscribed to a cable service and 29 percent of households were using a direct broadcast satellite (such as DirectTV or DISH).[39] Thus, the vast majority of Americans receive cable news in addition to their broadcast stations.

Cable and satellite providers also give consumers access to a less glitzy and more unfiltered source of news with C-SPAN, a cable channel that offers gavel-to-gavel coverage of congressional proceedings, as well as major public affairs events. C-SPAN (along with affiliated channels C-SPAN2 and C-SPAN3) benefits from having no sponsors distracting (with commercials or banners) or possibly affecting what it broadcasts. Because the content of C-SPAN can be erudite, technical, and sometimes downright tedious (such as the fixed camera shot of the Senate during a roll-call vote), audiences tend to be very small, but they are very loyal and give C-SPAN its place as a truly content-driven media source.

The latest development in television news is the growth in popularity of comedy news programs. *Saturday Night Live* and other late-night comedy programs such as those hosted by Jay Leno and David Letterman have mocked politicians and the news for years. More recent programs such as Jon Stewart's *The Daily Show* and Stephen Colbert's *Colbert Report*—a satire of FOX News's *The O'Reilly Factor*—are dedicated entirely to poking fun at world leaders and current events. One 2004 study conducted by the Annenberg Public Policy Center of the University of Pennsylvania revealed

VIDEO
ROUNDTABLE
**Soft News vs.
Hard News**

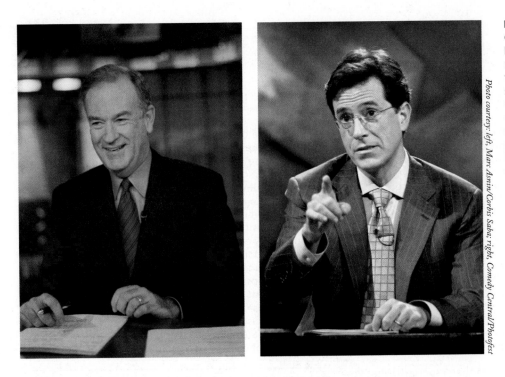

Photo courtesy: left, Marc Asnin/Corbis Saba; right, Comedy Central/Photofest

■ Bill O'Reilly, host of the FOX News Channel's *The O'Reilly Factor,* seen here at left, is one of the country's most visible conservative commentators. O'Reilly received some unforeseen competition from Comedy Central with the launch of Stephen Colbert's *Colbert Report*—a spin-off of *The Daily Show*—that lampoons O'Reilly's conservative views and blustering approach to commenting on the news.

comedy programs actually inform viewers as well as entertain them.[40] Regular viewers of *The Daily Show* were found to know more about world events than nonviewers, even when education, party identification, watching cable news, and other factors were taken into consideration.

THE NEW MEDIA

Increasingly, media consumers, especially those under the age of thirty-five, are abandoning traditional media outlets in favor of other sources (see Table 10.2). While ca-

TABLE 10.2 **THE NEWS GENERATION GAP**				
	Age 18–29 %	30–49 %	50–64 %	65+ %
Did yesterday				
Watched TV news	40	52	62	73
Local TV news	28	41	49	52
Nightly network news	17	25	38	46
Cable TV news	16	23	30	35
Morning news	11	16	21	27
Read a newspaper	26	37	52	59
Listened to radio news	34	49	42	29
No news	33	19	15	12
Watch/listen/read regularly				
Local TV news	46	54	64	69
Cable TV news	23	31	42	38
Nightly network news	19	23	45	53
Network TV magazines	15	22	30	33
Morning network news	16	22	23	31
Call-in radio shows	16	19	20	10
National Public Radio	14	18	15	11
Time/Newsweek/US News	12	13	15	13
Online news 3 + times/week	7	31	30	24

Source: Pew Research Center for the People and the Press, "Public's Habits Little Changed by September 11," June 9, 2002, http://people-press.org.

On Campus

WHERE DO COLLEGE STUDENTS GET THEIR CAMPAIGN NEWS?

In January 2004, the Pew Research Center for the People and the Press stated in a press release that Americans increasingly believed there is partisan bias in cable news.[a] Also buried in the release was the report that young voters (age eighteen to twenty-nine) increasingly rely on two sources for campaign news: the Internet and comedy television shows, such as *The Daily Show* and *Saturday Night Live*. Twenty-one percent of young voters, 16 percent of voters age thirty to forty-nine, and 7 percent of voters age fifty or older use the Internet for campaign news; 21 percent of young voters use comedy television shows, much higher than the 6 percent of those between thirty and forty-nine and 3 percent of those fifty or older. The fact that young voters might make voting decisions based on a quip from Steven Colbert or Seth Meyers's impression of John Kerry upset many in the media, generating a flurry of articles. One journalist called the age bracket "the Young and the Newsless."[b]

But there is more to the data than reported. What Pew actually revealed was that where voters get their news affects how well informed they are. For voters of all ages, if the regular source of 2004 campaign news was a television comedy show, they were very badly informed about the campaign. For voters using new Internet Web sites as their

regular source of campaign news, knowledge of the campaign was actually higher than average. Pew raises the issue of age because young voters use both comedy shows and the Internet more frequently than any other age demographic, a finding indicating that well-informed young voters gravitate to newer technologies for learning about politics. At the same time, while comedy viewers may claim to get their news from sketches and satire, it is clear that the content is only entertaining and not informing them.

So when Jon Stewart reminds the audience, as he often does, that he anchors a fake news show, the audience will listen and perhaps, after the "Moment of Zen" segment, check the headlines at a major news Web site or even pick up a local newspaper. After all, when told that *The Daily Show* could be confused with an old form of satire or a new kind of journalism, Stewart said, "Well, then, that either speaks to the sad state of comedy or the sad state of the news."[c]

[a]Pew Research Center for the People and the Press, "Cable and Internet Loom Large in Fragmented Political News Universe: Perceptions of Partisan Bias Seen as Growing, Especially by Democrats," January 11, 2004, http://www.pewinternet.org.

[b]Melanie McFarland, "Young People Turning Comedy Shows into Serious News Source," *Seattle Post-Intelligencer,* January 22, 2004, http://seattlepi.nwsource.com.

[c]Jon Stewart interview by Bill Moyers, *NOW,* July 11, 2003, http://www.pbs.org.

ble news networks are still the most regularly viewed, the Internet is gaining ground.[41] The Internet, which began as a Department of Defense project named Advanced Research Projects Agency Network (ARPANET) in the late 1960s, has grown into an unprecedented source of public information for people in all parts of the world. In 2000, 9 percent of Americans claimed to receive news from the Internet, whereas 24 percent did in 2005.[42] Of course, few people rely exclusively on the Internet for news, although it is likely in the future that many citizens will use the video components of the World Wide Web to substitute for television news watching or newspaper reading. Already, all major networks and most newspapers offer their news online. Major cable news stations, such as CNN, MSNBC, and FOX News, each have their own Web sites that are also used to promote their television programming as well as provide up-to-date news. The *New York Times* and *Washington Post* are available online for free to users who register. Access to older articles (and, in the case of the *Times,* op-ed pieces) requires a fee. Political magazines such as the conservative *National Review* and liberal *Nation* provide all online content free of charge; like the online newspapers, they earn revenue from advertising through pop-up and banner ads. (See On Campus: Where Do College Students Get Their Campaign News?)

In an attempt to assert an online presence, the U.S. government provides its own news, frequently publishing its press releases on Web sites it has set up for its major departments, as well as for both houses of Congress and the president. These Web sites offer basic information regarding the history, function, and current issues before the respective bodies. Web users who access the Senate or House site can enter their zip code to find out the identity of their elected representatives. Users can also access the complete voting record of individual members of Congress on the Senate and

House sites and use the contact information found there to contact any representative or senator.

The Internet also offers access to foreign news media previously unavailable to most Americans. The British Broadcasting Channel (BBC) has a Web site entirely devoted to news and available in over forty languages. International newspapers offer online content, although usually in their native languages. Al-Jazeera, a major Arabic television news source, has an English-language Web site providing news concerning the Middle East. (See Global Perspective: Al-Jazeera: The CNN of the Arab World?) Investigating alternative news sources like these allow individuals to gain a more nuanced and informed understanding of global issues.

Comparing News Media

CURRENT MEDIA TRENDS

The editors of the first partisan newspapers scarcely could have imagined what their profession would become more than two centuries later. Today, there are many thousands of daily and weekly newspapers, magazines, newsletters, and journals. Broadcast media encompass radio and television stations as well as satellite and cable media sources. The new media use the Internet and the latest technologies to blur the lines between all other forms of media and to create new opportunities for the dissemination of news. Several of the current trends are discussed below.

You Are the News Editor

The Influence of Media Giants Every newspaper, radio station, television station, and Web site is influential in its own area, and a handful of media outlets are influential nationally. The *New York Times, Wall Street Journal, USA Today,* and *Christian Science Monitor* are distributed nationally, and newspapers such as the *Washington Post* and *Los Angeles Times* also have substantial influence from coast to coast. These six newspapers have a pronounced effect on what the five major national **networks** (ABC, CBS, NBC, CNN, and FOX) broadcast on their evening news programs—or, in the case of cable news (MSNBC, CNBC, CNN, and FOX News), air on cable around the clock. In turn, these media giants influence regional and local media outlets. A major story that breaks in one of the major papers is nearly guaranteed to be featured on one or more of the network news shows and be discussed around the globe. The news shows are carried by hundreds of local stations—called **affiliates**—that are associated with the national networks and may choose to carry their programming. **Wire services** such as the Associated Press (AP), Reuters, and United Press International (UPI) distribute news around the globe. Most newspapers subscribe to at least one of these services, which not only produce their own news stories but also put on the wire major stories produced by other media outlets.

network
An association of broadcast stations (radio or television) that share programming through a financial arrangement.

affiliates
Local television stations that carry the programming of a national network.

wire service
An electronic delivery of news gathered by the news service's correspondents and sent to all member news media organizations.

Media Consolidation The news media in the United States are a multibillion-dollar for-profit business driven by the bottom line. Like all free-market enterprises, the pressure in privately owned media increasingly is to consolidate media ownership, so as to reap the benefits that come from larger market shares and fewer large-scale competitors.

Unlike traditional industries, where the primary concern associated with consolidation is the manipulation of prices made possible by monopolies or near monopolies, the consolidation of the media poses a far greater potential risk. Should the news media become dominated by a few mega corporations, the fear is that these groups could limit the flow of information and the free flow of ideas that comprise the very essence of a free society and that make democracy possible.

INCREASING USE OF EXPERTS

Most journalists know a little bit about many subjects but do not specialize in any one area and certainly do not possess enough knowledge to fill the hours of airtime made possible by cable's twenty-four-hour news cycle. Therefore, especially on cable stations, the news media like to employ expert consultants from a number of different disciplines

Global Perspective

AL-JAZEERA: THE CNN OF THE ARAB WORLD?

Few Americans other than those of Arabic descent had heard of al-Jazeera before October 7, 2001. On that day, less than one month following the 9/11 terrorist attacks on the World Trade Center and the Pentagon, Osama bin Laden spoke to the world for six and one-half minutes via a tape shown on al-Jazeera's television network. It was not the first time al-Jazeera carried bin Laden's image or his words, nor would it be the last. In June 1999 it broadcast a ninety-minute interview with him, and several bin Laden tapes have been aired since then. Some critics have taken these interviews, as well as the airing of graphic videos showing the execution of Western prisoners by al-Qaeda operatives in Iraq, as evidence that al-Jazeera is little more than a mouthpiece for al-Qaeda's anti-American propaganda, or at least an accomplice, but the answer is undoubtedly more complicated.

Al-Jazeera (which means "the island" or "the peninsula" in Arabic), is an independent station that broadcasts from the tiny, oil-rich, Islamic country of Qatar in the Persian Gulf. Qatar is a member of the Organization of Petroleum Exporting Countries (OPEC) and is ruled by a progressive emir (prince) who is pro-Western. The emir allowed American troops to use Qatar as a staging point for the 1991 Persian Gulf War and the invasion of Iraq. He funded al-Jazeera when it was founded in 1996. Al-Jazeera emerged out of the failure of a British Broadcasting Corporation (BBC) news service, after a Saudi Arabian–owned radio and television network reportedly terminated its financial support because the news service had aired a documentary about executions in Saudi Arabia.

Al-Jazeera immediately set a course that separated it from its competitors in the region. Most of them were owned either by Middle Eastern governments or by powerful individuals within those countries, and their standard offerings emphasized entertainment and limited news that amounted to state propaganda. A typical newscast would do little more than follow the morning-to-night public schedule of a leading official. Sensitive political and social issues were ignored for fear of the controversy they would create.

In contrast, the trail that al-Jazeera chose to follow was pioneered by Cable News Network (CNN). Like CNN, al-Jazeera focuses its political reporting on two staples. The first is on-the-scene coverage of conflicts or other world events. Just as CNN was the only television network to broadcast out of Baghdad in the Persian Gulf War,

al-Jazeera had a monopoly of live reporting from Kabul during the war in Afghanistan against the Taliban. Three Western news agencies, including CNN, also received permission from the Taliban government in 1999 to establish offices in Afghanistan, but only al-Jazeera did so. In 2001, al-Jazeera's office in Kabul was bombed by U.S. forces, as was the network's Baghdad office in 2003. In both cases, Pentagon officials insisted the bombings were accidents. Al-Jazeera also covers the Palestinian conflict extensively, receiving heavy criticism from the West for referring to Palestinians killed by Israeli forces as martyrs and showing extensive footage of Palestinian casualties.

A second programming staple is political talk shows that often feature call-ins from viewers. Among the most popular are *The Opposite Direction,* a live weekly two-hour show modeled after CNN's now defunct *Crossfire,* and *Without Frontiers,* in which an individual discusses a current topic in depth. Segments aired on these programs have often angered Middle Eastern governments where there is little tradition of a free press. Libya and Kuwait both threatened to recall their ambassadors to Qatar in protest over critical stories aired by al-Jazeera. Saudi Arabia did so and prohibited al-Jazeera from covering the annual pilgrimage to Mecca. The government of Algeria created a blackout in the capital city to prevent the airing of a story on its civil war. Saddam Hussein once criticized al-Jazeera's broadcasts as too "pro-American" and expelled two al-Jazeera reporters during the U.S.-led invasion of Iraq because of its coverage.

President George W. Bush, British Prime Minister Tony Blair, and U.S. government figures such as Colin Powell, Condoleezza Rice, and Donald Rumsfeld have all been interviewed by al-Jazeera. Osama bin Laden was interviewed after the 9/11 attacks, though the network decided against airing the interview when faced with strong criticism from U.S. officials. An interview with Israeli Prime Minster Ariel Sharon was cancelled because of criticism from Palestinian officials.

QUESTIONS

1. Spend some time looking at the English Web site of al-Jazeera (aljazeera.net). How does its coverage compare with that of American networks?
2. How do the sources quoted in al-Jazeera's articles differ from those quoted in U.S. news articles?

ranging from medical ethics to political campaigning. These experts, also referred to as pundits, or "talking heads," are hired to discuss the dominant issues of the day.

Scholars measuring the effects of televised experts have found that experts have a significant impact on shaping the views of Americans toward foreign policy. These scholars consider the findings concerning experts to be both good and bad for Americans. On the one hand, the "strong effects by commentators and experts are compatible with a picture of a public that engages in collective deliberation and takes expertise seriously." On the other hand, "one might argue that the potency of media commentators and of ostensibly nonpartisan TV 'experts' is disturbing. Who elected them to shape our views of the world? Who says they are insightful or even unbiased?"[43] The lesson is clear. Viewers and readers must rely on the networks and newspapers to choose experts wisely, and viewers must carefully examine the views expressed.

Narrowcasting In recent years, fierce competition to attract viewers and the availability of additional television channels made possible by cable and satellite television have led media outlets to move toward **narrowcasting**—targeting media programming at specific populations within society. Within the realm of cable news, the two ratings leaders, CNN and FOX News, have begun engaging in this form of niche journalism. The two stations divide audiences by ideology. FOX News emphasizes a conservative viewpoint and CNN increasingly stresses a more liberal perspective, although the FOX view is often more pronounced.[44]

narrowcasting
Targeting media programming at specific populations within society.

Technological Innovation Ironically, the same technology that has given rise to media giants also has the ability to increase the diversity of available news. **Blogs,** which have rapidly grown in popularity in recent years, are Web logs or journals that provide editorial and news outlets for citizens. They have become webs of information linking together people with common ideological or issue-specific interests. They also provide unprecedented access to events as they are unfolding. In some instances, information made public on blogs has been picked up by mainstream news outlets, revealing how the new media provide unprecedented opportunities for the flow of information.

blog
Web-based journal entries that provide an editorial and news outlet for citizens.

PARTICIPATION

Democracy and the Internet

While the future of the new media remains as unpredictable as the latest blog entry, it is likely that the new media will continue to blur the lines between print and broadcast, consumer and producer, commentary and fact, and entertainment and news. The distinction between the Internet and broadcast and cable news is likely to shrink as the technologies merge. Wireless handheld devices that allow users to send e-mail and text messages, make phone calls, browse the Internet, and download music and video clips are increasing in popularity. The growth of virtual social networks like MySpace and Facebook, as well as sites like YouTube that allow users to share videos, including campaign commercials and political commentary, are also affecting the ways in which Americans share and consume the news.

Rules Governing the Media

THE FIRST AMENDMENT to the U.S. Constitution, which prohibits Congress from abridging the freedom of the press, does not provide the media with unlimited print and broadcast freedom. A wide array of internal and external checks governs the behavior of the modern media.

JOURNALISTIC STANDARDS

The heaviest restrictions placed on reporters do not come from government regulations but from the industry's own professional norms and each journalist's level of integrity, as well as from the oversight provided by editors who are ultimately responsible for the accuracy of the news they produce. To help guide the ethical behavior of journalists, the Society of Professional Journalists publishes a detailed "Code of Ethics" for journalists that includes principles and standards governing issues such as avoiding conflicts of interest, dealing ethically with sources, and verifying the information being reported.

VIDEO DEBATE

Self-Censorship and the News

GOVERNMENT REGULATION OF THE ELECTRONIC MEDIA

The U.S. government regulates the electronic component of the media. Unlike radio or television, the print media are exempt from most forms of government regulation, although even print media must not violate community standards for obscenity, for instance. There are two reasons for this unequal treatment. First, the airwaves used by the electronic media are considered public property and are leased by the federal government to private broadcasters. Second, those airwaves are in limited supply; without some regulation, the nation's many radio and television stations would interfere with one another's frequency signals. It was not, in fact, the federal government but rather private broadcasters, frustrated by the numerous instances in which signal jamming occurred, that initiated the call for government regulation in the early days of the electronic media.

In 1996, Congress passed the sweeping Telecommunications Act, deregulating whole segments of the electronic media. The Telecommunications Act sought to provide an optimal balance of competing corporate interests, technological innovations, and consumer needs. The result of this deregulation was the sudden merger of previously distinct kinds of media in order to create a more "multimedia" approach to communicating information and entertainment. This gave us multimedia corporations such as Viacom, Time Warner and Comcast.

VIDEO DEBATE
Censorship and the FCC

In June 2003, the Federal Communications Commission (FCC) attempted to push through a series of reforms that would further deregulate the media by enabling media corporations to own more of different kinds of media in a given media market. Both Republicans and Democrats in Congress opposed the FCC changes, arguing that the country needs more and not less media diversification, given the increasing media outlet consolidation. Groups across the ideological spectrum also argued against media consolidation: conservative religious groups believe that large media corporations purvey immoral content, and liberal groups believe that less diversification kills community-based media. Finally, there was a general public outcry, with legislators receiving angry letters and e-mails demanding Congress stop the FCC action.[45] By July 2003, a huge bipartisan majority voted 400–21 to block the FCC policy changes. By December, Congress had passed an appropriations bill that raised the 35 percent cap on a national audience to 39 percent, a compromise that allowed the largest corporations to retain their current share—the largest corporation, Viacom, had 38.9 percent of the national audience—but prohibited any further expansion.[46]

CONTENT REGULATION

content regulation
Government attempts to regulate the substance of the mass media.

equal time rule
The rule that requires broadcast stations to sell airtime equally to all candidates in a political campaign if they choose to sell it to any.

The government also subjects the electronic media to substantial **content regulation** that, again, does not apply to the print media. Charged with ensuring that the airwaves "serve the public interest, convenience, and necessity," the FCC has attempted to promote equity in broadcasting. For example, the **equal time rule** requires that broadcast stations sell airtime equally to all candidates in a political campaign if they choose to sell it to any, which they are under no obligation to do. Political debates are exceptions to this rule. Stations may exclude less well-known and minor-party candidates from these events.

Until 2000, FCC rules required broadcasters to give candidates the opportunity to respond to personal attacks and to political endorsements by the station. In October 2000, however, a federal court of appeals found that these rules, long criticized by broadcasters as having a chilling effect on free speech, were unconstitutional.[47]

EFFORTS TO REGULATE MEDIA PRACTICES

In the United States, only government officials can be prosecuted for divulging classified information; no such law applies to journalists. Nor can the government, except under extremely rare and confined circumstances, impose prior restraints on the press—that is, the government cannot censor the press. This principle was clearly

American Values/American Voices

HOW MUCH FREEDOM SHOULD THE PRESS BE ALLOWED?

According to constitutional scholar Alexander Bickel in his analysis of the First Amendment's protections for the freedom of the press, "not everything is fit to print."[a] Bickel cautions against the press printing information that is inaccurate, indecent, or potentially dangerous to the national interest. What is the line to be drawn between national security and the freedom of the press? In 1943, Robert McCormick of the *Chicago Tribune*, a staunch political enemy of President Franklin D. Roosevelt, printed that the United States had broken secret Japanese military codes, thus potentially revealing to the enemy that the United States could read their secret communications. Under the Espionage Act of 1917, it was possible to prosecute journalists who endangered the defense of the country. When the Roosevelt administration decided against prosecuting the case so as not to draw more attention to the story, they helped to set a precedent against prosecuting journalists. In a democracy with strong protections for free speech and freedom of the press, there is an uneasy balance between the public's right to know and the government's interest in defending the country.

In 2006, the *New York Times* revealed that the Bush administration, in cooperation with a Belgian banking cooperative know as Swift, was secretly monitoring financial transactions. The *Times* had decided to print the article despite protests from the Bush administration. The administration reacted angrily to the story, stating that the *Times* had negatively affected the government's ability to fight terrorism. *Times* publisher Arthur Sulzberger Jr. defended the paper's decision to print the story based on the public's

right to know about the secret monitoring of financial transactions by the administration. *Times* executive editor Bill Keller and the editor of the *Los Angeles Times*, which also had printed the story, defended the decision to print the story in an editorial that ran in both papers, claiming they had the best interests of the country in mind and were doing their duty as journalists to let the public decide.[b] Quoting Justice Hugo Black's defense of the press's First Amendment rights in *New York Times Co.* v. *U.S.* (1971), they wrote, "The government's power to censor the press was abolished so that the press would remain forever free to censure the government. The press was protected so that it could bare the secrets of the government and inform the people."

The *Wall Street Journal* had also carried the story of the administration's monitoring. However, the *Journal*'s editorial board and other more right-leaning newspapers charged that the *Times* printed the story because of a political agenda against the Bush administration and its war on terrorism.[c] Meanwhile, the Bush administration wanted an investigation into who in the government had disclosed the information to the press. While there are no prosecutions pending in this case, the administration's reaction underlines the delicate balance that the press must consider as they make their daily decisions about what news is fit to print.

---

[a]Alexander Bickel, *The Morality of Consent* (New Haven, CT: Yale University Press, 1975).

[b]Dean Baquet and Bill Keller, "When Do We Publish a Secret?" *New York Times* (July 1, 2006).

[c]"Fit and Unfit to Print," *Wall Street Journal* (June 30, 2006).

---

established in *New York Times Co.* v. *U.S.* (1971). In this case, the Supreme Court ruled that the government could not prevent publication by the *New York Times* of the Pentagon Papers, classified government documents about the Vietnam War that had been stolen, photocopied, and sent to the *Times* and the *Washington Post* by Daniel Ellsberg, a government employee. "Only a free and unrestrained press can effectively expose deception in the government," Justice Hugo Black wrote in a concurring opinion for the Court. "To find that the President has 'inherent power' to halt the publication of news by resort to the courts would wipe out the First Amendment."[48]

Similar concerns arose in the United States during the 1991 Persian Gulf War. Reporters were upset that the military was not forthcoming about events on and off the battlefield, while some Pentagon officials and many persons in the general public accused the press of telling the enemy too much in their dispatches. The U.S. government attempted to isolate offending reporters by keeping them away from the battlefield. This maneuver was highly controversial and very unpopular with news correspondents because it directly interfered with their job of reporting the news.

Thus, during the 2003 invasion of Iraq, the Bush administration provided an interesting compromise to this dilemma when it gave journalists the opportunity to be embedded with various parts of the military and report about the experiences of each unit. Organizations such as the Project for Excellence in Journalism found that embedded journalists typically provided only anecdotal stories, lacked the overall context of the war, and stressed American successes without much coverage of Iraqi civilian casualties. While conceding these limitations, some scholars maintain that an embedded journalist is better than no journalist at all, especially since journalists of foreign news organizations, such as al-Jazeera, will cover the events from different perspectives.[49]

Whatever one's specific quarrel with the American press, most Americans would probably prefer that the media tell them too much rather than not enough. Totalitarian and authoritarian societies have a tame journalism, after all, so media excesses may be the price of popular sovereignty. (See American Values/American Voices: How Much Freedom Should the Press Be Allowed?)

How the Media Cover Politics

THE NEWS MEDIA focus an extraordinary amount of attention on our politicians and the day-to-day operations of our government. Since 1983, the number of print (newspaper and magazine) reporters accredited at the U.S. Capitol jumped from 2,300 to more than 4,100.[50] On the campaign trail, a similar phenomenon has occurred. Consequently, a politician's every public utterance is reported and intensively scrutinized and interpreted in the media. In this section, we will discuss media coverage of the political process and show how the tenor of this coverage has changed since the Watergate scandal of the early 1970s.

HOW THE PRESS AND PUBLIC FIGURES INTERACT

The type of communication between elected officials or public figures and the media may take different forms. A **press release** is a written document offering an official comment or position on an issue or news event; it is usually printed on paper and handed directly to reporters, or increasingly, released by e-mail or fax. A **press briefing** is a relatively restricted live engagement with the press, with the range of questions limited to one or two specific topics. In a press briefing, a press secretary or aide represents the elected official or public figure, who does not appear in person. In a full-blown **press conference,** an elected official appears in person to talk with the press at great length about an unrestricted range of topics. Press conferences provide a field on which reporters struggle to get the answers they need while public figures attempt to retain control of their message and spin the news and issues in ways favorable to them.

Politicians and media also interact in a variety of other ways. Politicians hire campaign consultants who use focus groups and polling in an attempt to gauge how to present the candidate to the media and to the public. Additionally, politicians can attempt to bypass the national news media through paid advertising and by appearing on talk shows and local news programs. (Some of these and other techniques for dealing with the media during a campaign are discussed in greater detail in chapter 12.) Politicians also use the media to attempt to retain a high level of name recognition and to build support for their ideological and policy ideas.

In the past, a reporter would think twice about filing a story critical of a politician's character, and the editors probably would have killed the story had the reporter been foolish enough to do so. The reason? Fear of a libel suit. (Recall from chapter 4 that libel is written defamation of character that unjustly injures a person's reputation.) The first question editors would ask about even an ambiguous or suggestive phrase about a public official was, "If we're sued, can you prove beyond a doubt what you've written?"

Such inhibitions were ostensibly lifted in 1964, when the Supreme Court ruled in *New York Times Co. v. Sullivan* that simply publishing a defamatory falsehood is not enough to justify a libel judgment.[51] Henceforth, a public official would have to prove

press release
A document offering an official comment or position.

press briefing
A relatively restricted session between a press secretary or aide and the press.

press conference
An unrestricted session between an elected official and the press.

VIDEO ROUNDTABLE

The Role of the Press

New York Times Co. v. Sullivan **(1964)**
The Supreme Court concluded that "actual malice" must be proved to support a finding of libel against a public figure.

"actual malice," a requirement extended three years later to all public figures, such as Hollywood stars and prominent athletes.[52] As discussed in chapter 4, the Supreme Court declared that the First Amendment requires elected officials and candidates to prove that the publisher either believed the challenged statement was false or at least entertained serious doubts about its truth and acted recklessly in publishing it in the face of those doubts. The actual malice rule has made it very difficult for public figures to win libel cases.

COVERING THE PRESIDENCY

The three branches of the U.S. government—the executive, legislative, and judicial—are roughly equal in power and authority, but in the world of media coverage the president is first among equals. All television cables lead to the White House, and a president can address the nation on all major networks almost at will.

Since Franklin D. Roosevelt's time, chief executives have used the office and presidential press conference as a bully pulpit to shape public opinion and explain their actions. The presence of the press in the White House enables a president to appear even on very short notice and to televise live, interrupting regular programming. The White House's press briefing room is a familiar sight on the evening news, not just because presidents use it fairly often, but also because the presidential press secretary has almost daily question-and-answer sessions there.

The post of press secretary to the president has existed only since Herbert Hoover's administration (1929–1933), and the individual holding it is the president's main disseminator of information to the press. For this vital position, some presidents choose close aides with whom they have worked previously and who are familiar with their thinking. Press secretaries must be very adept at dealing with the press; some worked as journalists prior to becoming a press secretary, and many go on to press jobs after their stint in the White House. For example, the first female press secretary, Dee Dee Myers, who served under President Bill Clinton, used her experience to launch a career in political punditry. Political journalist and FOX News contributor Tony Snow moved from the news media to the White House, becoming George W. Bush's third press secretary.

Photo courtesy Jim Young/Reuters/Landov

■ President George W. Bush chose former FOX News commentator Tony Snow as his third press secretary. Here, Snow fields questions in the White House press briefing room, which opened in 1970 on the former site of President Franklin D. Roosevelt's swimming pool. The briefing room was closed for extensive renovations in August of 2006. Given the traditionally testy relationship between presidential administrations and members of the press, some journalists reacted with suspicion to the renovation, worrying that they would be banned from the West Wing permanently.

While the president receives the vast majority of the press's attention, much of this focus is unfavorable. President Dwight D. Eisenhower once opened up a press conference by inviting the press to "nail him to the cross" as they usually did, and this approach suggests the way most presidents approach their formal encounters with the press. A study in the early 1990s found coverage of George Bush's handling of important national problems was almost solely negative.[53] Analysis of the coverage of Bill Clinton's turbulent presidency found a frenzy of negative media coverage immediately following the Monica Lewinsky scandal, followed by a longer period of more even-handed coverage.[54]

The media have faced a more difficult challenge in covering the administration of George W. Bush, a president who prides himself on the tight-lipped, no leaks nature of his White House. No member of his staff appears on television or in print without prior permission, while Bush himself held a record-low number of thirteen formal press conferences during his first term. The Bush communications team continues to keep the president's direct contact with the press to a minimum. The president's press conference the day after the 2006 midterm elections was only the eleventh of his second term. Compared to his father, who held sixty-four during his four years as president, Bush clearly has tried to control his image by controlling how much the press directly encounters him and by speaking at highly staged media events, quite often in military settings, where he delivers a scripted message and presents an interesting visual but answers no questions from the media.[55]

COVERING CONGRESS

With 535 voting members representing distinct geographic areas, Congress poses a challenge for the media. Nevertheless, the congressional press corps has more than 3,000 members.[56] Most news organizations solve the size and decentralization problems inherent in covering news developments in the legislative branch by concentrating coverage on three groups of individuals. First, the leaders of both parties in both houses receive the lion's share of attention because only they can speak for a majority of their party's members. Usually the majority and minority leaders in each house and the Speaker of the House are the preferred spokespersons, but the whips also receive a substantial share of airtime and column inches. Second, key committee chairs command center stage when subjects in their domain are newsworthy. Heads of the most prominent committees are guaranteed frequent coverage, but even the chairs and members of minor committees or subcommittees can achieve fame when the time and issue are right. Third, local newspapers and broadcast stations normally devote some resources to covering their local senators and representatives, even when these legislators are junior and relatively lacking in influence. Most office holders, in turn, are mainly concerned with meeting the needs of their local media contingents, since these reporters are the ones who directly and regularly reach the voters in their home constituencies.

As with coverage of the president, media coverage of Congress is disproportionately negative. Much media attention given to the House and Senate focuses on conflict among members. Some political scientists believe that such reporting is at least partially responsible for the public's negative perceptions of Congress.[57] As discussed earlier, coverage of Congress has been greatly expanded through cable channels C-SPAN, C-SPAN2, and C-SPAN3, which provide coverage of House and Senate sessions as well as many committee hearings. Americans can now watch their representatives in action without editing or interpretation.

One other area of congressional news coverage is worth noting: investigative committee hearings. Occasionally, a sensational scandal leads to televised congressional committee hearings that transfix and electrify the nation. In the early 1950s, Senator Joseph R. McCarthy (R–WI) held a series of hearings to root out what he claimed were Communists in the Department of State and other U.S. government agencies, as well as in Hollywood's film industry. The senator's style of investigation, which involved many wild charges made without proof and the smearing and labeling of opponents as Communists, gave rise to the term *McCarthyism*. In 2002, congressional committees investigated several high-profile corporate scandals. More recently, investigations addressed the abuse of detainees at the Abu Ghraib prison, the use of steroids in major league baseball, the government's response to Hurricane Katrina, and immigration. With the election of a Democratic Congress, the number and intensity of hearings is expected to rise.

COVERING THE SUPREME COURT

While the president and Congress interact with the media on a regular basis, the Supreme Court remains a virtual media vacuum. Despite persistent efforts by C-SPAN and other media outlets to gain access to the Court, television cameras have never been permitted to record Supreme Court proceedings. Citing the need to protect the public's perception of the Supreme Court as a nonpolitical and autonomous entity, the justices have given little evidence to suggest that they are eager to reverse their broadcast media ban. Instead, at the end of each term, they release written transcripts and audio recordings of the proceedings, which lack both the visuals and timeliness that could make them fodder for the modern press. Since 2000, however, reporters have been granted on a case-by-case basis the ability to make use of same-day audio recordings.

While print and broadcast reporters are granted access to the Court, even if their cameras are not, coverage of the Court remains severely limited when compared with coverage of the executive and legislative branches. There are less than a dozen full-time reporters covering the Supreme Court, and the amount of space dedicated to Court-related stories has continued to shrink. Court-related stories, involving complex legal issues, are simply not as easy to sell as graphic-intense stories related to Congress or the president.[58] Not surprisingly, Americans typically know less about the courts than any other branch of government.

The Media's Influence on the Public

THERE ARE MANY important questions concerning the media's influence on the public. For instance, how much influence do the media actually have on public opinion? Do the media have a discernible ideological bias, as some people suggest? Are people able to resist information that is inconsistent with their preexisting beliefs?

MEDIA EFFECTS

Some political scientists argue that the content of network television news accounts for a large portion of the volatility and change in policy preferences of Americans, when measured over relatively short periods of time.[59] These changes are called **media effects.** Let's examine how these media-influenced changes might occur.

First, reporting can sway people who are uncommitted and have no strong opinion in the first place. So, for example, the media have a greater influence on political independents than on strong partisans.[60] That said, the sort of politically unmotivated individual who is subject to media effects may not vote in a given election, and therefore the media influence tends to be of little particular consequence.

Second, it is likely that the media have a greater impact on topics far removed from the lives and experiences of their readers and viewers. News reports can probably

VISUAL LITERACY

Use of Media by the America Public

media effects
The influence of news sources on public opinion.

shape public opinion about events in foreign countries fairly easily. Yet, what the media say about domestic issues such as rising prices, neighborhood crime, or child rearing may have relatively little effect, because most citizens have personal experience of and well-formed ideas about these subjects.

Third, in a process often referred to as **agenda setting,** news organizations can help tell us what to think about, even if they cannot determine what we think. Indeed, the press often sets the agenda for a campaign or for government action by focusing on certain issues or concerns.

Fourth, the media influence public opinion through a subtle process referred to as **framing**—the process by which a news organization defines a political issue and consequently affects opinion about the issue. Finally, the media have the power to indirectly influence the way the public views politicians and government by emphasizing negative or positive aspects of issues important to voters.

MEDIA BIAS

Whenever the media break an unfavorable story about a politician, the politician usually counters with a cry of "biased reporting"—a claim that the press told an untruth, told only part of the truth, or reported facts out of context. Some research suggests that candidates may charge the media with bias as a strategy for dealing with the press, and that bias claims are part of the dynamic between elected officials and reporters. If a candidate can plausibly and loudly decry bias in the media as the source of his or her negative coverage, for example, reporters might temper future negative stories or give the candidate favorable coverage to mitigate the calls of bias.[61]

Are journalists biased? The answer is simple and unavoidable. Of course they are. Journalists, like all human beings, have values, preferences, and attitudes galore—some conscious, others subconscious—but all reflected at one time or another in the subjects selected for coverage or the portrayal of events or content communicated.

agenda setting
The process by which media coverage of key issues establishes national priorities.

framing
The process by which a news organization defines a political issue and consequently affects opinion about the issue.

PARTICIPATION
Are the Media Biased?

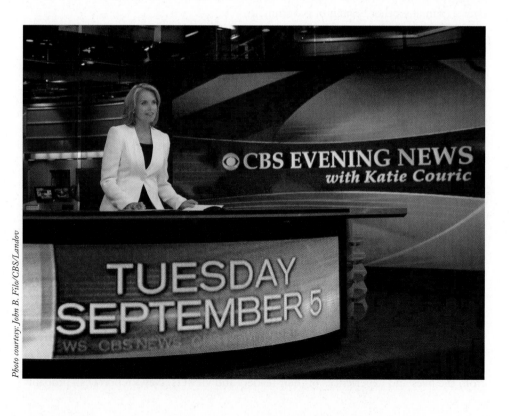

■ Celebrity journalist Katie Couric became anchor and managing editor of the CBS Evening News in September 2006.

Photo courtesy: John B. Filo/CBS/Landov

Given that the press is biased, in what ways is it biased and when and how are the biases shown?

For much of the 1980s and 1990s, the argument was that the media had a liberal bias because of the sheer number of journalists who leaned to the left. Studies in the 1980s showed that professional journalists were drawn heavily from the ranks of highly educated social and political liberals.[62] To this day, journalists are substantially Democratic in party affiliation and voting habits, progressive and anti-establishment in political orientation, and to the left of the general public on many economic, foreign policy, and social issues (such as abortion, affirmative action, gay rights, and gun control). Indeed, a 2004 survey revealed that, whereas 33 percent of the general public described themselves as being ideologically conservative, only 7 percent of those in the media did so.[63] Nevertheless, while many of the most influential reporters and executives who entered (or reentered) journalism after stints of partisan participation in campaigns or government worked for Democrats, an increasing number of them since 1994 have worked for Republicans..

Some scholars argue that corporate interests play a significant role in what journalists report and counter the liberal leanings of reporters.[64] Others argue that the deepest bias most political journalists have is the desire to get to the bottom of a good campaign story. Other human biases are also at work in reporting on politics. Whether the press likes or dislikes a candidate personally is often vital. So, too, is the increasing celebrity status of many people who report the news.

It seems, however, that much of the more recent media bias is intentional and a response to increasing fragmentation and competition among media. One-sided media, a type of narrowcasting, is gaining in popularity as networks intentionally market a one-sided message to secure a competitive edge in niche markets. A comprehensive study of the news media reports that audiences are aware of news bias and seek out particular perspectives in the news they consume. While "mainstream, general interest newspapers, network television and local television news" are slowly losing audiences, "online, ethnic and alternative media are growing markedly" and "share the same strength—the opportunity for audiences to select tailored content and, in the case of the Internet, to do it on demand."[65]

Media Bias

Summary

PUBLIC OPINION AND THE NEWS MEDIA are two factors that have a drastic impact on American politics and public policy. The first step in forming opinions occurs through a process called political socialization. Our family, school, peers, social groups—including religion, race, ethnicity, gender, and age—as well as where we live and the impact of events, affect how we view political events and issues.

Over the years, polling to measure public opinion has become increasingly sophisticated and more accurate because pollsters are better able to sample the public in their effort to determine their attitudes and positions on issues. Measuring public opinion, however, can be difficult. The most frequently used measure is the public opinion poll. Determining the content, phrasing the questions, selecting the sample, and choosing the right kind of poll are critical to obtaining accurate and useful data.

Myriad factors enter our minds as we form opinions about political matters. These include a calculation about the personal benefits involved, degree of personal political knowledge, and cues from leaders.

News media, a component of the larger mass media, provide the public with key information about subjects of public interest and play a crucial role in the political process. The news media consist of the print, radio, television, and new media.

Trends affecting the modern media include the growth of media conglomerates and an attendant consolidation of media outlets, the increasing use of experts, and narrowcasting in order to capture particular segments of the population. Increasingly, the lines between media types are blurred by technological innovations that continue to transform the way news is produced and distributed, as well as the way that the public perceives the media.

The government has gradually loosened restrictions on the media. The Federal Communications Commission (FCC) has reduced its regulation of licensees. Content regulations have also loosened, with the courts using a narrow interpretation of libel. The Telecommunications Act of 1996 further deregulated the communications landscape.

The media cover every aspect of the political process, including the executive, legislative, and judicial branches of government, though the bulk of media attention focuses on the president. Politicians have developed a symbiotic relationship with the media, both feeding the media a steady supply of news and occasionally being devoured by the latest media feeding frenzy.

By controlling the flow of information, framing issues in a particular manner, and setting the agenda, the media have the potential to exert influence over the public, though generally far less influence than people believe. While the media do possess biases, diverse news options are available in the United States, which provide savvy news consumers an unprecedented amount of information from which to choose.

KEY TERMS

affiliates, p. 301
agenda setting, p. 310
blog, p. 303
content regulation, p. 304
equal time rule, p. 304
exit polls, p. 291
framing, p. 310
mass media, p. 295
media effects, p. 309
muckraking, p. 297
narrowcasting, p. 303
network, p. 301
New York Times Co. v. *Sullivan* (1964), p. 306
news media, p. 295
political ideology, p. 294
political socialization, p. 278
press briefing, p. 306
press conference, p. 306
press release, p. 306
public opinion, p. 286
public opinion polls, p. 286
push polls, p. 290
random sampling, p. 289
sampling error, or margin of error, p. 292
stratified sampling, p. 289
straw polls, p. 287

tracking polls, p. 290
wire service, p. 301
yellow journalism, p. 295

SELECTED READINGS

Alvarez, R. Michael, and John Brehm. *Easy Answers, Hard Choices: Values, Information, and American Public Opinion.* Princeton, NJ: Princeton University Press, 2002.

Crouse, Timothy. *The Boys on the Bus,* reprint ed. New York: Random House, 2003.

Entman, Robert M. *Projections of Power: Framing News, Public Opinion, and U.S. Foreign Policy.* Chicago: University of Chicago Press, 2003.

Erikson, Robert S., and Kent L. Tedin. *American Public Opinion: Its Origins, Contents, and Impact,* 7th ed. New York: Longman, 2004.

Erikson, Robert S., Michael B. MacKuen, and James A. Stimson. *The Macro Polity.* New York: Cambridge University Press, 2002.

Graber, Doris A. *Mass Media and American Politics,* 7th ed. Washington, DC: CQ Press, 2005.

Hamilton, John Maxwell. *Hold the Press: The Inside Story on Newspapers,* reprint ed. Baton Rouge: Louisiana State University Press, 1997.

Jamieson, Kathleen Hall. *Everything You Think You Know About Politics . . . And Why You Were Wrong.* New York: Basic Books, 2000.

Jamieson, Kathleen Hall, and Paul Waldman. *The Press Effect: Politicians, Journalists, and the Stories That Shape the Political World.* Oxford: Oxford University Press, 2002.

Manza, Jeff, ed. *Navigating Public Opinion: Polls, Policy, and the Future of American Democracy.* New York: Oxford University Press, 2002.

McChesney, Robert W. *The Problem of the Media: U.S. Communication Politics in the Twenty-First Century.* New York: Monthly Review Press, 2004.

Mutz, Diana Carole. *Impersonal Influence: How Perceptions of Mass Collectives Affect Political Attitudes.* New York: Cambridge University Press, 1998.

Norrander, Barbara, and Clyde Wilcox, eds. *Understanding Public Opinion,* 2nd ed. Washington, DC: CQ Press, 2001.

Sabato, Larry J. *Feeding Frenzy: Attack Journalism and American Politics,* updated ed. Baltimore, MD: Lanahan, 2000.

Starr, Paul. *The Creation of the Media.* New York: Basic Books, 2004.

Warren, Kenneth F. *In Defense of Public Opinion Polling.* Boulder, CO: Westview, 2001.

West, Darrell M. *Air Wars: Television Advertising in Election Campaigns, 1952–1996.* Washington, DC: CQ Press, 2000.

WEB EXPLORATIONS

To learn more about the Gallup Organization and poll trends, see
http://www.gallup.com

To use NES data sets, see
http://www.umich.edu/~nes/

For the most recent Roper Center polls, see
http://www.ropercenter.uconn.edu

To test your own political knowledge, go to
http://www.ablongman.com/oconnor

To see an example of a nonstratified poll, go to
http://www.cnn.com

For examples of nineteenth-century yellow journalism, go to
http://alt.tnt.tv/movies/tntoriginals/roughriders/jour.home.html

To see how the media are diversifying and repackaging themselves
through the use of pundits, go to
http://www.publicagenda.org/specials/cjrpolls/cjrdec.htm

For examples of popular political blogs, go to
http://www.redstate.org

http://www.powerlineblog.com
http://www.dailykos.com
http://www.huffingtonpost.com/theblog
http://www.americablog.blogspot.com

To see which newspapers, magazines, and networks have a Web
presence and how that complements their standard coverage, go to
http://www.nationaljournal.com
http://www.washingtonpost.com
http://www.cnn.com

Photo courtesy: Victoria Arocho/AP Wide World Photos

POLITICAL PARTIES AND INTEREST GROUPS

11

IN JULY 2004, the Democrats used the city of Boston to formally launch the nomination of Senator John Kerry (D–MA) as their candidate for president of the United States. A few weeks later, from New York, the Republicans followed by renaming President George W. Bush their candidate. The televised convention proceedings and morning papers focused on the nominations of these two men and their personal attributes. Relatively little attention, however, was paid to the importance of the party platforms, the official statements that detail each party's positions on key public policy issues. Party platforms are often taken for granted, certainly by the news media, and even by many political activists. They are rarely noted by American voters, many of whom are cynical about the idea that parties stand for anything other than gaining power.

How wrong the cynics are. The Republicans' platform, entitled "A Safer World and a More Hopeful America," strongly defended the policies of the Bush administration, including the invasion of Iraq, a country they described as a "great and gathering" danger to American interests at home and abroad. The Democrats' platform, "Strong at Home, Respected in the World," pointed to the Bush administration's failure to find the weapons of mass destruction that had been said to constitute such a threat, and to the failure of the administration to bring peace to the region.

The platforms were filled with differing policy perspectives. The Republicans insisted that President Bush's 2001 and 2003 tax cuts were essential to rebuilding a weakened American economy. The Democrats argued that the tax cuts had created enormous national deficits to be paid off by future generations and had disproportionately benefited the richest Americans. The Republicans continued their strong pro-life stance on the issue of abortion, their most recent success being a federal ban on the late-term abortion procedure that pro-life groups call "partial birth abortion." Democrats made no mention of this ban but reiterated their commitment to a woman's right to make her own choices with regard to pregnancy and reproductive health.

The abortion issue had increased salience for the parties as Supreme Court vacancies were forecast by interest groups on both sides, and the future of abortion rights came into question. Republicans were opposed to same-sex marriages, and the party platform supported President Bush's call for a constitutional amendment to ban same-sex marriage. Democrats opposed amending the Constitution and asserted their belief that marriage should be defined at the state level. (See Table 11.1 for excerpts from the party platforms.)

Long after memories of the national conventions have faded, the issues embodied by the party platforms persist. In the first half of his second term, President Bush aggressively pursued the foreign policy objectives laid out in his party's platform by continuing the war on terrorism abroad and by pursuing an equally aggressive domestic policy against terrorism. Consistent with the party platform, the president fought for pro-business policies and a preservation of tax cuts, as well as the partial privatization of Social Security. He pursued the Republican Party's stated social issues, most notably by nominating conservative jurists John G. Roberts Jr. and Samuel A. Alito Jr. to fill vacancies on the Court.

In fact, the policy differences outlined in the platforms and pursued by the president stretch well beyond presidential politics, as these same themes echoed throughout the country in the 2006 midterm elections. Once again the parties differed on issues related to foreign policy and national security, taxation, and social issues such as same-sex marriage and abortion.

The extent to which individual party members personally embrace their party's platform varies, however, and the issues candidates emphasize are typically tailored to the concerns of their constituents. For example, Senator Bob Casey (D–PA), who defeated Senator Rick Santorum (R-PA) in 2006, emphasized his differences from his opponent on national security and tax issues, but like his opponent (and unlike the bulk of his party) is pro-life.

---

political party
A group of office holders, candidates, activists, and voters who identify with a group label and seek to elect to public office individuals who run under that label.

interest group
An organized group that tries to influence public policy.

WHEN JAMES MADISON warned of the dangers of faction in *Federalist No. 10*, he never envisioned the development of political parties, or the role that organized interests would eventually play in politics and policy making. It was not long after the ink was dry on the new Constitution that factions arose concerning the desirability to the new system of government that it created. And, soon after, political parties were formed to reflect those political divisions.

At the most basic level, a **political party** is a group of office holders, candidates, activists, and voters who identify with a group label and seek to elect to public office individuals who run under that label. Notice that the goal is to *win* office, not just compete for it. This objective is in keeping with the practical nature of Americans and the country's historical aversion to most ideologically driven, purist politics. Nevertheless, the group label—also called party identification—can carry with it clear messages about ideology and issue positions. Although these especially exist for minor, less broad-based parties that have little chance of electoral success, they also apply to the Democrats and the Republicans, the two national, dominant political parties in the United States.

In contrast to political parties, **interest groups,** which go by a variety of names—special interests, pressure groups, organized interests, political groups, lobby groups, and public interest groups—are organizations that "seek or claim to represent people or organizations which share one or more common interests or ideals."[1] Distinguished political scientist V. O. Key Jr. tried to differentiate political parties from interest groups by arguing that "interest groups promote their interests by attempting to influence government rather than by nominating candidates and seeking responsibility for the management of government.[2]

In this chapter we trace the evolution of the role of political parties and interest groups in America. First, we will examine the role of *political parties* in the American political process. Then, we will we turn to a discussion of *interest groups.*

TABLE 11.1 PARTY PLATFORMS: MODERATE BUT DIFFERENT

As most Americans have moderate political views and the aim of political parties is to attract voters, the platforms of the two dominant parties tend to be moderate in tone and sometimes similar in substance, though the differences below the rhetoric are often profound.

	Democratic Platform	*Republican Platform*
Environment	For generations, Americans of all political beliefs have understood that the protection of our environment and the stewardship of our land are vital to the strength of our nation. God gave America extraordinary natural gifts; it is our responsibility to protect them. The health of our families, the strength of our economy, and the well-being . of our worlds all depend upon a clean environment	Republicans know that economic prosperity is essential to environmental progress. That belief is supported by compelling historical evidence. For example, over the last 30 years, air pollution from the six major pollutants decreased substantially, even as our population grew, our energy consumption increased, and the economy expanded.
Abortion	We will defend the dignity of all Americans against those who would undermine it. Because we believe in the privacy and equality of women, we stand proudly for a women's right to choose, consistent with *Roe* v. *Wade*, and regardless of her ability to pay. We stand firmly against Republican efforts to undermine that right. At the same time, we strongly support family planning and adoption incentives. Abortion should be safe, legal, and rare.	As a country, we must keep our pledge to the first guarantee of the Declaration of Independence. That is why we say the unborn child has a fundamental individual right to life which cannot be infringed. We support a human life amendment to the Constitution and we endorse legislation to make it clear that the Fourteenth Amendment's protections apply to unborn children
Marriage	We support full inclusion of gay and lesbian families in the life of our nation and seek equal responsibilities, benefits, and protections for these families. In our country, marriage has been defined at the state level for 200 years, and we believe it should continue to be defined there. We repudiate President Bush's divisive effort to politicize the Constitution by pursuing a "federal Marriage Amendment." Our goal is to bring Americans together, not divide them apart.	We strongly support President Bush's call for a constitutional amendment that fully protects marriage, and we believe that neither federal nor state judges nor bureaucrats should force states to recognize other living arrangements as equivalent to marriage. We believe, and social science confirms, that the well-being of children is best accomplished in the environment of the home, nurtured by their mother and father anchored by the bonds of marriage.
Taxation	First, we must restore our values to our tax code. We want a tax code that rewards work and creates wealth for more people, not a tax code that hoards wealth for those who already have it. With the middle class under assault like never before, we simply cannot afford the massive Bush tax cuts for the very wealthiest.	We believe that good government is based on a system of limited taxes and spending. Furthermore, we believe that the federal government should be limited and restricted to the functions mandated by the United States Constitution. The taxation system should not be used to redistribute wealth or fund ever-increasing entitlements and social programs.

Note: Excerpts are taken directly from the relevant sections of the 2004 party platforms.

Sources: http://www.gop.com/media/2004platform.pdf and http://www.democrats.org/pdfs/2004platform.pdf

Political Parties

POLITICAL PARTIES HAVE EVOLVED CONSIDERABLY and changed form from time to time. Nevertheless, they usually have been reliable vehicles for mass participation in a representative democracy.

THE EVOLUTION OF THE AMERICAN PARTY SYSTEM

It is one of the great ironies of the early republic that George Washington's public farewell, which warned the nation against parties, marked the effective end of the brief era of partyless politics in the United States (see Figure 11.1). Washington's unifying influence ebbed as he stepped off the national stage, and his vice president and successor, John Adams, occupied a much less exalted position. To win the presidency in 1796, Adams narrowly defeated his arch-rival Thomas Jefferson, who according to the existing rules of the Constitution became vice president. Over the course of Adams's single term, two competing congressional factions, Federalists and Democratic-Republicans,

TIMELINE

Third Parties in American History

FIGURE 11.1 AMERICAN PARTY HISTORY AT A GLANCE

Note: Chart lists political parties that received at least 1 percent of the presidential vote.

Source: Harold W. Stanley and Richard G. Niemi, *Vital Statistics on American Politics, 2005–2006* (Washington, DC: CQ Press, 2006).

The Living Constitution

It is difficult to imagine modern American politics without the political parties, but where in the text of Constitution do we find the provision to establish them?

Nowhere in the Constitution do we find a provision establishing political parties. Some might point out that the First Amendment establishes the right to assemble as a Constitutional right, and this right certainly helps to preserve and protect parties from governmental oppression during rallies and conventions. However, the right to assembly is not the same as permission for two organizations to mediate elections. Furthermore, James Madison, in *Federalist No. 10*, feared that one of the greatest dangers to the new American republic was a majority tyranny created by the domination of a single faction fighting for one set of interests, so he hoped that extending the sphere of representation among many members of Congress would prevent a majority of representatives from coming together to vote as a bloc.

Of course, parties are *not* like the factions Madison describes. Parties today seem to embody Madison's principle of the extended sphere of representation. Neither of the two major political parties is monolithic in its beliefs; rather, both parties constantly reconsider their platforms in light of the changes of the various constituencies they try to represent. The Republicans have both Senator Olympia Snowe (ME), who is pro-choice and pro-environment, and Representative Roy Blunt (MO), who is pro-life and pro-business. Democrats have both Representative Dennis Kucinich (OH), who advocates withdrawal from the North American Free Trade Agreement, and Governor Bill Richardson (NM), who balances various racial/ethnic concerns and business interests while trying to protect the border between the U.S. and Mexico. Both comparisons yield differences in interests, the kind of things Madison wanted.

Finally, Madison himself actually belonged to two early American political parties during his public service, first the Federalists and later the Democratic-Republicans. In fact, it is because of the Federalist Party that we have a Constitution today. Federalists compromised with Anti-Federalists to provide a Bill of Rights so long as the Anti-Federalists would stop opposing ratification of the Constitution. So parties are not so much *in* the Constitution as *behind* the Constitution, first behind its ratification and, today, behind its preservation of diverse interests.

gradually organized around these clashing men and their principles: Adams and his Federalist allies supported a strong central government; the Democratic-Republicans of Thomas Jefferson and his allies inherited the mantle of the Anti-Federalists (see chapter 2) and preferred a federal system in which the states retained the balance of power. Jefferson actually preferred the simpler name "Republicans" for his faction, which was a very different group from today's party of the same name. Alexander Hamilton, however, a leading Federalist, insisted on calling the group "Democratic-

Republicans," in an attempt to disparage the group by linking them to the radical democrats of the French Revolution. In the presidential election of 1800, the Federalists supported Adams's reelection bid, but this time the Democratic-Republicans prevailed. Their nominee, Jefferson, then became the first U.S. president elected as the nominee of a political party (see The Living Constitution).

Jefferson was deeply committed to the ideas of his party, but not nearly as devoted to the idea of a party system. He regarded his party as a temporary measure necessary to defeat Adams, not a long-term political tool or an essential element of democracy. Jefferson's party never achieved widespread loyalty among the citizenry akin to that of today's Democrats and Republicans. Although Southerners were overwhelmingly partial to the Democratic-Republicans and New Englanders favored the Federalists, no broad-based party organizations existed to mobilize popular support. Rather, the congressional factions organized around Adams and Jefferson primarily were governmental parties designed to settle the dispute over how strong the new federal government would be.[3] Just as the nation was in its infancy, so, too, was the party system.

Early Parties Fade   What is sometimes called the second party system began around 1824, when Andrew Jackson ran for president. He lost to John Quincy Adams but was successful when he ran again in 1828. Around this time, party membership broadened along with the electorate. After receiving criticism for being elitist and undemocratic, the small caucuses of congressional party leaders that had previously nominated candidates gave way to nominations at large party conventions. In 1832, the Democratic Party, which succeeded the old Jeffersonian Democratic-Republicans, held the first national presidential nomination convention. Formed around President Andrew Jackson's popularity, the Democratic Party attracted most of the newly enfranchised voters, who were drawn to Jackson's charismatic style. His strong personality helped to polarize politics, and opposition to the president coalesced into the Whig Party. Among the Whig Party's early leaders was Henry Clay, the Speaker of the House from 1811 to 1820. The incumbent Jackson defeated Clay in the 1832 presidential contest. Jackson was the first chief executive who won the White House as the nominee of a truly national, popularly based political party.

The Whigs and the Democrats continued to strengthen after 1832, establishing state and local organizations almost everywhere. Their competition usually was fierce and closely matched, and they brought the United States the first broadly supported two-party system in the Western world.[4] Unfortunately for the Whigs, the issue of slavery sharpened the many divisive tensions within the party, which led to its gradual dissolution and replacement by the new Republican Party. Formed in 1854 by anti-slavery activists, the Republican Party set its sights on the abolition (or at least the containment) of slavery. After the losing presidential effort of John C. Frémont in 1856, the party was able to assemble enough support primarily from former Whigs and anti-slavery northern Democrats to win the presidency for Abraham Lincoln in a fragmented 1860 election. In that year, the South voted solidly Democratic, beginning a tradition so strong that not a single southern state voted Republican for president again until 1920.

Democrats and Republicans: The Golden Age   From the presidential election of 1860 to this day, the same two major parties, the Republicans and the Democrats, have dominated elections in the United States, and control of an electoral majority has seesawed between them. Party stability, as the dominance of party organizations in local and state governments, and the impact of those organizations on the lives of millions of voters, were the central traits of the era called the "Golden Age" of political parties.

This era, occurred as emigration from Europe (particularly from Ireland, Italy, and Germany) fueled the development in America of big-city party organizations that gained control of local and state government. These big-city party organizations were called **machines.** A political machine is a party organization that uses tangible incentives such as jobs and favors to win loyalty among voters. Machines are also characterized by a high degree of leadership control over member activity. Party machines were a central element of life for millions of people in the United States during the Golden Age. For city-dwellers, their party and their government were virtually interchangeable during this time. Party organizations sponsored community events and provided social services to those in immediate need, all in exchange for loyalty to party bosses and their candidates.

Political parties thus not only served the underlying political needs of the society but also supplemented the population's desire for important services. In addition to providing housing, employment, and even food to many voters, parties in most major cities provided entertainment by organizing torchlight parades, weekend picnics, socials, and the like. Many citizens—even those who weren't particularly "political—attended, thereby gaining some allegiance to one party or the other. The parties offered immigrants not just services but also the opportunity for upward social mobility as they rose in the organization. As a result, parties engendered intense devotion among their supporters and office holders that helped to produce startlingly high voter turnouts—75 percent or better in all presidential elections from 1876 to 1900—compared with today's 50–60 percent.[5]

The Modern Era The modern era seems very different from the Golden Age of parties. Many social, political, technological, and governmental changes have contributed to changes in the nature of the national parties since the 1920s. Historically, the government's gradual assumption of important functions previously performed by the parties, such as printing ballots, conducting elections, and providing social welfare services, had a major impact. Beginning in the 1930s with Franklin D. Roosevelt's New Deal, social services began to be seen as a right of citizenship rather than as a privilege extended in exchange for a person's support of a party. Also, as the flow of immigrants slowed dramatically in the 1920s, party organizations gradually shrank in many places.

A **direct primary** system, in which party nominees were determined by the ballots of qualified voters rather than at party conventions, gained widespread adoption by the states in the first two decades of the twentieth century. Direct primaries, which were championed by individuals in groups that made up the Progressive movement, which flourished in the first two decades of the twentieth century, removed the power of nomination from party leaders and workers and gave it instead to a much broader and more independent electorate, thus loosening the tie between party nominees and the party organization.

Additional Progressive movement reforms also contributed to reduced party influence in the United States. **Civil service laws,** for example, which require appointment on the basis of merit and competitive examinations, removed opportunities for much of the patronage used by the parties to reward their followers (see chapter 8).

In the post–World War II era, extensive social changes also contributed to the move away from strong parties. A weakening of the party system gave rise to candidate and **issue-oriented politics,** politics that focuses on the individuals running for office and specific issues, such as civil rights, tax cutting, or environmentalism, rather than on party platforms. Interest groups and lobbyists have stepped into the void that weaker parties have left behind, and candidates compete for endorsements and contributions from a variety of single- and multi-issue organizations. Issue politics tends to cut across party lines and encourages voters to **ticket-split**—to vote for candidates of different parties in the same election (a phenomenon we discuss in greater depth in chapter 12). Parties' diminished control over issues and campaigns have also left candidates considerable power in how they conduct themselves during election season

machine
A party organization that recruits voter loyalty with tangible incentives and is characterized by a high degree of control over member activity.

direct primary
The selection of party candidates through the ballots of qualified voters rather than at party nomination conventions.

civil service laws
These acts removed the staffing of the bureaucracy from political parties and created a professional bureaucracy filled through competition.

issue-oriented politics
Politics that focuses on specific issues rather than on party, candidate, or other loyalties.

ticket-split
To vote for candidates of different parties for various offices in the same election.

candidate-centered politics
The shift in focus away from party control over platforms and fundraising toward candidates running more independently, and with voters attentions focused on particular candidates rather than party affiliation.

party realignment
A shifting of party coalition groupings in the electorate that remains in place for several elections.

critical election
An election that signals a party realignment through voter polarization around new issues.

and how they seek resources. This new **candidate-centered politics** is an outgrowth of voters focusing directly on the candidates, their particular issues and character, rather than on their party affiliation.

Another post–World War II social change that has affected the parties is the shift from urban to suburban locales. Millions of people have moved from the cities to the suburbs, where a sense of privacy and detachment can deter the most energetic party organizers. In addition, population growth in the last half-century has created districts with far more people, making it less feasible to knock on every door or shake every hand.

Realignment   Periodically in national elections, voters make dramatic shifts in partisan preference that drastically alter the political landscape. During these **party realignments,** existing party affiliations are subject to upheaval: many voters may change parties, and the youngest age group of voters may permanently adopt the label of the newly dominant party.[6]

Preceding a major realignment are one or more **critical elections,** which may polarize voters around new issues and personalities in reaction to crucial developments, such as a war or an economic depression. Three tumultuous eras in particular have produced noteworthy critical elections. First, Thomas Jefferson, in reaction against the Federalist Party's agenda of a strong, centralized federal government, formed the Democratic-Republican Party, which took the presidency and Congress in 1800. Second, in reaction to the growing crisis over slavery, the Whig Party gradually dissolved and the Republican Party gained strength and ultimately won the presidency in 1860. Third, the Great Depression of the 1930s caused large numbers of voters to repudiate Republican Party policies and embrace the Democratic Party. Each of these cases resulted in fundamental and enduring alterations in the party equation.

The last confirmed major realignment, then, happened in the 1928–1936 period, as Republican Herbert Hoover's presidency was held to one term because of voter anger about the Depression. In 1932, Democrat Franklin D. Roosevelt swept to power as the electorate decisively rejected Hoover and the Republicans. This dramatic vote of "no confidence" was followed by substantial changes in policy by the new president. The majority of voters responded favorably to Roosevelt's New Deal policies, accepted his vision of society, and ratified their choice of the new president's party in subsequent presidential and congressional elections.

The idea that party realignments occurred on a predictable, periodic basis beguiled many political scientists in the 1960s and 1970s, and much attention was focused on awaiting the next sea change in partisan alignment.[7] However, no uniform shift in partisan alignment has occurred in American politics since the election of Franklin D. Roosevelt in 1932. In fact, divided partisan government has been a dominant outcome of elections since World War II. Many scholars today question the value of party realignments in understanding partisanship and policy change. While each critical election shares some degree of similarity, they are each precipitated by distinctive political changes that are linked to particular periods and issues.[8] Nonetheless, party realignments offer a useful basis for understanding how pivotal elections may lastingly alter the direction of American politics.

A critical election is not the only occasion when changes in partisan affiliation are accommodated. In truth, every election produces realignment to some degree, since some individuals undoubtedly are pushed to change parties by events and by their reactions to the candidates. Research suggests that partisanship is much more responsive to current issues and personalities than had been believed earlier, and that major realignments are just extreme cases of the kind of changes in party loyalty registered every year.[9]

Secular Realignment   Although the term *realignment* is usually applied only if momentous events such as war or economic depression produce enduring and substantial alterations in the party coalitions, political scientists have long recognized that a more gradual rearrangement of party coalitions can occur.[10] Called **secular realignment,** this piecemeal process depends not on convulsive shocks to the political system, but on slow, almost barely discernible demographic shifts—the shrinking of one party's base of support and the enlargement of the other's, for example—or simple generational replacement (that is, the dying off of the older generation and the maturing of the younger generation). According to one version of this theory, in an era of weaker party attachments (such as we currently are experiencing), a dramatic, full-scale realignment may not be possible.[11] Still, a critical mass of voters may be attracted for years to one party's banner in waves or streams, if that party's leadership and performance are consistently examplary.

The prospect of a national realignment is unlikely as long as party ties remain tenuous for so many voters.[12] However, regionally there have been slow but stable partisan realignments that have affected the power bases of the major parties. During the 1990s, the southern states, traditionally Democratic stalwarts since the Civil War, have shifted dramatically toward the Republican Party. The Northeast, a longtime reliable voting bloc for Republicans, has become increasingly Democratic during the same period. Many factors have contributed to these gradual regional shifts in party allegiance. Southern Democrats were the most conservative of the New Deal coalition, favoring the social status quo and opposing civil rights reform. As the Democratic Party shifted its platform toward more liberal social causes such as civil rights and social welfare spending, many southern voters and politicians shifted their allegiance toward the Republican Party. In a region where voting for a Republican once was considered taboo, the South is now one of the most reliable blocs of Republican voters.[13]

THE FUNCTIONS OF THE AMERICAN TWO-PARTY SYSTEM

For 150 years, the two-party system has served as the mechanism American society uses to organize and resolve social and political conflict. Political parties often are the chief agents of change in our political system. They provide vital services to society, and it would be difficult to envision political life without them.

Mobilizing Support and Gathering Power Party affiliation is enormously helpful to elected leaders. Therefore the parties aid office holders by giving them room to develop their policies and by mobilizing support for them. When the president addresses the nation and requests support for his policies, for example, his party's members are usually the first to respond to the call, perhaps by flooding Congress with e-mails and phone calls urging action on the president's agenda. Moreover, because there are only two major parties, citizens who are interested in politics or public policy are mainly attracted to one or the other party, creating natural majorities or near majorities for party office holders to command. The party generates a community of interests that bond disparate groups over time into **coalitions.**

A Force for Stability and Moderation The parties encourage stability in the type of coalitions they form. There are inherent contradictions in these coalitions that, oddly enough, strengthen the nation even as they strain party unity. President Franklin D. Roosevelt's Democratic New Deal coalition, for example, included many African Americans and most southern whites, opposing groups nonetheless joined in common political purpose by economic hardship and, in the case of better-off Southerners, in longtime voting habits.

secular realignment
The gradual rearrangement of party coalitions, based more on demographic shifts than on shocks to the political system.

VIDEO DEBATE
Poverty and Political Parties

coalition
A group of interests or organizations that join forces for the purpose of electing public officials.

Unity, Linkage, and Accountability   Parties provide the glue to hold together disparate elements of the U.S. governmental and political apparatus. The Framers designed a system that divides and subdivides power, making it possible to preserve individual liberty but difficult to coordinate and produce action in a timely fashion. Parties help compensate for this drawback in the executive and legislative branches. Although rivalry between these two branches of U.S. government is inevitable, the partisan affiliations of the leaders of each branch constitute a common basis for cooperation, as the president and his fellow party members in Congress usually demonstrate daily.

The party's linkage function does not end there. Party identification and organization foster communication between the voter and the candidate, as well as between the voter and the office holder. The party connection is one means of increasing accountability in election campaigns and in government. Candidates on the campaign trail and elected party leaders in office are required from time to time to account for their performance at party-sponsored forums, nominating primaries, and conventions.

The Electioneering Function   The election, proclaimed author H. G. Wells, is "democracy's ceremonial, its feast, its great function," and the political parties assist this ceremony in essential ways. First, the parties help to funnel eager, interested individuals into politics and government. While most candidates are self-recruited, some are also recruited each year by the two parties, as are many of the candidates' staff members—the people who manage the campaigns and go on to serve in key governmental positions once the election has been won.

Elections can have meaning in a democracy only if they are competitive, and in the United States they probably could not be competitive without the parties. (When we use the term *competitive*, we mean that both parties have sufficient organization, money, and people to run a vigorous election campaign, and to sustain their arguments through the period of governance.)

Currently, both major political parties have supplemented labor-intensive, person-to-person operations with modern technological and communication strategies, and both parties are similar in the objectives they pursue to achieve political power. Nevertheless, each party has its strengths and weaknesses.

The contemporary national Republican Party has considerable organizational prowess, often surpassing the Democrats in fund-raising by large margins (see Figure 11.2). In recent election cycles, Democrats have worked hard to compete with the Republican Party fund-raising machine, which is fueled by a large number of wealthy donors. In 2004, the Republican Party outraised the Democratic Party, but the Democrats came closer to matching the Republicans than in any other modern election season.

The parties raise so much money because they have developed networks of donors reached by a variety of methods. Both parties have highly successful mail solicitation lists. Republicans also pioneered the use of interactive technologies to attract voters. But, former Democratic presidential candidate and current Democratic National Committee (DNC) chair Howard Dean used an Internet Web site to coordinate "meet-ups" and to bring in unprecedented campaign contributions online. When his presidential candidacy ended in defeat in the 2004 primaries, Dean and his network of activist-contributors became a fund-raising resource for Democrats, a fact that Dean later trumpeted during his successful bid to chair the DNC.

The Republican National Committee (RNC) also manages a sophisticated fund-raising data base, as well as helping to coordinate national get out the vote (GOTV) efforts. Many observers credit the success of the Bush campaign in 2004 to a well-organized and costly GOTV effort by the Republican Party. Because Democrats were the majority party in Congress for decades throughout the twentieth century, they have been late in creating similar programs. Recent electoral defeats made Democrats realize that their party must change to survive, that it must dampen internal ideologi-

FIGURE 11.2 POLITICAL PARTY FINANCES, 1991–2006

Note how the Republican Party has consistently taken in higher receipts than their Democratic competitors and how the receipts for both parties have substantially increased over time, even following the 2002 Bipartisan Campaign Reform Act (BCRA) which outlawed soft money contributions (shown in the top graph) to the parties.

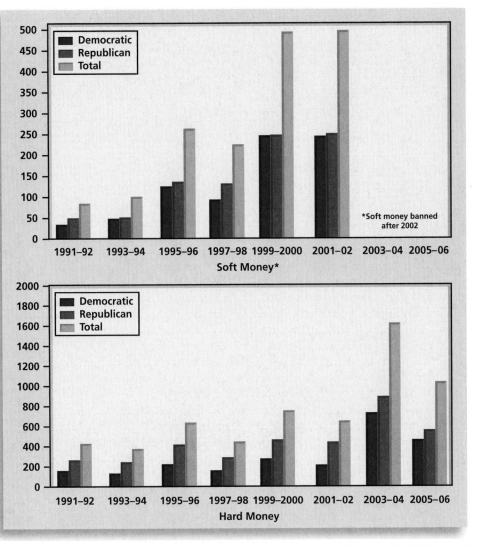

Sources: 2003–2006 from Center for Responsive Politics, http://www.opensecrets.org, and earlier years from Harold W. Stanley and Richard G. Niemi, *Vital Statistics on American Politics 2003–2004* (Washington, DC: CQ Press, 2004).

cal disputes and begin to revitalize its organization. Thus was born, with the Republican Party's accomplishments as a model, the commitment to technological and fund-raising modernization that drives the Democratic Party today. In 2006, Democrats focused on fielding competitive candidates in nearly every race and the DNC provided organizing funds to Democrats in traditionally Republican states as part of a 50-state grassroots organizing effort. These strategies, along with low approval ratings for President Bush and the Republican-led Congress, resulted in significant Democratic victories in 2006.

Legislative Organization In no segment of U.S. government is the party more visible or vital than in the Congress. In this century, political parties have dramatically increased the sophistication and impact of their internal congressional organizations. Prior to the beginning of every session, the parties in both houses of Congress gather (or "caucus") separately to select party leaders (House Speaker and majority and minority leaders, Senate majority and minority leaders, party whips, and so on) and to arrange for the appointment of members of each chamber's committees. In effect, then, the parties organize and operate the Congress, as discussed in chapter 6.

To promote their policy positions, the leaders of each party in Congress try to advance legislation to further their interests. Party labels, in fact, consistently have been the most powerful predictor of congressional roll-call voting. In the last few years, party voting has increased noticeably, as reflected in the upward trend by both Democrats and Republicans shown in Figure 11.3. Although not invariably predictive, a member's party affiliation proved to be the indicator of his or her votes more than 90 percent of the time in 2005; that is, the average representative or senator sided with his or her party on about 90 percent of the votes that divided a majority of Democrats from a majority of Republicans that year. In most recent years, unanimous party-line votes have become increasingly common, with Democrats providing a record 151 unanimous roll-call votes in 2005.[14]

There are many reasons for the recent growth of congressional party unity. Both congressional parties, for instance, gradually have become more ideologically homogeneous and internally consistent. Southern Democrats today typically are moderate or liberal like their counterparts in other regions of the nation. Similarly, the vast majority of Republicans in Congress identify themselves as conservative. Partisan gerrymandering, redrawing congressional lines so as to create safe districts, has also increased party cohesion, as members of Congress increasingly represent congressional districts that strongly favor a single party. The political party campaign committees have also played a role in this renewed cohesiveness. Each national party committee has been recruiting and training House and Senate candidates as never before, and devising themes and issues aimed at targeted districts. With the numbers so close in both chambers of Congress, each party has a singular focus on electing a majority of legislators.

Party as a Voting and Issue Cue A voter's party identification can act as an invaluable filter for information, a perceptual screen that affects how he or she digests political news. Parties try to cultivate a popular image and help inform the public about issues through advertising and voter contact. Therefore, party affiliation provides a use-

FIGURE 11.3 CONGRESSIONAL PARTY UNITY SCORES, 1959–2005

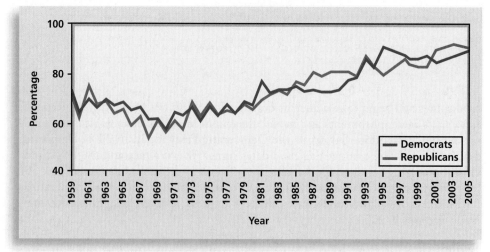

Note how party-based voting has increased conspicuously since the 1970s.

Source: *Congressional Quarterly Almanacs* (Washington, DC: CQ Press).

ful cue for voters, particularly for the least informed and least interested, who can use the party label as a shortcut or substitute for interpreting issues and events they may not fully comprehend. Better-educated and more involved voters also find party identification helpful. After all, no one has the time to study every issue carefully or to become fully knowledgeable about every candidate seeking public office.

Policy Formulation and Promotion The **national party platform** is the most visible instrument that parties use to formulate, convey, and promote public policy. Every four years before the presidential nominating conventions, each party writes a lengthy platform explaining its positions on key issues. Platforms have significant impact, as discussed in the opening vignette. Typically, about two-thirds of the promises in the victorious party's presidential platform are completely or mostly implemented. Moreover, about one-half or more of the pledges of the losing party also tend to find their way into public policy, a trend that no doubt reflects the effort of both parties to support broad policy positions that enjoy widespread support in the general public.[15]

The party platform also has great influence on a new presidential administration's legislative program and on the president's State of the Union Address. While party affiliation is normally the single most important determinant of voting in Congress and in state legislatures, the party–vote relationship is even stronger when party platform issues come up on the floor of Congress.[16]

Besides mobilizing Americans on a permanent basis, then, the parties convert the cacophony of hundreds of identifiable social and economic groups into a two-part semi-harmony that is much more comprehensible, if not always on key and pleasing to the ears. The simplicity of two-party politics may be deceptive, given the enormous variety in public policy choices, but a sensible system of representation in the American context might be impossible without it.

Crashing the Party: Minor Parties in the American Two-Party System Despite their lack of electoral strength, minor parties based on causes often neglected by the major parties have had an important impact on American politics. Third parties find their roots in sectionalism (as did the South's states' rights Dixiecrat Party, made up of members who broke away from the Democrats in 1948), in economic protest (such as the agrarian revolt that fueled the Populists, an 1892 prairie-states party), in specific issues (such as the Green Party's support of the environment), in ideology (the Socialist, Communist, and Libertarian Parties are examples), and in appealing, charismatic personalities (Theodore Roosevelt's affiliation with the Bull Moose Party in 1912 is perhaps the best case). Many minor parties have drawn strength from a combination of these sources. The American Independent Party in 1968 enjoyed a measure of success because of a dynamic leader (George Wallace), a firm geographic base (the South), and an emotional issue (civil rights). In 1992, Ross Perot, the billionaire with a folksy Texas manner, was a charismatic leader whose campaign was fueled by the deficit issue (as well as by his personal fortune).

Minor-party and independent candidates are not limited to presidential elections. Many also run in congressional elections, and the numbers appear to be growing. In the 2006 congressional elections, for example, nearly 350 minor-party and independent candidates ran for seats in the House and Senate—almost three and half times as many as in 1968 and one and a half times the number that ran in 1980. Two members of the 109th Congress, Representative Bernie Sanders and Senator Jim Jeffords of Vermont, were independents and both caucused with the Democratic Party. The 110th Congress also has two independents caucusing with the Democratic Party: Sanders won the Vermont Senate race as an independent and Senator Joe Lieberman won reelection as an independent in Connecticut after losing the Democratic primary. Minor-party candidates for the House are most likely to emerge under three conditions: (1) when a House seat becomes open; (2) when a minor-party candidate has previously competed in the district; and, (3) when partisan competition between the two major parties in the district is close.[17]

national party platform
A statement of the general and specific philosophy and policy goals of a political party, usually promulgated at the national convention.

VIDEO ROUNDTABLE

Third Parties

328   CHAPTER 11   ★   POLITICAL PARTIES AND INTEREST GROUPS

Above all, third parties make electoral progress in direct proportion to the failure of the two major parties to incorporate new ideas or alienated groups or to nominate attractive candidates as their standard-bearers. Third parties do best when declining trust in the two major political parties plagues the electorate.[18] Usually, though, third parties are eventually co-opted by one of the two major parties, each of them eager to take the politically popular issue that gave rise to the third party and make it theirs to secure the allegiance of the third party's supporters.

THE PARTY ORGANIZATION

Although the distinctions might not be as clear today as they were two or three decades ago, the two major parties remain fairly loosely organized, with national, state, and local branches (see Figure 11.4). The different levels of each party represent diverse interests in Washington, D.C., state capitals, and local governments throughout the nation.

National Committees The first national party committees were skeletal and formed some years after the creation of the presidential nominating conventions in the 1830s. First the Democrats in 1848 and then the Republicans in 1856 established national governing bodies—the Democratic National Committee, or DNC, and the Republican National Committee, or RNC—to make arrangements for the national

FIGURE 11.4 POLITICAL PARTY ORGANIZATION IN AMERICA: FROM BASE TO PINNACLE

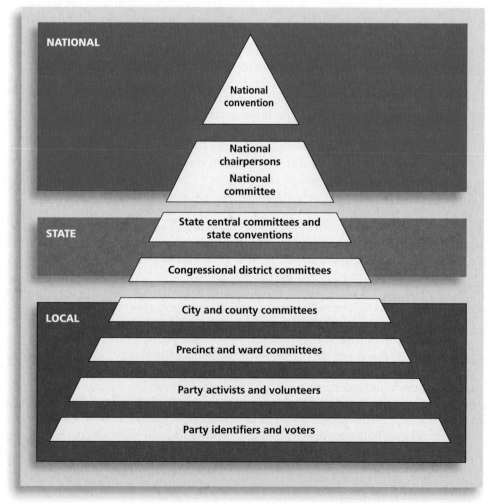

conventions and to coordinate the subsequent presidential campaigns. In addition, to serve their interests, the party caucuses in the House and Senate organized their own national committees, loosely allied with the DNC and RNC.

There is an informal division of labor among the national committees. Whereas the DNC and RNC focus primarily on aiding presidential campaigns and conducting general party-building activities, the congressional campaign committees work primarily to maximize the number of seats held by their respective parties in Congress. In the past two decades, all of the national committees have become major, service-oriented organizations.[19]

Leadership The key national party official is the chairperson of the national committee. Although the chair is formally elected by the national committee, he or she is usually selected by the sitting president or newly nominated presidential candidate, who is accorded the right to name the individual for at least the duration of his or her campaign. The chair often becomes the prime spokesperson and arbitrator for the party during the four years between elections. He or she is called on to minimize factionalism, negotiate candidate disputes, raise money, and prepare the machinery for the next presidential election. Balancing the interests of all potential White House contenders is a particularly difficult job, and strict neutrality is expected from the chair.

National Conventions Every four years, each party holds a **national convention** to nominate its presidential and vice presidential candidates. In addition to nominating the presidential ticket, the convention also fulfills its role as the ultimate governing body for the party. The rules adopted and the party platform that is passed serve as durable guidelines that steer the party until the next convention.

States and Localities Although national committee activities of all kinds attract most of the media attention, the party is structurally based not in Washington, D.C., but in the states and localities. With the notable exception of the campaign finance arena, virtually all government regulation of political parties is left to the states. Most importantly, the vast majority of party leadership positions are filled at subnational levels.

The arrangement of party committees provides for a broad base of support. The smallest voting unit, the precinct, usually takes in a few adjacent neighborhoods and is the fundamental building block of the party. There are more than 100,000 precincts in the United States. Precinct committee members are the foot soldiers of any party, and their efforts are supplemented by party committees above them in the wards, cities, counties, towns, villages, and congressional districts.

The state governing body supervising this collection of local party organizations is usually called the state central (or executive) committee. Its members come from all major geographic units, as determined by and selected under state law. Generally, state parties are free to act within the limits set by their state legislatures without interference from the national party, except in the selection and seating of presidential convention delegates.

Informal Groups The formal structure of party organization is supplemented by numerous official and semi-official groups that

national convention
A party meeting held in the presidential election year for the purposes of nominating a presidential and vice presidential ticket and adopting a platform.

VISUAL LITERACY

Political Parties: State Control and National Platforms

■ The president is generally the most visible party leader. Here, Republican President Dwight D. Eisenhower is shown in 1952 surrounded by Republican Committee women from eleven states.

Photo courtesy: Bettmann/Corbis

■ State parties often provide valuable financial assistance to party organizations at the local level. Here, Florida Republican Party Chair Carole Jean Jordan presents Jefferson County Republicans with a check for $7,000 in matching funds for party development.

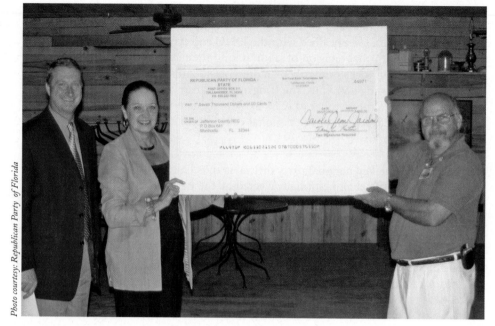

Photo courtesy: Republican Party of Florida

SIMULATION
You Are an Informed Voter

think tank
Institutional collection of policy-oriented researchers and academics who are sources of policy ideas.

party identification
A citizen's personal affinity for a political party, usually expressed by his or her tendency to vote for the candidates of that party.

attempt to affect politics through the formal party organization. Both the DNC and RNC have affiliated organizations of state and local party women (the Democrats' Women's Leadership Circle and National Federation of Democratic Women, and the National Federation of Republican Women), as well as numerous college campus organizations, including the College Democrats of America and the College Republican National Committee. The youth divisions (the Young Democrats of America and the Young Republicans' National Federation) have a generous definition of "young," up to and including age thirty-five. State governors have their own party associations, too: the Democratic Governors Association and Republican Governors Association.

Just outside the party orbit are the supportive interest groups and associations that often provide money, labor, or other forms of assistance to the parties. Labor unions, progressive political action committees (PACs), teachers, African American and liberal women's groups, and the Americans for Democratic Action are some of the Democratic Party's organizational groups. Business PACs, the U.S. Chamber of Commerce, fundamentalist Christian organizations, and some anti-abortion and anti-gay groups work closely with the Republicans.

Each U.S. party also has several institutionalized sources of policy ideas. Though unconnected to the parties in any official sense, these **think tanks** (institutional collections of policy-oriented researchers and academics) influence party positions and platforms.

SOURCES OF PARTY IDENTIFICATION

Most American voters identify with a party but do not belong to it. (See Politics Now: A Purple Electorate?) Universal party membership does not exist in the United States: the voter pays no prescribed dues; no formal rules govern an individual's party activities; and voters assume no enforceable obligations to the party even when they consistently vote for its candidates. A party has no real control over its adherents, and the party's voters subscribe to few or none of the commonly accepted tenets of organizational membership, such as regular participation and some measure of responsibility for the group's welfare. Rather, **party identification** or affiliation is a somewhat informal and impressionistic exercise whereby a citizen acquires a party label and accepts its standard as a summary of his or her political views and preferences.

Politics Now

A PURPLE ELECTORATE?

Journalists and pundits generally have assumed that the growing political divisions in the United States are between so-called "blue" and "red" states. Blue states are largely composed of New England, New York, the Pacific Coast, and a few Midwestern states. Red States make up the South, the Midwest, Southwest, the Rockies, and Alaska. The electoral map of the 2000 presidential election reflected this striking geographical continuity, which was generally duplicated in the 2004 presidential election. Many suppose that the stark regional contrast indicates a growing division among the American people, but the reality is that Americans are not as ideologically rigid as the map might indicate. Polling from after the 2004 election indicates that most Americans do not fit neatly into the categories of liberal or conservative, with most respondents demonstrating inconsistent or ambivalent views on many issues that clearly divide partisans. Increasingly pundits and scholars are referring to the American political landscape as being more "purple," or a complex combination of both liberal and conservative beliefs.

There is a tendency for people to pay more attention to those who make the most noise; subsequently, activists and extremists receive more attention, giving us the impression that everyone is an activist and an extremist. Looking at the survey results at right, it's clear that Americans are more in sync with regard to social issues like the death penalty, making English the official language, and school vouchers than one would otherwise suppose. Still, the results below reveal that there are some important differences between voters in red and blue states. Red state voters tend to be somewhat more conservative and more likely to be evangelical Christians than blue state voters. With results like these, it is hard to discount entirely the belief in a cultural division among Americans.

RED VERSUS BLUE

Survey responses from voters in "red states" (states won by the Republican George W. Bush) and "blue states" (states won by the Democrat Al Gore) in the 2000 presidential election.

	Blue	Red
Party		
Democratic self-ID	40	32
Republican self-ID	25	34
Ideology		
Liberal	20	11
Conservative	24	31
Religion		
Evangelical Christian	28	45
Religion is important	62	74
Issues		
Do whatever it takes to protect the environment	70	64
Homosexuality should be accepted in society	57	45
Favor death penalty	70	77
Abortion always legal	48	37
Stricter gun control	64	52
Make English official language	70	66
Favor school vouchers	51	54

Sources: National survey, Pew Research Center for the People and the Press (2000); and Morris P. Fiorina et al., *Culture War? The Myth of a Polarized America* (New York: Longman, 2005).

For those Americans who do firmly adopt a party label, their party often becomes a voter's central political reference symbol and perceptual screen, a prism or filter through which the world of politics and government flows and is interpreted. For these partisans, party identification is a significant aspect of their political personality and a way of defining and explaining themselves to others. The loyalty generated by the label can be as intense as any enjoyed by sports teams and alma maters.

PARTICIPATION

Deciding on a Political Party

Individual party identifications are reinforced by the legal institutionalization of the major parties. Because of restrictive ballot laws, campaign finance rules, the powerful inertia of political tradition, and many other factors, voters for all practical purposes are limited to a choice between a Democrat and a Republican in almost all elections—a situation that naturally encourages the pragmatic choosing up of sides. About half of the states require a voter to state a party preference (or independent status) when registering to vote, and they restrict voting in a party primary only to registrants in that particular party, making it an incentive for voters to affiliate themselves with a party.[20]

Like individuals, groups vary in the degree to which they identify with the Democratic Party or the Republican Party. (See Table 11.2.) In modern American politics

TABLE 11.2 PARTY IDENTIFICATION BY GROUP AFFILIATION

		Democratic Party	Independent Party	Republican Party
Region	North East	30	43	22
	North Central	29	30	30
	South	35	29	30
	West	30	35	30
Gender	Male	25	38	30
	Female	37	29	38
Race	Asian	18	39	36
	Black	61	33	2
	Hispanic	36	36	15
	White	25	32	36
Age	<30	31	42	21
	30-49	29	32	30
	50 +	34	30	31
Income	<35,000	33	35	25
	35,000-69,999	34	29	33
	70,000 +	26	30	38
Education	High School or	32	36	25
	College	29	30	34
	Advanced Degree	39	25	32
Union Member	Yes	36	38	20
Religion Type	Protestant	31	31	32
	Catholic	32	33	30
	Jewish	60	20	17
Religious Attendance	Weekly or >	31	29	34
	Monthly	31	32	32
	< Monthly	38	31	25
Marital Status	Married	28	29	36
	Single	32	42	20
	Divorced	33	35	25
Ideology	Conservative	18	28	48
	Moderate	29	37	30
	Liberal	51	39	6

Note: In this table, independent leaners are collapsed into the independent column. Partisans and strong partisans are collapsed into the party columns. Due to rounding, not all rows equal 100 percent.

Source: National Election Study 2004.

VIDEO ROUNDTABLE
The Difference Between Democrats and Republicans

the geographic regions are closely contested between the parties. A gender gap also persists in American politics. In 2004, for example, exit polls showed that women favored Democrats, and men favored Republicans. George W. Bush received 55 percent of the men's vote versus 44 percent for Kerry, while Bush received 48 percent of the female vote versus Kerry's 51 percent.

Race and ethnicity are extremely significant factors in determining party affiliation. African Americans, for example, almost always are Democrats. Hispanics supplement African Americans as Democratic Party stalwarts; by more than three to one, Hispanics prefer the Democratic Party. Voting patterns of Puerto Ricans are very similar to African Americans, while Mexican Americans also favor the Democrats, but by smaller margins. An exception is the Cuban American population, whose anti–Fidel Castro tilt leads to support for the Republican Party.

Age has long been associated with party identification, with most voters developing their partisan affiliations based on formative political experiences growing up. For example, many voters who were alive during the Great Depression identify strongly with the Democratic Party, whereas many who were young during the Reagan years today identify with the Republican Party. Today, generally the very youngest and very oldest voters tend to prefer the Democratic Party, while middle-age voters favor the Republican Party.

Occupation, income, and education also influence party affiliation. The GOP remains predominant among executives, professionals, and white-collar workers, whereas the Democrats lead substantially among trial lawyers, educators, and blue-collar workers. Labor union members are also Democratic by two to one. Women who do not work outside the home are less liberal and Democratic than those who do. Occupation, income, and education are closely related, of course, so many of the same partisan patterns appear in all three classifications. Democratic support generally decreases as one climbs the income scale. Those with a college education tend to support the Republican Party, while those with advanced degrees tend to be nonpartisan.

Party preferences by religion are also traditional, but with modern twists. White Protestants—especially Methodists, Presbyterians, and Episcopalians—favor Republicans, whereas Catholics and, even more so, Jewish voters tend to favor the Democratic Party. Decreased polarization is apparent all around, though.[21] Democrats have made inroads among many liberal Protestant denominations over the past three decades, and Republicans can now sometimes claim up to 25 percent of the Jewish population and a nearly equal share of the Catholic vote. Evangelical Christians are somewhat less Republican than commonly believed. The GOP usually has just a 10 percent edge among them, primarily because so many African Americans, who are strongly pro-Democrat, are also members of this group.

Ideologically, there are few surprises. Liberals are overwhelmingly Democratic and conservatives are staunchly Republican in most surveys and opinion studies.

THE FUTURE OF PARTY POLITICS

Over the past two decades, numerous political scientists as well as other observers, journalists, and party activists have become increasingly anxious about **dealignment,** a general decline in partisan identification and loyalty in the electorate.[22] Since parties traditionally provide political information and serve as an engine of political participation, it has been feared that weakening party attachments are undermining political involvement. Many public opinion surveys have shown an increase in independents at the expense of the two major parties. The Center for Political Studies/Survey Research Center (CPS/SRC) of the University of Michigan has charted the rise of self-described independents from a low of 19 percent in 1958 to a peak of 40 percent in 2000.

From 1952 to 1964 about three-fourths or more of the electorate volunteered a party choice without prodding, but since 1970 an average of less than two-thirds has been willing to do so. Professed independents have increased from around one-fifth of the electorate in the 1950s to over one-third during the last three decades. In recent years the numbers of voters who identify with parties has stabilized, but the numbers still lag far behind historical norms.

Nevertheless, the parties' decline can easily be exaggerated. Although political parties have evolved considerably and changed form from time to time, they usually have been reliable vehicles for mass participation in a representative democracy. The parties' journeys through U.S. history have been characterized by the same ability to adapt to prevailing conditions that is often cited as the genius of the Constitution. Both major parties exhibit flexibility and pragmatism, which help ensure their survival and the success of the society they serve.

Despite massive changes in political conditions and frequent dramatic shifts in the electorate's mood, the two major parties not only have achieved remarkable longevity but also have almost always provided strong competition for each other and the voters at the national level. (See Global Perspective: The Emergence of New Parties for information on how America's experience with parties differs from most European nations.) Of the thirty presidential elections from 1884 to 2004, for instance, the Republicans won seventeen and the Democrats fourteen.

The sharp rise in party unity scores in Congress discussed earlier in the chapter suggests the party in government is alive and well, while the unprecedented fund-raising of the party organizations suggests that political parties are here to stay. Perhaps most of all,

dealignment
A general decline in partisan identification and loyalty in the electorate.

Declining Political Parties

Global Perspective

THE EMERGENCE OF NEW PARTIES

As we have seen in this chapter, the American political party system essentially is a two-party system. Occasionally, third parties or independent candidates surface and make a bid to win public office, but for all practical purposes, Americans remain wedded to the Republican and Democratic parties. Such long-standing allegiances are not the case in Western Europe. There, support for new political parties (those founded since 1960) has been growing steadily over the past four decades at the expense of older established political parties, regardless of whether we look at presidential systems or parliamentary ones. The emergence of these new parties is tied to voter dissatisfaction with existing parties and the ability of new parties to tap into very specific complaints and concerns on the part of citizens.

In the 1960s, new parties received only 3.9 percent of the vote across Western Europe. They were most successful in France (16.3 percent) and least successful in Great Britain (0 percent) and Ireland (0.3 percent). Their percentage of the vote increased to 9.7 percent in the 1970s and to 15.3 percent in the 1980s. In the 1990s, new parties received 23.7 percent of all votes cast in Western Europe—a 19.8 percent increase.

The following table shows the growth of support for new parties in selected Western European states. Only in Great Britain have they failed to increase their share of the vote.

MEAN PERCENTAGE OF VOTE RECEIVED BY NEW PARTIES

	1960s	1970s	1980s	1990s
Finland	1.6	8.2	13.7	22.3
France	16.3	29.1	27.1	41.7
Germany	4.3	0.5	7.5	13.9
Great Britain	0	0.8	11.6	2.3
Italy	9.5	3.3	7.1	66.8
Netherlands	2.3	26.6	44.5	45.9

Even more significant than the growth in support for new parties in Western Europe is the growing support over the past two decades for extremist parties—political parties at the ideological ends of the political spectrum. Those on the political left are most easily identified today as Green parties. They advocate a clearly defined and aggressive pro-environmental agenda. Those on the political right tend to be more difficult to classify. Many of the most visible ones, such as the National Front in France or the Freedom Party in Austria, advocate strongly nationalistic and anti-immigration policies that critics characterize as racist and anti-Semitic.

Jean-Marie Le Pen, leader of the French National Front, scored a surprising 16.86 percent of the vote in the 2002 presidential elections, enough for Le Pen to go on to a second round of voting with the incumbent Jacques Chirac. Having such a marginal and extreme party make it to a second round of voting was a first for French politics and sent shock waves throughout Europe and the world. Le Pen and the National Front's fortunes did not last far beyond the first round of voting, however, as Chirac easily won the second round with a convincing 82 percent of the vote. In Austria, the Freedom Party, led by Jörg Haider, gradually gained support during the 1990s, eventually becoming part of a coalition government in 2000. Many outside of Austria, especially Jewish groups, fear the Freedom Party's influence because of its strident anti-immigrant, anti-European Union, and nationalistic political history. While the party lost a good deal of support in the 2002 elections, and Haider has stepped down as leader, the party persists. In 2004 Haider was elected governor of the Austrian province of Carinthia with over 42 percent of the vote.

MEAN PERCENTAGE OF VOTE RECEIVED BY EXTREMIST PARTIES

	Green Vote		Right-Wing Vote	
	1980s	1990s	1980s	1990s
Finland	2.7	7.0	0	0.3
France	0.9	8.4	6.7	14.2
Germany	5.1	6.4	0.3	2.5
Great Britain	0.3	0.3	0.1	0
Italy	1.3	2.7	6.6	20.9
Netherlands	1.1	5.6	0.6	1.8

QUESTIONS

1. Under what conditions might new parties develop in the United States and get the type of support that they have in Western Europe?
2. Which type of extremist parties are more likely to become electorally successful in the United States, ones on the political left or the political right? Why?

Source: Hans Keman, ed., *Comparative Democratic Politics* (London: Sage, 2002), 134, 137.

Comparing Political Parties

history teaches us that the development of parties in the United States has been inevitable. The Framers' utopian hopes for the avoidance of partisan faction, Madison's chief concern, have given way to an appreciation of the parties' constructive contributions to conflict definition and resolution throughout the history of the American republic. Political parties have become the primary means by which society addresses its irreconcilable differences, and as such they play an essential role in democratic society.

Interest Groups

THE FACE OF INTEREST GROUP POLITICS in the United States is changing as quickly as laws, political consultants, and technology allow. Big business and trade groups are increasing their activities and engagement in the political system at the same time that there is conflicting evidence concerning whether ordinary citizens join political groups. In an influential 1995 essay and later in a 2000 book, political scientist Robert Putnam argued that fewer Americans are joining groups, a phenomenon he labelled "bowling alone."[23] Others have faulted Putnam, concluding that America is in the midst of an "explosion of voluntary groups, activities and charitable donations [that] is transforming our towns and cities."[24] Although bowling leagues, which were a very common means of bringing people together, have withered, other groups such as volunteer groups, soccer associations, health clubs, and environmental groups are flourishing. Older groups such as the Elks Club and the League of Women Voters, whose membership was tracked by Putnam, no longer are attracting members, but this does not necessarily mean that people aren't joining groups; they just aren't joining the ones studied by Putnam,

Why is this debate so important? Political scientists believe that involvement in these kinds of community groups and activities enhances the level of **social capital,** "the web of cooperative relationships between citizens that facilitates resolution of collective action problems."[25] The more social capital that exists in a given community, the more citizens are engaged in its governance and well-being, and the more likely they are to work for the collective good.[26] This tendency to form small-scale associations for the public good, or **civic virtue,** as Putnam calls it, creates fertile ground within communities for improved political and economic development.[27] Thus, if Americans truly are joining fewer groups, we might expect the overall quality of government and its provision of services to suffer.

Interest groups are also important because they give the unrepresented or underrepresented an opportunity to have their voices heard, thereby making the government and its policy-making process more representative of diverse populations and perspectives.

WHY AND HOW INTEREST GROUPS FORM AND MAINTAIN THEMSELVES

Interest groups go by various names: special interests, pressure groups, organized interests, nongovernmental organizations (NGOs), political groups, lobby groups, and public interest groups. David B. Truman, one of the first political scientists to study interest groups, defines an organized interest as "any group that, on the basis of one or more shared attitudes, makes certain claims upon other groups in society for the establishment, maintenance, or enhancement of forms of behavior that are implied by shared attitudes."[28] Interest groups are differentiated from political parties largely by the fact that interest groups do not directly run candidates for office. Truman explained the formation of interest groups through what he termed **disturbance theory.** He hypothesized that groups arise, in part, to counteract the activities of other groups or of organized special interests.

Political scientist Robert Salisbury expanded on Truman's theories by arguing that groups form when resources—be they clean air, women's rights, or rights of the unborn, for example—are inadequate or scarce. Unlike Truman, Salisbury stresses the role that leaders, or what he terms "entrepreneurs," play in the formation of groups.[29]

Political scientists have studied several phenomena that contribute in varying degrees—individually and collectively—to particular groups' successes. These include: (1) leaders; (2) patrons and funding; and, (3) a solid membership base.

Interest group theorists frequently acknowledge the key role that leaders play in the formation, viability, and success of interest groups while noting that leaders often vary from rank-and-file members on various policies.[30] The role of an interest-group leader

social capital
The myriad relationships that individuals enjoy that facilitate the resolution of community problems through collective action.

civic virtue
The tendency to form small-scale associations for the public good.

**Comparing
Interest Groups**

disturbance theory
Political scientist David B. Truman's theory that interest groups form in part to counteract the efforts of other groups.

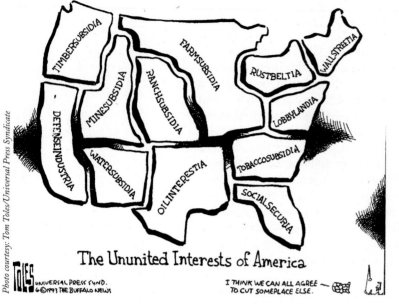

The Ununited Interests of America

I THINK WE CAN ALL AGREE —
TO CUT SOMEPLACE ELSE.

UNIVERSAL PRESS SYND.
©1993 THE BUFFALO NEWS

Photo courtesy: Tom Toles/Universal Press Syndicate

■ Geography often determines the kinds of special interests that are most common in a given region.

VIDEO ROUNDTABLE

Pluralism

patron
Person who finances a group or individual activity.

collective good
Something of value that cannot be withheld from a nonmember of a group, for example, a tax write-off or a better environment.

free rider problem
Potential members fail to join a group because they can get the benefit, or collective good, sought by the group without contributing the effort.

is similar to that of an entrepreneur in the business world. Leaders of groups must find ways to attract members. As in the marketing of a new product, an interest-group leader must offer something attractive to persuade members to join. Potential members of the group must be convinced that the benefits of joining outweigh the costs.

All interest groups require adequate funding to build their memberships as well as to advance their policy objectives. Governments, foundations, and wealthy individuals can serve as **patrons,** providing crucial start-up funds for groups, especially public interest groups.[31] Advertising, litigating, and lobbying are expensive. Without financiers, few public interest groups could survive their initial start-up period.

Organizations usually are composed of three kinds of members. At the top are a relatively small number of leaders who devote most of their energies to the single group. The second tier of members is generally involved psychologically as well as organizationally. They are the workers of the group—they attend meetings, pay dues, and chair committees to see that things get done. In the bottom tier are the rank and file, members who don't actively participate. They pay their dues and call themselves group members, but they do little more. Most group members fall into this last category.

Groups vary tremendously in their ability to enroll what are called potential members. According to economist Mancur Olson Jr., all groups provide some **collective good**—that is, something of value, such as money, a tax write-off, a good feeling, or a better environment, that can't be withheld from a nonmember.[32] If one union member at a factory gets a raise, for example, all other workers at that factory will, too. Therefore, those who don't join or work for the benefit of the group still reap the rewards of the group's activity. The downside of this phenomenon is called the **free rider problem.** As Olson asserts, potential members may be unlikely to join a group because they realize that they will receive many of the benefits the group achieves, regardless of their participation. Not only is it irrational for free riders to join any group, but the bigger the group, the greater the free rider problem. Thus, groups need to provide a variety of other incentives to convince potential members to join. These can be newsletters, discounts, or simply a good feeling.

THE ORIGINS AND DEVELOPMENT OF AMERICAN INTEREST GROUPS

Although all kinds of local groups proliferated throughout the colonies and in the new states, it was not until the 1830s, as communications networks improved, that the first groups national in scope emerged. Many of these first national groups were single-issue groups deeply rooted in the Christian religious revivalism that was sweeping the nation. Concern with humanitarian issues such as temperance (total abstinence from alcoholic beverages), peace, education, and slavery led to the founding of numerous associations dedicated to solving these problems. Among the first of these groups was the American Anti-Slavery Society, founded in 1833 by William Lloyd Garrison.

After the Civil War, more groups were founded. For example, the Women's Christian Temperance Union (WCTU) was created in 1874 with the goal of outlawing the sale of liquor. Its members, many of them quite religious, believed that the consumption of alcohol was an evil injurious to family life because many men drank away their paychecks, leaving no money to feed or clothe their families.

Business interests began to play even larger roles in both state and national politics. A popular saying of the day noted that the Standard Oil Company did everything to the Pennsylvania legislature except refine it. Increasingly large trusts, monopolies, business combinations, and corporate conglomerations in the oil, steel, and sugar industries became sufficiently powerful to control many representatives in the state and national legislatures.

By the 1890s, a profound change had occurred in the nation's political and social outlook. Rapid industrialization, an influx of immigrants, and monopolistic business practices created a host of problems, including crime, poverty, squalid and unsafe working conditions, and widespread political corruption. Many Americans began to believe that new measures would be necessary to impose order on this growing chaos and to curb some of the more glaring problems. The political and social movement that grew out of these concerns was called the Progressive movement.

In response to the pressure applied by Progressive-era groups, the national government began to regulate business. Because businesses had a vested interest in keeping wages low and costs down, more business groups organized to consolidate their strength and to counter Progressive moves. Not only did governments have to mediate Progressive and business demands, but they also had to accommodate the role of organized labor, which often allied itself with Progressive groups against big business.

The National Association of Manufacturers (NAM) was founded in 1895 by manufacturers who had suffered business reverses in the economic panic of 1893 and who believed that they were being affected adversely by the growth of organized labor. The second major business organization came into being in 1912, when the U.S. Chamber of Commerce was created with the assistance of the Department of Commerce and Labor. (The chamber was created before that department was split into the Department of Commerce and the Department of Labor.)

Until the creation of the American Federation of Labor (AFL) in 1886, there was not any real national union activity. The AFL brought skilled workers from several trades together into one stronger national organization for the first time. As the AFL grew in power, many business owners began to press individually or collectively to quash the unions. As business interests pushed states for what are called open shop laws to outlaw unions in their factories, the AFL became increasingly political. It also was forced to react to the success of big businesses' use of legal injunctions to prohibit union organization. In 1914, massive lobbying by the AFL and its members led to passage of the Clayton Act, which labor leader Samuel Gompers hailed as the Magna Carta of the labor movement. This law allowed unions to organize free from prosecution and also guaranteed their right to strike, a powerful weapon against employers. Membership in labor unions held steady throughout the early and mid-1900s and then skyrocketed toward the end of the Depression. By then, organized labor began to be a potent political force as it was able to turn out its members in support of particular political candidates. Labor became a stronger force in U.S. politics when the American Federation of Labor merged with the Congress of Industrial Organizations in 1955. Concentrating its efforts largely on the national level, the new AFL-CIO immediately turned its energies to pressuring the government to protect concessions won from employers at the bargaining table and to other issues of concern to its members, including minimum wage laws, the environment, civil rights, medical insurance, and health care.

More recently, the once fabled political clout of organized labor has been on the wane at the national level. Union membership has plummeted as the nation has changed from a land of manufacturing workers and farmers to a nation of white-collar professionals and service workers. Thus, unions and agricultural organizations no longer have the large memberships or the political clout once held in governmental circles. Even worse for the future of the labor movement in the United States, at least in the short run, is the split that occurred at the AFL-CIO's 2005 annual meeting. Plagued by continuing hemorrhaging of its membership, and mired in disagreement of how much money to devote to the campaigns of Democrats at a time when Republicans controlled all three branches of government, three of the largest member

Join the Debate

SHOULD THERE BE LIMITS ON INTEREST GROUP PARTICIPATION?

OVERVIEW: The First Amendment to the Constitution guarantees the right to freedom of speech, press, association and the right to "petition the government for a redress of grievances." These are necessary rights in a democracy because they guarantee the right of the people—within the framework of law—to have their voice heard by the government. Grievances can be political or social in nature, and all citizens have the right to petition the government to have their (sometimes narrow) interest or issue addressed. This right includes expressing policy preferences. While political speech and activity as well as the actions of government are regulated by law to prevent the encroachment of undue influence and corruption, the line between appropriate regulation and rights violations often is difficult to discern. Additionally, in order for government to fulfill its functions, it must attempt to balance fairly the claims of very diverse competing interests. Because the framework within which interest groups and government must operate is contentious, regulation is necessary. But, when a group lobbies to change government policies, can the government require full disclosure of the group's activities and finances?

Depending on what is done with the information gathered from interest group disclosure requirements, the government may be acting in the public interest. For example, part of the mandate from the Lobbying Disclosure Act of 1995 (LDA) is to facilitate public access to information about lobbying groups as well as about the government's knowledge of their activities. The goal is to allow concerned citizens to verify accountability of both group and government activity—this allows government watchdog groups such as OpenSecrets to correlate lobbying activities with perceived government response. Moreover, insisting that groups disclose information allows both government and the public to know what individuals or groups are behind a lobby's agenda.

The political nature of lobbying activity may mean that interest groups are subject to a higher standard of disclosure and scrutiny. Just as the American people demand transparency in government activity, it seems reasonable that they be provided with information regarding those interest groups monitoring (or supporting) the government. To that end, requiring disclosure of group information is rational. But, what about the right to privacy? Should interest groups have the same right to privacy as individuals? After all, citizens are not required to disclose the reasons behind their votes or why they engage in political activity the way they do. Why should interest groups be denied this standard of privacy?

ARGUMENTS FOR REGULATING INTEREST GROUP ACTIVITIES

- **Interest groups are not given a constitutional role to make or influence policy.** Though individuals and groups have the right to lobby the government, they have no unrestricted right to do so. Given literally thousands of interests, the government must have some means to prioritize and determine the legitimacy of various groups. For example, should a local 4H group have the same voice and access to national policy makers as the National Dairy Association?

unions seceded from the AFL-CIO. The Service Employees International Union (SEIU), the Teamsters, and the United Food and Commercial Workers Union left to form the Change to Win Coalition.[33] This split, coupled with the fact that 84 percent of all labor union members live in but twelve states, continues to make it difficult to predict any renewed labor presence nationwide.[34]

The Rise of the Interest Group State During the 1960s and 1970s, the Progressive spirit reappeared in the rise of public interest groups. **Public interest groups** are organizations "that seek a collective good, the achievement of which will not selectively and materially benefit the membership or activists of the organization.[35] Many Progressive era groups were created to solve the varied problems of new immigrants and the poor. Today, civil rights and liberties groups such as the NAACP and the American Civil Liberties Union (ACLU), environmental groups, good government groups such as Common Cause, peace groups, church groups, groups that speak out for those who cannot (such as children, the mentally ill, or animals), and

public interest group
An organization that seeks a collective good that will not selectively and materially benefit the members of the group.

■ **Regulation is necessary to ensure the public knows why and in what capacity an interest group is acting.** LDA's regulatory mandate is to ensure accountability in the lobbying process. The American public needs to know about corruption or misinformation not only coming from the government, but coming from interest groups as well. For instance, the Rainbow Push Coalition has been implicated in lobbying the City of Chicago to keep a dangerous after-hours dance club open in which a fire subsequently caused twenty-one deaths. The club owners, Rainbow Push, and certain Chicago politicians were known to have a business relationship.

■ **Regulation of interest groups allows the government to level the playing field.** Research published by the American Political Science Association (APSA) contends that inequality and unequal access to wealth harms the American democratic process. APSA implies that wealthier groups have a larger voice and thus more access to policy makers. By regulating interest groups, the federal government can ensure relative equality of access—and voice—to policy makers.

ARGUMENTS AGAINST REGULATING INTEREST GROUP ACTIVITIES

■ **Government regulation of interest groups may stifle political speech.** For example, the U.S. Supreme Court upheld the Bipartisan Campaign Reform Act's provision prohibiting groups from issue advertising sixty days prior to a general election. Many scholars and legal experts believe that this is a fundamental violation of political speech rights, as it is now believed that money gives "voice" to the political process—and to deny groups the right to political advertisement is to deny political speech.

■ **Regulation of groups essentially creates approved speech and politics.** By using regulation to determine which groups have the right to lobby the government, the government is in effect establishing which groups are legitimate (in both their activities and speech) and which are not. It is not the government's role to conclude whether a group's political activity and speech are more or less legitimate or important.

■ **Government regulation of interest groups is not necessary.** In an open, pluralistic society, interest groups are subject to market dynamics. That is, those groups that truly represent broad or important interests will have their views heard over those that do not. Thus, a natural voice is given to those groups deemed by the American people to represent important interests and issues.

QUESTIONS

1. Is compelling disclosure of group information a violation of privacy rights? How can this be reconciled with the public's right to know?
2. Does the political nature of lobbyist activity demand a higher level of governmental scrutiny?

SELECTED READINGS

Herrnson, Paul S., Ronald G. Shaiko, and Clyde Wilcox, editors. *The Interest Group Connection,* Second Edition. Washington, D.C.: CQ Press, 2004.

Rozell, Mark J., Clyde Wilcox, David Madland. *Interest Groups in American Campaigns: The New Face of Electioneering,* Second Edition. Washington, D.C.: CQ Press, 2005.

organizations such as Concerned Women for America are examples of public interest groups. Generally, liberal public interest groups devote themselves to representing the interests of African Americans, women, the elderly, the poor, and consumers, or to working on behalf of the environment. Many of their leaders and members were active in the civil rights and anti–Vietnam War movements of the 1960s.

The civil rights and anti-war struggles left many Americans feeling cynical about a government that they believed failed to respond to the will of the majority. They also believed that if citizens banded together, they could make a difference. Thus, two major new public interest groups—Common Cause and Public Citizen, Inc.—were founded. Common Cause, a good-government group that acts as a watchdog over the federal government, is similar to some of the early Progressive movement's public interest groups. Common Cause effectively has challenged aspects of the congressional seniority system, successfully urged the passage of sweeping campaign financing reforms, and played a major role in the enactment of legislation authorizing federal financing of presidential campaigns. Perhaps more well known than Common Cause is

SIMULATION

You Are a Member of Concerned Citizens for World Justice

On Campus

SPEAKING UP

Many conservative college students believe that their voices are being stifled on campuses across the United States. Some charge that there is discrimination by professors and a lack of respect of diverse views in the classroom. Others say that the hiring process favors liberal professors. Some charge a bias in the selection of campus speakers and funding of groups.

A 2002 study by the Center for the Study of Popular Culture revealed that at the nation's top thirty-two universities, Democratic professors greatly outnumbered Republicans. Said Harvey Mansfield, a conservative Harvard political scientist, "We have sixty members in the department of government. Maybe three are Republicans. How could that be just by chance? How could that be fair?"[a]

The Center for the Study of Popular Culture has drafted an Academic Bill of Rights that it is urging colleges and universities to adopt. This document requests institutions of higher learning to "include both liberal and conservative viewpoints in their selection of campus speakers and syllabuses for courses and to choose faculty members 'with a view toward fostering a plurality of methodologies and perspectives.'"[b] It also notes a variety of ways in which students' academic freedom can be compromised, including:

■ Mocking national or religious leaders.
■ Forcing students to take a particular point of view in assignments.
■ Requiring readings that cover only one side of an issue.

University administrators and the American Association of University Professors (AAUP) have been nearly unanimous in their disapproval of the center's proposed Academic Bill of Rights. "The danger of such guidelines," says the AAUP, "is that they invite diversity to be measured by political standards that diverge from the academic criteria of the scholarly profession." The AAUP points out that to comply with this Academic Bill of Rights, a professor professing a Nazi philosophy would need to be hired even "if that philosophy is not deemed a reasonable scholarly option within the discipline."[c]

Former Reagan White House lawyer David Horowitz, president of the Center for the Study of Popular Culture in California, has penned *The Professors: The 101 Most Dangerous Academics in America,* profiling the professors he considers among the most liberal in America and accusing them of "poisoning the minds of today's college students."[d] His group, Students for Academic Freedom, has chapters on more

than 150 college campuses around the nation and works to pass state academic freedom legislation. It also works with many campus College Republican chapters. Its work has proven effective, especially in drawing the attention of conservative lawmakers to the problems that Horowitz and many other conservatives see as the liberal orthodoxy on college campuses. The Pennsylvania legislature, for example, approved a resolution calling on its fourteen state colleges to make sure that their campuses are free from what the center calls "the imposition of ideological orthodoxy."[e]

At some schools, including the University of Colorado, students can post alleged discrimination by liberal professors on special student-created Web sites.[f] The University of Texas at Austin has a "Professor Watch List," and Students for Academic Freedom and NoIndoctrination.org allow students from all over the country to post complaints about particular professors. Many professors view this as a form of blacklisting similar to that which existed in the 1950s when professors who were suspected of being members of or sympathetic to the Communist Party were barred from teaching positions.

QUESTIONS

1. On some campuses, rewards of up to $100 have been posted for lecture notes and recordings of liberal professors' lectures. Are these legitimate interest group tactics or violations of basic principles of academic freedom?
2. Getting issues on the public agenda is often as important for groups as the actual passage of legislation or rules. How successful have conservative student groups been on your campus in having issues of classroom bias addressed?

[a]Quoted in Yilu Zhao, "Taking the Liberalism Out of Liberal Arts," *New York Times* (April 3, 2004): B9.
[b]Zhao, "Taking the Liberalism Out."
[c]http://www.aaup.org.
[d]David Horowitz, *The Professors: The 101 Most Dangerous Academics in America* (New York: Regnery, 2006).
[e]Bob Kemper, "Conservatives Gain Foothold on Campus," *Atlanta Journal-Constitution* (October 9, 2005): 1C.
[f]Dave Curtin, "Students' Site Solicits Allegations of CU Bias," *Denver Post* (January 20, 2004): A1.

Public Citizen, Inc., the collection of groups headed by Ralph Nader (who later went on to run as a candidate for president in 1996, 2000, and 2004).

Conservative Response: Religious and Ideological Groups
During the 1960s and 1970s, various public interest groups and civil rights and women's rights movements grew and achieved success in shaping and defining the public agenda. Conservatives, concerned by the activities of these liberal groups, responded by

forming religious and ideological groups that became a potent force in U.S. politics. In 1978, the Reverend Jerry Falwell founded the first major new religious group, the Moral Majority. The Moral Majority was widely credited with assisting in the election of Ronald Reagan as president in 1980 as well as with the defeats of several liberal Democratic senators that same year. Falwell claimed to have sent 3 to 4 million newly registered voters to the polls.[36]

In 1990, televangelist Pat Robertson, host of the popular television program *The 700 Club*, formed a new group, the Christian Coalition. Since then, it has grown in power and influence. The Christian Coalition played an important role in the Republicans' winning control of the Congress in 1994. In 2004, the group distributed more than 100 million voter guides in churches throughout the United States. The Christian Coalition also lobbies Congress and the White House. The group had the sympathetic ear of President George W. Bush, whom it helped elect. In fact, one of Bush's first moves as president was to create an Office of Faith-Based and Community Initiatives to work with religious groups to effect policy change.

The Christian Coalition is not the only conservative interest group to play an important role in the policy process as well as in elections at the state and national level. The National Rifle Association (NRA), an active opponent of gun control legislation, saw its membership rise in recent years (see Figure 11.5), as well as its importance in Washington, D.C. The NRA and its political action committee spent $20 million to reelect President George W. Bush in 2004. Conservative interests are also pressed by student groups. (See On Campus: Speaking Up.)

VIDEO ROUNDTABLE
Successful Interest Groups

FIGURE 11.5 NRA MEMBERSHIP

The National Rifle Association (NRA), a single-issue interest group, lobbies against any law that would restrict an individual's right to bear arms. NRA membership tends to increase in reaction to proposed gun control legislation or near an election. Interestingly, following the 1999 Columbine High School shooting in Colorado, in which twelve people were killed and several others were wounded, membership increased dramatically. Its membership also took a jump after the 9/11 terrorist attacks.

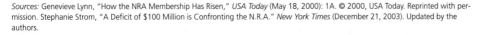
Sources: Genevieve Lynn, "How the NRA Membership Has Risen," *USA Today* (May 18, 2000): 1A. © 2000, USA Today. Reprinted with permission. Stephanie Strom, "A Deficit of $100 Million is Confronting the N.R.A." *New York Times* (December 21, 2003). Updated by the authors.

WHAT DO INTEREST GROUPS DO?

Interest groups are involved in myriad activities. They lobby all three branches of government, and engage in grassroots lobbying. They also participate in protest activities, and many are actively engaged in the campaign process, among other activities.

lobbying
The activities of a group or organization that seeks to influence legislation and persuade political leaders to support the group's position.

lobbyist
Interest group representative who seeks to influence legislation that will benefit his or her organization through political persuasion.

**You Are a
Lobbyist**

Lobbying Most interest groups put lobbying at the top of their agendas. **Lobbying** is the process by which interest groups attempt to assert their influence on the policy-making process. The term **lobbyist** refers to any representative of a group that attempts to influence a policy maker by one or more of the tactics listed in Table 11.3. Almost all interest groups lobby by testifying at hearings and contacting legislators. Other groups also provide information that decision makers might not have the time, opportunity, or interest to gather on their own.

Lobbying Congress Today, efforts to reform lobbying continue to plague members of Congress, who are the targets of a wide variety of lobbying activities: congressional testimony on behalf of a group, individual letters from interested constituents, campaign contributions, trips, and speaking fees (see Figure 11.6). The outright payment of money for votes is illegal, of course, but there are numerous documented instances of money changing hands for votes. Because, as discussed in chapter 6, lobbying plays such an important role in Congress, many effective lobbyists often are former members of that body, former staff aides, former White House officials or Cabinet officers, or other Washington insiders.

Lobbying the Executive Branch Groups often target one or more levels of the executive branch because there are so many potential access points, including the president, White House staff, and the numerous levels of the executive-branch bureau-

TABLE 11.3 GROUPS AND LOBBYISTS USING EACH LOBBYING TECHNIQUE (PERCENTAGE)

Technique	STATE-BASED GROUPS		WASHINGTON, D.C.-BASED GROUPS (n = 175)
	Lobbyists (n = 595)	Organizations (n = 301)	
1. Testifying at legislative hearings	98	99	99
2. Contacting government officials directly to present point of view	98	97	98
3. Helping to draft legislation	96	88	85
4. Alerting state legislators to the effects of a bill on their districts	96	94	75
5. Having influential constituents contact legislator's office	94	92	80
6. Consulting with government officials to plan legislative strategy	88	84	85
7. Attempting to shape implementation of policies	88	85	89
8. Mounting grassroots lobbying efforts	88	86	80
9. Helping to draft regulations, rules, or guidelines	84	81	78
10. Raising new issues and calling attention to previously ignored problems	85	83	84
11. Engaging in informal contacts with officials	83	81	95
12. Inspiring letter-writing or telegram campaigns	82	83	84
13. Entering into coalitions with other groups	79	93	90
14. Talking to media	73	74	86
15. Serving on advisory commissions and boards	58	76	76
16. Making monetary contributions to candidates	—	45	58
17. Attempting to influence appointment to public office	44	42	53
18. Doing favors for officials who need assistance	41	36	56
19. Filing suit or otherwise engaging in litigation	36	40	72
20. Working on election campaigns	—	29	24
21. Endorsing candidates	—	24	22
22. Running advertisements in media about position	18	21	31
23. Engaging in protests or demonstrations	13	21	20

Sources: State-Based Groups: Anthony J. Nownes and Patricia Freeman, "Interest Group Activity in the States," *Journal of Politics* 60 (1998): 92. Washington, D.C.-Based Groups: Kay Lehman Schlozman and John Tierney, "More of the Same: Washington Pressure Group Activity in a Decade of Change," *Journal of Politics* 45 (1983): 358.

FIGURE 11.6 TOP LOBBYING EXPENDITURES

For most interest groups, lobbying is their most important activity. Successful lobbying efforts require spending large amounts of money, as shown in the bar graph.

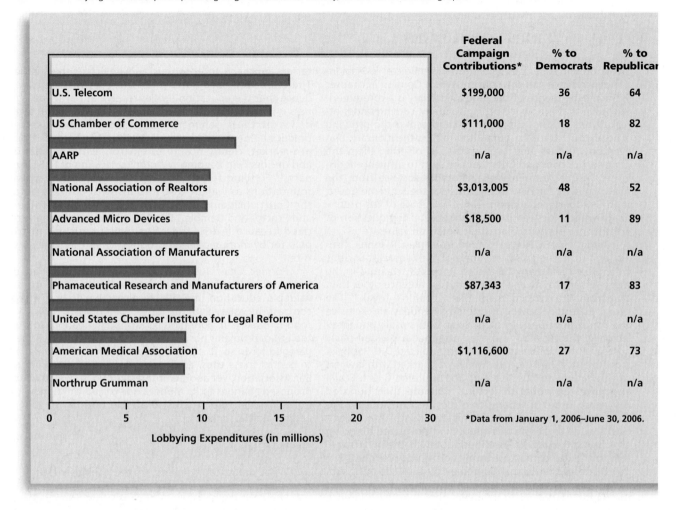

	Federal Campaign Contributions*	% to Democrats	% to Republican
U.S. Telecom	$199,000	36	64
US Chamber of Commerce	$111,000	18	82
AARP	n/a	n/a	n/a
National Association of Realtors	$3,013,005	48	52
Advanced Micro Devices	$18,500	11	89
National Association of Manufacturers	n/a	n/a	n/a
Phamaceutical Research and Manufacturers of America	$87,343	17	83
United States Chamber Institute for Legal Reform	n/a	n/a	n/a
American Medical Association	$1,116,600	27	73
Northrup Grumman	n/a	n/a	n/a

Lobbying Expenditures (in millions)

*Data from January 1, 2006–June 30, 2006.

Sources: Political Moneyline, http://www.tray.com; Center for Responsive Politics, http://www.opensecrets.org.

cracy. Groups try to work closely with the administration to influence policy decisions at their formulation and later implementation stages. As with congressional lobbying, the effectiveness of a group often depends on its ability to provide decision makers with important information and a sense of where the public stands on the issue.

An especially strong link exists between interest groups and regulatory agencies (see chapter 8). Because of the highly technical aspects of much regulatory work, many groups employ Washington attorneys and lobbying firms to deal directly with the agencies. So great is interest group influence in the decision-making process of these agencies that many people charge that the agencies have been captured by the interest groups.

VIDEO ROUNDTABLE

Lobbyists

Lobbying the Courts The courts, too, have proved a useful target for interest groups.[37] (See American Values/American Voices: Trips for Judges.) Although you might think that the courts decide cases that affect only the parties involved or that they should be immune from political pressures, interest groups for years have recognized the value of lobbying the courts, especially the Supreme Court, and many political scientists view it as a form of political participation.[38] As shown in Table 11.3,

American Values/American Voices

TRIPS FOR JUDGES

As noted in American Values/American Voices: Judicial Independence and the Court of World Opinion in chapter 9, the independence of the federal judiciary is a core American value that is now, according to many, coming under attack. What was not discussed in chapter 8 is the growing concern that interest groups are affecting the judiciary, and even how judges and justices vote, by offering them the same sort of trips and gifts that are used to influence legislators. Justice Antonin Scalia's notable absence from the swearing in of the new Chief Justice of the Supreme Court, John G. Roberts Jr., added fuel to the debate of the propriety of what critics call judicial junkets and the question of whether or not they violate basic American values.

Although ABC News recorded Scalia playing tennis, fishing, and socializing with members of the Federalist Society, when asked later why he missed Roberts's swearing in, he was reluctant to say any more about his absence other than that he had a "commitment that I couldn't break." The event invitation, however, offered attendees an exclusive and "rare opportunity to spend time, both socially and intellectually, with Scalia."[a] He even attended a cocktail party hosted by the lobbying firm where indicted D.C. lobbyist Jack Abramoff had worked, which was packed with lawyers who regularly do business with the Supreme Court. Scalia also gave ten hours of lectures to more than hundred lawyers on issues of separation of powers.[b] He appeared to have no second thoughts about his attendance at the event, even though earlier he was resoundingly criticized for going on a hunting trip with Vice President Dick Cheney just before the Court heard a case involving the vice president.

Disclosure forms that Supreme Court justices must submit annually reveal that five of the justices accepted "tens of thousands of dollars in valuable gifts." Justice Clarence Thomas, for example, accepted golf club memberships, scholarships to help pay for his nephew's education, and even a rare Bible estimated to be worth nearly $20,000.[c] Interestingly, rules about what kinds of gifts jurists can accept apply only to lower federal court judges, but many critics believe that the justices of the Supreme Court should, by action and public pronouncements, follow a higher ethical standard.

The Community Rights Counsel (CRC), a liberal group that tracks what it calls "junketing judges," notes that it is conservative, anti-regulatory organizations that dominate the provision of exclusive, free trips for judges. The "big three"—the Law and Economics Center (LEC), the Foundation for Research on Economics and the Environment (FREE), and the Liberty Fund—provided trips for 125 judges and have conducted seminars, attended by about 14 percent of federal judiciary, that advance a conservative/liber-

tarian approach to economic and environmental issues.[d] The CRC's Web page notes that "there is considerable evidence that the education judges receive at Big Three seminars is influencing judicial opinions." It believes that attendance at these seminars makes judges more likely to practice a "new strand of judicial activism that is distinctly pro-market, clearly hostile to environmental regulations and decidedly in keeping with the curriculum of FREE seminars."[e] Funding for all three groups comes from private foundations as well as corporations with business before the Court, including Exxon Mobile, Ford Motor Company, and Proctor and Gamble.[f] The CRC, however, has been criticized because it does not offer similar criticisms of trips paid for by more moderate groups such as the Aspen Institute.[g]

Former Chief Justice William H. Rehnquist had defended these conferences, saying that judges "are getting valuable education unavailable elsewhere."[h] In a sharply contrasting voice, Senator Russell Feingold (D–WI) asked John G. Roberts Jr. during his confirmation hearings to study the ethics problems posed by these seminars. While Roberts pledged to do so, it is unlikely that any moves will be made to restrict these trips. While many looked to the American Bar Association, yet another interest group, to weigh in with proposed changes to its Model Code of Judicial Conduct to tighten travel rules, its first draft did nothing to suggest ending judicial junkets.[i]

QUESTIONS

1. What value can you see to these kinds of trips for judges?
2. Should there be an equal time rule requiring judges to attend courses offered by groups on both sides of the ideological divide, or should judges continue to attend courses of their own choosing?

[a]Brian Ross, "Supreme Court Ethics Problem?" *Nightline,* ABC News, January 23, 2006.

[b]Karen Abbott, "Scalia Takes Heat for 'Junket'; Lawyers Defend His Teaching of a Course at Colorado Resort," *Rocky Mountain News* (January 25, 2006): 9A.

[c]Abbott, "Scalia Takes Heat for 'Junket.'"

[d]"Who's Junketing the Judges," Trips for Judges, http://tripsforjudges.com.

[e]"Why Junkets Matter," Trips for Judges, http://tripsforjudges.com.

[f]"Funding Sources and Litigations Ties," Trips for Judges, http://tripsforjudges.com.

[g]"Judicial Seminars Are Not Always Junkets," *Tampa Tribune* (May 25, 2006): 16.

[h]"Rehnquist Defends Groups' Trips for Judges," *Milwaukee Journal Sentinel* (May 15, 2001): 4A.

[i]"Time to Ban Judicial Junkets," *New York Times* (October 15, 2005): A18; and Dorothy Samuels, "Judiciary, Too, Has a Lobbying Scandal," *Sacramento Bee* (January 22, 2006): E4.

72 percent of the Washington-based groups surveyed participated in litigation as a lobbying tool.

Generally, interest group lobbying of the courts can take two forms: direct sponsorship or the filing of *amicus curiae* briefs. Most major Supreme Court cases noted in this book have been sponsored by an interest group, or one or both of the parties in the case have been supported by one or more *amicus curiae* briefs.

Grassroots Lobbying As the term implies, grassroots lobbying is a form of pressure-group activity that attempts to involve individuals who contact their representatives directly in an effort to affect policy.[39] Although it often involves door-to-door informational or petition drives—a tried and true method of lobbying—the term also encompasses more modern forms such as fax and Internet lobbying of lawmakers.

Interest groups regularly try to inspire their members to engage in grassroots activity, hoping that lawmakers will respond to those pressures and the attendant publicity. In essence, the goal of many organizations is to persuade ordinary voters to serve as their advocates. In the world of lobbying, there are few things more useful than a list of committed supporters. Interest groups now run carefully targeted and costly television advertisements pitching one side of an argument. Some of these undefined masses, as they join together on the Internet or via faxes, may be mobilized into one or more groups.

Regulating Lobbying Practices For the first 150 years of our nation's history, federal lobbying practices went unregulated. While this continues to remain largely true in the courts, reforms have altered the state of affairs in Congress and the executive branch. In 1946, in an effort to limit the power of lobbyists, Congress passed the Federal Regulation of Lobbying Act, which required anyone hired to lobby any member of Congress to register and file quarterly financial reports. For years, few lobbyists actually filed these reports and numerous good government groups continued to argue for the strengthening of lobbying laws. Until 1995, however, their efforts were blocked by civil liberties groups such as the ACLU, who argued that registration provisions violate the First Amendment's freedom of speech and the right of citizens to petition the government.

Interest Groups and Campaign Finance

But, by 1995, public opinion polls began to show that Americans believed that the votes of members of Congress were available to the highest bidder. Thus, in late 1995, after nearly fifty years of inaction, Congress passed the first effort to regulate lobbying since the 1946 act. The Lobbying Disclosure Act employs a strict definition of lobbyist (one who devotes at least 20 percent of a client's or employer's time to lobbying activities). It also requires lobbyists to: (1) register with the clerk of the House and the secretary of the Senate; (2) report their clients and issues and the agency or house they lobbied; and, (3) estimate the amount they are paid by each client. (See Join the Debate: Should There Be Limits on Interest Group Participation?) These reporting requirements make it easier for watchdog groups or the media to monitor lobbying activities. In fact, a comprehensive analysis by the Center for Responsive Politics revealed that by June 2005, 32,890 lobbyists were registered. Nearly $4 million was spent on lobbying for every member of Congress.[40]

Formal lobbying of the executive branch is not governed by these restrictions. Executive branch employees are, however, constrained by the 1978 Ethics in Government Act. This act, enacted in the wake of the Watergate scandal, attempted to curtail questionable moves by barring members of the executive branch from representing any clients before their agency for one year after leaving governmental service. Thus, someone who worked in air pollution policy for the Environmental Protection Agency and then went to work for the Environmental Defense Fund would have to wait a year before lobbying his or her old agency.

Protest Activities An occasional though highly visible tactic used by some groups is protest activity. Although it is much more usual for a group's members to opt for more conventional forms of lobbying or to influence policy through the electoral process, when these forms of pressure-group activities are unsuccessful some groups (or individuals within groups) resort to more forceful legal as well as illegal measures to attract attention to their cause. Since the Revolutionary War, violent, illegal protest has been one tactic of organized interests. The Boston Tea Party, for example, involved breaking all sorts of laws, although no one was hurt physically. Other forms of protest, such as Shays's Rebellion, ended in tragedy for some participants. Much more recently, anti-war protestors have been willing to march and risk detention and jail in the United States. And, protesters regularly try to picket or protest meetings of the International Monetary Fund or the World Bank. Political conventions as well as inaugurations also routinely are targeted by protesters. Animal rights activists such as People for the Ethical Treatment of Animals (PETA), for example, often rely on illegal protest activities to draw attention to their cause. Members of the Animal Liberation Front, for example, stalked the wife of a pharmaceutical executive, broke into her car, stole her credit cards, and then made over $20,000 in unauthorized charitable donations.[41] Some radical groups post the names of people they believe to be engaging in wrongful activity on the Web, along with their addresses and threats. As a result, some groups have faced federal terrorism charges.

Election Activities In addition to trying to achieve their goals (or at least draw attention to them) through conventional and unconventional forms of lobbying, many interest groups also become involved more directly in the electoral process.

Candidate Recruitment and Endorsements Many interest groups claim to be nonpolitical. But, some interest groups recruit, endorse, and/or provide financial or other forms of support for political candidates. EMILY's List (EMILY stands for "Early money is like yeast—it makes the dough rise") was founded to support pro-choice Democratic Congressional women candidates, especially during party primary election contests. It now, however, like its Republican counterpart the WISH List (WISH stands for Women in the House and Senate), recruits and trains candidates at all levels in addition to contributing to their campaigns.

Getting Out the Vote Many interest groups believe that they can influence public policy by putting like-minded representatives in office. To that end, many groups across the ideological spectrum, such as the Christian Coalition and EMILY's List, launch massive get out the vote (GOTV) efforts. These include identifying prospective voters and getting them to the polls on Election Day. Well-financed interest groups such as MoveOn.org and Progress for America often produce issue-oriented ads for newspapers, radio, and television designed to educate the public as well as increase voter interest in election outcomes.

VIDEO DEBATE

Political Action Committees

Rating the Candidates or Office Holders Many liberal and conservative ideological groups rate candidates to help their members (and the general public) evaluate the voting records of members of Congress. The American Conservative Union (conservative) and the Americans for Democratic Action (liberal)—two groups at ideological polar extremes—routinely rate candidates and members of Congress based on their votes on key issues. (See Analyzing Visuals: Interest Group Ratings of Selected Members of Congress.) These scores help voters know more about their representatives' votes on issues that concern them.

political action committee (PAC)
Federally mandated, officially registered fund-raising committee that represents interest groups in the political process.

VISUAL LITERACY

PACS and the Money Trail

Political Action Committees As discussed in chapter 12, corporations, labor unions, and interest groups are allowed to form **political action committees (PACs)**. PACs allow these interests to raise money to contribute to political candidates in national elections. Unlike some contributions to interest groups, contributions to PACs are not tax deductible, and PACs generally don't have members who call legislators; instead, PACs have contributors who write checks specifically for the purpose of campaign donations. PAC money plays a significant role in the campaigns of many congressional incumbents, often averaging over half a House candidate's total campaign spending. PACs generally contribute to those who have helped them before and who serve on committees or subcommittees that routinely consider legislation of concern to that group.

Analyzing Visuals

INTEREST GROUP RATINGS OF SELECTED MEMBERS OF CONGRESS

Among the election activities of interest groups are the endorsement of candidates for public office and the rating of candidates and incumbents. Interest groups inform their members, as well as the public generally, of the voting records of office holders, helping voters make an informed voting decision. The table below displays the 2005 ratings of selected members of Congress by eight interest groups that vary greatly in their ideological tendencies. Each group rates the members of Congress on issues that are important to the group. For example, the AFL-CIO bases its rating on a member's votes in support of labor unions. After reviewing the table, answer the following critical thinking questions: Which members of the Senate would you consider the most liberal? Which groups' ratings did you use to reach your conclusion? Which members of the House would you consider the most conservative? Which groups' ratings did you use to reach your conclusion? Would it be important to know which of a representative's votes were used by each group to determine the rating? Explain your answer.

Member	ACU	ACLU	ADA	AFL-CIO	CC	CoC	LCV	NARAL
Senate								
Dianne Feinstein (D–CA)	12	78	95	69	0	50	90	100
Mitch McConnell (R-KY)	100	25	5	7	100	94	0	0
Kay Bailey Hutchison (R–TX)	95	22	15	7	100	94	5	20
Ted Kennedy (D–MA)	0	86	95	100	0	28	95	100
House								
John Boehner (R–OH)	100	0	0	13	91	88	0	0
Sheila Jackson Lee (D–TX)	14	95	100	93	7	56	61	100
Ileana Ros-Lehtinen (R–FL)	88	17	10	20	80	93	11	0
Henry Waxman (D–CA)	0	95	100	93	15	38	100	100

Key
ACU = American Conservative Union
ACLU = American Civil Liberties Union
ADA = Americans for Democratic Action
AFL-CIO = American Federation of Labor–Congress of Industrial Organizations
CC = Christian Coalition
CoC = Chamber of Commerce
LCV = League of Conservation Voters
NARAL = NARAL Pro-Choice America

Members are rated on a scale from 1 to 100, with 1 being the lowest and 100 being the highest support of a particular group's policies.

Interest Groups and Representation

Summary

A POLITICAL PARTY is an organized effort by office holders, candidates, activists, and voters to pursue their common interests by gaining and exercising power through the electoral process. The goal is to win office so as to exercise power and pursue common policy objectives.

The evolution of U.S. political parties has been remarkably smooth, and the stability of the Democratic and Republican groupings is a wonder, considering all the social and political tumult in U.S. history. For 150 years, the two-party system has served as the mechanism American society uses to organize and resolve social and political conflict. The Democratic and Republican Parties, through lengthy nominating processes, provide a screening mechanism for those who aspire to office, helping to weed out unqualified individuals, expose and test candidates' ideas on important policy questions, and ensure a measure of long-term continuity and accountability.

The basic structure of the major parties is complex and amorphous. The state and local parties are generally more important than the national ones, though campaign technologies and fund-raising concentrated in Washington, D.C., have helped to centralize power within national party committees.

While dealignment, a general decline in partisan identification and loyalty in the electorate, has undoubtedly occurred over the last fifty years, the future of the party system is not in doubt. Parties remain strong, adaptive, and essential players in the political process and are likely to remain so in the future.

Interest groups lie at the heart of the American social and political system. Those who study interest groups have offered a variety of definitions to explain what they are. Most definitions revolve around notions of associations or groups of individuals who share some sort of common interest or attitude and who try to influence or engage in activity to affect governmental policies or the people in government.

Interest groups, national in scope, did not begin to emerge until around the 1830s. Later, from 1890 to 1920, the Progressive movement emerged. The 1960s saw the rise of a wide variety of liberal interest groups. By the 1970s through the 1980s, legions of conservatives were moved to form new groups to counteract those efforts. Business groups, corporations, and unions established their presence in Washington, D.C.

Interest groups give Americans opportunities to make claims, as a group, on government. The most common activity of interest groups is lobbying, which takes many forms. Groups routinely pressure members of Congress and their staffs, the president and the bureaucracy, and the courts; they use a variety of techniques to educate and stimulate the public to pressure key governmental decision makers. Interest groups also attempt to influence the outcome of elections; some run their own candidates for office. Others rate elected officials to inform their members how particular legislators stand on issues of importance to them or establish political action committees (PACs).

KEY TERMS

candidate-centered politics, p. 322
civic virtue, p. 335
civil service laws, p. 321
coalition, p. 323
collective good, p. 336
critical election, p. 322
dealignment, p. 333
direct primary, p. 321
disturbance theory, p. 335
free rider problem, p. 336
interest group, p. 316
issue-oriented politics, p. 321
lobbying, p. 342
lobbyist, p. 342
machine, p. 321
national convention, p. 329
national party platform, p. 327
party identification, p. 330
party realignment, p. 322
patron, p. 336
political action committee (PAC), p. 346

political party, p. 316
public interest group, p. 338
social capital, p. 335
secular realignment, p. 323
think tank, p. 330
ticket-split, p. 321

SELECTED READINGS

Aldrich, John Herbert. *Why Parties? The Origin and Transformation of Political Parties in America.* Chicago: University of Chicago Press, 1995.

Baumgartner, Frank, and Beth Leech. *Basic Interests.* Princeton, NJ: Princeton University Press, 1998.

Berry, Jeffrey M. *The Interest Group Society*, 4th ed. New York: Addison Wesley, 2001.

Cigler, Allan J., and Burdett A. Loomis, eds. *Interest Group Politics*, 8th ed. Washington, DC: CQ Press, 2007.

Corrado, Anthony, et al. *The New Campaign Finance Sourcebook.* Washington, DC: Brookings Institution, 2005.

Cox, Gary W., and Mathew McCubbins, *Setting the Agenda.* New York: Cambridge University Press, 2005.

Hershey, Marjorie Randon. *Party Politics in America*, 12th ed. New York: Pearson Longman, 2007.

Key, V. O., Jr. *Politics, Parties, and Pressure Groups*, 5th ed. New York: Crowell, 1964.

Kollman, Ken. *Outside Lobbying: Public Opinion and Interest Group Strategies.* Princeton, NJ: Princeton University Press, 1998.

Maisel, L. Sandy, ed. *The Parties Respond*, 4th ed. Boulder, CO: Westview, 2002.

McGlen, Nancy E., et al. *Women, Politics, and American Society*, 4th ed. Upper Saddle River, NJ: Prentice Hall, 2004.

Nownes, Anthony. *Total Lobbying: What Lobbyists Want (And How They Try to Get It).* New York: Cambridge University Press, 2006.

Olson, Mancur, Jr. *The Logic of Collective Action: Public Good and the Theory of Groups.* Cambridge, MA: Harvard University Press, 1965.

Reichley, James. *The Life of the Parties: A History of American Political Parties.* Lanham, MD: Rowman and Littlefield, 2000.

Sabato, Larry J., and Bruce A. Larson. *The Party's Just Begun: Shaping Political Parties for America's Future*, 2nd ed. New York: Longman, 2002.

Schattschneider, E. E. *Party Government.* New York: Holt, Rinehart and Winston, 1942.

Sirota, David. *Hostile Takeover: How Big Money and Corruption Conquered Our Government—And How We Take It Back.* New York: Crown, 2006.

Wattenberg, Martin P. *The Decline of American Political Parties, 1952–1996.* Cambridge, MA: Harvard University Press, 1998.

WEB EXPLORATIONS

To evaluate how the "Big Two" political parties portray their platform issues and use political language to present their policies, go to
http://www.democrats.org
http://www.rnc.org
To learn about the campaign finances of the political parties, go to
http://www.tray.com

To explore the partisan and ideological agendas of unaffiliated think tanks and search for connections to specific parties or politicians, go to

http://www.heritage.org

http://www.cato.org

http://www.ppionline.org

http://www.moveon.org

To compare the planks of several minor parties and find one that represents your views, go to

http://www.reformparty.org

http://www.gp.org

http://www.lp.org

For more on NOW and the NRA, see

http://www.now.org

http://www.nra.org

For more about Common Cause and Public Citizen, Inc., see

http://www.commoncause.org

http://www.publiccitizen.org

For more on the Christian Coalition of America and other conservative Christian groups, see

http://www.cc.org

For more on the AFL-CIO and SEIU, see

http://www.aflcio.org

http://www.seiu.org

OFFICE TITLE		1 PRESIDENTIAL ELECTORS FOR Vote for One	2 MEMBER OF THE HOUSE OF REPRESENTATIVES 8th Congressional District Vote for One	3 SHERIFF Vote for One	4 COUNTY CLERK Vote for One	5 MEMBER OF THE BOARD OF CHOSEN FREEHOLDERS Vote for Two	6	7	8
CARGO		1 ELECTORES PRESIDENCIALES PARA Vote por Uno	2 MIEMBRO DE LA CASA DE REPRESENTATIVOS 8th Dístrito Congresional Vote por Uno	3 ALGUACIL Vote por Uno	4 SECRETARIO DEL CONDADO Vote por Uno	5 MIEMBRO DE LA JUNTA DE PROPIETARIOS Voten por Dos	6	7	8
REPUBLICAN REPUBLICANO	A	1A George W. BUSH Dick CHENEY ⊠	2A George AJJAN ⊠	3A Mark J. MICHALSKI ⊠	4A Ronni D. NOCHIMSON ⊠	5A Michael G., Jr. MECCA ⊠	6A Walter PORTER ⊠		
DEMOCRAT DEMOCRATA	B	1B John F. KERRY John EDWARDS ⊠	2B Bill, Jr. PASCRELL ⊠	3B Jerry SPEZIALE ⊠	4B Karen BROWN ⊠	5B Terry DUFFY ⊠	6B Pat LEPORE ⊠		
NOMINATION BY PETITION NOMINACION POR PETICION	C								
NOMINATION BY PETITION NOMINA	D								

12

VOTING, ELECTIONS, AND CAMPAIGNS

DURING THE MONTHS leading up to the 2004 presidential election, no one doubted that the race between Republican President George W. Bush and the Democratic challenger, Massachusetts Senator John Kerry, would be close. The question everyone wanted answered was exactly how close it would be. Although presidential elections are national, both candidates focused on specific states that showed either narrow margins or even ties. Many of these so-called "battleground states" were located in the Rust Belt—Wisconsin, Michigan, Ohio, and Pennsylvania. Others such as Minnesota, Iowa, Florida, New Hampshire, New Mexico, and Hawaii were spread across the country.

Of these several battleground states, three stood out because of their razor-thin margins of victory in 2000 and their large number of electoral votes. Pennsylvania, a state the 2000 Democratic candidate Al Gore won by 220,000 votes, had twenty-one electoral votes. Florida, had twenty-seven electoral votes up for grabs. Finally, there was Ohio with twenty electoral votes, a state no Republican candidate has lost and still been able to go on to win the presidency. By Election Day, it was conventional wisdom that a candidate had to win at least two of these three states to win the election. By early evening, it was clear that Bush would take Florida by a much wider margin than in 2000, and Kerry would narrowly win Pennsylvania. This left the election up to Ohio, which both candidates had visited more than twenty-five times he had won it in 2004. Throughout the night, Bush appeared to hold a 2 percent voter margin over Kerry, leading some networks—FOX News and NBC—to call the state for Bush, while others—such as ABC, CBS, and CNN—left it too close to call. However, fears that Ohio might become the 2004 version of Florida quickly abated when it became clear that Kerry could not rely on provisional and absentee ballots to overtake Bush's voter lead. By the morning after Election Day, Bush was declared the winner in Ohio.

Bush also won the battleground states of New Mexico and Iowa (states Gore carried in 2000), but he lost New Hampshire to Kerry. The remaining

CHAPTER OUTLINE

⭐ Voting Behavior

⭐ Presidential Elections

⭐ Congressional Elections

⭐ The Media's Role in the Campaign Process

⭐ Campaign Finance

⭐ Bringing It Together: The 2004 Presidential Campaign and Election battleground states also went to Kerry, but they did not collectively have enough Electoral College votes for him to win. When considering how the 2004 Electoral College map changed from the 2000 map, one can see that the division of coastal "blue" (Democratic) states and "red" (Republican) states became even more contiguous. Like the Pacific states (except Alaska), New England is now completely Democratic in terms of Electoral College votes, while the South from Florida to Arizona is solidly Republican.

The general regional divisions between red and blue remained in 2006. Still, Republicans lost ground across the country in the 2006 midterm elections, with upsets in red states like Virginia, Texas, and Florida providing Senate and House Democrats with control of both chambers for the first time since 1994.

Comparing Voting and Elections

EVERY FOUR YEARS, on the Tuesday following the first Monday in November, a plurality of voters, simply by casting ballots peacefully across a continent-sized nation, reelects or replaces politicians at all levels of government—from the president of the United States, to members of the U.S. Congress, to state legislators. Americans tend to take this process for granted, but in truth it is a marvel. Many other countries do not enjoy the benefit of competitive elections and the peaceful transition of political power made possible through the electoral process. American political institutions have succeeded in maintaining peaceful elections, even when they are closely contested, as was the case with the 2000 presidential election. Elections take the pulse of average people and gauge their hopes and fears, they provide direction for government action, and they hold the nation's leaders accountable.

Today, the United States, judging from its frequent elections at all levels of government is committed to democracy. The nation has steadily increased the size of the electorate (those citizens eligible to vote) by removing restrictions based on property ownership, religion, race, and gender. But despite the increased access of all voters to the ballot box, and the various direct democratic devices such as primaries and initiatives opened to the public in the last century, voter turnout remains historically low. After all the blood spilled and energy expended to expand voting rights, little more than half of eligible voters bother to go to the polls.

This chapter focuses on the purposes served by elections, the various kinds of elections held in the United States, and patterns of voting over time. After an examination of voting behavior, we will look at the types of elections held in the United States, specifically presidential and congressional elections. We will discuss the outcome of the 2006 midterm elections and then will explore the media's role in defining campaigns as well as efforts to reform campaign finance. We will conclude with the story of the 2004 presidential election, which demonstrates how these elements come together in the world of national politics.

Voting Behavior

Voting Turnout: Who Votes?

RESEARCH ON VOTING BEHAVIOR seeks primarily to explain two phenomena: voter turnout (that is, what factors contribute to an individual's decision to vote or not to vote) and vote choice (once the decision to vote has been made, what leads voters to choose one candidate over another).

PATTERNS IN VOTER TURNOUT

turnout
The proportion of the voting-age public that votes.

Turnout is the proportion of the voting-age public that votes. About 40 percent of the eligible adult population in the United States votes regularly, whereas 25 percent are occasional voters and thirty-five percent rarely or never vote. (For a comparison

Global Perspective

POLITICAL PARTICIPATION AROUND THE WORLD

The table shows the average percentage of the voting age population that voted in national elections between 1945 and 2005.

Country	Vote Percentage
Italy	93
Iceland	90
New Zealand	86
Netherlands	85
Australia	84
Denmark	84
Sweden	83
Germany	81
Israel	80
Norway	80
Finland	79
Romania	77
Spain	77
Ireland	75
United Kingdom	75
Japan	69
Canada	68
France	67
India	61
Switzerland	49
United States	48

Source: International Institute for Democracy and Electoral Assistance, "Global Database," http://www.idea.int/vt/survey/voter_turnout_pop2.cfm.

From a global perspective, voting rates in the United States are embarrassingly low. While other Western democracies have average voting rates that often exceed 70 percent, the number generally is less than 50 percent for the United States. Italy, the nation with the highest average voting rate since 1945, exceeds 90 percent, while the average voting rate among all the countries in the International Institute for Democracy and Electoral Assistance data base was 65 percent.

While voting rates in the United States are unquestionably low, the figures might not be as discouraging as they suggest. Voting in the United States remains a voluntary activity, but voting is compulsory in a number of countries—for example, in Australia, Italy, Uruguay, Belgium, and Cyprus, all of which enjoy rates of over 70 percent participation. Few countries with compulsory voting laws have strict enforcement requirements, however, with the most strict penalties usually being only a modest fine. Moreover, voters in the United States and Switzerland, with their lower turnout numbers, are called on to vote far more often than in other nations. Between 1945 and 2005, the United States held thirty national elections in addition to several local and state elections, while Italy held only fourteen, Iceland held sixteen, and Portugal held nine. Switzerland's canton system holds countless local elections for a variety of candidates and issues. And, while voting rates are low in the United States for any given election, when one takes into account the number of elections that take place in the United States, Americans are frequent participators in the electoral process.

There is additional evidence to suggest that voting rates in the United States are not as dismal as they first appear. The 2000 and 2004 presidential elections saw increases in voter participation. In the 2004 presidential race, more than 122 million Americans cast ballots, more than in any other election in U.S. history, though the voting rate as a percentage of eligible voters remained relatively low, at 57 percent. In comparison, in 1960, the year with the highest voter participation rate in the twentieth century (65 percent), fewer than 69 million people voted in the presidential race. Moreover, through the 1970s, there were substantial differences between the voting rates in the American South and the rest of the nation, differences that have been dramatically reduced in recent elections.

QUESTIONS

1. How often should elections be held? Can they be held too frequently? Explain your reasoning.
2. Should the United States make voting compulsory, as it is in Australia and Belgium? Why or why not?

with other countries, see Global Perspective: Political Participation Around the World.) Some of the factors known to influence voter turnout include education, income, age, gender, race and ethnicity, and interest in politics.

Education People who vote usually are more highly educated than nonvoters. People with more education tend to learn more about politics, are less hindered by registration requirements, and are more self-confident about their ability to affect public life. Therefore, one might argue that institutions of higher education provide citizens with opportunities to learn about and become interested in politics.

Income There is also a strong relationship between income and voting. A considerably higher percentage of citizens with annual incomes over $65,000 vote than do citizens with incomes under $35,000. Income level, to some degree, is connected to education level, as wealthier people tend to have more opportunities for higher education, and more education also may lead to higher income. Wealthy citizens are more likely than poor ones to think that the "system" works for them and that their votes make a difference.

By contrast, lower-income citizens often feel alienated from politics, possibly believing that conditions will remain the same no matter who holds office. American political parties may contribute to this feeling of alienation. Unlike parties in many other countries that tend to associate themselves with specific socioeconomic classes, U.S. political parties are less directly linked to socioeconomic class. One consequence of "classless" parties is that the poor may feel their interests are unrepresented, feeding feelings of alienation and apathy.

VIDEO ROUNDTABLE

Political Participation and the Young

■ Citizen Change is one of many organizations that endeavors to educate, register, and turn out young voters in national elections. Here, Sean "Diddy" Combs is seen wearing a shirt featuring the group's much-publicized slogan.

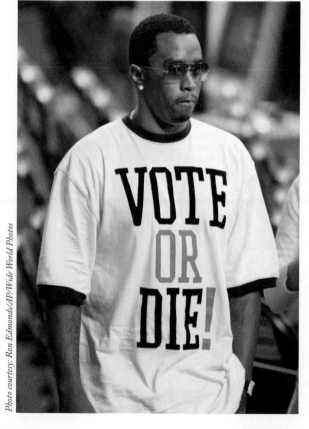

Photo courtesy: Ron Edmonds/AP/Wide World Photos

Age A strong correlation exists between age and voter participation rates. As discussed in the chapter 2 opening vignette, the Twenty-Sixth Amendment, ratified in 1971, lowered the voting age to eighteen. While this amendment obviously increased the number of *eligible* voters, it did so by enfranchising the group that is least likely to vote. A much higher percentage of citizens age thirty and older vote than do citizens younger than thirty, although voter turnout decreases over the age of seventy, primarily due to the difficulties some older voters have getting to the polling location. Regrettably, less than half of eligible eighteen- to twenty-four-year-olds are even registered to vote. However, record numbers of young people voted in 2004. (See On Campus: Increasing the Youth Vote.)

Gender It is generally accepted that in the period following ratification of the Nineteenth Amendment in 1920, women voted at a lower rate than men. Recent polls suggest that today women vote at the same or a slightly higher rate than men. Since women comprise slightly more than 50 percent of the U.S. population, they now account for a majority of the American electorate.

Race and Ethnicity Despite substantial gains in voting rates among minority groups, especially African Americans, race remains an important factor in voter participation. Whites still tend to vote more regularly than do African Americans, Hispanics, and members of other minority groups.

Several factors help to explain the persistent difference in voting rates between white and black voters. One reason is the relative income and educational levels of the two racial groups. African Americans tend to be poorer and to have less formal education than whites; as mentioned earlier, both of these factors affect voter turnout. Significantly, though, highly educated and wealthier African Americans are as likely to vote as whites of similar background, and sometimes more likely.[1] Another explanation focuses on the long term consequence of the voting barriers that African Americans historically faced in the United States, especially in areas of the Deep South (see chapter 6).

Race also helps explain why the South has long had a lower turnout than the rest of the country. As discussed in chapter 6, in the wake of Reconstruction, the southern states made it extremely difficult for African Americans to register to vote, and only a small percentage of the eligible African American population was registered throughout the South through the 1960s.

On Campus

STUDENTS AND VOTING

In the 2004 presidential election, 47% of eligible voters aged 18–24 voted—11% more than in the 2000 presidential election.[a] While midterm elections typically draw fewer voters than presidential elections, exit polls suggested that the "surge" in the youth vote continued in 2006, when 26% of young people voted—two million more than in the 2002 midterms.[b] Still, when compared to the approximately 66% of voters 25 and over who voted in the last presidential election, 47% can only be described as low.

This low level of turnout should disturb young voters, since their low turnout directly impacts what issues state and federal governments address. Ongoing military action in Iraq and Afghanistan, the federal deficit, concerns about rising health costs, and concerns about the long-term financial stability of Social Security are all issues likely to affect young voters—if not now then in the future. Rising tuition costs and the extent to which government supports higher education are issues that hit even closer to home, since many students already must work to pay their tuition bills and are likely to have loans to repay when they graduate. The stakes are high for young voters, so why aren't they voting?

According to one survey, young voters said they did not vote because they believed their vote does not make a difference, they did not have enough information to make a decision, or they were too busy.[c] Nearly half of the students sampled claimed not to discuss politics with their parents, and over half of them said schools did not sufficiently educate them on how to vote! Of course, if you do not know how to vote, then you do not vote, and if you never vote, then you never discover that your vote does make a difference.

A number of get out the vote efforts focus on informing young voters about how to vote. Rock the Vote, for instance, provides young voters with registration kits and election schedules. However, those with the most to gain from securing the young vote, the two major political parties, remain on the sidelines. Another study shows that over 53 percent of undergraduates claim that neither party contacted them during the 2004 presidential campaign.[d] If one of the parties chooses to fill this gap, it could tilt the balance in their favor in future elections. That would be good not only for the party but for young voters, since they could use their influence to affect legislation.

[a]National Election Pool exit polls, http://www.cnn.com/ELECTION/2004/pages/results/states/US/P/00/epolls.0.html

[b]See http://www.civic youth.org/quick/youth_voting.htm for information on youth voting drawn from exit poll results in 2002, 2004, and 2006.

[c]http://www.stateofthevote.org/factsheet.html.

[d]Richard Niemi and Michael Hamner, Circle Fact Sheet: College Students in the 2004 Election, http://www.civicyouth.org/PopUps/FactSheets/FS_College_Voting.pdf.

The Voting Rights Act (VRA) of 1965 helped to change this situation. VRA was intended to guarantee voting rights to African Americans nearly a century after passage of the Fifteenth Amendment. Often now heralded as the most successful piece of civil rights legislation ever passed, the VRA key provisions of which were extended for an additional twenty-five years in 2006, targets states that had used literacy or morality tests or poll taxes to exclude blacks from the polls. The act bans any voting device or procedure that interferes with a minority citizen's right to vote and requires approval for any changes in voting qualifications or procedures in certain areas where minority registration was not in proportion to the racial composition of the district. It also authorizes the federal government to monitor all elections in areas where discrimination was found to be practiced or where less than 50 percent of the voting-age public was registered to vote in the 1964 election.

The 2000 Census revealed that the Hispanic community in the United States is slightly larger in size than the African American community; thus, Hispanics have the potential to wield enormous political power. In California, Texas, Florida, Illinois, and New York, five key electoral states, Hispanic voters have emerged as powerful allies for candidates seeking office. However, voter turnout among Hispanics is even lower than turnout among African Americans.[2]

Like any voting group, Hispanics are not easily categorized and voting patterns cannot be neatly generalized. However, several major factors play out as key decision-making variables: one's point of origin, length of time in the United States, and income levels. Although Hispanics share a common history of Spanish colonialism and similar patterns of nation building, they differ in political processes and agendas.

Despite having U.S. citizenship, Puerto Ricans can vote in a presidential election only if they live on the mainland and establish residency. Cuban Americans are concentrated in south Florida and tend to be conservative and vote for GOP candidates. Mexican American voters are more likely to vote for Democrats, but as a group they are very issue-oriented and their voting patterns vary according to income levels, length of time in the United States, and age.[3]

Interest in Politics An interest in politics must also be included as an important factor for voter turnout. Many citizens who vote have grown up in families interested and active in politics. There is also a strong relationship between interest in politics and age, income, and education, factors discussed above that are also known to increase the likelihood of voter participation.

People who are highly interested in politics constitute only a small minority of the U.S. population. For example, the most politically active Americans—party and issue-group activists—make up less than 5 percent of the country's more than 300 million people. Those who contribute time or money to a party or a candidate during a campaign make up only about 10 percent of the total population. On the other hand, although these percentages appear low, they translate into millions of Americans who contribute more than just votes to the system.

WHY IS VOTER TURNOUT SO LOW?

The United States has one of the lowest voter participation rates of any nation in the industrialized world. In 1960, 62 percent of the eligible electorate voted in the presidential election, but by 1996, American voter participation had fallen to a record low of 48.8 percent—the lowest general presidential election turnout in modern times. In 2004, participation climbed to 57 percent, the highest it has been since 1968. (See

FIGURE 12.1 REASONS GIVEN FOR NOT VOTING
According to the U.S. Census Bureau's Current Population Survey taken after the 2004 elections, "too busy" was the single biggest reason Americans gave for not voting on Election Day. Anger toward politicians and disenchantment with the current political system also drove Americans away from the polls.

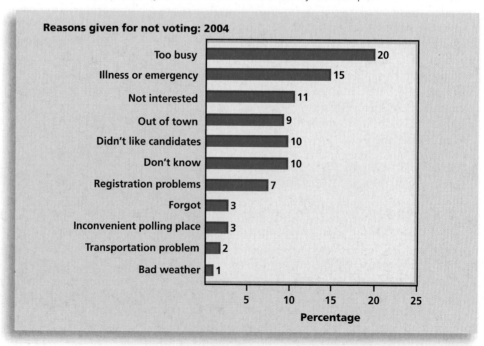

Reasons given for not voting: 2004

Reason	Percentage
Too busy	20
Illness or emergency	15
Not interested	11
Out of town	9
Didn't like candidates	10
Don't know	10
Registration problems	7
Forgot	3
Inconvenient polling place	3
Transportation problem	2
Bad weather	1

Source: U.S. Census Bureau, Current Population Survey, November 2004.

Join the Debate: Does Low Turnout Matter?) Figure 12.1 shows several reasons U.S. nonvoters give for not voting. A number of contributing factors are discussed below.

Too Busy Over 90 million eligible voters did not cast a ballot in the 2004 presidential election. According to the U.S. Census Bureau, 20 percent of registered nonvoters reported they did not vote in a recent election because they were too busy or had conflicting work or school schedules. Another 15 percent said that they did not vote because they were ill, disabled, or had a family emergency. While these reasons seem to account for a large portion of the people surveyed, they may also reflect the respondents' desire not to seem uneducated about the candidates and issues or apathetic about the political process.

VIDEO DEBATE
Compulsory
Voting

Difficulty of Registration Of those citizens who are registered, the overwhelming majority vote. A major reason for lack of participation in the United States remains the relatively low percentage of the adult population that is registered to vote (see Figure 12.2 for an overview of the percentage of registered voters by age, race, and gender). There are several reasons for the low U.S. registration rate. First, while nearly every other democratic country places the burden of registration on the government rather than on the individual, in the United States the registration process still requires individual initiative—a daunting impediment in this age of political apathy. Thus, the cost (in terms of time and effort) of registering to vote is higher in the United States than it is in other industrialized democracies. Second, many nations automatically register all of their citizens to vote. In the United States, however, citizens must jump the extra hurdle of remembering on their own to register.

FIGURE 12.2 PERCENTAGE OF REGISTERED VOTERS BY AGE, RACE/ETHNICITY, AND GENDER, 2004

	Unregistered	Registered
Age: 18–24	57%	43%
25–44	45%	55%
45–64	31%	69%
65 and over	24%	76%
Race/Ethnicity: White	32%	68%
Black	38%	62%
Asian and Pacific Islander	51%	49%
Hispanic (of any race)	47%	53%
Gender: Men	35%	65%
Women	32%	68%

Source: U.S. Census Bureau, Current Population Survey.

Join the Debate

DOES LOW VOTER TURNOUT MATTER?

OVERVIEW: While voting rates in the United States have spiked during the last two presidential elections, they remain significantly lower than in other Western democracies and abysmally low in nonpresidential years. It is not uncommon for candidates in midterm elections to win office with support from less than 20 percent of the eligible voters.

In 2004, nationwide voter turnout was just over 60 percent of the voting-age population, nearly 10 percentage points up from 51 percent in 2000.

In 2006, a post-election analysis from American University's Center for the Study of the American Electorate estimated that 40.4 percent of the electorate voted in the 2006 midterm elections—up from 39.7 percent in the 2002 midterms and the highest turnout since 1982.

The 2004 surge in voter turnout, which seems to have continued somewhat in 2006, was the product of considerable effort and unique circumstances. The major political parties and nonpartisan groups had been registering voters throughout the year and in unprecedented numbers. Voters also had much to motivate them with the election predicted to be as close as in 2000 and featuring critical issues such as the war in Iraq, the fate of Social Security, and possible appointments to the Supreme Court. Even under these extraordinary circumstances, nearly 40 percent of eligible voters, a figure that equates to almost 90 million people, chose not to participate in 2004. Does the nation's persistently low level of political participation pose a threat to democracy in America?

ARGUMENTS THAT LOW VOTER PARTICIPATION IS NOT A PROBLEM

■ **The preferences of nonvoters are not much different from those who do vote.** While higher voting rates are desirable in theory, in practice they might not make a difference in election outcomes and are unlikely to justify the expense associated with costly reform plans designed to increase voter participation.

Indeed, it is no coincidence that voter participation rates dropped markedly after reformers, desiring to combat voter fraud, pushed through strict voter registration laws in the early part of the twentieth century. Correspondingly, recent studies of the effects of relaxed state voter registration laws show that easier registration leads to higher levels of turnout. When states adopted Election Day registration of new voters, large and significant improvements in turnout occurred among younger voters and the poor.[4] The National Voter Registration Act of 1993, commonly known as the Motor Voter Act, was a recent attempt to ease the bureaucratic hurdles associated with registering to vote. The law requires states to provide the opportunity to register through drivers' license agencies, public assistance agencies, and through the mail. While a large number of Americans have yet to take advantage of the Motor Voter Act, it is likely that the law is at least partially responsible for the increases in voter participation experienced in 2000 and 2004. (For more on the effects of ballots and election law, see American Values/American Voices: Protecting the Electoral Process.)

Difficulty of Absentee Voting Stringent absentee ballot laws are another factor in low voter turnout for the United States. Many states, for instance, require citizens to apply in person for absentee ballots, a burdensome requirement given that one's inability to be present in his or her home state is often the reason for absentee balloting in the first place.

Number of Elections Another explanation for low voter turnout in this country is the sheer number and frequency of elections. According to a study by the International Institute for Democracy and Electoral Assistance, the United States typically holds twice as many national elections as other western democracies, a consequence of the relatively short two-year term of office for members of the House of Representatives.[5] American federalism (see chapter 3), with its separate elections at the local, state,

- **Legal barriers that once restricted voting among disenfranchised groups (African Americans, women, and those eighteen to twenty years old) have been eliminated.** In the absence of restrictions, nonvoting is voluntary and indicates an acceptance of things as they are.
- **Low voter turnout increases the quality of voter participation.** Since nonvoters tend to be less well educated and less informed than voters, low voting rates might increase the quality of political participation in the United States.

ARGUMENTS THAT LOW VOTER PARTICIPATION IS A PROBLEM

- **Voters do not represent the interests of nonvoters.** The socioeconomic composition and attitudes of present-day nonvoters are significantly different from those of voters. Even if their expressed preferences about politics do not look very distinctive, their objective circumstances and their need for government services differ from the majority of those who do vote.

- **Low voting rates perpetuate racial imbalances within government.** Since voting rates remain lower for Hispanic, African American, and other minority groups than for whites, the racial composition of elected officials remains far from representative of the nation as a whole.
- **Low voter rates delegitimize the political process.** Voting rates that dip below 50 percent challenge the very legitimacy of the political system, as elected officials cannot claim a clear mandate, or even the support of a substantial segment of society.

SELECTED READINGS

Conway, M. Margaret. *Political Participation in the United States,* 3rd ed. Washington, DC: CQ Press, 2000.
Patterson, Thomas E. *The Vanishing Voter: Public Involvement in an Age of Uncertainty.* New York: Vintage, 2003.

and national levels, and use of primary elections for the selection of candidates, also contributes to the number of elections in which Americans are called on participate.

PATTERNS IN VOTE CHOICE

Just as there are certain predictable patterns when it comes to American voter turnout, so, too, are there predictable patterns of vote choice. Some of the most prominent correlates of vote choice include partisan identification, race and ethnicity, gender, income, ideology, issues, and campaign-specific developments.

Party Identification   As discussed in chapter 11, party identification is a long-term force in American politics. Party identification, which is dependent on a variety of factors noted in chapter 11, often acts as a lens that shapes how an individual perceives a particular candidate.[6] It also affects how one processes information about candidates and political issues.

Issues   Individual issues also have important effects on vote choice in any given election year. In 1992 when Bill Clinton's chief political adviser, James Carville, established "it's the economy stupid" as Clinton's campaign mantra, he was confirming a well established idea in American politics: perceptions of the economy drive voter decisions.[7] Simply put, voters tend to reward the party in government, usually the president's party, during good economic times and punish the party in government during periods of economic downturn. When this occurs, the electorate is exercising **retrospective judgments;** that is, voters are rendering judgment on the performance of the party in power by judging whether the economy has improved under its governance. At other times, voters might use **prospective judgments;** that is, they vote based on what they perceive to be the future direction of the economy. By looking

retrospective judgment
A voter's evaluation of the performance of the party in power.

prospective judgment
A voter's evaluation of a candidate based on what he or she pledges to do about an issue if elected.

■ President George W. Bush greets members of the NAACP after addressing organization members at their annual convention on July 20, 2006, the same day that the Senate approved a 25-year extension of the Voting Rights Act. Up until this occasion, Bush had been the first president since Herbert Hoover to refuse to address the group.

Photo courtesy: Win McNamee/Getty Images

primary election
Election in which voters decide which of the candidates within a party will represent the party in the general election.

closed primary
A primary election in which only a party's registered voters are eligible to vote.

open primary
A primary in which party members, independents, and sometimes members of the other party are allowed to vote.

crossover voting
Participation in the primary of a party with which the voter is not affiliated.

raiding
An organized attempt by voters of one party to influence the primary results of the other party.

runoff primary
A second primary election between the two candidates receiving the greatest number of votes in the first primary.

general election
Election in which voters decide which candidates will actually fill elective public offices.

forward, voters can evaluate if a party's positions are likely to serve their interests, while not holding the ruling party accountable for economic conditions that might be beyond the party's control (for example, the economic effects of a hurricane or terrorist attack). Whether using retrospective or prospective judgments, there is little doubt that perceptions about the economy are consistently among the most important issues in voters' minds.

TYPES OF ELECTIONS

In the U.S. system, elections happen at various levels and come in numerous types. In **primary elections,** voters decide which of the candidates within a party will represent the party's ticket in the general elections. There are different kinds of primaries. For example, **closed primaries** allow only a party's registered voters to cast a ballot, and **open primaries** allow independents and sometimes members of the other party to participate. Closed primaries are considered healthier for the party system because they prevent members of one party from influencing the primaries of the opposition party. Studies of open primaries indicate that **crossover voting** — participation in the primary of a party with which the voter is not affiliated—occurs frequently.[8] Nevertheless, the research shows little evidence of much **raiding** — an *organized* attempt by voters of one party to influence the primary results of the other party.[9]

When none of the candidates in the initial primary secures a majority of the votes, most states have a **runoff primary,** a contest between the two candidates with the greatest number of votes. Louisiana has a novel twist on the primary system. There, all candidates for office appear on the ballot, and if one candidate receives over 50 percent of the vote, the candidate wins and no general election is necessary. If no candidate wins a majority of the vote, the top two candidates, even if they belong to the same party, face each other in a runoff election.

Once party members vote for their party candidates for various offices, each state holds its general election. In the **general election,** voters decide which candidates actually will fill the nation's elective public offices. These elections are held at many levels, including municipal, county, state, and national. Whereas primaries are contests

American Values/American Voices

PROTECTING THE ELECTORAL PROCESS

Fair and open elections are the bedrock upon which the legitimacy of any democratic system rests. Are American elections as secure and free of fraud and corruption as many would like to believe?

Following the contentious presidential election of 2000, Democrats and Republicans alike have been quick to allege fraud and tampering in closely contested races. In 2002, the Republican Party decried what they claimed was widespread fraud in registering Native American voters in the South Dakota senatorial election. Meanwhile, in the closely contested 2002 New Hampshire Senate race, state Republican efforts to jam a Democratic phone bank led to a guilty plea and prison term for the New Hampshire Republican Party's executive director and a Virginia-based Republican consultant. In 2004, Democratic groups, especially Internet bloggers, cried foul about a host of alleged vote fraud and voter intimidation in Ohio and other states. While these are isolated examples, many groups worry that increased use of mail-in ballots and electronic voting machines, and proposals for Internet voting, will open American elections to a host of abuses.

There have been some famous examples of vote fraud in American history. In the late nineteenth century, political bosses such as William Marcy Tweed—better known as Boss Tweed—were found to have bought votes, stuffed ballot boxes, and generally abuse the trust of voters in New York and other major cities. The end of machine politics in big cities did not end vote fraud, however. In the 1960 presidential election, the campaigns of both John F. Kennedy and Richard M. Nixon were accused of questionable activities in Illinois and Texas, pivotal states in the closest election of the century. However, while a handful of convictions were handed down in Chicago for election fraud, subsequent investigations were unable to find enough electoral misdeeds to change the outcome of the election.[a]

In the 2004 presidential election, many Democrats accused Republicans and the Bush campaign of organized voter intimidation or ballot manipulation in several states. Kathy Dopp, a mathematician and Webmaster of ustogether.org, was quick to point to gains for Bush in traditionally Democratic counties in Florida where new optical scanning equipment was in use.[b] Subsequent investigations by a group of academics found that these patterns were not evidence of fraud, and that there was "no current evidence of irregularities of sufficient magnitude or scope to change the popular vote."[c]

The recent trend in the Northwest toward mail-in balloting has opened up potential for fraud. In 2004, in the incredibly close Washington State gubernatorial election, where 129 votes ended up determining the winner, several irregularities plagued the recount. Several boxes of ballots were unsecured or misplaced and went uncounted initially, while a handful of ballots were found to have been sent in fraudulently. As more states begin to adopt mail-in balloting, electronic voting, and other new technologies, the potential for misconduct will continue to rise. However, despite some incompetence and certain isolated incidents of fraud, most modern elections in the United States appear to be free and fair.

QUESTIONS

1. Some have suggested that allowing voters to use the Internet to cast their ballots would encourage many more to participate. Do you think the Internet is a safe and responsible technology to use for elections? What is the potential for fraud and abuse?

2. Since partisans usually run state elections and oversee the election process, is there too much potential for conflicts of interest in counting and administering elections? Should there be a nonpartisan government agency to oversee U.S. elections? Why or why not?

---

[a]David Greenberg, "Was Nixon Robbed? The Legend of the Stolen 1960 Presidential Election," *Slate* (October 16, 2000).

[b]Tom Zeller Jr., "Vote Fraud Theories, Spread by Blogs, Are Quickly Buried," *New York Times* (November 12, 2004).

[c]National Research Commission on Elections and Voting, "Alleged Irregularities in the United States Presidential Election of 2 November 2004" (New York: Social Science Research Council, 2004).

---

between the candidates within each party, general elections are contests between the candidates of opposing parties.

Three other types of elections are the initiative, the referendum, and the recall. An **initiative** is a process that allows citizens to propose legislation or state constitutional amendments by submitting them directly to the state electorate for popular vote, provided the initiative supporters receive a certain number of signatures on petitions supporting the placement of the proposal on the ballot. The initiative process is used in twenty-four states and the District of Columbia. A **referendum** is an election whereby the state legislature submits proposed legislation or state constitutional amendments to the state's voters for approval. Although both the

initiative
An election that allows citizens to propose legislation and submit it to the state electorate for popular vote.

referendum
An election whereby the state legislature submits proposed legislation to the state's voters for approval.

■ Senator Joseph I. Lieberman of Connecticut, seen here celebrating his reelection with his wife, Hadassah, lost the Democratic primary in 2006 and ran and won the general election as an independent. After the 2006 election, the slim margin held by Senate Democrats hinged on Lieberman, who describes himself as an Independent Democrat, and Bernie Sanders, a Vermont independent. The fragility of this margin as well as the importance of every member was thrown into even sharper relief in December of 2006, when Senator Tim Johnson (D-SD) had emergency brain surgery. .

Photo courtesy: Ruth Fremson/The New York Times

referendum and the initiative provide for more direct democracy, they are not free from controversy.

The third type of election (or "deelection") found in many states is the **recall,** in which voters can remove an incumbent from office prior to the next scheduled election. Recall elections are very rare, and sometimes they are thwarted by the official's resignation or impeachment prior to the vote.

recall
An election in which voters can remove an incumbent from office by popular vote.

The Initiative and Referendum

Presidential Elections

VARIETY ASIDE, no U.S. election can compare to the presidential contest. This spectacle, held every four years, brings together all the elements of politics and attracts the most ambitious and energetic politicians to the national stage. Voters in a series of state contests that run through the winter and spring of the election year select delegates who will attend each party's national convention. Following the national convention for each party, held in mid and late summer, there is a final set of fifty separate state elections all held on the Tuesday after the first Monday in November to select the president. This lengthy process exhausts candidates and voters alike, but it allows the diversity of the United States to be displayed in ways a shorter, more homogeneous presidential election process could not.

THE NOMINATION CAMPAIGN

The **nomination campaign** begins as soon as the candidate has decided to run—sometimes years prior to an official announcement—and ends the night of the party primary or convention. (For more on Constitutional requirements for holding federal office, see The Living Constitution.) During the nomination campaign, the candidate targets the leaders and activists who choose nominees in primaries or conventions. Party leaders are concerned with electability, while party activists are often ideologically and issue oriented, so a candidate must appeal to both bases.

nomination campaign
That part of a political campaign aimed at winning a primary election.

You Are a Presidential Campaign Consultant

Primaries Versus Caucuses The mix of preconvention contests has changed over the years, with the most pronounced trend being the shift from caucuses to primary elections. Only seventeen states held presidential primaries in 1968; the

The Living Constitution

No Person shall be a Representative who shall not have attained to the Age of twenty five Years.

—ARTICLE I, SECTION 2

No Person shall be a Senator who shall not have attained to the Age of thirty Years.

—ARTICLE I, SECTION 3

. . . neither shall any person be eligible to that Office [of the Presidency] who shall not have attained to the Age of thirty five Years.

—ARTICLE II, SECTION 1

There was little debate among the Framers at the Constitutional Convention that elected officials should have enough experience in life and in politics before being qualified to take on the responsibility of representing the interests of the nation and of their district or state. It is likely that they concurred, as they so often did, with John Locke, who stated in section 118 of his *Second Treatise of Government*, "*a Child is born a Subject of no Country or Government. He is under his Father's Tuition and Authority, till he come to Age of Discretion.*" However, a minor, who is not subject to the authority of the state in the same way as a full citizen, also could not possibly be qualified to vote. The Framers added age requirements higher than the age when one becomes a full citizen as a guarantee that individuals with the necessary experience would be elected. Notice how the age limits scale upward according to the amount of deliberation and decision making that the position involves. House members need to be only twenty-five, but the president must be at least thirty-five, giving whoever would run for that office plenty of time to acquire the political experience necessary for the central role he or she will play.

State governments usually employ similar requirements. For instance, Virginia requires that candidates for the state's House of Delegates and Senate be at least twenty-one years old, while candidates for the state's three most powerful executive positions—governor, lieutenant governor, and attorney general—must be at least thirty years old. South Dakota, however, sets the minimum age limit for its most important executive officers—governor and lieutenant governor—at twenty-one.

Amazingly, the Framers did not impose an age limit on Supreme Court justices, not even the chief justice. Perhaps the Framers thought that the president was not likely to appoint minors to the bench, or at least that they would not be approved by the Senate. Looking at the nine justices today, it is obvious that the Framers were right not to worry.

number increased to thirty-eight in 1992, forty-two in 1996, forty-three in 2000, and thirty eight in 2004. In recent years, the vast majority of delegates to each party's national convention have been selected through the primary system.

The caucus is the oldest, most party-oriented method of choosing delegates to the national conventions. Traditionally, the caucus was a closed meeting of party activists in each state who selected the party's choice for presidential candidate. In the late-nineteenth and early twentieth centuries, however, many people viewed these caucuses as elitist and anti-democratic, and reformers succeeded in replacing them with direct primaries in most states. Although there are still presidential nominating caucuses today (in Iowa, as noted above), they are now more open and attract a wider range of the party's membership. Indeed, new participatory caucuses more closely resemble primary elections than they do the old, exclusive party caucuses.[10]

front loading
The tendency of states to choose an early date on the primary calendar.

The primary schedule has been altered by a phenomenon often referred to as **front-loading,** the tendency of states to choose an early date on the primary calendar. Seventy percent of all the delegates to both party conventions are now chosen before the end of March. This trend is hardly surprising, given the added press emphasis on the first contests and the voters' desire to cast their ballots before the competition is decided. The focus on early contests (such as the Iowa caucus and the New Hampshire primary), coupled with front-loading, can result in a party's selecting a nominee too quickly. Front-loading has also had other important effects on the nomination process. First, a front-loaded primary schedule generally benefits the front-runner, since opponents have little time to turn the contest around once they fall behind. Second, front-loading gives an advantage to the candidate who can raise the bulk of the money *before* the nomination season begins, since there will be little opportunity to raise money once the primaries begin and since candidates will need to finance campaign efforts simultaneously in many states. In 2004, Internet fund-raising emerged as a means to soften this advantage; its use expanded in 2006 and will continue to expand in future elections. Finally, front-loading has amplified the importance of the "invisible primary"—the year or so prior to the start of the official nomination season when candidates begin raising money and unofficially campaigning.[11]

The Party Conventions   The seemingly endless nomination battle does have a conclusion: the national party conventions held in the summer of presidential election years. The out-of-power party traditionally holds its convention first, in late July, followed in mid-August by the party controlling the White House. Preempting an hour or more of prime-time network television for four nights and monopolizing the cable networks such as CNN, FOX News, and C-SPAN, these remarkable conclaves give the civically engaged viewer a chance to learn about party candidates.

Yet, the conventions once were much more: they were composed of party members who made actual decisions, where party leaders held sway, and deals were sometimes cut in "smoke-filled rooms" to deliver nominations to little-known contenders called "dark horses." This era predated the modern emphasis on reform, primaries, and proportional representation, all of which have combined to make conventions the place where parties choose one of several nominees who has been pre-selected through the various primaries and caucuses.[12]

Delegate Selection   The selection of delegates to the conventions is no longer the function of party leaders but of primary elections and grassroots caucuses. Moreover, recent reforms, especially by the Democratic Party, have generally weakened any remaining control by local party leaders over delegates. In fact, most delegates are popularly elected and come to their party's convention already committed to supporting a particular candidate.

Who the delegates are, a topic that is less important today than it was when delegates enjoyed more power in the selection process, still reveals interesting differences between the political parties. Both parties draw their delegates from an elite group whose income and educational levels are far above the average American's. Nearly 40 percent of delegates at the 2004 Democratic convention were members of a minority

TABLE 12.1 HISTORIC MOMENTS FOR WOMEN AT THE CONVENTIONS

Since 1980, Democratic Party rules have required that women constitute 50 percent of the delegates to its national convention. The Republican Party has no similar quota. Nevertheless, both parties have tried to increase the role of women at the convention. Some "firsts" and other historic moments for women at the national conventions include:

1876	First woman to address a national convention
1890	First women delegates to conventions of both parties
1940	First woman to nominate a presidential candidate
1951	First woman asked to chair a national party
1972	First woman keynote speaker
1984	First major-party woman nominated for vice president (Democrat Geraldine Ferraro)
1996	Wives of both nominees make major addresses
2000	Daughter of a presidential candidate nominates her father
2004	Both candidates introduced by their daughters

Source: Center for American Women in Politics. Updated by authors.

group, and half were women. (For some historic "firsts" for women at the conventions, see Table 12.1.) Only 17 percent of the delegates to the Republican convention were minority group members; however, this actually marks the GOP's concerted effort to increase minority representation at its convention, since only 9 percent of the 2000 delegates were minority group members.

THE GENERAL ELECTION CAMPAIGN

After earning the party's nomination, candidates embark on the **general election campaign.** They must seek the support of interest groups and a majority of voters and decide on the issues they will emphasize. When courting interest groups, a candidate seeks both money and endorsements, although the results are mainly predictable: liberal, labor, and minority groups usually back Democrats, while social conservatives and business organizations support Republicans. The most active groups often coalesce around emotional issues such as abortion and gun control, and these organizations can produce a bumper crop of money and activists for favored candidates.

Virtually all candidates adopt a brief theme, or slogan, to serve as a rallying cry in their quest for office. Most slogans can fit many candidates ("He's on our side," "She

general election campaign
That part of a political campaign aimed at winning a general election.

Comparing Political Campaigns

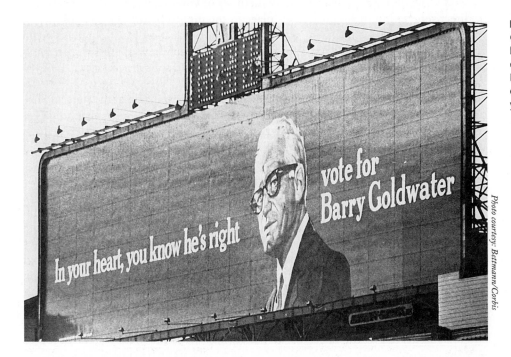

■ 1964 Republican candidate Barry Goldwater's famous slogan, "In your heart, you know he's right," was quickly lampooned by incumbent Democratic opponent President Lyndon B. Johnson's campaign as "In your guts, you know he's nuts."

Photo courtesy: Bettmann/Corbis

hears you," "New Leadership for a Change"). Candidates try to avoid controversy in their selection of slogans, and some openly eschew ideology. The clever candidate also attempts to find a slogan that cannot be lampooned easily.

THE KEY PLAYERS IN A PRESIDENTIAL CAMPAIGN

Most observers agree that the most important aspect of any campaign is the quality of the candidate and the attributes of the campaign team. The ability to convey ideas in a persuasive manner, the cornerstone of all political campaigns, ultimately rests in the hands of the candidate. The ability to package and project the candidate's message in the most effective and persuasive manner, the work of the campaign staff, requires expertise in media and public relations. The ability to raise funds, which in turn provide volume to the campaign message, requires the combined effort of a strong candidate and experienced campaign staff.

SIMULATION

You Are a Professional Campaign Manager

voter canvass
The process by which a campaign reaches individual voters, either by door-to-door solicitation or by telephone.

get out the vote (GOTV)
A push at the end of a political campaign to encourage supporters to go to the polls.

campaign manager
The individual who travels with the candidate and coordinates the many different aspects of the campaign.

finance chair
A professional who coordinates the fund-raising efforts for the campaign.

pollster
A professional who takes public opinion surveys that guide political campaigns.

direct mailer
A professional who supervises a political campaign's direct-mail fund-raising strategies.

communications director
The person who develops the overall media strategy for the candidate, blending the free press coverage with the paid TV, radio, and mail media.

press secretary
The individual charged with interacting and communicating with journalists on a daily basis.

The Candidate Before there can be a campaign there must be candidates. Candidates run for office for any number of reasons, including personal ambition, the desire to promote ideological objectives or to pursue specific public policies, or simply because they think they can do a better job than their opponents.[13] In any case, all successful candidates must be prepared to spend a considerable amount of time and energy in pursuit of their desired office, and all candidates must be prepared to expose themselves to public scrutiny and the chance of rejection by the voters.

The Campaign Staff Paid staff, political consultants, and dedicated volunteers work behind the scenes to support the candidate. Collectively, they plan strategy, conduct polls, write speeches, craft the campaign's message, organize dinners and other fund-raising events, and design television advertisements, radio spots, and direct-mail pieces. The staff, professional and volunteer, keeps the candidate on message and manages the campaign's near-infinite details. Presidential campaign organizations, not surprisingly, have the most elaborate structures.

Volunteers are the lifeblood of every national, state, and local campaign. Volunteers answer phone calls, staff candidate booths at festivals and county fairs, copy and distribute campaign literature, and serve as the public face of the campaign. They go door to door to solicit votes, or use computerized telephone banks to call targeted voters with scripted messages, two primary methods of **voter canvass.** Most canvassing, or direct solicitation of support, takes place in the month before the election, when voters are most likely to be paying attention. Closer to Election Day, volunteers begin vital **get out the vote (GOTV)** efforts, calling and e-mailing supporters to remind them to vote and arranging for their transportation to the polls if necessary.

The Candidate's Professional Staff Nearly every campaign at the state and national level is run by a **campaign manager,** who coordinates and directs the campaign. The campaign manager is the person closest to the candidate, the person who delivers the good and bad news about the condition of the campaign and makes the essential day-to-day decisions, such as whom to hire and when to air which television advertisement. The campaign manager helps to determine the campaign's overall strategy, and equally important, works to keep the campaign on message throughout the race.

Other key paid positions, depending on the race, include the **finance chair,** who is responsible for bringing in the large contributions that fund the campaign, the **pollster,** who takes public opinion surveys to learn what issues voters want candidates to address in speeches, and the **direct mailer,** who supervises direct-mail fund-raising.

The **communications director** develops the overall media strategy for the candidate, carefully blending press coverage with paid TV, radio, and mail media, not to mention advertisements on Web sites visited by those likely to favor the candidate's positions.

The **press secretary** or the communications director is charged with interacting and communicating with journalists on a daily basis. It is the press secretary's job to be quoted in the newspapers or on TV explaining the candidate's positions or reacting to the actions of the opposing candidate. Good news is usually announced by the candidate. Bad news, including responding to attacks from the other side, is the preserve of the press secretary (better to have someone not on the ballot doing the dirty work of the campaign).

An increasingly indispensable part of modern political campaigns is the campaign's **Internet team,** which manages the campaign's communications, outreach, and fund-raising via the Internet, and increasingly tries to manage the candidate's visibility on blogs popular with the party faithful. Since making an online appeal for campaign contributions costs significantly less than raising funds through expensive direct-mail campaigns or pricey fund-raising events—the standard means of attaining campaign resources—the Internet is radically altering the way candidates raise funds for their campaigns. The importance of the Internet team is likely to expand in future elections.

Campaign consultants are the private-sector professionals and firms who sell the technologies, services, and strategies many candidates need to get elected. Consultants' numbers have grown exponentially since they first appeared in the 1930s, and their specialties and responsibilities have increased accordingly, to the point that campaign consultants are now an obligatory part of campaigns at the state and national level.[14] Candidates generally hire specialized consultants who focus on only one or two areas, such as fund-raising, polling, mass mailings, media relations, advertising, Internet outreach, and speech writing.

Media consultants design TV, radio, and direct-mail advertisements. More than one consultant or even an advertising company or two may be assigned to this fundamental part of the modern political campaign. The communications director, with frequent involvement from the campaign manager, pollster, and sometimes even the candidate, works with the media consultant to craft the campaign's advertising message and address key issues.

THE ELECTORAL COLLEGE: HOW PRESIDENTS ARE ELECTED

The campaign for the presidency has many facets, but the object of the exercise is clear: winning a majority of the **Electoral College.** This uniquely American institution consists of representatives of each state who cast the final ballots that actually elect a president. The total number of **electors**—the members of the Electoral College—for each state is equivalent to the number of senators and representatives that state has in the U.S. Congress. And, the District of Columbia is accorded three electoral votes.

The Electoral College was the result of a compromise between those Framers who argued for selection of the president by the Congress and those who favored selection by direct popular election. The Electoral College compromise, although not a perfect solution, had practical benefits. Since there were no mass media in those days, common citizens, even reasonably informed ones, were unlikely to know much about a candidate from another state. On the one hand, this situation could have left voters with no choice but to vote for someone from their own state, thus making it improbable that any candidate would secure a national majority. On the other hand, the electors would be men of character with a solid knowledge of national politics who were able to identify, agree on, and select prominent national statesmen.

There are three essentials to understanding the Framers' design of the Electoral College. The system was constructed: (1) to work without political parties; (2) to cover both the nominating and electing phases of presidential selection; and, (3) to produce a nonpartisan president.

The Electoral College machinery as originally designed by the Framers was somewhat complex. Each state designated electors (through appointment or popular vote) equal in number to the sum of its representation in the House and Senate. The

SIMULATION

You Are a Media Consultant to a Politcial Candidate

Internet team

Campaign staff that makes use of Web-based resources to communicate with voters, raise funds, organize volunteers, and plan campaign events.

campaign consultant

The private-sector professionals and firms who sell to a candidate the technologies, services, and strategies required to get that candidate elected.

media consultant

A professional who produces candidates' television, radio, and print advertisements.

Electoral College

Representatives of each state who cast the final ballots that actually elect a president.

elector

Member of the Electoral College chosen by methods determined in each state.

VIDEO ROUNDTABLE

The Electoral College

electors met in their respective states. Each elector had two votes to cast in the Electoral College's selection for the president and vice president, although electors could not vote for more than one candidate from their state. The rules of the college stipulated that each elector was allowed to cast only one vote for any single candidate, and by extension obliged each elector to use his second vote for another candidate. There was no way to designate votes for president or vice president; instead, the candidate with the most votes (provided he also received votes from a majority of the electors) won the presidency and the runner-up won the vice presidency. If two candidates received the same number of votes and both had a majority of electors, the election was decided in the House of Representatives, with each state delegation acting as a unit and casting one vote. If no candidate secured a majority, the election would also be decided in the House, with each state delegation casting one vote for any of the top five electoral vote-getters. In both these scenarios, the candidate needed a majority of the total number of states for victory.

The Electoral College in the Nineteenth Century

The republic's fourth presidential election revealed a flaw in the Framers' Electoral College plan. In 1800, Thomas Jefferson and Aaron Burr were, respectively, the presidential and vice presidential candidates advanced by the Democratic-Republican Party, and supporters of the Democratic-Republican Party controlled a majority of the Electoral College. Accordingly, each Democratic-Republican elector in the states cast one of his two votes for Jefferson and the other one for Burr, a situation that resulted in a tie for the presidency between Jefferson and Burr, since there was no way under the constitutional arrangements for electors to earmark their votes separately for president and vice president. Even though most understood Jefferson to be the actual choice for president, the Constitution mandated that a tie be decided by the House of Representatives. It was, of course, and in Jefferson's favor, but only after much energy was expended to persuade lame-duck Federalists not to give Burr the presidency.

The Twelfth Amendment, ratified in 1804 and still the constitutional foundation for presidential elections, was an attempt to remedy the confusion between the selection of vice presidents and presidents that beset the election of 1800. The amendment provided for separate elections for each office, with each elector having only one vote to cast for each. In the event of a tie or when no candidate received a majority of the total number of electors, the election still went to the House of Representatives; now, however, each state delegation would have one vote to cast for one of the three candidates who had received the greatest number of electoral votes.

The Electoral College modified by the Twelfth Amendment has fared better than the college as originally designed, but it has not been problem free. On three occasions during the nineteenth century, the electoral process resulted in the selection of a president who received fewer votes than his opponent. This instance occurred in 1824 when neither John Quincy Adams nor Andrew Jackson secured a majority of electoral votes, throwing the election into the House. Although Jackson had more electoral and popular votes than Adams, the House voted for the latter as president. In the 1876 contest between Republican Rutherford B. Hayes and Democrat Samuel J. Tilden, no candidate received a majority of electoral votes; the House decided in Hayes's favor even though he had only one more (disputed) electoral vote and 250,000 fewer popular votes than Tilden. In the election of 1888, President Grover Cleveland secured about 100,000 more popular votes than did Benjamin Harrison, yet Harrison won a majority of the Electoral College vote, and with it the presidency.

VISUAL LITERACY

American Electoral Rules: How Do They Influence Campaigns?

The Electoral College in the Twentieth and Twenty-First Centuries

Several near crises pertaining to the Electoral College occurred in the twentieth century. The election of 1976 was almost a repeat of those nineteenth-century contests in which the candidate with fewer popular votes won the presidency. Even though Democrat Jimmy Carter received about 1.7 million more popular votes than Republican Gerald Ford, a switch of some 8,000 popular votes in Ohio and Hawaii would have

Politics Now

SHOULD WE ABOLISH THE ELECTORAL COLLEGE?

Since the passage of the Twelfth Amendment to the U.S. Constitution in 1804, there has been no major constitutional change to the system of electing the president. The original system the Framers envisioned to manage the choice of president, the Electoral College is still in place. Many at the Constitutional Convention worried that unscrupulous men who would incite the people and destroy liberty could be elected president if the election were based on the popular vote. As Alexander Hamilton remarked, the Constitution would prevent politicians with "talents for low intrigue, and the little arts of popularity" from ever attaining the office of president. It is also the case that the drafters of the Constitution, under the idea of federalism, understood the states as electing the president, either through their legislatures or through a popular vote within the state, not individual voters through their status as U.S. citizens. At various times, however, there have been calls to abolish the Electoral College in favor of a national popular vote, with the loudest shouts coming in the wake of the Florida voting debacle in 2000.

A group called National Popular Vote (NPV) has been working within several states to get state legislatures and federal elected officials to endorse abolishing the Electoral College and instituting fully popular elections in its place. Because of the extreme difficulty associated with gathering enough support for a constitutional amendment, and the opposition from smaller states that fear a dilution of their representation, serious attempts have rarely been successful. However, NPV has devised a clever way to circumvent the necessity of an amendment. The group proposes that states change their election laws to give their electoral votes not to the winners in their states, but the winner of the popular vote in all fifty states. If NPV can convince enough state legislatures—enough to reach a combined total of at least 270 electoral votes, the number needed to elect a president—this would eliminate the power of the Electoral College to determine a president. A total of 29 states, including California, have sponsors lined up to introduce NPV legislation in 2007. The California Legislature actually approved NPV legislation in 2006, but the bill was vetoed by Governor Arnold Schwarzenegger.

QUESTIONS

1. Should we still value the Framers' concerns about unscrupulous or dangerous candidates potentially inciting and haranguing the people and gaining the office of president? Or has the nature of politics or the sophistication of the American people changed sufficiently to eliminate the need for the Electoral College? Explain your answer.
2. Given the election disaster in Florida in 2000 over a handful of votes, do you think electing a president through the popular vote would cause a nationwide political disaster if another close election were to occur? Why or why not?

Sources: National Popular Vote, http://www.nationalpopularvote.com/; FairVote: The Center for Voting and Democracy, http://www.fairvote.org/.

---

secured for Ford enough votes to win the Electoral College, and hence the presidency. Had Ross Perot stayed in the 1992 presidential contest, he could have thrown the election into the House of Representatives. His support had registered from 30 percent to 36 percent in the polls in early 1992, prior to his dropping out of the race. When he reentered the race, some of that backing had evaporated, and he finished with 19 percent of the vote and carried no states. However, Perot drained a substantial number of Republican votes from George Bush, thus splitting the GOP base and enabling Bill Clinton to win many normally GOP-leaning states.[15]

Throughout the 2000 presidential campaign, many analysts foresaw that the election would likely be the closest since the 1960 race between John F. Kennedy and Richard M. Nixon. Few realized, however, that the election would be so close that the winner would not be officially declared for more than five weeks after Election Day. And, no one could have predicted that the Electoral College winner, George W. Bush, would lose the popular vote and become president after a controversial U.S. Supreme Court decision *Bush* v. *Gore* (2000), stopped the recount in Florida. With the margin of the Electoral College results so small (271 for Bush, 267 for Gore), a Gore victory in any number of closely contested states could have given him a majority in the Electoral College. As it turned out, Al Gore became only the fourth person to win the popular vote and lose the presidency. (See Politics Now: Should We Abolish the Electoral College?)

TIMELINE
And the Winner Is . . . Close Calls in Presidential Elections

VIDEO DEBATE
The 2000 Presidential Election

reapportionment
The reallocation of the number of seats in the House of Representatives after each decennial census.

PARTICIPATION

The Electoral College Debate

Keep in mind that through **reapportionment,** representation in the House of Representatives, and consequently in the Electoral College, is altered every ten years to reflect population shifts. Reapportionment is simply the reallocation of congressional seats that takes place after each decennial census. The number of congressional seats has been fixed at 435 since 1910. Since that time, the average size of congressional districts has tripled in population, from 211,000 following the 1910 Census to 647,000 in the 2000 Census. Following the 2000 Census, Arizona, Florida, Georgia, and Texas each gained two congressional districts, and therefore two additional seats in the House of Representatives and two additional votes in the Electoral College. California, Colorado, Nevada, and North Carolina each picked up one seat and one vote. Two states, New York and Pennsylvania, each lost two seats and two votes, while eight states each lost a single seat and electoral vote. The 2000 Census shows a sizeable population shift from the Northeast to the South and West. (See Figure 12.3.)

Recent reapportionment has favored the Republicans. With the exception of California, George W. Bush carried all of the states that gained seats in 2000. Had Bush won the same states in 2004 that he won in 2000, he would have gained six additional electoral votes.

FIGURE 12.3 THE STATES DRAWN IN PROPORTION TO THEIR ELECTORAL COLLEGE VOTES

This map visually represents the respective electoral weights of the fifty states in the 2004 presidential election. For each state, the gain or loss of Electoral College votes based on the 2000 Census is indicated in parentheses.

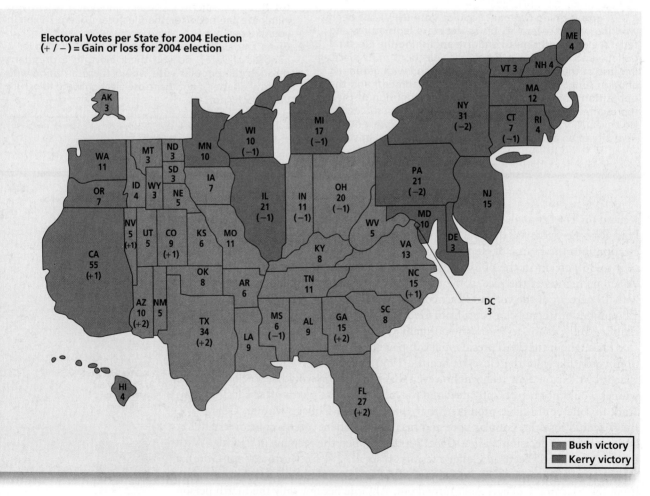

Note: States drawn in proportion to number of electoral votes. Total electoral votes: 538.

Source: New York Times 2004 Election Guide, http://www.nytimes.com.

Congressional Elections

COMPARED WITH PRESIDENTIAL ELECTIONS, congressional elections receive scant national attention. Unlike major-party presidential contenders, most candidates for Congress labor in relative obscurity. There are some celebrity nominees for Congress—television stars, sports heroes, even local TV news anchors. In 2000, First Lady Hillary Rodham Clinton made history with her Senate campaign and gained the nation's attention by becoming the only first lady to win elective office. The vast majority of party nominees for Congress, however, are little-known state legislators and local office holders who receive remarkably limited coverage in many states and communities. For them, just establishing name identification in the electorate is the biggest battle.

THE INCUMBENCY ADVANTAGE

The current circumstances enhance the advantages of **incumbency** (that is, already being in office). As discussed in chapter 6, those people in office tend to remain in office. Reelection rates for sitting House members have exceeded 95 percent in recent election years, while the reelection rate for incumbent senators is slightly less, but also high, usually in the mid 80 percent range.[16] In a "bad" year for House incumbents, such as the Democratic wave of 2006, "only" 94 percent of incumbents will win, but the senatorial reelection rate can drop much lower on occasion (79 percent in 2006). To the political novice, these reelection rates might seem surprising, as public trust in government and satisfaction with Congress has remained remarkably low during the very period that reelection rates have been on the rise.

incumbency
The holding of an office.

REDISTRICTING

Because the Constitution requires that representation in the House be based on state population, and that each state have at least one representative, congressional districts must be redrawn by state legislatures to reflect population shifts, so that each member in Congress will represent approximately the same number of residents. This process of redrawing congressional districts to reflect increases or decreases in seats allotted to the states, as well as population shifts within a state, is called **redistricting.** Redistricting is a largely political process that the majority party in a state uses to ensure formation of voting districts that protect their majority.

This redistricting process often involves what is called **gerrymandering.** The term is a derived by combining the last name of the Massachusetts governor first credited with politicizing the process, Elbridge Gerry, and the word salamander, which signifies the oddly shaped district that Gerry created. Because of enormous population growth, the partisan implications of redistricting, and the requirement under the Voting Rights Act for minorities to get an equal chance to elect candidates of their choice, legislators end up drawing oddly shaped districts to achieve their goals.[17]

Redistricting plans routinely meet with court challenges across the country. Following the 2000 Census and the subsequent redistricting in 2002, the courts threw out legislative maps in a half-dozen states, primarily because of state constitutional concerns about compactness. The circuitous boundaries of improper districts often cut across county lines or leap over natural barriers and split counties and long-standing communities.[18]

Over the years, the Supreme Court has ruled that:

- Congressional as well as state legislative districts must be apportioned on the basis of population.[19]
- District lines must be contiguous; you must be able to draw the boundaries of the district with one unbroken line.
- Purposeful gerrymandering of a congressional district to dilute minority strength is illegal under the Voting Rights Act of 1965.[20]

VIDEO ROUNDTABLE
Redistricting

redistricting
The redrawing of congressional districts to reflect population changes or for political advantage.

gerrymandering
The legislative process through which the majority party in each statehouse tries to assure that the maximum number of representatives from its political party can be elected to Congress through the redrawing of legislative districts.

You Are Redrawing the Districts in Your State

■ Redrawing of districts for obvious racial purposes to enhance minority representation is constitutional if race is not the "predominate" factor over all other factors that are part of traditional redistricting, including compactness.[21] In *LULAC et. al.* v. *Perry* (2006), the Supreme Court reinforced these decisions by upholding most of the 2003 political gerrymander of Texas by state Republicans, but declaring one district unconstitutional because it violated federal voting rights protections for Hispanics.

THE IMPACT OF SCANDALS

Scandals come in many varieties in this age of investigative journalism. The old standby of financial impropriety has been supplemented by other forms of career-ending incidents, such as sexual improprieties. Incumbents implicated in scandals typically do not lose reelections—because they simply choose to retire rather than face defeat.[22] The power of incumbency is so strong, however, that many legislators survive even serious scandal to win reelection. For example, Louisiana Representative William J. Jefferson was alleged by the FBI to have taken $100,000 in bribe money, but won reelection in 2006 with 57% of the vote. Jefferson, a Democrat, was far luckier than Republican colleagues implicated in a variety of 2006 scandals, however. Incumbent Republican Senator George Allen of Virginia lost his seat in part due to his use of a racially charged term on the campaign trail. Representative Mark Foley (R–FL) resigned shortly before the 2006 elections after newspaper reports that he had sent sexually explicit instant messages and emails to underage male congressional pages. Foley's seat in a normally safe Republican district was won by a Democrat, and accusations that a number of members of the Republican House leadership may have known about the e-mails for some time resulted in an embarrassing series of ethics hearings conducted in the run-up to the elections.

PRESIDENTIAL COATTAILS

The defeat of a congressional incumbent can occur as a result of the presidential coattail effect. Successful presidential candidates usually carry into office congressional candidates of the same party in the year of their election.

MIDTERM ELECTIONS

midterm election
Election that takes place in the middle of a presidential term.

Elections in the middle of presidential terms, called **midterm elections,** present a threat to incumbents of the president's party. Just as the presidential party usually gains seats in presidential election years, it usually loses seats in off years (see Table 12.2). The problems and tribulations of governing normally cost a president some popularity, alienate key groups, or cause the public to want to send the president a message of one sort or another. An economic downturn or presidential scandal can underline and expand this circumstance, as the Watergate scandal of 1974 and the recession of 1982 demonstrated. The 2002 midterm elections, however, bucked that trend, marking the first time since 1934 that a first-term president gained seats for his party in a midterm election. The 2002 election was likely an anomaly, as it was the first election following the 2001 terrorist attacks, and voters most likely sought political stability by supporting the president's party.

Most apparent is the tendency of voters to punish the president's party much more severely in the sixth year of an eight-year presidency, a phenomenon associated with retrospective voting. After only two years, voters are still willing to "give the guy a chance," but after six years, voters are often restless for change. Senate elections are less inclined to follow these off-year patterns than are House elections. The idiosyncratic nature of Senate contests is due to their intermittent scheduling (only one-third of the seats come up for election every two years) and the existence of well-funded, well-known candidates who can sometimes swim against the political tide.

After the 2004 election, Republicans increased their majorities to twenty-nine seats in the House and ten seats in the Senate. In what was seen as a referendum on

TABLE 12.2 CONGRESSIONAL ELECTION RESULTS, 1948–2006

The party of the president in power almost always loses seats in midterm elections, especially in the midterm election of the second term. In the "sixth-year itch," voters often are tired of the incumbent president and reward the opposition party with big gains in Congress. The few recent exceptions, during the Clinton and Bush administrations, showed the American people's unhappiness with the impeachment scandal and their concerns related to the war on terrorism.

Gain (+) or Loss (–) for President's Party

President	Presidential Election Years			Nonpresidential Election Years		
	Year	House	Senate	Year	House	Senate
Truman (D)	1948	+76	+9	1950	−29	−6
Eisenhower (R)	1952	+24	+2	1954	−18	−1
Eisenhower (R)	1956	−2	0	1958	−48	−13
Kennedy (D)	1960	−20	−2	1962	−4	+3
Johnson (D)	1964	+38	+2	1966	−47	−4
Nixon (R)	1968	+7	+5	1970	−12	+2
Nixon (R)	1972	+13	−2	Ford (R): 1974	−48	−5
Carter (D)	1976	+2	0	1978	−15	−3
Reagan (R)	1980	+33	+12	1982	−26	+1
Reagan (R)	1984	+15	−2	1986	−5	−8
G. Bush (R)	1988	−3	−1	1990	−9	−1
Clinton (D)	1992	−10	0	1994	−52	−9[a]
Clinton (D)	1996	+10	−2	1998	+5	0
G. W. Bush (R)	2000	−2	−4	2002	+6	+2
G. W. Bush (R)	2004	+3	+4	2006	−30	−6

[a]Includes the switch from Democrat to Republican of Alabama U.S. Senator Richard Shelby.

President George W. Bush's policy in Iraq, however, the Republican Party lost control of both chambers of Congress in the 2006 election. This midterm election was typical of the sixth-year itch, with voters looking for a change and punishing the incumbent president's party in Congress.

Throughout the 2006 campaign season, many Democrats ran on a decidedly anti-Iraq war platform. Public disapproval with the ongoing war and a series of ethics scandals had begun to take its political toll on the Republican Party. With President Bush's job approval averaging 39% in the months leading to the election, many analysts were seeing the signs of a Democratic wave that would sweep over the midterm elections.

Democrats' convincing sweep of the House in 2006 saw a takeover of far more seats they had needed to win control of the chamber. Democrats captured eight open Republican seats and defeated 22 GOP incumbents, including many moderate Republican officeholders from northeastern states. Democrats picked up more than the fifteen seats they needed to win a House majority in just six states east of the Mississippi: Connecticut (2), Florida (2), Indiana (3), New Hampshire (2), New York (3), and Pennsylvania (4).

While a Democratic takeover of the House was all but assured prior to election day, the battle for control of the Senate was far from certain. Of the 33 seats up for election in 2006, Democrats needed not only to hold control of competitive seats in New Jersey and Maryland, but they also needed to pick up six of seven Republican-held seats to create a majority. On election night, four Republican incumbents became early casualties of the sixth-year itch. The hotly contested open seat race in Tennessee stayed in the GOP column. Two races remained too close to call on election night: Democrats needed to win in both Virginia and Montana to take control of the Senate. On Wednesday, Democrat John Tester claimed a narrow victory over Republican Conrad Burns in Montana, and the next day, Republican George Allen of Virginia conceded defeat to Democratic challenger Jim Webb. Including the seats of Joe Lieberman of Connecticut and Bernie Sanders of Vermont, who ran as independents, the Democrats won a governing majority of 51 seats, reclaiming the U.S. Senate for the first time since 2002, and overall control of Congress for the first time in twelve years.

VIDEO ROUNDTABLE

Mid-Term Elections 2006

TABLE 12.3 RESULTS OF SELECTED ELECTIONS, 2006

State	Contest	Winner	Loser	Significance
Arizona	House	Harry Mitchell(D)	J.D. Hayworth (R)	Challenger Harry Mitchell received high-profile Republican endorsements and had momentum throughout the very bitter race. Hayworth, a leading supporter of immigration reform, suffered from the late push by Democrats in Arizona.
Florida	House	Tim Mahoney (D)	Joe Negron (R)	Joe Negron's defeat in a highly Republican district was largely due to the negative stigma associated with Mark Foley's name appearing on the ballot. Negron's campaign used the slogan "Punch Foley for Joe" to great last-minute effect, but it simply was not enough.
Illinois	House	Peter Roskam (R)	Tammy Duckworth (D)	Tammy Duckworth, a disabled Iraq war veteran, drew national attention in her House bid, but Roskam pulled out the win in a traditionally Republican district.
Massachusetts	Governor	Deval Patrick (D)	Kerry Healey (R)	Deval Patrick made history by becoming only the second African American to be elected governor of any state, following seventeen years after Doug Wilder's victory in Virginia in 1989.
Missouri	Senate	Claire McCaskill (D)	Jim Talent (R)	In the "Show Me" state, the advantage of a stem cell research question on the ballot (and not a same-sex marriage question) helped Democrat Claire McCaskill defeat incumbent Jim Talent.
Montana	Senate	Jon Tester (D)	Conrad Burns (R)	Conrad Burns, an embattled incumbent with ties to indicted lobbyist Jack Abramoff, portrayed Jon Tester as well left of Montana's mainstream, but the taint of scandal proved insurmountable for Burns in this nail-biter.
North Carolina	House	Heath Shuler (D)	Charles Taylor (R)	Ex-Redskins quarterback Heath Shuler, a conservative Blue Dog Democrat, hammered incumbent Charles Taylor over ethical issues and picked up an important seat for Democrats in the South.
Ohio	Senate	Sherrod Brown (D)	Mike DeWine (R)	DeWine's defeat serves as the best example of just how drastically the Republican Party's fortunes faded over the course of 2006. Brown's aggressive campaign benefited from voter dissatisfaction with scandals associated with Republican Gov. Bob Taft and Rep. Bob Ney.
New York	Governor	Eliot Spitzer (D)	John Faso (R)	Attorney General Eliot Spitzer has been preparing his bid for governor for many years, and a decisive win put the New York governorship back in Democratic hands following 12 years of Republican rule.
Tennessee	Senate	Bob Corker (R)	Harold Ford (D)	Although Ford proved a more charismatic candidate than Corker, his race and single status – highlighted by a controversial RNC ad – may have hurt him in the closing weeks of this very tough campaign.
Texas	House	Nick Lampson (D)	Shelley Sekula-Gibbs (R)	In another scandal-plagued House race, Republican majority leader Tom DeLay resigned from Congress too late for an official replacement to be placed on the ballot. Former Democratic congressman Nick Lampson defeated Republican Shelley Sekula-Gibbs's write-in campaign.
Virginia	Senate	Jim Webb (D)	George Allen (R)	Allen's missteps and allegations of racial insensitivity throughout the campaign gave Webb, a former Navy Secretary under Reagan, a big win for Democrats and control of the Senate.

As a result of the 2006 midterm elections, it is clear that both parties will need to be responsive to the mandate from voters to address the situation in Iraq. As discussed in chapter 6, the 110th Congress will see its very first female Speaker of the House in Nancy Pelosi (D–CA). The ability of Speaker Pelosi and the Democrats to accomplish domestic legislative goals in a closely divided Congress will have a tangible impact as their party tries to capture the presidency in 2008.

paid media
Political advertisements purchased for a candidate's campaign.

free media
Coverage of a candidate's campaign by the news media.

new media
Technologies such as the Internet that blur the line between media sources and create new opportunities for the dissemination of news and other information

The Media's Role in the Campaign Process

WHAT VOTERS ACTUALLY SEE AND HEAR of the candidate is primarily determined by the **paid media** that the campaign creates and pays to have disseminated, the **free media** that result from stories about the campaign that the media choose to broadcast, and the **new media** that blur the lines between paid and free media sources. The campaign staff and media consultants discussed above determine the amount, form, and content of paid media. Free media coverage consists of independent press coverage—all the media outlets covering the candidate and his or her run for office. Coverage by the new media, made possible by a wide array of technological innovations, is generated in part by the campaign but is also driven by individuals from outside the campaign who either contribute to the candidate's existing online effort or who maintain Web sites and blogs of their own.

PAID MEDIA

Positive ads stress the candidate's qualifications, family and personal ties, and issue positions with no direct reference to the opponent. Positive ads are usually favored by the incumbent candidate. **Negative ads** attack the opponent's character and platform and, with the exception of the candidate's brief, legally required statement that he or she approved the ad, may not even mention the candidate who is paying for the airing. **Contrast ads** compare the records and proposals of the candidates, with a bias toward the candidate sponsoring the ad. Most paid advertisements are short **spot ads** that range from ten to sixty seconds long, though in the past, when airtime was less expensive, some ads ran as long as thirty minutes and took the form of documentaries.

Before the 1980s, well-known incumbents usually ignored negative attacks from their challengers, believing that the proper stance was to be above the fray. But, after some well-publicized defeats of incumbents in the early 1980s in which negative television advertising played a prominent role, incumbents began attacking their challengers in earnest.[23] The new rule of politics became "An attack unanswered is an attack agreed to." In a further attempt to stave off brickbats from challengers, incumbents began anticipating the substance of their opponents' attacks and airing **inoculation ads** early in the campaign to protect themselves in advance from the other side's spots.

FREE MEDIA

While candidates have control over what advertisements are run (paid media), they have little control over how journalists will cover their campaigns and convey them to voters. During campaign season, the news media constantly report political news. What they report is largely based on news editors' decisions of what is newsworthy or "fit to print." The press often reports what candidates are doing, such as giving speeches, holding fundraisers, or meeting with party leaders. Even better from the candidate's perspective, the news media may report on a candidate's success, perhaps giving that candidate the brand of a "winner," making him or her that much more difficult to beat. Reporters may also investigate rumors of a candidate's misdeeds or unflattering personal history, such as run-ins with the law or a failed marriage.

The media's expectations and their focus on the political horse race can have an effect on how the public views the candidates. Using poll data, journalists often predict the margins by which they expect contenders to win or lose. A clear victory of 5 percentage points can be judged a setback if the candidate had been projected to win by 12 or 15 points. The tone of the media coverage—that a candidate is either gaining or losing support in polls—can affect whether people decide to give money and other types of support to a candidate.[24]

THE NEW MEDIA

Contemporary campaigns have an impressive new array of weapons at their disposal: faster printing technologies, reliable data bases, automatic dialing, instantaneous Internet publishing and mass e-mail, fax machines, video technology, and enhanced telecommunications and teleconferencing. As a result, candidates can gather and disseminate information better and faster than ever.

One outcome of these changes is the ability of candidates to employ "rapid-response" techniques: the formulation of prompt and informed responses to changing

positive ad
Advertising on behalf of a candidate that stresses the candidate's qualifications, family, and issue positions, without reference to the opponent.

negative ad
Advertising on behalf of a candidate that attacks the opponent's platform or character.

contrast ad
Ad that compares the records and proposals of the candidates, with a bias toward the sponsor.

spot ad
Television advertising on behalf of a candidate that is broadcast in sixty-, thirty-, or ten-second duration.

inoculation ad
Advertising that attempts to counteract an anticipated attack from the opposition before the attack is launched.

Television and Presidential Campaigns

Photos courtesy: left, Bettmann/Corbis; right, Rich Wilking/Reuters/Corbis

■ Presidential debates have come a long way—at least in terms of studio trappings—since the ill-at-ease Richard M. Nixon was visually bested by John F. Kennedy in the first televised debate. John Kerry's strong performances in the three presidential debates of 2004 helped him stay within striking distance of President Bush's lead going into the final weeks of the campaign.

events on the campaign battlefield. In response to breaking news of a scandal or issue, for example, candidates can conduct background research, implement an opinion poll and tabulate the results, devise a containment strategy and appropriate "spin," and deliver a reply. This makes a strong contrast with the campaigns of the 1970s and early 1980s, dominated primarily by radio and TV advertisements, which took much longer to prepare and had little of the flexibility enjoyed by the contemporary e-campaign.[25]

The first widespread use of the Internet in national campaigning came in 1996. Republican presidential candidate Bob Dole urged voters to log onto his Web site, and many did. According to one source, during the 2004 election 37 percent of the adult population and 61 percent of all Americans with Internet access regularly logged on to get campaign and election information.[26] All of the candidates for the 2004 presidential campaign made use of Web sites, even when their candidacies were only in the exploratory stage. With the advent of blogs, a candidate's Web site can take on a life of its own. Blogs enable supporters and the occasional stealthy opponent to post messages on the candidate's Web site and to engage in a nearly contemporaneous exchange of ideas with other supporters and with the candidate's Internet team. Even after the campaign has concluded, online networks can persist and keep supporters abreast of a candidate's future direction.

Campaign Finance

THE UNITED STATES has struggled to achieve effective campaign finance rules for well over one hundred years. In the early 1970s, for example, Congress enacted its most ambitious round of campaign laws to date, the Federal Election Campaign Act (FECA). FECA and its later amendments established disclosure requirements, established the Presidential Public Funding Program, which provides partial public funding for presidential candidates who meet certain criteria, and created the Federal Elections Commission (an independent federal agency tasked with enforcing the nation's election laws).

The most recent bout of reforms were set in motion by Senators John McCain (R–AZ) and Russell Feingold (D–WI), who co-sponsored the 2002 **Bipartisan Campaign Reform Act** (BCRA) in the Senate, while Representatives Chris Shays (R–CT) and Martin Meehan (D–MA) sponsored the House version. BCRA includes a "fast track" provision that any suits challenging the constitutionality of the reforms will be immediately placed before a U.S. district court, and it gives appellate powers to the U.S. Supreme Court. The reason for this provision was simple: to thwart the numerous lobbying groups and several high-profile elected officials who threatened to tie up BCRA in

Bipartisan Campaign Reform Act (2002)
Legislation that prohibits soft-money contributions to political parties and limits amounts individuals can give.

the courts for as long as they could. No sooner did President George W. Bush sign BCRA than U.S. Senator Mitch McConnell (R–KY) and the National Rifle Association separately filed lawsuits claiming that BCRA violated free speech rights.

In May 2003, a three-judge panel of the U.S. District Court for the District of Columbia found that the BCRA restrictions on soft-money donations violated free speech rights, although the BCRA restrictions on political advertising did not.[27] The decision was immediately appealed to the Supreme Court. After oral arguments in September, the Court handed down its 5–4 decision, *McConnell* v. *FEC* (2003), in December, concluding that the government's interest in preventing political-party corruption overrides the free speech rights to which the parties would otherwise be entitled. In other words, the Supreme Court very narrowly upheld the BCRA measures restricting speech both in the form of political contributions (the soft-money ban) and in political advertising.[28]

PARTICIPATION

The Debate Over Campaign Finance Reform

CURRENT RULES

The Court's decision in *McConnell* means that political money is now regulated by the federal government under the terms of the Bipartisan Campaign Reform Act, which supplanted most of the provisions of the Federal Election Campaign Act. Table 12.4 summarizes key provisions of this law, which outlaws unlimited and unregulated contributions to parties, known as soft money, and limits the amounts that individuals, interest groups, and political parties can give to candidates for president, U.S. senator, and U.S. representative. The goal of all limits is the same: to prevent any single group or individual from gaining too much influence over elected officials, who naturally feel indebted to campaign contributors.

Individual Contributions Individual contributions are donations from individual citizens. The 2006 maximum allowable contribution under federal law for congressional and presidential elections is $2,100 per election to each candidate, adjusted biannually for inflation, with primary and general elections considered separately. Individuals are also limited to a total of $50,700 in gifts to all candidates, PACs, and parties combined in each calendar year. Most candidates receive a majority of all funds directly from individuals, and most individual gifts are well below the maximum level. Finally, individuals who spend over $10,000 to air "electioneering communication," that is, "any broadcast, cable, or satellite communication which refers to a clearly identified candidate for Federal office" within sixty days of a general election or thirty days of a primary election, are now subject to a strict disclosure law. The rationale behind the last regulation is that spending on an ad favoring a candidate is effectively the same as a contribution to the candidate's campaign and requires the same scrutiny as other large donations.

Political Action Committee (PAC) Contributions When interest groups such as labor unions, corporations, and ideological issue groups seek to make donations to campaigns, they must do so by establishing **political action committees (PACs).** PACs are officially recognized fund-raising organizations that are allowed by federal law to participate in federal elections. (Some states have similar requirements for state elections.) Under current rules, a PAC can give no more than $5,000 per candidate per election (primary, general, and special election), and $15,000 each year to each of the units of the national parties.

Approximately 4,000 PACs are registered with the Federal Election Commission—the governmental agency charged with administering the election laws. In 2004, PACs contributed $294 million to Senate and House candidates, while individuals donated $693 million. (See Figure 12.4.) On aver-

political action committee (PAC)
Federally mandated, officially registered fund-raising committee that represents interest groups in the political process.

TABLE 12.4	INDIVIDUAL CONTRIBUTION LIMITS PER ELECTION CYCLE BEFORE AND AFTER BIPARTISAN CAMPAIGN REFORM ACT (2002)	
	Before	*After**
Contributions per candidate	$1,000	$2,100
Contributions per national party committee	$20,000	$26,700
Total contributions per two-year cycle	$50,000	$101,400
Soft money	Unlimited	Banned

*These limits are for 2006. BCRA limits are adjusted in odd-numbered years to account for inflation.
Source: Campaign Finance Institute: http://www.cfinst.org.

FIGURE 12.4 EXPENDITURES BY PACS IN THE 2004 ELECTION CYCLE

PACs contributed a total of $290 million to candidates competing in the 2004 election. Notice how PACs used a majority of their expenditures to support congressional candidates and how PAC spending has a slight bias toward Republican candidates and a strong bias toward incumbents.

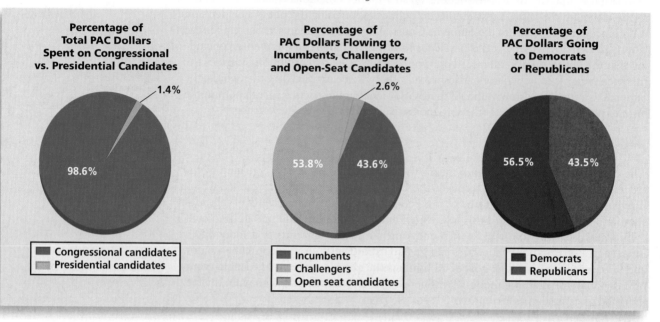

Percentage of Total PAC Dollars Spent on Congressional vs. Presidential Candidates

1.4%
98.6%

- Congressional candidates
- Presidential candidates

Percentage of PAC Dollars Flowing to Incumbents, Challengers, and Open-Seat Candidates

2.6%
53.8%   43.6%

- Incumbents
- Challengers
- Open seat candidates

Percentage of PAC Dollars Going to Democrats or Republicans

56.5%   43.5%

- Democrats
- Republicans

Source: Federal Election Commission.

age, PAC contributions account for 57 percent of the war chests (campaign funds) of House candidates and 67 percent of the treasuries of Senate candidates. Incumbents benefit the most from PAC money; incumbents received $228 million, much more than the $66 million given to challengers during the 2004 election cycle.[29] By making these contributions, PACs hope to secure entrée to the candidate after he or she has been elected to influence them on issues important to the PAC. Corporate PACs give primarily to incumbents because incumbents tend to win, and lobbyists want to guarantee access for their clients. Single-issue and more ideologically based PACs are often willing to support challengers and more untried candidates who pledge to support their positions if elected.[30]

Because donations from a small number of PACs make up such a large proportion of campaign war chests, PACs have influence disproportionate to that of individuals. Studies, in fact, have shown that PACs effectively use contributions to punish legislators and affect policy, at least in the short run.[31] Legislators who vote contrary to the wishes of a PAC see their donations withheld, but those who are successful in legislating as the PAC wishes are rewarded with even greater donations.[32] However, contribution limits keep the influence of PACs to $5,000 per candidate per year, and while this amount may substantially aid an incumbent's reelection, it pales in comparison to the total budget required for victory in federal elections.

In an attempt to control PACs, the BCRA has a limit on the way PACs attempt to influence campaigns. The law strictly forbids PACs from using corporate or union funds for the electioneering communications discussed earlier. PACs can use corporate or labor contributions only for administrative costs. The purpose of the limit is to prevent corporations or unions from having an undue influence on the outcome of elections, as they have in the past, by heavily advertising toward specific audiences in the weeks leading up to elections.

Political Party Contributions   Candidates also receive donations from the national and state committees of the Democratic and Republican Parties. As mentioned in chapter 11, political parties can give substantial contributions to their congressional nominees. Under the current rules, national parties can give up to $5,000 to a House candidate in their general election and $37,000 to a Senate candidate.

In 2006, the Republican and Democratic parties funneled over million to their standard-bearers, via direct contributions and coordinated expenditures. In competitive races, the parties may provide 15–17 percent of their candidates' total war chests. In addition to helping elect party members, campaign contributions from political parties have another, less obvious benefit: helping to ensure party discipline in voting. One study of congressional voting behavior for instance, found that those members who received a large percentage of their total campaign funds from their party voted with their party more often than they were expected to.[33]

Member-to-Candidate Contributions

In Congress and in state legislatures, well-funded, electorally secure incumbents now often contribute campaign money to their party's needy incumbent and non-incumbent legislative candidates.

This activity began in some state legislatures (notably California), but it is now well-established at the congressional level.[34] Generally, members establish their own PACs—informally dubbed "leadership" PACs—through which they distribute campaign support to candidates. Members largely give their contributions to the same candidates who receive the bulk of congressional campaign committee resources. Thus, member contributions at the congressional level have emerged as a major supplement to the campaign resources contributed by the party campaign committees.

Candidates' Personal Contributions

Candidates and their families may donate to the campaign. The U.S. Supreme Court ruled in *Buckley* v. *Valeo* (1976) that no limit could be placed on the amount of money candidates can spend from their own families' resources, since such spending is considered a First Amendment right of free speech.[35]

For wealthy politicians, this allowance may mean personal spending in the millions. In 2006, for example, the top two self-financers were candidates for the Senate, Republican Pete Ricketts of Nebraska and Democrat Ned Lamont of Connecticut. Both lost their bids despite each spending over $10 million of their own money on their campaigns. While Lamont ran a competitive campaign, Ricketts only managed to receive 36% of the vote against incumbent Democrat Ben Nelson. While self-financed candidates often garner a great deal of attention, most candidates commit much less than $100,000 in family resources to their election bids.[36]

Public Funds

Public funds are donations from general tax revenues. Only presidential candidates (and a handful of state and local contenders) receive public funds. Under the terms of the FECA (which first established public funding of presidential campaigns), a candidate for president can become eligible to receive public funds during the nominating contest by raising at least $5,000 in individual contributions of $250 or less in each of twenty states. The candidate can apply for federal **matching funds,** whereby every dollar raised from individuals in amounts less than $251 increments is matched by the federal treasury on a dollar-for-dollar basis. Of course, this assumes there is enough money in the Presidential Election Campaign Fund to do so. The fund is accumulated by taxpayers who designate $3 of their taxes for this purpose each year when they send in their federal tax returns. (Only about 20 percent of taxpayers check off the appropriate box, even though participation does not increase their tax burden.)

For the general election, the two major-party presidential nominees can accept a $75 million lump-sum payment from the federal government after the candidate accepts his or her nomination. If the candidate accepts the money, it becomes the sole source for financing the campaign. A candidate could refuse the money and be free from the spending cap the government attaches to it, though this has never happened. Because the Democratic convention occurred five weeks before the Republican convention in 2004, John Kerry actually had five weeks more than Bush during which he had to stretch out the $75 million the government provided. Kerry first considered

public funds
Donations from the general tax revenues to the campaigns of qualifying presidential candidates.

matching funds
Donations to presidential campaigns from the federal government that are determined by the amount of private funds a qualifying candidate raises.

VIDEO DEBATE

Public Campaign Financing

Analyzing Visuals

THE TEN MOST ACTIVE 527 GROUPS IN 2004

After the Bipartisan Campaign Reform Act of 2002 outlawed soft-money contributions to political parties, Democratic and Republican political operatives were quick to find alternative ways to funnel money into the political process. The tool of choice following the 2002 reforms was the previously underutilized 527 political committees, named after their designation in the Internal Revenue Service code. Looking at the

information in the table, what conclusions can you draw about the relative success of Democratic and Republican fund-raising efforts with regard to 527 groups? Given what you know about some of the individual 527s listed below, a number of which are discussed in the text, what conclusions can you draw about the effectiveness of various 527 strategies with regard to the 2004 presidential election?

Committee	Expenditures	Pro-Democratic	Pro-Republican
America Coming Together	$78,040,480	X	
Joint Victory Campaign 2004	$72,588,053	X	
Media Fund	$57,694,580	X	
Service Employees International Union	$47,730,761	X	
Progress for America	$35,631,378		X
American Federation of State/County/Municipal Employees	$26,170,411	X	
Swift Boat Veterans for Truth	$22,565,360		X
MoveOn.org	$21,565,803	X	
College Republican National Committee	$17,260,655		X
New Democrat Network	$12,524,063	X	

Source: http://www.opensecrets.org.

forgoing the public funding and later considered not accepting his party's nomination until after the Republican convention, but neither option proved popular and he eventually decided to accept the public funding and abide by the spending limit.[37]

A third-party candidate receives a smaller amount proportionate to his or her November vote total if that candidate gains a minimum of 5 percent of the vote. Note that in such a case, the money goes to third-party campaigns only the *after* the election is over; no money is given in advance of the general election.

THE FALL OF THE SOFT-MONEY LOOPHOLE AND THE RISE OF THE 527 LOOPHOLE

soft money
The virtually unregulated money funneled by individuals and political committees through state and local parties.

Soft money is campaign money raised and spent by political parties for expenses such as overhead and administrative costs and for grassroots activities such as political education and get out the vote efforts. Soft-money donations are prohibited under BCRA, and third-party issue ads, if coordinated with a federal candidate's campaign, can now be considered campaign contributions and are thus regulated by the FEC. The last election cycle for the parties to use soft money was 2001–2002, and the amount raised, nearly $430 million for Republican and Democrats combined, highlights why the reform seemed necessary.[38] Republicans raised $219 million in soft money from pharmaceutical, insurance, and energy companies. Democrats came in just under $211 million in soft money from unions and law firms. With soft money banned, the hope was that wealthy donors and interest groups would be deprived of their privileged and potentially corrupting influence on parties and candidates. The hope was that like every other citizen, they would have to donate within the hard-money limits placed on individuals and PACs. Unfortunately, these reforms have not worked and the 2004 election revealed the latest campaign finance loophole.

The most significant unintended result of BCRA was the emergence of political entities known as **527 political committees.** Their name comes from the number of the provision of the Internal Revenue tax code that establishes their legal status. The 527s are essentially unregulated interest groups that focus on specific causes or policy positions and attempt to influence voters. (See Analyzing Visuals: The Ten Most Active 527 Groups in 2004.)

According to the tax code, 527s may not directly engage in advocacy for or against a candidate but can advocate on behalf of political issues. This allowed them to circumvent the direct advocacy prohibition by creating what detractors call "sham issue ads"—ads that name a particular candidate and state how the candidate supported or harmed a particular interest without directly stating the 527 group's opinion on how to vote in the election. Thus, money that would have entered the system as unregulated soft money in previous election cycles ended up in the hands of 527 organizations in 2004, funding several television advertisements and direct mailings.[39] BCRA now forbids the airing of these ads thirty days before a primary and sixty days before a general election to limit their influence on voters.

The 527s exist in both political camps, though the Democrats, the party out of power, were first to pursue them aggressively in 2004. Two of the largest pro-Democratic committees in the 2004 election were the Media Fund and Americans Coming Together (ACT). Both raised millions of dollars from people eager to see a Democrat in the White House. These committees bought TV, radio, and print advertising to sell their message, focusing on the battleground or "swing" states that were not firmly in the Bush or Kerry camps. Even though most political observers predicted that President George W. Bush would easily outspend Senator John Kerry (D–MA) in the presidential contest, the Democratic 527s considerably aided the Democratic campaign. Through the end of the 2004 election, pro-Democratic 527 groups spent more than $200 million, more than double that of their Republican counterparts. Groups on both sides saw large donations from wealthy individuals, including billionaire George Soros, who gave $23.4 million to Democratic organizations, and Texas developer Bob Perry, who donated $8 million to Republican groups.[40] As fund-raising records in almost every category were shattered in 2004, the campaign reform law clearly had no effect on overall spending or in limiting the amount that wealthy individuals can contribute to influence the process. 527 committees contributed almost $300 million to House and Senate candidates in 2006, with the Service Employees International Union's 527 contributing the most at over $26 million. Bob Perry's 527 topped the list of individual contributors, giving over $5 million to Republican groups.

It is very likely that reformers will once again attempt to reform their reforms. The abolition of 527s is highly unlikely—and the money supporting them would most likely reappear in some other way. Overall, however, one lesson of BCRA is obvious: no amount of clever legislating will rid the American system of campaign money. Interested individuals and groups will always find ways to have their voices heard. The challenge is to find a way to force contributors to disclose their contributions in a timely fashion, so that the public may take this information into account when deciding how to vote.

527 Political Committees
Nonprofit and unregulated interest groups that focus on specific causes or policy positions and attempt to influence voters.

VIDEO ROUNDTABLE
Campaign Finance Reform

Bringing It Together: The 2004 Presidential Campaign and Election

THE 2004 PRESIDENTIAL ELECTION may go down in history for how extremely it divided the nation. An entire month before the election, polls showed that only 3 percent of Americans remained undecided on a candidate. Despite his status as an incumbent, implementation of tax cuts, and reputation for decisiveness, President George W. Bush faced an incredibly heated race against Massachusetts Senator John Kerry. At the most basic level, Americans knew that John Kerry had the knowledge and experience to serve in the highest office in the nation. Many were also unhappy with the situation in Iraq, job losses, and health care costs. However, Americans were casting their first presidential vote after the September 11, terrorist attacks, and they also had reservations about electing a president whose leadership during a national security crisis had not yet been proven.

THE PARTY NOMINATION BATTLE

Although few Americans were aware of it, the Republican Party *did* hold presidential primaries in 2004. Few noticed, as is usually the case when there is an incumbent candidate, because there was no significant opposition within the party to George W. Bush's reelection.

The Democrats, meanwhile, had ten candidates competing for their party's nomination. Democratic Party veterans Representative Dick Gephardt (MO), Senator and 2000 vice presidential nominee Joseph Lieberman (CT), Senator Bob Graham (FL), and Senator John Kerry (MA) joined the five other "original" candidates, Senator John Edwards (NC), former Illinois Senator and Ambassador Carol Moseley Braun (the first African American woman in the Senate), former Vermont Governor Howard Dean, Representative Dennis Kucinich (OH), and the Reverend Al Sharpton, an African American activist from New York. Retired General Wesley Clark entered late in the race after some Democrats ran a "Draft Clark" effort.

The Democratic candidates spent the spring and summer of 2003 in the typical primary season fashion: fund-raising, debating, giving speeches, and concentrating on the key states of Iowa and New Hampshire. By autumn, a full year prior to the general election, Senator Graham had dropped out of the race, citing fund-raising problems and proving the old adage that the first votes in any campaign are cast with dollars, not ballots. Autumn also brought the rise of the once "fringe" candidate Howard Dean. Dean's solid stance against the Iraq War and pointed criticism of President Bush appealed to Democratic partisans, providing him with impressive grassroots support and a large war chest. Although in the spring of 2003 Democratic insiders were predicting that John Kerry would emerge as the front-runner, the fall brought Howard Dean the endorsements of party leaders such as Iowa Senator Tom Harkin and former Vice President Al Gore.

Initially, the Democrats' campaigns were focused on contrasting themselves with President Bush. However, as Dean emerged as the apparent front-runner, his rivals

■ At a debate held in Phoenix, Arizona, on October 3, 2003, several members of the Democratic primary field discussed their ideas with the audience.

Photo courtesy: Matt York/AP Wide World Photos

began aiming many of their attacks in his direction rather than at the president. The former governor's third-place finish in the Iowa caucuses, behind both John Kerry and John Edwards, may be partially attributed to these attacks. Others blamed the Iowa upset on the campaign's mismanagement of Dean's resources—not spending enough on ads and appearances and overspending on other items. Dean would win only one primary, in Vermont, and he dropped out of the race in February.

After Iowa, the race centered on Kerry and Edwards. Edwards, the charismatic first-term senator from North Carolina, hoped to energize the party and find support in the South. Edwards gave one of the most memorable stump speeches of the 2004 presidential election. In this speech, called "The Two Americas," Edwards discussed how the wealthy minority of Americans live in stark contrast to the majority of working and middle-class Americans. The contrast was not to provoke a "hate the rich" politics of envy but to demonstrate how the disparity between the two groups was detrimental to American democracy and could be closed only by improving state services, repealing tax breaks for the rich, and giving greater tax relief to the middle class.

Kerry relied on his experience and his support among party loyalists, capitalizing on anti-Bush sentiment and the perception that he was the best candidate to defeat Bush in the general election. In the end, Democratic voters sided with Kerry, and Edwards dropped out of the race in March, leaving Kerry as the "presumptive" Democratic candidate. Democrats appeared united, at least in their determination to defeat George W. Bush in the general election. For this reason, many suggest, they chose a candidate quickly and channeled their energies toward winning in the fall.

THE DEMOCRATIC CONVENTION

With Kerry entering the national convention in a virtual tie with George W. Bush, he and Edwards, now on the ticket as the vice presidential hopeful, would take this opportunity to define their candidacy, woo new voters, and rally their party faithful at the July 26–29 Democratic National Convention. The convention was held in Boston, Massachusetts, Kerry's home state and solid Democratic territory.

The overarching theme of the convention was "Respected abroad, stronger at home." This emphasis on national security was most prominent on the final night of the convention, which featured testimonials from former Senator Max Cleland and Kerry's Vietnam Swiftboat crewmates. In Kerry's speech, foreign affairs and his personal biography vastly overshadowed other topics. The biographical portion was most likely in response to polls that showed Kerry as not yet having established a personal connection with Americans. Kerry also used his speech as an opportunity to defend against GOP accusations that he was a "flip-flopper" on key issues. In one of his most direct attacks on the integrity of President Bush, Kerry pledged that his leadership would "start by telling the truth to the American people."

Despite what most analysts considered a solid performance, Kerry did not receive a significant post-convention "bounce." In their candidate's defense, the Kerry campaign argued that challengers historically run behind incumbents by about 15 points heading into a convention, whereas Kerry entered the convention already polling neck and neck with Bush.

THE REPUBLICAN CONVENTION

The Republican National Convention was held from August 30 to September 2, beginning a full month after the Democratic National Convention ended. It was held in Madison Square Garden in New York City, considered one of the most heavily liberal, Democratic locales in the nation and most certainly Kerry territory. It was clear that the GOP picked New York City not to win over its residents but rather in an effort to use the symbolism of the 9/11 terrorist attacks to their advantage.

Under the theme "A Nation of Courage," the 2004 Republican National Convention had an unmistakable focus on showcasing moderate Republicans. The right-wing branch of the Republican Party that had captured the stage at past conventions would stand aside as the more moderate Arnold Schwarzenegger, Rudy Giuliani, and John McCain spoke on behalf of their party and President Bush. The convention would be a delicate balancing act between reaching out to the swing voters (who were charmed in 2000 by Bush's "compassionate conservative" agenda) without alienating the socially conservative Republican base.

The 2004 Republican National Convention was not only a depiction of the Republican Party's agenda and campaign strategy but also a vivid demonstration of how polarized the nation had become. Thousands of New Yorkers and protesters from other states took to the streets during the convention for primarily peaceful protests against Bush, the Iraq War, and the Republican Party. Still, the GOP had reason to be pleased with its convention performance. Whereas the Democratic National Convention did not give Kerry a bounce in public opinion polls, Bush left New York with the prize of a modest 2 percent post-convention bounce, giving him the support of 52 percent of likely voters.

THE PRESIDENTIAL DEBATES

The first presidential debate took place on September 30, 2004, at the University of Miami in Coral Gables, Florida. During the discussion on foreign policy, Bush and Kerry clashed sharply on the war in Iraq and on fighting terrorism. Television ratings were exceptionally high, with the first debate being watched by 62.5 million viewers, the most since 1992. Viewers generally found Kerry to have won the debate, and many pundits commented on Bush's lack of energy and focus.

A town hall format was used for the second presidential debate, wherein voters found to be undecided by the Gallup polling organization were allowed to ask questions of each candidate in turn. Reacting against the criticism that he seemed tired and unfocused, Bush was extremely forthright and energetic throughout the night. The candidates met for the last time on October 13 in Tempe, Arizona. This debate followed a structure similar to that for the first debate, with the candidates standing behind podiums and answering questions. For the first time during the debates, the questions were geared toward domestic issues. The public and media commentators generally considered the last debate to have been won by Kerry. Ultimately, Kerry—with his debate performances—seemed to even the playing field going into the final days of the campaign.

THE FALL CAMPAIGN AND GENERAL ELECTION

In the final weeks of the campaign, public opinion was deadlocked, and many Americans began to fear that the closeness and uncertainty of 2000 were again possible in 2004. There was even the real possibility of a tie in the Electoral College, which would throw the election into the House of Representatives. The election was especially close in the key battleground states of Ohio, Florida, Pennsylvania, New Mexico, Iowa, and Wisconsin.

Bush stayed on message during the last days of the campaign, emphasizing the need to continue the effort in Iraq and to strongly prosecute the war on terrorism. Kerry continued to hack away at the president's choice to invade Iraq as misguided and without a plan for victory. Kerry especially criticized Bush's handling of foreign relations, mentioning the bad blood in Europe and around the world created out of his Iraq policy. Kerry promised a change in international relations in which the United States would be more attuned to the concerns of allies and would expend more effort building alliances to fight the global war on terrorism. In a number of television commercials, and in public appearances, Bush fought back, continuing to paint Kerry as a "flip-flopper" who frequently switched his positions to follow public opinion. To attack Kerry's credibility on defense,

Bush also used a *New York Times* interview in which Kerry likened terrorism before 9/11 to a "nuisance" like illegal gambling or prostitution.

Despite the efforts of each campaign, public opinion remained very divided in key states like Ohio and Florida up until the election. Realizing this, both candidates made a marathon sprint through battleground states in the last few days before the election. Bush covered several states in the final week but spent seven consecutive days traveling through Ohio, including Election Day. Kerry visited Michigan, Wisconsin, Florida, and Ohio in the final days of the campaign. After voting in his home state of Texas, Bush flew back to Washington to await the election results. Kerry returned to Massachusetts to cast his vote and follow an Election Day tradition of lunch at a Boston oyster bar. With the election close, and both candidates confident of their chances, the afternoon wore on in anticipation of the first exit polls.

ELECTION RESULTS

Network and cable news bureaus proceeded with caution on election night and did not call states for one candidate or another until the outcome was clear. As the night wore on and more states began to close their polls, Bush began to show a convincing lead in the key battleground state of Florida. However, the networks remained extremely cautious. As Election Day approached midnight, Florida had been called for Bush, but Ohio still remained too close to call for some networks, despite a significant lead by the president. By early the next morning, neither candidate had yet to capture the necessary 270 electoral votes. Despite a lead of over 100,000 votes for Bush in Ohio, the Kerry campaign believed there might be enough late votes to turn the tide.

By later that morning, the Bush campaign was confident that they had carried the election, and they informed the Kerry campaign that they would be declaring victory. Allowing Kerry the courtesy of giving his concession speech first, the Bush campaign waited until the early afternoon for Kerry to speak. Kerry then conceded formally at historic Faneuil Hall in Boston, emphasizing the need for unity after such a divisive campaign. About an hour later, Bush gave his victory speech at the Ronald Reagan building in Washington, D.C., also speaking of the need for unity but emphasizing his victory as ratification by the people of his policies.

ANALYZING THE OUTCOME OF THE 2004 ELECTION

One distinguishing characteristic of the 2004 election was that it had the highest voter turnout rate since 1968, with 60.7 percent of eligible citizens participating, or an estimated 122 million votes. Millions more Americans voted in 2004 than in 2000, despite long lines that kept some voters waiting for over seven hours. Not surprisingly, the largest turnouts occurred in swing states, where a majority of campaign time and resources were spent. The major partisan divide is seen as a primary cause for such high numbers.

In many ways, the 2004 presidential election was similar to the 2000 election. For the most part, "red states" remained red and "blue states" remained blue. Most of the action, and campaign spending, took place in the handful of competitive states, which once again determined the outcome of the election. While 2004 was the most expensive presidential race in the nation's history, this too was merely a continuation of long-standing modern trends. And after years of debating campaign finance reform and enacting the much touted Bipartisan Campaign Reform Act of 2002, the spending by interest groups and wealthy individuals continued unabated.

Perhaps the most amazing aspect of the election was that while 60 million people left the election disappointed, some profoundly so, as their preferred candidate was defeated, the event unfolded without incident. Americans continue to accept and take comfort in the results of their nation's democratic process.

Summary

VOTING, ELECTIONS, AND CAMPAIGNS are essential parts of American government and the democratic principles we hold dear. Whether they are casting ballots in congressional or presidential elections, voters behave in certain distinct ways and exhibit unmistakable patterns to political scientists who study them.

Elections in the United States include primary elections, general elections, initiatives, referenda, and recall elections.

No U.S. election can compare to the presidential contest. This spectacle, held every four years, brings together all the elements of politics and attracts the most ambitious and energetic politicians to the national stage. No longer closed affairs dominated by deals cut in "smoke-filled rooms," today's conventions are more open made-for-television events in which the party platform is drafted and adopted, and the presidential ticket is formally nominated.

Compared with presidential elections, which are played out on the national stage, congressional elections are a different animal. Most candidates for Congress labor in relative obscurity. The 2006 midterm elections resulted in Democrats gaining control of both chambers of Congress for the first time since 1994.

The media play an important role in defining the landscape of all elections. Candidates rely on both free media and paid media, purchasing ad time on television and ad space in print media. The Internet plays an increasingly important role in defining candidate perceptions.

As a result of the rise of soft money, Congress passed the Bipartisan Campaign Finance Reform Act, in 2002. BCRA was promptly challenged but was upheld with very few exceptions by the Supreme Court. Though BCRA was successful in banning the unregulated soft-money that flowed through the political parties, it exposed another loophole in the existing campaign finance laws, the unregulated money that now flows through 527 groups.

The events of the 2004 election demonstrate how all of the components of voting, elections and campaigns come together in modern politics.

KEY TERMS

527 political committees, p. 380
Bipartisan Campaign Reform Act (2002), p. 376
campaign consultant, p. 367
campaign manager, p. 366
closed primary, p. 360
communications director, p. 366
contrast ad, p. 374
crossover voting, p. 360
direct mailer, p. 366

elector, p. 367
Electoral College, p. 367
finance chair, p. 366
free media, p. 374
front-loading, p. 364
general election, p. 360
general election campaign, p. 365
gerrymandering p. 371
get out the vote (GOTV), p. 366
incumbency, p. 371
initiative, p. 361
inoculation ad, p. 374
Internet team, p. 367
matching funds, p. 379
media consultant, p. 367
midterm election, p. 372
negative ad, p. 374
new media, p. 374
nomination campaign, p. 362
open primary, p. 360
paid media, p. 374
political action committee (PAC), p. 377
pollster, p. 366
positive ad, p. 374
press secretary, p. 366
primary election, p. 360
prospective judgment, p. 359
public funds, p. 379
raiding, p. 360
reapportionment, p. 370
recall, p. 362
redistricting, p. 371
referendum, p. 361
retrospective judgment, p. 359
runoff primary, p. 360
soft money, p. 379
spot ad, p. 374
turnout, p. 352
voter canvass, p. 366

SELECTED READINGS

Abramson, Paul R., John H. Aldrich, and David W. Rohde. *Change and Continuity in the 2000 and 2002 Elections.* Washington, DC: CQ Press, 2003.

Ansolabehere, Stephen, and Shanto Iyengar. *Going Negative: How Political Ads Shrink and Polarize the Electorate.* New York: Free Press, 1997.

Campbell, Angus, Philip E. Converse, Warren E. Miller, and Donald E. Stokes, reprint ed. *The American Voter.* Chicago: University of Chicago, 1980.

Fenno, Richard F., Jr. *Senators on the Campaign Trail: The Politics of Representation.* Norman: University of Oklahoma Press, 1998.

Herrnson, Paul S. *Congressional Elections: Campaigning at Home and in Washington,* 4th. ed. Washington, DC: CQ Press, 2003.

Holbrook, Thomas M. *Do Campaigns Matter?* Thousand Oaks, CA: Sage, 1996.

Jacobson, Gary C. *The Politics of Congressional Elections*, 5th ed. New York: HarperCollins, 2000.

Key, V. O., Jr., with Milton C. Cummings. *The Responsible Electorate*. Cambridge, MA: Harvard University Press, 1966.

Nelson, Michael, ed. *The Elections of 2004*. Washington, DC: CQ Press, 2005.

Nie, Norman H., Sidney Verba, and John R. Petrocik. *The Changing American Voter*. Cambridge, MA: Harvard University, 1980.

Patterson, Thomas E. *The Vanishing Voter: Public Involvement in an Age of Uncertainty*. New York: Vintage, 2003.

Sabato, Larry J. *Divided States of America: The Slash and Burn Politics of the 2004 Presidential Election*. New York: Longman, 2005.

Sabato, Larry J. *The Sixth Year Itch: The Rise and Fall of George W. Bush's Presidency*. New York: Longman, 2007.

Teixeira, Ruy. *The Disappearing American Voter*. Washington, DC: Brookings Institution, 1992.

Thurber, James A., and Candice J. Nelson. *Campaign Warriors: Political Consultants in Elections*. Washington, DC: Brookings Institution, 2000.

Verba, Sidney, Kay Lehman Schlozman, and Henry E. Brady. *Voice and Equality: Civic Voluntarism in American Politics*. New York: Belknap Press, 1996.

Wayne, Stephen J. *The Road to the White House*. 6th ed. New York: Wadsworth, 2003.

WEB EXPLORATIONS

To learn about the functions of the Federal Election Commission, the government agency that monitors and enforces campaign finance and election laws, see
http://www.fec.gov

To access the most up-to-date, high-quality data on voting, public opinion, and political participation, go to
http://www.gallup.com

To learn more about the Electoral College, go to
http://www.fec.gov/pages/ecmenu2.htm

To explore campaign contributions and election results, see
http://www.opensecrets.org

To learn more about candidates you have supported in the past or to familiarize yourself with other political candidates so you can make informed choices, go to
http://www.vote-smart.org

To look at what voters said before going to the polls and whom they actually voted for, go to
http://www.pollingreport.com

Photo courtesy: Mark Wilson/Getty Images

SOCIAL AND ECONOMIC POLICY

13

IN 2003, the United States federal government assumed a new major responsibility in the area of health care for its citizens. Following years of agitation and national debate over the high cost of prescription drugs, President George W. Bush signed into law the Medicare Prescription Drug, Improvement, and Modernization Act. Hotly debated in Congress because of its expensive price tag and its controversial aspects, the legislation was hailed by President Bush as "the greatest advance in health care coverage for America's seniors since the founding of Medicare."[1] Seniors choosing to participate received drug discount cards in 2004, with the more extensive subsidized prescription benefit taking effect in 2006. The estimated cost for the first ten years of this new government benefit originally was projected at $400 million, but shortly after the legislation was signed, the cost was recalculated to be significantly higher.

This was not the first time the federal government took on health care responsibilities. In 1965, the expensive new programs of Medicare (for the elderly) and Medicaid (for the poor) were established as part of an overall expansion of the governmental programs to promote social welfare as part of President Lyndon's B. Johnson's Great Society program (see chapter 3). Medicare became a sacred program in the decades that followed, and it achieved considerable success in improving the health of the nation's senior citizens.

However, the absence of a drug benefit as part of Medicare left many older Americans with decreased ability to pay for the prescription drugs they depend on to maintain their well-being. Prescription drug costs rose at double-digit rates in the late 1990s, and it was estimated in 2002 that approximately two-fifths of American retirees were without insurance to help pay for the escalating cost of essential medicine. This led to increasing demand for government action. Letters, calls, e-mails, and petitions from constituents pressed members of Congress to act on the high cost of prescription drugs. Media stories about older Americans going bankrupt to pay for needed medications pushed the issue further onto center stage, and public hearings by

Congress provided an additional spotlight. President Bush signed the prescription drug benefit into law in December 2003, and today millions of seniors are enrolled in the federal government's program.

While getting the prescription drug bill into law was an arduous task, implementing the legislation has proven even more challenging. The provisions of the plan have been difficult for many senior citizens become accustomed to, and states have struggled with administering the program. As the prescription benefits went into effect in early 2006, senior citizens expressed considerable disillusionment with the program. According to a survey by the Kasier Family Foundation, American seniors were almost twice as likely to say they view the prescription drug benefit unfavorably (45 percent) as favorably (23 percent).[2] Such attitudes from the very individuals that the program was designed to assist had to be discouraging to the Bush administration, which had banked on the program as a key component of its domestic policy agenda.

Does establishing such an expensive new government program serve the national interest? For many seniors the answer was yes: it appeared that the passage of this new benefit meant that Congress and the president finally were addressing a serious concern in their lives. Other observers, however, were more skeptical: where will the money come from to pay the hundreds of billions of dollars this prescription drug benefit will cost just over its first ten years? According to one critic, "The drug benefit is a blatant pitch for the votes of the elderly that worsens the long-term budget outlook and will be paid for by the young."[3] Some opponents of the program argued that the new drug benefit was really a boon to pharmaceutical and insurance companies and didn't provide enough help to seniors. Was the government being responsible or irresponsible in making public policy establishing this new program? What obligation does the government owe to promoting the social welfare of its people?

---

public policy
An intentional course of action followed by government in dealing with some problem or matter of concern.

PUBLIC POLICY IS A PURPOSIVE COURSE of action followed by government in dealing with some problem or matter of concern.[4] Public policies are governmental policies based on law; they are authoritative and binding on people. Individuals, groups, and government agencies that do not comply with policies can be penalized through fines, loss of benefits, or even jail terms. As the phrase "course of action" implies, policies develop or unfold over time. They involve more than a legislative decision to enact a law or a presidential decision to issue an executive order. Also important is how the law or executive order is carried out. Whether a policy is vigorously enforced, enforced in only some instances, or not enforced at all helps determine its meaning and impact.

In this chapter, we will discuss social and economic policy. Policies in both areas follow similar patterns, in what is called the policy-making process. After considering the nature of the policy-making process, we will examine social welfare policy and the government's involvement in the economy. Finally, we will examine the government's role in stabilizing the economy.

The Policy-making Process

POLITICAL SCIENTISTS and other social scientists have developed many theories and models to explain the formation of public policies. Here, we present a widely used model of the policy-making process that views it as a sequence of stages or functional activities. (See Figure 13.1.) Public policies do not just happen; rather, they are typically the products of a predictable pattern of events. Models for analyzing the policy-making process do not always explain *why* public policies take the specific forms that they do, however. That depends on the political struggles over particular policies. Nor do models necessarily tell us *who* dominates or controls the formation of public policy.

FIGURE 13.1 STAGES OF THE PUBLIC POLICY PROCESS

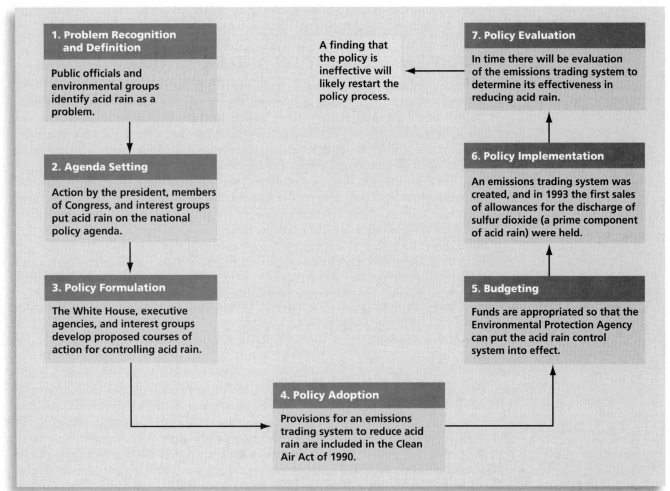

Despite the limitations of models, however, public policy making frequently does follow a sequence of stages. Sometimes some of the stages may merge, such as the policy formulation and adoption stages. Another instance of stages merging occurs when administrative agencies such as the Occupational Safety and Health Administration (OSHA) make policy through rule making at the same time that they implement it. Finally, we need to recognize that what happens at one stage of the policy-making process affects action at later stages, and sometimes such action is done deliberately in anticipation of these effects. Thus, particular provisions may be included in a law either to help or hinder its implementation, depending on the interests of the provisions' proponents.

STAGES OF THE POLICY PROCESS

The policy process has seven steps: (1) A *problem* that disturbs the people and leads them to call for governmental intervention. Individual or group efforts are then made to get the problem (2) placed on a governmental *agenda*. If successful, this step is followed by (3) *formulation* of alternative approaches to addressing the problem. (4) *Policy adoption* involves the formal enactment of a policy. (5) *Budgeting* allocates the resources to provide for the proper implementation of public policies. (6) *Policy implementation*, the actual administration or application of public policies to their targets, may then be followed by (7) *policy evaluation* to determine a policy's accomplishments, consequences, or shortcomings. Evaluation may restart the process by identifying a new problem and touching off an attempt to modify or terminate the policy.

PROBLEM RECOGNITION AND DEFINITION

At any given time, there are many conditions that disturb or distress people: polluted air and water, the outsourcing of jobs overseas, rising rates of childhood obesity, natural disasters, the rising cost of college tuition, lewdness or violence on television, and possible terrorist attacks. All disturbing conditions do not automatically become problems in need of public policy solutions, however. Some of them may be accepted as trivial, inevitable, or beyond the control of government.

For a condition to become a problem, there must be some criterion—a standard or value—that leads people to believe that the condition does not have to be accepted or acquiesced to and, further, that it is something with which government can deal effectively and appropriately. For example, natural disasters such as hurricanes are unlikely to be identified as a policy problem because there is little that government can do about them directly. The consequences of hurricanes—the human distress and property destruction that they bring—are another matter. Relief from the devastation of natural disasters can be a focus of government action, and agencies such as the Federal Emergency Management Agency (FEMA) have been set up to reduce these hardships. When these agencies fail to fulfill their roles, as FEMA did in the wake of Hurricane Katrina in 2005, the public requires answers for why government has not done its job.

Usually there is not a single, agreed-on definition of a problem. Indeed, political struggle often occurs at this stage because how the problem is defined helps determine what sort of action is appropriate. For instance, it is more difficult to tackle problems that affect large numbers of people or that require behavioral change than problems that have more focused solutions. (See Politics Now: The Politics of Immigration Reform.)

Note that public policies themselves are frequently viewed as problems or the causes of other problems. Thus, for some people, gun control legislation is a solution to gun violence. To the National Rifle Association (NRA), however, any law that restricts gun ownership is a problem because the NRA views such laws as inappropriately infringing on an individual's constitutional right to keep and bear arms. To social conservatives, legal access to abortion is a problem; for social liberals, laws restricting abortion access fall into the problem category.

AGENDA SETTING

Once a problem is recognized and defined as such by a significant segment of society, it must be brought to the attention of public officials and it must secure a place on an **agenda,** a set of issues to be discussed or given attention. In the area of public policy there are two basic types of agendas: the systemic agenda and the governmental or institutional agenda. The **systemic agenda** is essentially a discussion agenda; it comprises "all issues that are commonly perceived by the members of the political community as meriting public attention and as involving matters within the legitimate jurisdiction" of governments.[5] Every political community—national, state, and local—has a systemic agenda.

A **governmental** or **institutional agenda** includes only problems to which legislators or other public officials feel obliged to devote active and serious attention. Not all the problems that attract the attention of officials are likely to have been widely discussed by the general public, or even the "attentive" public—those who follow certain issues closely. Problems or issues (an issue emerges when disagreement exists over what should be done about a problem) may move onto an institutional agenda, whether from the systemic agenda or elsewhere, in several ways. These include crisis situations, political campaigns, and interest group lobbying, among many others.

agenda
A set of issues to be discussed or given attention.

systemic agenda
All public issues that are viewed as requiring governmental attention; a discussion agenda.

governmental (institutional) agenda
The changing list of issues to which governments believe they should address themselves.

Politics Now

THE POLITICS OF IMMIGRATION REFORM

On May 1, 2006, the streets of America's cities were filled with nearly a million individuals protesting initiatives in Congress that would crack down on illegal immigration in the United States. In addition to marching, many of these protesters did not go to work that day and boycotted shopping to call attention to the positive economic impact that immigrants have on the nation. As Congress considered tightening the borders and stiffening penalties on illegal aliens, members of many immigrant communities sought to demonstrate the numerous contributions that immigrants, both legal and illegal, bring to the quality of life in the United States. Indeed, there is evidence that the estimated 12 million illegal immigrants living in the United States do make substantial contributions to the U.S. economy.[a] By working primarily for low wages, illegal immigrants help to keep down the costs of many goods and services in the United States, including agricultural products, construction, and restaurant meals. In turn, these lower costs increase consumer demand, and the overall economy is enhanced. In addition, some argue that illegal immigrants often take jobs that Americans do not want, and therefore help to provide valuable labor that would not otherwise be available. The Pew Hispanic Center has found that a majority of Americans believe that illegal immigrants are taking jobs that their fellow citizens won't do.[b]

But even as most economists agree that the proliferation of low-wage illegal immigrants helps to keep prices down in the United States, there are also significant costs incurred by the presence of undocumented laborers in America. Harvard economist George Borjas contends that the primary losers in regard to illegal immigration are U.S. citizens who do not have high school diplomas, particularly poorer African Americans and native-born Hispanic Americans. Others contend that the biggest burden of illegal immigration

falls on American taxpayers who pay for government programs that benefit both illegal immigrants and their dependents. The Center for Immigration Studies (CIS), a Washington-based group that advocates tougher immigration policies, used Census Bureau figures to argue that illegal immigrants contribute far less in taxes than the cost of government services they use. According to a 2004 CIS report, households headed by illegal aliens accounted for more than $26 billion in costs to the federal government in 2002 through government services, including Medicaid, medical treatment for the uninsured, food assistance programs, and federal aid to public schools.[c]

There have been many proposals to limit government services to illegal aliens. In 2005 and 2006, numerous bills were taken up by state legislatures to limit illegal immigrant access to taxpayer-funded social services such as drug rehabilitation, childcare programs, and mental health centers. Meanwhile, Congress focused more of its efforts on trying to stop the entry of illegal aliens by passing legislation to construct a wall along the U.S.-Mexican border. President Bush signed this bill into law in 2006.

The overall impact of illegal immigration on the nation's economic, fiscal, and social well-being will in all likelihood remain a subject of heated debate. What is certain is that the political controversies surrounding illegal immigration will continue to occupy a prominent role in American politics in both the near and long term.

[a]Mary Fitzgerald, "Illegal Immigrants' Cost to Government Studied," *Washington Post* (August 26, 2004): A21 and Nell Henderson, "Effect of Immigration on Jobs, Wages Is Difficult for Economists to Nail Down," *Washington Post* (April 15, 2006): D1.

b The Pew Hispanic Center, "The State of American Public Opinion on Illegal Immigration in Spring 2006," http://pewhispanic.org/files/factsheets/18.pdf.

c Center for Immigration Studies, *The High Cost of Cheap Labor: Illegal Immigration and the Federal Budget,* http://www.cis.org/articles/2004/fiscalexec.html.

POLICY FORMULATION

Policy formulation is the crafting of appropriate and acceptable proposed courses of action to ameliorate or resolve public problems. It has both political and technical components. The political aspect of policy formulation involves determining generally what should be done to reduce acid rain, for example—whether standard setting and enforcement or emissions testing should be used. The technical facet involves correctly stating in specific language what one wants to authorize or accomplish, so as to adequately guide those who must implement policy and to prevent distortion of legislative intent. Political scientist Charles O. Jones suggests that formulation may take different forms.[6]

Routine formulation is "a repetitive and essentially changeless process of reformulating similar proposals within an issue area that is well established on the government agenda." For instance, the formulation of policy for veterans' benefits represents a standard process of drafting proposals similar to those established in the past.

policy formulation
The crafting of appropriate and acceptable proposed courses of action to ameliorate or resolve public problems.

Analogous formulation handles new problems by drawing on experience with similar problems in the past. What has been done in the past to cope with the activities of terrorists? What has been done in other states to deal with child abuse, divorce law reform, or same-sex marriage?

Creative formulation involves attempts to develop new or unprecedented proposals that represent a departure from existing practices and that will better resolve a problem. For example, plans to develop an anti-missile defense system to shoot down incoming missiles represents a departure from previous defense strategies of mutual destruction.

Policy formulation may be undertaken by various players in the policy process: the president, presidential aides, agency officials, specially appointed task forces and commissions, interest groups, private research organizations (or "think tanks"), and legislators and their staffs. The people engaged in formulation usually are looking ahead toward policy adoption.

POLICY ADOPTION

policy adoption
The approval of a policy proposal by the people with the requisite authority, such as a legislature.

Policy adoption is the approval of a policy proposal by the people with requisite authority, such as a legislature or chief executive. This approval gives the policy legal force. Because most public policies in the United States result from legislation, policy adoption frequently requires the building of majority coalitions necessary to secure the enactment of legislation.

In chapter 6, we discuss how power is diffused in Congress and how the legislative process comprises a number of roadblocks or obstacles—House subcommittees, House full committees, the House Rules Committee, and so on—that a bill must navigate successfully before it becomes law. A majority is needed to clear a bill through each of these obstacles; hence, not one majority but a series of majorities is needed for congressional policy adoption. To secure the needed votes, a bill may be watered down or modified at each of these decision points. Or, the bill may fail to win a majority at one of them and die, at least for the time being.

The adoption of major legislation, such as the Medicare Prescription Drug Act discussed in the opening vignette, requires much negotiation, bargaining, and compromise. In some instances, years or even decades may be needed to secure the enactment of legislation on a controversial matter. Congress considered federal aid to public education off and on over several decades before it finally won approval in 1965. At other times, the approval process may move quickly.

SIMULATION
You Are a State Legislator

Not all policy adoption necessitates formation of majority coalitions. Presidential decision making on foreign affairs, military actions, and other matters is often unilateral. Although a president has many aides and advisers and is bombarded with information and advice, the final decision rests with him or her. Ultimately, too, it is the president who decides whether to veto a bill passed by Congress. Sometimes a president can get concessions from Congress by threatening to veto legislation. For example, following the September 11, 2001, terrorist attacks, George W. Bush was able to secure some changes to a spending bill simply by raising the specter of a veto.

BUDGETING

Most policies require money to be carried out; some policies, such as those providing income security, essentially involve the transfer of money from taxpayers to the government and back to individual beneficiaries. Funding for most policies and agencies is provided through the budgetary process. Whether a policy is well funded or poorly funded has a significant effect on its scope, impact, and effectiveness.

A policy can be nullified by a refusal to fund, which was the fate of the Homeownership and Opportunity for People Everywhere (Hope VI) program. In 2006, the Bush administration decided not to seek funds for HOPE VI, a program within the

Department of Housing and Urban Development (HUD) that demolishes obsolete and severely distressed public housing, while introducing community service and self-sufficiency initiatives. President Bush had tried to eliminate HOPE VI twice before by not funding it, but each time Congress directed financial resources to HUD to keep the program alive. However, in 2006 Congress followed the president's lead, and HOPE VI was terminated.[7]

Other policies or programs often suffer from inadequate funding. Thus, the Occupational Safety and Health Administration (OSHA) can afford to inspect annually only a small fraction of the workplaces within its jurisdiction. Similarly, the Department of Housing and Urban Development has funds sufficient to provide rent subsidies only to approximately 20 percent of the eligible low income families.

The budgetary process also gives the president and the Congress an opportunity to review the government's many policies and programs, to inquire into their administration, to appraise their value and effectiveness, and to exercise some influence on their conduct. Not all of the government's hundreds of programs are fully examined every year. But, over a period of several years, most programs come under scrutiny.

Where the Money Goes

POLICY IMPLEMENTATION

Policy implementation is the process of carrying out public policies, most of which are implemented by administrative agencies. Some, however, are enforced in other ways. Product liability and product dating are two examples. Product liability laws such as the Food and Drug Act of 1906, the National Traffic and Motor Vehicle Safety Act of 1966, and the Consumer Product Safety Act of 1972 are typically enforced by lawsuits initiated in the courts by injured consumers or their survivors. In contrast, state product-dating laws are implemented more by voluntary compliance when grocers take out-of-date products off their shelves or by consumers when they choose not to buy food products after the use dates stamped on them. The courts also get involved in implementation when they are called on to interpret the meaning of legislation, review the legality of agency rules and actions, and determine whether institutions such as prisons and mental hospitals conform to legal and constitutional standards.

Administrative agencies may be authorized to use a number of techniques to implement the public policies within their jurisdictions. These techniques can be categorized as authoritative, incentive, capacity, and hortatory techniques, depending on the behavioral assumptions on which they are based.[8]

Authoritative techniques for policy implementation rest on the notion that people's actions must be directed or restrained by government to prevent or eliminate activities or products that are unsafe, unfair, evil, or immoral. Consumer products must meet certain safety regulations, and radio stations can be fined heavily or even have their broadcasting licenses revoked if they broadcast obscenities.

Many governmental agencies have authority to issue rules and set standards to regulate such matters as meat and food processing, the discharge of pollutants into the environment, the healthfulness and safety of workplaces, and the safe operation of commercial airplanes. Compliance with these standards is determined by inspection and monitoring, and penalties may be imposed on people or companies that violate the rules and standards set forth in a particular policy. For example, under Title IX, the federal government can terminate funds to colleges or universities that discriminate against female students. Its detractors sometimes stigmatize this pattern of action as "command and control regulation," although in practice it often involves much education, bargaining, and persuasion in addition to the exercise of authority. In the case of Title IX, for instance, the Department of Education will try to negotiate with a school to bring it into compliance before funding is terminated.

Incentive techniques for policy implementation encourage people to act in their own best interest by offering payoffs or financial inducements to get them to comply

policy implementation
The process of carrying out public policy through governmental agencies and the courts.

with public policies. Such policies may provide tax deductions to encourage charitable giving, or the purchase of alternative fuel vehicles such as hybrid automobiles. Farmers receive subsidies to make their production (or nonproduction) of wheat, cotton, and other goods more profitable. Conversely, sanctions such as high taxes may discourage the purchase and use of such products as tobacco or liquor, and pollution fees may reduce the discharge of pollutants by making this action more costly to businesses.

Capacity techniques provide people with information, education, training, or resources that will enable them to participate in desired activities. The assumption underlying the provision of these techniques is that people have the incentive or desire to do what is right but lack the capacity to act accordingly. Job training may enable able-bodied people to find work, and accurate information on interest rates will enable people to protect themselves against interest-rate gouging. Financial assistance can help the needy acquire better housing and warmer winter coats and perhaps lead more comfortable lives.

Hortatory techniques encourage people to comply with policy by appealing to people's "better instincts" in an effort to get them to act in desired ways. In this instance, the policy implementers assume that people decide how to act according to their personal values and beliefs on matters such as right and wrong, equality, and justice. During the Reagan administration, First Lady Nancy Reagan implored young people to "Just say no" to drugs. Hortatory techniques also include the use of highway signs that tell us "Don't Be a Litterbug" and "Don't Mess with Texas" to discourage littering. Slogans such as "Only You Can Prevent Forest Fires" are meant to encourage compliance with fire and safety regulations in national parks and forests.

You Are an Environmental Activist

Effective administration of public policies depends partly on whether an agency is authorized to use appropriate implementation techniques. Many other factors also come into play, including the clarity and consistency of policies' statutory mandates, adequacy of funding, political support, and the will and skill of agency personnel. Often government will turn to a combination of authoritative, incentive, capacity, and hortatory approaches to reach their goals. For example, public health officials employ all of these tools in their efforts to reduce tobacco use. These techniques include laws prohibiting smoking in public places, taxes on the sales of tobacco products, warning labels on packs of cigarettes, and anti-smoking commercials on television. There is no easy formula that will guarantee successful policy implementation; in practice, many policies only partially achieve their goals.

POLICY EVALUATION

policy evaluation
The process of determining whether a course of action is achieving its intended goals.

Practitioners of **policy evaluation** seek to determine what a policy is actually accomplishing. They may also try to determine whether a policy is being fairly or efficiently administered. Policy evaluation may be conducted by a variety of players: congressional committees, through investigations and other oversight activities; presidential commissions; administrative agencies themselves; university researchers; private research organizations, such as the Brookings Institution and the American Enterprise Institute; and the Government Accountability Office (GAO).

The GAO, created in 1921, is an important evaluator of public policies. Every year, the GAO conducts hundreds of studies of government agencies and programs, either at the request of members of Congress or on its own initiative. The titles of three of its 2006 evaluations convey a notion of the breadth of its work: *Military Housing: Management Issues Require Attention as the Privatization Program Matures; Ryan White Care Act: Changes Needed to Improve Distribution of Funding; Internal Control: Improvements Needed in Federal Drug Administration's Post-market Decision-making and Oversight Process.*

Social scientists and qualified investigators design studies to measure the societal impact of programs and to determine whether these programs are achieving their specified goals or objectives. The national executive departments and agencies often have officials and units responsible for policy evaluation; so do state governments. Evaluation research and studies can stimulate attempts to modify or terminate policies and thus restart the policy process. Legislators and administrators may formulate and advocate amendments designed to correct problems or shortcomings in a policy. In 1988, for example, legislation was adopted to correct weaknesses in the enforcement of the Fair Housing Act of 1968, which banned discrimination in the sale or rental of most housing. Policies are also terminated as a result of the evaluation process; for example, through the Airline Deregulation Act of 1978, Congress eliminated the Civil Aeronautics Board and its program of economic regulation of commercial airlines. This action was taken on the assumption that competition in the marketplace would better protect the interests of airline users. Competition has indeed reduced the cost of flying on many popular routes.

The demise of programs is relatively rare, however; more often, a troubled program is modified or allowed to limp along because it provides a popular service. For example, the nation's passenger rail system Amtrak has been consistently unable to survive without significant government subsidies. While its Northeast lines are financially self-sufficient, many of Amtrak's longer distance routes are unable to operate without significant subsidies. Nevertheless, the more rural routes remain popular with legislators in western states, and thus, Amtrak continues to receive federal support.[9]

VIDEO ROUNDTABLE

Energy Policy

While policy evaluation has become more rigorous, systematic, and objective over the past few decades, judgments by policy makers still are often based on anecdotal and fragmentary evidence rather than on solid facts and thorough analyses. Sometimes a program is judged to be a good program simply because it is politically popular or fits the ideological beliefs of an elected official. For example, despite very limited empirical evidence that "abstinence only" education reduces the level of sexual engagement among teenagers, the administration of President George W. Bush has sought increased federal funding for this approach to fight teen pregnancy.[10]

Social Welfare Policy

SOCIAL WELFARE POLICY IS A TERM that designates a broad and varied range of government programs designed to protect people from want and deprivation, to improve their health and physical well-being, provide educational and employment training opportunities, and otherwise enable them to lead more satisfactory, meaningful, and productive lives. The issue of who is deserving and what they deserve is at the heart of the debate over social welfare programs. Over time, the focus of social welfare programs has expanded from providing minimal assistance to the destitute to helping the working poor attain a degree of security and provide for their health, nutrition, income security, employment, and education needs. Another aspect of social welfare policy is discussed in On Campus: Student Loan Relief.

social welfare policy
Government programs designed to improve quality of life.

THE ORIGINS OF SOCIAL WELFARE POLICY

Most social welfare programs in the United States are largely a product of the twentieth century, although their origins can be traced far into the nation's past. As U.S. society became more urban and industrial, self-sufficiency declined and people became more interdependent and reliant on a vast system of production, distribution, and exchange. The ostentation of the very wealthy and the suffering of the many on the bottom rung of the social ladder created fears of an economic revolution if the gap between rich and poor was not reduced. The Great Depression of the 1930s reinforced the notion that hard work alone would not provide economic security for everyone and showed that the state governments and private charities lacked adequate resources

TIMELINE

The Evolution of Social Welfare Policy

On Campus

STUDENT LOAN RELIEF

If you are reading this book as a student at an American college, you are likely to be the recipient of some form of student financial aid. In the 2004–2005 academic year, $129 billion in aid was distributed to students at higher education institutions in the United States. These funds were needed to help college students keep up with the soaring costs of a post-secondary education. According to the College Board, the cost of tuition for a public university increased by 7 percent between 2004 and 2005, and the costs of a private university rose by 5.9 percent. While these increases are substantial, they are actually smaller than the double-digit increases in tuition that students have experienced in most years since 2000.[a]

With higher tuition burdens facing college students, financial aid demands have escalated in recent years. Government has continued to help students meet their financial needs, but in a different manner than in the past. Between 1996 and 2002, students increasingly received financial aid in the form of grants-in-aid rather than student loans. In 2004–2005, the percentage of total undergraduate aid in the form of grants declined for the third year in a row, with loans accounting for a greater share of aid than grants for the first time since 1997.

Greater dependence on loans to finance higher education has implications for both students and the broader society. Obviously, increased levels of student loans mean increased financial burdens for students as they enter the workforce. In 2004, two out of three public university graduates had student loan debt, with the median amount of money borrowed topping $15,000. The level of debt is even higher for the three out of four graduates of private universities who take out loans, with median debt burdens just under $20,000 in 2004.[b]

Student loan debt may be seen as a great long-term investment for individuals because of the beneficial effect of a college degree on lifetime earnings. Census Bureau statistics from 2000 indicate that college graduates earn nearly twice as much as high school graduates, making higher loan levels a necessary evil for many students.[c] But, growing student loan debt may be excluding graduates from taking jobs in low-paying public service jobs. Faced with the prospect of repaying student loans shortly after graduation, financially constrained individuals will most likely seek higher paying jobs in the private sector rather than lower paying jobs in government or nonprofit organizations.

To make public service more financially attainable to students with high levels of debt, the federal government has created numerous incentive programs. In 2001, the federal government's Office of Personnel Management (OPM) enacted rules that allowed federal agencies to set up debt relief programs for specific employees. Agencies such as the Department of Energy, General Services Administration, NASA, and the Department of Health and Human Services adopted the programs in efforts to attract or retain talented individuals. Under the new OPM rules, federal government agencies could relieve as much as $6,000 a year in a person's student loan obligations. To receive benefits, applicants would have to sign an agreement to remain in the service of the agency for at least three years.[d]

Other debt relief programs are available. For workers who provide services to low-income, high-risk children and their families, debt would be completely cancelled after five years. Loan relief is also available for individuals who teach in high-demand fields such as math, science, foreign languages, and bilingual education, and to workers in career fields such as nursing, law enforcement, corrections, and medicine. Members of the U.S. armed forces can have up to 50 percent of their loans canceled if they serve in hazardous areas. Vista and Peace Corps volunteers also qualify for debt relief. Through these programs, government may be able to persuade a critical mass of young professionals to take on jobs that serve the greater public interest.

---

[a]College Board, "2005–2006 College Costs," http://www.collegeboard.com.

[b]Steven Barr, "Repayment Program's Slow Start May Be a Matter of Timing," *Washington Post* (July 2, 2002): B2.

[c]Kimberly Lankford, "Fringe Benefit," *Kiplinger's Personal Finance* 56 (July 2002): 94.

[d] Beth Kobliner, "Learn Now, Pay Back (Somewhat Less) Later," *New York Times* (June 30, 2002): A12, and Jim McTague, "Sallie Forth," *Barron's* 82 (June 24, 2002): 35.

---

to alleviate economic want and distress. Beginning with the Social Security Act of 1935, which we will describe below, a variety of national programs aimed at providing economic security have emerged.

Social Security Act
A 1935 law that established old-age insurance (Social Security) and assistance for the needy, children, and others, and unemployment insurance.

Income Security Passage of the **Social Security Act** in 1935 represented the beginning of a permanent welfare state in America and a dedication to the ideal of greater equity.[11] The act consisted of three major components: (1) old-age insurance (what we now call Social Security); (2) public assistance for the needy, aged, blind, and families with dependent children (later, people with disabilities were added); and, (3) unemployment insurance and compensation.

The core of the Social Security Act was the creation of a compulsory old-age insurance program funded equally by employer and employee contributions. The act imposed a payroll tax, collected from the employer, initially equal to 1 percent from both employee and employer starting in 1937. The Social Security Act also addressed the issue of unemployment, requiring employers to pay 3 percent of a worker's salary into an insurance fund. If workers became unemployed, they could draw from this fund for a given period of time. During the time laid-off workers drew from the insurance fund, they were required to seek other jobs. This component of the Social Security Act served two basic purposes: on the individual level, it provided income to laid-off workers, expanding the social safety net; on the broader economic level, it acted as an automatic stabilizer, increasing the amount of money in the nation's economy when financial resources were scarce.

Photo courtesy: Bettmann/Corbis

■ The Great Depression, beginning in late 1929 and continuing throughout the 1930s, dramatically pointed out to average Americans the need for a broad social safety net and gave rise to a host of income, health, and finance legislation.

Social Security is credited with replacing a piecemeal collection of local programs with a national system. This national system was widely praised but also was perceived to contain two basic flaws: the payroll tax was regressive (the tax fell disproportionately on lower-income contributors) because of limits on the amount of income taxed for Social Security purposes, and some workers were excluded from the program. Over the next decades, Social Security was expanded to include a much greater percentage of American workers. The program also became one of the most successful and popular governmental programs. In the 1930s, poverty rates were highest among the elderly. Today, seniors have the lowest rate of poverty among any age group in the United States.

Health Care Governments in the United States have long been active in the health care field. Local governments began to establish public health departments in the first half of the nineteenth century, and state health departments followed in the second half. Discoveries related to the bacteriological causes of diseases and human ailments discovered in the late nineteenth and early twentieth centuries led to significant advances in improving public health. Public sanitation and clean-water programs, pasteurization of milk, immunization programs, and other activities reduced greatly the incidence of infectious and communicable diseases. Public health policies have also been highly effective in reducing the incidence of infectious diseases such as measles, infantile paralysis (poliomyelitis), and smallpox. The increase in the average American's life expectancy from forty-seven in 1900 to nearly seventy-eight in 2006 is tightly linked to public health programs.

Beginning in 1798 with the establishment of the National Marine Service (NMS) for "the relief of sick and disabled seamen," which was the forerunner of the Public Health Service, the national government has provided health care for some segments of the population. Efforts have been made over the years to expand coverage of health care to more and more Americans. The current Medicare and Medicaid programs that provide hospital benefits for the elderly (in the case of Medicare) and medical costs for the poor (in the case of Medicaid) were first passed by Congress in 1965. The national government's role in health care expanded dramatically with the enactment of these two programs. The share of health care expenditures financed by public spending rose from under 25 percent in 1960 to almost 40 percent in 1970.

During this time, public expenditures on health care as a percent of total gross domestic product (GDP) rose by more than 100 percent, from 1.3 percent to 2.7 percent. Total expenditures rose from 5.3 percent of GDP in 1960 to 7.4 percent in 1970.[12]

SOCIAL WELFARE POLICIES TODAY

Income security and health care encompass many complex policies and programs. While all levels of government (national, state, and local) are involved with the development and implementation of social welfare policies, we emphasize the national government's role. However, new programs are giving states greater control over public welfare and health care programs.

Income security programs protect people against loss of income because of retirement, disability, unemployment, or death or absence of the family breadwinner. Although cases of total deprivation are now rare, many people are unable to provide a minimally decent standard of living for themselves and their families. They are poor in a relative if not an absolute sense. In 2006, the poverty threshold for a four-person family unit was $19,307.[13]

Income security programs fall into two general categories. Social insurance programs are **non-means-based programs** that provide cash assistance to qualified beneficiaries. **Means-tested programs** require that people must have incomes below specified levels to be eligible for benefits. Benefits of means-tested programs may come either as cash or in-kind benefits, such as food stamps.

Non-Means-Based Programs
Non-means-based social insurance programs operate in a manner somewhat similar to private automobile or life insurance. Contributions are made by or on behalf of the prospective beneficiaries, their employers, or both. When a person becomes eligible for benefits, the monies are paid as a matter of right, regardless of the amount of wealth or unearned income (for example, from dividends and interest payments) belonging to the recipient.

Old Age, Survivors, and Disability Insurance   This program began as old-age insurance, providing benefits only to retired workers. Its coverage was extended to survivors of covered workers in 1939 and to the permanently disabled in 1956. Customarily called Social Security, it is not, as many people believe, a pension program that collects contributions from workers, invests them, and then returns them with interest to beneficiaries. Instead, current workers pay taxes that go directly toward providing benefits for retirees. In 2006, an employee tax of 7.65 percent was levied on the first $94,200 of wages or salaries and placed into the Social Security Trust Fund. An equal tax was levied on employers. Nearly all employees and most of the self-employed (who pay a 15.3 percent tax) are now covered by Social Security. People earning less than $94,200 pay a greater share of their income into the Social Security Fund, since wages or salaries above that amount are not subject to the Social Security tax. The Social Security tax therefore is considered a regressive tax because it captures larger proportions of incomes from lower- and middle-income individuals than from high-wage earners.

People born before 1938 are eligible to receive full retirement benefits at age sixty-five. The full retirement age gradually rises until it reaches sixty-seven for persons born in 1960 or later. Individuals can opt to receive reduced benefits as early as age sixty-two. In January 2006, the average monthly Social Security benefit for all retired workers was $1,002, with the maximum monthly benefit set at $2,053. Social Security is the primary source of income for many retirees and keeps them from living in poverty. However, eligible people are entitled to Social Security benefits regardless of how much *unearned* income (for example, dividends and interest payments) they also receive.

Beginning with a change in 2004, Social Security recipients between the ages of sixty-two and sixty-four had one dollar withheld from their earnings for every two

**Comparing
Social Welfare
Policy**

non-means-based program
Program such as Social Security where benefits are provided irrespective of the income or means of recipients.

means-tested program
Income security program intended to assist those whose incomes fall below a designated level.

dollars earned after a specific amount of earnings was reached. One dollar for every three dollars earned was withheld from a sixty-five-year-old recipient's earnings after the earnings threshold was reached. A Social Security recipient older than sixty-five was allowed to earn an unlimited amount of money without any reduction in Social Security benefits.[14]

The trustees of the Social Security Trust Fund predicted in 2006 that, starting about 2010, Social Security Fund expenditures would begin to increase rapidly as those born in the two decades immediately following World War II begin to reach retirement age. It was estimated that by 2017, payments would exceed revenues collected. Viewing costs and revenues as a proportion of taxable payrolls (to correct for the value of the dollar over time), one can see that projected revenues remain relatively constant over time, while costs are projected to rise substantially (see Figure 13.2). Aside from the retirement of those born after World War II, other factors pressuring the fund include increased life expectancies and low fertility rates. In other words, Americans are living longer and having fewer children who as workers would contribute to the Social Security Fund.

After George W. Bush was elected president in 2000, he promoted his vision of privatizing Social Security through investments in stocks and bonds, and he created a President's Commission to Strengthen Social Security. This panel consisted of sixteen members and was co-chaired by the former Senator Daniel Patrick Moynihan (D–NY) and Richard Parsons, co-chief operating officer of AOL Time Warner. By the end of 2001, the panel disappointed proponents of privatization with their set of recommendations. The panel provided three options: (1) allowing workers to invest up to 2 percentage points of their payroll tax in personal accounts; (2) allowing workers to invest up to 4 percentage points of their payroll tax in personal accounts, to a maximum of $1,000 per year; and, (3) allowing workers to invest an additional 1 percent of their earnings in a personal account. Proponents of privatization had hoped for a single recommendation. Congress ignored the recommendations, no doubt influenced by the slump in the stock market and the unpopular panel observations. The panel believed that ultimately benefits would have to be cut or more money would have to be assigned to the program. Following his reelection in 2004, Bush reaffirmed his support for Social Security privatization.

FIGURE 13.2 SOCIAL SECURITY COSTS AND REVENUES, 1970–2080

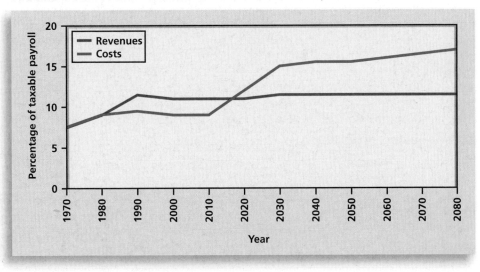

Source: Status of the Social Security and Medicare Programs. A Summary of the 2004 Annual Reports, http://www.ssa.gov/OACT/TRSUM/trsummary.html.

Despite controlling both houses of Congress and the presidency after the 2004 elections, Republicans were unable to achieve any substantial reform of Social Security. This may be explained by continued public skepticism regarding the president's plan. According to a 2005 poll by the Pew Research Center for the People and the Press, only about 4 in 10 Americans supported the concept of individualized accounts as part of the Social Security system.[15] Given the central role that these accounts have played in Bush's reform efforts, it was not a surprise that his plan was unable to gather the necessary support in Congress. Simply put, many Republican legislators could not risk aligning themselves with the President because of the possibility of a backlash at the polls. In fact, Democratic candidates used President Bush's support for Social Security privatization against their Republican opponents with some success in the 2006 midterm elections. While the future of the Social Security system is quite uncertain, it is not a risky prediction to contend that Social Security will continue to be an election issue well beyond 2006.

Unemployment Insurance As mentioned earlier, unemployment insurance is financed by a payroll tax paid by employers. The program pays benefits to workers who are covered by the government plan and are unemployed through no fault of their own. The Social Security Act provided that if a state set up a comparable program and levied a payroll tax for its support, most of the federal tax would be forgiven (not collected). The states were thus accorded a choice: either set up and administer an acceptable unemployment program, or let the national government handle the matter. Within a short time, all states had their own programs.

Unemployment insurance covers employers of four or more people, but not part-time or occasional workers. Benefits are paid to unemployed workers who have neither been fired for personal faults nor quit their jobs, and who are willing and able to accept suitable employment. State unemployment programs differ considerably in levels of benefits, length of benefit payment, and eligibility for benefits. For example, in 2004, average weekly benefit payments ranged from $508 in Massachusetts and $496 in Washington to $210 in both Alabama and Mississippi.[16] In general, less generous programs exist in southern states, where labor unions are less powerful. Nationwide, only about half of the people who are counted as unemployed at any given time are receiving benefits.

In July 2006, the unemployment rate stood at 4.8 percent (see Analyzing Visuals: Unemployment Rates by State). While unemployment rates under five percent are considered good by historical standards, there is considerable difference in employment conditions across the nation. In Hawaii and Wyoming, unemployment rates were three percent. Conversely, levels of unemployment in states such as Michigan, Mississippi, and Alaska were over 6.5 percent. There is also considerable variation in unemployment rates across race, gender, and age. For example, levels of unemployment for African American males are approximately twice that of white males, with unemployment rates of 25 percent or greater common among young African American males.[17]

Means-Tested Programs Means-tested income security programs are intended to help the needy, that is, individuals or families whose incomes fall below specified levels, such as a percentage of the official poverty line. Included in the means-tested categories are the Supplemental Security Income (SSI), Temporary Assistance for Needy Families (TANF), and food stamp programs.

Supplemental Security Income This program began under the Social Security Act as a grant-in-aid program to help the needy aged or blind. Grants were financed jointly by the national and state governments, but the states played a major role in determining standards of eligibility and benefit levels. In 1950, Congress extended coverage to needy people who were permanently and totally disabled. With the support

Analyzing Visuals

UNEMPLOYMENT RATES BY STATE

This map shows the rates of unemployment across the United States in the summer of 2006. According to the Bureau of Labor Statistics, the U.S. unemployment rate was 4.8 percent percent in July 2006, down from a high of 6 percent in 2003. As can be seen on the map, certain states and regions have rates far higher than the national average. Based on your analysis of this map and your understanding of the chapter dis-cussion, answer the following critical thinking questions: Which states are currently suffering from the highest levels of unemployment, and why do you think that is so? Why do you think unemployment rates vary substantially from state to state? Do you detect any similarities among states with the lowest rates of unemployment? What role do you think the un-employment rate will play in the 2008 presidential elections?

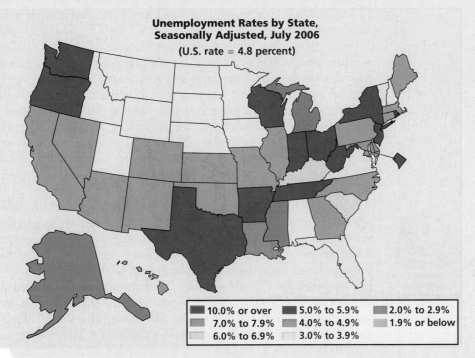

Unemployment Rates by State, Seasonally Adjusted, July 2006
(U.S. rate = 4.8 percent)

10.0% or over	5.0% to 5.9%	2.0% to 2.9%
7.0% to 7.9%	4.0% to 4.9%	1.9% or below
6.0% to 6.9%	3.0% to 3.9%	

Source: Bureau of Labor Statistics, Local Area Unemployment Statistics, http://www.bls.gov/lau/#tables.

of the Nixon administration, Congress reconfigured the grant programs into the Sup-plemental Security Income (SSI) program in 1974. Primary funding for SSI is pro-vided by the national government, which sets uniform benefit levels throughout the nation. In 2006, monthly SSI payments were about $603 for an individual and $904 for a married couple.[18] The states may choose to supplement the federal benefits, and forty-eight states do.

For years, this program generated little controversy, as modest benefits go to peo-ple who obviously cannot provide for themselves. However, in 1996, access to SSI and other programs was limited by legislation.

Family and Child Support In 1950, Aid to Families with Dependent Children (AFDC), the predecessor to the Temporary Assistance for Needy Families (TANF) program, was broadened to include not only dependent children without fathers but also mothers themselves or other adults with whom dependent children were living. The AFDC rolls expanded greatly since 1960 because of the increasing numbers of children born to unwed mothers, the growing divorce rate, and the migration of poor people to cities, where they are more likely to apply for and be provided with benefits.

Because of its clientele, the AFDC program was the focus of much controversy. Critics who pointed to the rising number of recipients claimed that it encouraged promiscuity, out-of-wedlock births, and dependency that resulted in a permanent class of welfare families. In what was hailed as the biggest shift in social policy since the Great Depression, a new welfare bill, the Personal Responsibility and Work Opportunity Reconciliation Act (PRWORA) of 1996, created the Temporary Assistance for Needy Families (TANF) program to replace AFDC. The shift from AFDC to TANF was meant to foster a new philosophy of work rather than welfare dependency. The most fundamental change enacted in the new law was the switch in funding for welfare from an open-ended matching program to a block grant to the states. PRWORA also gave states more flexibility in reforming their welfare programs toward work-oriented goals.

Significant features of the welfare plan included: (1) a requirement that single mothers with a child over five years of age work within two years of receiving benefits; (2) a provision that required unmarried mothers under the age of eighteen to live with an adult and attend school to receive welfare benefits; (3) a five-year lifetime limit for aid from block grants; (4) a requirement that mothers must provide information about a child's father to receive full welfare payments; (5) an end to food stamps and Supplemental Security Income for legal immigrants; (6) an end to cash welfare benefits and food stamps for convicted drug felons; and, (7) a limit on food stamps to three months in a three-year period for persons eighteen to fifty years old who are not raising children and not working.[19]

Making a Difference: Welfare Reform

In 2002, the George W. Bush administration released a detailed plan for TANF reauthorization. The plan proposed to strengthen work rules to ensure that all welfare families were engaged in meaningful activities that would lead to self-sufficiency. These meaningful activities included not only work, but also allowed "individuals participating in substance abuse treatment, rehabilitative services, and work-related training" to qualify for TANF benefits.[20] The administration proposed increasing the proportion of TANF families that would have to participate in work activities and increasing the number of hours of required work.[21] Between 2002 and 2006, Congress passed a number of extensions to keep the TANF program in operation, with President Bush signing a reauthorization in February 2006. This reauthorization did not address the issue of increased work hours but did strengthen enforcement of child support provisions and provided over $150 million to encourage married couples to remain together.[22]

Food Stamp Program The initial food stamp program (1939–1943) was primarily an effort to expand domestic markets for farm commodities. Food stamps provided the poor with the ability to purchase more food, thus increasing the demand for American agricultural produce. Attempts to reestablish the program during the Eisenhower administration failed, but in 1961, a $381,000 pilot program began under the Kennedy administration. It was made permanent in 1964 and extended nationwide in 1974. Although strongly opposed by Republicans in Congress, Democrats put together a majority coalition when urban members agreed to support a wheat and cotton price support program wanted by rural and southern Democrats in return for their support of food stamps.

In the beginning, recipients had to pay cash for food stamps, but this practice ceased in 1977. Benefiting low-income families, the program has helped to combat hunger and reduce malnutrition. Food stamps went to more than 25 million beneficiaries in 2005 at a cost of $31 billion. The average participant received $93 worth of stamps per month.[23] In 2005, families of four earning less than $2,043 in gross monthly income or $1,571 in net monthly income qualified for food stamps.[24]

The national government operates several other food programs for the needy. These programs include a special nutritional program for women, infants, and children (WIC); a school breakfast and lunch program; and an emergency food assistance program.

The Effectiveness of Income Security Programs Many of the income security programs, including Social Security, Supplemental Security Income, and food stamps, are **entitlement programs.** That is, Congress sets eligibility criteria—such as disability, age, income level, or unemployment—and those who meet the criteria are legally "entitled" to receive benefits. Unlike such programs as public housing, military construction, and space exploration, spending for entitlement programs is mandatory. Year after year, funds *must* be provided for them unless the laws creating the programs are changed. This feature of entitlement programs has made it difficult to control spending for them.

Income security programs have not eliminated poverty and economic dependency, but they have improved the lives of large numbers of people. Millions of elderly people in the United States would be living below the poverty line were it not for Social Security. While often a matter of considerable debate, a range of income security programs is a characteristic of all democratic industrial societies.

Photo courtesy: Tony Savino/The Image Works

■ Food stamps remain an important component of the federal government's safety net for low-income Americans.

entitlement program
Income security program to which all those meeting eligibility criteria are entitled.

HEALTH CARE

Currently, many millions of people receive medical care through the medical branches of the armed forces, the hospitals and medical programs of the Department of Veterans Affairs, and the Indian Health Service. The government spent $69.2 billion in 2004 for health and human service, and estimated that it would spend $68.9 billion in the 2006 fiscal year for health and human services, the construction and operation of facilities, and the salaries of doctors and other medical personnel.[25]

The national government finances most medical research, primarily through the National Institutes of Health (NIH) and Centers for Disease Control and Prevention (CDC), which are a part of the U.S. Department of Health and Human Services. NIH institutes and centers spend more than $10 billion annually on biomedical research. Most Americans accept and support extensive government spending on medical research. Congress, in fact, often appropriates more money for medical research than the president recommends.

The United States spends significant sums of money on public health, a larger proportion of its gross domestic product than most other industrialized democracies. Much of the increase in funding for health care has gone to the Medicare and Medicaid programs. Reasons for growth in medical spending include the third-party payment system, the public's increased expectations, increased demand for services, advances in health care technology, and the perception of health care as a right.[26] (See American Values/American Voices: Liberty and Health Care for All.) In many ways the issue of soaring health care costs underlies most of the current problems affecting the American health care system and limits the range of alternatives available to government officials.

American Values/ American Voices

LIBERTY AND HEALTH CARE FOR ALL

Americans hate to be told what to do. As noted in chapter 1, personal liberty is one of the most important characteristics of American democracy. Since the nation's founding, its citizens have been vigilant about keeping government from interfering in their ability to make their own choices. In recent years, this deep cultural attachment to individual liberty has played a major role in the area of health care provision.

According to the U.S. Census Bureau, 45.8 million Americans lacked health care insurance in 2004. Among these uninsured were millions of individuals who worked full time but did not receive health insurance from their employers and were ineligible for Medicaid because they earned too much. The current number of uninsured is higher than at any time since the 1930s, and the number of uninsured Americans has been growing for some time.

During the early 1990s, the Clinton administration proposed a major federal policy that would provide at least some health insurance coverage to all Americans. Despite public opinion polls that supported federal efforts to address the problem of the uninsured, Clinton's plan ended in a notable defeat for his administration. Among the main causes of its demise was a rise in public concern over the impact of the plan on the ability of individuals to choose their own physicians. In order to reach its goal of universal health care coverage, the Clinton reform called for restrictions on individual choices in order to help control the spiraling costs of health services. The declining public support for the Clinton plan was undoubtedly aided by a series of television ads funded by the health insurance industry that warned Americans they would lose control of their health care under the Clinton proposal. Arguments against the Clinton plan were summed up in a statement by then Republican Senator Bob Dole, who told the *Washington Post*, "More cost. Less choice. More taxes. Less quality. More government control. Less control for you and your family. That's what the president's government-run plan is likely to give you."[a]

Since the demise of the Clinton health care plan, the problems of the health care system have not gone away. In fact, the costs of health care have risen even faster than in the early 1990s, and the number of uninsured has increased by millions. With the public's deep-seated resistance to losing personal liberty narrowing the choices available to policy makers in the area of health care reform, government officials have had to come up with creative options to address the ongoing problem.

In 2006, Massachusetts passed a state law requiring every individual in the Commonwealth to purchase health insurance by July 1, 2007. For the approximately 500,000 individuals who were uninsured in Massachusetts, this will mean different things. First, about 100,000 state residents are eligible for Medicaid but are not receiving this benefit because they have not enrolled in the program. Another 200,000 residents who made too much money to get Medicaid but have been unable to afford health insurance will receive assistance on an income-based sliding scale to buy insurance policies without deductibles. Another 200,000 Massachusetts residents with incomes above the federal poverty line will be able to purchase lower-cost policies in the private market. The financial assistance for health insurance will be financed by redirecting much of the $1 billion spent by state government on the uninsured.

But, how can government make someone purchase health insurance, especially given the American attachment to personal liberty? The answer is through economic disincentives. Beginning in 2008, failure by individuals to purchase health insurance will result in the loss of their state tax refund equal to 50 percent of an affordable health insurance premium. Thus, failure to use the government assistance will actually come at a price for those without health insurance.

While it is too early to say if the Massachusetts health insurance reforms will work, the approach taken in the Bay State may be a model for national reform. The Massachusetts plan does place limits on personal choice, but only among those without health insurance. The plan does not limit options for the majority of individuals who already have insurance, and thus it did not draw the same harsh public reaction that the Clinton reform plan received in the 1990s. This may explain why the legislation was approved by a bipartisan 154–2 margin in the Massachusetts House of Representatives and a 37–0 vote in the state Senate.

QUESTIONS

1. What major factors have led to the high number of Americans without any form of health insurance?
2. Do you support the Massachusetts health insurance plan? Why or why not?

---

[a]Ann Devroy , "President Insists Congress Enact Reforms in Welfare, Health Care," *Washington Post* (January 26, 1994): A1.

Sources: U.S. Census Bureau, "Income, Poverty, and Health Insurance Coverage in the United States: 2004," August 2005, http://www.census.gov; Theda Sckopol, *Boomerang: Health Care Reform and the Turn Against Government* (New York: Norton, 1997); Ann Devroy, "President Insists Congress Enact Reforms in Welfare, Health Care," *Washington Post* (January 26, 1994): A1; Kaiser Commission on Medicaid and the Uninsured, "Massachusetts Health Care Reform Fact Sheet," http://www.kff.org/uninsured/upload/7494.pdf; Steve LeBlanc, "Mass Lawmakers Pass Bill to Require Health Insurance for All," *Boston Globe* (April 4, 2006).

A quick review of the increase in health care costs over the past fifteen years helps to demonstrate the magnitude of the problem. Per capita spending on health care in the United States increased by 123 percent in the fourteen-year period between 1990 and 2004. Comparatively, per capita income in America increased by only 59 percent during the same time frame, meaning that individual financial resources grew at less than half the rate of the cost of health care. Behind this dramatic increase in health care costs are a number of important factors. First, more people are living longer and are requiring costly and extensive care in their declining years. Second, the range and sophistication of diagnostic practices and therapeutic treatments, which are often quite expensive, have increased. Third, the expansion of private health insurance, along with Medicare and Medicaid, has reduced the direct costs of health care to most people and increased the demand for services. More people, in short, can afford care. They may also be less aware of the costs of care. Fourth, the costs of health care have also increased because of its higher quality and because labor costs have outpaced productivity in the provision of hospital care.[27] Fifth, U.S. health care focuses less on preventing illnesses and more on curing them, which is more costly.

While all areas of health care experienced significant increases in cost since 1990, there were areas within the broader health field that underwent the sharpest spike in prices. Prescription drug costs increased at rates even greater than those for physicians and hospital stays, thus increasing the pressure for the federal government to adopt the prescription drug program discussed at the beginning of this chapter. Because government health care programs such as Medicare and Medicaid are directly affected by soaring prices, policy makers have been challenged to keep these programs fully funded. In 2005, national expenditures for both the Medicare and Medicaid programs were $515 billion. Projected increases for Medicare and Medicaid are expected to grow between 2005 and 2011 at a faster pace than other key areas of the federal budget.

The Growth of the Budget and Federal Spending

Medicare **Medicare,** which covers persons receiving Social Security benefits, is administered by the Center for Medicare and Medicaid Services in the Department of Health and Human Services. Medicare coverage has two components, Parts A and B. Benefits under Part A come to all Americans automatically at age sixty-five, when they qualify for Social Security. It covers hospitalization, some skilled nursing care, and home health services. Individuals have to pay about $700 in medical bills before they are eligible for Part A benefits. Medicare is financed by a payroll tax of 1.45 percent paid by both employees and employers on the total amount of one's wages or salary.

Part B, which is optional, covers payment for physicians' services, outpatient and diagnostic services, X-rays, and some other items not covered by Part A. Excluded from coverage are the cost of eyeglasses, hearing aids, and dentures. This portion of the Medicare program is financed partly by monthly payments from beneficiaries and partly by general tax revenues.

As noted in the opening vignette, a new Medicare benefit available since January 2006 provides some prescription drug coverage for recipients who opt to participate. Those who enroll pay a monthly premium of approximately $35; after a $250 annual deductible, 75 percent of their prescription drug costs are paid. For those whose annual prescription drug costs exceed $5,100, the new program will pay 95 percent of the costs over that amount. There are some odd gaps in the prescription drug coverage, however. Many congressional Democrats found the bill too weak to help the average senior and claimed its primary beneficiaries would be the pharmaceutical and insurance industries. But, even some Democrats voted for its final passage, as they agreed with the leaders of the American Association of Retired Persons (AARP) that it was time to do something, and this seemed the only plan with a chance to pass.[28]

The addition of the prescription drug benefit troubled many budget conservatives because of the added costs it is projected to impose on a system that, whatever its merits, is extraordinarily expensive. And, it was later revealed that the actual costs of this new program were seriously understated during the congressional debate. That leads many to wonder how the federal budget can withstand the additional pressure. Medicare itself has become a costly program because people live longer, the elderly need more hospital and physicians' services, and medical care costs are rising rapidly. Attempts to limit or cap expenditures for the program have had only marginal effects.

Medicare
The federal program established in the Lyndon B. Johnson administration that provides medical care to elderly Social Security recipients.

Medicaid

An expansion of Medicare, this program subsidizes medical care for the poor.

Medicaid Enacted into law at the same time as Medicare, the **Medicaid** program provides comprehensive health care to all who qualify as needy under TANF and SSI. In 2005, Medicaid served over 52 million people at a cost of $184.2 billion.[29] Nursing facility services, in-patient general hospital services, home health services, and prescription drugs represent major categories of spending within the Medicaid program.

The national government pays 50 to 79 percent of Medicaid costs, based on average per capita income, and thus awards more financial support to poorer states. Each state is responsible for the administration of its own program and sets specific standards of eligibility and benefit levels for Medicaid recipients within the boundaries set by national guidelines. In some states, nearly all needy people are covered by Medicaid, while in others, only one-third or so of the needy are protected. Some states also award coverage to the "medically indigent," that is, to people who do not qualify for welfare but for whom large medical expenses would constitute a severe financial burden.

While the average amount paid for by the states varies, the portion of state budgets going to Medicaid is similar—ever upward. If Medicaid expenditures continue to grow at their present rate, the ability of the states and the national government to fund other social welfare programs will be compromised.

Economic Policy

DURING THE NATION'S FIRST CENTURY, the states were responsible for managing economic affairs. The national government defined its economic role narrowly, although it did collect tariffs (taxes on imported goods), fund public improvements, and encourage private development (see The Living Constitution). Congress became active in setting economic policy and enacting economic regulation only after people realized that the states alone could not solve the problems affecting the economy.

THE ORIGINS OF ECONOMIC POLICY

Comparing Economic Policy

Although the U.S. economic system is a mixed free-enterprise system characterized by the private ownership of property, private enterprise, and marketplace competition, the national government has long played an important role in fostering economic development through its tax, tariff, public lands disposal, and public works policies, and also through the creation of a national bank (see chapter 3). For much of the nineteenth century, however, national regulatory programs were few and were restricted to such tasks as steamboat inspection and the regulation of trade with the Native American tribes.

Following the Civil War, the United States entered a period of rapid economic growth and extensive industrialization. Small business owners, Reformers, and farmers in the Midwest pressured the government to control these new forces. After nearly two decades of pressure from farmers, owners of small businesses, and reformers in the cities, Congress adopted the Interstate Commerce Act in 1887 to regulate the railroad industry. Enforced by the new Interstate Commerce Commission (ICC), the act required that railroad rates should be "just and reasonable."[30]

Three years later, Congress dealt with the problem of "trusts," the name given to large-scale, monopolistic businesses that dominated many industries, including oil, sugar, whiskey, salt, and meatpacking. The Sherman Anti-trust Act of 1890 prohibits all restraints of trade, including price-fixing, bid-rigging, and market allocation agreements. It also prohibits all monopolization or attempts to monopolize, including domination of a market by one company or a few companies. The Interstate Commerce Act and the Sherman Anti-trust Act were the key legislative responses of the national government to the new industrialization.

The Living Constitution

The Congress shall have power to lay and collect taxes on incomes, from whatever source derived, without apportionment among the several States, and without regard to any census or enumeration.

—SIXTEENTH AMENDMENT

Ratified on February 3, 1913, the Sixteenth Amendment modified the Article I prohibition against levying a "direct tax" on individual property, unless the tax in question addresses the rule of apportionment as set forth in Article I, sections 2 and 9. This amendment was yet another revision made to the Constitution in response to a U.S. Supreme Court decision, namely the 1895 *Pollock* v. *Farmers' Loan & Trust Co.*—a judgment in which a divided Court held that Congress could not tax incomes uniformly throughout the United States.

The authority to tax is one of the fundamental rights inherent in legitimate government, and it is the hallmark of good and just governance to tax citizens fairly and equitably. The Constitution gives the House of Representatives sole authority to originate revenue bills, since the Framers believed the House, as the institution that directly represents the people, should determine how taxes should be raised and apportioned. Indeed, during the ratification debates, concern was expressed in regard to the Senate's ability to amend revenue bills as being a potential means for unjust taxation, since the Senate would not directly represent the people in its political capacity.

As the nineteenth century drew to a close, the Supreme Court became aware that in the new industrial age, the *Pollock* decision could threaten national solvency. As a result, the Court began to redefine "direct taxation" so as to help the federal government adapt to the new era. For example, the Court held in 1911 that corporate income could be taxed as an "excise measured by income." And, in its first appraisal of the newly ratified Sixteenth Amendment, the Court began to view income taxes as a form of indirect taxation. The Sixteenth Amendment has thus guaranteed the federal government a consistent and continuous revenue stream, and it is up to the Congress and the president to ensure fair taxation for all Americans.

THE PROGRESSIVE ERA AND THE NEW DEAL

The Progressive movement drew much of its support from the middle class and sought to reform the political, economic, and social systems of U.S. society. There was a desire to bring corporate power under the control of government and make it more responsive to democratic ends. Progressive administrations under presidents Theodore Roosevelt and Woodrow Wilson established or strengthened regulatory programs to protect consumers and to control railroads, business, and banking. The Pure Food and Drug Act and the Meat Inspection Act, both enacted in 1906, marked the beginning of consumer protection as a major responsibility of the national government. These laws prohibited adulteration and mislabeling of food and drugs and set sanitary standards for the food industry.

■ Here, a political cartoonist depicts how the U.S. government was perceived by some as being dominated by various trusts in the nineteenth century.

Photo courtesy: Bettmann/Corbis

laissez-faire
A French term literally meaning "to allow to do, to leave alone." It is a hands-off governmental policy that is based on the belief that governmental involvement in the economy is wrong.

interventionist state
Alternative to the *laissez-faire* state; the government takes an active role in guiding and managing the private economy.

PARTICIPATION
Farm Subsidies and Domestic Policy

The Depression and the New Deal marked a major turning point in U.S. history in general and in U.S. economic history in particular. During the 1930s, the **laissez-faire** state, the doctrine in which the government mostly provided a framework of rules within which the economy was left alone to operate, was replaced with an **interventionist state,** in which the government began to play an active and extensive role in guiding and regulating the private economy. The New Deal established the national government as a major regulator of private businesses and as ultimately responsible for maintaining a stable economy. It brought about a number of reforms in almost every area, including finance, agriculture, labor, and industry.

Financial Reforms Major New Deal banking laws included the Glass-Steagall Act (1933), which required the separation of commercial and investment banking and set up the Federal Deposit Insurance Corporation (FDIC) to insure bank deposits, originally for $5,000 per account. Legislation was also passed to control abuses in the stock markets. The Securities Act (1933) required that prospective investors be given full and accurate information about the stocks or securities being offered to them. The Securities Exchange Act (1934) created the Securities and Exchange Commission (SEC), an independent regulatory commission. The SEC was authorized to regulate the stock exchanges, to enforce the Securities Act, and to reduce the number of stocks bought on margin (that is, with borrowed money).

Agriculture and Labor During the New Deal, Congress passed several laws designed to boost farm income by restricting agriculture production in order to bring it into better balance with demand. At the same time, Congress passed the National Labor Relations Act, better known as the Wagner Act after its sponsor, Senator Robert Wagner (D–NY). This statute guaranteed workers' rights to organize and bargain collectively through unions of their own choosing. The act prohibited a series of "unfair labor practices," such as discriminating against employees because of their union activities. The National Labor Relations Board (NLRB) was created to implement the act and to conduct elections to determine which union, if any, employees wanted to represent them. Unions prospered under the protection provided by the Wagner Act.

The last major piece of New Deal economic legislation passed by Congress was the Fair Labor Standards Act (FLSA) of 1938. Intended to protect the interests of low-paid workers, the law set twenty-five cents per hour and forty-four hours per week as initial minimum standards. Within a few years, wages rose to forty cents per hour, and hours declined to forty per week. The act also banned child labor.

Industry Regulations During the New Deal, Congress established new or expanded regulatory programs for several industries. The Federal Communications Commission (FCC), created in 1934 to replace the old Federal Radio Commission, was given extensive jurisdiction over the radio, telephone, and telegraph industries. The Civil Aeronautics Board (CAB) was put in place in 1938 to regulate the commercial aviation industry. The Motor Carrier Act of 1935 put the trucking industry under the jurisdiction of the Interstate Commerce Commission (ICC). As with railroads, regulation of industries such as trucking and commercial aviation extended to such matters as entry into the business, routes of service, and rates.

ECONOMIC AND SOCIAL REGULATIONS

Economists and political scientists frequently distinguish between economic regulation and social regulation. **Economic regulation** focuses on such matters as control of entry into a business, prices or rates businesses charge, and service routes or areas. Economic regulation is usually tailored to the conditions of particular industries, such as railroads or stock exchanges. In contrast, **social regulation** sets standards for the quality and safety of products and the conditions under which goods are produced and services rendered. Social regulation strives to protect and enhance the quality of life.

Most of the regulatory programs established through the 1950s fell into the category of economic regulation. From the mid-1960s to the mid-1970s, however, the national government passed social regulatory legislation affecting consumer protection, health and safety, and environmental protection. Congress based this legislation on its commerce clause authority.

As a consequence of this flood of social regulation, many industries that previously had limited dealings with government found they now had to comply with government regulation in the conduct of their operations. For example, the automobile industry, which previously had been lightly touched by anti-trust, labor relations, and other general statutes, found that its products were now affected by motor vehicle emissions standards and federally mandated safety standards.

DEREGULATION

Deregulation is the reduction in market controls (such as price fixing, subsidies, or controls on who can enter the field) in favor of market-based competition. Beginning in the 1950s, advocates of deregulation contended that regulation often encouraged lack of competition and monopolistic exploitation, discrimination in services, and inefficiency in operation of regulated industries. For instance, regulatory standards meant that no new major commercial airline was permitted to enter the industry after the Civil Aeronautics Board (CAB) began to regulate the industry in 1938. Consequently, consumers paid higher prices for airfares and had fewer choices than they would in a more competitive market. Supporters of deregulation contended that regulatory commissions such as the CAB and Interstate Commerce Commission were more responsive to the interests of the regulated firms than to the public interest.

For some time, there were no changes in economic regulation despite these criticisms. In the mid-1970s, however, Republican President Gerald R. Ford decided to make deregulation a major objective of his administration. He saw regulation as one cause of the high inflation that existed at the time. At about this time, Senator

economic regulation
Governmental regulation of business practices, industry rates, routes, or areas serviced by particular industries.

social regulation
Governmental regulation of the quality and safety of products as well as the conditions under which goods and services are produced.

deregulation
A reduction in market controls (such as price fixing, subsidies, or controls on who can enter a field) in favor of market-based competition.

Photo courtesy: Dave Einsel/Getty Images

■ One of the most noted recent scandals to rock the corporate world involved the Houston-based energy giant Enron. In 2006, the company's former CEO, Jeffrey Skilling (seen here, center left, leaving court), was found guilty on nineteen counts of fraud and conspiracy related to his work at Enron and sentenced to over 24 years in prison. The Enron scandal, along with others at World-Com and Global Crossing, served as a catalyst for tighter federal government oversight of business and accounting practices in the United States.

Edward M. Kennedy (D–MA) became chair of a subcommittee of the Senate Judiciary Committee. Kennedy decided to use his new position to hold hearings on airline deregulation. The combined actions of Ford and Kennedy put deregulation on the national policy agenda and got the deregulatory movement underway. Democrats and Republicans, liberals and conservatives all found deregulation an appealing political issue.[31]

Deregulation was also a high priority for Ford's successor, Democratic President Jimmy Carter. Legislation that deregulated commercial airlines, railroads, motor carriers, and financial institutions was enacted during Carter's term as president. All successive presidents have maintained an active deregulatory agenda. But, the effects of deregulation have been mixed. The Airline Deregulation Act of 1978, for example, completely eliminated economic regulation of commercial airlines over several years, and although many new passenger carriers flocked into the industry when barriers to entry were first removed, they were unable to compete successfully with existing major airlines. All of the original new entrants have now disappeared, as have some of the major airlines that were operating at the time of deregulation. Consequently, there are now fewer major carriers than under the regulatory regime, although new airlines, such as JetBlue, continue to emerge. Competition has lowered some passenger rates, but there is disagreement as to the extent to which passengers have benefited. For example, by 2002, it was clear that since enactment of the Airline Deregulation Act, small communities were losing service. Despite Congress's promise to maintain service to small communities, thirty-eight communities lost air service between 1978 and 2002.[32]

In spite of the mixed record of economic deregulation, it has remained a top policy priority among American politicians. The same cannot be said of deregulation efforts in the social sphere. Strong support continues for social regulation to protect consumers, workers, and the environment. Moreover, in some areas in which economic deregulation occurred, there have been calls to "reregulate." This has occurred in the airline industry because of concern about safety and domination by a small number of companies. Join the Debate: File Sharing and Protecting Intellectual Property Rights discusses another aspect of regulation.

STABILIZING THE ECONOMY

VIDEO ROUNDTABLE

Deficit Spending

Although there continues to be disagreement about the degree to which governments, especially the national government, should be involved, few question the important role that government plays in the economic stability in the nation, which is critical to the success of domestic and national policy. **Economic stability** is a condition in which there is economic growth, a rising national income, high employment, and a steadiness in the general level of prices. (See Global Perspective: Economic Freedom Around the World.) Conversely, economic instability involves either inflation or recession. **Inflation** occurs when there is too much demand for the available supply of goods and services, with the consequence that general price levels rise as buyers compete for the available supply. Prices may also rise if large corporations and unions have sufficient economic power to push prices and wages above competitive levels. A **recession** is marked by a decline in the economy. Investment sags, production falls off, and unemployment increases.

The government manages the economy through monetary and fiscal policies. Monetary policies influence the economy through changes in the money supply, while fiscal policies influence the behavior of consumers and businesses through government spending and taxing decisions.

economic stability
A situation in which there is economic growth, rising national income, high employment, and steadiness in the general level of prices.

inflation
A rise in the general price levels of an economy.

recession
A short-term decline in the economy that occurs as investment sags, production falls off, and unemployment increases.

Monetary Policy: Controlling the Money Supply

Monetary Policy: Controlling the Money Supply The government conducts **monetary policy** by managing the nation's money supply and influencing interest rates. In an industrialized economy, all those making exchanges—consumers, businesses, and government—use money. That is, prices of goods and services are set in **money** units (dollars), and the amount of money in circulation influences the quantity of goods and services demanded, the number of workers hired, the decisions to build factories, and so on. Money is more than just the currency and coin in our pockets: it includes balances in our checkbooks, deposits in bank accounts, and the value of other assets.

Created in 1913 to adjust the money supply to the needs of agriculture, commerce, and industry, the Federal Reserve System comprises the Federal Reserve Board (FRB) (formally, the Board of Governors of the Federal Reserve System; informally, "the Fed"), the Federal Open Market Committee (FOMC), the twelve Federal Reserve Banks in regions throughout the country, and other member banks.[33]

The **Federal Reserve Board** (FRB) has responsibility for the formation and implementation of monetary policy because of its ability to control the credit-creating and lending activities of the nation's banks. When individuals and corporations deposit their money in financial institutions such as commercial banks and savings and loan associations, these deposits serve as the basis for loans to borrowers. In effect, the loaning of money creates new deposits or financial liabilities—new money that did not previously exist.

The Federal Reserve System's primary monetary policy tools are the setting of reserve requirements for member banks, control of the discount, and open market operations. Formally, authority to use these tools is allocated to the FRB, the Federal Reserve Bank boards of directors, and the FOMC, respectively. In actuality, however, all three are dominated by the FRB, which, in recent decades, has been under the sway of its chair. Paul Volcker and Alan Greenspan (past chairs) and Ben S. Bernanke, the current chair, are influential and respected policy makers. Public officials and the financial community pay great attention to the utterances of the Fed's chair for clues to the future course of monetary policy.

Reserve requirements set by the Federal Reserve Board designate the portion of the banks' deposits that most banks must retain as backing for their loans. The reserves determine how much or how little banks can lend to businesses and consumers. For example, if the FRB changed the reserve requirements and allowed banks to keep $10 on hand rather than $15 for every $100 in deposits that it held, it would free up some additional money for loans. The **discount rate** is the rate of interest at which the FRB lends money to member banks. In **open market operations,** the FRB buys and sells government securities in the open market. The FRB can also use "moral suasion" to influence the actions of banks and other members of the financial community by suggestion, exhortation, and informal agreement. Because of its commanding position as a monetary policy maker, the media, economists, and market observers pay attention to verbal signals about economic trends and conditions emitted by the FRB and its chair.

How the FRB uses these tools depends in part on its views of the state of the economy. If inflation appears to be the problem, then the Fed would likely restrict or tighten the money supply. If a recession with rising unemployment appears to threaten the economy, then the FRB would probably act to loosen or expand the money supply in order to stimulate the economy.

Fiscal Policy: Taxing and Spending

Fiscal Policy: Taxing and Spending **Fiscal policy** is the deliberate use of the national government's taxing and spending policies to influence the

monetary policy
A form of government regulation in which the nation's money supply and interest rates are controlled.

money
A system of exchange for goods and services that includes currency, coins, and bank deposits.

Federal Reserve Board
A seven-member board that sets member banks' reserve requirements, controls the discount rate, and makes other economic decisions.

reserve requirements
Governmental requirements that a portion of member banks' deposits must be retained to back loans made.

discount rate
The rate of interest at which member banks can borrow money from their regional Federal Reserve Bank.

open market operations
The buying and selling of government securities by the Federal Reserve Bank in the securities market.

fiscal policy
Federal government policies on taxes, spending, and debt management, intended to promote the nation's macroeconomic goals, particularly with respect to employment, price stability, and growth.

■ Ben S. Bernanke, center, after President Bush announced Bernanke's nomination to replace Federal Reserve Board Chair Alan Greenspan, at left.

Join the Debate

FILE SHARING AND PROTECTING INTELLECTUAL PROPERTY RIGHTS

OVERVIEW: The U.S. Constitution, in Article I, section 8, gives Congress the authority to "promote the Progress of Science and the useful Arts, by securing to Authors and Inventors the exclusive Right to their respective Writings and Discoveries." According to legal scholars, the idea behind this clause is twofold: first, it recognizes that works of the mind, such as those produced in the arts and sciences, can bring great benefits to society at large; second, it recognizes not only that intellectual property can greatly impact the nation's finances in terms of real property (just think what the personal computer has done to revolutionize the economy), but also that inventors and artists should reap the rewards of their efforts. The government must balance competing claims with regard to what constitutes legitimate intellectual property and what belongs to the public domain. In some instances, this balancing act may have dramatic consequences for the nation in general. The controversy involving the entertainment industry and those (by some estimates) 60 million Americans engaged in peer-to-peer file sharing illustrates how the government must balance these competing claims. Peer-to-peer file sharing bypasses the need for central servers by allowing all computers to communicate and share resources as equals. This technology has allowed for a boom in music file sharing and instant messaging.

The Recording Industry Association of America (RIAA) testified that file sharing cost the music industry an 8 percent loss in sales in 2002 and a 9 percent drop in CD unit sales during that same period. In part due to perceived economic losses owing to file-sharing activity, the RIAA sued Internet service providers in order to gain access to users who were file sharing illegally. In *Verizon* v. *RIAA* (2003), the RIAA won access to peer-to-peer programs and the ability to sue—without the approval of a judge—those engaged in illegal file sharing. Users, for their part, argue that hard drives are personal property and are subject to requisite privacy rights, and what they do with their personal property (as long as no one is "harmed") is not the business of RIAA or government.

In *Metro-Goldwyn-Mayer Studios Inc. et al.* v. *Grokster, Ltd. et al.* (2005), a case brought by twenty-eight of the world's largest entertainment companies against the manufacturers of Morpheus, Grokster, and Kazaa file-sharing software, the Supreme Court's unanimous ruling was a defeat for the manufacturers of peer-to-peer interface software that allows for sharing music and video files. Justice Souter wrote the majority opinion: "We hold that one who distributes a device with the object of promoting its use to infringe copyright, as shown by clear expression or other affirmative steps taken to foster infringement, is liable for the resulting acts of infringement."[a] The debate over the decision continues today, since many have argued that such an interpretation of copyright laws will stifle innovation. In effect, the Supreme Court deemed that Grokster was liable for inducing copyright infringement. As one advocacy group inquired: "When should the distributor of a multi-purpose tool be held liable for the infringements that may be committed by end-users of the tool?"[b] The broader question is whether an innovator is responsible for all infringements by the end user.

As the above case shows, the rapid pace of change in computer, Internet, and affiliated technologies has created questions regarding rights, economics, and law that are difficult to answer. These technologies have dramatically altered and enlarged the public domain. What constitutes intellectual property? What constitutes the public domain? What are the implications of an unregulated Internet? How

VISUAL LITERACY

Evaluating Federal Spending and Economic Policy

overall operation of the economy and maintain economic stability. The president and Congress formulate fiscal policy and conduct it through the federal budget process. The powerful instruments of fiscal policy are budget surpluses and deficits. These are achieved by manipulating the overall or "aggregate" levels of revenue and expenditures.

According to standard fiscal policy, there is a level of total or aggregate spending at which the economy will operate at full employment. Total spending is the sum of consumer spending, private investment spending, and government spending. If consumer and business spending does not create demand sufficient to cause the economy to operate at full employment, then the government should make up the shortfall by much regulation will suffocate creative, intellectual, and economic activity?

ARGUMENTS FOR ALLOWING FILE SHARING

- **File sharing fosters creativity and innovation.** Once an idea is out in the public domain, others can take the original concept and improve it. This may improve a social good and increase economic productivity as well. For example, the first personal computers could not multitask and could run only one application at a time. The development of multitasking greatly increased the viability of the computer as a tool and means of communication to increase economic productivity.
- **Files are private property.** Hard-drive files are created by the user. Once a user creates a file, it becomes his or her property and should have the legal protection of such. The right to privacy and property are understood to be two fundamental rights in the American system, and the Fourth Amendment's prohibition against unwarranted searches and seizures should apply.
- **Peer-to-peer file sharing improves the quality of life for the economically disadvantaged.** What better way to ensure that the economically disadvantaged have access to music, entertainment, and information than to allow services such as Kazaa and Napster? File sharing allows those without means to access programs not only for entertainment but for work and productivity as well.

ARGUMENTS AGAINST ALLOWING FILE SHARING

- **Sharing entertainment, literature, and software files constitutes theft of intellectual property.** The products of artists and inventors are protected by federal copyright law. To use a product under copyright protection without permission or payment may be a criminal offense. The fine for copyright violation when downloading music can be a maximum of $150,000 per song.

- **File sharing without paying for service or content reduces incentives for innovators to create.** Free-market economic theory contends that those who do not benefit from their efforts, whether artists, writers, musicians, or software engineers, are more likely to switch to other employment to meet their living needs. This may deprive society of artistic, intellectual, or technological goods.
- **Illegal peer-to-peer file sharing constitutes "free riding" and causes economic harm.** Those who download or upload music files that they have not bought are benefiting from purchases by other consumers and are lowering income and incentives for those who produce intellectual property. This has the effect of reducing resources devoted to producing content. Paying customers are crucial to spur investment in content and technology.

QUESTIONS

1. Does peer-to-peer file sharing increase innovation and productivity? Why, or why not?
2. Does intellectual property need added or different protections? What makes intellectual property different from real property?

SELECTED READINGS

Bouchoux, Deborah. *Protecting Your Company's Intellectual Property: A Practical Guide to Trademarks, Copyrights, Patents, and Trade Secrets.* New York: American Management Association, 2001.

Lessig, Lawrence. *The Future of Ideas: The Fate of the Commons in the Connected World.* New York: Vintage, 2002.

[a]"Supreme Court Rules Against File Swapping," http://news.com.com/Supreme+Court+rules+against+file+swapping/2100-1030_3-5764135.html.

[b]*MGM v. Grokster,* 545 U.S. _____ (2005).

increasing spending in excess of revenues. This was essentially what Roosevelt's New Deal policies accomplished during the Great Depression. If inflation is the problem confronting policy makers, then government can reduce demand for goods and services by reducing its expenditures and running a budget surplus.[34]

Discretionary fiscal policy involves deliberate decisions by the president and Congress to run budget surpluses or deficits. This can be done by increasing or decreasing spending while holding taxes constant, by increasing or cutting taxes while holding spending stable, or by some combination of changes in taxing and spending. For example, President Reagan in 1981 and President George W. Bush in 2001 and 2003 pushed tax cuts through Congress in part to stimulate a faltering economy.

SIMULATION

You Are Trying to Get a Tax Cut

Global Perspective

ECONOMIC FREEDOM AROUND THE WORLD

Economic globalization is blurring the territorial boundaries that separate countries. In the process, it is creating a single world economy. Significant differences still remain among countries, however, in regard to their political and economic systems. These differences are important to investors because they affect investors' ability to earn profits and their decisions on where to set up new businesses or expand existing ones. Important considerations include tax rates, communication and transportation systems, regulations governing investments, and labor costs. The last of these has been particularly influential for certain businesses. Between 2000 and 2003, the United States lost 455,000 jobs in the computer and electronics industry. It is not hard to understand why. Salaries for computer programmers in the United States, for example, ranged from $60,000 to $80,000 per year. In Ireland, the range was $23,000 to $34,000; in India, it was $5,880 to $11,000. A more recent evaluation of data published by the Bureau of Labor Statistics, however, suggests a more optimistic picture: the IT unemployment rate was 2.5 percent in early 2006, the lowest it has been since early 2001. The analysis provided by *Information Week* suggests that there has been a 20 percent decline in computer programmer employment in the United States, while the number of software engineers employed increased by 15 percent. The former requires less expertise and can be outsourced with greater ease.[a]

Outsourcing, of course, is a concern for all countries that stress economic freedom. Market friendly legislation and institutions in developing countries help attract much needed foreign investments to promote economic development. Developing countries face economic and political pressure from donor countries and organizations such as the World Bank and the International Monetary Fund to promote economic freedom. We can get a quick picture of how hospitable a country is to business by looking at its ranking on the *Economic Freedom of the World* index prepared by the Economic Freedom Network. The group's 2006 report (based on 2004 data) evaluated 130 countries on a 10-point scale, with 10 being the highest score.[b] The measure scores a country's performance on thirty-seven different dimensions, including a legal system that protects an individual's private property, a stable currency, patent rights protections, the freedom to compete in labor and product markets, and tax policies that encourage investment. According to the study, economic freedom does not lead to greater income inequality and tends to appear where there are high individual income levels, high rates of economic growth, and long life expectancy. The 2006 report found that the average economic freedom score was 6.5 in 2004—up from 5.99 in 1995. Overall, economic freedom declined during the 1970s and reached a low of 5.1 in 1980. Since then, economic freedom has been on the rise, especially with the collapse of the Soviet Union.

In 2004, Hong Kong, a special trade area within China, had the highest economic freedom ranking (8.7). The United States ranked third (8.2). Mexico was sixtieth (6.6). The highest-ranking South American country was Chile at twentieth (7.4). African and Latin American countries as well as countries that emerged from the former Soviet Union tended to congregate at the bottom of the rankings. Botswana was the highest-ranking African country at Thirty-fifth (7.1).

The 2006 report found that nations in the top quartile in economic freedom have an average per capita GDP of $24,402, compared to only $2,998 for those countries in the bottom quartile. Similarly, the nations in the top quartile far outperform those in the bottom quartile in terms of life expectancy, employment rates, and other quality of life indicators.

QUESTIONS

1. What political factors most directly impact a nation's economic performance?
2. What is the difference between economic freedom and political freedom?

---

[a]Eric Chabrow, "More U.S. Workers Have IT Jobs Than Ever Before," *Information Week,* April 24, 2006, http://www.informationweek.com.

[b]Economic Freedom of the World, 2005 Annual Report: Executive Summary, http://www.freetheworld.com.

Summary

THIS CHAPTER EXAMINED the policy-making process, social welfare policies, and economic policies. The policy-making process can be viewed as a sequence of functional activities beginning with the identification and definition of public problems. Once identified, problems must get on the governmental agenda. Other stages of the process include policy formulation, policy adoption, budgeting for policies, policy implementation, and the evaluation of policy.

The origins of social welfare policy can be traced back to early initiatives in the nation's history. Only after the Great Depression, however, was a public-sector role in the delivery of social services broadly accepted. Most income security programs generally take two forms: non-means-based programs and means-based programs, which indicate that all people who meet eligibility requirements are automatically entitled to receive benefits. Governments in the United States have a long history of involvement in the health of Americans. Most state and local governments have health departments, and the U.S. government has several public health and medical research divisions. Medicare and Medicaid are the two most prominent national programs. As the cost of health care has risen, however, new demands have been made to restrain the rate of growth in costs.

Efforts by the national government to regulate the economy began with anti-monopoly legislation during the Progressive era. Then, during the New Deal, a host of new programs were created by Congress and the president to correct the lingering effects of the Great Depression. Full employment, employee-employer relations, and social regulation became new concerns of government even before social regulation, which involves the reduction in market controls, emerged as an attractive political issue.

The national government continues to shape monetary policy by regulating the nation's money supply and interest rates. Monetary policy is controlled by the Federal Reserve Board. Fiscal policy, which involves the deliberate use of the national government's taxing and spending policies, is another tool of the national government and involves the president and Congress setting the national budget.

KEY TERMS

agenda, p. 392
deregulation, p. 411
discount rate, p. 413
economic regulation, p. 411
economic stability, p. 412
entitlement program, p. 405
Federal Reserve Board, p. 413
fiscal policy, p. 413
governmental (institutional) agenda, p. 392
inflation, p. 412
interventionist state, p. 410
laissez-faire, p. 410
Medicaid, p. 408
Medicare, p. 407
means-tested program, p. 400
monetary policy, p. 413
money, p. 413
non-means-based program, p. 400
open market operations, p. 413
policy adoption, p. 394
policy evaluation, p. 396
policy formulation, p. 393
policy implementation, p. 395
public policy, p. 390
recession, p. 412
reserve requirements, p. 413
social regulation, p. 411
Social Security Act, p. 398
social welfare policy, p. 397
systemic agenda, p. 392

SELECTED READINGS

Chernow, Ron. *Alexander Hamilton.* New York: Penguin, 2004.

Gilens, Martin. *Why Americans Hate Welfare: Race, Media, and the Politics of Antipoverty Policy.* Chicago: University of Chicago Press, 2001.

Kettl, Donald F. *Deficit Politics: Public Budgeting in Its Institutional and Historical Context.* New York: Macmillan, 1992.

Krugman, Paul. *The Great Unraveling: Losing Our Way in the New Century.* New York: Norton, 2003.

Lindbloom, Charles E., and Edward J. Woodhouse. *The Policy-Making Process,* 3rd ed. Englewood Cliffs, NJ: Prentice Hall, 1993.

Mead, Lawrence M., ed. *The New Paternalism: Supervisory Approaches to Poverty.* Washington, DC: Brookings Institution, 1997.

Oberlander, Jonathan. *The Political Life of Medicare.* Chicago: University of Chicago Press, 2003.

Phillips, Kevin. *Wealth and Democracy: A Political History of the American Rich.* New York: Broadway Books, 2002.

Rubin, Robert E., with Jacob Weisberg. *In an Uncertain World: Tough Choices from Wall Street to Washington.* New York: Random House, 2003.

Sherraden, Michael. *Inclusion in the American Dream: Assets, Poverty, and Public Policy.* Oxford: Oxford University Press, 2005.

Skocpol, Theda. *The Missing Middle: Working Families and the Future of American Social Policy.* New York: Norton, 2000.

Thompson, Frank, and John Dilulio Jr. *Medicaid and Devolution: A View from the States.* Washington, DC: Brookings Institution, 1998.

Thurmaier, Kurt M., and Katherine G. Willoughby. *Policy and Politics in State Budgeting.* Armonk, NY: M. E. Sharpe, 2001.

Tonelson, Alan. *The Race to the Bottom: Why a Worldwide Worker Surplus and Uncontrolled Free Trade Are Sinking American Living Standards.* Boulder, CO: Westview, 2002.

Weil, Alan, and Kenneth Finegold, eds. *Welfare Reform: The Next Act.* Washington, DC: Urban Institute, 2002.

WEB EXPLORATIONS

To understand how public policies are prioritized and analyzed, go to
http://www.ncpa.org

To see an overview of the legislative process for public policy, go to
http://www.house.gov/house/Tying_it_all.html

To understand how public policy laws are made, go to
http://thomas.loc.gov/home/lawsmade.toc.html

To learn about the research institutes and organizations that evaluate policies, go to
http://www.aei.org
http://www.brookings.org

To learn more about the most current Social Security benefits and statistics, go to
http://www.ssa.gov

To learn more about current welfare provisions, go to
http://www.progress.org

For other health care policy initiatives and consumer health information, go to
http://www.nih.gov

To learn about the government bureau for economic analysis, go to
http://www.bea.doc.gov

To compare various business cycle indicators, go to
http://www.tcb-indicators.org

To access the most current labor and wages data for your state or region, go to
http://www.bls.gov/ncs

To learn about current economic policy, go to
http://www.nber.org

To learn more about regulation of financial markets via the Federal Reserve Board, go to
http://www.federalreserve.gov

To compare the current fiscal budget with budgets from prior years, go to
http://www.whitehouse.gov/omb

To compare the federal budget with the national debt, go to
http://www.gpoaccess.gov/usbudget/fy04/index.html

Photo courtesy: Kevin LaMarque/Reuters/Corbis

FOREIGN AND DEFENSE POLICY

14

THE U.S. WAR ON TERRORISM is a multifaceted, global undertaking that includes military action overseas, increased security measures at home, cooperation among domestic and international intelligence agencies, diplomacy, and the prevention of terrorists' access to weapons of mass destruction. It involves both domestic strategies, such as efforts to improve homeland security, and international activities, such as the promotion of democracy abroad, military strikes against terrorist organizations and the states that sponsor them, and diplomatic initiatives designed to thwart the spread of religious extremism. In the context of the war on terrorism, the division of U.S. policies into "foreign affairs" and "domestic affairs" is somewhat artificial.

After the terrorist attacks of September 11, 2001, striking the appropriate balance between foreign and domestic affairs so that American interests and objectives are achieved and the American public is protected remains a continuing challenge for the president and others involved in the foreign and defense policy process. For example, three days after the events of 9/11, President George W. Bush authorized the National Security Administration (NSA) to eavesdrop on telephone calls and e-mails between American citizens and foreigners suspected of terrorist ties without first seeking a court warrant. The NSA's spying program created a great deal of controversy because the 1978 Foreign Intelligence Surveillance Act (FISA) requires a special court to approve any interception of communications involving U.S. citizens. The program has generated debate in Congress over the legality of President Bush's decision to order the NSA to conduct warrantless surveillance of Americans' communications. The Justice Department has argued that the president's constitutional role as commander in chief provides adequate justification for his authorization of such a program. Critics argue that the program violates U.S. law, that the president is unnecessarily extending the reach of the federal government, and that the NSA's limited resources should be targeted at more precise threats to national security.

CHAPTER OUTLINE

- ⭐ The Origins of U.S. Foreign and Defense Policy

- ⭐ Foreign Policy Decision Making

- ⭐ Twenty-First-Century Challenges

The debate has intensified in the wake of revelations of a much larger data-mining project designed to track the domestic phone records of millions of ordinary U.S. citizens and analyze them for signs that Americans are communicating with suspected terrorists. President Bush has strongly defended his administration's surveillance and monitoring efforts: "We're not mining or trolling through the personal lives of millions of innocent Americans," he publicly stated. "Our efforts are focused on links to al Qaeda and their known affiliates."[1] But, the NSA's domestic surveillance program blurs the distinction between domestic and foreign policies and raises complicated constitutional questions about the reach of the federal government in the context of combating terrorism.

Domestic issues, such as the privacy rights of ordinary Americans, have become part of the discussion of how best to pursue a defense policy that effectively thwarts terrorism here and abroad. The war on terrorism has dramatically changed how the United States conducts foreign and defense policy; ushering in a period of unprecedented unilateral military action abroad, aggressive detention processes for those suspected of terrorist activities, and controversial spying programs at home.

isolationism

A national policy of avoiding participation in foreign affairs.

unilateralism

A national policy of acting without consulting others.

moralism

The policy of emphasizing morality in foreign affairs.

pragmatism

The policy of taking advantage of a situation for national gain.

■ General Michael V. Hayden defends the NSA eavesdropping program in 2006.

Photo courtesy: Lauren Victoria Burke/AP Wide World Photos

FOLLOWING THE END OF THE COLD WAR, the collapse of the Soviet Union, and the expulsion of Iraqi forces from Kuwait in the 1991 Persian Gulf War, U.S. foreign policy began a period of transition. Many wondered what role the United States would play in a multipolar world with only one remaining superpower. Most hoped that the world would be a safer place in the new millennium. After September 11, however, the United States recognized a new and deadly adversary: terrorism. More Americans began to pay attention to foreign policy and defense issues. Many wondered how the United States, with its superior military resources and unchallenged supremacy in the world order, could be susceptible to a devastating series of terrorist attacks on a single fateful day.

Like social and economic policy, U.S. foreign and defense policy has evolved. Today, the United States still is the most powerful and influential country in the world. No other country has as large an economy, as powerful a military, or plays as influential a role in world affairs as the United States. It was not always this way. When the United States was founded, it was a weak country on the margins of world affairs, with an uncertain future. (See The Living Constitution.)

Even so, the United States was fortunate. Separated from Europe and Asia by vast oceans, it had abundant resources and industrious people. The United States often stood apart from world engagements, following a policy of **isolationism,** that is, avoiding participation in foreign affairs. However, isolationism was rarely total. Even in its early years, the United States engaged in foreign affairs, and it always was a trading nation. Another consistent hallmark of U.S. policy was **unilateralism,** that is, acting without consulting others. **Moralism** was also central to U.S. self-image in foreign policy, with most Americans believing their country had higher moral standards than European and other countries. Many Americans were also proud of their **pragmatism**—their ability to find ways to take advantage of a situation. Thus, when Europe was at war, Americans sold goods to both sides and profited handsomely. When opportunities to acquire more land arose, Americans aggressively pursued them.

In this chapter, we first will trace the origins of current U.S. foreign and defense policy in the years since the United States became a world power. After studying foreign and defense policy decision making, we will discuss twenty-first-century foreign policy challenges.

The Living Constitution

To provide for calling forth the Militia to execute the Laws of the Union, suppress Insurrections and repel Invasions;

To provide for organizing, arming, and disciplining, the Militia, and for governing such Part of them as may be employed in the Service of the United States, reserving to the States respectively, the Appointment of the Officers, and the Authority of training the Militia according to the discipline proscribed by Congress;

—ARTICLE I, SECTION 8

With the Constitution's Article I militia clauses, a significant defect of the Articles of Confederation was corrected. A fundamental weakness of the earlier document was that it did not grant the central U.S. government adequate means for national defense, and this defect was understood to hamper the Revolutionary War effort. In the view of the Framers, a government without the force to administer its laws or to defend its citizens was either a weak government or no government at all, and these clauses consequently give the federal government authority to call up the state militias in times of national emergency or distress.

Joseph Story, an associate justice of the Supreme Court from 1812 to 1845, commented that the militia clauses passed the Constitutional Convention "by a declared majority" because the delegates understood that the power to call up the militia would be necessary in providing for the common defense and in securing domestic peace. The clauses address the understanding that military training, proficiency, and organization should be uniform across state and national forces so as to ensure effectiveness and efficiency in military operations.

Many Anti-Federalists, however, were concerned that the federal government could call together the state militias for unjust ends. They held the position that state governments should control their militias in order to prevent any perfidy on the part of the federal government. To this end, the states were given authority to name militia officers and train their forces. During the War of 1812—to the consternation of President James Madison—two state governments withheld their militias, because they believed it was the purview of the state to set the terms for the use of its guards. The Supreme Court has since held that, except for constitutional prohibitions, the Congress has "unlimited" authority over the state militias. The National Defense Act of 1916 mandated the use of the term "National Guard" and gave the president the authority to mobilize the National Guard during times of national emergency or war.

Throughout U.S. history, the National Guard has proved effective and essential in defending the United States. With the extensive use of the National Guard to assist American efforts in Iraq and in the struggle against terrorism, its role has expanded. The militia clauses ensure the unity, effectiveness, and strength of the United States military not only during wartime, but also during other national emergencies.

VIDEO ROUNDTABLE

Unilateralism and Multilateralism

SIMULATION

You Are President John F. Kennedy

Cuban Missile Crisis
The 1962 confrontation that nearly escalated into war between the United States and the Soviet Union over Soviet deployment of medium-range ballistic missiles in Cuba.

The Origins of Current U.S. Foreign and Defense Policy

THROUGHOUT THE 1950S AND INTO THE 1960S, the world seemed divided into two camps, one led by the United States and the other by the communist Soviet Union. John F. Kennedy became president in 1961 during this Cold War period. Kennedy brought a sense of optimism and activism to the United States that captivated many Americans. "Ask not what your country can do for you," Kennedy urged Americans in his inaugural address, "but what you can do for your country."

Containing the Soviet Union while at the same time establishing cordial relations with it to lessen the peril of nuclear war was high on President Kennedy's foreign and military policy agenda. Thus, in 1961, Kennedy met Soviet President Nikita Khrushchev in Vienna, Austria. The meeting, on neutral soil, did not go well. Both leaders returned to their respective countries and immediately increased military spending. In 1962, the Soviet Union began to deploy intermediate-range ballistic missiles in Cuba, only ninety miles from Florida, leading to the **Cuban Missile Crisis.**[2] The United States reacted strongly, placing a naval blockade around Cuba and warning the Soviet Union to withdraw the missiles or suffer the consequences. After several days during which the world was closer to nuclear war than it had ever been, Khrushchev backed down and withdrew the missiles. The world breathed a sigh of relief.

The Cuban Missile Crisis led to a period of improved U.S.-Soviet relations. During the crisis, the United States and the Soviet Union had marched to the edge of nuclear war, and neither liked what they saw. Thus, in 1963, the two nations concluded a partial nuclear test ban treaty and installed a "hot line" between Washington, D.C., and Moscow to allow the leaders of the two countries to talk directly during crises.

The Cuban Missile Crisis confirmed the majority of Americans' belief that the Soviet Union was an expansionist power. Despite its dangers, most Americans believed that containment was the correct strategy, and that the United States remained the moral defender of liberty and justice, acting pragmatically but always with restraint to prevent communist expansion. Few questioned the morality of containment, the necessity for pragmatism, or the need for internationalism and American-led multilateralism.

Then came the Vietnam War.[3] The United States sought to contain communism from spreading from North Vietnam into South Vietnam starting in the 1950s. It was in the mid-1960s, however, that U.S. bombing and ground operations began, and they escalated quickly. While many in South Vietnam were grateful for U.S. assistance, others actively supported the communists. The United States became embroiled in a civil war in which it was difficult to determine friend from foe. Eventually, the U.S. presence in Vietnam grew to more than 500,000 troops, 58,000 of whom ultimately were killed. As deaths mounted and costs grew, many Americans asked questions they had rarely asked before. Was the United States on the side of justice in Vietnam, or had it only replaced France there as a colonial power? How much killing and how great a cost would the United States bear to prevent the expansion of communism? Was communism still the enemy it had been? Increasingly, U.S. citizens became less persuaded that their mission in Vietnam was moral or that communism was universally dangerous. By the end of the 1960s, Americans were not as sure of their moral superiority as they had been, nor were they sure that containment was the proper strategy on which to base their foreign and military policy. President Lyndon B. Johnson, who had presided over the massive U.S. military escalation in Vietnam, became so unpopular by 1968 that he chose not to run for reelection.

■ Many Americans continue to visit the Vietnam War Memorial in Washington, D.C., to grieve for those in the U.S. military who gave their lives during the conflict in Southeast Asia.

Photo courtesy: Bachman/The Image Works

DÉTENTE AND HUMAN RIGHTS: 1969–1981

When Richard M. Nixon was inaugurated as president in 1969, he declared it was time to move from "an era of confrontation" to "an era of negotiation" in relations with the Soviet Union. Recognizing that nuclear war would destroy life as it existed, searching for a way to exit Vietnam, and trying to improve East–West relations without conceding international leadership or renouncing containment, Nixon undertook policies that began this transformation. The improvement in U.S.-Soviet relations was called **détente.**[4]

As Nixon calculated how to achieve these objectives, some criticized his approach as cynical. Emphasizing pragmatism to the virtual exclusion of moralism, Nixon's approach reminded many of old-style European power politics that the United States had rejected since its earliest days. Critics pointed to the **Nixon Doctrine**—that the United States would provide military aid to countries but not do the fighting for them—as evidence of this cynicism. Under the Nixon Doctrine, the United States expanded military aid to South Vietnam and accelerated bombing even as negotiations for American withdrawal proceeded. To many, this showed that Nixon ignored morality. Others supported Nixon's approach, arguing that it would get the United States out of Vietnam, open relations with China, and improve relations with the Soviet Union.

The changed nature of U.S.-Soviet relations brought about by détente was best illustrated by the frequency of summit meetings. From 1972 to 1979, American and Soviet leaders met six times, but détente was more than summitry. It also included increased trade, arms control agreements such as the Strategic Arms Limitation Treaty and the Anti-Ballistic Missile Treaty, and cultural exchanges. Détente improved East–West relations in Europe as well. For example, the heads of government of almost every nation in Europe and North America attended a meeting in Helsinki, Finland, in 1975.

When Jimmy Carter became president in 1977, he too intended to pursue détente. However, he rejected Nixon's foreign policy cynicism. Carter instead emphasized **human rights,** that is, the protection of people's basic freedoms and needs. This found a sympathetic ear among many Americans. Once again, they believed, the

détente
The relaxation of tensions between the United States and the Soviet Union that occurred during the 1970s.

Nixon Doctrine
The policy implemented at the end of the Vietnam War that the United States would provide arms and military equipment to countries but not do the fighting for them.

human rights
The belief that human beings have inalienable rights such as freedom of speech and freedom of religion.

United States would emphasize morality in foreign policy. Some American critics wondered, however, if Carter's emphasis on human rights was misdirected and was weakening the United States.

Concern about American weakness grew in 1979 when radical Iranians, with the support of Iran's fundamentalist Islamic government, overran the U.S. embassy in Tehran and held the embassy staff captive. The **Iranian hostage crisis** eroded Carter's support in the United States. For over a year, the country was powerless to win the hostages' release. A failed rescue attempt added to American humiliation. (The hostages were not released until the day that Carter left office in 1981.)

Détente finally died in 1979 when the Soviet Union invaded Afghanistan. Described by Carter as "the most serious strategic challenge since the Cold War began," the Soviet invasion led to an immediate increase in U.S. defense spending. Carter also adopted a more hard-line approach to foreign policy, announcing the **Carter Doctrine** under which the United States would fight to prevent any further Soviet expansion toward the Persian Gulf and its nearby oil fields.

CONTAINMENT REVISITED AND RENEWED: 1981–1989

The tense U.S.-Soviet relations during Jimmy Carter's last year as president became confrontational during President Ronald Reagan's first term in office. Reagan accelerated the U.S. arms buildup and initiated an activist foreign policy in response to Soviet influence in developing countries. He sent U.S. troops into Grenada, a small pro-Soviet island in the Carribean and supported the Contras, an insurgency attempting to overthrow the pro-Soviet Sandinista government in Nicaragua. In addition, Reagan emphasized morality in American foreign policy and pushed to create an open international economic system.[5]

By 1984, however, relations between the United States and the Soviet Union were beginning to improve. The two countries upgraded their hotlines and agreed to expand arms-control talks. Most importantly, the rhetoric from both capitals deescalated. What happened? First, although most Americans supported the arms buildup, they were concerned about confrontation with the Soviets. Thus, Reagan moderated his anti-Soviet rhetoric leading up to the 1984 U.S. presidential election. Second, U.S. foreign and military policy initiatives had an impact on Moscow as, in addition to its arms buildup, the United States implemented the **Reagan Doctrine,** under which the United States provided arms to anti-Soviet movements fighting pro-Soviet governments in Afghanistan, Angola, and Mozambique as well as Nicaragua. These programs increased the cost of Soviet involvement there and led Soviet leaders to rethink their foreign policy. Finally, the Soviet Union had serious internal problems. Its economy was performing poorly and it suffered from a leadership crisis when three Soviet leaders died between 1982 and 1985. These problems had to be addressed. To do this, the Soviet Union needed a less confrontational relationship with the United States.

Recognizing these problems, Soviet President Mikhail Gorbachev worked with Reagan to improve relations. Even before Gorbachev's reforms took hold, he and Reagan laid the groundwork for a transformation in relations.[6] At the third of five summit meetings, the two leaders signed an agreement to

Iranian hostage crisis
Crisis during the Carter administration when Iranian students with support of the Iranian government took over the U.S. embassy in Tehran, holding all the personnel hostage.

Carter Doctrine
Policy announced after the 1979 Soviet invasion of Afghanistan that the Persian Gulf area was a vital U.S. interest and the United States would fight to maintain access to it.

Reagan Doctrine
Policy that the United States would provide military assistance to anti-communist groups fighting against pro-Soviet governments.

■ After several tense years in U.S.-Soviet relations, the emergence of Mikhail Gorbachev as Soviet president in 1985 led to the adoption of stunning reforms in the Soviet Union and a series of increasingly friendly summit meetings between Gorbachev and U.S. President Ronald Reagan.

Photo courtesy: Tannen Murray/The Image Works

destroy all intermediate-range nuclear weapons. Gorbachev introduced reforms in domestic, foreign, and military policies that transformed the Soviet Union and U.S.-Soviet relations. Although the reforms were intended to address the serious problems that the Soviet Union faced, they eventually led to the end of the Cold War and the demise of the Soviet Union.[7]

SEARCHING FOR A NEW INTERNATIONAL ORDER: 1989–2000

George Bush assumed the United States presidency in 1989 pledging to continue Reagan's foreign policy directions. However, the pace and scope of change in Eastern Europe and the Soviet Union raised questions about the entire direction of U.S. foreign policy. The first question came from Eastern Europe. In 1989, the people of many Eastern European states revolted against their governments. During previous rebellions, Soviet troops stationed in Eastern Europe subdued the rebellions. This time, Gorbachev ordered Soviet troops to remain in their barracks. The rebellions continued, and in every communist country in Eastern Europe, the government fell.

The United States was not quite sure how to respond. At first, Bush proceeded cautiously. As it became clear that the revolutions were irreversible, the United States and other democratic states helped the new noncommunist Eastern European states try to establish democratic political and free market economic systems. Remarkably, in a matter of months, the "Iron Curtain" dividing Eastern and Western Europe had collapsed, with almost no serious bloodshed.

The 1990 Iraqi invasion of Kuwait in the Middle East produced a new challenge. The Bush administration believed that the invasion threatened vital U.S. interests, and the United Nations passed a resolution authorizing the use of force to expel Iraq from Kuwait. Shortly after Congress voted to support the use of military force against Iraq, the Persian Gulf War began in January 1991. In an attack called Operation Desert Storm, U.S. and allied forces defeated Iraq in a matter of weeks. The objective—expelling Iraq from Kuwait—was achieved with few U.S. casualties.[8] The conduct of Operation Desert Storm reflected the principles of the **Powell Doctrine** articulated by Colin Powell, President Bush's chair of the Joint Chiefs of Staff.

Meanwhile, startling events were unfolding in the Soviet Union. Under Gorbachev, the Soviet Union posed less and less of a threat as it and the United States forged an increasingly close relationship. Weakened by a failed coup attempt against Gorbachev in the summer of 1991, its economy in shambles, and torn by internal dissent and the desires of nationalities for independence, the Soviet Union collapsed.[9] The Cold War was over, as was the need for containment. Once again Americans asked questions: What would U.S. strategy now be? With the Cold War over, should the United States cut defense spending, and if so, how much? How much aid should the United States send to its former enemy to help it survive its collapse? What criteria would guide decisions about where and when to employ U.S. forces abroad in a world with only one remaining superpower?

These were the complex questions Bill Clinton faced when he assumed the presidency in 1993. Defining the American role in this world presented a challenge. Clinton's agenda centered on implementing engagement and enlargement, shaping new international economic relationships, deciding when U.S. armed forces should be used overseas, and puzzling over what role the United States should play in the post–Cold War world. **Engagement** meant that the United States would not retreat into isolationism as it did after World War I and for a short time after World War II. Engagement implied that the United States relied on negotiations and cooperation rather than confrontation and conflict, although it would use force when necessary. **Enlargement** meant that the United States would promote democracy, open markets, and other Western political, economic, and social values. In practice, engagement and enlargement led to the implementation of the Partnership for Peace program with

From Stand-Alone to Superpower: The Evolution of American Foreign Policy

Powell Doctrine

An all-or-nothing approach to military intervention advocated by Colin Powell: use overwhelming force for quick, decisive victory, and have an exit strategy before any intervention.

engagement

Policy implemented during the Clinton administration that the United States would remain actively involved in foreign affairs.

enlargement

Policy implemented during the Clinton administration that the United States would actively promote the expansion of democracy and free markets throughout the world.

Politics Now

THE UNITED STATES AND THE INTERNATIONAL CRIMINAL COURT

In 1998, a United Nations conference finalized a treaty establishing an International Criminal Court (ICC) that would have jurisdiction over crimes against humanity, war crimes, and genocide once sixty states ratified it. By 2001, 139 states had signed the treaty. The United States was not one of them.

The United States opposes crimes against humanity, war crimes, and genocide. In the mid-1990s, it deployed thousands of troops to Bosnia to help prevent genocide. In the late 1990s, it supported the creation of a UN tribunal that indicted Yugoslav President Slobodan Milosevic for war crimes and convicted other Serbs of crimes against humanity for their ethnic-cleansing campaign against Bosnian Muslims. In 1999, the United States contributed most of the armed forces for NATO's military operation against ethnic cleansing in Kosovo.

Why then did the United States not support the ICC? Some conservative Americans believed that the powers the ICC statutes gave the court might lead to politically motivated prosecutions of U.S. military personnel involved in peacekeeping missions, fearing that frivolous charges might be made against U.S. personnel engaged in legitimate activities. For example, Senator Jesse Helms (R–NC) argued that a government that committed human rights abuses against its citizens might charge that a member of the U.S. armed forces trying to prevent such abuses was violating the rights of its citizens and bring charges against him or her in the ICC. Defenders of the ICC asserted that this could not occur, because the ICC statutes allowed the United States and other peacekeeping states to preempt the ICC by first trying anyone so accused in their own national courts.

The United States under President Bill Clinton signed the treaty in 2000, but the Senate never ratified it. When George W. Bush took office in 2001, he renounced the treaty. As the International Criminal Court neared operational status in 2002, Bush threatened to oppose all UN peacekeeping missions if the ICC began operations, to refuse to provide U.S. funding for such operations if approved, and to refuse to have U.S. forces participate in any peacekeeping efforts. The Bush administration also initiated an extensive diplomatic offensive designed to conclude one-on-one agreements with other countries that they would not prosecute or bring changes against U.S. peacekeepers. The United States threatened to cut off military aid to countries that refused to sign bilateral agreements. By 2004, ninety-two countries had signed such agreements.

The U.S. diplomatic effort was widely criticized outside the United States as an attempt to circumvent the ICC. For example, the European Union and many of its members chastised the United States, and Amnesty International called the effort an attempt to undermine the ICC.

Despite U.S. resistance, the ICC was established at the Hague, in the Netherlands, and prepared to conduct investigations, trials, and appeals procedures for cases involving war crimes and other crimes against humanity. By 2006, the Court completed elections for eighteen judgeships organized into three divisions: pre-trial, trial, and appeals. On March 17, 2006, Thomas Lubanga Dyilo, a Congolese national accused of war crimes, was arrested and transferred to the International Criminal Court where he awaits a trial. He is the first person to be arrested and transferred to the court since its entry into force in 2002. The ICC has also issued arrest warrants for several Ugandan individuals and is investigating allegations of genocide in the Darfur region of Sudan as requested by the United Nations Security Council.

former communist states in Eastern Europe and the former Soviet Union and the expansion of the North Atlantic Treaty Organization (NATO), a defense alliance established during the Cold War.

Deciding when to use U.S. armed forces overseas is a vexing problem. As we have seen, from the end of World War II to the collapse of the Soviet Union, U.S. military intervention was usually tied to containing communism. With the Soviet Union gone, this easy benchmark for deciding when to intervene no longer existed. Thus, the Clinton administration had to clarify when and under what conditions the United States would intervene. The administration faced different types of crises in countries in Africa, Eastern Europe, Asia, the Middle East, and the Carribean and intervened militarily in a number of those countries, but no pattern was evident about the use of U.S. military force overseas. In some cases, the U.S. response was largely humanitarian. Other situations dictated peacekeeping or peace enforcement efforts; still others involved combat activities.

International economic issues were another focus of Clinton's activities. With help from members of his own Democratic Party as well as Senate Republicans, he guided the **North American Free Trade Agreement (NAFTA)** into law, establishing the free flow of goods among Canada, Mexico, and the United States. The United States under Clinton played a major role in initiating the Free Trade Area of the Americas and the Asia-Pacific Economic Cooperation agreement, as well as in creating the **World Trade Organization (WTO),** charged with overseeing world trade, judging trade disputes, and lowering tariffs.[10]

THE WAR ON TERRORISM: 2001 TO THE PRESENT

During his first months as president, George W. Bush conducted an active foreign policy, traveling to other countries and ordering several changes to policy. (See Politics Now: The United States and the International Criminal Court.) As a Texan, Bush placed high priority on U.S. relations with Mexico and other Latin American states. Indeed, his first trip outside the United States as president was to Mexico to discuss immigration, anti-drug policies, economic development, and border issues.

By September 2001, the Bush administration had a full foreign policy agenda. Relations with Latin America, Europe, Russia, and China all loomed large, as did security, international economics, immigration, drugs, and the environment. However, the new administration had not sorted through this considerable agenda to determine the items it considered most important. Suddenly and unexpectedly, on the morning of September 11, 2001, the Bush administration's foreign and defense priorities became clear.

On September 11, members of **al-Qaeda,** the terrorist network founded by Muslim fundamentalist Osama bin Laden, hijacked four jetliners, flying two into the twin towers of New York's World Trade Center. The impact and the subsequent collapse of the towers killed almost 3,000 people. Another hijacked plane slammed into the Pentagon, killing 189. The fourth plane, headed toward Washington, D.C., crashed into a field in Pennsylvania after passengers charged the hijackers and forced them to lose control of the plane.[11]

North American Free Trade Agreement (NAFTA)
Agreement that promotes free movement of goods and services among Canada, Mexico, and the United States.

World Trade Organization (WTO)
International governmental organization created in 1995 that manages multilateral negotiations to reduce barriers to trade and settle trade disputes.

al-Qaeda
Worldwide terrorist organization led by Osama bin Laden; responsible for numerous terrorist attacks against U.S. interests, including September 11, 2001, attacks against the World Trade Center and the Pentagon.

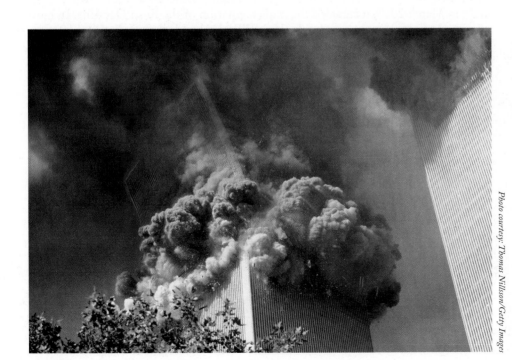

■ The south tower of the World Trade Center collapses September 11, 2001, after it was struck by a hijacked airplane. The north tower, also struck by a hijacked plane, collapsed shortly after. The tragic September 11 terrorist attacks caused enormous loss of life and had a profound impact on U.S. foreign and defense policy.

Photo courtesy: Thomas Nillsson/Getty Images

9-11-2001

war on terrorism
Initiated by George W. Bush after the September 11, 2001, attacks to weed out terrorist operatives throughout the world, using diplomacy, military means, improved homeland security, stricter banking laws, and other means.

Taliban
Fundamentalist Islamic government of Afghanistan that provided terrorist training bases for al-Qaeda.

Bush Doctrine
Policy advocated by President George W. Bush of using preemptive military action against a perceived threat to U.S. interests.

weapons of mass destruction (WMDs)
Biological, chemical, and nuclear weapons, which present a sizeable threat to U.S. security.

■ President George W. Bush holds a meeting with his national security team on September 12, 2001. From left are Secretary of Defense Donald Rumsfeld, Secretary of State Colin Powell, Bush, Vice President Dick Cheney, and Henry Shelton, chair of the Pentagon Joint Chiefs of Staff.

After the attacks, President Bush launched the **war on terrorism** and organized a coalition of nations to identify and combat terrorist threats. He also demanded that Afghanistan's **Taliban** government, which had provided safe haven for bin Laden and al-Qaeda's terrorist training camps, turn bin Laden over to the United States. When the Taliban refused, the Bush administration launched Operation Enduring Freedom in October 2001. The military operation included air strikes against Taliban and al-Qaeda targets and support for the Northern Alliance, an Afghani opposition force battling Taliban control. By the end of 2001, the Taliban were overthrown and the United States began an open-ended commitment to peace enforcement and assistance with the transition to a democratic government in Afghanistan.

Ironically, the September 11 attacks drew the United States and Russia closer together as Russia helped the United States gain access to military bases in Central Asia. The United States also muted its criticism of Russian policies in Russia's breakaway province of Chechnya, and Russian President Vladimir Putin indicated a willingness to modify the 1972 Anti-Ballistic Missile Treaty, thereby removing ballistic missile defense as a stumbling block in U.S.-Russian relations. The United States and Russia made so much progress on strategic arms discussions that during Bush's May 2002 trip to Moscow, the United States and Russia signed the Strategic Offensive Arms Reduction Treaty, under which both sides agreed to cut their strategic nuclear arsenals to the lowest total in decades.[12]

The terrorist attacks of September 11, had a profound impact on U.S. foreign policy. Despite its superpower status and nuclear superiority, the United States appeared vulnerable in a way it had not previously. President Bush responded to the crisis on U.S. soil by inaugurating a global campaign against terrorists and their supporters. Like other presidents before him, George W. Bush began to put his distinctive stamp on how the country should address threats to national security. Bush and his foreign policy team concluded that a more ambitious, "muscular" posture was needed to fight threats to U.S. interests. Instead of relying on the reactive strategies of deterrence and containment, the Bush administration advocated a proactive doctrine of preemptive military action. This bold but controversial strategy is commonly referred to as the **Bush Doctrine.**

When the United States launched its war against Saddam Hussein's Iraqi government in March 2003, it signaled the implementation of the Bush Doctrine. In most past conflicts of this magnitude, the United States had intervened militarily in response to a direct attack (such as Japan's attack on Pearl Harbor in the Hawaiian Islands in 1941), or to defend other countries that had been invaded (such as South Korea or Kuwait). The 2003 U.S.-led invasion of Iraq was part of a new strategy that sought to promote American security through preemptive military strikes against potentially dangerous nations. Believing that Iraq was secretly developing **weapons of mass destruction (WMDs)**—nuclear, chemical, or biological that it was a safe harbor and potential breeding ground for terrorists, the U.S. government chose to act. The

Photo courtesy: Kevin LaMarque/Reuters

U.S. action, however, did not have the support of the **United Nations (UN),** the international governmental organization created near the end of World War II to guarantee the security of nations and promote global economic, physical, and social well-being. The UN Security Council refused to endorse the recourse to war. The failure of the United States to win approval from the Security Council for the 2003 invasion of Iraq led to vigorous debate at home and abroad, and U.S. actions created hard feelings among many of America's traditional allies. (See Join the Debate: Should the United States Pull Out of the United Nations?)

The overthrow of Saddam Hussein's government in the spring of 2003 was relatively quick. The U.S.-led bombing campaign destroyed much of the military and governmental infrastructure in Iraq within days, and Hussein's forces seemed helpless and disorganized. Within weeks, U.S. and other allied forces had entered Hussein's palaces, torn down statues of the dictator around the country, and began to create a post-Saddam government in Iraq. American forces ultimately captured Saddam Hussein himself on December 13, 2003.

Over time, coalition forces failed to find evidence of a nuclear weapons program in Iraq—the original justification provided by the Bush administration for a preemptive military strike—but it is clear that Hussein possessed chemical weapons, engaged in genocide, and brutally oppressed the Shiite majority in Iraq.[13] As evidence of WMDs failed to materialize, the Bush administration changed its justification for the war and argued that Saddam Hussein posed a severe danger to the world because of his long history of brutality and emphasized the goal of promoting democracy in the Middle East through his removal from power.

In the months after President Bush declared an end to major combat, soldiers from the United States and its allies found themselves under attack from mortar fire, roadside bombings, and suicide missions by various insurgents. As the American military presence in Iraq continued, American war deaths and injuries mounted. By December of 2006, more than 2,900 U.S. service men and women had lost their lives in Iraq, and thousands more had been injured.

In January 2005, Iraq had held a legislative election in which the Iraqi people chose representatives for a newly formed 275-member Iraqi National Assembly. The election marked an important step in the process of turning over control of the country from U.S. and coalition forces to the Iraqis themselves. But as civil unrest grew, hopes for the withdrawal of U.S. troops were dashed. On August 14, 2005, the *Washington Post* quoted a dismal assessment of the situation in Iraq from an anonymous U.S. senior official: "the United States no longer expects to see a model new democracy, a self-supporting oil industry, or a society in which the majority of people are free from serious security or economic challenges. . . . What we expected to achieve was never realistic given the timetable or what unfolded on the ground."[14] Throughout 2006, frequent terrorist attacks and sectarian violence continued to define conditions in Iraq, and many observers agreed that the country was embroiled in a civil war. The resignation of Secretary of Defense Donald Rumsfeld after the 2006 elections suggests the administration intends to adjust its policy in Iraq in response to rising violence and waning public support.

The September 11 attacks gave the United States two overarching foreign and defense policy priorities: defense of the homeland and pursuing the global war on terrorism. Few Americans disagree with these priorities. However, other foreign and defense policy issues, such as the threat of a nuclear North Korea and Iran, hostilities between Israel and Lebanon, and the humanitarian crisis in Sudan, have also captured the public's attention.

Having discussed the history of U.S. foreign policy during the twentieth century and the new direction foreign policy has taken during the presidency of George W. Bush, we turn to a discussion of how foreign policy is made and describe the major players involved.

United Nations (UN)

The international governmental organization created near the end of World War II to guarantee the security of nations and to promote global economic, physical, and social well-being.

Americans in Iraq

Join the Debate

SHOULD THE UNITED STATES PULL OUT OF THE UNITED NATIONS?

OVERVIEW: The United Nations came into existence in 1945 in the wake of two world wars and the desire of most nations for an international organization dedicated to pursuing global justice, peace, and human rights. To back up its mandate, the United States and the United Nations have worked together to help maintain relative global security. For example, UN member nations helped defend South Korea from invasion by North Korea, provided a blueprint to help mediate peace in the Middle East, and voted for sanctions against South Africa to help end racial apartheid. The UN has also helped millions living in famine, as well as aided countless refugees fleeing war and natural disasters by providing food, shelter, clothing, and medical relief.

Since the end of the Cold War, the United States and the United Nations have developed competing and sometimes antagonistic views with regard to the UN's mandate and global role. In 1992, for example, the UN released a bold initiative—the Agenda for Peace—to recast the UN's peacekeeping role. The move was viewed by some U.S. policy makers as giving the UN control over U.S. military and foreign policy resources and it received a great deal of criticism in Congress.

Furthermore, due to disagreements with the United States over a variety of issues, including its military and foreign policy role in the Middle East, its refusal to ratify the Kyoto climate change treaty, and its opposition to a treaty to abolish land mines, the UN voted the United States off the UN Human Rights Commission in 2001. This action infuriated the Bush administration, because countries that engage in human rights violations, such as Sudan, Libya, and Cuba, retained their seats on the commission. The United States walked out of the UN conference on racism in 2001 because it objected to criticisms of Israel in a draft of the conference's final declaration. The strain between the Bush administration and the United Nations increased even more in 2003 when the UN Security Council refused to sanction military action against Iraq. The UN also faced criticism for a major financial scandal involving its Oil for Food program, which had been created during Saddam Hussein's regime in order to give the Iraqi people humanitarian aid while sanctions against Hussein's government were in place. Nearly $1 billion disappeared into hidden bank accounts and fake corporations, and the U.S. Congress launched an investigation into where the money went.

To what extent should the United States support the diplomatic and peacekeeping efforts of the United Nations? Should the United States have a dominant role in determining UN policy and actions, given its dominant role in the world? Many U.S. conservatives support a full U.S. withdrawal from the United Nations. Would this decision help or hurt the United States' interests in the long run?

ARGUMENTS IN FAVOR OF THE UNITED STATES PULLING OUT OF THE UNITED NATIONS

- **It is difficult for the United Nations to act, and even when it does, it is incapable of enforcing its own resolutions.** In 2006, Iran made public its intention to develop nuclear weapons, but the UN could not forge a consensus regarding how to respond. China and Russia balked at imposing sanctions on Iran, creating an impasse within the Security Council. Getting the global community to act with one voice can be extremely difficult, given the diverse interests of the countries that are represented on the Security Council and within the larger UN body.

Foreign Policy Decision Making

THE EXECUTIVE BRANCH is the most powerful branch of government in the formulation and implementation of U.S. foreign and military policy. Other groups, including Congress, the military-industrial complex, the news media, and the public, also influence and shape American foreign and military policy.

THE EXECUTIVE BRANCH

The executive branch is the locus for creating and implementing U.S. foreign and military policy; within the executive branch, the president is the most important individual.

- **The United States is not accountable to international organizations when pursuing its own interests.** The United States and the United Nations have divergent interests and understandings of international law and diplomacy. Placing members of the American armed forces under UN command cedes control to an organization that may not always act in the best interests of the United States. The United States must maintain its ability to act in whatever way it sees fit to defend its interests at home and abroad.
- **Adhering to UN resolutions results in giving up American sovereignty.** Some supporters of U.S. withdrawal from the United Nations believe the UN is attempting to create a "world government" and that to accede to UN mandates and resolutions is to relinquish U.S. sovereignty and U.S. control over its own citizens. Many see the UN as one more instance of the international community trying to institute international government.

ARGUMENTS AGAINST THE UNITED STATES PULLING OUT OF THE UNITED NATIONS

- **The UN engages in peacekeeping and nation building when the United States will not.** The UN is currently engaged in about fifteen peacekeeping operations, with more than 72,000 uniformed personnel from member nations in places such as Lebanon, Haiti, and Sudan. The UN can provide peacekeeping support when the United States is either unable or unwilling, thus preventing humanitarian disaster and conflict. This is an essential function if global security and stability are to be maintained.
- **The United States must lead by example.** Because the United States has a unique world, military, and economic position, it can use its various strengths and principles to promote global peace and justice. Why should other nations respond to UN resolutions and decrees when the United States does not? By acceding to UN requests, the United States can set an example for other nations to follow, and this may help facilitate other nations' compliance with UN wishes to ensure global security.
- **International institutions provide global stability and promote peaceful conflict resolution.** Since the establishment of the United Nations, there have been no worldwide wars. The UN was able to provide security for South Korea and it acts as an international forum for conflict mediation. Though imperfect, the UN affords a medium in which human rights policy is debated and developed and international security and stability discussed. For example, the UN has taken on the cause of disarmament and elimination of WMDs and thereby provides legitimacy in this policy domain, whereas the United States cannot. Because the United States is a world power, its membership in the UN gives the organization credibility and validity.

QUESTIONS

1. Does adhering to UN mandates mean giving up national sovereignty? Explain.
2. What can be done to reconcile U.S. and UN interests? Do the United States and the United Nations have similar interests? If not, what is to be done?

SELECTED READINGS

Jett, Dennis. *Why Peacekeeping Fails.* New York: Palgrave Macmillan, 2001.

Weiss, Thomas, ed. *United Nations and Changing World Politics.* Boulder, CO: Westview, 2004.

Among executive departments, the Department of State is primarily responsible for diplomatic activity and the Department of Defense for military policy. Other executive agencies, such as the National Security Council, the Joint Chiefs of Staff, and the Central Intelligence Agency, provide additional resources for the president. In some cases, the relatively new Department of Homeland Security (see chapter 8) has a role to play in foreign policy decision making as well.

The President   The president is preeminent in foreign and military policy for several reasons. The president alone is in charge of all executive-branch resources. The president has greater access to and control over information, and the president alone can act with little fear that his actions will be countermanded. American presidents

Department of State
Chief executive-branch department responsible for formulation and implementation of U.S. foreign policy.

Department of Defense
Chief executive-branch department responsible for formulation and implementation of U.S. military policy.

Joint Chiefs of Staff
Advisory body to the president that includes the chief of staff of the army, chief of staff of the air force, chief of naval operations, and marine commandant.

Central Intelligence Agency (CIA)
Executive agency responsible for collection and analysis of information and intelligence about foreign countries and events.

National Security Council (NSC)
Executive agency responsible for advising the president about foreign and defense policy and events.

■ General Peter Pace, head of the Joint Chiefs of Staff, testifying at a hearing before the Senate Armed Services Committee. To his right are Secretary of Defense Donald Rumsfeld and General John Abizaid, Head of U.S. Central Command.

have often used their authority to order U.S. armed forces to engage in actions without seeking approval from others. President Ronald Reagan ordered air strikes against Libya and the invasion of Grenada, President George Bush ordered the invasion of Panama, and President Bill Clinton ordered cruise missile attacks against Afghanistan, Iraq, and Sudan, all on their own authority. Although these presidents informed congressional leaders of their intended actions, they made the decision and undertook the action on their own. For far more extensive and serious military commitments—such as the 1991 Persian Gulf War and the use of force against Iraq in 2003—the president sought and received congressional approval in advance.

The Departments of State and Defense The Departments of State and Defense have responsibility for implementing U.S. diplomatic and military policy, respectively. The **Department of State** is the oldest executive department, established originally in 1781 under the Articles of Confederation and reorganized during President George Washington's administration. Today there are more than 30,000 personnel within the Department of State who gather information on foreign political, economic, social, and military situations, represent the United States in negotiations and international organizations, staff U.S. embassies and consulates in more than 180 countries, and manage numerous international assistance programs.

The **Department of Defense** contributes to policy formulation and provides the forces to undertake military operations. It was created after World War II when Congress consolidated the Departments of War, Army, Navy, and Air Force into a single department. Under the secretary of defense and other appointed civilian officials, the Department of Defense directs U.S. forces from the Pentagon, a complex across the Potomac River from Washington, D.C. With thousands of civilian employees and millions of active-duty, National Guard, and reserve military personnel, the Department of Defense is among the most influential executive departments.

Within the Defense Department, the **Joint Chiefs of Staff** represents an important advisory body to the president, the secretary of defense, and the National Security Council. The Joint Chiefs of Staff provides a link between senior civilian leadership in the department and the professional military and often assists with the coordination of the various branches of the armed forces.

The **Central Intelligence Agency (CIA)** and the **National Security Council (NSC)** were established by Congress in 1947 to collect, collate, and analyze information necessary to meet national security requirements and to advise the president on foreign and military affairs. The CIA is the most well-known intelligence agency, but it is one of fifteen agencies engaged in intelligence work. Many of these reside within the Department of Defense, but the Departments of State, Homeland Security, Treasury, and Energy also maintain intelligence units. The CIA is an independent agency and its head, the director of central intelligence, reports directly to the president. The Intelligence Reform and Terrorism Prevention Act of 2004 established a director of national intelligence who oversees the entire intelligence community.

During the Cold War, the CIA ran covert operations to try to alter political events in many countries.[15] At times, these operations undermined broader U.S. objectives by supporting assassinations, corruption, and other scandalous activities. In the 1970s, Congress criticized the CIA and mandated changes in procedures to provide more congressional oversight to its secret operations. In the 1990s, the CIA's failure to predict the fall of the Soviet Union and the penetration of the agency by foreign agents raised congressional interest in reforming the CIA. After the September 11 terrorist attacks, the CIA and the rest of the intelligence community were criticized for failing to identify clues that could have prevented the attacks and for relying too heavily on electronic means of gathering intelligence and not heavily enough on human sources. Controversy over faulty intelligence about Iraq, the agency's serious lack of human intelligence sources, and its connection to secret prisons has generated a great deal of criticism on Capitol Hill and among the public.[16]

The National Security Council was set up to institutionalize the system by which the U.S. government integrates foreign and military policy and to coordinate U.S. activities on a range of foreign policy and military issues. The NSC includes the president, the vice president, the secretaries of state and defense, the chair of the Joint Chiefs of Staff, and the director of the CIA. The special assistant for national security affairs manages the NSC and is often one of the president's closest advisers.

The Department of Homeland Security

Following the September 11 terrorist attacks on the United States, the Office of Homeland Security was created by executive order and tasked to coordinate the executive branch's efforts to "detect, prepare for, prevent, protect against, respond to, and recover from terrorist attacks against the United States." Legislation in late 2002 converted this office into the cabinet-level **Department of Homeland Security (DHS).** This was the largest reorganization of the federal government since the creation of the Department of Defense in 1947. The homeland security reorganization process brought the functions of twenty-two existing agencies, approximately thirty newly created agencies or offices, and 180,000 employees under a single department. The mission of the DHS is to protect the American public from future acts of terror by engaging in activities designed to thwart terrorist activities and respond to any future crises.

The DHS is the locus for federal, state, and local homeland security coordination. DHS staff work with state, local, and private-sector partners to identify threats, determine vulnerabilities, and target resources. The DHS organization includes the Transportation Security Administration (TSA), the organization responsible for aviation security; the Federal Emergency Management Agency (FEMA), the primary federal disaster relief organization; Customs and Border Protection; the Coast Guard; the Secret Service; and immigration services and enforcement.

VIDEO ROUNDTABLE

The Department of Homeland Security

Department of Homeland Security
Cabinet department created after the September 11, 2001, terrorist attacks to coordinate domestic U.S. security efforts against terrorism.

CONGRESS

The Constitution gave Congress fewer responsibilities in foreign and defense policy than the president. Nevertheless, it plays an important role in the foreign policy process. Most would agree that Congress is the second most important actor in shaping American foreign and military affairs.[17] Congress influences foreign and defense policy through its congressional leadership, oversight, approval of treaties and appointments, appropriations, and the War Powers Act.

From World War II until the late 1960s, Congress deferred to the president and the military on foreign and military issues and rarely exercised its oversight responsibilities outside appropriations. The Vietnam War changed this. As questions emerged about U.S. policy toward Vietnam, Congress questioned executive leadership in other areas of foreign and military policy as well. This expanded oversight is now the norm. For example, in 2005 and 2006, the Senate Foreign Relations Committee questioned Bush administration officials and military leaders about growing sectarian violence in Iraq and the NSA's domestic spying program.

The Constitution gives the U.S. Senate explicit power to approve treaties, but the Senate has rejected treaties only twenty times in U.S. history. The Senate's power to approve treaties is not inconsequential, however. Presidents want to avoid the embarrassment of Senate rejection of a treaty, the delay of a filibuster, or senatorial refusal to consider a treaty, and they often adjust treaties accordingly. Presidents can avoid the treaty process by using executive agreements, which unlike treaties do not require Senate approval. (Table 7.2 in chapter 7 illustrates the increasing use of executive agreements.)

Although the Constitution gives the president the power to appoint ambassadors and others involved in foreign and military policy, it gives the Senate the responsibility to provide advice and consent on these appointments. This gives Congress influence over key executive-branch foreign and defense policy makers. In 2005, President Bush nominated John R. Bolton to serve as the U.S. ambassador to the United Nations. Bolton has close ties to the Bush family and participated in the 2000 presidential vote recount in Florida. His nomination caused a prolonged filibuster by Senate Democrats, who opposed Bolton for a number of reasons, including his skepticism of the UN, his opposition to the International Criminal Court, and his aggressive management tactics. Ultimately, President Bush installed Bolton via a congressional recess appointment that expired at the end of the 109th Congress in 2006. Bolton chose to resign at the end of his appointment rather than trying to win confirmation from the Senate's Democratic majority.

Congress also has a key role in shaping foreign and military policy through its power to appropriate funds and influence when and where the United States fights through its control of the budget. While the power to go to war is shared by the executive and legislative branches of government, the power to appropriate funds belongs to the legislature alone (see Figure 14.1 for information on U.S. defense spending since 1940).

VISUAL LITERACY

Evaluating Defense Spending

FIGURE 14.1 U.S. DEFENSE SPENDING, 1940–2004

The figure shows the percentage change from the prior year in the amount of current dollars spent on U.S. defense. As the figure illustrates, nothing in modern American history compares to the increase in spending after the United States entered World War II in 1941. Other significant increases in defense spending were related to the Cold War in the early 1950s and the Vietnam War in the mid to late 1960s. President George W. Bush's defense increases after 2001 are the highest since the end of the Cold War in the 1980s.

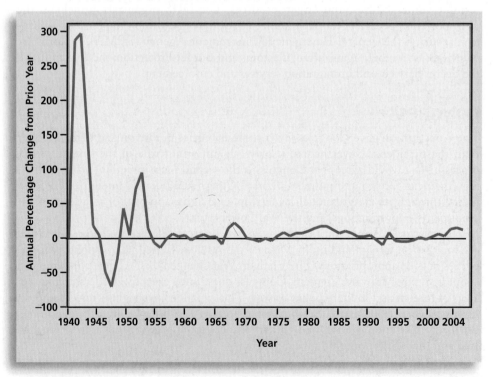

Source: Harold W. Stanley and Richard G. Niemi, eds., *Vital Statistics on American Politics, 2005–2006* (Washington, DC: CQ Press, 2006). Reprinted by permission.

Throughout American history, there have been cases where Congress and the executive branch disagreed on U.S. military actions overseas. During the Vietnam War, however, Congress tried to define and limit the president's and the executive branch's ability to engage in military action overseas by passing the **War Powers Act.** The act requires the president to consult with Congress before deploying American troops into hostile situations. Under certain conditions, the president is required to report to Congress within forty-eight hours of deployment. A presidential report can trigger a sixty-day clock that requires congressional approval for any continued military involvement past the sixty-day window. If Congress does not give explicit approval within sixty days, the president then has thirty days to withdraw the troops. Under the act, the president could respond to an emergency, such as rescuing endangered Americans, but could not engage in a prolonged struggle without congressional approval. The War Powers Act is controversial and has not proven to be an effective restraint on presidential military adventurism.

War Powers Act
Passed by Congress in 1973; the president is limited in the deployment of troops overseas to a sixty-day period in peacetime (which can be extended for an extra thirty days to permit withdrawal) unless Congress explicitly gives its approval for a longer period.

THE MILITARY-INDUSTRIAL COMPLEX

President Dwight D. Eisenhower, a former general who commanded the allied forces during World War II, warned in his 1961 farewell address that the United States had developed a **military-industrial complex** that included the military and defense industries. This complex, Eisenhower feared, could become an increasingly dominant factor in U.S. politics with "potential for the disastrous rise of misplaced power."[18]

The military-industrial complex has power for several reasons. First, it has economic clout. During the Cold War, as much as 7 percent of the U.S. gross national product was spent on defense. Second, it has access to technical expertise and political information. Third, the military and defense industries share many interests. For example, both benefited economically when tensions between the United States and Soviet Union increased. Fourth, personal and professional relationships between the military and defense industries are close, and many retired military officers go to work for defense industries. Finally, military and defense industry officials work closely with legislators and their staffs. Planned or unplanned, undue influence can accompany close working relations.

military-industrial complex
The grouping of the U.S. armed forces and defense industries.

PARTICIPATION

Economic Sanctions and Cuba

THE NEWS MEDIA

The news media are important to our understanding of foreign and defense policy because media reports provide information on government actions and policy initiatives. From World War II to the Vietnam War, the press tended to support the president in foreign and military policy. As a rule, editors assumed that government statements were true and printed them as fact. In the mid-1960s, this changed as U.S. involvement in Vietnam grew and reporters based in Vietnam realized that the daily military briefings sometimes were untrue. This led many journalists to investigate government statements as opposed to accepting them.

Some observers complain that since the Vietnam War and the Watergate scandal during President Richard M. Nixon's administration, the news media have become too intent on investigating and challenging the government. But, others argue that freedom of the press is a crucial, constitutionally protected right in the United States, and that investigative reporting is critical for a full accounting of government activities.

During the 1991 Persian Gulf War, the military provided the media extensive access to marines in landing ships off the shore of Kuwait. The Pentagon hoped that Iraq would monitor the broadcasts and that the news coverage would convince Iraq to keep its best divisions on the Kuwaiti coast, awaiting the marines while the actual attack came far inland. The ruse worked. Iraq monitored the broadcasts and kept its best divisions on the coast, waiting for the landing that never came. The assault far inland went perfectly. The U.S. government had used the media to gain a military advantage.

More recently, in Iraq, the media broke the news about abuse of prisoners at Abu Ghraib prison by military personnel, launching a public outcry and government in-

Analyzing Visuals

ABU GHRAIB PRISONER ABUSE

Photos of American soldiers demeaning, taunting, and torturing Iraqi detainees in the Abu Ghraib prison shocked the world when they were published in 2004. The resulting scandal led to investigations by both Congress and the Pentagon and a series of trials and guilty verdicts against the alleged abusers, most of whom were young, lower-level soldiers. It has not been determined whether these soldiers were following orders from army personnel higher in the chain of command. All such acts violate the Geneva conventions of warfare, to which the United States adheres. In the photo at right, which quickly became emblematic of the scandal, a hooded detainee is being forced to stand barefoot on a small box and has been hooked up to wires, probably to make the prisoner believe that he is going to be electrocuted. Under what, if any, circumstances should such treatment be condoned? What limits should be placed on American military personnel when they are in charge of detainees in the war on terrorism?

Photo courtesy: The New Yorker Magazine

vestigations. (See Analyzing Visuals: Abu Ghraib Prisoner Abuse.) Media outlets also revealed that the Department of Defense paid Pentagon contractors to plant articles written by American soldiers in Iraqi publications, and in some instances Iraqi journalists were paid to provide positive coverage of conditions in the country and U.S. reconstruction efforts. The Department of Defense has since launched an investigation of this practice because it undermines the concept of a free press in Iraq and distorts the journalistic process into a propaganda effort.[19]

As discussed in chapter 11, the media are able to influence what issues the public thinks about with regard to foreign policy, although it does not necessarily influence people's opinions on those topics except where a person knows little about the issue and has not already formed an opinion. And, even in cases where the media raise public awareness about a topic that leads to a public outcry, the media do not determine policy. For example, despite extensive media coverage, ethnic cleansing in Bosnia and Kosovo went on for years before the United States responded militarily. Our opening vignette in chapter 5 describing government policies toward Darfur also underscores this view.

THE PUBLIC

Public opinion also influences U.S. foreign and defense policy. However, as a rule, the American public is more interested in domestic affairs than foreign and defense policy (see Figure 14.2).

In the United States and other democracies, foreign policy or defense crises generally increase presidential popularity, but sometimes the increase is temporary. Presi-

FIGURE 14.2 THE MOST IMPORTANT PROBLEM: DOMESTIC OR FOREIGN, 1947–2005

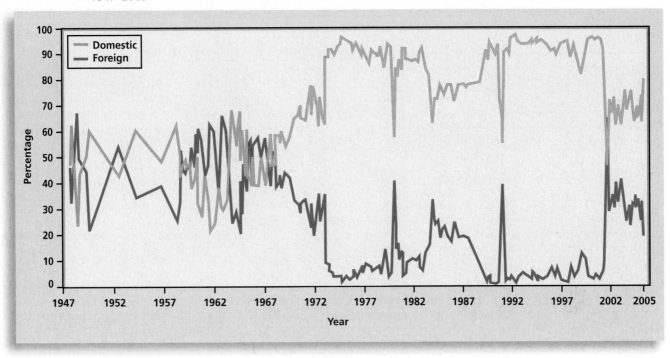

Note: Typical question: "What do you think is the most important problem facing this country today?"

Source: Harold W. Stanley and Richard G. Niemi, eds., *Vital Statistics on American Politics, 2005–2006* (Washington, DC: CQ Press, 2006). Reprinted by permission.

dent George W. Bush's approval ratings skyrocketed from 51 percent to 86 percent shortly after the September 11 terrorist attacks—the largest "rally effect" ever reported by the Gallup polling organization. Bush's popularity remained high during the war in Afghanistan, fell somewhat at the beginning of the war in Iraq in 2003, and then declined significantly as the war dragged on following the president's "Mission Accomplished" declaration in May 2003. By 2006, Bush's job approval rating had fallen to a low of 31 percent. Experts agree that the president's precipitous fall in the polls is due in large part to difficulties in managing growing civil conflict in Iraq and the federal government's poor response to Hurricane Katrina.

In addition to public opinion, the American public affects foreign and defense policy through elections and public action. Political activists especially influence U.S. policy when they join or work with **nongovernmental organizations (NGOs),** international organizations that have members from several countries who seek a set of objectives but are not formally connected to a government. Amnesty International, for example, monitors human rights violations worldwide and seeks to galvanize world opinion to influence the behaviors of oppressive governments.

nongovernmental organization (NGO)
An organization that is not tied to a government.

Twenty-First-Century Challenges

THROUGHOUT THE POST–WORLD WAR II ERA, most Americans agreed that it was in the United States's national interest to attain economic prosperity, defend the homeland, and protect American values. Further, with occasional exceptions such as the Vietnam War, they generally agreed with the policies put into place to attain these interests. In the post–Cold War era, prosperity, homeland defense, and protecting na-

Global Perspective

U.S. FOREIGN POLICY AND THE UNITED NATIONS

Most American presidents have had what amounts to a love-hate relationship with the United Nations (UN) since its creation following World War II. More than one U.S. administration has simultaneously been drawn to the UN and turned its back on it—in large part because of the different perspectives on U.S. foreign policy goals and the role of the UN. The United States sees itself as an international reformer and understands that the UN can be an important ally in democracy promotion. Viewed in this light, the United States and United Nations have similar policy goals: the Declaration of Independence, the U.S. Constitution, and the United Nations' Universal Declaration of Human Rights espouse a commitment to securing freedom, justice, and consensual government as positive human goods.

In March 2006, the Bush administration released its National Security Strategy in which it noted that the goal of U.S. foreign policy is to end tyranny and secure human dignity. To pursue these ends, the president advocated a policy of diplomacy, but with the option of using preemptive military force if diplomatic efforts failed. Similarly, at the end of the Cold War, the United Nations delivered its Agenda for Peace, a 1992 policy statement in which the United Nations declared that its post–Cold War mission is to help secure freedom, justice, and human rights. Though they have congruent goals, the United States and the United Nations are often at odds on how much of a say the United States, the world's one remaining superpower, should have in the UN's peacekeeping missions.

When the UN was founded, it was hoped that the permanent members of the Security Council—the United States, Great Britain, France, China, and the Soviet Union—would be able to work together to keep international peace. This hope was soon dashed by the outbreak of the Cold War. In the mid 1950s, in an effort to lessen the intensity of the Cold War in the developing world and to reestablish a role for itself in settling international disputes, the UN moved forward with the twin ideas of preventive diplomacy and peacekeeping. Before a conflict turned into open fighting, the UN would try to mediate and settle the dispute. If its efforts failed, it could send UN peacekeeping forces to stabilize a situation. The presence of UN peacekeepers, known as "blue helmets," was governed by three rules. First, UN peacekeepers must be invited into a country by its government. Second, they must be neutral in the conflict. Third, they must leave when asked. Both the United States and the Soviet Union were willing to accept the presence of UN peacekeepers as a second-best solution in a conflict. It meant that although neither side had won, neither side had lost to the other.

With the end of the Cold War, U.S.-Soviet rivalry for influence around the world diminished. Conflicts between states and within states, however, continued. Some states devolved into chaos, with citizens caught between warring factions. To address such crises, the UN reworked the ground rules of peacekeeping. Under it, UN blue helmets would not have to be invited into a country by the government or have to leave when asked. Once in a country, they are not expected to be neutral and stay above the conflict. They are there to help bring an end to hostilities and reestablish peace and order. Though the United States provides the bulk of financial and material support, American policy makers believe that other nations can make up for their relative lack of monetary support by providing the necessary troops—and this they in fact do.

As the table highlights, an inherent tension is built into UN peacekeeping efforts. The states that provide the most money for peacekeeping are not those that provide the most troops. Both sets of states believe they should have the major say in how these troops are used.

Top Five Providers of Assessed Contributions to UN Peacekeeping Budget as of January 1, 2006	
United States	27%
Japan	19%
Germany	9%
United Kingdom	7%
France	7%

Top Five Troop Contributors to UN Missions as of March 31, 2006	
Bangladesh	10,255 troops
Pakistan	9,638 troops
India	9,061 troops
Jordan	3,723 troops
Nepal	3,498 troops

Source: United Nations Department of Peacekeeping Operations Fact Sheet, http://www.un.org.

QUESTIONS

1. Who should have the most say in UN peacekeeping operations, those who contribute the money for them or those who provide the personnel? Why?
2. Under what circumstances is the United States likely to support UN interventions? Under what circumstances is the United States likely to pursue its own military solutions?

tional interests remain key elements of U.S. foreign policy. (See Global Perspective: U.S. Foreign Policy and the United Nations.)

Before the September 11 terrorist attacks, there was disagreement about what policies should be adopted to attain these interests. Subsequent consensus regarding

American Values/American Voices

MULTILATERALISM AND UNILATERISM IN AMERICAN FOREIGN POLICY

Since its creation, the United States has considered itself an exceptional nation. Established against great odds, to this day the nation represents a beacon of hope for the oppressed, disenfranchised, or those people simply searching for a better life. The fact that the nation currently reigns as the world's only superpower adds to America's sense of exceptionalism. The conduct of American foreign policy is rooted in the belief that the United States represents a role model for the rest of the world and its values and ideals are universal and worthy of emulation by others. President Ronald Reagan often referred to America as "the shining house on the hill"—an example of what other countries should strive to achieve.

The fall of the Soviet Union and the end of communism in Eastern Europe fueled numerous foreign policies designed to advance democracy and democratic principles abroad. President Bill Clinton emphasized "enlargement of democracy" through the promotion, militarily and economically, of democratic governments around the world. His successor, President George W. Bush, identified "the global expansion of democracy" as a key pillar of American security. In the context of Afghanistan and Iraq, President Bush has vigorously pursued the exportation of democracy as a central component of American foreign policy.

While the presidencies of George Bush, Bill Clinton, and George W. Bush all share an interest in the global promotion of democratic values, compared to his father's presidency and that of Clinton, George W. Bush has relied to a much greater degree on unilateral action to accomplish his foreign policy goals—including the spread of democracy to the Middle East. Whereas his two predecessors emphasized a multilateral approach—what one scholar has called "the preference for seeking international consensus and multilateral implementation of solutions to world problems"— George W. Bush has often pursued a strategy of unilateralism when dealing with global issues—"the preference for seeking *American* solutions to international problems, even if these are at odds with international norms."[a]

The unilateralist approach is evident in the Bush administration's 2001 renunciation of the Kyoto Protocol, an international agreement that commits industrialized nations to reductions in greenhouse emissions; its 2002 refusal to participate in the International Criminal Court despite legal obligations arising from President Clinton's signature on the treaty that established the court; and the 2003 decision to withdraw a resolution requesting United Nations approval for U.S. military action against Saddam Hussein because of international opposition to an American invasion of Iraq. In an address to the nation on March 19, 2003, when preemptive U.S. military action commenced against Iraq, President Bush announced that the United States was acting unilaterally "to disarm Iraq, to free its people, and to defend the world from grave danger." In response to criticism of his go-it-alone approach, Bush declared in his 2004 State of the Union Address that the United States would never ask the international community for a "permission slip" to act in defense of national interests.

Proponents of the unilateralist approach argue that when American interests collide with those of the international community, the United States must be willing to engage in unilateral action in order to protect vital national interests—regardless of the level of opposition to those activities by other countries. Unilateralism provides the president with a great deal more flexibility in crafting and executing foreign policy than does a multilateral approach and is certainly an important option during times of a national emergency. Multilateralism requires a commitment to a process of give-and-take with regard to international consensus building and awareness that the United States will not always be able to dictate the rules of play. Critics of the Bush administration's unilateralist tendencies argue that preemptive military action in Iraq has done little to dampen the nuclear ambitions of Iran and North Korea. During his second administration, Bush has begun to move away from unilateralism and has made diplomatic overtures to Iran and emphasized a multilateral approach to dealing with North Korea's missile tests.

QUESTIONS

1. Under what conditions is a unilateralist approach to the conduct of foreign policy more suitable than a multilateral solution? When might multilateralism be a more suitable approach?
2. Does the United States have a special responsibility to lead the rest of the world, or is it simply one of several important world leaders such as China, Russia, and the European community?

[a]Snow, Donald M. *United States Foreign Policy: Politics Beyond the Water's Edge,* 3rd ed. Belmont, CA: Thomson Wadsworth, 2005.

the need for strong homeland defense and for effective prosecution of the war on terrorism has largely eclipsed earlier debates about which foreign policy to prioritize. Nevertheless, the Bush administration's support of preemptive military action has generated debate about how to address emerging threats. Saber-rattling from North Korea, Iran's quest for enriched uranium, humanitarian crises such as the genocide in

Comparing Foreign and Security Policies

the Darfur region of Sudan, and the reemergence of the Taliban and its regime of violent intimidation in rural regions of Afghanistan are just some examples of continuing major foreign policy problems.

In the twenty-first century, the United States remains the world's only superpower, but it is vulnerable to terrorist attack even as it confronts other foreign and defense policy challenges. How the United States manages homeland defense, the war on terrorism, and appropriate responses to future international crises is the greatest challenge for twenty-first-century U.S. policy makers. Lessons learned from the war in Iraq will likely have a profound influence over how U.S. foreign policy evolves. Notably, most Americans still accept internationalism, multilateralism, moralism, and pragmatism as the basis for U.S. foreign and defense policy. (See American Values/American Voices: Multilateralism and Unilateralism in American Foreign Policy.) Most also recognize that the United States faces foreign policy and defense challenges in addition to terrorism.

Summary

FOREIGN AND MILITARY POLICY making is an important function of the U.S. government. From the earliest days, isolationism, unilateralism, moralism, and pragmatism were central elements of U.S. foreign and military policy. After World War II, foreign and military policy often dominated the American political agenda, and defense spending became one of the biggest items in the national budget. Foreign policy and national defense became major concerns, especially issues such as U.S.-Soviet relations, nuclear weapons, and the Vietnam War. Despite debate, an underlying consensus existed that American policy should focus on containing the Soviet Union. After the Soviet Union collapsed, no immediate consensus emerged on the direction of U.S. foreign policy until the September 11 terrorist attacks elevated homeland defense and the global war on terrorism to the top of the U.S. foreign and defense policy agenda.

Balances found in other parts of the U.S. political system are generally absent in foreign and military policy. The executive branch of government dominates foreign and military policy, with the Departments of State and Defense being particularly important. Within the executive branch, the president predominates.

Institutions outside the executive also play a role in U.S. foreign and military policy. These include Congress, the military-industrial complex, the news media, and the public.

The United States faces major challenges in foreign and military policy during the twenty-first century, especially homeland defense and the global war on terrorism.

KEY TERMS

al-Qaeda, p. 427
Bush Doctrine, p. 428

Carter Doctrine, p. 424
Central Intelligence Agency (CIA), p. 432
Cuban Missile Crisis, p. 422
Department of Defense, p. 432
Department of Homeland Security, p. 433
Department of State, p. 432
détente, p. 423
engagement, p. 425
enlargement, p. 425
human rights, p. 423
Iranian hostage crisis, p. 424
isolationism, p. 420
Joint Chiefs of Staff, p. 432
military-industrial complex, p. 435
moralism, p. 420
National Security Council (NSC), p. 432
Nixon Doctrine, p. 423
nongovernmental organization (NGO), p. 437
North American Free Trade Agreement (NAFTA), p. 427
Powell Doctrine, p. 425
pragmatism, p. 420
Reagan Doctrine, p. 424
Taliban, p. 428
unilateralism, p. 420
United Nations, p. 429
war on terrorism, p. 428
War Powers Act, p. 435
weapons of mass destruction (WMDs), p. 428
World Trade Organization (WTO), p. 427

SELECTED READINGS

Ambrose, Stephen, and Douglas Brinkley (contributor). *Rise to Globalism: American Foreign Policy Since 1938,* 8th ed. New York: Penguin, 1997.

Axelrod, Alan. *American Treaties and Alliances.* Washington, DC: CQ Press, 2000.

Bacevich, Andrew J. *American Empire: The Realities and Consequences of U.S. Diplomacy.* Cambridge: Harvard University Press, 2002.

Boot, Max. *The Savage Wars of Peace: Small Wars and the Rise of American Power.* New York: Basic Books, 2002.

Byman, Daniel, and Matthew C. Waxman. *The Dynamics of Coercion: American Foreign Policy and the Limits of Military Might.* Cambridge: Cambridge University Press, 2002.

Clarke, Richard A. *Against All Enemies: Inside America's War on Terror.* New York: Free Press, 2004.

Ervin, Clark Kent. *Open Target: Where America Is Vulnerable to Attack.* New York: Palgrave Macmillan, 2006.

Forsythe, David P., Patrice C. McMahon, and Andrew Wedeman. *American Foreign Policy in a Globalized World.* New York: Routledge, 2006.

Halberstam, David. *War in a Time of Peace: Bush, Clinton, and the Generals.* New York: Scribner's, 2001.

Hook, Steven W. *U.S. Foreign Policy: The Paradox of World Power.* Washington, DC: CQ Press, 2005.

Howard, Russell D., James J. F. Forest, and Joanne C. Moore, *Homeland Security and Terrorism: Readings and Interpretations.* New York: McGraw Hill, 2006.

Huntington, Samuel P. *The Clash of Civilizations and the Remaking of World Order.* New York: Touchstone, 1998.

Johnson, Loch K. *Seven Sins of American Foreign Policy,* New York: Longman, 2007.

Kissinger, Henry. *Diplomacy.* New York: Touchstone, 1995.

Lowenthal, Mark M. *Intelligence: From Secrets to Policy,* 2nd ed. Washington, DC: CQ Press, 2003.

Mann, Robert A. *A Grand Delusion: America's Descent into Vietnam.* New York: Basic Books, 2001.

Nye, Joseph S., Jr. *The Paradox of American Power: Why the World's Only Superpower Can't Go It Alone.* New York: Oxford University Press, 2002.

———. *The Impact of September 11 on Contemporary International Relations.* New York: Longman, 2003.

Talbott, Strobe, and Nayan Chanda, eds. *The Age of Terror: America and the World After September 11.* New York: Basic Books, 2002.

WEB EXPLORATIONS

To see the reach and worldwide involvement of the United Nations, go to http://www.unsystem.org

To learn more about U.S. military operations around the globe, go to
http://www.defenselink.mil

To learn more about the CIA and the larger intelligence community, go to
http://www.cia.gov

To learn more about key congressional committees in military and foreign affairs, go to
http://www.house.gov/hasc
http://www.senate.gov/~armed_services/
http://www.house.gov/international_relations
http://www.senate.gov/~foreign

To visit the official site of the International Criminal Court, go to
http://www.icc-cpi.int

To learn more about the Kyoto Protocol and its implementation, go to
http://unfccc.int

To learn more about strategic security, nuclear nonproliferation, and weapons of mass destruction, among other national security issues, visit the Federation of American Scientists at
http://www.fas.org

The Declaration of Independence

In Congress, July 4, 1776
The Unanimous Declaration of the Thirteen United States of America

When in the Course of human events it becomes necessary for one people to dissolve the political bands which have connected them with another, and to assume, among the powers of the earth, the separate and equal station to which the Laws of Nature and of Nature's God entitle them, a decent respect to the opinions of mankind requires that they should declare the causes which impel them to the separation.

We hold these truths to be self-evident, that all men are created equal, that they are endowed by their Creator with certain unalienable Rights, that among these are Life, Liberty and the pursuit of Happiness. That to secure these rights, Governments are instituted among Men, deriving their just powers from the consent of the governed. That whenever any Form of Government becomes destructive of these ends, it is the Right of the People to alter or to abolish it, and to institute new Government, laying its foundation on such principles and organizing its powers in such form, as to them shall seem most likely to effect their Safety and Happiness. Prudence, indeed, will dictate that Governments long established should not be changed for light and transient causes; and accordingly all experience hath shewn that mankind are more disposed to suffer, while evils are sufferable, than to right themselves by abolishing the forms to which they are accustomed. But when a long train of abuses and usurpations, pursuing invariably the same Object evinces a design to reduce them under absolute Despotism, it is their right, it is their duty, to throw off such Government, and to provide new Guards for their future security.—Such has been the patient sufferance of these Colonies; and such is now the necessity which constrains them to alter their former Systems of Government. The history of the present King of Great Britain is a history of repeated injuries and usurpations, all having in direct object the establishment of an absolute Tyranny over these States. To prove this, let Facts be submitted to a candid world.

He has refused his Assent to Laws, the most wholesome and necessary for the public good.

He has forbidden his Governors to pass Laws of immediate and pressing importance, unless suspended in their operation till his Assent should be obtained; and when so suspended, he has utterly neglected to attend to them.

He has refused to pass other Laws for the accommodation of large districts of people, unless those people would relinquish the right of Representation in the Legislature, a right inestimable to them and formidable to tyrants only.

He has called together legislative bodies at places unusual, uncomfortable, and distant from the depository of their Public Records, for the sole purpose of fatiguing them into compliance with his measures.

He has dissolved Representative Houses repeatedly, for opposing with manly firmness his invasions on the rights of the people.

He has refused for a long time, after such dissolutions, to cause others to be elected; whereby the Legislative Powers, incapable of Annihilation, have returned to the People at large for their exercise, the State remaining in the mean time exposed to all the dangers of invasion from without, and convulsions within.

He has endeavored to prevent the population of these States; for that purpose obstructing the Laws of Naturalization of Foreigners; refusing to pass others to encourage their migration hither, and raising the conditions of new Appropriations of Lands.

He has obstructed the Administration of Justice, by refusing his Assent to Laws for establishing Judiciary powers.

He has made Judges dependent on his Will alone, for the tenure of their offices, and the amount and payment of their salaries.

He has erected a multitude of New Offices, and sent hither swarms of Officers to harass our people, and eat out their substance.

He has kept among us, in times of peace, Standing Armies without the Consent of our legislatures.

He has affected to render the Military independent of and superior to the Civil power.

He has combined with others to subject us to a jurisdiction foreign to our constitution, and unacknowledged by our laws, giving his Assent to their Acts of pretended Legislation:

For quartering large bodies of armed troops among us:

For protecting them, by a mock Trial, from punishment for any Murders which they should commit on the Inhabitants of these States:

For cutting off our Trade with all parts of the world:

For imposing Taxes on us without our Consent:

For depriving us in many cases, of the benefits of Trial by Jury:

For transporting us beyond Seas to be tried for pretended offences:

For abolishing the free System of English Laws in a neighboring Province, establishing therein an Arbitrary government, and enlarging its Boundaries so as to render it at once an example and fit instrument for introducing the same absolute rule into these Colonies:

For taking away our Charters, abolishing our most valuable Laws, and altering fundamentally the Forms of our Governments:

For suspending our own Legislatures, and declaring themselves invested with power to legislate for us in all cases whatsoever.

He has abdicated Government here, by declaring us out of his Protection and waging War against us.

He has plundered our seas, ravaged our Coasts, burnt out towns, and destroyed the lives of our people.

He is at this time transporting large Armies of foreign Mercenaries to compleat the works of death, desolation and tyranny, already begun with circumstances of Cruelty and perfidy scarcely paralleled in the most barbarous ages, and totally unworthy the Head of a civilized nation.

He has constrained our fellow Citizens taken Captive on the high Seas to bear Arms against their Country, to become the executioners of their friends and Brethren, or to fall themselves by their Hands.

He has excited domestic insurrections amongst us, and has endeavored to bring on the inhabitants of our frontiers, the merciless Indian Savages, whose known rule of warfare, is an undistinguished destruction of all ages, sexes and conditions.

In every stage of these Oppressions We have Petitioned for Redress in the most humble terms: Our repeated Petitions have been answered only by repeated injury: A Prince, whose character is thus marked by every act which may define a Tyrant, is unfit to be the ruler of a free people.

Nor have We been wanting in attention to our British brethren. We have warned them from time to time of attempts by their legislature to extend an unwarrantable jurisdiction over us. We have reminded them of the circumstances of our emigration and settlement here. We have appealed to their native justice and magnanimity; and we have conjured them by the ties of our common kindred to disavow these usurpations, which would inevitably interrupt our connections and correspondence. They too have been deaf to the voice of justice and consanguinity. We must, therefore, acquiesce in the necessity, which denounces our Separation, and hold them, as we hold the rest of mankind, Enemies in War, in Peace Friends.

We, therefore, the Representatives of the United States of America, in General Congress, Assembled, appealing to the Supreme Judge of the world for the rectitude of our intentions, do, in the Name, and by Authority of the good People of these Colonies, solemnly publish and declare, That these United Colonies are, and of Right ought to be Free and Independent States; that they are Absolved from all Allegiance to the British Crown, and that all political connection between them and the State of Great Britain, is and ought to be totally dissolved: and that as Free and Independent States, they have full power to levy War, conclude Peace, contract Alliances, establish Commerce, and to do all other Acts and Things which Independent States may of right do. And for the support of this Declaration, with a firm reliance on the protection of Divine Providence, we mutually pledge to each other our Lives, our Fortunes and our sacred Honor.

JOHN HANCOCK

NEW HAMPSHIRE
Josiah Bartlett
William Whipple
Matthew Thornton

MASSACHUSETTS BAY
Samuel Adams
John Adams
Robert Treat Paine
Elbridge Gerry

RHODE ISLAND
Stephen Hopkins
William Ellery

CONNECTICUT
Roger Sherman
Samuel Huntington
William Williams
Oliver Wolcott

NEW YORK
William Floyd
Philip Livingston
Francis Lewis
Lewis Morris

NEW JERSEY
Richard Stockton
John Witherspoon
Francis Hopkinson
John Hart
Abraham Clark

PENNSYLVANIA
Robert Morris
Benjamin Rush
Benjamin Franklin
John Morton
George Clymer
James Smith
George Taylor
James Wilson
George Ross

DELAWARE
Caesar Rodney
George Read
Thomas McKean

MARYLAND
Samuel Chase
William Paca
Thomas Stone
Charles Carroll

VIRGINIA
George Wythe
Richard Henry Lee
Thomas Jefferson
Benjamin Harrison
Thomas Nelson, Jr.
Francis Lightfoot Lee
Carter Braxton

NORTH CAROLINA
William Hooper
Joseph Hewes
John Penn

SOUTH CAROLINA
Edward Rutledge
Thomas Heyward, Jr.
Thomas Lynch, Jr.
Arthur Middleton

GEORGIA
Button Gwinnett
Lyman Hall
George Walton

Federalist No. 10

November 22, 1787
James Madison

TO THE PEOPLE OF THE STATE OF NEW YORK.

Among the numerous advantages promised by a well constructed Union, none deserves to be more accurately developed than its tendency to break and control the violence of faction. The friend of popular governments, never finds himself so much alarmed for their character and fate, as when he contemplates their propensity to this dangerous vice. He will not fail therefore to set a due value on any plan which, without violating the principles to which he is attached, provides a proper cure for it. The instability, injustice and confusion introduced into the public councils, have in truth been the mortal diseases under which popular governments have every where perished; as they continue to be the favorite and fruitful topics from which the adversaries to liberty derive their most specious declamations. The valuable improvements made by the American Constitutions on the popular models, both ancient and modern, cannot certainly be too much admired; but it would be an unwarrantable partiality, to contend that they have as effectually obviated the danger on this side as was wished and expected. Complaints are every where heard from our most considerate and virtuous citizens, equally the friends of public and private faith, and of public and personal liberty; that our governments are too unstable; that the public good is disregarded in the conflicts of rival parties; and that measures are too often decided, not according to the rules of justice, and the rights of the minor party; but by the superior force of an interested and over-bearing majority. However anxiously we may wish that these complaints had no foundation, the evidence of known facts will not permit us to deny that they are in some degree true. It will be found indeed, on a candid review of our situation, that some of the distresses under which we labor, have been erroneously charged on the operation of our governments; but it will be found, at the same time, that other causes will not alone account for many of our heaviest misfortunes; and particularly, for that prevailing and increasing distrust of public engagements, and alarm for private rights, which are echoed from one end of the continent to the other. These must be chiefly, if not wholly, effects of the unsteadiness and injustice, with which a factious spirit has tainted our public administrations.

By a faction I understand a number of citizens, whether amounting to a majority or minority of the whole, who are united and actuated by some common impulse of passion, or of interest, adverse to the rights of other citizens, or to the permanent and aggregate interests of the community.

There are two methods of curing the mischiefs of faction: the one, by removing its causes; the other, by controlling its effects.

There are again two methods of removing the causes of faction: the one by destroying the liberty which is essential to its existence; the other, by giving to every citizen the same opinions, the same passions, and the same interests.

It could never be more truly said than of the first remedy, that it is worse than the disease. Liberty is to faction, what air is to fire, an aliment without which it instantly expires. But it could not be a less folly to abolish liberty, which is essential to political life, because it nourishes faction, than it would be to wish the annihilation of air, which is essential to animal life, because it imparts to fire its destructive agency.

The second expedient is as impracticable, as the first would be unwise. As long as the reason of man continues fallible, and he is at liberty to exercise it, different opinions will be formed. As long as the connection subsists between his reason and his self-love, his opinions and his passions will have a reciprocal influence on each other; and the former will be objects to which the latter will attach themselves. The diversity in the faculties of men from which the rights of property originate, is not less an insuperable obstacle to a uniformity of interests. The protection of these faculties is the first object of Government. From the protection of different and unequal faculties of acquiring property, the possession of different degrees and kinds of property immediately results: and from the influence of these on the sentiments and views of the respective proprietors, ensues a division of the society into different interests and parties.

The latent causes of faction are thus sown in the nature of man; and we see them every where brought into different degrees of activity, according to the different circumstances of civil society. A zeal for different opinions concerning religion, concerning Government and many other points, as well of speculation as of practice; an attachment to different leaders ambitiously contending for pre-eminence and power; or to persons of other descriptions whose fortunes have been interesting to the human passions, have in turn divided mankind into parties, inflamed them with mutual animosity, and rendered them much more disposed to vex and oppress each other, than to cooperate for their common good. So strong is this propensity of mankind to fall into mutual animosities, that where no substantial occasion presents itself, the most frivolous and fanciful distinctions have been sufficient to kindle their unfriendly passions, and excite their most violent conflicts. But the most common and durable source of factions, has been the various and unequal distribution of property. Those who hold, and those who are without property, have ever formed distinct interests in society. Those who are creditors, and those who are debtors, fall under a like discrimination. A landed interest, a manufacturing interest, a mercantile interest, a monied interest, with many lesser interests, grow up of necessity in civilized nations, and divide them into different classes, actuated by different sentiments and views. The regulation of these various and interfering interests forms the principal task of modern Legislation, and involves the spirit of party and faction in the necessary and ordinary operations of Government.

No man is allowed to be a judge in his own cause; because his interest would certainly bias his judgment, and, not improbably, corrupt his integrity. With equal, nay with greater reason, a body of men, are unfit to be both judges and parties, at the same time; yet, what are many of the most important acts of legislation, but so many judicial determinations, not indeed concerning the rights of single persons, but concerning the rights of large bodies of citizens, and what are the different classes of legislators, but advocates and parties to the causes which they determine? Is a law proposed concerning private debts? It is a question to which the creditors are parties on one side, and the debtors on the other. Justice ought to hold the balance between them. Yet the parties are and must be themselves the judges; and the most numerous party, or, in other words, the most powerful faction must be expected to prevail. Shall domestic manufactures be encouraged, and in what degree, by restrictions on foreign manufactures? are questions which would be differently decided by the landed and the manufacturing classes; and probably by neither, with a sole regard to justice and the public good. The apportionment of taxes on the various descriptions of property, is an act which seems to require the most exact impartiality; yet, there is perhaps no legislative act in which greater opportunity and temptation are given to a predominant party, to trample on the rules of justice. Every shilling with which they over-burden the inferior number, is a shilling saved to their own pockets.

It is in vain to say, that enlightened statesmen will be able to adjust these clashing interests, and render them all subservient to the public good. Enlightened statesmen will not always be at the helm: Nor, in many cases, can such an adjustment be made at all, without taking into view indirect and remote considerations, which will rarely prevail over the immediate interest which one party may find in disregarding the rights of another, or the good of the whole.

The inference to which we are brought, is, that the *causes* of faction cannot be removed; and that relief is only to be sought in the means of controlling its *effects*.

If a faction consists of less than a majority, relief is supplied by the republican principle, which enables the majority to defeat its sinister views by regular vote: It may clog the administration, it may convulse the society; but it will be unable to execute and mask its violence under the forms of the Constitution. When a majority is included in a faction, the form of popular government on the other hand enables it to sacrifice to its ruling passion or interest, both the public good and the rights of other citizens. To secure the public good, and private rights, against the danger of such a faction, and at the same time to preserve the spirit and the form of popular government, is then the great object to which our enquiries are directed: Let me add that it is the great desideratum, by which alone this form of government can be rescued from the opprobrium under which it has so long labored, and be recommended to the esteem and adoption of mankind.

By what means is this object attainable? Evidently by one of two only. Either the existence of the same passion or interest in a majority at the same time, must be prevented; or the majority, having such co-existent passion or interest, must be rendered, by their number and local situation, unable to concert and carry into effect schemes of oppression. If the impulse and the opportunity be suffered to coincide, we well know that neither moral nor religious motives can be relied on as an adequate control. They are not found to be such on the injustice and violence of individuals, and lose their efficacy in proportion to the number combined together; that is, in proportion as their efficacy becomes needful.

From this view of the subject, it may be concluded, that a pure Democracy, by which I mean, a Society, consisting of a small number of citizens, who assemble and administer the Government in person, can admit of no cure for the mischiefs of faction. A common passion or interest will, in almost every case, be felt by a majority of the whole; a communication and concert results from the form of Government itself; and there is nothing to check the inducements to sacrifice the weaker party, or an obnoxious individual. Hence it is, that such Democracies have ever been spectacles of turbulence and contention; have ever been found incompatible with personal security, or the rights of property; and have in general been as short in their lives, as they have been violent in their deaths. Theoretic politicians, who have patronized this species of Government, have erroneously supposed, that by reducing mankind to a perfect equality in their political rights, they would, at the same time, be perfectly equalized and assimilated in their possessions, their opinions, and their passions.

A republic, by which I mean a government in which the scheme of representation takes place, opens a different prospect, and promises the cure for which we are seeking. Let us examine the points in which it varies from pure democracy, and we shall comprehend both the nature of the cure and the efficacy which it must derive from the union.

The two great points of difference, between a democracy and a republic, are, first, the delegation of the government, in the latter, to a small number of citizens, elected by the rest; secondly, the greater number of citizens, and greater sphere of country, over which the latter may be extended.

The effect of the first difference is, on the one hand, to refine and enlarge the public views, by passing them through the medium of a chosen body of citizens, whose wisdom may best discern the true interest of their country, and whose patriotism and love of justice, will be least likely to sacrifice it to temporary or partial considerations. Under such a regulation, it may well happen, that the public voice, pronounced by the representatives of the people, will be more consonant to the public good, than if pronounced by the people themselves, convened for the purpose. On the other hand the effect may be inverted. Men of factious tempers, of local prejudices, or of sinister designs, may by intrigue, by corruption, or by other means, first obtain the suffrages, and then betray the interest of the people. The question resulting is, whether small or extensive republics are most favorable to the election of proper guardians of the public weal, and it is clearly decided in favor of the latter by two obvious considerations.

In the first place, it is to be remarked that, however small the republic may be, the representatives must be raised to a certain number, in order to guard against the cabals of a few; and that however large it may be, they must be limited to a certain number, in order to guard against the confusion of a multitude. Hence, the number of representatives in the two cases not being in proportion to that of the constituents, and being proportionally greatest in the small republic, it follows, that if the proportion of fit characters be not less in the large than in the small republic, the former will present a greater option, and consequently a greater probability of a fit choice.

In the next place, as each Representative will be chosen by a greater number of citizens in the large than in the small Republic, it will be more difficult for unworthy candidates to practise with success the vicious arts, by which elections are too often carried; and the suffrages of the people being more free, will be more likely to center on men who possess the most attractive merit, and the most diffusive and established characters.

It must be confessed, that in this, as in most other cases, there is a mean, on both sides of which inconveniences will be found to lie. By enlarging too much the number of electors, you render the representatives too little acquainted with all their local circumstances and lesser interests; as by reducing it too much, you render him unduly attached to these, and too little fit to comprehend and pursue great and national objects. The Federal Constitution forms a happy combination in this respect; the great and aggregate interests being referred to the national, the local and particular, to the state legislatures.

The other point of difference is, the greater number of citizens and extent of territory which may be brought within the compass of Republican, than of Democratic Government; and it is this circumstance principally which renders factious combinations less to be dreaded in the former, than in the latter. The smaller the society, the fewer probably will be the distinct parties and interests composing it; the fewer the distinct parties and interests, the more frequently will a majority be found of the same party; and the smaller the number of individuals composing a majority, and the smaller the compass within which they are placed, the more easily will they concert and execute their plans of oppression. Extend the sphere, and you take in a greater variety of parties and interests; you make it less probable that a majority of the whole will have a common motive to invade the rights of other citizens; or if such a common motive exists, it will be more difficult for all who feel it to discover their own strength, and to act in unison with each other. Besides other impediments, it may be remarked, that where there is a consciousness of unjust or dishonorable purposes, communication is always checked by distrust, in proportion to the number whose concurrence is necessary.

Hence it clearly appears, that the same advantage, which a Republic has over a Democracy, in controlling the effects of faction, is enjoyed by a large over a small Republic—is enjoyed by the Union over the States composing it. Does this advantage consist in the substitution of Representatives, whose enlightened views and virtuous sentiments render them superior to local prejudices, and to schemes of injustice? It will not be denied, that the Representation of the Union will be most likely to possess these requisite endowments. Does it consist in the greater security afforded by a greater variety of parties, against the event of any one party being able to outnumber and oppress the rest? In an equal degree does the increased variety of parties, comprised within the Union, increase this security? Does it, in fine, consist in the greater obstacles opposed to the concert and accomplishment of the secret wishes of an unjust and interested majority? Here, again, the extent of the Union gives it the most palpable advantage.

The influence of factious leaders may kindle a flame within their particular States, but will be unable to spread a general conflagration through the other States: a religious sect, may degenerate into a political faction in a part of the Confederacy but the variety of sects dispersed over the entire face of it, must secure the national Councils against any danger from that source: a rage for paper money, for an abolition of debts, for an equal division of property, or for any other improper or wicked project, will be less apt to pervade the whole body of the Union, than a particular member of it; in the same proportion as such a malady is more likely to taint a particular county or district, than an entire State.

In the extent and proper structure of the Union, therefore, we behold a Republican remedy for the diseases most incident to Republican Government. And according to the degree of pleasure and pride, we feel in being Republicans, ought to be our zeal in cherishing the spirit, and supporting the character of Federalists.

PUBLIUS

Federalist No. 51

February 6, 1788
James Madison

TO THE PEOPLE OF THE STATE OF NEW YORK.

To what expedient then shall we finally resort for maintaining in practice the necessary partition of power among the several departments, as laid down in the constitution? The only answer that can be given is, that as all these exterior provisions are found to be inadequate, the defect must be supplied, by so contriving the interior structure of the government, as that its several constituent parts may, by their mutual relations, be the means of keeping each other in their proper places. Without presuming to undertake a full development of this important idea, I will hazard a few general observations, which may perhaps place it in a clearer light, and enable us to form a more correct judgment of the principles and structure of the government planned by the convention.

In order to lay a due foundation for that separate and distinct exercise of the different powers of government, which to a certain extent, is admitted on all hands to be essential to the preservation of liberty, it is evident that each department should have a will of its own; and consequently should be so constituted, that the members of each should have as little agency as possible in the appointment of the members of the others. Were this principle rigorously adhered to, it would require that all the appointments for the supreme executive, legislative, and judiciary magistracies, should be drawn from the same fountain of authority, the people, through channels, having no communication whatever with one another. Perhaps such a plan of constructing the several departments would be less difficult in practice than it may in contemplation appear. Some difficulties however, and some additional expense, would attend the execution of it. Some deviations therefore from the principle must be admitted. In the constitution of the judiciary department in particular, it might be inexpedient to insist rigorously on the principle; first, because peculiar qualifications being essential in the members, the primary consideration ought to be to select that mode of choice, which best secures these qualifications; secondly, because the permanent tenure by which the appointments are held in that department, must soon destroy all sense of dependence on the authority conferring them.

It is equally evident that the members of each department should be as little dependent as possible on those of the others, for the emoluments annexed to their offices. Were the executive magistrate, or the judges, not independent of the legislature in this particular, their independence in every other would be merely nominal.

But the great security against a gradual concentration of the several powers in the same department, consists in giving to those who administer each department, the necessary constitutional means, and personal motives, to resist encroachments of the others. The provision for defense must in this, as in all other cases, be made commensurate to the danger of attack. Ambition must be made to counteract ambition. The interest of the man must be connected with the constitutional right of the place. It may be a reflection on human nature, that such devices should be necessary to control the abuses of government. But what is government itself but the greatest of all reflections on human nature? If men were angels, no government would be necessary. If angels were to govern men, neither external nor internal controls on government would be necessary. In framing a government which is to be administered by men over men, the great difficulty lies in this: You must first enable the government to control the governed; and in the next place, oblige it to control itself. A dependence on the people is no doubt the primary control on the government; but experience has taught mankind the necessity of auxiliary precautions.

This policy of supplying by opposite and rival interests, the defect of better motives, might be traced through the whole system of human affairs, private as well as public. We see it particularly displayed in all the subordinate distributions of power; where the constant aim is to divide and arrange the several offices in such a manner as that each may be a check on the other; that the private interest of every individual, may be a sentinel over the public rights. These inventions of prudence cannot be less requisite in the distribution of the supreme powers of the state.

But it is not possible to give to each department an equal power of self defense. In republican government the legislative authority, necessarily, predominates. The remedy for this inconveniency is, to divide the legislature into different branches; and to render them by different modes of election, and different principles of action, as little connected with each other, as the nature of their common functions, and their common dependence on the society, will admit. It may even be necessary to guard against dangerous encroachments by still further precautions. As the weight of the legislative authority requires that it should be thus divided, the weakness of the executive may require, on the other hand, that it should be fortified. An absolute negative, on the legislature, appears at first view to be the natural defense with which the executive magistrate should be armed. But perhaps it would be neither altogether safe, nor alone sufficient. On ordinary occasions, it might not be exerted with the requisite firmness; and on extraordinary occasions, it might be perfidiously abused. May not this defect of an absolute negative be supplied, by some qualified connection between this weaker department, and the weaker branch of the stronger department, by which the latter may be led to support the constitutional rights of the former, without being too much detached from the rights of its own department? If the principles on which these observations are founded be just, as I persuade myself they are, and they be applied as a criterion, to the several state constitutions, and to the federal constitution, it will be found, that if the latter does not perfectly correspond with them, the former are infinitely less able to bear such a test.

There are moreover two considerations particularly applicable to the federal system of America, which place that system in a very interesting point of view.

First. In a single republic, all the power surrendered by the people, is submitted to the administration of a single government; and usurpations are guarded against by a division of the government into distinct and separate departments. In the compound republic of America, the power surrendered by the people, is first divided between two distinct governments, and then the portion allotted to each, subdivided among distinct and separate departments. Hence a double security arises to the rights of the people. The different governments will control each other; at the same time that each will be controlled by itself.

Second. It is of great importance in a republic, not only to guard the society against the oppression of its rulers; but to guard one part of the society against the injustice of the other part. Different interests necessarily exist in different classes of citizens. If a majority be united by a common interest, the rights of the minority will be insecure. There are but two methods of providing against this evil: The one by creating a will in the community independent of the majority, that is, of the society itself, the other by comprehending in the society so many separate descriptions of citizens, as will render an unjust combination of a majority of the whole, very improbable, if not impracticable. The first method prevails in all governments possessing an hereditary or self appointed authority. This at best is but a precarious security; because a power independent of the society may as well espouse the unjust views of the major, as the rightful interests, of the minor party, and may possibly be turned against both parties. The second method will be exemplified in the federal republic of the United States. While all authority in it will be derived from and dependent on the society, the society itself will be broken into so many parts, interests and classes of citizens, that

the rights of individuals or of the minority, will be in little danger from interested combinations of the majority. In a free government, the security for civil rights must be the same as for religious rights. It consists in the one case in the multiplicity of interests, and in the other, in the multiplicity of sects. The degree of security in both cases will depend on the number of interests and sects; and this may be presumed to depend on the extent of country and number of people comprehended under the same government. This view of the subject must particularly recommend a proper federal system to all the sincere and considerate friends of republican government: Since it shows that in exact proportion as the territory of the union may be formed into more circumscribed confederacies or states, oppressive combinations of a majority will be facilitated, the best security under the republican form, for the rights of every class of citizens, will be diminished; and consequently, the stability and independence of some member of the government, the only other security, must be proportionally increased. Justice is the end of government. It is the end of civil society. It ever has been, and ever will be pursued, until it be obtained, or until liberty be lost in the pursuit. In a society under the forms of which the stronger faction can readily unite and oppress the weaker, anarchy may as truly be said to reign, as in a state of nature where the weaker individual is not secured against the violence of the stronger: And as in the latter state even the stronger individuals are prompted by the uncertainty of their condition, to submit to a government which may protect the weak as well as themselves: So in the former state, will the more powerful factions or parties be gradually induced by a like motive, to wish for a government which will protect all parties, the weaker as well as the more powerful. It can be little doubted, that if the state of Rhode Island was separated from the confederacy, and left to itself, the insecurity of rights under the popular form of government within such narrow limits, would be displayed by such reiterated oppressions of factious majorities, that some power altogether independent of the people would soon be called for by the voice of the very factions whose misrule had proved the necessity of it. In the extended republic of the United States, and among the great variety of interests, parties and sects which it embraces, a coalition of a majority of the whole society could seldom take place on any other principles than those of justice and the general good; and there being thus less danger to a minor from the will of the major party, there must be less pretext also, to provide for the security of the former, by introducing into the government a will not dependent on the latter; or in other words, a will independent of the society itself. It is no less certain than it is important, notwithstanding the contrary opinions which have been entertained, that the larger the society, provided it lie within a practicable sphere, the more duly capable it will be of self government. And happily for the *republican cause,* the practicable sphere may be carried to a very great extent, by a judicious modification and mixture of the *federal principle.*

PUBLIUS

Presidents, Congresses, and Chief Justices: 1789–2007

Term	President and Vice President	Party of President	Congress	Majority Party		Chief Justice of the United States
				House	Senate	
1789–1797	**George Washington** John Adams	None	1st 2nd 3rd 4th	(N/A) (N/A) (N/A) (N/A)	(N/A) (N/A) (N/A) (N/A)	John Jay (1789–1795) John Rutledge (1795) Oliver Ellsworth (1796–1800)
1797–1801	**John Adams** Thomas Jefferson	Federalist	5th 6th	(N/A) Fed	(N/A) Fed	Oliver Ellsworth (1796–1800) John Marshall (1801–1835)
1801–1809	**Thomas Jefferson** Aaron Burr (1801–1805) George Clinton (1805–1809)	Democratic-Republican	7th 8th 9th 10th	Dem-Rep Dem-Rep Dem-Rep Dem-Rep	Dem-Rep Dem-Rep Dem-Rep Dem-Rep	John Marshall (1801–1835)
1809–1817	**James Madison** George Clinton (1809–1812)[a] Elbridge Gerry (1813–1814)[a]	Democratic-Republican	11th 12th 13th 14th	Dem-Rep Dem-Rep Dem-Rep Dem-Rep	Dem-Rep Dem-Rep Dem-Rep Dem-Rep	John Marshall (1801–1835)
1817–1825	**James Monroe** Daniel D. Tompkins	Democratic-Republican	15th 16th 17th 18th	Dem-Rep Dem-Rep Dem-Rep Dem-Rep	Dem-Rep Dem-Rep Dem-Rep Dem-Rep	John Marshall (1801–1835)
1825–1829	**John Quincy Adams** John C. Calhoun	National-Republican	19th 20th	Nat'l Rep Dem	Nat'l Rep Dem	John Marshall (1801–1835)
1829–1837	**Andrew Jackson** John C. Calhoun (1829–1832)[c] Martin Van Buren (1833–1837)	Democratic	21st 22nd 23rd 24th	Dem Dem Dem Dem	Dem Dem Dem Dem	John Marshall (1801–1835) Roger B. Taney (1836–1864)
1837–1841	**Martin Van Buren** Richard M. Johnson	Democratic	25th 26th	Dem Dem	Dem Dem	Roger B. Taney (1836–1864)
1841	**William H. Harrison**[a] John Tyler (1841)	Whig				Roger B. Taney (1836–1864)
1841–1845	**John Tyler** (VP vacant)	Whig	27th 28th	Whig Dem	Whig Whig	Roger B. Taney (1836–1864)
1845–1849	**James K. Polk** George M. Dallas	Democratic	29th 30th	Dem Whig	Dem Dem	Roger B. Taney (1836–1864)
1849–1850	**Zachary Taylor**[a] Millard Fillmore	Whig	31st	Dem	Dem	Roger B. Taney (1836–1864)

Term	President and Vice President	Party of President	Congress	Majority Party		Chief Justice of the United States
				House	Senate	
1850–1853	**Millard Fillmore** (VP vacant)	Whig	32nd	Dem	Dem	Roger B. Taney (1836–1864)
1853–1857	**Franklin Pierce** William R. D. King (1853)[a]	Democratic	33rd 34th	Dem Rep	Dem Dem	Roger B. Taney (1836–1864)
1857–1861	**James Buchanan** John C. Breckinridge	Democratic	35th 36th	Dem Rep	Dem Dem	Roger B. Taney (1836–1864)
1861–1865	**Abraham Lincoln**[a] Hannibal Hamlin (1861–1865) Andrew Johnson (1865)	Republican	37th 38th	Rep Rep	Rep Rep	Roger B. Taney (1836–1864) Salmon P. Chase (1864–1873)
1865–1869	**Andrew Johnson** (VP vacant)	Republican	39th 40th	Union Rep	Union Rep	Salmon P. Chase (1864–1873)
1869–1877	**Ulysses S. Grant** Schuyler Colfax (1869–1873) Henry Wilson (1873–1875)[a]	Republican	41st 42nd 43rd 44th	Rep Rep Rep Dem	Rep Rep Rep Rep	Salmon P. Chase (1864–1873) Morrison R. Waite (1874–1888)
1877–1881	**Rutherford B. Hayes** William A. Wheeler	Republican	45th 46th	Dem Dem	Rep Dem	Morrison R. Waite (1874–1888)
1881	**James A. Garfield**[a] Chester A. Arthur	Republican	47th	Rep	Rep	Morrison R. Waite (1874–1888)
1881–1885	**Chester A. Arthur** (VP vacant)	Republican	48th	Dem	Rep	Morrison R. Waite (1874–1888)
1885–1889	**Grover Cleveland** Thomas A. Hendricks (1885)[a]	Democratic	49th 50th	Dem Dem	Rep Rep	Morrison R. Waite (1874–1888) Melville W. Fuller (1888–1910)
1889–1893	**Benjamin Harrison** Levi P. Morton	Republican	51st 52nd	Rep Dem	Rep Rep	Melville W. Fuller (1888–1910)
1893–1897	**Grover Cleveland** Adlai E. Stevenson	Democratic	53rd 54th	Dem Rep	Dem Rep	Melville W. Fuller (1888–1910)
1897–1901	**William McKinley**[a] Garret A. Hobart (1897–1899)[a] Theodore Roosevelt (1901)	Republican	55th 56th	Rep Rep	Rep Rep	Melville W. Fuller (1888–1910)
1901–1909	**Theodore Roosevelt** (VP vacant, 1901–1905) Charles W. Fairbanks (1905–1909)	Republican	57th 58th 59th 60th	Rep Rep Rep Rep	Rep Rep Rep Rep	Melville W. Fuller (1888–1910)
1909–1913	**William Howard Taft** James S. Sherman (1909–1912)[a]	Republican	61st 62nd	Rep Dem	Rep Rep	Melville W. Fuller (1888–1910) Edward D. White (1910–1921)
1913–1921	**Woodrow Wilson** Thomas R. Marshall	Democratic	63rd 64th 65th 66th	Dem Dem Dem Rep	Dem Dem Dem Rep	Edward D. White (1910–1921)
1921–1923	**Warren G. Harding**[a] Calvin Coolidge	Republican	67th	Rep	Rep	William Howard Taft (1921–1930)
1923–1929	**Calvin Coolidge** (VP vacant, 1923–1925) Charles G. Dawes (1925–1929)	Republican	68th 69th 70th	Rep Rep Rep	Rep Rep Rep	William Howard Taft (1921–1930)
1929–1933	**Herbert Hoover** Charles Curtis	Republican	71st 72nd	Rep Dem	Rep Rep	William Howard Taft (1921–1930) Charles Evans Hughes (1930–1941)

Term	President and Vice President	Party of President	Congress	Majority Party		Chief Justice of the United States
				House	Senate	
1933–1945	**Franklin D. Roosevelt**[a] John Nance Garner (1933–1941) Henry A. Wallace (1941–1945) Harry S Truman (1945)	Democratic	73rd 74th 75th 76th 77th 78th	Dem Dem Dem Dem Dem Dem	Dem Dem Dem Dem Dem Dem	Charles Evans Hughes (1930–1941) Harlan F. Stone (1941–1946)
1945–1953	**Harry S Truman** (VP vacant, 1945–1949) Alben W. Barkley (1949–1953)	Democratic	79th 80th 81st 82nd	Dem Rep Dem Dem	Dem Rep Dem Dem	Harlan F. Stone (1941–1946) Frederick M. Vinson (1946–1953)
1953–1961	**Dwight D. Eisenhower** Richard M. Nixon	Republican	83rd 84th 85th 86th	Rep Dem Dem Dem	Rep Dem Dem Dem	Frederick M. Vinson (1946–1953) Earl Warren (1953–1969)
1961–1963	**John F. Kennedy**[a] Lyndon B. Johnson (1961–1963)	Democratic	87th	Dem	Dem	Earl Warren (1953–1969)
1963–1969	**Lyndon B. Johnson** (VP vacant, 1963–1965) Hubert H. Humphrey (1965–1969)	Democratic	88th 89th 90th	Dem Dem Dem	Dem Dem Dem	Earl Warren (1953–1969)
1969–1974	**Richard M. Nixon**[b] Spiro Agnew (1969–1973)[c] Gerald R. Ford (1973–1974)[d]	Republican	91st 92nd	Dem Dem	Dem Dem	Earl Warren (1953–1969) Warren E. Burger (1969–1986)
1974–1977	**Gerald R. Ford** Nelson A. Rockefeller[d]	Republican	93rd 94th	Dem Dem	Dem Dem	Warren E. Burger (1969–1986)
1977–1981	**Jimmy Carter** Walter Mondale	Democratic	95th 96th	Dem Dem	Dem Dem	Warren E. Burger (1969–1986)
1981–1989	**Ronald Reagan** George Bush	Republican	97th 98th 99th 100th	Dem Dem Dem Dem	Rep Rep Rep Dem	Warren E. Burger (1969–1986) William H. Rehnquist (1986–2005)
1989–1993	**George Bush** Dan Quayle	Republican	101st 102nd	Dem Dem	Dem Dem	William H. Rehnquist (1986–2005)
1993–2001	**Bill Clinton** Al Gore	Democratic	103rd 104th 105th 106th	Dem Rep Rep Rep	Dem Rep Rep Rep	William H. Rehnquist (1986–2005)
2001–2009	**George W. Bush** Dick Cheney	Republican	107th 108th 109th 110th	Rep Rep Rep Dem	Dem Rep Rep Dem	William H. Rehnquist (1986–2005) John G. Roberts Jr. (2005–)

[a]Died in office.
[b]Resigned from the presidency.
[c]Resigned from the vice presidency.
[d]Appointed vice president.

Selected Supreme Court Cases

- *Agostini* v. *Felton* (1997): The Court agreed to permit public school teachers to go into parochial schools during school hours to provide remedial education to disadvantaged students because it was not an excessive entanglement of church and state.

- *Ashcroft* v. *Free Speech Coalition* (2002): The Court ruled that the Child Online Protection Act of 1998 was unconstitutional because it was too vague in its reliance on "community standards" to define what is harmful to minors.

- *Atkins* v. *Virginia* (2002): Execution of the mentally retarded is prohibited by the Eighth Amendment's cruel and unusual punishment clause.

- *Ayotte* v. *Planned Parenthood of Northern New England* (2006): A New Hampshire abortion law that did not provide an exception for the woman's health was unconstitutional.

- *Batson* v. *Kentucky* (1986): Peremptory challenges cannot be used to exclude all people of a given race (in this case, African Americans) from a jury pool.

- *Benton* v. *Maryland* (1969): Incorporated the Fifth Amendment's double jeopardy clause.

- *Board of Regents* v. *Southworth* (2000): Unanimous ruling from the Supreme Court which stated that public universities could charge students a mandatory activities fee that could be used to facilitate extracurricular student political speech so long as the programs are neutral in their application.

- *Bowers* v. *Hardwick* (1986): Unsuccessful attempt to challenge Georgia's sodomy law. The case was overturned by *Lawrence* v. *Texas* in 2003.

- *Brandenburg* v. *Ohio* (1969): The Court fashioned the direct incitement test for deciding whether certain kinds of speech could be regulated by the government. This test holds that advocacy of illegal action is protected by the First Amendment unless imminent action is intended and likely to occur.

- *Brown* v. *Board of Education* (1954): Supreme Court decision holding that school segregation is inherently unconstitutional because it violates the Fourteenth Amendment's guarantee of equal protection; marked the end of legal segregation in the United States.

- *Brown* v. *Board of Education II* (1955): Follow-up to *Brown* v. *Board of Education*, this case laid out the process for school desegregation and established the concept of dismantling segregationist systems "with all deliberate speed."

- *Brown University* v. *Cohen* (1997): Landmark Title IX case that put all colleges and universities on notice that discrimination against women would not be tolerated, even when, as in the case of Brown University, the university had tremendously expanded sports opportunities for women.

- *Buckley* v. *Valeo* (1976): The Court ruled that money spent by an individual or political committee in support or opposition of a candidate (but independent of the candidate's campaign) was a form of symbolic speech, and therefore could not be limited under the First Amendment.

- *Bush* v. *Gore* (2000): Controversial 2000 election case that made the final decision on the Florida recounts, and thus determined the result of the 2000 election.

- *Cantwell* v. *Connecticut* (1940): The case in which the Supreme Court incorporated the freedom of religion, ruling that the freedom to believe is absolute, but the freedom to act is subject to the regulation of society.

- *Chicago, B&Q R.R. Co.* v. *Chicago* (1897): Incorporated the Fifth Amendment's just compensation clause.

- *Civil Rights Cases* (1883): Name attached to five cases brought under the Civil Rights Act of 1875. In 1883, the Supreme Court decided that discrimination in a variety of public accommodations, including theaters, hotels, and railroads, could not be prohibited by the act because it was private and not state discrimination.

- *Clinton* v. *City of New York* (1998): The Court ruled that the line-item veto was unconstitutional because it gave powers to the president denied him by the U.S. Constitution.

- *Colorado Republican Federal Campaign Committee* v. *Federal Election Commission* (1996): The Supreme Court extended its ruling in *Buckley* v. *Valeo* to also include political parties.

- *Cooper* v. *Aaron* (1958): Case wherein the Court broke with tradition and issued a unanimous decision against the Little Rock School Board, ruling that the district's evasive schemes to avoid the *Brown II* decision were illegal.

- *Craig* v. *Boren* (1976): The Court ruled that keeping drunk drivers off the roads may be an important governmental objective, but allowing women aged eighteen to twenty-one to drink alcoholic beverages while prohibiting men of the same age from drinking is not substantially related to that goal.

- *DeJonge* v. *Oregon* (1937): Incorporated the First Amendment's right to freedom of assembly.

- *Dred Scott* v. *Sandford* (1857): Concluded that the U.S. Congress lacked the constitutional authority to bar slavery in the territories; this decision narrowed the scope of national power while it enhanced that of the states. This case marks the first time since *Marbury* v. *Madison* that the Supreme Court found an act of Congress unconstitutional.

- *Duncan* v. *Louisiana* (1968): Incorporated the Sixth Amendment's trial by jury clause.

- *Furman* v. *Georgia* (1972): The Supreme Court used this case to end capital punishment, at least in the short run. (The case was overturned by *Gregg* v. *Georgia* in 1976.)

- *Garcia* v. *San Antonio Metropolitan Transport Authority* (1985): In this case, the court ruled that Congress has the broad power to impose its will on state and local governments, even in areas that have traditionally been left to state and local discretion.

- *Georgia* v. *Randolph* (2006): The Court ruled that both residents of a home must consent to a search before that search is regarded as constitutional.

- *Gibbons* v. *Ogden* (1824): The Court upheld broad congressional power over interstate commerce.

- *Gideon* v. *Wainwright* (1963): Granted indigents the right to counsel.

- *Gitlow* v. *New York* (1925): Incorporated the free speech clause of the First Amendment, ruling that the states were not completely free to limit forms of political expression.

- *Gonzales* v. *O Centro Espirita Beneficente União do Vegetal* (2006): Under the Religious Freedom Restoration Act, the government has to make an exception to the Controlled Substances Act for a substance used in religious services.

- *Gonzales* v. *Raich* (2005): Upheld power of Congress to ban and prosecute the possession and use of marijuana for medical purposes, even in states that permitted it.

- *Gregg* v. *Georgia* (1976): Overturning *Furman* v. *Georgia*, the case ruled that Georgia's rewritten death penalty statute is constitutional.

- *Griswold* v. *Connecticut* (1965): Supreme Court case that established the Constitution's implied right to privacy.

- *Grutter* v. *Bollinger* (2003): The Court voted to uphold the constitutionality of the University of Michigan law school's affirmative action policy, which gave preference to minority students.

- *Hamdan* v. *Rumsfeld* (2006): The Court ruled that detainees in the war on terrorism were entitled to the protections of the Geneva Convention and the procedural rights of the Uniform Code of Military Justice, since Congress had not approved of President George W. Bush's system of military tribunals. Congress passed the Military Commissions Act in 2006 to address the Court's ruling in *Hamdan*.

- *Hamdi et al* v. *Rumsfeld* (2004): The government does not have the authority to detain a U.S. citizen charged as an enemy combatant in the war on terrorism without providing basic due process protections under the Fifth Amendment.

- *Harris* v. *Forklift Systems* (1993): The Court ruled that a federal civil rights law created a "broad rule of workplace equality."

- *Hill* v. *McDonough* (2006): Challenging the form of execution prescribed in a defendant's sentence is not a proper use of a *habeas corpus* petition.

- *House* v. *Bell* (2006): A Tennessee death-row inmate who had otherwise exhausted his federal appeals was provided an exception due to the availability of DNA evidence suggesting his innocence; the case recognized the potential exculpatory power of DNA evidence.

- *Kelo* v. *New London* (2004): The Court ruled that government could take private property and then sell it to private developers so long as that property was slated for economic development that would benefit the surrounding community.

- *Klopfer* v. *North Carolina* (1967): Incorporated the Sixth Amendment's right to a speedy trial.

- *Korematsu* v. *U.S.* (1944): In this case, the Court ruled that the internment of Japanese Americans during World War II was not unconstitutional.

- *Lawrence* v. *Texas* (2003): The Court reversed its 1986 ruling in *Bowers* v. *Hardwick* by finding a Texas statute that banned sodomy to be unconstitutional.

- *League of United Latin American Citizens et al.* v. *Perry* (2006): Part of the 2004 Texas redistricting plan violated the Voting Rights Act because it deprived Hispanic citizens of the right to elect a representative of their choosing.

- *Lemon* v. *Kurtzman* (1971): The Court determined that direct government assistance to religious schools is unconstitutional. In the majority opinion, the Court created what has become known as the "Lemon Test" for deciding if a law is in violation of the establishment clause.

- *Malloy* v. *Hogan* (1964): Incorporated the Fifth Amendment's self-incrimination clause.

- *Mapp* v. *Ohio* (1961): Incorporated a portion of the Fourth Amendment by establishing that illegally obtained evidence cannot be used at trial.

- *Marbury* v. *Madison* (1803): Case in which the Court first asserted the power of judicial review in finding that a congressional statute extending the Court's original jurisdiction was unconstitutional.

- *McConnell* v. *FEC* (2003): Generally speaking, the Bipartisan Campaign Finance Reform Act of 2002 does not violate the First Amendment.

- *McCreary County* v. *ACLU of Kentucky* (2005): The Court ruled that the display of the Ten Commandments in public schools and courthouses violated the establishment clause.

- *McCulloch* v. *Maryland* (1819): The Court upheld the power of the national government and denied the right of a state to tax the bank. The Court's broad interpretation of the necessary and proper clause paved the way for later rulings upholding expansive federal powers.

- *Miller* v. *California* (1973): Case wherein the Supreme Court began to formulate rules designed to make it easier for states to regulate obscene materials and to return to communities a greater role in determining what is obscene.

- *Miranda* v. *Arizona* (1966): The Fifth Amendment requires that individuals arrested for a crime must be advised of their right to remain silent and to have counsel present.

- *Muller* v. *Oregon* (1908): Case that ruled Oregon's law barring women from working more than ten hours a day was constitutional; also an attempt to define women's unique status as mothers to justify their differential treatment.

- *Near* v. *Minnesota* (1931): By ruling that a state law violated the freedom of the press, the Supreme Court incorporated the free press provision of the First Amendment.

- *New York Times Co.* v. *Sullivan* **(1964):** Supreme Court ruling that simply publishing a defamatory falsehood is not enough to justify a libel judgment. "Actual malice" must be proved to support a finding of libel against a public figure.

- *New York Times Co.* v. *U.S.* **(1971):** Also called the Pentagon Papers case; the Supreme Court ruled that any attempt by the government to prevent expression carried "a heavy presumption" against its constitutionality.

- *In re Oliver* **(1948):** Incorporated the Sixth Amendment's right to a public trial.

- *Palko* v. *Connecticut* **(1937):** Set the Court's rationale of selective incorporation, a judicial doctrine whereby most but not all of the protections found in the Bill of Rights are made applicable to the states via the Fourteenth Amendment.

- *Parker* v. *Gladden* **(1966):** Incorporated the Sixth Amendment's right to an impartial trial.

- *Planned Parenthood* v. *Casey* **(1992):** This case was an unsuccessful attempt to challenge Pennsylvania's restrictive abortion regulations.

- *Plessy* v. *Ferguson* **(1896):** *Plessy* challenged a Louisiana statute requiring that railroads provide separate accommodations for blacks and whites. The Court found that separate but equal accommodations did not violate the equal protection clause of the Fourteenth Amendment.

- *Pointer* v. *Texas* **(1965):** Incorporated the Sixth Amendment's right to confrontation of witnesses.

- *Quilici* v. *Village of Morton Grove* **(1983):** The Supreme Court refused to review a lower court's ruling upholding the constitutionality of a local ordinance banning handguns against a Second Amendment challenge.

- *Regents of the University of California* v. *Bakke* **(1978):** A sharply divided Court concluded that the university's rejection of Bakke as a student had been illegal because the use of strict affirmative action quotas was inappropriate.

- *Reno* v. *American Civil Liberties Union* **(1997):** The Court ruled that the 1996 Communications Decency Act prohibiting transfer of obscene or indecent materials over the Internet to minors violated the First Amendment because it was too vague and overbroad.

- *Reynolds* v. *Sims* **(1964):** The Court decided that every person should have an equally weighted vote in electing governmental representatives.

- *Robinson* v. *California* **(1962):** Incorporated the Eighth Amendment's right to freedom from cruel and unusual punishment.

- *Roe* v. *Wade* **(1973):** The Supreme Court found that a woman's right to an abortion was protected by the right to privacy that could be implied from specific guarantees found in the Bill of Rights and the Fourteenth Amendment.

- *Romer* v. *Evans* **(1996):** A Colorado constitutional amendment precluding any legislative, executive, or judicial action at any state or local level designed to bar discrimination based on sexual preference was ruled not rational or reasonable.

- *Tennessee* v. *Lane* **(2004):** Upheld application of the Americans with Disabilities Act to state courthouses.

- *Texas* v. *Johnson* **(1989):** The Court overturned the conviction of a Texas man found guilty of setting fire to an American flag.

- *U.S.* v. *Miller* **(1939):** The last time the Supreme Court addressed the constitutionality of the Second Amendment; ruled that the amendment was only intended to protect a citizen's right to own ordinary militia weapons.

- *U.S.* v. *Morrison* **(2000):** The Court ruled that Congress has no authority under the commerce clause to enact a provision of the Violence Against Women Act providing a federal remedy to victims of gender-motivated violence.

- *U.S. v. Nixon* **(1974):** In a case involving President Richard M. Nixon's refusal to turn over tape recordings of his conversations, the Court ruled that executive privilege does not grant the president an absolute right to secure all presidential documents.

- *Webster v. Reproductive Health Services* **(1989):** In upholding several restrictive abortion regulations, the Court opened the door for state governments to enact new restrictions on abortion.

- *Weeks v. U.S.* **(1914):** Case wherein the Supreme Court adopted the exclusionary rule, which bars the use of illegally obtained evidence at trial.

- *Wolf v. Colorado* **(1949):** The Court ruled that illegally obtained evidence did not necessarily have to be eliminated from use during trial.

- *Zelman v. Simmons-Harris* **(2002):** The Court concluded that governments can give money to parents to allow them to send their children to private or religious schools.

★★★ Notes

CHAPTER 1

1. Thomas Byrne Edsall, "The Era of Bad Feelings," *Civilization* (March/April 1996): 37.
2. Jack C. Plano and Milton Greenberg, *The American Political Dictionary*, 6th ed. (New York: Holt, Rinehart and Winston, 1982).
3. The United States Agency for International Development, "Agency Objectives: Civil Society."
4. Susan A. MacManus, *Young v. Old: Generational Combat in the 21st Century* (Boulder, CO: Westview Press, 1995), 3.
5. Dennis Cauchon, "Who Will Take Care of an Older Population?" *USA Today* (October 25, 2005): 1–2B.
6. FOX News/Opinion Dynamics Poll, April 6, 2006, Lexis-Nexis RPOLL.
7. CBS News Poll, February 27, 2006, http://www.cbsnews.com.
8. Terrence Ball and Richard Dagger, *Political Ideologies and the Democratic Ideal* (New York: Longman, 2004), 2.
9. Isaiah Berlin, *The Crooked Timber of Humanity: Chapters in the History of Ideas* (New York: Vintage, 1992), 1.
10. Jack C. Plano and Milton Greenberg, *The American Political Dictionary*, 9th ed. (Fort Worth, TX: Harcourt Brace, 1993), 16.
11. Philip E. Converse, "The Nature of Belief Systems in Mass Publics," in David E. Apter, ed., *Ideology and Discontent* (New York: Free Press, 1964), 206–21.
12. Roper Center for Public Opinion Research, University of Connecticut, June 29, 2005, Lexis-Nexis RPOLL.

CHAPTER 2

1. See Richard B. Bernstein with Jerome Agel, *Amending America* (New York: New York Times Books, 1993), 138–40.
2. *Oregon* v. *Mitchell*, 400 U.S. 112 (1970).
3. Bernstein with Agel, *Amending America*, 139.
4. For an account of the early development of the colonies, see D. W. Meining, *The Shaping of America*, vol. 1: *Atlantic America, 1492–1800* (New Haven, CT: Yale University Press, 1986).
5. For an excellent chronology of the events leading up to the writing of the Declaration of Independence and the colonists' break with Great Britain, see Calvin D. Lonton, ed., *The Bicentennial Almanac* (Nashville, TN: Thomas Nelson, 1975).
6. See Garry Wills, *Inventing America: Jefferson's Declaration of Independence* (New York: Random House, 1978). Wills argues that the Declaration was signed solely to secure foreign aid for the ongoing war effort.
7. See Gordon S. Wood, *The Creation of the American Republic, 1776–1787*, reissue ed. (New York: Norton, 1993).
8. For more about the Articles of Confederation, see Merrill Jensen, *The Articles of Confederation* (Madison: University of Wisconsin Press, 1940).
9. Charles A. Beard, *An Economic Interpretation of the Constitution of the United States*, reissue ed. (Mineola, NY: Dover, 2004).
10. John Patrick Diggins, "Power and Authority in American History: The Case of Charles A. Beard and His Critics," *American Historical Review* 86 (October 1981): 701–30; Robert Brown, *Charles Beard and the Constitution: A Critical Analysis of "An Economic Interpretation of the Constitution"* (Princeton, NJ: Princeton University Press, 1956).
11. Jackson Turner Main, *The Anti-Federalists: Critics of the Constitution, 1781–1788* (Chapel Hill: University of North Carolina, 2004).
12. Wood, *Creation of the American Republic*.
13. For more on the political nature of compromise at the convention, see Calvin C. Jillson, *Constitution Making: Conflict and Consensus in the Federal Constitution of 1787* (New York: Agathon, 1988).
14. Bernard Bailyn, *The Ideological Origins of the American Revolution* (Cambridge, MA: Belknap Press, 1967).

15. Richard E. Neustadt, *Presidential Power: The Politics of Leadership from FDR to Carter* (New York: Macmillan, 1980), 26.
16. Federal Republicans favored a republican or representative form of government (do not confuse this term with the modern Republican Party, which came into being in 1854; see chapter 11). Ultimately, the word *federal* referred to the form of government embodied in the new Constitution, and *confederation* referred to a "league of states," as under the Articles, and later was applied in the "Confederacy" of 1861–1865.
17. See Ralph Ketcham, ed., *The Anti-Federalist Papers and the Constitutional Debates* (New York: New American Library, 1986).
18. See Herbert J. Storing, *What the Anti-Federalists Were For* (Chicago: University of Chicago Press, 1981), for a fuller discussion of Anti-Federalist views.
19. See Alan P. Grimes, *Democracy and the Amendments to the Constitution* (Lexington, MA: Lexington Books, 1978).
20. David E. Kyvig, *Repealing National Prohibition* (Chicago: University of Chicago Press, 1978).
21. See Jane J. Mansbridge, *Why We Lost the ERA* (Chicago: University of Chicago Press, 1986).
22. *Marbury* v. *Madison*, 5 U.S. 137 (1803).
23. Speech by Attorney General Edwin Meese III before the American Bar Association, July 9, 1985, Washington, DC. See also Antonin Scalia and Amy Gutman, eds. *A Matter of Interpretation: Federal Courts and the Law* (Princeton, NJ: Princeton University Press, 1998).
24. Speech by Associate Justice William J. Brennan Jr. at Georgetown University Text and Teaching Symposium, October 10, 1985, Washington, DC.
25. Bruce Ackerman, *We the People: Foundations* (Cambridge, MA: Belknap Press, 1991).

CHAPTER 3

1. Evan Thomas, "How Bush Blew It," *Newsweek* (September 19, 2005), http://www.msnbc.msn.com.
2. See Spencer S. Hsu, "Katrina Report Spreads Blame: Homeland Security, Chertoff Singled Out," *Washington Post* (January 12, 2006): A1.
3. John Mountjoy, "Interstate Cooperation: Interstate Compacts Make a Comeback," *Council of State Governments*, available online at http://www.csg.org.
4. *McCulloch* v. *Maryland*, 17 U.S. 316 (1819).
5. *Gibbons* v. *Ogden*, 22 U.S. 1 (1824).
6. *Dred Scott* v. *Sandford*, 60 U.S. 393 (1857).
7. *Plessy* v. *Ferguson*, 163 U.S. 537 (1896).
8. *Panhandle Oil Co.* v. *Knox*, 277 U.S. 218, 223 (1928).
9. *Indian Motorcycle Co.* v. *U.S.*, 238 U.S. 570 (1931).
10. *Pensacola Telegraph* v. *Western Union*, 96 U.S. 1 (1877).
11. *Pollock* v. *Farmers Loan and Trust*, 157 U.S. 429 (1895); and *Springer* v. *U.S.*, 102 U.S. 586 (1881).
12. John O. McGinnis, "The State of Federalism," testimony before the Senate Government Affairs Committee, May 5, 1999.
13. *NLRB* v. *Jones and Laughlin Steel Co.*, 301 U.S. 1 (1937).
14. *U.S.* v. *Darby Lumber Co.*, 312 U.S. 100 (1941).
15. *Wickard* v. *Filburn*, 317 U.S. 111 (1942).
16. Morton Grodzins, "Centralization and Decentralization in the American Federal System," in Robert A. Goldwin, ed., *A Nation of States* (Chicago: Rand McNally, 1963), 3–4.
17. Alice M. Rivlin, *Reviving the American Dream* (Washington, DC: Brookings Institution, 1992), 92.
18. Rivlin, *Reviving the American Dream*, 98.
19. Richard P. Nathan et al., *Reagan and the States* (Princeton, NJ: Princeton University Press, 1987), 4.
20. Richard Wolf, "States Bracing for Leaner Times," *USA Today* (July 10, 2000): 1A.

21. Marianne Arneberg, "Cuomo Assails Judicial Hodgepodge," *Newsday* (August 15, 1990): 15.
22. *Webster* v. *Reproductive Health Services*, 492 U.S. 490 (1989).
23. *Stenberg* v. *Carhart*, 530 U.S. 914 (2000).
24. *Ayotte* v. *Planned Parenthood of Northern New England* 546 U.S. _____ (2006).
25. *U.S.* v. *Lopez*, 514 U.S. 549 (1995).
26. *Seminole Tribe* v. *Florida*, 517 U.S. 44 (1996).
27. *Boerne* v. *Flores*, 521 U.S. 507 (1997).
28. *Printz* v. *U.S.*, 521 U.S. 898 (1997).
29. *Florida Prepaid* v. *College Savings Bank*, 527 U.S. 627 (1999).
30. Linda Greenhouse, "The Rehnquist Court and Its Imperiled States' Rights Legacy," *New York Times* (June 12, 2005): A3.
31. *Nevada Department of Human Resources* v. *Hibbs*, (2003).
32. *Gonzales* v. *Raich*, 545 U.S. 1 (2005).
33. *Gonzales* v. *Oregon*, 547 U.S. _____ (2005).

CHAPTER 4

1. Sudarsan Raghaven, "Crisis in Darfur Is Expected to Draw Thousands to Mall; Rallies Promoting End to Genocide Planned in 17 other Cities," *Washington Post* (April 30, 2006): C3.
2. Raghaven, "Crisis in Darfur Is Expected to Draw Thousands to Mall."
3. Sudarsan Raghaven, "Divisions Cast Aside in Cry for Darfur; Mall Rally Highlights Growing Concern," *Washington Post* (May 1, 2006): A1.
4. Farah Stockman, "Americans Rally for Darfur; Protests Push Action on Genocide," *Boston Globe* (May 1, 2006): A1.
5. The absence of a bill of rights led Mason to refuse to sign the proposed Constitution, noting that he "would sooner chop off his right hand than put it to the Constitution as it now stands." Quoted in Eric Black, *Our Constitution: The Myth That Binds Us* (Boulder, CO: Westview, 1988), 75.
6. *Barron* v. *Baltimore*, 32 U.S. 243 (1833).
7. *Allgeyer* v. *Louisiana*, 165 U.S. 578 (1897).
8. *Gitlow* v. *New York*, 268 U.S. 652 (1925).
9. *Near* v. *Minnesota*, 283 U.S. 697 (1931). For more about *Near* see Fred W. Friendly, *Minnesota Rag: The Dramatic Story of the Landmark Case That Gave New Meaning to Freedom of the Press* (New York: Random House, 1981).
10. *Palko* v. *Connecticut*, 302 U.S. 319 (1937).
11. *Zobrest* v. *Catalina Foothills School District*, 506 U.S. 813 (1992).
12. *Engel* v. *Vitale*, 370 U.S. 421 (1962).
13. *Lee* v. *Weisman*, 505 U.S. 577 (1992).
14. *Santa Fe Independent School District* v. *Doe*, 530 U.S. 290 (2000).
15. *Lemon* v. *Kurtzman*, 403 U.S. 602 (1971).
16. "An Eternal Debate," *Omaha World-Journal* (November 27, 2002): 6B.
17. *Widmar* v. *Vincent*, 454 U.S. 263 (1981).
18. *Rosenberger* v. *University of Virginia*, 515 U.S. 819 (1995).
19. *Agostini* v. *Felton*, 521 U.S. 203 (1997).
20. *Mitchell* v. *Helms*, 530 U.S. 793 (2000).
21. *Zelman* v. *Simmons-Harris*, 536 U.S. 639 (2002).
22. *McCreary County* v. *ACLU of Kentucky*, 545 U.S. _____ (2005).
23. Alan Cooperman, "Judge Bars Tax-Funded Religious Jail Project," *Washington Post* (June 3, 2006): A2.
24. *Employment Division, Dept. of Human Resources of Oregon* v. *Smith*, 494 U.S. 872 (1990).
25. *Boerne* v. *Flores*, 521 U.S. 507 (1997).
26. *Gonzales* v. *O Centro Espirita Beneficiente Uniao Do Vegetal*, 546 U.S. _____ (2006).
27. Tony Mauro, "Stern's Raunch Is Better than Silence," *USA Today* (May 12, 2004): 13A.
28. *Ex parte McCardle*, 74 U.S. 506 (1869).
29. David M. O'Brien, *Constitutional Law and Politics*, vol. 2: *Civil Rights and Civil Liberties* (New York: Norton, 1991), 345.
30. See Frederick Siebert, *The Rights and Privileges of the Press* (New York: Appleton-Century, 1934), 886, 931–40.
31. *Schenck* v. *U.S.*, 249 U.S. 47 (1919).
32. *Brandenburg* v. *Ohio*, 395 U.S. 444 (1969).

33. *New York Times Co.* v. *U.S.*, 403 U.S. 713 (1971).
34. *Nebraska Press Association* v. *Stuart*, 427 U.S. 539 (1976).
35. *Abrams* v. *U.S.*, 250 U.S. 616 (1919).
36. *Stromberg* v. *California*, 283 U.S. 359 (1931).
37. *Tinker* v. *Des Moines Independent Community School District*, 393 U.S. 503 (1969).
38. *Texas* v. *Johnson*, 491 U.S. 397 (1989).
39. *U.S.* v. *Eichman*, 496 U.S. 310 (1990).
40. *R.A.V.* v. *City of St. Paul*, 505 U.S. 377 (1992).
41. *Virginia* v. *Black*, 538 U.S. 343 (2003).
42. *Chaplinsky* v. *New Hampshire*, 315 U.S. 568 (1942).
43. *New York Times Co.* v. *Sullivan*, 376 U.S. 254 (1964).
44. *Chaplinsky* v. *New Hampshire*, 315 U.S. 568 (1942).
45. *Cohen* v. *California*, 403 U.S. 15 (1971).
46. *Regina* v. *Hicklin*, L.R. 2 Q.B. 360 (1868).
47. *Roth* v. *U.S.*, 354 U.S. 476 (1957).
48. *Miller* v. *California*, 413 U.S. 15 (1973).
49. *Barnes* v. *Glen Theater*, 501 U.S. 560 (1991).
50. *Reno* v. *American Civil Liberties Union*, 521 U.S. 844 (1997).
51. *Ashcroft* v. *Free Speech Coalition*, 535 U.S. 234 (2002).
52. David G. Savage, "Ban on 'Virtual' Child Porn Is Upset by Court," *Los Angeles Times* (April 17, 2002): A1; Lyle Denniston, "Court Puts 2D Pornography Law on Hold: A Majority Doubt Giving Localities an Internet Veto," *Boston Globe* (May 14, 2002): A2.
53. Nick Anderson and Elizabeth Levin, "Crime Bill Passes Easily in Congress: Measure Includes Expansion of Amber Alert System," *Los Angeles Times* (April 11, 2003): A36.
54. *Ashcroft* v. *American Civil Liberties Union*, 542 U.S. 656 (2004).
55. *DeJonge* v. *Oregon*, 229 U.S. 353 (1937).
56. *Barron* v. *Baltimore*, 32 U.S. 243 (1833).
57. *Dred Scott* v. *Sandford*, 60 U.S. 393 (1857).
58. *U.S.* v. *Miller*, 307 U.S. 174 (1939).
59. *Quilici* v. *Village of Morton Grove*, 104 U.S. 194 (1983).
60. *Printz* v. *U.S.*, 514 U.S. 898 (1997).
61. *Wilson* v. *Arkansas*, 514 U.S. 927 (1995).
62. *Hudson* v. *Michigan*, 547 U.S. _____ (2006).
63. *U.S.* v. *Sokolov*, 490 U.S. 1 (1989).
64. *U.S.* v. *Knights*, 534 U.S. 112 (2001).
65. *Georgia* v. *Randolph*, 547 U.S. _____ (2006).
66. *Johnson* v. *U.S.*, 333 U.S. 10 (1948).
67. *Winston* v. *Lee*, 470 U.S. 753 (1985).
68. *South Dakota* v. *Neville*, 459 U.S. 553 (1983).
69. *Michigan* v. *Tyler*, 436 U.S. 499 (1978).
70. *Hester* v. *U.S.*, 265 U.S. 57 (1924).
71. *Carroll* v. *U.S.*, 267 U.S. 132 (1925).
72. *U.S.* v. *Arvizu*, 534 U.S. 266 (2002).
73. *Skinner* v. *Railway Labor Executives' Association*, 489 U.S. 602 (1989).
74. *Vernonia School District* v. *Acton*, 515 U.S. 646 (1995).
75. *Board of Education of Independent School District No. 92 of Pottawatomie County* v. *Earls*, 536 U.S. 822 (2002).
76. *Ferguson* v. *City of Charleston*, 532 U.S. 67 (2001).
77. *Counselman* v. *Hitchcock*, 142 U.S. 547 (1892).
78. *Brown* v. *Mississippi*, 297 U.S. 278 (1936).
79. *Dickerson* v. *U.S.*, 530 U.S. 428 (2000).
80. *Smith* v. *Massachusetts*, 543 U.S. _____ (2005).
81. *Weeks* v. *U.S.*, 232 U.S. 383 (1914).
82. *Mapp* v. *Ohio*, 367 U.S. 643 (1961).
83. *U.S.* v. *Grubbs*, 547 U.S. _____ (2006).
84. *Johnson* v. *Zerbst*, 304 U.S. 458 (1938).
85. *Gideon* v. *Wainwright*, 372 U.S. 335 (1963).
86. *Argersinger* v. *Hamlin*, 407 U.S. 25 (1972).
87. *Scott* v. *Illinois*, 440 U.S. 367 (1979).
88. *Alabama* v. *Shelton*, 536 U.S. 654 (2002).
89. *Rompilla* v. *Beard*, 545 U.S. _____ (2005).
90. *Strauder* v. *West Virginia*, 100 U.S. 303 (1880).
91. *Taylor* v. *Louisiana*, 419 U.S. 522 (1975).
92. *Batson* v. *Kentucky*, 476 U.S. 79 (1986).
93. *J.E.B.* v. *Alabama*, 511 U.S. 127 (1994).
94. *Maryland* v. *Craig*, 497 U.S. 836 (1990).

95. See Michael Meltsner, *Cruel and Unusual: The Supreme Court and Capital Punishment* (New York: Random House, 1973).
96. *Furman v. Georgia*, 408 U.S. 238 (1972).
97. *Gregg v. Georgia*, 428 U.S. 153 (1976).
98. *House v. Bell*, 547 U.S. _____ (2006).
99. *Hill v. McDonough*, 547 U.S. _____ (2006).
100. *Olmstead v. U.S.*, 277 U.S. 438 (1928).
101. *Griswold v. Connecticut*, 381 U.S. 481 (1965).
102. *Eisenstadt v. Baird*, 410 U.S. 113 (1972).
103. *Roe v. Wade*, 410 U.S. 113 (1973).
104. *Webster v. Reproductive Health Services*, 492 U.S. 490 (1989).
105. *Planned Parenthood of Southeastern Pennsylvania v. Casey*, 502 U.S. 1056 (1992).
106. Karen O'Connor, *No Neutral Ground: Abortion Politics in an Age of Absolutes* (Boulder, CO: Westview, 1996).
107. *Stenberg v. Carhart*, 530 U.S. 914 (2000).
108. *Bowers v. Hardwick*, 478 U.S. 186 (1986).
109. *Lawrence v. Texas*, 539 U.S. 558 (2003).
110. *Cruzan v. Director, Missouri Dept. of Health*, 497 U.S. 261 (1990).
111. *Vacco v. Quill*, 521 U.S. 793 (1997).
112. Office of the Attorney General, Memorandum for Asa Hutchinson, Administrator, the Drug Enforcement Administration, November 6, 2001.
113. William McCall, "Oregon Suicide Law Gets Longer Reprieve: Court Allows US Senate 5 Months to Ready Arguments," *Boston Globe* (November 21, 2001): A8.
114. *Oregon v. Ashcroft*, 192 F. Supp. 2d 1077 (2002); and Kim Murphy, "U.S. Cannot Block Oregon Suicide Law, Judge Rules," *Los Angeles Times* (April 18, 2002): A1.
115. Attorney General's petition for a writ of certiorari, *Gonzales v. Oregon*, 547 U.S. _____ 2005.

CHAPTER 5

1. Dan Eggen, "Civil Rights Focus Shift Roils Staff at Justice," *Washington Post* (December 13, 2005):/A1. This vignette draws heavily from this article.
2. Eggen, "Civil Rights Focus Shift Roils Staff at Justice."
3. Dan Eggen, "Politics Alleged in Voting Cases," *Washington Post* (January 23, 2006):/A1.
4. David E. Rosenbaum et al., "New Twist in Texas Districting Dispute," *New York Times* (December 3, 2005).
5. *LULAC et al. v. Perry*, 547 U.S. _____ (2006).
6. *Minor v. Happersett*, 88 U.S. 162 (1875).
7. *Civil Rights Cases*, 109 U.S. 3 (1883).
8. *Plessy v. Ferguson*, 163 U.S. 537 (1896).
9. *Williams v. Mississippi*, 170 U.S. 213 (1898); *Cummins v. Richmond County Board of Education*, 175 U.S. 528 (1899).
10. *Missouri ex rel. Gaines v. Canada*, 305 U.S. 337 (1938).
11. *Sweatt v. Painter*, 339 U.S. 629 (1950); *McLaurin v. Oklahoma*, 339 U.S. 637 (1950).
12. *Brown v. Board of Education*, 347 U.S. 483 (1954).
13. But see Gerald Rosenberg, *The Hollow Hope: Can Courts Bring About Social Change?* (Chicago: University of Chicago Press, 1991).
14. Juan Williams, *Eyes on the Prize: America's Civil Rights Years, 1954–1965* (New York: Penguin, 1987), 10.
15. *Brown v. Board of Education II*, 349 U.S. 294 (1955).
16. Quoted in Williams, *Eyes on the Prize*, 37.
17. *Cooper v. Aaron*, 358 U.S. 1 (1958).
18. Jo Freeman, *The Politics of Women's Liberation* (New York: Longman, 1975), 57.
19. *Hoyt v. Florida*, 368 U.S. 57 (1961).
20. *Reed v. Reed*, 404 U.S. 71 (1971).
21. *Craig v. Boren*, 429 U.S. 190 (1976).
22. *Mississippi University for Women v. Hogan*, 458 U.S. 718 (1982).
23. *Craig v. Boren*, 429 U.S. 190 (1976).
24. *Orr v. Orr*, 440 U.S. 268 (1979).
25. *JEB v. Alabama ex rel. TB*, 440 U.S. 268 (1979).
26. *U.S. v. Virginia*, 518 U.S. 515 (1996).
27. *Nguyen v. INS*, 533 U.S. 53 (2001).
28. *Rostker v. Goldberg*, 453 U.S. 57 (1981).
29. *Michael M. v. Superior Court of Sonoma County*, 450 U.S. 464 (1981).
30. *Rostker v. Goldberg*, 453 U.S. 57 (1981).
31. *U.S. v. Virginia*, 518 U.S. 515 (1996).
32. *Meritor Savings Bank v. Vinson*, 477 U.S. 57 (1986).
33. *Oncale v. Sundowner Offshore Services, Inc.*, 523 U.S. 75 (1998).
34. *Hishon v. King & Spalding*, 467 U.S. 69 (1984).
35. *Johnson v. Transportation Agency*, 480 U.S. 616 (1987).
36. Christine Marie Sierra, "Hispanics and the Political Process," in Pastora San Juan Cafferty and David W. Engstrom, eds., *Hispanics in the United States* (New Brunswick, NJ: Transaction, 2000), ch. 10.
37. F. Chris Garcia, *Latinos and the Political System* (Notre Dame, IN: University of Notre Dame Press, 1988), 1.
38. *White v. Register*, 412 U.S. 755 (1973).
39. *San Antonio Independent School District v. Rodriguez*, 411 U.S. 1 (1973).
40. *Edgewood Independent School District v. Kirby*, 777 SW.2d 391 (1989).
41. "MALDEF 'Pleased with Settlement of California Public Schls Inequity Case, *Williams v. California*," August 13, 2004.
42. "U.S. Supreme Court to Hear MALDEF's Appeal of Texas Redistricting Case," MALDEF, December 12, 2005.
43. *LULAC et al. v. Perry*, 547 U.S. _____ (2006).
44. "Best-Selling Book Challenges Long-Held Theories About Life in America," *Voice of America News*, October 7, 2005.
45. Rennard Strickland, "Native Americans," in Kermit Hall, ed., *The Oxford Companion to the Supreme Court of the United States* (New York: Oxford University Press, 1992), 579.
46. *Cobell v. Norton*, 204 F.3d 1081 (2001). For more on the Indian trust, see http://www.indiantrust.com/overview.cfm.
47. Richard Luscombe, "Tribes Go on Legal Warpath," *The Observer* (April 25, 2004): 20.
48. Diane Helene Miller, *Freedom to Differ: The Shaping of the Gay and Lesbian Struggle for Civil Rights* (New York: New York University Press, 1998).
49. Sarah Brewer, David Kaib, and Karen O'Connor, "Sex and the Supreme Court: Gays, Lesbians, and Justice," in Craig A. Rimmerman, Kenneth D. Wald, and Clyde Wilcox, eds., *The Politics of Gay Rights* (Chicago: University of Chicago Press, 2000).
50. Evan Gerstmann, *The Constitutional Underclass: Gays, Lesbians, and the Failure of Class-Based Equal Protection* (Chicago: University of Chicago Press, 1999).
51. Deborah Ensor, "Gay Veternas Working for Change," *San Diego Union* (April 13, 2002): B1.
52. John White, "'Don't Ask' Costs More than Expected," *Washington Post* (February 14, 2006): A4.
53. *Romer v. Evans*, 517 U.S. 620 (1996).
54. *Lawrence v. Texas*, 539 U.S. 558 (2003).
55. David Pfeiffer, "Overview of the Disability Movement: History, Legislative Record and Political Implications," *Policy Studies Journal* (Winter 1993): 724–42; and "Understanding Disability Policy," *Policy Studies Journal* (Spring 1996): 157–74.
56. Joan Biskupic, "Supreme Court Limits Meaning of Disability," *Washington Post* (June 23, 1999): A1.
57. *Sutton v. United Air Lines, Inc.*, 527 U.S. 471 (1999).
58. *Tennessee v. Lane*, 541 U.S. 509 (2004).
59. American Association of People with Disabilities, http://www.aapd-dc.org.
60. *Regents of the University of California v. Bakke*, 438 U.S. 265 (1978).
61. *Grutter v. Bollinger*, 539 U.S. 306 (2003).
62. *Gratz v. Bollinger*, 539 U.S. 306 (2003).
63. Victoria Colliver, "Class Action Considered in Wal-Mart Suit," *San Francisco Chronicle* (September 25, 2003): B1.
64. "Wal-Mart's Immigrant Labor Problem," *Tampa Tribune* (November 14, 2003): 10.

CHAPTER 6

1. For an outstanding account of Pelosi's campaign for the whip post, see Juliet Eilperin, "The Making of Madam Whip: Fear and Loathing—

and Horse Trading—The Race for the House's No. 2 Democrat," *Washington Post* (January 6, 2002): W27.

2. "Mother of All Whips," *Pittsburgh Post-Gazette* (February 9, 2002): A11.

3. "What Is the Democratic Caucus?" http://dcaucusweb.house.gov/about/what_is.asp.

4. Charles Babbington, "Pelosi Seeks House Minority 'Bill of Rights,' Hastert Dismisses Democrats' Complaint, Saying GOP Record Is Better than Foes,'" *Washington Post* (June 24, 2004): A23.

5. Barbara Sinclair, "The Struggle over Representation and Law-making in Congress: Leadership Reforms in the 1990s," in James A. Thurber and Roger H. Davidson, eds., *Remaking Congress: Change and Stability in the 1990s* (Washington, DC: CQ Press, 1995), 105.

6. Woodrow Wilson, *Congressional Government: A Study in American Government* (New York: Meridian Books, 1956; originally published in 1885), 79.

7. Roger H. Davidson, "Congressional Committees in the New Reform Era: From Combat to the Contract," in Thurber and Davidson, *Remaking Congress*, 28.

8. For more about committees, see Christopher Deering and Steven S. Smith, *Committees in Congress*, 3rd ed. (Washington, DC: CQ Press, 1997).

9. Woodrow Wilson, *Congressional Government* (New York: Houghton Mifflin, 1885).

10. Kenneth A. Shepsle, *The Giant Jigsaw Puzzle: Democratic Committee Assignments in the Modern House* (Chicago: University of Chicago Press, 1978).

11. Tim Groseclose and Charles Stewart III, "The Value of Committee Seats in the House, 1947–91," *American Journal of Political Science* 42 (April 1998): 453–74.

12. Gary W. Cox and Jonathan N. Katz, "Why Did the Incumbency Advantage in U.S. House Elections Grow?" *American Journal of Political Science* 40 (May 1996): 478–97; Kenneth N. Bickers and Robert M. Stein, "The Electoral Dynamics of the Federal Pork Barrel," *American Journal of Political Science* 40 (November 1996): 1300–26; and Diana Evans, *Greasing the Wheels: Using Pork Barrel Projects to Build Majority Coalitions in Congress* (NY: Cambridge University Press, 2004).

13. Marjorie Randon Hershey, "Congressional Elections," in Gerald M. Pomper et al., *The Election of 1992: Reports and Interpretations* (Chatham, NJ: Chatham House, 1993), 159.

14. Alan I. Abramowitz, "Incumbency, Congressional Spending, and the Decline of Competition in House Elections," *Journal of Politics* 53 (February 1991): 34–56.

15. Amy Keller, "The Roll Call 50 Richest: For Richer or Poorer Thanks to Spouses, Kerry Keeps Top Spot and Clinton Joins List," *Roll Call* (September 9, 2002).

16. *Congressional Quarterly Weekly Report* (January 6, 2001).

17. Norman Ornstein, "GOP Moderates Can Impact Policy—If They Dare," *Roll Call* (February 12, 2003).

18. Byron York, "Bored by Estrada? Owen May Be a Reprise," *The Hill* (March 19, 2003): 43.

19. See L. Martin Overby, "The Senate and Justice Thomas: A Note on Ideology, Race, and Constituent Pressures," *Congress and the Presidency* 21 (Autumn 1994): 131–6.

20. Ken Kollman, "Inviting Friends to Lobby: Interest Groups, Ideological Bias, and Congressional Committees," *American Journal of Political Science* 41 (April 1997): 519–44. See also Marie Hojnacki and David C. Kimball, "Organized Interests and the Decision of Whom to Lobby in Congress," *American Political Science Review* 92 (December 1998): 775–90.

21. Barbara S. Romzek and Jennifer A. Utter, "Congressional Legislative Staff: Political Professionals or Clerks?" *American Journal of Political Science* 41 (October 1997): 1251–79; Susan Webb Hammond, "Recent Research on Legislative Staffs," *Legislative Studies Quarterly* (November 1996): 543–76.

22. Keith Krehbiel, "Cosponsors and Wafflers from A to Z." *American Journal of Political Science* 39 (November 1995): 906–23.

23. William F. West, "Oversight Subcommittees in the House of Representatives," *Congress and the Presidency* 25 (Autumn 1998): 147–60.

24. This discussion draws heavily on Steven J. Balla, "Legislative Organization and Congressional Review," paper delivered at the 1999 meeting of the Midwest Political Science Association.

25. *Wall Street Journal* (April 13, 1973): 10.

26. Craig Gilbert, "Use of Force Is President's Call," *Milwaukee Journal Sentinel* (April 18, 2002): A8.

CHAPTER 7

1. "Two Hundred Years of Presidential Funerals," *Washington Post* (June 10, 2004): C14.

2. "The Fold: Presidential Funerals; Farewell to the Chiefs," *Newsday* (June 9, 2004): A38.

3. Gail Russell Chaddock, "The Rise of Mourning in America," *Christian Science Monitor* (June 11, 2004): 1.

4. Richard E. Neustadt, *Presidential Power and the Modern Presidency* (New York: Free Press, 1991).

5. Winston Solberg, *The Federal Convention and the Formation of the Union of the American States* (Indianapolis, IN: Bobbs-Merrill, 1958), 235.

6. James P. Pfiffner, "Recruiting Executive Branch Leaders," *Brookings Review* 19 (Spring 2001): 41–43.

7. Benjamin I. Page and Mark P. Petracca, *The American Presidency* (New York: McGraw-Hill, 1983), 262.

8. Jim Lobe, "Bush 'Unsigns' War Crimes Treaty," AlterNet.com, May 6, 2002; and Lincoln P. Bloomfield Jr., "The U.S. Government and the International Criminal Court," address to the Parliamentarians for Global Action, United Nations, September 12, 2003.

9. "War Powers: Resolution Grants Bush Power He Needs," *Rocky Mountain News* (September 15, 2001): B6.

10. *Public Papers of the Presidents* (1963), 889.

11. Quoted in Neustadt, *Presidential Power and the Modern Presidency*, 9.

12. Quoted in Page and Petracca, *The American Presidency*, 57.

13. See Louis Fisher, *Constitutional Conflicts Between Congress and the President*, 4th ed. (Lawrence: University Press of Kansas, 1997).

14. Franklin D. Roosevelt, Press Conference, July 23, 1937.

15. See Lance LeLoup and Steven Shull, *The President and Congress: Collaboration and Conflict in National Policymaking*, 2nd ed. (Boston: Allyn and Bacon, 2003).

16. See Cary Covington, J. Mark Wrighton, and Rhonda Kinney, "A 'Presidency-Augmented' Model of Presidential Success on House Roll Call Votes," *American Journal of Political Science* 39 (November 1995): 1001–24; and Wayne P. Steger, "Presidential Policy Initiation and the Politics of Agenda Control," *Congress and the Presidency* 24 (Spring 1997): 102–14.

17. Quoted in Thomas E. Cronin, *The State of the Presidency*, 2nd ed. (Boston: Little, Brown, 1980), 169.

18. Robert A. Caro, *Master of the Senate: The Years of Lyndon Johnson* (New York: Knopf, 2002).

19. Mary Leonard, "Bush Begins Talks on Human Cloning," *Boston Globe* (January 17, 2002): A6.

20. Samuel Kernell, *New Strategies of Presidential Leadership*, 2nd ed. (Washington, DC: CQ Press, 1993), 3.

21. Jeffrey Cohen, "Presidential Rhetoric and the Public Agenda," *American Journal of Political Science* 39 (February 1995): 87–107.

22. George Reedy, *The Twilight of the Presidency* (New York: New American Library), 38–39.

23. Neustadt, *Presidential Power*, 1–10.

24. Samuel Kernell, *Going Public: New Strategies of Presidential Leadership*, 3rd ed. (Washington, DC: CQ Press, 1997).

25. William E. Gibson, "Job Approval Ratings Steady: Personal Credibility Takes a Hit," *News and Observer* (August 19, 1998): A16.

CHAPTER 8

1. Gardiner Harris, "Bush Plan Shows U.S. Is Not Ready for Deadly Flu," *New York Times* (October 8, 2005).

2. Anita Manning and David Jackson, "Bird Flu Plan Lacks a Key Detail," *USA Today* (May 4, 2006): 2A.

3. Harris, "Bush Plan Shows U.S. Is Not Ready for Deadly Flu."
4. Harris, "Bush Plan Shows U.S. Is Not Ready for Deadly Flu."
5. Stephen Barr, "Users Mostly Rate Agencies Favorably," *Washington Post* (April 13, 2000): A29.
6. Harold D. Lasswell, *Politics: Who Gets What, When and How* (New York: McGraw-Hill, 1938).
7. David Osborne and Ted Gaebler, *Reinventing Government* (Reading, MA: Addison-Wesley, 1992), 20–21.
8. Office of Personnel Management, *The Fact Book,* http://www.opm.gov/feddata/factbook/2005/factbook2005.pdf.
9. Stephen Barr, "Some Trainees Voice Frustration with Presidential Management Intern Program," *Washington Post* (November 26, 2001): B2.
10. Kenneth J. Cooper, "U.S. May Repay Loans for College," *Washington Post* (December 13, 2001): A45.
11. "A Century of Government Growth," *Washington Post* (January 3, 2000): A17. On the difficulty of counting the exact number of government agencies, see David Nachmias and David H. Rosenbloom, *Bureaucratic Government: U.S.A* (New York: St. Martin's, 1980).
12. The classic work on regulatory commissions is Marver Bernstein, *Regulating Business by Independent Commission* (Princeton, NJ: Princeton University Press, 1955).
13. H. H. Gerth and C. Wright Mills, *From Max Weber* (New York: Oxford University Press, 1958).
14. Karen DeYoung, "Saudis Detail Steps on Charities; Kingdom Seeks to Quell Record on Terrorist Financing," *Washington Post* (December 3, 2002): A1.
15. Mike Allen, "White House to Defer to NASA Investigation; Work on Space Policy to Await Probe's End," *Washington Post* (February 5, 2003): A14.
16. Michael Lipsky, *Street-Level Bureaucracy: Dilemmas of the Individual in Public Services* (New York: Russell Sage Foundation, 1980).
17. Cornelius M. Kerwin, *Rulemaking: How Government Agencies Write Law and Make Policy,* 2nd ed. (Washington, DC: CQ Press, 1999), xv.
18. George A. Krause, "Presidential Use of Executive Orders, 1953–1994," *American Politics Quarterly* 25 (October 1997): 458–81.
19. Irene Murphy, *Public Policy on the Status of Women* (Lexington, MA: Lexington Books, 1974).
20. Rosemary O'Leary, *Environmental Change: Federal Courts and the EPA* (Philadelphia: Temple University Press, 1993).
21. James F. Spriggs II, "The Supreme Court and Federal Administrative Agencies: A Resource-Based Theory and Analysis of Judicial Impact," *American Journal of Political Science* 40 (November 1996): 1122.
22. Wendy Hansen, Renee Johnson, and Isaac Unah, "Specialized Courts, Bureaucratic Agencies, and the Politics of U.S. Trade Policy," *American Journal of Political Science* 39 (August 1995): 529–57.

CHAPTER 9

1. *Hamdan* v. *Rumsfeld* 549 U.S. _____ (2006).
2. Charles Lane, "High Court Rejects Detainees Tribunals," *Washington Post* (June 30, 2006): A1.
3. Joan Biskupic and Laura Parker, "Justices Reject Gitmo Tribunals," *USA Today* (June 30, 2006): A1.
4. *Marbury* v. *Madison,* 5 U.S. 137 (1803).
5. *Martin* v. *Hunter's Lessee,* 14 U.S. 304 (1816).
6. Oliver Ellsworth served from 1796 to 1800.
7. *Marbury* v. *Madison,* 5 U.S. 137 (1803).
8. This discussion draws heavily on Jack C. Plano and Milton Greenberg, *The American Political Dictionary,* 10th ed. (Fort Worth, TX: Harcourt Brace, 1996), 247.
9. David W. Neubauer, *Judicial Process: Law, Courts, and Politics* (Pacific Grove, CA: Brooks/Cole, 1991), 57.
10. Cases involving citizens from different states can be filed in state or federal court.
11. Sheldon Goldman and Elliot E. Slotnick, "Clinton's First Term Judiciary: Many Bridges to Cross," *Judicature* (May/June 1997): 254–55.
12. Quoted in Lawrence Baum, *The Supreme Court,* 3rd ed. (Washington, DC: CQ Press, 1989), 108.
13. John Brigham, *The Cult of the Court* (Philadelphia: Temple University Press, 1987).
14. Stephen L. Wasby, *The Supreme Court in the Federal Judicial System,* 4th ed. (Chicago: Nelson-Hall, 1988), 194.
15. Wasby, *The Supreme Court in the Federal Judicial System,* 194.
16. Wasby, *The Supreme Court in the Federal Judicial System,* 199. Much of this change occurred as the result of an increase in state criminal cases, of which nearly 100 percent concerned constitutional questions.
17. Data compiled by authors for 2001–2002 term of the Court.
18. Justice Stevens chooses not to join this pool. According to one former clerk, "He wanted an independent review," but Stevens examines only about 20 percent of the petitions, leaving the rest to his clerks. Tony Mauro, "Ginsburg Plunges into the Cert Pool," *Legal Times* (September 6, 1993): 8.
19. Paul Wahlbeck, James F. Spriggs II, and Lee Sigelman, "Ghost-writers on the Court? A Stylistic Analysis of U.S. Supreme Court Opinion Drafts," *American Politics Research* 30 (March 2002): 166–92. Wahlbeck, Spriggs, and Sigelman note that "between 1969 and 1972—the period during which the justices each became entitled to a third law clerk . . . the number of opinions increased by about 50 percent and the number of words tripled."
20. Richard A. Posner, *The Federal Courts: Crisis and Reform* (Cambridge, MA: Harvard University Press, 1985), 114.
21. Todd C. Peppers, *Courtiers of the Marble Palace: The Rise and Influence of the Supreme Court Law Clerk* (Palo Alto, CA: Stanford University Press, 2006).
22. Edward Lazarus, *Closed Chambers: The First Eyewitness Account of the Epic Struggles Inside the Supreme Court* (New York: Random House, 1998).
23. "Retired Chief Justice Warren Attacks . . . Freund Study Group's Composition and Proposal," *American Bar Association Journal* 59 (July 1973): 728.
24. Kathryn Werdegar, "The Solicitor General and Administrative Due Process," *George Washington Law Review* (1967–1968): 482.
25. Rebecca Mae Salokar, *The Solicitor General: The Politics of Law* (Philadelphia: Temple University Press, 1992), 3.
26. Richard C. Cortner, *The Supreme Court and Civil Liberties* (Palo Alto, CA: Mayfield, 1975), vi.
27. Gregory A. Caldeira and John R. Wright, "*Amicus Curiae* Before the Supreme Court: Who Participates, When and How Much?" *Journal of Politics* 52 (August 1990): 803.
28. See also John R. Hermann, "American Indians in Court: The Burger and Rehnquist Years," Ph.D. dissertation, Emory University, 1996.
29. Linda Greenhouse, "With O'Connor Retirement and a New Chief Justice Comes an Awareness of Change," *New York Times* (January 28, 2006): A10.
30. Donald L. Horowitz, *The Courts and Social Policy* (Washington, DC: Brookings Institution, 1977), 538.
31. *Webster* v. *Reproductive Health Services,* 492 U.S. 490 (1989).
32. See, for example, Tracey E. George and Lee Epstein, "On the Nature of Supreme Court Decision Making," *American Political Science Review* 86 (1992): 323–37; Melinda Gann Hall and Paul Brace, "Justices' Responses to Case Facts: An Interactive Model," *American Politics Quarterly* (April 1996): 237–61; Lawrence Baum, *The Puzzle of Judicial Behavior* (Ann Arbor: University of Michigan Press, 1997); and Gregory N. Flemming, David B. Holmes, and Susan Gluck Mezey, "An Integrated Model of Privacy Decision Making in State Supreme Courts," *American Politics Quarterly* 26 (January 1998): 35–58.
33. Jeffrey A. Segal and Harold J. Spaeth, *The Supreme Court and the Attitudinal Model Revisited* (New York: Cambridge University Press, 2002).
34. Gerard Gryski, Eleanor C. Main, and William Dixon, "Models of State High Court Decision Making in Sex Discrimination Cases," *Journal of Politics* 48 (1986): 143–55; and C. Neal Tate and Roger Handberg, "Time Binding and Theory Building in Personal Attribute Models of Supreme Court Voting Behavior, 1916–1988," *American Political Science Review* 35 (1991): 460–80.
35. Donald R. Songer and Sue Davis, "The Impact of Party and Region on Voting Decisions in the U.S. Courts of Appeals, 1955–86," *Western Political Quarterly* 43 (1990): 830–44.

36. See, generally, Lee Epstein and Jack Knight, "Field Essay: Toward a Strategic Revolution in Judicial Politics: A Look Back, a Look Ahead," *Political Research Quarterly* 53 (September 2000): 663–76.

37. Thomas R. Marshall, "Public Opinion, Representation and the Modern Supreme Court," *American Politics Quarterly* 16 (1988): 296–316.

38. Timothy R. Johnson and Andrew D. Martin, "The Public's Conditional Response to Supreme Court Decisions," *American Political Science Review* 92 (June 1998): 299–309.

39. *Korematsu* v. *U.S.*, 323 U.S. 214 (1944).

40. *Youngstown Sheet & Tube Co.* v. *Sawyer*, 343 U.S. 579 (1952).

41. The Supreme Court ruled that President Truman's seizure and operation of U.S. steel mills in the face of a strike threat were unconstitutional, because the Constitution implied no such broad executive power. See Alan Westin, *Anatomy of a Constitutional Law Case* (New York: Macmillan, 1958); and Maeva Marcus, *Truman and the Steel Seizure Case* (New York: Columbia University Press, 1977).

42. *U.S.* v. *Nixon*, 418 U.S. 683 (1974).

43. Gallup Poll, *Public Opinion Online.* (May 21–24, 2004).

44. "Supreme Court Cases Overruled by Subsequent Decision," U.S. Government Printing Office, http://www.gpoaccess.gov/constitution/pdf/con041.pdf.

45. *Reynolds* v. *Sims*, 377 U.S. 533 (1964).

46. *Mississippi University for Women* v. *Hogan*, 458 U.S. 718 (1982).

CHAPTER 10

1. Robert D. Hess and David Easton, "The Child's Changing Image of the President," *Public Opinion Quarterly* 14 (Winter 1960): 632–42; and Fred I. Greenstein, *Children and Politics* (New Haven, CT: Yale University Press, 1965).

2. Laura Pappano, "Potential War Poses Threat to Teachers," *Boston Globe* (March 9, 2003): B9.

3. James Simon and Bruce D. Merrill, "Political Socialization in the Classroom Revisited: The Kids Voting Program," *Social Science Journal* 35 (1998): 29–42.

4. Simon and Merrill, "Political Socialization in the Classroom Revisited."

5. *Statistical Abstract of the United States, 1997* (Washington, DC: Government Printing Office, 1997), 1011.

6. Princeton Research Survey Associates Poll, December 19, 2003–January 3, 2004.

7. Princeton Research Survey Associates Poll, March 17–21, 2004.

8. Steven M. Cohen and Charles S. Liebman, "American Jewish Liberalism," *Public Opinion Quarterly* 61 (1997): 405–30.

9. *USA Today* and CNN/Gallup Tracking Poll, USAToday.com.

10. Edward S. Greenberg, "The Political Socialization of Black Children," in Edward S. Greenberg, ed., *Political Socialization* (New York: Atherton Press, 1970), 181.

11. Elaine J. Hall and Myra Marx Ferree, "Race Differences in Abortion Attitudes," *Public Opinion Quarterly* 50 (Summer 1986): 193–207; and Jon Hurwitz and Mark Peffley, "Public Perceptions of Race and Crime: The Role of Racial Stereotypes," *American Journal of Political Science* 41 (April 1997): 375–401.

12. Elaine S. Povich, "Courting Hispanics: Group's Votes Could Shift House Control," *Newsday* (April 21, 2002): A4.

13. Alejandro Portes and Rafael Mozo, "The Political Adaptation Process of Cubans and Other Ethnic Minorities in the United States: A Preliminary Analysis," in F. Chris Garcia, ed., *Latinos and the Political System* (Notre Dame, IN: University of Notre Dame Press, 1988), 161.

14. Pamela Johnston Conover and Virginia Sapiro, "Gender, Feminist Consciousness and War," *American Journal of Political Science* 37 (November 1993): 1079–99.

15. Margaret Trevor, "Political Socialization, Party Identification, and the Gender Gap," *Public Opinion Quarterly* 63 (Spring 1999): 62–89.

16. Alexandra Marks, "Gender Gap Narrows over Kosovo," *Christian Science Monitor* (April 30, 1999): 1.

17. Pew Research Center for the People and the Press, 2002, http://people-press.org.

18. Susan A. MacManus, *Young v. Old: Generational Combat in the 21st Century* (Boulder, CO: Westview, 1995).

19. "Church Pews Seat More Blacks, Seniors, and Republicans," http://www.gallup.com/POLL_ARCHIVES/970329.html.

20. Allan M. Winkler, "Public Opinion," in Jack Greene, ed., *The Encyclopedia of American Political History* (New York: Charles Scribner's Sons, 1988), 1038.

21. *Literary Digest* 122 (August 22, 1936): 3.

22. *Literary Digest* 125 (November 14, 1936): 1.

23. Robert S. Erikson, Norman Luttbeg, and Kent Tedin, *American Public Opinion: Its Origin, Contents, and Impact* (New York: Wiley, 1980), 28.

24. Francis J. Connolly and Charley Manning, "What 'Push Polling' Is and What It Isn't," *Boston Globe* (August 16, 2001): A21.

25. Michael W. Traugott, "The Polls in 1992: Views of Two Critics: A Good General Showing, but Much Work Needs to Be Done," *Public Perspective* 4 (November/December 1992): 14–16.

26. Suzanne Soule, "Will They Engage? Political Knowledge, Participation and Attitudes of Generations X and Y," paper prepared for the 2001 German and American Conference, quoting Richard G. Niemi and Jane Junn, *Civic Education* (New Haven, CT: Yale University Press, 1998).

27. Quoted in Everett Carll Ladd, "Fiskin's 'Deliberative Poll' Is Flawed Science and Dubious Democracy," *Public Perspective* (December/January 1996): 41.

28. Tamara Henry, "Kids Get 'Abysmal' Grade in History," *USA Today* (May 10, 2002): 1A.

29. "Don't Know Much About . . ." *Christian Science Monitor* (May 16, 2002): 8.

30. V. O. Key Jr., *The Responsible Electorate: Rationality in Presidential Voting, 1936–1960* (Cambridge, MA: Belknap Press of Harvard University, 1966).

31. Richard Nodeau et al., "Elite Economic Forecasts, Economic News, Mass Economic Judgments and Presidential Approval," *Journal of Politics* 61 (February 1999): 109–35.

32. Michael Towle, Review of *Presidential Responsiveness and Public Policymaking: The Public and the Policies* by Jeffrey E. Cohen, *Journal of Politics* 61 (February 1999): 230–2.

33. John E. Mueller, *War, Presidents, and Public Opinion* (New York: Wiley, 1973), 69.

34. See Mitchell Stephens, *A History of News: From the Drum to the Satellite* (New York: Viking, 1989).

35. For a delightful rendition of this episode, see Shelley Ross, *Fall from Grace* (New York: Ballantine, 1988), ch. 12.

36. Doris A. Graber, *Mass Media and American Politics*, 3rd ed. (Washington, DC: CQ Press, 1989), 12. Also see Thomas C. Leonard, *The Power of the Press: The Birth of American Political Reporting* (New York: Oxford University Press, 1986).

37. Pew Research Center for the People and the Press, "Cable and Internet Loom Large in Fragmented Political News Universe: Perceptions of Partisan Bias Seen as Growing, Especially by Democrats," January 11, 2004.

38. Pew Research Center, "Cable and Internet Loom Large."

39. Katy Bachman, "Direct Broadcast Satellite Gains Users; Cable Wanes," mediaweek.com, April 7, 2004.

40. Annenberg National Election Study, 2004, http://www.annenbergpublicpolicycenter.org.

41. Pew Research Center for the People and the Press, Political Communications Study, January 11, 2004, http://people-press.org.

42. Pew Research Center, "Public More Critical of Press, but Goodwill Persists," June 26, 2005.

43. Donald L. Lorand and Benjamin I. Page, "Shaping Foreign Policy Opinions: The Role of TV News," *Journal of Conflict Resolution* 36 (June 1992): 227–41.

44. Andrew Kohut, *The Biennial Pew Media Survey: How News Habits Changed in 2004,* Brookings/Pew Research Center Forum, Washington, DC, June 8, 2004, http://www.brookings.edu.

45. Christopher Stern, "FCC Chairman's Star a Little Dimmer," *Washington Post* (July 25, 2003): E01, http://www.washingtonpost.com.

46. Mark K. Miller. "On Hold; Rankings Change Little as Regulatory Uncertainty Keeps Station Trading in Neutral," *Broadcasting and Cable* (April, 19, 2004): 50.

47. *RTNDA* v. *FCC*, 299 F.3d 269 (DC Cir. 2000).

48. *New York Times Co.* v. *U.S.*, 403 U.S. 713 (1971).

49. Jillian Harrison, "Embedded Journalism Limited in Perspective, Tufts U. Professors Say," *University Wire*, April 15, 2003.

50. U.S. Senate press gallery and U.S. House of Representatives radio-television correspondents gallery.

51. *New York Times Co.* v. *Sullivan*, 376 U.S. 254 (1964). See also Steven Pressman, "Libel Law: Finding the Right Balance," *Editorial Research Reports* 2 (August 18, 1989): 462–71.

52. *Curtis Publishing Co.* v. *Butts*, 388 U.S. 130 (1967); *Associated Press* v. *Walker*, 388 U.S. 130 (1967).

53. Thomas Patterson, *Out of Order* (New York: Vintage, 1994).

54. John R. Zaller, "Monica Lewinsky's Contribution to Political Science," *PS: Political Science and Politics* 31 (June 1998): 182–89.

55. Lori Robertson, "In Control," *American Journalism Review*, (February/March 2005).

56. Harold W. Stanley and Richard G. Niemi, *Vital Statistics on American Politics*, 4th ed. (Washington, DC: CQ Press, 1994), 28.

57. John R. Hibbing and Elizabeth Theiss-Morse, *Congress as Public Enemy: Political Attitudes Toward American Political Institutions* (New York: Cambridge University Press, 1995).

58. Karen Aho, "Broadcasters Want Access, but Will They Deliver Serious Coverage?" *Columbia Journalism Review* 5 (September/October), http://www.cjr.org.

59. Benjamin I. Page, Robert Y. Shapiro, and Glenn R. Dempsey, "What Moves Public Opinion?" *American Political Science Review* 81 (March 1987): 23–44.

60. Shanto Iyengar and Donald R. Kinder, *News That Matters* (Chicago: University of Chicago Press, reprint ed., 1989).

61. David Domke, David P. Fan, Dhavan V. Shah, and Mark D. Watts, "The Politics of Conservative Elites and the 'Liberal Media' Argument," *Journal of Communication* 49 (Fall 1999): 35–58.

62. American Society of Newspaper Editors, *The Changing Face of the Newsroom* (Washington, DC: ASNE, 1989), 33; William Schneider and I. A. Lewis, "Views on the News," *Public Opinion* 8 (August/September 1985): 6–11, 58–59; and S. Robert Lichter, Stanley Rothman, and Linda S. Lichter, *The Media Elite* (Bethesda, MD: Adler and Adler, 1986).

63. Pew Research Center for the People and the Press, "How Journalists See Journalists 2004."

64. Martin Gilens and Craig Hertzman, "Corporate Ownership and News Bias: Newspaper Coverage of the 1996 Telecommunication Act," *Journal of Politics* 62 (May 2000), 369–86.

65. See http://www.stateofthenewsmedia.org/narrative_overview_audience.asp?media=1.

CHAPTER 11

1. Graham Wilson, *Interest Groups in the United States* (New York: Oxford University Press, 1981), 4.

2. V. O. Key, *Politics, Parties, and Pressure Groups* (New York, Crowell, 1942), 23.

3. John H. Aldrich, *Why Parties? The Origin and Transformation of Party Politics in America* (Chicago: University of Chicago Press, 1995).

4. By contrast, Great Britain did not develop truly national, broad-based parties until the 1870s.

5. See *Historical Statistics of the United States: Colonial Times to 1970*, part 2, series Y-27-28 (Washington, DC: Government Printing Office, 1975), based on unpublished data prepared by Walter Dean Burnham.

6. On the subject of party realignment, see Walter Dean Burnham, *Critical Elections and the Mainsprings of American Politics* (New York: Norton, 1970); Kristi Andersen, *The Creation of a Democratic Majority* (Chicago: University of Chicago Press, 1979); and John R. Petrocik, "Realignment: New Party Coalitions and the Nationalization of the South," *Journal of Politics* 49 (May 1987): 347–75.

7. See Walter Dean Burnham, *Critical Elections and the Mainsprings of American Politics* (New York: W. W. Norton, 1970) for a defense of realignment theory.

8. For a perspective on reconsidering the relevance and validity of critical realignments, see David Mayhew, *Electoral Realignments* (New Haven, CT: Yale University Press, 2004).

9. Morris P. Fiorina, *Retrospective Voting in American National Elections* (New Haven, CT: Yale University Press, 1981); and Charles H. Franklin and John E. Jackson, "The Dynamics of Party Identification," *American Political Science Review* 77 (1983): 957–73.

10. See, for example, V. O. Key Jr., "A Theory of Critical Elections," *Journal of Politics* 17 (February 1955): 3–18.

11. See Everett Carll Ladd, "The Brittle Mandate: Electoral Dealignment and the 1980 Presidential Election," *Political Science Quarterly* 96 (1981): 1–25.

12. Everett Carll Ladd, "Like Waiting for Godot: The Uselessness of 'Realignment' for Understanding Change in Contemporary American Politics," in Byron Shafer, ed., *The End of Realignment? Interpreting American Electoral Eras* (Madison: University Wisconsin Press, 1991).

13. For a discussion of secular realignment in the south, See Jeffrey M. Stonecash, "Class and Party: Secular Realignment and the Survival of Democrats Outside the South," *Political Research Quarterly* 53 (December 2000): 731–52.

14. Martin Kady II, "Party Unity: Learning to Stick Together," *CQ Weekly* (January 9, 2006) 92.

15. See David E. Price, *Bringing Back the Parties* (Washington, DC: CQ Press, 1984), 284–8.

16. See, for example, Sarah McCally Morehouse, "Legislatures and Political Parties," *State Government* 59 (1976): 23.

17. Christian Collet and Martin P. Wattenberg, "Strategically Unambitious: Minor Party and Independent Candidates in the 1996 Congressional Elections," in John C. Green and Daniel M. Shea, eds., *The State of the Parties: The Changing Role of Contemporary American Parties*, 3rd ed. (Lanham, MD: Rowman and Littlefield, 1999).

18. Marc J. Hetherington, "The Effect of Political Trust on the Presidential Vote, 1968–1992," *American Political Science Review* 93 (1999): 311–26.

19. John Clifford Green, Paul S. Herrnson, and John C. Green, eds., *Responsible Partisanship: The Evolution of American Political Parties Since the 1950s* (Lawrence, KS: University Press of Kansas, 2003).

20. See Steven E. Finkel and Howard A. Scarrow, "Party Identification and Party Enrollment: The Difference and the Consequence," *Journal of Politics* 47 (May 1985): 620–42.

21. The presidential election of 1960 may be an extreme case, but John F. Kennedy's massive support among Catholics and Nixon's less substantial but still impressive backing by Protestants demonstrates the polarization that religion could produce. See Philip E. Converse, "Religion and Politics: The 1960 Election," in Angus Campbell et al., *Elections and the Political Order* (New York: Wiley, 1966), 96–124.

22. For a discussion of recent trends in party strength see Morris P. Fiorina, "Parties and Partisanship: A 40-Year Retrospective," *Political Behavior* 24 (2002), 93–115.

23. Robert D. Putnam, "Bowling Alone: America's Declining Social Capital," *Journal of Democracy* 6 (1995): 650–65; and Putnam, *Bowling Alone: The Collapse and Revival of American Community* (New York: Simon and Schuster, 2000).

24. Everett Carll Ladd, quoted in Richard Morin, "Who Says We're Not Joiners," *Washington Post* (May 2, 1999): B5.

25. John Brehm and Wendy Rahn, "Individual-Level Evidence for the Causes and Consequences of Social Capital," *American Journal of Political Science* 41 (July 1997): 999.

26. Mark Schneider et al., "Institutional Arrangements and the Creation of Social Capital: The Effects of Public School Choice," *American Political Science Review* 91 (March 1997): 82–93.

27. Nicholas Lemann, "Kicking in Groups," *Atlantic Monthly* (April 1996), NEXIS.

28. David B. Truman, *The Governmental Process: Political Interests and Public Opinion* (New York: Knopf, 1951), 33.

29. Robert H. Salisbury, "An Exchange Theory of Interest Groups," *Midwest Journal of Political Science* 13 (1969): 1–32.

30. See, for example, Lee Ann Banaszak, *Why Movements Succeed or Fail: Opportunity, Culture, and the Struggle for Woman Suffrage* (Princeton: Princeton University Press, 1996); Frank R. Baumgartner and Beth L. Leech, *Basic Interests: The Importance of Groups in Politics and in Political Science* (Princeton: Princeton University Press, 1999).

31. Jack Walker, *Mobilizing Interest Groups in America: Patrons, Professions, and Social Movements* (Ann Arbor: The University of Michigan Press, 1991).

32. Mancur Olson Jr., *The Logic of Collective Action: Public Goods and the Theory of Groups* (Cambridge, MA: Harvard University Press, 1965).

33. Chris Kutalik, "What Does the AFL-CIO Split Mean?" Labor Notes, September 2005, http://www.labornotes.org.

34. Thomas B. Edsall, "Labor's Divisions Widen As Membership Declines," *Washington Post* (March 7, 2005): A2.

35. Jeffrey M. Berry, *Lobbying for the People: The Political Behavior of Public Interest Groups* (Princeton, NJ: Princeton University Press, 1977), 7.

36. Peter Steinfels, "Moral Majority to Dissolve: Says Mission Accomplished," *New York Times* (June 12, 1989): A14.

37. Some political scientists speak of "iron rectangles," reflecting the growing importance of a fourth party, the courts, in the lobbying process.

38. Clement E. Vose, "Litigation As a Form of Pressure Group Activity," *Annals* 319 (September 1958): 20–31.

39. Robert A. Goldberg, *Grassroots Resistance: Social Movement in Twentieth Century America* (Belmont, CA: Wadsworth, 1991).

40. Center for Responsive Politics, http://www.opensecrets.org.

41. Michelle Garcia, "Animal Rights Activists Step Up Attacks in N.Y.," *Washington Post* (May 9, 2005): A3.

CHAPTER 12

1. Thomas M. Guterbock and Bruce London, "Race, Political Orientation, and Participation: An Empirical Test of Four Competing Theories," *American Sociological Review* 48 (1983): 439–53.

2. Carol A, Cassel, "Hispanic Turnout: Estimates from Validated Voting Data," *Political Science Quarterly* 55 (June 2002): 391–408.

3. League of United Latin American Citizens, http://www.lulac.org.

4. Stephen Knack and J. White, "Election-Day Registration and Turnout Inequality," *Political Behavior* 22 (March 2000): 29–44.

5. International Institute for Democracy and Electoral Assistance, "Global Database," http://www.idea.int/vt/survey/voter_turnout_pop2.cfm.

6. Charles E. Smith Jr. et al., "Party Balancing and Voting in Congress in the 1996 National Election," *American Journal of Political Science* 43 (July 1999): 737–64.

7. Michael S. Lewis-Beck and Mary Stegmaier, "Economic Determinants of Electoral Outcomes," *Annual Review of Political Science* 3 (2000): 183–219.

8. Paul Allen Beck, *Party Politics in America,* 8th ed. (New York: Longman, 1998); David Adamany, "Cross-over Voting and the Democratic Party's Reform Rules," *American Political Science Review* 70 (1976): 536–41; Ronald Hedlund and Meredith W. Watts, "The Wisconsin Open Primary: 1968 to 1984," *American Politics Quarterly* 14 (1986): 55–74; and Gary D. Wekken, "The Conceptualization and Measurement of Crossover Voting," *Western Political Quarterly* 41 (1988): 105–14.

9. Todd L. Cherny and Stephan Kroll, "Crashing the Party: An Experimental Investigation of Strategic Voting in Primary Elections," *Public Choice* 114 (2003): 387–420; and Gary D. Wekken, "Why Crossover Voters Are Not 'Mischievous' Voters," *American Politics Quarterly* 19 (1991): 229–47.

10. Elaine Ciulla Kamarck and Kenneth M. Goldstein, "The Rules Matter: Post-Reform Presidential Nominating Politics," in L. Sandy Maisel, *The Parties Respond: Changes in American Parties and Campaigns* (Boulder, CO: Westview, 1994), 174.

11. Larry J. Sabato, "Presidential Nominations: The Front-loaded Frenzy of 1996," in Larry J. Sabato, ed., *Toward the Millennium: The Elections of 1996* (New York: Allyn and Bacon, 1997).

12. Byron Shafer, *Bifurcated Politics: Evolution and Reform in the National Party Convention* (Cambridge, MA: Harvard University Press, 1988).

13. See "Candidates and Nominations" in Paul S. Herrnson, *Congressional Elections: Campaigning at Home and in Washington,* 4th ed. (Washington, D.C.: CQ Press, 2004), 35–68.

14. Dennis W. Johnson, *No Place for Amateurs: How Political Consultants Are Reshaping American Democracy* (New York: Routledge, 2001).

15. R. Michael Alvarez and Jonathan Nagler, "Economics, Issues, and the Perot Candidacy: Voter Choice in the 1992 Presidential Election," *American Journal of Political Science* 39 (1995): 714–44.

16. Common Cause, redistricting issues, http//:www.commoncause.org.

17. "How to Rig an Election," *Economist* (April 25, 2002).

18. Matthew Mosk and Lori Montgomery, "Md. Court Spurns Assembly Map: Glendening Plan Ruled Unconstitutional; Judges to Redraw Lines," *Washington Post* (June 12, 2002).

19. *Wesberry v. Sanders,* 376 U.S. 1 (1964).

20. *Thornburg v. Gingles,* 478 U.S. 30 (1986).

21. *Shaw v. Reno,* 113 S.Ct. 2816 (1993).

22. Gary C. Jacobson and Michael A. Dimock, "Checking Out: The Effects of Bank Overdrafts on the 1992 House Elections," *American Journal of Political Science* 38 (1994): 601–24; and Paul S. Herrnson, *Congressional Elections: Campaigning at Home and in Washington,* 2nd ed. (Washington, DC: CQ Press, 1998).

23. Five liberal Democratic U.S. senators, including George McGovern of South Dakota, were defeated in this way in 1980, for example.

24. Diana C. Mutz, "Effects of Horse-Race Coverage on Campaign Coffers: Strategic Contributing in Presidential Primaries," *Journal of Politics* 57 (November 1995): 1015–42.

25. See "Media, Old and New," in Johnson, *No Place for Amateurs,* 115–47.

26. Pew Internet and American Life Project, www.pewinternet.org/pdfs/PIP_2004_Campaign.pdf.

27. *McConnell v. Federal Election Commission* 251 F. Supp. 2d 176, 251 F. Supp. 2d 948 (2003).

28. *McConnell v. Federal Election Commission* 540 U.S. 93 (2003).

29. See http://www.opensecrets.org/overview/stats.asp?cycle=2004.

30. See "The Interests Campaign" in Herrnson (2004).

31. Steven T. Engel and David J. Jackson, "Wielding the Stick Instead of its Carrot: Labor PAC Punishment of Pro-NAFTA Democrats," *Political Research Quarterly* 51 (September 1998): 813–28.

32. Janet M. Box-Steffensmeier and J. Tobin Grant, "All in a Day's Work: The Financial Rewards of Legislative Effectiveness," *Legislative Studies Quarterly* 24 (November 1999): 511–23.

33. Kevin M. Leyden and Stephen A. Borrelli, "An Investment in Goodwill: Party Contributions and Party Unity Among U.S. House Members in the 1980s," *American Politics Quarterly* 22 (October 1994): 421–52.

34. Amy Keller, "Helping Each Other Out: Members Dip into Campaign Funds for Fellow Candidates," *Roll Call* (June 15, 1998): 1. For member contribution activity at the state level, see Jay K. Dow, "Campaign Contributions and Intercandidate Transfers in the California Assembly," *Social Science Quarterly* 75 (1994): 867–80. For member contribution activity at the congressional level, see Bruce A. Larson, "Ambition and Money in the U.S. House of Representatives: Analyzing Campaign Contributions from Incumbents' Leadership PACs and Reelection Committees" (Ph.D. dissertation, University of Virginia, 1998). For a briefer account, see Paul S. Herrnson, "Money and Motives: Spending in House Elections," in Lawrence C. Dodd and Bruce J. Oppenheimer, eds., *Congress Reconsidered,* 6th ed. (Washington, DC: CQ Press, 1997).

35. *Buckley v. Valeo,* 424 U.S. 1 (1976).

36. Jeffrey Milyo and Tim Groseclose, "The Electoral Effects of Incumbent Wealth," *Journal of Law and Economics* 42 (1999), 699–722.

37. Marisa Katz, "Matching Funds," *New Republic Online* (July 13, 2004), http://www.tnr.com.

38. See http://www.commoncause.org/laundromat/stat/topdonors0.1.htm.

39. Federal Election Commission Release, "Party Financial Activity Summarized," December 14, 2004, http://www.fec.gov.

40. Michael Janofsky, "Advocacy Groups Spent Record Amount on 2004 Election," *New York Times* (December 17, 2004).

CHAPTER 13

1. "President Signs Medicare Legislation," White House news release, December 8, 2003, http://www.whitehouse.gov.
2. Kaiser Family Foundation, Kaiser Health Poll Report Survey, Selected Findings on Seniors' Views of the Medicare Prescription Drug Benefit, February 17, 2006, http://www.kff.org.
3. Robert J. Samuelson, "Medicare as Pork Barrel," *Newsweek* (December 1, 2003): 47.
4. James E. Anderson, *Public Policymaking: An Introduction*, 4th ed. (Boston: Houghton Mifflin, 2000). This discussion draws on Anderson's study.
5. Roger W. Cobb and Charles D. Elder, *Participation in American Politics: The Dynamics of Agenda-Building*, 2nd ed. (Baltimore, MD: Johns Hopkins University Press, 1983), ch. 5.
6. Charles O. Jones, *An Introduction to the Study of Public Policy*, 3rd ed. (Monterey, CA: Brooks/Cole, 1984), 87–89.
7. Judy Sarasohn, "Bush's '06 Budget Would Scrap or Reduce 154 Programs," *Washington Post* (February 22, 2005): A13.
8. This discussion draws on Anne Schneider and Helen Ingram, "Behavioral Assumptions of Policy Tools," *Journal of Politics* 52 (May 1990): 510–29.
9. Government Accountability Office, Amtrak Management: Systematic Problems Require Actions to Improve Efficiency, Effectiveness, and Accountability, GAO-06-145, April 2005, http://www.gao.gov.
10. Douglas Kirby, *Emerging Answers: Research Findings on Programs to Reduce Teen Pregnancy* (Washington, DC: National Campaign to Prevent Teen Pregnancy, 2001).
11. Ronald Edsforth, *The New Deal: America's Response to the Great Depression* (Oxford: Blackwell, 2000), 231.
12. Robert Rich and William White, "Health Care Policy and the American States: Issues of Federalism," in R. Rich and W. White, eds., *Health Policy, Federalism, and the American States* (Washington, DC: Urban Institute, 1996), 20.
13. U.S. Department of Health and Human Services, http://aspe.hhs.gov.
14. Social Security Fact Sheet, http://www.ssa.gov.
15. Pew Research Center for the People and the Press, "Survey Finds Bush Failing in Social Security Reform," March 3, 2005.
16. Economic Policy Institute, "State Unemployment Insurance Policies as of June 2004," http://www.epinet.org.
17. Bureau of Labor Statistics, *Employment Situation Summary*, http://www.bls.gov.
18. Social Security Administration, http://ssa-custhelp.ssa.gov.
19. Steven G. Koven, Mack C. Shelley II, and Bert E. Swanson, *American Public Policy: The Contemporary Agenda* (Boston: Houghton Mifflin, 1998), 271.
20. The White House, "Working Toward Independence," February 2002, http://www.whitehouse.gov.
21. Nanette Relave, "TANF Reauthorization and Work Requirements," *The Reauthorization Resource*, February 2002, http://www.welfareinfo.org.
22. U.S. Department of Health and Human Services, "Welfare Reform Reauthorized," February 8, 2006, http://www.hhs.gov.
23. U.S. Department of Agriculture, "Food Stamp Program Annual Summary," March 24, 2006, http://www.fns.usda.gov.
24. U.S. Department of Agriculture, "Food Stamp Program," October 1, 2005, http://www.fns.usda.gov.
25. Office of Management and Budget, "Fiscal Year 2006: Mid-Session Review Budget of the U.S. Government," July 13, 2005, http://www.whitehouse.gov.
26. Mark Rushefsky and Kant Patel, *Politics, Power, and Policy Making* (Armonk, NY: M. E. Sharpe, 1998), 27.
27. Henry J. Aaron, *Serious and Unstable Condition: Financing America's Health Care* (Washington, DC: Brookings Institution, 1991), ch. 2.
28. John F. Dickerson, "Can We Afford All This?" *Time* (December 8, 2004), 48–51; Edward Walsh and Bill Brubaker, "Drug Benefits Impact Detailed," *Washington Post* (December 8, 2003): A10.
29. Congressional Budget Office, "Medicaid: Federal Outlays in Billions of Dollars," 2005, http://www.house.gov; Kaiser Family Foundation, "HIV/AIDS Policy Fact Sheet," September 2005, http://www.kff.org.
30. After 108 years of operation, the ICC expired at the end of 1995 as part of the effort by congressional Republicans to reduce federal regulations and allow market forces more freedom in which to operate.
31. Martha Derthick and Paul J. Quirk, *The Politics of Deregulation* (Washington, DC: Brookings Institution, 1985); Dorothy Robyn, *Braking the Special Interests: Trucking Deregulation and the Politics of Policy Reform* (Chicago: University of Chicago Press, 1987).
32. "Is Small Community Air Service Near Extinction?" *Commuter/Regional Airline News* 20:23, 1, http://proquest.umi.com/pdqweb/.
33. About 38 percent of the nation's commercial banks are members of the Federal Reserve System.
34. James E. Anderson, David W. Brady, Charles S. Bullock III, and Joseph Stewart Jr., *Public Policy and Politics in America*, 2nd ed. (Monterey, CA: Brooks/Cole, 1984), 38–40.

CHAPTER 14

1. "President Bush Discusses NSA Surveillance Program," White House press briefing, May 11, 2006. Full text available at www.whitehouse.gov/news/releases.
2. See Graham Allison, *Essence of Decision: Explaining the Cuban Missile Crisis* (Boston: Little, Brown, 1971).
3. For a discussion of U.S., Soviet, and Chinese views of the Vietnam War, see Daniel S. Papp, *Vietnam: The View from Moscow, Beijing, Washington* (Jefferson, NC: McFarland, 1981).
4. Michael Froman, *The Development of the Idea of Détente* (New York: St. Martin's Press, 1982).
5. See Colin S. Gray, "Strategic Forces," in Joseph Kruzel, ed., *1986–1987 American Defense Annual* (Lexington, MA: Lexington Books, 1986). For a discussion of Reagan's early international economic policies, see Jeffrey E. Garten, "Gunboat Economics," *Foreign Affairs* 63 (1985): 538–99.
6. See Stephen E. Ambrose, *Rise to Globalism: American Foreign Policy Since 1938*, 8th revised ed. (New York: Penguin Books, 1998); Steven W. Hook and John Spanier, *American Foreign Policy Since World War II*, 15th ed. (Washington, DC: CQ Press, 2000); Richard Mandelbaum and Strobe Talbott, *Reagan and Gorbachev* (New York: Vintage Books, 1987); and Richard A. Melanson, *American Foreign Policy Since the Vietnam War*, 3rd ed. (Armonk, NY: M. E. Sharpe, 2000).
7. Karen Brutents and Larisa Galperin, "Origins of the New Thinking," *Russian Social Science Review* 47 (2006): 73–102; David Laibman, "The Soviet Demise: Revisionist Betrayal, Structural Defect, or Authoritarian Distortion?" *Science & Society* 69 (2005) 594–606; John Muelle, "What Was the Cold War About? Evidence from Its Ending," *Political Science Quarterly* 119 (2004/2005): 609–31.
8. See William Head and Earl H. Tilford Jr., *The Eagle in the Desert: Looking Back on U.S. Involvement in the Persian Gulf War* (Westport, CT: Praeger, 1996).
9. See Geoffrey Hosking, *The Awakening of the Soviet Union* (Cambridge, MA: Harvard University Press, 1990); David Remnick, *Lenin's Tomb: The Last Days of the Soviet Empire* (New York: Random House, 1993); and Jeffrey T. Checkel, *Ideas and International Political Change: Soviet/Russian Behavior and the End of the Cold War* (New Haven, CT: Yale University Press, 1997).
10. Jeffrey J. Schott, *The WTO After Seattle* (Washington, DC: Institute for International Economics, 2000); and Bhagirath L. Das, *World Trade Organization: A Guide to New Frameworks for International Trade* (New York: St. Martin's, 2000).
11. See Daniel S. Papp, *The Impact of September 11 on Contemporary International Relations* (New York: Pearson, 2003).
12. "Strategic Offensive Arms Reduction Treaty," U.S. Department of State, May 24, 2002.
13. Dana Priest and Walter Pincus, "U.S. 'Almost All Wrong' on Weapons," *Washington Post* (October 7, 2004): A1; Hans Blix, *Disarming Iraq* (New York: Pantheon Books, 2004); Richard A. Clarke, *Against All Enemies: Inside America's War on Terror* (New York: Free Press, 2004); Kenneth M. Pollack, *The Threatening Storm: The Case for Invading Iraq* (New York: Random House, 2002).

14. Robin Wright and Ellen Knickmeyer, "U.S. Lowers Sights On What Can Be Achieved in Iraq," *Washington Post* (August 14, 2005): A1.

15. See Loch K. Johnson, *America's Secret Power: The CIA in a Democratic Society* (New York: Oxford University Press, 1989).

16. United States Senate, Select Committee on Intelligence, *Report of the Select Committee on Intelligence on the U.S. Intelligence Community's Prewar Intelligence Assessments on Iraq,* (Washington, DC: Government Printing Office), 2004; Josh Meyer and Greg Miller, "The Prisoner Problem," *Los Angeles Times* (September 7, 2006): A1; David Stout, "Senate Panel Defies Bush on Detainee Bill," *New York Times* (September 14, 2006): A10.

17. James M. Lindsay, "Congress, Foreign Policy, and the New Institutionalism," *International Studies Quarterly* 38 (June 1994): 281–304.

18. For Eisenhower's thoughts on the subject, see Dwight D. Eisenhower, *The White House Years* (Garden City, NY: Doubleday, 1963–1965).

19. David S. Cloud, "U.S. Urged to Stop Paying Iraqi Reporters," *New York Times* (May 24, 2006).

A

administrative adjudication: A quasi-judicial process in which a bureaucratic agency settles disputes between two parties in a manner similar to the way courts resolve disputes.

administrative discretion: The ability of bureaucrats to make choices concerning the best way to implement congressional intentions.

advisory referendum: A process in which voters cast nonbinding ballots on an issue or proposal.

affiliates: Local television stations that carry the programming of a national network.

affirmative action: Policies designed to give special attention or compensatory treatment to members of a previously disadvantaged group.

agenda: A set of issues to be discussed or given attention.

agenda setting: The constant process of forming the list of issues to be addressed by government.

al-Qaeda: Worldwide terrorist organization led by Osama bin Laden, responsible for numerous attacks against U.S. interests, including 9/11 attacks against the World Trade Center and the Pentagon.

American dream: An American ideal of a happy, sucessful life, which often includes wealth, a house, a better life for one's children, and, for some, the ability to grow up to be president.

amicus curiae: "Friend of the court"; a third party to a lawsuit who files a legal brief for the purpose of raising additional points of view in an attempt to influence a court's decision.

Anti-Federalists: Those who favored strong state governments and a weak national government; opposed the ratification of the U.S. Constitution.

appellate courts: Courts that generally review only findings of law made by lower courts.

appellate jurisdiction: The power vested in an appellate court to review and/or revise the decision of a lower court.

apportionment: The process of allotting congressional seats to each state following the decennial census according to their proportion of the population.

Articles of Confederation: The compact among the thirteen original states that was the basis of their government. Written in 1776, the Articles were not ratified by all the states until 1781.

B

bicameral legislature: A legislature divided into two houses; the U.S. Congress and the state legislatures are bicameral except Nebraska, which is unicameral.

bill: A proposed law.

bill of attainder:
A law declaring an act illegal without a judicial trial.

Bill of Rights: The first ten amendments to the U.S. Constitution, which largely guarantee specific rights and liberties.

Bipartisan Campaign Reform Act (2002): Legislation that prohibits soft-money contributions to political parties and limits amounts individuals can give.

Black Codes: Laws denying most legal rights to newly freed slaves; passed by southern states following the Civil War.

block grant: Broad grant with few strings attached; given to states by the federal government for specified activities, such as secondary education or health services.

Blog: A Web log; Web-based journal entries that provide an editorial and news outlet for citizens.

brief: A document containing the legal written arguments in a case filed with a court by a party prior to a hearing or trial.

Brown v. Board of Education (1954): U.S. Supreme Court decision holding that school segregation is inherently unconstitutional because it violates the Fourteenth Amendment's guarantee of equal protection; marked the end of legal segregation in the United States.

bureaucracy: A set of complex hierarchical departments, agencies, commissions, and their staffs that exist to help a chief executive officer carry out his or her duties. Bureaucracies may be private organizations of governmental units.

Bush Doctrine: Policy advocated by President George W. Bush of using preemptive military action against a perceived threat to U.S. interests.

C

Cabinet:
The formal body of presidential advisers who head the fifteen executive departments. Presidents often add others to this body of formal advisers. **campaign consultant:** The private-sector professionals and firms who sell to a candidate the technologies, services, and strategies required to get that candidate elected.

campaign manager: The individual who travels with the candidate and coordinates the many different aspects of the campaign.

Carter Doctrine: Policy announced after the 1979 Soviet invasion of Afghanistan that the Persian Gulf area was a vital U.S. interest and the United States would fight to maintain access to it.

categorical grant: Grant for which Congress appropriates funds for a specific purpose.

Central Intelligence Agency: Executive agency responsible for collection and analysis of information and intelligence about foreign countries and events.

checks and balances: A governmental structure that gives each of the three branches of government some degree of oversight and control over the actions of the others.

citizen: Member of the political community to whom certain rights and obligations are attached.

civic virtue: The tendency to form small-scale associations for the public good.

civil law: Codes of behavior related to business and contractual relationships between groups and individuals.

civil liberties: The personal guarantees and freedoms that the federal government cannot abridge by law, constitution, or judicial interpretation.

civil rights: The government-protected rights of individuals against arbitrary or discriminatory treatment by governments or individuals based on categories such as race, sex, national origin, age, religion, or sexual orientation.

Civil Rights Act of 1964: Legislation passed by Congress to outlaw segregation in public facilities and racial discrimination in employment, education, and voting; created the Equal Employment Opportunity Commission.

Civil Rights Cases (1883): Name attached to five cases brought under the Civil Rights Act of 1875. In 1883, the Supreme Court decided that discrimination in a variety of public accommodations, including theaters, hotels, and railroads, could not be prohibited by the act because it was private, not state, discrimination.

civil service laws: These acts removed the staffing of the bureaucracy from political parties and created a professional bureaucracy filled through competition.

civil service system: The system created by civil service laws by which many appointments to the federal bureaucracy are made.

civil society: Society created when citizens are allowed to organize and express their views publicly as they engage in an open debate about public policy.

clear and present danger test: Test articulated by the Supreme Court in *Schenck v. U.S.* (1919) to draw the line between protected and unprotected speech; the Court looks to see "whether the words used…" could "create a clear and present danger that they will bring about substantive evils" that Congress seeks "to prevent."

closed primary: A primary election in which only a party's registered voters are eligible to vote.

cloture: Mechanism requiring sixty senators to vote to cut off debate.

coalition: A group made up of interests or organizations that join forces for the purpose of electing public officials.

collective good: Something of value that cannot be withheld from a nonmember of a group, for example, a tax write-off or a better environment.

collective security: The concept that peace would be secured if all countries collectively opposed any country that invaded another.

Committees of Correspondence: Organizations in each of the American colonies created to keep colonists abreast of developments with the British; served as powerful molders of public opinion against the British.

communications director: The person who develops the overall media strategy for the candidate, blending the free press coverage with the paid TV, radio, and mail media.

concurrent powers: Authority possessed by both the state and national governments that may be exercised concurrently as long as that power is not exclusively within the scope of national power or in conflict with national law.

confederation: Type of government where the national government derives its powers from the states; a league of independent states.

conference committee: Joint committee created to iron out differences between Senate and House versions of a specific piece of legislation.

congressional review: A process whereby Congress can nullify agency regulations by a joint resolution of legislative disapproval.

conservative: One thought to believe that a government is best that governs least and that big government can only infringe on individual, personal, and economic rights.

constitution: A document establishing the structure, functions, and limitations of a government.

constitutional courts: Federal courts specifically created by the U.S. Constitution or by Congress pursuant to its authority in Article III.

containment: Strategy to oppose expansion of Soviet power, particularly in Western Europe and East Asia, with military power, economic assistance, and political influence.

content regulation: Governmental attempts to regulate the electronic media.

contrast ad: Ad that compares the records and proposals of the candidates, with a bias toward the sponsor.

cooperative federalism: The relationship between the national and state governments that began with the New Deal.

criminal law: Codes of behavior related to the protection of property and individual safety.

critical election: An election that signals a party realignment through voter polarization around new issues.

crossover voting: Participation in the primary of a party with which the voter is not affiliated.

Cuban Missile Crisis: The 1962 confrontation that nearly escalated into war between the United States and Soviet Union over Soviet deployment of medium-range ballistic missiles in Cuba.

D

Declaration of Independence: Document drafted by Thomas Jefferson in 1776 that proclaimed the right of the American colonies to separate from Great Britain.

delegate: Role played by elected representatives who vote the way their constituents would want them to, regardless of their own opinions.

democracy: A system of government that gives power to the people, whether directly or through elected representatives.

department: Major administrative unit with responsibility for a broad area of government operations. Departmental status usually indicates a permanent national interest in a particular governmental function, such as defense, commerce, or agriculture.

Department of Defense: Chief executive-branch department responsible for formulation and implementation of U.S. military policy.

Department of Homeland Security: Cabinet department created after the 9/11 attacks to coordinate domestic U.S. security efforts against terrorism.

Department of State: Chief executive-branch department responsible for formulation and implementation of U.S. foreign policy.

deregulation: A reduction in market controls (such as price fixing, subsidies, or controls on who can enter a field) in favor of market-based competition.

détente: The relaxation of tensions between the United States and the Soviet Union that occurred during the 1970s.

direct democracy: A system of government in which members of the polity meet to discuss all policy decisions and then agree to abide by majority rule.

direct incitement test: A test articulated by the Supreme Court in *Brandenberg* v. *Ohio* (1969) that holds that advocacy of illegal action is protected by the First Amendment unless imminent lawless action is intended and likely to occur.

direct mailer: A professional who supervises a political campaign's direct-mail fund-raising strategies.

direct primary: The selection of party candidates through the ballots of qualified voters rather than at party nomination conventions.

discharge petition: Petition that gives a majority of the House of Representatives the authority to bring an issue to the floor in the face of committee inaction.

discount rate: The rate of interest at which member banks can borrow money from their regional Federal Reserve Bank.

disturbance theory: Political scientist David B. Truman's theory that interest groups form in part to counteract the efforts of other groups.

divided government: The political condition in which different political parties control the White House and Congress.

domestic dependent nation: A type of sovereignty that makes an Indian tribe in the United States outside the authority of state governments but reliant on the federal government for the definition of tribal authority.

double jeopardy: Part of the Fifth Amendment that protects individuals from being tried twice for the same offense.

dual federalism: The belief that having separate and equally powerful levels of government is the best arrangement.

due process clause: Clause contained in the Fifth and Fourteenth Amendments. Over the years, it has been construed to guarantee to individuals a variety of rights ranging from economic liberty to criminal procedural rights to protection from arbitrary governmental action.

due process rights: Procedural guarantees provided by the Fourth, Fifth, Sixth, and Eighth Amendments for those accused of crimes.

E

economic regulation: Government regulation of business practices, industry rates, routes, or areas serviced by particular industries.

economic stability: A situation in which there is economic growth, rising national income, high employment, and steadiness in the general level of prices.

Eighth Amendment: Part of the Bill of Rights that states: "Excessive bail shall not be required, nor excessive fines imposed, nor cruel and unusual punishments inflicted."

elector: Member of the Electoral College chosen by methods determined in each state.

Electoral College: Representatives of each state who cast the final ballots that actually elect a president.

Embargo Act: Passed by Congress in 1807 to prevent U.S. ships from leaving U.S. ports for foreign ports without the approval of the federal government.

engagement: Policy implemented during the Clinton administration that the United States would remain actively involved in foreign affairs.

enlargement: Policy implemented during the Clinton administration that the United States would actively promote the expansion of democracy and free markets throughout the world.

entitlement program: Income security program to which all those meeting eligibility criteria are entitled.

enumerated powers: Seventeen specific powers granted to Congress under Article I, section 8, of the U.S. Constitution; these powers include taxation, coinage of money, regulation of commerce, and the authority to provide for a national defense.

Equal Employment Opportunity Commission: Federal agency created to enforce the Civil Rights Act of 1964, which forbids discrimination on the basis of race, creed, national origin, religion, or sex in hiring, promotion, or firing.

equal protection clause: Section of the Fourteenth Amendment that guarantees that all citizens receive "equal protection of the laws."

Equal Rights Amendment: Proposed amendment that would bar discrimination against women by federal or state governments.

equal time rule: The rule that requires broadcast stations to sell airtime equally to all candidates in a political campaign if they choose to sell it to any.

establishment clause: The first clause in the First Amendment; it prohibits the national government from establishing a national religion.

ex post facto **law:** Law passed after the fact, thereby making previously legal activity illegal and subject to current penalty; prohibited by the U.S. Constitution.

exclusionary rule: Judicially created rule that prohibits police from using illegally seized evidence at trial.

executive agreement: Formal government agreement entered into by the president that does not require the advice and consent of the U.S. Senate.

Executive Office of the President (EOP): Establishment created in 1939 to help the president oversee the executive branch bureaucracy.

executive order: Rule or regulation issued by the president that has the effect of law. All executive orders must be published in the *Federal Register*.

executive privilege: An implied presidential power that allows the president to refuse to disclose information regarding confidential conversations or national security to Congress or the judiciary.

exit polls: Polls conducted at selected polling places on Election Day.

F

federal budget deficit: The amount by which federal expenditure exceeds federal revenue.

Federal Employees Political Activities Act: 1993 liberalization of the Hatch Act. Federal employees are now allowed to run for office in nonpartisan elections and to contribute money to campaigns in partisan elections.

Federal Reserve Board: A seven-member board that sets member banks' reserve requirements, controls the discount rate, and makes other economic decisions.

federal system: System of government where the national government and state governments share some powers, derive all authority from the people, and the powers of the national government are specified in a constitution.

The Federalist Papers: A series of eighty-five political papers written by John Jay, Alexander Hamilton, and James Madison in support of ratification of the U.S. Constitution.

Federalists: Those who favored a stronger national government and supported the proposed U.S. Constitution; later became the first U.S. political party.

Fifteenth Amendment: One of the three Civil War amendments; specifically enfranchised newly freed male slaves.

Fifth Amendment: Part of the Bill of Rights that imposes a number of restrictions on the federal government with respect to the rights of persons suspected of committing a crime. It provides for indictment by a grand jury, protection against self-incrimination, and prevents the national government from denying a person life, liberty, or property without the due process of law. It also prevents the national government from taking property without fair compensation.

fighting words: Words that, "by their very utterance inflict injury or tend to incite an immediate breach of peace." Fighting words are not subject to the restrictions of the First Amendment.

filibuster: A formal way of halting action on a bill by means of long speeches or unlimited debate in the Senate.

finance chair: A professional who coordinates the fund-raising efforts for the campaign.

First Amendment: Part of the Bill of Rights that imposes a number of restrictions on the federal government with respect to the civil liberties of the people, including freedom of religion, speech, press, assembly, and petition.

First Continental Congress: Meeting held in Philadelphia from September 5 to October 26, 1774, in which fifty-six delegates (from every colony except Georgia) adopted a resolution in opposition to the Coercive Acts.

fiscal policy: Federal government policies on taxes, spending, and debt management, intended to promote the nation's macroeconomic goals, particularly with respect to employment, price stability, and growth.

527 political committees: Nonprofit and unregulated interest groups that focus on specific causes or policy positions and attempt to influence voters.

Fourteenth Amendment: One of the three Civil War amendments; guarantees equal protection and due process of the laws to all U.S. citizens.

Fourth Amendment: Part of the Bill of Rights that reads: "The right of the people to be secure in their persons, houses, papers, and effects, against unreasonable searches and seizures, shall not be violated, and no Warrants shall issue, but upon probable cause, supported by Oath or affirmation, and particularly describing the place to be searched, and the persons or things to be seized."

framing: The process by which a news organization defines a political issue and consequently affects opinion about the issues.

free exercise clause: The second clause of the First Amendment. It prohibits the U.S. government from interfering with a citizen's right to practice his or her religion.

free media: Coverage of a candidate's campaign by the news media.

free rider problem: Potential members fail to join a group because they can get the benefit, or collective good, sought by the group without contributing to the effort.

front-loading: The tendency of states to choose an early date on the primary calendar.

full faith and credit clause: Section of Article IV of the Constitution that ensures judicial decrees and contracts made in one state will be binding and enforceable in any other state.

G

General Agreement on Tariffs and Trade: Devised shortly after World War II as an interim agreement until a World Trade Organization could be created to help lower tariffs and increase trade.

general election: Election in which voters decide which candidates will actually fill elective public offices.

general election campaign: That part of a political campaign aimed at winning a general election.

gerrymandering: The legislative process through which the majority party in each statehouse tries to assure that the maximum number of representatives from its political party can be elected to Congress through the redrawing of legislative districts.get out the vote

(GOTV): A push at the end of a political campaign to encourage supporters to go to the polls.

Gibbons v. *Ogden* **(1824):** The Court upheld broad congressional power over interstate commerce. The Court's broad interpretation of the Constitution's commerce clause paved the way for later rulings upholding expansive federal powers.

government: The formal vehicles through which policies are made and affairs of state are conducted.

government corporation: A business established by Congress that performs functions that can be provided by a private business (such as the U.S. Postal Service).

governmental (institutional) agenda: The changing list of issues to which governments believe they should address themselves.

governmental party: The office holders and candidates who run under a political party's banner.

governor: Chief elected executive in state government.

grandfather clause: Voting qualification provision in many Southern states that allowed only those whose grandfathers had voted before Reconstruction to vote unless they passed a wealth or literacy test.

Great Compromise: A decision made during the Constitutional Convention to give each state the same number of representatives in the Senate regardless of size; representation in the House was determined by population.

H

Hatch Act: Law enacted in 1939 to prohibit civil servants from taking activist roles in partisan campaigns. This act prohibited federal employees from making political contributions, working for a particular party, or campaigning for a particular candidate.

hold: A tactic by which a senator asks to be informed before a particular bill is brought to the floor. This stops the bill from coming to the floor until the hold is removed.

human rights: The belief that human beings have inalienable rights such as freedom of speech and freedom of religion.

I

impeachment: The power delegated to the House of Representatives in the Constitution to charge the president, vice president, or other "civil officers," including federal judges, with "Treason, Bribery, or other High Crimes and Misdemeanors." This is the first step in the constitutional process of removing such government officials from office.

implementation: The process by which a law or policy is put into operation by the bureaucracy.

implied powers: Powers derived from the enumerated powers and the necessary and proper clause. These powers are not stated specifically but are considered to be reasonably implied through the exercise of delegated powers.

impressment: The British practice in the early eighteenth century of stopping ships at sea to seize sailors suspected of having deserted the Royal Navy.

incorporation doctrine: An interpretation of the Constitution that holds that the due process clause of the Fourteenth Amendment requires that state and local governments also guarantee those rights.

incumbency: The holding of an office.

independent executive agency: Governmental unit that closely resembles a Cabinet department but has a narrower area of responsibility (such as the Central Intelligence Agency) and is not part of any Cabinet department.

independent regulatory commission: An agency created by Congress that is generally concerned with a specific aspect of the economy.

indirect (representative) democracy: A system of government that gives citizens the opportunity to vote for representatives who will work on their behalf.

inflation: A rise in the general price levels of an economy.

inherent powers: Powers that belong to the national government simply because it is a sovereign state.

initiative: A process that allows citizens to propose legislation and submit it to the state electorate for popular vote.

inoculation ad: Advertising that attempts to counteract an anticipated attack from the opposition before the attack is launched.

interagency council: A working group created to facilitate coordination of policy making and implementation across a host of governmental agencies.

interest group: An organized group that tries to influence public policy.

international governmental organization (IGO): An organization created by the governments of at least two and often many countries that operates internationally with the objectives of achieving the purposes that the member countries agree on.

International Monetary Fund: International governmental organization created shortly before the end of World War II to stabilize international financial relations through fixed monetary exchange rates.

Internet team: Campaign staff that uses Web-based resources to communicate with voters, raise funds, organize volunteers, and plan events.

interstate compacts: Contracts between states that carry the force of law; generally now used as a tool to address multistate policy concerns.

interventionist state: Alternative to the laissez-faire state; the government takes an active role in guiding and managing the private economy.

Iranian hostage crisis: Crisis during the Carter administration when Iranian students with support of the Iranian government took over the U.S. embassy in Tehran, holding all the personnel hostage.

iron triangle: The relatively stable relationship and pattern of interaction that occurs among an agency, interest groups, and congressional committees or subcommittees.

isolationism: A national policy of avoiding participation in foreign affairs.

issue network: The loose and informal relationship that exists among a large number of actors who work in broad policy areas.

issue-oriented politics: Politics that focuses on specific issues rather than on party, candidate, or other loyalties.

J

Joint Chiefs of Staff: Advisory body to the president that includes chief of staff of the army, chief of staff of the air force, chief of naval operations, and marine commandant.

joint committee: Includes members from both houses of Congress, conducts investigations or special studies.

judicial activism: A philosophy of judicial decision making that argues judges should use their power broadly to further justice, especially in the areas of equality and personal liberty.

judicial implementation: Refers to how and whether judicial decisions are translated into actual public policies affecting more than the immediate parties to a lawsuit.

judicial restraint: A philosophy of judicial decision making that argues courts should

allow the decisions of other branches of government to stand, even when they offend a judge's own sense of principles.

judicial review: Power of the courts to review acts of other branches of government and the states.

Judiciary Act of 1789: Established the basic three-tiered structure of the federal court system.

jurisdiction: Authority vested in a particular court to hear and decide the issues in any particular case.

L

laissez-faire: A French term literally meaning "to allow to do, to leave alone." It is a hands-off governmental policy that is based on the belief that government involvement in the economy is wrong.

League of Nations: Created in the peace treaty that ended World War I, it was an international governmental organization dedicated to preserving peace.

legislative courts: Courts established by Congress for specialized purposes, such as the Court of Military Appeals.

libel: False written statements or written statements tending to call someone's reputation into disrepute.

liberal: One considered to favor extensive governmental involvement in the economy and the provision of social services and to take an activist role in protecting the rights of women, the elderly, minorities, and the environment.

libertarian: One who favors a free market economy and no governmental interference in personal liberties.

lobbying: The activities of a group or organization that seeks to influence legislation and persuade political leaders to support the group's position.

lobbyist: Interest group representative who seeks to influence legislation that will benefit his or her organization through political persuasion.

logrolling: Vote trading; voting yea to support a colleague's bill in return for a promise of future support.

M

machine: A party organization that recruits its members with tangible incentives and is characterized by a high degree of control over member activity.

majority leader: The elected leader of the party controlling the most seats in the House of Representatives or the Senate; is second in authority to the Speaker of the House and in the Senate is regarded as its most powerful member.

majority party: The political party in each house of Congress with the most members.

majority rule: The central premise of direct democracy in which only policies that collectively garner the support of a majority of voters will be made into law.

manager: A professional executive hired by a city council or county board to manage daily operations and to recommend policy changes.

manifest destiny: Theory that the United States was divinely mandated to expand across North America to the Pacific Ocean.

Marbury v. *Madison* (1803): Supreme Court first asserted the power of judicial review in finding that the congressional statute extending the Court's original jurisdiction was unconstitutional.

markup: A process in which legislative committee members offer changes to a bill before it goes to the floor in either house for a vote.

Marshall Plan: European Recovery Program, named after Secretary of State George C. Marshall, of extensive U.S. aid to Western Europe after World War II.

mass media: The entire array of organizations through which information is collected and disseminated to the general public.

matching funds: Donations to presidential campaigns from the federal government that are determined by the amount of private funds a qualifying candidate raises.

McCulloch v. *Maryland* (1819): The Supreme Court upheld the power of the national government and denied the right of a state to tax the bank. The Court's broad interpretation of the necessary and proper clause paved the way for later rulings upholding expansive federal powers.

means-tested program: Income security program intended to assist those whose incomes fall below a designated level.

media consultant: A professional who produces political candidates' television, radio, and print advertisements.

media effects: The influence of news sources on public opinion.

Medicaid: An expansion of Medicare, this program subsidizes medical care for the poor.

Medicare: The federal program established in the Lyndon B. Johnson administration that provides medical care to elderly Social Security recipients.

mercantilism: An economic theory designed to increase a nation's wealth through the development of commercial industry and a favorable balance of trade.

merit system: The system by which federal civil service jobs are classified into grades or levels, to which appointments are made on the basis of performance on competitive examinations.

midterm election: Election that takes place in the middle of a presidential term.

military-industrial complex: The grouping of the U.S. armed forces and defense industries.

minority leader: The elected leader of the party with the second highest number of elected representatives in the House of Representatives or the Senate.

minority party: The political party in each house of Congress with the second most members.

Miranda **rights:** Statements that must be made by the police informing a suspect of his or her constitutional rights protected by the Fifth Amendment, including the right to an attorney provided by the court if the suspect cannot afford one.

Miranda v. *Arizona* (1966): A landmark Supreme Court ruling that held the Fifth Amendment requires that individuals arrested for a crime must be advised of their right to remain silent and to have counsel present.

monarchy: A form of government in which power is vested in hereditary kings and queens who govern in the interests of all.

monetary policy: A form of government regulation in which the nation's money supply and interest rates are controlled.

money: A system of exchange for goods and services that includes currency, coins, and bank deposits.

Monroe Doctrine: President James Monroe's 1823 pledge that the United States would oppose attempts by European states to extend their political control into the Western Hemisphere.

moralism: The policy of emphasizing morality in foreign affairs.

muckraking: A form of journalism, in vogue in the early twentieth century, concerned with reforming government and business conduct.

multilateralism: The U.S. foreign policy that actions should be taken in cooperation with other states after consultation.

N

narrowcasting: Targeting media programming at specific populations within society.

national convention: A party conclave (meeting) held in the presidential election year for the purposes of nominating a presidential and vice presidential ticket and adopting a platform.

national party platform: A statement of the general and specific philosophy and policy goals of a political party, usually promulgated at the national convention.

National Security Agency (NSA): Intelligence agency responsible for gathering intelligence from electronic and other sources and for code breaking.

National Security Council (NSC): Executive agency responsible for advising the president about foreign and defense policy and events.

natural law: A doctrine that society should be governed by certain ethical principles that are part of nature and, as such, can be understood by reason.

necessary and proper clause: The final paragraph of Article I, section 8, of the U.S. Constitution, which gives Congress the authority to pass all laws "necessary and proper" to carry out the enumerated powers specified in the Constitution; also called the elastic clause.

negative ad: Advertising on behalf of a candidate that attacks the opponent's platform or character.

network: An association of broadcast stations (radio or television) that share programming through a financial arrangement.

New Deal: The name given to the program of "Relief, Recovery, Reform" begun by President Franklin D. Roosevelt in 1933 to bring the United States out of the Great Depression.

new federalism: Federal/state relationship proposed by Reagan administration during the 1980s; hallmark is returning administrative powers to the state governments.

New Jersey Plan: A framework for the Constitution proposed by a group of small states; its key points were a one-house legislature with one vote for each state, the establishment of the acts of Congress as the "supreme law" of the land, and a supreme judiciary with limited power.

new media: Technologies such as the Internet that blur the line between media sources and create new opportunities for the dissemination of news and other information.

New York Times Co. v. *Sullivan* (1964): The Supreme Court concluded that "actual malice" must be proved to support a finding of libel against a public figure.

Nineteenth Amendment: Amendment to the Constitution that guaranteed women the right to vote.

Ninth Amendment: Part of the Bill of Rights that reads "The enumeration in the Constitution, of certain rights, shall not be construed to deny or disparage others retained by the people."

Nixon Doctrine: The policy implemented at the end of the Vietnam War that the United States would provide arms and military equipment to countries but not do the fighting for them.

nomination campaign: That part of a political campaign aimed at winning a primary election.

nongovernmental organization (NGO): An organization that is not tied to a government.

non-means-based program: Program such as Social Security where benefits are provided irrespective of the income or means of recipients.

North American Free Trade Agreement (NAFTA): Agreement that promotes free movement of goods and services among Canada, Mexico, and the United States.

O

Office of Management and Budget (OMB): The office that prepares the president's annual budget proposal, reviews the budget and programs of the executive departments, supplies economic forecasts, and conducts detailed analyses of proposed bills and agency rules.

oligarchy: A form of government in which the right to participate is conditioned on the possession of wealth, social status, military position, or achievement.

open market operations: The buying and selling of government securities by the Federal Reserve Bank in the securities market.

open primary: A primary in which party members, independents, and sometimes members of the other party are allowed to vote.

organizational party: The workers and activists who staff the party's formal organization.

original jurisdiction: The jurisdiction of courts that hear a case first, usually in a trial. Courts determine the facts of a case under their original jurisdiction.

oversight: Congressional review of the activities of an agency, department, or office.

P

paid media: Political advertisements purchased for a candidate's campaign.

pardon: The authority of a government to cancel someone's conviction of a crime by a court and to eliminate all sanctions and punishments resulting from conviction.

party caucus or conference: A formal gathering of all party members.

party identification: A citizen's personal affinity for a political party, usually expressed by his or her tendency to vote for the candidates of that party.

party in the electorate: The voters who consider themselves allied or associated with the party.

party realignment: A shifting of party coalition groupings in the electorate that remains in place for several elections.

patron: Person who finances a group or individual activity.

patronage: Jobs, grants, or other special favors that are given as rewards to friends and political allies for their support.

Pearl Harbor: Naval base in Hawaii attacked by Japan on December 7, 1941, initiating U.S. entry into World War II.

Pendleton Act: Reform measure that created the Civil Service Commission to administer a partial merit system. The act classified the federal service by grades, to which appointments were made based on the results of a competitive examination. It made it illegal for federal political appointees to be required to contribute to a particular political party.

personal liberty: A key characteristic of U.S. democracy. Initially meaning freedom from governmental interference, today it includes demands for freedom to engage in a variety of practices free from governmental discrimination.

Plessy v. Ferguson (1896): Plessy challenged a Louisiana statute requiring that railroads provide separate accommodations for blacks and whites. The Court found that separate but equal accommodations did not violate the equal protection clause of the Fourteenth Amendment.

pocket veto: If Congress adjourns during the ten days the president has to consider a bill passed by both houses of Congress, without the president's signature, the bill is considered vetoed.

policy adoption: The approval of a policy proposal by the people with the requisite authority, such as a legislature.

policy evaluation: The process of determining whether a course of action is achieving its intended goals.

policy formulation: The crafting of appropriate and acceptable proposed courses of action to ameliorate or resolve public problems.

policy implementation: The process of carrying out public policy through governmental agencies and the courts.

political action committee (PAC): Federally mandated, officially registered fund-raising committee that represents interest groups in the political process.

political culture: Commonly shared attitudes, beliefs, and core values about how government should operate.

political equality: The principle that all citizens should participate equally in government; implied by the phrase "one person, one vote."

political ideology: A coherent set of values and beliefs about the purpose and scope of government.

political party: A group of office holders, candidates, activists, and voters who identify with a group label and seek to elect to public office individuals who run under that label.

political socialization: The process through which individuals acquire their political beliefs and values.

politico: Role played by elected representatives who act as trustees or as delegates, depending on the issue.

politics: The study of who gets what, when, and how—or how policy decisions are made.

poll tax: A tax levied in many southern states and localities that had to be paid before an eligible voter could cast a ballot.

pollster: A professional who takes public opinion surveys that guide political campaigns.

popular consent: The idea that governments must draw their powers from the consent of the governed.

popular sovereignty: The notion that the ultimate authority in society rests with the people.

pork: Legislation that allows representatives to bring home the bacon to their districts in the form of public works programs, military bases, or other programs designed to benefit their districts directly.

positive ad: Advertising on behalf of a candidate that stresses the candidate's qualifications, family, and issue positions, without reference to the opponent.

Powell Doctrine: An all-or-nothing approach to military intervention advocated by Colin Powell: use overwhelming force for quick, decisive victory, and have an exit strategy before any intervention.

pragmatism: The policy of taking advantage of a situation for national gain.

precedent: Prior judicial decision that serves as a rule for settling subsequent cases of a similar nature.

preemption: A concept derived from the Constitution's supremacy clause that allows the national government to override or preempt state or local actions in certain areas.

president pro tempore: The official chair of the Senate; usually the most senior member of the majority party.

press briefing: A relatively restricted session between a press secretary or aide and the press.

press conference: An unrestricted session between an elected official and the press.

press release: A document offering an official comment or position.

press secretary: The individual charged with interacting and communicating with journalists on a daily basis.

primary election: Election in which voters decide which of the candidates within a party will represent the party in the general election.

prior restraint: Constitutional doctrine that prevents the government from prohibiting speech or publication before the fact; generally held to be in violation of the First Amendment.

privileges and immunities clause: Part of Article IV of the Constitution guaranteeing that the citizens of each state are afforded the same rights as citizens of all other states.

prospective judgment: A voter's evaluation of a candidate based on what he or she pledges to do about an issue if elected.

public funds: Donations from the general tax revenues to the campaigns of qualifying presidential candidates.

public interest group: An organization that seeks a collective good that will not selectively and materially benefit the members of the group.

public opinion: What the public thinks about a particular issue or set of issues at any point in time.

public opinion polls: Interviews or surveys with samples of citizens that are used to estimate the feelings and beliefs of the entire population.

public policy: An intentional course of action followed by government in dealing with some problem or matter of concern.

push polls: "Polls" taken for the purpose of providing information on an opponent that would lead respondents to vote against that candidate.

R

raiding: An organized attempt by voters of one party to influence the primary results of the other party.

random sampling: A method of poll selection that gives each person in a group the same chance of being selected.

Reagan Doctrine: Policy that the United States would provide military assistance to anti-communist groups fighting against pro-Soviet governments.

reapportionment: The reallocation of the number of seats in the House of Representatives after each decennial census.

recall: An election in which voters can remove an incumbent from office by popular vote.

recession: A short-term decline in the economy that occurs as investment sags, production falls off, and unemployment increases.

redistricting: The redrawing of congressional districts to reflect population changes or for political advantage.

referendum: An election whereby the state legislature submits proposed legislation to the state's voters for approval.

regulations: Rules that govern the operation of a particular government program that have the force of law.

republic: A government rooted in the consent of the governed; a representative or indirect democracy.

reservation land: Land designated in a treaty that is under the authority of an Indian nation and is exempt from most state laws and taxes.

reserve (or police) powers: Powers reserved to the states by the Tenth Amendment that lie at the foundation of a state's right to legislate for the public health and welfare of its citizens.

reserve requirements: Government requirements that a portion of member banks' deposits must be retained to back loans made.

retrospective judgment: A voter's evaluation of the performance of the party in power.

right to privacy: The right to be let alone; a judicially created doctrine encompassing an individual's decision to use birth control or secure an abortion.

Roe v. *Wade* **(1973):** The Supreme Court found that a woman's right to an abortion was protected by the right to privacy that could be implied from specific guarantees found in the Bill of Rights applied to the states through the Fourteenth Amendment.

Roosevelt Corollary: Concept developed by President Theodore Roosevelt early in the twentieth century that it was the U.S. responsibility to assure stability in Latin America and the Caribbean.

rule making: A quasi-legislative administrative process that has the characteristics of a legislative act.

Rule of Four: At least four justices of the Supreme Court must vote to consider a case before it can be heard.

runoff primary: A second primary election between the two candidates receiving the greatest number of votes in the first primary.

S

sampling error or margin of error: A measure of the accuracy of a public opinion poll.

Second Continental Congress: Meeting that convened in Philadelphia on May 10, 1775, to make one last effort to avert conflict with England. It adopted the Declaration of Independence in 1776.

secular realignment: The gradual rearrangement of party coalitions, based more on demographic shifts than on shocks to the political system.

select (or special) committee: Temporary committee appointed for specific purpose, such as conducting a special investigation or study.

selective incorporation: A judicial doctrine whereby most but not all of the protections found in the Bill of Rights are made applicable to the states via the Fourteenth Amendment.

senatorial courtesy: Process by which presidents, when selecting district court judges, defer to senators of their own party who represent the state where the vacancy occurs; also the process by which a governor, when selecting an appointee, defers to the state senator in whose district the nominee resides.

seniority: Time of continuous service on a committee, or within the House or Senate.

separation of powers: A way of dividing power among three branches of government in which members of the House of Representatives, members of the Senate, the president, and the federal courts are selected by and responsible to different constituencies.

Seventeenth Amendment: Made senators directly elected by the people; removed their selection from state legislatures.

Sixteenth Amendment: Authorized Congress to enact a national income tax.

Sixth Amendment: Part of the Bill of Rights that sets out the basic requirements of procedural due process for federal courts to follow in criminal trials. These include speedy and public trials, impartial juries, trials in the state where crime was committed, notice of the charges, the right to confront and obtain favorable witnesses, and the right to counsel.

slander: Untrue spoken statements that defame the character of a person.

social capital: The myriad relationships that individuals enjoy that facilitate the resolution of community problems through collective action.

social conservative: One who believes that traditional moral teachings should be supported and furthered by the government.

social contract theory: The belief that people are free and equal by God-given right and that this in turn requires that all people give their consent to be governed; espoused by John Locke and influential in the writing of the Declaration of Independence.

social regulation: Government regulation of the quality and safety of products as well as the conditions under which goods and services are produced.

Social Security Act: A 1935 law that established old-age insurance (Social Security) and assistance for the needy, children, and others, and unemployment insurance.

social welfare policy: Government programs designed to improve quality of life.

soft money: The virtually unregulated money funneled by individuals and political committees through state and local parties.

solicitor general: The fourth-ranking member of the Department of Justice; responsible for handling all appeals on behalf of the U.S. government to the Supreme Court.

sovereign immunity: The right of a state to be free from lawsuit unless it gives permission to the suit. Under the Eleventh Amendment, all states are considered sovereign.

Spanish-American War: Brief 1898 war against Spain because of Spanish policies and presence in Cuba and U.S. desire to attain overseas territory.

Speaker of the House: The only officer of the House of Representatives specifically mentioned in the Constitution; elected at the beginning of each new Congress by the entire House; traditionally a member of the majority party.

spoils system: The firing of public-office holders of a defeated political party and their replacement with loyalists of the newly elected party.

spot ad: Television advertising on behalf of a candidate that is broadcast in sixty-, thirty-, or ten-second duration.

Stamp Act Congress: Meeting of representatives of nine of the thirteen colonies held in New York City in 1765, during which representatives drafted a document to send to the king listing how their rights had been violated.

standing committee: Committee to which proposed bills are referred.

stare decisis: In court rulings, a reliance on past decisions or precedents to formulate decisions in new cases.

stratified sampling: A variation of random sampling; Census data are used to divide a country into four sampling regions. Sets of counties and standard metropolitan statistical areas are then randomly selected in proportion to the total national population.

straw polls: Unscientific surveys used to gauge public opinion on a variety of issues and policies.

strict constructionist: An approach to constitutional interpretation that emphasizes the Framers' original intentions.

strict scrutiny: A heightened standard of review used by the Supreme Court to determine the constitutional validity of a challenged practice.

substantive due process: Judicial interpretation of the Fifth and Fourteenth Amendments' due process clause that protects citizens from arbitrary or unjust laws.

suffrage movement: The drive for voting rights for women that took place in the United States from 1890 to 1920.

supremacy clause: Portion of Article VI of the U.S. Constitution mandating that national law is supreme to (that is, supercedes) all other laws passed by the states or by any other subdivision of government.

suspect classification: Category or class, such as race, that triggers the highest standard of scrutiny from the Supreme Court.

symbolic speech: Symbols, signs, and other methods of expression generally also considered to be protected by the First Amendment.

systemic agenda: All public issues that are viewed as requiring governmental attention; a discussion agenda.

T

Taliban: Fundamentalist Islamic government of Afghanistan that provided terrorist training bases for al-Qaeda.

tariffs: Taxes on imports used to raise government revenue and to protect infant industries.

Tenth Amendment: Part of the Bill of Rights that reiterates powers not delegated to the national government are reserved to the states or to the people.

Thirteenth Amendment: One of the three Civil War amendments; specifically bans slavery in the United States.

Three-Fifths Compromise: Agreement reached at the Constitutional Convention stipulating that each slave was to be counted as three-fifths of a person for purposes of determining population for representation in the U.S. House of Representatives.

Title IX: Provision of the Educational Amendments of 1972 that bars educational institutions receiving federal funds from discriminating against female students.

totalitarianism: A form of government in which power resides in a leader who rules according to self-interest and without regard for individual rights and liberties.

tracking polls: Continuous surveys that enable a campaign to chart its daily rise or fall in support.

trial courts: Courts of original jurisdiction where a case begins.

Truman Doctrine: U.S. policy initiated in 1947 of providing economic assistance and military aid to countries fighting against communist revolutions or political pressure.

trustee: Role played by elected representatives who listen to constituents' opinions and then use their best judgment to make final decisions.

turnout: The proportion of the voting-age public that votes.

Twenty-Fifth Amendment: Adopted in 1967 to establish procedures for filling vacancies in the office of president and vice president as well as providing for procedures to deal with the disability of a president.

Twenty-Second Amendment: Adopted in 1951, prevents a president from serving more than two terms or more than ten years if he came to office via the death or impeachment of his predecessor.

U

unfunded mandates: National laws that direct states or local governments to comply with the federal rules or regulations (such as clean air or water standards) but contain no federal funding to defray the cost of meeting these requirements.

unilateralism: A national policy of acting without consulting others.

unitary system: System of government where the local and regional governments derive all authority from a strong national government.

United Nations (UN): The international governmental organization created shortly before the end of World War II to guarantee the security of nations and to promote global economic, physical, and social well-being.

U.S. v. Nixon **(1974):** Key Supreme Court ruling on power of the president, finding that there is no absolute constitutional executive privilege to allow a president to refuse to comply with a court order to produce information needed in a criminal trial.

V

veto: The formal, constitutional authority of the chief executive to reject bills passed by both houses of the legislative body, thus preventing their becoming law without further legislative action.

veto power: The formal, constitutional authority of the president to reject bills passed by both houses of Congress, thus preventing their becoming law without further congressional action.

Virginia Plan: The first general plan for the Constitution, proposed by James Madison and Edmund Randolph. Its key points were a bicameral legislature, an executive chosen by the legislature, and a judiciary also named by the legislature.

voter canvass: The process by which a campaign gets in touch with individual voters, either by door-to-door solicitation or by telephone.

W

war on terrorism: Initiated by President George W. Bush after the 9/11 attacks to weed out terrorist operatives throughout the world, using diplomacy, military means, improved homeland security, stricter banking laws, and other means.

War Powers Act: Passed by Congress in 1973; the president is limited in the deployment of troops overseas to a sixty-day period in peacetime (which can be extended for an extra thirty days to permit withdrawal) unless Congress explicitly gives its approval for a longer period.

weapons of mass destruction: Biological, chemical, and nuclear weapons, which present a sizeable threat to U.S. security.

whip: One of several representatives who keep close contact with all members and take nose counts on key votes, prepare summaries of bills, and in general act as communications links within the party.

wire service: An electronic delivery of news gathered by the news service's correspondents and sent to all member news media organizations.

World Bank: International governmental organization created shortly before the end of World War II to provide loans for large economic development projects.

World Trade Organization: International governmental organization created in 1995 that manages multilateral negotiations to reduce barriers to trade and settle trade disputes.

writ of *certiorari:* A request for the Court to order up the records from a lower court to review the case.

writ of *habeas corpus:* A court order in which a judge requires authorities to prove that a prisoner is being held lawfully and that allows the prisoner to be freed if the judge is not persuaded by the government's case. *Habeas corpus* rights imply that prisoners have a right to know what charges are being made against them.

Y

yellow journalism: A form of newspaper publishing in vogue in the late-nineteenth century that featured pictures, comics, color, and sensationalized, oversimplified news coverage.